JONATHAN COE

LIKE A FIERY ELEPHANT

THE STORY OF B. S. JOHNSON

continuum

NEW YORK

2005

First U.S. Edition

The Continuum International Publishing Group Inc
15 East 26 Street, New York, NY 10010

www.continuumbooks.com

First published in the United Kingdom in 2004 by Picador,
an imprint of Pan Macmillan Ltd.

Printed in the United States of America

Library of Congress Cataloging-in-Publication Data

  Coe, Jonathan.
    Like a fiery elephant : the story of B.S. Johnson / Jonathan Coe.—1st U.S. ed.
      p. cm.
    Includes bibliographical references (p.) index.
    ISBN 0-8264-1735-3 (hardcover : alk. paper)
    1. Johnson, B. S. (Bryan Stanley), 1933-1973. 2. Novelists, English—20th
century—Biography. 3. Experimental fiction, English—History and
criticism. I. Title.
  PR6060.O3Z64 2005
  823'.912—dc22   2005003277

I. M.

Joyce Yates (1916–2002)

and

Julia Trevelyan Oman (1930–2003)

'Telling stories is telling lies'

B. S. JOHNSON, *Albert Angelo*

I looked up from my writing,
    And gave a start to see,
As if rapt in my inditing,
    The moon's full gaze on me.

Her meditative misty head
    Was spectral in its air,
And I involuntarily said,
    'What are you doing there?'

'Oh, I've been scanning pond and hole
    And waterway hereabout
For the body of one with a sunken soul
    Who has put his life-light out.

'Did you hear his frenzied tattle?
    It was sorrow for his son
Who is slain in brutish battle,
    Though he has injured none.

'And now I am curious to look
    Into the blinkered mind
Of one who wants to write a book
    In a world of such a kind.'

Her temper overwrought me,
    And I edged to shun her view,
For I felt assured she thought me
    One who should drown him too.

THOMAS HARDY

CONTENTS

INTRODUCTION

THE INDUSTRIOUS BIOGRAPHER

AN EXPOSITION WITHOUT WHICH YOU MIGHT HAVE FELT UNHAPPY

> *I · · always with I · · one starts from · ·*
> *one and I share the same character · · are one ·*
> *· · · · one always starts with I · · one · ·*
> *· · · alone · · · · · · · sole · · · ·*
> *· · · · · · · single · · · · · · · · ·*
> *· · I*

I was thirteen years and almost three months old on 12 November 1974. It was a day on which Denis Healey, the Chancellor of the Exchequer, had announced that VAT on petrol was to go up from eight per cent to twenty-five per cent. A warrant had been issued for the arrest of Lord Lucan. The Jewish Defence League had pledged to assassinate Yasser Arafat, the leader of the PLO. A man of twenty-six had been shot dead while playing table tennis in a Belfast convent and an essay published by the Institute for the Study of Conflict had predicted the reunification of Ireland and the withdrawal of British troops within fifteen years. None of which weighed very heavily on my mind as I settled down with my family to watch television after the *News at Ten*. It was a Tuesday night during the school term, so normally I would have been getting ready for bed at this time. But there was a special programme showing this evening, something that none of us wanted to miss. It was going out on ITV (a channel we rarely watched, as a rule), was called *Fat Man on a Beach*, and although we had never heard of the man presenting it, and although its description in the television listings of the *Daily Telegraph* was enigmatic to say the least, there was no doubt in our minds that it constituted essential viewing. It was a documentary about Porth Ceiriad bay, a beach on the Lleyn peninsula in Gwynedd, north Wales. The place where we had taken our holidays every year for the last decade or more. A place with which we were so familiar that I even believe we had somehow come to feel – in a way not untypical of English holidaymakers in Wales – that we owned it. That it belonged to us.

What did we expect from this programme? We expected to be flattered, I imagine: to have our sense of familiarity and ownership flattered, played up to, with shots of readily identifiable landmarks which would have us squawking, 'There's the path to the caravan site!' and 'There's the shop where we get the milk!' Perhaps we were even prepared, in a spirit of Reithian open-mindedness, to absorb a certain amount of information about Welsh customs and the local population, which we were at great pains to avoid during the two or three weeks of every year we spent caravanning on the peninsula.

In the event, anyway, we got none of these things.

Instead we were expected to watch forty minutes of a fat man sitting in various positions on the beach, and talking to us. And worse still, reading poetry! This man appeared, on the surface, to be jolly enough: in looks and manner I have since heard him compared variously to Max Bygraves, Tony Hancock and Tommy Cooper. His eyes seemed somehow wary and serious, though ('The first thing I saw of him when I opened the door was his eyes [...] their look that struck me as sad and *afraid*'[1]) and the things that he spoke about, when they were not simply baffling, were often gloomy. He told a long story about a man being thrown off his motorbike, his body being cut in two by a wire fence 'like a cheese cutter through cheese', and described this story as 'a metaphor for the way the human condition seems to treat humankind'. He wandered off into philosophical digressions, telling us that life was 'really all chaos ... I cannot prove it is chaos any more than anyone else can prove there is a pattern, or there is some sort of deity, but even if it is all chaos, then let's celebrate the chaos. Let's celebrate the accidental. Does that make us any the worse off? Are we any the worse off? There is still love; there is still humour.' Somehow the man sounded uncertain of this, of the notion that chaos could be 'celebrated'. It was not said in a very celebratory way. There was also some footage of a dead sheep, zooming in to a close shot of its bloodied head.

We didn't like this at all. We got up and turned the television off before the programme had ended. I made my way dutifully up to bed.

And that was my first glimpse of B. S. Johnson. I had no idea then, of course, that I would later spend seven years of my life trying to uncover the story of his. Nor did I know, as I watched his ruefully clownish performance on television that evening, that his life had ended abruptly little more than two weeks after the making of this film; a year almost to the day before it was broadcast. So full of life and energy did he seem on that beach, it's hard to believe that I had already been looking at a dead man.

*

'Aren't you rather young to be writing his memoirs?' someone might object, on learning that I was barely able to read when B. S. Johnson was beginning to do his most important work. And it's true that, even when I was a thirteen-year-old – and an unnaturally studious and introverted thirteen-year-old, at that – the appeal of radical experimentalism in the English novel had not exactly hit me like a thunderclap. I liked *Monty Python*, but that was about as far as it went, where the subversion of aesthetic conventions was concerned. I simply had no idea who B. S. Johnson was, or where he was coming from, when I saw *Fat Man on a Beach* for the first time. And no doubt, even now, there are people holding this book in their expectant hands who are in a very similar state of ignorance. Perhaps for these readers, if for no one else, a few words of general introduction might be appropriate.

And so:

B. S. Johnson was, if you like, Britain's one-man literary avant-garde of the 1960s. Yes, of course there were other avant-garde writers around at the time (Alan Burns, Eva Figes, Ann Quin, Christine Brooke-Rose spring immediately to mind). But they were not as famous as he was, they were not as good at putting their names about, they did not appear on television as often as he did, they did not argue their case as passionately or fight their corner as toughly as he did, and there is not – as far as I can see, anyway – the same stubborn residue of public interest in their lives and work, at the time of my writing this, some thirty or forty years after the event. B. S. Johnson was different. B. S. Johnson was special.

He was a working-class Londoner, born in Hammersmith in 1933, whose childhood was defined by the trauma of wartime evacuation and his failure to pass the eleven-plus. In his late teens he was shunted into banking and accountancy jobs until he forced himself to learn Latin at evening classes and then won places at Birkbeck College and King's College London. During the rest of his short lifetime he published six novels: *Travelling People, Albert Angelo, Trawl, The Unfortunates, House Mother Normal* and *Christie Malry's Own Double-Entry*. A seventh novel, *See the Old Lady Decently*, which was to have been the first of a trilogy, was not published until two years after his death. In addition, he wrote enough poetry to fill two slim volumes, several full-length plays (mostly unperformed) and wrote or directed more than a dozen short films (mostly for television). He was a busy sports reporter, too, covering tennis and soccer for the national papers, to say nothing of pouring out a torrent of book reviews and polemical articles for anyone who would print them. And he worked tirelessly for the trade union movement, making documentaries and propaganda films, anonymously, under the Freeprop banner. All this, and more, squeezed into a working life that lasted little more than a decade.

On the face of things, Johnson had a high reputation. His books won prizes, his films won prizes, and throughout his career he received plenty of favourable reviews. But he was always angry, and hurt, and unhappy at his treatment by the literary establishment. One of his press releases described him as 'the most important young English novelist now writing',[2] but it galled him that not everybody accepted this view. (And besides, he wrote that press release himself.) At an early age, with the publication of his first novel, *Travelling People*, he adopted an uncompromising, oppositional stance to the efforts of his fellow novelists. What these people were all writing, essentially, was 'the nineteenth-century narrative novel', an exercise which he regarded, in a post-Joycean universe, as the literary equivalent of travelling by horse and cart when there were cars and trains available.

Johnson, by contrast, set himself the not inconsiderable task of re-inventing the novel with every book he wrote. Starting, in *Travelling People*, with devices adapted from his beloved *Tristram Shandy* – pages shading to grey, then to black, to convey the experience of a character having a heart attack – he went on to cut holes through the pages of a book, so that readers could see forward to a future event (*Albert Angelo*), and present the chapters of one novel unbound in a box, so that readers could shuffle them and recreate the randomness of experience for themselves (*The Unfortunates*). And so, at a time when the lightly ironic, social-realist novels of Kingsley Amis, John Wain and William Cooper set the dominant literary tone, it was Johnson himself, if anyone, who looked like the anachronism: an old-style modernist, who firmly believed that literary tradition could be kept alive only by radically redefining it, who conceived of literature (borrowing his metaphor from Nathalie Sarraute) as 'a relay race, the baton of innovation passing from one generation to another', but was dismayed to see that 'the vast majority of British novelists has dropped the baton, stood still, turned back, or not even realised that there is a race'.[3]

It is hard to overestimate how much, or on how many different counts, Johnson – who began his creative life as a poet, then wanted to be a playwright, before finally turning his hand to novel-writing – disliked not just most contemporary fiction, but almost everything, in fact, about the novel as a form. Dialogue, characterization and plot as you might expect to encounter them in almost any English novelist from Fielding to Ian McEwan are all pretty much absent from his books. His preferred mode was the interior monologue: what dialogue there is in his novels, he hedges around with ironical disclaimers. His preferred central character was himself, unapologetic and undisguised: when presenting 'fictional' characters he makes it clear that they are authorial puppets, with no pretence of inner reality; Johnson's novels were always written 'without any question of destroying the reader's suspension of disbelief, since such suspension was not to be attempted'.[4] And he disdained plot because 'Life does not tell stories. Life is chaotic, fluid, random; it leaves myriads of ends untied, untidily. Writers can extract a story from life only by strict, close selection, and this must mean falsification. Telling stories really is telling lies.'[5]

Johnson was not the first person to hold this view. Mistrust of the imagination, and of the falsehoods into which it threatens to lead us, goes back a long way: as far back as Plato, at the very least. It's an extreme position, all the same, and not one which you would expect to sit comfortably with the role of novelist. But then, Johnson wasn't interested in making life easy for himself. He took up other extreme positions, both in his professional and his personal life. Ultimately, these positions – and the chain of random circumstances with which they disastrously intersected – proved destructive. He took his own life at the age of forty, in November 1973.

*

B. S. Johnson was a vigorous polemicist, and when I next discovered him – ten years after that first, uncomprehending encounter with his televised image in my parents' living room – I fell powerfully under his spell. I had emerged from the experience of reading English at Cambridge only lightly scathed and imbued with a thriving, unshakeable contempt for anyone who had had the temerity to attempt the writing of literature in the last seventy or eighty years. It's true that there were one or two figures whose presumption in this regard was forgiven by the cartel of dons whose job it had been to oversee the development of my undergraduate mind: pre-eminent among these was Samuel Beckett, who despite having the bad manners to remain alive at this date had already been thoroughly canonized by the Cambridge cardinals. Beckett, you were allowed to admit, was a genius. Well, I couldn't see it with his later stuff, and still can't, but I obediently fell in love with his early novels, and a couple of years later, when I was installed at Warwick University writing a thesis on the safely deceased Henry Fielding, I had thrust upon me a paperback called *Christie Malry's Own Double-Entry*, written by someone I had never heard of, B. S. Johnson, and saw that the cover was emblazoned, incredibly, with a puff from the great man, Samuel Beckett, himself! This seemed extraordinary. Surely Beckett did not normally give jacket quotations?* I read the novel in a couple of hours – as it can be read and as indeed it was intended to be read – and then devoured

---

* It's true, he didn't. See below, p. 353. Incidentally it was my friend Andrew Brewerton who lent me his copy of Johnson's novel. Public credit where it's long overdue.

everything else I could find by B. S. Johnson. Which, at any other place in Britain in the mid-1980s, would have been very little (his work being almost entirely out of print by then). But Bernard Bergonzi, then a professor in the Warwick English department, had been a friendly critic of Johnson's in the 1960s* and had seen to it that the university library had a complete set of his books, even the unbound *Unfortunates*. So I was in luck.

Knowing almost nothing about contemporary British writing, and having thoroughly mastered, at Cambridge, the art of the sweeping, uninformed dismissal, I was more than ready to concur with B. S. Johnson's theories about the modern novel. Yes, of course it was all hopeless and old-fashioned. Of course there was no point in writing anything that didn't follow straight on from *Ulysses* and *The Unnamable*. (Although this did not stop me, on the sly, from working on my own essentially social-realist novels when I should have been writing my thesis.) More recently, needless to say, this conviction has slipped out of my grasp, along with most of the other certainties of youth. If I think about it at all, I see the high modernism of Joyce and Beckett as a straitjacket the novel had to break out of – just as late twentieth-century composers, if classical music was ever going to move forward again, had to make a decisive break with the twelve-tone system. Stories – those 'lies' which are not lies at all because they are shared, because they are part of an honest pact in which both writer and reader are complicit – remain the bedrock of the novel; narrative curiosity (dismissed by Johnson as 'that primitive, vulgar and idle curiosity of the reader to know "what happens next"') remains the centrifugal force which draws readers back to the novel and therefore keeps it alive. In the three decades since Johnson's death, the British novel has reinvigorated itself in other ways, ways which he did not foresee: not by 'making it new' with ever more radical attempts at formal innovation, but by recognizing the multi-ethnicity of modern Britain and opening itself to influences from other cultures; by tapping into the energies of popular film, music and television; by turning its back on modernist elitism and rediscovering the pleasures of humour, storytelling, demotic, and so on. All of which is not to say that the British novel is in better shape than it was in 1973, merely that it has survived, and will continue to survive, even while *Finnegans Wake* and Beckett's *Trilogy* come to seem less and less like meaningful points of reference for most of its practitioners. On this point, it would seem, I've parted company with B. S. Johnson: for the time being, at any rate. Perhaps I shall come round to him again in my twilight years.

More importantly, there are so many other things to admire in Johnson's work, even if you reject his dogma: his command of language, his freshness,

---

* See below, p. 231.

his formal ingenuity, the humanity that shines through even his most rigorous experiments, his bruising honesty. For all of these, he remains one of my greatest literary heroes. And above all, I suppose, for the simple reason that he took himself, and his art – or craft, vocation, call it what you will – so seriously. Because, in spite of what he said, it's not the reactionaries or the old fogeys who pose the greatest threat to the novel. It's the dilettantes. The gentlemen (and -women) amateurs. The resting actors and the bored journalists and the ubiquitous media people hungry for kudos and the talented but directionless Oxbridge graduates who've all got agents queuing up to take them out to lunch. And because it's so easy for these people to get published, we end up with bookshops piled from floor to ceiling with novels that aren't really novels at all, written by people who haven't given the form and its possibilities a tenth of the thought that B. S. Johnson gave to it before he even set pen to paper.

I wasn't planning to use this introduction as a soapbox. Really I have found myself writing the above to try to explain the apparent paradox of a novelist who loves (traditional) novels writing the biography of a novelist who seemed to hate them. But for all that I now disagree with much of what he wrote and believed, I have to say that, in the course of preparing this book, I have found myself empathizing with B. S. Johnson more closely than ever before. This is because I have finally come to know, over the last few years, what it's like to force yourself to work within a set of assumptions that you fundamentally distrust. In my case, these are the assumptions that underpin the writing of – and public appetite for – literary biography.

Like B. S. Johnson, I have a strong puritanical streak, and it remains one of my core beliefs that a work of literature should speak for itself, without the need for glossing, interpreting or contextualizing by reference to its writer's life. But how naive that sounds, even as I write it down! We live in a culture of radio and television interviews, newspaper profiles, public readings with question-and-answer sessions, which has ensured that novels themselves – far from being seen as self-contained statements, as having anything remotely *final* about them – have merely become one (early) stage in a larger process: a process devoted, essentially, to the scrutiny and interrogation of writers' lives in the name of that insatiable curiosity which feeds on anyone reckless enough to set themselves up as a public figure. No one retains any real sense of the novel itself, in other words, as a reliable model of human nature: we have lost all semblance of that kind of faith in literature, or in the trustworthiness of writers. Which means, in effect, that we no longer *read* literature at all: we cross-examine it, forensically, in the light of its writers' lives, assuming that it's in the gaps, the interstices, the shortfalls between theory and practice that the real truths about human nature will emerge. This has brought about a radical change of emphasis, enabling a situation in which people know far more about Philip Larkin's political beliefs, or Ted Hughes's treatment of his wife, than they know (or care) about their poetry. A situation in which the actor Kate Winslet can declare, triumphantly and without irony, that she is a 'huge fan' of Iris Murdoch even though she has never read any of her books.

It seems, nowadays, that literature is discussed more than ever before; but at the same time, it has never been less valued. And literary biography (for which the British have a unique passion) has had a large part to play in making this state of affairs possible. Milan Kundera predicted as much more than a decade ago, when he dismissed the whole genre by pointing out that

> the novelist destroys the house of his life and uses its stones to build the house of his novel. A novelist's biographers thus undo what a novelist has done, and redo what he undid. All their labour cannot illuminate either the value or the meaning of a novel, can scarcely even identify a few of the bricks. The moment Kafka attracts more attention than Joseph K., Kafka's posthumous death begins.[6]

And yes, this is a truth I hold to be self-evident; but it doesn't quite apply, in B. S. Johnson's case. Slippery as the relationship is between Kafka and Joseph K, the relationship between B. S. Johnson the novelist and 'B. S. Johnson' the – hero? central character? subject? – of his own novels is more slippery still. This is a man who wrote novels only about *himself*, with passionate honesty: or at least convinced himself that he did. He also wrote novels 'especially to exorcise, to remove from myself, from my mind, the burden [of] having to bear some pain, the hurt of some experience: in order that it may be over there, in a book, and not here in my mind'.[7] It's banal, admittedly, to state that in Johnson's case, considering the manner of his death, this endeavour did not work. But doesn't this dreadful fact raise an important question about the novel, about what it can and can't achieve? About the limits of its ability to console us? I think I've finally realized that it's my need to answer this question – or to establish once and for all that there is no answer – that has seen me (just about) through the often uncomfortable process of sifting through the private archives of a man I now know better than most of my closest friends, but who somehow still remains, for all his novelistic candour, a perfect stranger to me.

Anyway, that is why the book you're about to read has the look, at times, more of a dossier than a conventional literary biography. It contains its fair share of guesswork, and was compiled with plenty of selectivity; but my guiding principle – given that I am dealing here with events that were sometimes barely understood by those who lived through them, and are now barely remembered by those who have survived (let alone by me, who was still in short trousers at the time, and living hundreds of miles away) –

has been to tell the story as much as I can in Johnson's own words, quoting directly, and in the words of those who have spoken to me about him. The result will be fragmentary, unpolished. There will be gaps, where through misfortune or obstruction or sometimes sheer inertia I will not have been able to find out as much as I would have liked. And where I lapse into speculation, I shall try to be upfront about it. I shall try to be honest. That much at least Johnson himself would have appreciated.

My strategy will be this. Many of the people picking up this book will not (regrettably) have read anything by B. S. Johnson before. Revered though he is by a few, he is unknown nowadays to most British readers under forty. So I shall begin by explaining, in a little more detail, what it was that he wrote and that I think he achieved. After that, *pace* Milan Kundera, I shall have to bring myself to knock down the walls of his house and we shall take a wander together through the rubble, perhaps shaking our heads in awe and wonderment at the melancholy grandeur of the ruins we find there. Then, by way of interlude, we shall listen to some different people talking about B. S. Johnson, arguing amongst themselves even though these are – in most cases – people who have never actually met each other. And last of all, a short coda. In which I shall attempt to put forward my own, highly personal – and, yes, speculative – thoughts about the forces that may have been driving him in his last few days and hours: a 'transcursion into his mind' – to use Johnsonian language – or even (the phrase is from his fifth novel, *House Mother Normal*) 'a diagram of certain aspects of the inside of his skull', as he gets ready to compose his final message to the world; to write his very last word.

Before we get that far, however, I hope there will be plenty to enjoy along the way. We're talking about novels, after all, and novels, even gloomy ones, are supposed to cheer us up, to provide recompense, when life isn't all that it should be. Supposed, in short, to give us pleasure.

Aren't they?

A LIFE IN SEVEN NOVELS

One of the last important things B. S. Johnson wrote, about six months before he died, was an introduction to his collection of 'shorter prose', *Aren't You Rather Young To Be Writing Your Memoirs?*. This essay became, and remains, probably the most famous and frequently quoted item in the Johnson oeuvre: a belligerent critique of the conservatism of modern British writing, and an impassioned apologia for his own methods.

Here he lambasted those figures who continued to write 'as though the revolution that was *Ulysses* had never happened', insisting that any attempt, in the early 1970s, to follow the practice of the great nineteenth-century novelists was 'anachronistic, invalid, irrelevant and perverse'. 'Present-day reality', he argued, 'is markedly different from [. . .] nineteenth-century reality. Then it was possible to believe in pattern and eternity, but today what characterises reality is the possibility that chaos is the most likely explanation'. He went on to quote Samuel Beckett:

> What I am saying does not mean that there will henceforth be no form in art. It only means that there will be new form, and that this form will be of such a type that it admits the chaos, and does not try to say that the chaos is really something else. [. . .] To find a form that accommodates the mess, that is the task of the artist now.

Towards the end of the essay, Johnson also drew up a short list of the contemporary British writers for whom he felt some sort of qualified admiration or affinity. But he did not specifically state that he had chosen them because their work was 'experimental' (a word he came to dislike) or even innovative or unconventional. The reason he gave, instead, was that they were people 'who are writing as though it mattered, as though they meant it, as though they meant it to matter'.

This is a subjective criterion, of course. But if we are to make a case for B. S. Johnson as one of the most significant writers of the 1960s, I think that these are the terms we should use, first of all. Johnson maintained that the neo-Dickensian novel was dead, and that writers who did not follow loyally in the footsteps of Joyce and the other modernists were deluding themselves. As I have said, I'm no longer convinced that this is a very helpful position to take up: but as for whether *he* wrote as though it mattered, as though he meant it, as though he meant it to matter – well, that's an easy one. The 1960s throw up few bodies of work as compelling, as coherent, as intelligent and deeply felt as B. S. Johnson's. Let us set aside for a moment his poetry, his films, his stage and television plays, and look solely at the seven novels which were his crowning achievement. Together, they constitute a frank and courageous (if incomplete) spiritual autobiography; a gloomy meditation on the treacherous randomness of life (the unreliability of human relationships, the body's propensity to decay); and, not least impressively – again, to quote Johnson himself, writing in his penultimate novel – a 'continuous dialogue with form', a pained examination of his own role as novelist which is anything but academic and self-referential.

To make this case more fully, let's look at each of these novels in turn. Always with the proviso that any readers who feel that they already know them inside out, or who are – for various perfectly sound reasons of their own – not interested in my critical judgements, can fast-forward to the second part of this book, where they will perhaps find more to engage them.

1: *TRAVELLING PEOPLE*

Written 1959–61 (Johnson's age at time of writing: 26–8)

First published 1963: Constable hardback

Other editions 1964: Corgi paperback; 1967: Panther paperback

In his first novel, we find Johnson testing the water: it contains plenty of experiments with form, but they are not radical. Each chapter is written in a different mode (third-person, epistolary, film script, stream of consciousness, and so on), but this veneer of stylistic adventurousness hides a conventional enough Bildungsroman, based closely on some of Johnson's own most recent experiences, and featuring a central character who is a routinely fictionalized version of the author himself.

This character is called Henry Henry, and as the novel opens he has just graduated in philosophy from London University. Hitch-hiking from London to Holyhead en route to Dublin, he explains to one of the drivers who picks him up that 'I've just finished a university course, and I want very much to relax after the strain of finals.' The driver, whose name is Trevor, offers him a temporary job helping out at an exclusive country club in Aberfyllin, north Wales, called the Stromboli Club, which caters for wealthy businesspeople from the Midlands and the north of England (what we would nowadays call the nouveau riche). Henry accepts the offer, and arrives at the club one month later after a brief holiday in Dublin with his friend Robert.

Once installed at the Stromboli Club, Henry finds himself caught up in the rivalry between Trevor, the manager, and the punningly named Maurie Bunde, the ageing playboy who owns the club and uses it to live out the fantasy that he is still young and attractive to the opposite sex. Maurie is secretly sharing a bed with Kim, another young member of the staff, who soon strikes up a rapport (platonic, at first) with Henry. The ensuing personal and romantic tensions are explored at some considerable length – this being the longest of Johnson's novels – until events arrive at a climax of sorts with the death of Maurie, due to a combination of athletic and sexual overexertion. This frees up Kim to have a brief but ecstatic physical relationship with Henry, after which they decide that they are not right for each other. They both leave the club ('Adam and Eve,' as Henry puts it, 'cast out of the Garden of Gorgeous Hydrangeas!') and resume their separate travels. The last we see of Henry, he is sitting in a working-class transport cafe, 'replete but feeling he had never enjoyed a meal less', and reflecting that, after a whole summer spent watching the idle rich at play in supposedly Edenic surroundings, he would rather be sitting down to an indifferent meal in the company of lorry drivers. '*This* is paradise,' he tells himself, looking around.

Johnson would later refer to *Travelling People* as a 'disaster', and claim that he did not want it to be reprinted. But this was a moral, not a literary judgement: he came to dislike it because it mingled fiction with autobiography in a way which he regarded as dishonest. In many ways, however, it is one of his most engaging novels. The constant shifting between different forms, styles and points of view creates a rich, satisfying texture. The characters are solid, well drawn. And the novel is full of incidental passages, throwaway detail, which prove that, even at this early stage in his development, Johnson was a rigorous, alert, imaginative prose stylist, with a poet's exactitude and respect for language; something which even his most virulent detractors have never tried to deny:

> The curious wind turning over the pages of a newspaper caught his eye; Henry went over and picked it up, and as he did so his legs protested that they had not been rested for over half an hour now. Henry accordingly tore out the only section of a newspaper that interested him, that column devoted to those fortunate enough to have died but unfortunate enough to have left something behind by which to be remembered, and spread out the rest on a sloping stratum of exposed granite; calculating that he could depend upon approximately ten minutes' sit before the porosity of the paper transmitted the dampness of the rock to his trousers, he began to read.

What unbalances *Travelling People*, what makes it an oddly misshapen novel, is the discrepancy between Johnson's elaborate attention to form and the essential thinness of the narrative material. Perhaps this is to say nothing more than that it is a first novel by a bright English graduate fresh out of university, who at that point in his life had done more reading than living. But considering the hugeness of the themes Johnson would take on in some of his later, shorter books, it seems excessive that he should devote more than 100,000 words here to a story of personal infighting at a high-class holiday resort. Grander claims have been made for the novel's preoccupations: in a personal letter written a few years later, Johnson insisted that 'TP is about old age, illusion and reality'.[1] But it's hard to see how the book does anything more than glance in this direction: Maurie Bunde, who provides the only real example of self-deceiving old age, is a minor character compared to Henry Henry. The narrative focuses almost exclusively on Henry's own sentimental education, and in substance this theme is both lightweight and entirely conventional.

Now out of print for more than thirty years, *Travelling People* remains very enjoyable, both for its narrative high spirits (which Johnson would not recapture until the jet-black comedy of *Christie Malry's Own Double-Entry*, a full decade later) and for the energy with which it kicks off his lifelong 'dialogue with form'. It is a good first novel, which from today's vantage point – considering that it was published in the same year as Thomas Pynchon's *V*, and one year after *A Clockwork Orange* and *The Golden Notebook* – nonetheless scarcely seems like a groundbreaking piece of work.

2: *ALBERT ANGELO*

Written Autumn 1962 to July 1963 (Johnson's age at time of writing: 29–30)

First published 1964: Constable hardback

Other editions 1967: Panther paperback; 1987: New Directions paperback; 2004: Picador (as part of *B. S. Johnson Omnibus*)

Johnson's second novel draws on his experiences as a supply teacher in a series of tough north London state schools in the early 1960s. At this point in his life he still considered his poetry to be more important than his novels: poetry, he believed, was his true vocation, and supply teaching was the deeply unsatisfactory means by which he was obliged to support it. In *Albert Angelo* he fictionalizes this situation through the character of Albert, a frustrated architect who lives – as B. S. Johnson did at the time – in a rented room in an early Victorian square in the Angel district of north London.

Johnson's dissatisfaction with traditional novelistic 'plots' was already complete by this stage, and the narrative of *Albert Angelo* is entirely fragmentary and episodic. We see Albert at his drawing board, attempting to design buildings; we see him conducting lessons, attempting to get his pupils interested in geology while his own thoughts are somewhere else altogether; in some of the most vivid passages, we see him travelling through north London's nocturnal, multi-ethnic cityscape, drifting from late-night cafe to late-night cafe in the company of his friend Terry, both of them single and embittered by what they consider to be 'betrayals' by their respective girlfriends. Albert, in particular, is morosely preoccupied by a failed affair with a woman called Jenny, and he spends much of the novel picking over the bones of the relationship with miserable obsessiveness. All the time, meanwhile, his pupils grow more and more violent and unruly. Previous teachers have committed suicide or had nervous breakdowns, and in the book's one concession to narrative tension there seems to be a slow-burning threat that the class might be planning to do something unspeakable to Albert himself.

And so the novel proceeds, for 161 of its 178 pages. Suddenly, however, its progress is disrupted by a colossal authorial intervention – 'OH, FUCK ALL THIS LYING' – and we are plunged into a section called 'Disintegration'. Here, in what seems to be nothing less than a gesture of profound moral disgust, Johnson sloughs off all the pretences which he has been sustaining throughout the rest of the book. The voice moves into an urgent, almost unpunctuated present tense:

> — fuck all this lying look what im really trying to write about it is writing not all this stuff about architecture trying to say something about writing about my writing im my hero though what a useless appellation my first character then im trying to say something about me through him albert an architect when whats the point in covering up covering up covering over pretending pretending I can say anything through him that is anything that I would be interested in saying

> — so an almighty aposiopesis

> — Im trying to say something not tell a story telling stories is telling lies and I want to tell the truth about me about my experience about my truth about my truth to reality about sitting here writing looking out across Claremont Square trying to say something about the writing and nothing being an answer to the loneliness to the lack of loving ...

> — look, I'm trying to tell you something of what I feel about being a poet in a world where only poets care anything real about poetry, through the objective correlative of an architect who has to earn his living as a teacher.

this device you cannot have failed to see creaking, ill-fitting at many places, many places, for architects *manqués* can earn livings very nearly connected with their art, and no poet has ever lived by his poetry, and architecture has a functional aspect quite lacking in poetry, and, simply, architecture is just not poetry.

This section concludes with Johnson advising his readers to 'Go elsewhere for their lies. Life is not like that, is just not like that.' But he provides some conciliation by adding, 'even I [...] would not leave such a mess, such a mess, so many loose ends.' And so there follows a perfunctory return to fiction in the one-and-a-half-page 'Coda', which finds Albert's pupils throwing him into the local canal and leaving him there to drown.

For Johnson, this novel marked an irreversible breakthrough in terms of his personal aesthetic. 'I really discovered what I should be doing with *Albert Angelo* ... where I broke through the English disease of the objective correlative to speak truth directly if solipsistically in the novel form, and heard my own small voice.'[2] He prefaced the book with an extract from *The Unnamable* by Samuel Beckett, to whose theory and practice of the novel he maintained, throughout his life, a slavish devotion, and chose a passage in which Beckett describes the time he has spent creating fictional characters as 'wasted [...] when I had me, on the premises, within easy reach'. 'There is nothing else,' the extract continues, 'let us be lucid for once, nothing else but what happens to me.' And this, from now on, would become Johnson's extraordinary, rigorous, constraining rule as a novelist: to write about 'nothing else but what happens to me'.

It should be added that *Albert Angelo*, for all its downbeat subject matter (and it is, essentially, the self-portrait of a depressive personality), is for the most part an extremely exuberant novel. The fragments of subversive and sometimes wildly surreal schoolboy essays Johnson presents are very funny; there is an appealing knockabout bleakness to Albert and Terry's nocturnal jaunts; and the book, which is even more 'experimental' in form than *Travelling People*, contains some of Johnson's most ingenious devices. The most famous of these is a rectangular hole cut through two of the recto pages (pages 147 and 149) so that the reader can see through to a future event described on page 151. As with the earlier novel, the variety of styles, voices and techniques is recognizably part of a lucid attempt to capture the multifaceted nature of empirical reality. With deadly seriousness (which is not the same as earnestness) Johnson was setting out to capture the 'truth' by any and every means available.

3: *TRAWL*

Written June to December 1965 (Johnson's age at time of writing: 32)

First published 1966: Secker & Warburg hardback

Other editions 1968: Panther paperback;
2004: Picador (as part of *B. S. Johnson Omnibus*)

Trawl finds Johnson, for the first time, not even toying with the fictional and quasi-fictional trappings which had started to disgust him so much in his two previous novels. It is, according to the author himself, 'all interior monologue, a representation of the inside of my mind but at one stage removed; the closest one can come in writing'. His publisher at that time, Fred Warburg of Secker & Warburg, considered it to be not a novel but an autobiography. Johnson disagreed: 'It is a novel, I insisted and could prove; what it is not is fiction.'³ Quite how he would have gone about 'proving' this remains unclear. There is at the very least, then, a formal ambiguity about the book which makes it hard to summarize in conventional terms.

Trawl contains no plot and no invented characters, although some of the names of real people were changed for legal reasons. It describes, in the first person, a three-week voyage Johnson himself undertook as a supernumerary on a deep-sea fishing trawler in the Barents Sea. Intercut with these descriptions are numerous flashbacks, recalling incidents from Johnson's past, many of them romantic or sexual, most of them unhappy or unsatisfactory. In particular we are told a great deal about his long, lonely periods of evacuation during the Second World War, and his failed romance at King's College London with a fellow undergraduate. (The same woman who appears in *Albert Angelo*, first as Jenny and then – under her real name – as Muriel. In *Trawl* she is called Gwen.)

On the third page of the book, the narrator gives his reasons for having made the voyage: 'to shoot the narrow trawl of my mind into the vasty sea of my past'. The journey is a conscious, willed attempt to provoke recollection, reflection and finally, it is hoped, understanding of the narrator's abiding sense of failure and isolation. B. S. Johnson the novelist, however, and B. S. Johnson the narrator and central character of *Trawl* cannot be exactly the same person, because when Johnson himself undertook this voyage in October 1963 he had a second reason for doing so: to provide himself, quite deliberately and specifically, with material for a novel. No mention is made in *Trawl* of this motive, or indeed of the novel-writing process itself, which took place two years later, despite the fact that the book is narrated in the present tense. There are therefore two 'B. S. Johnsons' present within the book, existing in an uneasy and shifting relationship with one another. Perhaps this was what he meant when he described the novel as operating 'at one stage removed; the closest one can come in writing'.

Johnson may have been adamant that *Trawl* was a bona fide novel, not an autobiography, but he was also quite happy to see it described as a long narrative poem. This designation seemed to him perfectly accurate. It is, of all his novels, the one in which his prose is at its most lyrical, charged and inventive, and the passages evoking life aboard the trawler are among the best he ever wrote.

> The first real sunset of the trip, as well, today: great blazing streamers bar the sky like long banners at a tourney, the light alchemizes the brass of the bridge into winedark gold: now the short northern autumn day closes quickly: the coast, of Norway is it, or of Russia, appears only as a formal change in the pattern of clouds on our port side. Down below on the deck the lights steadily illuminate no activity but the swell of the water in the washer, and the way starfish and the white bellies of dabs move unnaturally in the bilges. A fishgut hangs like a hank of hair from the iron grill in a pound board [...] The green bleep from the fishfinder now catches the Skipper's intentness as he sits over this talismanic yet scientific aid to fishing, brighter now than the sun · · · · · ·
> Yes, it has been a good day. I shall sleep tonight.

The novel concludes, rather unusually for Johnson, on a tentative grace note of hope. Shortly before making the voyage on which *Trawl* was based, he had begun a relationship with Virginia Kimpton, the beautiful daughter of affluent middle-class parents. 'Ginnie', as he called her, appears at the end of the novel, her identity undisguised, waiting unexpectedly on the quayside to greet her lover as the trawler comes into port. Just before glimpsing her, the narrator realizes that his voyage has been a success, and he feels purged of his memories: 'It is as though I have at last paid off some vast emotional debt that I had incurred through all my years: that I have earned enough to repay that debt, in these last three weeks.' He now feels capable of clinging to some 'vision of a future not more than five years off: Ginnie as wife, a child, a son, perhaps, the chyme sliding down his chin, freedom to work as I have to work, a home: in the far hope of that happiness, I give life one more chance.'

When he wrote these words, Johnson might already have felt that the vision had been realized (he and Virginia did have a son by then, for instance); but our knowledge of what happened to him later gives the passage a terrible retrospective poignancy. We might think, as well, that to 'give life one more chance' simply because of a new relationship is to impose a terrible burden of expectation upon your latest partner. Bearing all of which in mind, it feels somehow heartless to pass *literary* judgement on the ending of *Trawl*. But our business, for the moment, is with literature only, and it needs to be remarked that there is something forced, something *unachieved*, about the way that *Trawl* finally abandons its mode of anguished recollection for this qualified stirring of optimism. It coincides with the ship's return to England a little too patly and there seems to have been no actual breakthrough in the narrator's process of self-examination, no real moment of catharsis, to prepare us for it. But this is one of the few blemishes in a novel which otherwise ranks as one of Johnson's finest.

4: *THE UNFORTUNATES*

Written Spring to September 1967 (Johnson's age at time of writing: 34)

First published 1969: Panther in association with Secker & Warburg

Other editions 1999: Picador

This is B. S. Johnson's most famous – or notorious – novel: the one in which the twenty-seven sections are presented, unbound, in a small box, to be shuffled and read in whichever random order the reader happens to take them. It was his most extreme attempt to remain faithful to reality – the defining characteristic of which he now saw to be chaos.

Its subject matter, however, is orthodox enough. While still an undergraduate at King's College London, Johnson had been editor of the student magazine *Lucifer*, and had once made a trip to Nottingham to make friendly contact with the editorial board of that university's magazine. On this trip he had been introduced to a Nottingham undergraduate called Tony Tillinghast, and the two became close friends. The friendship was spiky and combative: Tony was a serious, assiduous scholar, bent on an academic career; Johnson professed to despise academia, claiming that the work of literary critics and historians was only worthwhile if it helped writers to produce better books. Taking up this challenge, Tony had read *Travelling People* in manuscript, chapter by chapter as Johnson wrote it, scribbling copious annotations in the margin. The novel had been dedicated to him and his wife June. And then, in late 1962, Tony had been diagnosed with cancer. Two years later he was dead, at the age of just twenty-nine. *The Unfortunates* is Johnson's telling of the story of this friendship, and this death.

In terms of its narrative mode, the novel follows on almost seamlessly from *Trawl*: again, it is 'all interior monologue', with episodes from the past intercut with present-tense action. This time, the scenes in the present take place at a football match in an unnamed English provincial city. As in *Albert Angelo*, Johnson was here drawing on another aspect of his professional life:

in the mid-1960s, after giving up supply teaching, he supported himself by various kinds of journalism including sports reporting. For a while he was a soccer reporter for the *Observer*, and the starting point of *The Unfortunates* is that he has, in this capacity, been sent out one Saturday afternoon to cover a match; when he arrives at his destination, he realizes that it is the same city where Tony studied as a postgraduate, and where Johnson himself used to visit him. For the rest of that afternoon, as the narrator attempts to concentrate on the task of reporting the football game, memories of Tony keep recurring, resurfacing, interposing themselves.

This, to Johnson's way of thinking, posed a very specific technical problem:

> The memories of Tony and the routine football reporting, the past and the present, interwove in a completely random manner, without chronology. This is the way the mind works, my mind anyway [... But] this randomness was directly in conflict with the technological fact of the bound book: for the bound book imposes an order, a fixed page order, on the material. I think I went some way towards solving this problem by writing the book in sections and having those sections not bound together but loose in a box.[4]

Christine Brooke-Rose – a writer who might have been expected to sympathize with Johnson's enterprise (he did, after all, include her in his highly selective roll-call of honour in the introduction to *Aren't You Rather Young To Be Writing Your Memoirs?*) – declared herself unimpressed by *The Unfortunates*. She thought it was not as original as Burroughs's cut-up experiments, where the 'random element is introduced at source, as part of the creative process', and she concluded that 'in whatever order one reads *The Unfortunates*, it is still a realistic and dreary novel of a football player returning to his Midlands home-town.'[5] Quite apart from the fact that this ungenerous verdict is based on a misremembering of the novel's subject matter, it also – rather more tellingly – fails even to recognize that the book might be intended to have an emotional impact. Certainly there is nothing very sophisticated about Johnson's central conceit: randomly ordered pages as a tangible metaphor for the random interplay of memories and impressions in the human mind (and also, let us not forget, for football itself, where the play proceeds randomly within a framework of rules and conventions). Other writers of the period – including Christine Brooke-Rose herself, along with Alan Burns and Rayner Heppenstall – may have been ringing far more cerebral changes on the novel's possibilities. But if Johnson's work stands up better today than most of the writing of his 'experimental' peers, this has everything to do with the fact that he refused – or was unable – to sacrifice intensity of feeling on the altar of formal ingenuity, and *The*

Unfortunates is the supreme example of this. To read it is to be drawn, inexorably, by the coiled, unyielding threads of Johnson's prose, into a vortex of shared grief. On this level it is a challenging and deeply affecting novel: though more thoroughly lacking in humour than any of the others, except perhaps *Trawl.*

It is also the first of Johnson's books to be concerned with disease and bodily decay, themes which would come to trouble and preoccupy him more and more from this point onwards. The physical descriptions of Tony's cancer-ravaged body are unsparing:

> His cheeks sallowed and collapsed round the insinuated bones, the gums shrivelled, was it, or shrunken, his teeth now standing free of each other in the unnatural half yawn of his mouth, yes, the mouth that had been so full-fleshed, the whole face, too, now collapsed, derelict, the thick-framed glasses the only constant, the mouth held open as in a controlled scream, but no sound, the head moving only slightly, the white dried and sticky saliva, the last secretions of those harassed glands, cauterized into deficiency . . .

If the whole novel had proceeded in this vein it might have been unbearable. As it is, while the book never becomes exactly cheery, there are incidental pleasures along the way: the frustrations and compromises of the football reporter's art evoked with comic accuracy, some fine descriptions of provincial architecture (the city, though never named, was in fact Nottingham), and above all a modest, deep-rooted, intellectually vibrant friendship celebrated in conscientious detail. Johnson's assurance to the dying Tony had been, 'I'll get it all down, mate.' *The Unfortunates* was his faithful and loving fulfilment of that promise.

5: *HOUSE MOTHER NORMAL*

Written February to July 1970 (Johnson's age at time of writing: 37)

First published 1971: Trigram Press and Collins, simultaneous editions

Other editions 1973: Quartet; 1986: Bloodaxe; 1986: New Directions paperback;
2004: Picador paperback (as part of *B. S. Johnson Omnibus*)

Three years passed between the writing of *The Unfortunates* and *House Mother Normal,* the longest interval between novels in Johnson's career. His fifth novel also marked a decisive and somewhat surprising change of mode, away from first-person confessional. What we have here is precisely the opposite, in fact: a novel which shows one single (and fictional!) event from ten different points of view.

House Mother Normal is set inside an old people's home. The nine inmates are sitting down to dinner, along with the House Mother herself, and Johnson gives us ten interior monologues, each purporting to offer a transcription of one character's thoughts as the evening's entertainment unfolds. One of the dark jokes at the heart of the novel is that each successive character is more infirm than the last, so that the monologues get more and more fragmented, partial and incoherent as the book progresses. Thus Sarah Lamson, who is aged seventy-four, with her hearing seventy-five per cent intact and a maximum CQ count* of ten, thinks more or less lucidly and coherently; by the time we've got to George Hedbury, aged eighty-nine and with a CQ count of only two (and also suffering from incontinence, advanced senile depression and intermittent renal failure among other complaints), we are reduced to a few disconnected words strewn apparently at random over the page. Finally we get the House Mother's own version of events, which turns out to be even more unreliable – or at least bizarre – than those of her elderly charges. Johnson's intention was that we should be left wondering, at the end of the book, who is the more 'normal': a decrepit old man whose perceptions have become blurred through senility, or the callously uncaring young woman who is supposed to be looking after him?

House Mother Normal is the novel Johnson fans can wave in front of his detractors when they accuse him of being a limited novelist, lacking in sympathy for anyone but himself, his imagination circumscribed by a lifelong introversion bordering on solipsism. This criticism does not hold water, where his fifth novel is concerned. It is the one book in which he does 'characterization' (albeit through the medium of his beloved interior monologue), and certainly the only one in which he attempts to think himself, with some degree of plausibility, into the minds of his female characters. But what's even more impressive, to my mind, is that this unaccustomed breadth of human sympathy coexists with – even arises out of – a technical 'experiment' that is as rigorous and audacious as anything he attempted. Taking his cue from Philip Toynbee's novel *Tea with Mrs Goodman,*[†] he divides the book into ten sections of twenty-one pages each, and ensures that in every section, the same event (and the characters' differing responses to it) occurs not just on the same page but at precisely the same point on that page: so that the whole book becomes – to use a musical analogy – richly polyphonic, fugal, a novel that can be read 'verti-

---

* As Johnson explains in the text, a CQ count is 'the total of correct answers … given in response to the ten classic questions … for senile dementia'. The questions are: Where are you now? What is this place? What day is this? What month is it? What year is it? How old are you? What is your birthday? In what year were you born? Who is on the throne now – king or queen? Who was on the throne before?

† Published in 1947: see below, pp. 296–8.

cally' as well as 'horizontally'. And while with some avant-garde novelists (Toynbee himself, for instance) such an experiment might seem chilly and over-calculated, Johnson miraculously avoids this pitfall. His characteristic forthrightness, his inability to mask his emotions at any time – which may well have been part of his downfall, in his real-life dealings with other people – here guarantees that technical brilliance is never given precedence over a humane and proper response to the characters' pitiable situation.

Johnson had been planning to write *House Mother Normal* for many years. The idea came to him while writing *Travelling People*, he said, but 'the subsequent three personal novels interposed themselves, demanded to be written first'.[6] But *Albert Angelo*, *Trawl* and *The Unfortunates* form so coherent a sequence, in the way they show Johnson moving towards and then adhering to his highly specific concept of novelistic truth, that it feels as though *House Mother Normal* is the book that 'interposes itself'. What has happened to his Beckettian resolve to write about 'nothing else but what happens to me'? His fifth novel contains a gesture towards it, nothing more. As I said, each of the interior monologues is twenty-one pages long – apart from the House Mother's. She is allowed twenty-two pages, and on the last of these, Johnson makes her come forward and speak to the reader in her own voice: 'Thus you see I too am the puppet or concoction of a writer (you always knew there was a writer behind it all? Ah, there's no fooling you readers!), a writer who has me at present standing in the post-orgasmic nude but who still expects me to be his words without embarrassment or personal comfort. So you see this is from his skull. It is a diagram of certain aspects of the inside of his skull! What a laugh!'

The implication here is a contradictory one: it *is* permissible to fictionalize, to make things up, apparently, but only if you come clean about it in the end. And yet, as Johnson's own words make clear, there is actually no need to come clean about it, because 'there's no fooling you readers!': he already recognizes, in other words, that readers are sophisticated beings who are quite capable of deciding for themselves what is true and what isn't.

Quite apart from this contradiction there is suddenly a new and disturbing note of weariness in Johnson's writing. You can hear it in the shoulder-shrugging admission that 'there's no fooling you readers!' and in the tired sarcasm of 'What a laugh!' It's a note which seems even more pronounced in the shorter prose he was writing at around the same time. It's the sound, I think, of a writer beginning to give up on his own art; becoming bored by it; ceasing to believe, as he might once have believed, that it might somehow compensate him for the pain of living.

But now I am getting ahead of myself.

6: *CHRISTIE MALRY'S OWN DOUBLE-ENTRY*

Written December 1970 to March 1972 (Johnson's age at time of writing: 37–9)
First published 1973: Collins
Other editions 1974: Quartet; 1984: Penguin;
1985: New Directions paperback; 2001: Picador

Despite its decisive rejection of linear narrative, *House Mother Normal* found Johnson excelling, for once, at one of the traditional novelistic virtues: of all his books, it is the one with the greatest number of clearly delineated fictional characters. His sixth novel is even more approachable for the non-experimentally inclined reader. It is a brilliant, fast-paced black comedy, and is usually the point at which newcomers to B. S. Johnson are encouraged to start.

Christie Malry is a young accounts clerk at a confectionery factory in Hammersmith, west London. The era is unspecified, but seems to fall somewhere between the London of the 1970s and the drabber, more benighted city of the early 1950s. (Johnson himself had been an accounts clerk at just such a factory at the age of nineteen, in 1952.) Frustrated by the petty injustices and frustrations which seem to beset his life, and particularly by the behaviour of anyone in authority, Christie evolves a unique way of taking his revenge on society: a system of *moral* double-entry bookkeeping. This means that for every offence society commits against him, Christie feels entitled to exact recompense in order to balance the moral books: '*Every Debit must have its Credit, the First Golden Rule*', according to Fra Luca Bartolomeo Pacioli, the fifteenth-century Tuscan monk who invented double-entry bookkeeping and whose writings are quoted extensively throughout the novel.

At first Christie's grievances are small, and the payment he demands is correspondingly modest: resenting the presence of an office block which stands in his path, Christie claims recompense from the builder's heirs by scratching a line down its stone facing with the edge of a coin. When his office supervisor shows no sympathy over the death of his mother, Christie responds by destroying an important letter and landing him in trouble with a local restaurant owner. But before long, the campaign has become more sinister. In a particularly inventive move, Johnson generates suspense in this novel not within the narrative proper, but by reproducing a succession of the balance sheets from Christie's account book. Thus the reader is able to watch, with increasingly appalled fascination, as the figure for unpaid debt in the Recompense column – 'Balance owing to Christie carried forward to next Reckoning' – grows bigger and bigger.

Soon we realize that we are watching the development of a terrorist mentality. Small-scale atrocities (a bomb planted outside Hythe House, the office of the Collector of Taxes) and even larger ones (the killing of 20,000 west Londoners by adding poison to their water supply) cannot provide adequate recompense for such perceived offences as 'General diminution of Christie's life by advertising' and 'Socialism not given a chance' (which alone is estimated to be worth £311,398 in the Debit column). It becomes apparent that we are dealing with a man whose ingrained sense of personal and social injustice can never be mollified. Someone like this stands outside the norms of conventional literature just as he does outside the norms of society, so there seems no possible method of resolving the book's thematic tensions; and indeed Johnson doesn't attempt to. Reverting to his preoccupation with bodily decay and terminal illness, he has Christie abruptly develop cancer and die from it. The novel closes with this narrative whimper and the last thing we see is a chilling 'Final Reckoning' which includes a figure of £352,392 for 'Balance written off as Bad Debt'. The words 'Account Closed' are scrawled across the bottom.

Christie Malry's Own Double-Entry was the last full-length piece of work that B. S. Johnson completed to his own satisfaction. The bulk of the novel seems to have been written very quickly (mostly in February 1972), which might partly account for the mood of narrative high spirits which had not been apparent in his work since the closing chapters of *Travelling People* (also written in a feverish rush). *Christie Malry*'s distinctive tone arises from the tension between these high spirits and the overwhelmingly grim – not to mention nihilistic – vision of society Johnson offers. Although seemingly throwaway and spontaneous, this is not an easy trick to pull off, and somehow the novel's gleeful melange of humour and pessimism managed to curdle into something much more dampening in the recent feature film adaptation.[7] But Johnson, at least, knew exactly what he was doing, and the rejection of orthodox novelistic methods which was expressed in *House Mother Normal* with such tired contempt here feels radical and invigorating.

Nonetheless, there is a valedictory quality to some of the novel's later passages: a sense that the narrator is saying goodbye not just to Christie, his terminally ill hero, but to something else, more abstract but just as precious – his own terminally ill commitment to the novel as a form:

> 'Yes, Christie, you go on to the end,' I assured him, and myself went on: 'Surely no reader will wish me to invent anything further, surely he or she can extrapolate only too easily from what has gone before?'
>
> 'If there is a reader,' said Christie. 'Most people won't read it.'
>
> 'Politicians, policemen, some educators and many others treat "most people" as idiots.'
>
> 'So writers may too?'

'On the contrary. "Most people" are right not to read novels today.'
'You've said all this before.'
'I'm very likely to say it again, since it's true.'
A pause. Then suddenly Christie said:
'Your work has been a continuous dialogue with form?'
'If you like,' I replied diffidently.

When a writer has come to see so few possibilities left for the art form in which he has chosen to work, and is able to look back so dispassionately on his own achievement, it's hard not to feel that the end of his involvement with it must be almost in sight. And yet, remarkably, shortly after writing this passage, Johnson was to embark upon his most ambitious and personally demanding literary project yet.

7: *SEE THE OLD LADY DECENTLY*

Written December 1972 to September 1973 (Johnson's age at time of writing: 39–40)

First published 1975: Hutchinson

Other editions none

The scenes in *Christie Malry's Own Double-Entry* that show the hero dying of cancer were written within a few months of Johnson's own mother's death from the same disease. Profoundly affected, even devastated, by her death, Johnson seems almost immediately to have started thinking about how he could best memorialize her in a novel.

Like *House Mother Normal*, *Christie Malry* had grown out of a very early idea for a book, one which Johnson said he might have written towards the beginning of his career if his more personal novels had not 'interposed themselves' first. But now, with these two ideas out of the way, it was time to return to the journey he had first embarked upon almost ten years before when he declared, in *Albert Angelo*, that 'telling stories is telling lies'. The difference, this time, was that he was going to tell the truth about somebody else's life, not just his own.

The scheme Johnson proposed to himself was dizzyingly large and complex. He envisioned a trilogy, the three volumes to be called *See the Old Lady Decently*, *Buried Although* and *Amongst Those Left Are You*: the titles would run continuously across the three books' spines to form a single sentence. The focus of the trilogy would be a complete narrative of his mother's life, but two other, grander themes were to run concurrently: these were to be 'the decay of the mother country' and 'the renewal aspect of motherhood'.[8] After the rather small-scale, solipsistic authenticity he had achieved in *Trawl* and *The Unfortunates*, then, he was planning to give this new project not only a political dimension, but also – for want of a better word – a spiritual one. This marked a huge step forward in Johnson's literary ambition. His political views (like his views on everything else) were strong, but in his novels he had rarely done more than mention them in passing: now he was planning to compose a sustained critique of Britain's imperial and post-war decline, taking in most of the historical landmarks of the twentieth century.

It's even more intriguing that he was intending to write about 'the renewal aspect of motherhood' and in particular the Mother Goddess, drawing on the work of Jung and Erich Neumann. This aspect of the trilogy might seem surprising to those readers who are familiar only with Johnson the militant atheist of the previous six novels. Certainly he felt a hatred for established religion and especially – perhaps simply because it was closest to home – the Church of England; but this did not make him a complete rationalist. He had a fascination with paganism, witchcraft and the pre-Christian religions generally, which by and large he managed to keep at a safe distance from his work. But there are signs that by the time of 'The Matrix Trilogy' (as it was to be called), and indeed the film *Fat Man on a Beach*, he was beginning to feel ready – perhaps compelled, even – to address this topic head-on in his writing. In this respect the last two volumes, had he lived to complete them, might well have been the most challengingly self-revealing things he ever wrote.

In the meantime, we are left with only the first instalment, *See the Old Lady Decently*. It was published posthumously, and exactly as Johnson had delivered it even though, just a few days before he died, the publishers had expressed strong reservations about the novel in its present form. It is the most diverse and fragmentary of all his books. Imagined scenes from his mother's early life as a waitress, written in the lively comic idiom of *Christie Malry*, are interwoven with much more low-key, verbatim transcripts of taped recollections from Johnson's father. Poems about motherhood alternate with sections written in the manner of a guided tour of Great Britain, describing its imperial rise and fall while leaving occasional blanks in the text for readers to fill in the details as they see fit. The last few pages provide a breathtaking, virtuoso description of Johnson's own conception and development from embryo to newborn baby. And perhaps the most affecting passages are those that allow us glimpses of the author himself, trying to work on the book we are currently reading and fighting off distractions from the outside world and the younger members of his own family:

> During the above my daughter came up to my room, practising her writing before going to bed. BOOTS and SNOW are the words she likes

best, at the moment. Then she went down for her supper. Afterwards she came up and gave me a delicious café Liègois [*sic*], or rather the remains of one. Mummy had the cream, she informed me. Spaghetti for lunch, green peppers, café Liègois, whatever became of England? Now she is drawing round her hand [*sic*], one at a time, with my red pens, one after the other. Do you like this? She is fluttering the paper at my elbow, demanding attention. I give it her, telling her to put it where I can find an envelope for it in the morning. Suddenly she leaves the room, not saying *Night Night,* and the loss is noticeable. I call her, she does not return. The loss is

Johnson's determination to incorporate accounts of the writing process into the novel itself marks an advance on *Trawl* and *The Unfortunates,* which unsatisfactorily purported to offer present-tense transcripts of mental processes that the reader knew full well had taken place some years previously. In this respect, Johnson seems here to have been approaching closer to his ideal of the totally honest, totally truthful novel. But in other ways his attempts to stay faithful at all times to the multiplicity of reality were causing his art to fracture. 'Does it matter?' he asks himself at one point, questioning the accuracy of his own re-creation of a London hotel kitchen in the 1920s:

Does anything matter? The thing is that all seems very similar. Nothing seems capable of being new, I feel as old as the whole of history, knowing everything that mankind can. Except the details.

It must be an illusion. My mind must be going.

It may even have been as simple as that.

Later in the book, this suspicion that the novel may be a futile, impotent form, entirely unequipped to deal with the complexities of human history and experience, begins to assume a note of desperation:

All this [the events of 1928] is very difficult to comprehend. Look, there were millions of people, thousands of peoples, hundreds of countries, all of them going in every direction and performing every kind of significant and insignificant act. How could anyone impose order on that multitudinous discontinuity? History must surely be lying, of one kind or another, no more true than what used to be called fiction? How can any one mind comprehend it? And would there be any point if it could?

See the Old Lady Decently is, then, in many ways, the work of a writer reaching the end of his artistic tether. In another context I have described it as being characterized by 'an air of strain and imprecision, weariness even'.[9] This seems unjust to me now, or at least inaccurate. It would be better to say that B. S. Johnson, sworn disciple of Joyce and Beckett, was here coming close to writing his own *Finnegans Wake* or *How It Is*: the work which would announce, once and for all, that he was parting company irrevocably with the conventional novel, driven almost to distraction by its inadequacies and evasions. Of course Johnson, arguably, did not have the single-mindedness and conviction of either Joyce or Beckett. He could not, at this point, see where his radical aesthetic must inevitably take him: either towards Beckettian minimalism or to a sort of insane Joycean inclusiveness. He was reluctant to go down either path (despite being a fan of everything Joyce wrote up to *Ulysses*, and everything Beckett wrote up to *The Unnamable*, he never showed much interest in their later work). As a result, *See the Old Lady Decently* is full of compromise: it is a statement of the literary problems Johnson felt himself to be facing, rather than a bold step forward on the journey towards solving them artistically.

Nevertheless, at least he recognized those problems; and at least he was – to use his own favourite word – honest about them. Few other writers, either during Johnson's lifetime or subsequently, have thought so hard about the novel as a form, have been prepared to put its possibilities to such intelligent scrutiny. Here perhaps is one working definition of 'writing as though it mattered', and it's hard not to feel that in this respect Johnson might have felt just as isolated, and just as embattled, in today's English literary culture as he did thirty years ago. Watching him pour scorn on his unnamed fellow writers 'imitating the act of being nineteenth-century novelists', we can imagine his line on lad-lit, chick-lit and the new phenomenon of the celebrity novel. For all his inconsistencies and self-contradictions, he cuts an impressive figure in that last, fiercely combative essay: commanding, resolute; a man who has already chosen his direction in the literary relay race, seized the baton of innovation and left most of his contemporaries standing. His faith in his own theories seems unshakeable.

A LIFE IN 160 FRAGMENTS

THE GODDESS

'Life does not tell stories. Life is chaotic, fluid, random; it leaves myriads of ends untied, untidily. Writers can extract a story from life only by strict, close selection, and this must mean falsification. Telling stories really is telling lies.'

How, then, can a biography be anything other than one big lie, from start to finish? If (as I have discovered) even to condense the details of a comparatively short life such as B. S. Johnson's into five hundred pages requires grotesque, enormous acts of compression and selection, what hope is there for the whole enterprise? One of the most bracing things for any reader coming face to face with Johnson's work is the realization that it immediately throws down gauntlets like this, forces you to question your most fundamental assumptions about any kind of writing process. He is the most *challenging* of literary figures, in that respect. How to begin, with the thought of such careful, uncompromising scrutiny hanging over you? 'B. S. Johnson was born on 5 February 1933.' And then what? His first word? Footstep? Nappy change? But think of all the life-events I will have missed out in between!

Of course, writing itself becomes simply impossible if you subject it to standards like that. Better to go to the other extreme: no pretence of inclusiveness, no aspirations towards objectivity. The biography as creative enterprise, artwork: the chaos of reality rigorously sifted through, selected and moulded into appealing narrative shapes: broad paths hacked through the undergrowth, for readers to stroll along at their ease. Isn't that what they pay us writers for, after all? In which case, I shouldn't worry about chronology, or correctness. The important thing is to bring Johnson to life, to *find* the man, somehow, in among the pile of material I've accumulated while writing this book and which now threatens to bury rather than illuminate him.

That material consists, partly, of interview transcripts, conversations with the people who knew him best. But the bulk of it did not have to be sought out in this way: it was left for me. When Johnson died he left some forty boxes of papers, mostly filed and in good order, at his home in Islington, north London. They sat there for twenty-three years, largely unexamined, until his widow Virginia gave me permission to come and start looking through them. I became an irregular visitor to this house for more than seven years. Towards the end, I was almost a resident.

The vast majority of the archive comprised working papers, manuscript drafts, literary correspondence. All of it fascinating, and invaluable, of course, for the light it threw on Johnson's working methods, and his relationships with agents and publishers. Almost everything I read of this nature confirmed the portrait of Johnson I had already sketched out in my head: a portrait I had reconstructed, largely, from my reading of that famously aggressive and dogmatic introduction to *Aren't You Rather Young To Be Writing Your Memoirs?*. A man utterly sure of himself, confident of his own talents and strategies, capable of the most magisterial pronouncements on literary methodology: 'Joyce is the Einstein of the novel.' 'I am not interested in telling lies in my own novels.' 'If form were the aim then one would have formalism; and I reject formalism.' My assumption that this essay was an expression of Johnson's personality as well as his literary opinions seemed to be confirmed by Zulfikar Ghose,* who once wrote that, 'the polemical, belligerent tone of that piece, the posture of deliberately provoking offence and the suggestion that the writer is in exclusive possession of the truth and the reader contemptibly stupid if he does not accept that truth echo the way he used to argue. The voice rising, getting more irritated and excited. There was something of the bully in him.' And everything I found in the archive seemed, at first, to confirm this impression to a greater or lesser degree. Here were records of literary quarrels, letters of indignant rebuke fired off to publishers, clippings files full of reviews in which Johnson pushed the same polemical line about the traditional novel being washed up, and so on. The portrait of the self-assured man of letters – the high modernist: serious, single-minded, uncompromising – became more and more solid, and persuasive. Which was disappointing, in a way. Because I didn't want to be proved right about B. S. Johnson. I wanted to be surprised. I wanted to be astonished. I wanted to find something, in short, that would undermine the received idea and *bring him to life for me*.

So I thought that perhaps I should start this book with the discovery that first had this effect. The moment when I realized that Johnson was in fact more complex, more troubling than that: that there was more to him than the man brilliantly described by his friend Gordon Williams as being 'wracked by self-certainties'. The moment when, sitting in the quiescence

---

* Poet and novelist, born in Pakistan in 1935. Throughout the 1960s, he was Johnson's closest friend and ally in literary London.

and solitude of his empty house, sifting through that interminable paper-work, I came across something new, something that gave me the stirrings of a sense, at last, of what an *ambiguous* figure Johnson might have been. And it was in that ambiguity that I felt him flicker to life for the first time, and was able to murmur to his ghost (borrowing the phrase from one of Johnson's own plays), 'So, after all – *You're Human Like the Rest of Them*'.

It was in a diary that I found it – a diary from autumn 1961. This had been a difficult time in Johnson's life. He was twenty-eight years old, had graduated from King's College London more than a year ago and was now working as a supply teacher in the north London area. He had completed his first novel, *Travelling People*, but couldn't find a publisher for it. He was single and lonely: none of his relationships seemed to be working out, and his latest inamorata (an Irish folk singer by the name of Kate) had just jilted him. One of his closest friends from King's, Stuart Crampin, had suffered a near-fatal climbing accident, which affected Johnson deeply. What's more, after spending the summer working on a farm in North Wales, he was feeling guilty that he'd done no writing while he was there, and towards the end of that period had undergone a strange occult experience (later described in a story called 'Sheela-na-gig') which suggested – at the very least – that he was run down and depressed. It all started to get on top of him and he lapsed, temporarily, into a kind of paralysed, introverted despair. A keen amateur gunsman in his youth, he still had a shooting rifle back at his parents' house, and he went to retrieve it. 'I considered suicide as the only thing which would relieve me,' he wrote in that diary. 'It seems possible that I would have done so had my rifle been at home and not at Barnes. I have fetched it now, and seem [...] much more secure in the knowledge it is a few seconds away.'

The diary entry sprawls over several densely written pages. Towards the end, it shifts from being a record of Johnson's latest crisis to something more wide-ranging. Like the novel *Trawl*, which he would conceive in less than two years' time, it becomes one man's attempt 'to discover why he has felt himself to be isolated all his life: an attempt to resolve his problems which is desperate in its seriousness'. In these final, opaque, fragmentary pages, Johnson starts to look back over the last six years of his life, picking out some of the most important happenings, the events that have defined him. This is what he wrote.

1: EXTRACT FROM DIARY/NOTEBOOK *(1 October 1961)*

(Jan 55) Physical manifestation of Goddess; indicates my servitude to her; death at 29; never able to have happy love/marriage as She was so jealous; but reward as writer; poetry really starts from then; NO BLACK

MAGIC – BUT EQUALLY CERTAINLY NOT XTIAN. (Mar 55) Meeting with Michael;* confirmation of all this; unified concept of art and life; M on life, I on art – conflict; M wanted to go too deep and I was too scared to follow him; (Aug 55) break which freed me, broke him; real conflict; Bach; went to Rome; own version; pursued own art-course; went to college as my way of following; directed first by Joyce then by Muriel.†

Homosexuality would be such an affront to the Goddess that I am tempted, merely to see if she would destroy me.

If only I could prove Her wrong by finding a woman who would love me completely, then Her spell would be broken: time is so short (there are four months left of my 29th year) and that is why I talk about Kate as the last chance.

The 'devil' I 'saw' was her punishment for not serving her in Wales. A vision of punishment, now made real.

[...]
DONA NOBIS PACEM

Bach link with Michael: the constant, ever-fixed mark, the centre around which it is possible to build an intellectual life.

Because of the seriousness of all this, I have built up an enormous protection of laughter: there is nothing that I cannot laugh at – this has been my reaction, and people often hate me for it. Really, laughter is the most wonderful thing on earth!

God is either dead, or has become indifferent, or has opted out, or treats it all as a big joke – on us; the smaller gods and powers seem to me to have taken over.

[...]
Michael probably *sees* me going out with Morgan le Fay.

I *am* all these conflicting people.

[...]
Now, Kate, you understand my preoccupation with time, now you understand my despair at meeting you just before I had to go away; now you understand the intellectual pace and fury at which I live.

---

* See below, p. 41.
† Joyce Yates (see below, pp. 72–5) and Muriel Starkey (see below, pp. 82–5).

The first time I read this, I didn't know what to make of it. Apart from registering that here was a very different voice to the forceful, confident theorizer of *Aren't You Rather Young To Be Writing Your Memoirs?*, I simply felt myself adrift in a sea of references I couldn't understand. Who or what, for instance, was the 'Goddess' Johnson claimed to have encountered in a 'physical manifestation'?

I didn't work that one out until several people whom I interviewed made me aware – rather unexpectedly, I have to say – that Joyce's *Ulysses* was not, in fact, the book that had the greatest influence on B. S. Johnson. That accolade has to go to Robert Graves's *The White Goddess* – that mad, brilliant 'historical grammar of poetic myth', first published in 1948, in which Graves set out to argue that the language of true poetry was 'a magical language bound up with popular religious ceremonies in honour of the Moon-goddess or Muse, some of them dating from the Old Stone Age'. In his first chapter, Graves described this Goddess as 'a lovely, slender woman with a hooked nose, deathly pale face, lips red as rowan-berries, startlingly blue eyes and long fair hair', and added that 'I cannot think of any true poet from Homer onwards who has not independently recorded his experience of her. The test of a poet's vision, one might say, is the accuracy of his portrayal of the White Goddess and of the island over which she rules.'[1] It's clear that this book had a profound and complex effect on B. S. Johnson, and that he saw many ways in which its themes intersected with his own life. We are talking about more than a simple literary or aesthetic influence. This was a book which seduced him so thoroughly that he even believed himself to have seen a 'physical manifestation' of the figure of the White Goddess shortly before his twenty-second birthday: round about the time that he seriously began writing poetry himself. (Throughout his life, incidentally, he regarded himself as a poet first and a novelist second: 'poet' was how he described his occupation on his passport.) This encounter, whatever form it took, was perfectly real to him. He believed in it all his life, although no doubt the strength of this belief fluctuated with his moods, and it was probably strongest when he was most depressed.

Piecing together friends' recollections, along with fragments of unpublished poetry and other writing, I gradually learned that when this 'Goddess' appeared to him in a 'physical manifestation', she warned him that he would never be happy in a romantic relationship, and that he would die before he reached the age of thirty.* Hence, in the extract quoted above, Johnson's desire to 'prove Her wrong by finding a woman who would love me completely', his sense that 'time is so short', his description of Kate as 'the

---

* Though this may have been a confirmation of something he believed already: see below, pp. 56–8.

last chance' (although of course he also says this about Virginia in *Trawl*) and his comment about 'the intellectual pace and fury at which I live'.

What, then, of 'the "devil" I "saw"', which was 'her punishment for not serving her in Wales'?

I can only assume this refers to the incident which Johnson described in 'Sheela-na-gig', a piece of short prose included in his collection *Statement Against Corpses*, co-written with Zulfikar Ghose and published in 1964. The background to this was as follows: Johnson had been spending the summer of 1961 on the Lleyn peninsula in North Wales, 'on a kind of working holiday: I stayed at David's farm [...] and helped with the harvest and anything else there was to help with.' One evening he had to drive to Dorset to fetch a spare part for a damaged combine harvester. He had stopped off at Kilpeck and visited the famous church there, with its grotesque carvings including the Sheela-na-gig: 'narrow face, huge eyes, thin lips, skeletal ribs, legs haunched high and wide, stick-like arms outside and under the thighs for the hands to hold open an enormously exaggerated vulva'. The Sheela-na-gig, he noted, was a pre-Christian and pre-Celtic figure, symbolic of both death and procreation. And then, driving back to Wales the next night across a 'desolate, hardly inhabited tract of land', he picked up a female hitchhiker who, on being told where he was going, replied, 'I know,' and on being asked where she was going, replied 'You know.' When, after about twenty minutes' silent driving, she told him to stop the car and climbed out, leaving the door open, Johnson 'leant across to close it, straightened up, and there she was, sitting down in the road facing me, just inside the headlights' range. She raised her knees, and suddenly she *was* the *sheela-na-gig*, just as the one at Kilpeck, but living, *living*.

'I felt an elemental oneness, union, unity, with the moon, the lights, the road, the moor, the sheep, the van, the stones, and, above all, with her.

'I began to feel disembodied again.'[2]

Of course, I had read the 'Sheela-na-gig' story before, and because Johnson was rarely – even at this early stage of his career – in the habit of *making things up*, I already assumed that it was based on some kind of personal experience. What I hadn't suspected was that it might tie in so directly with something else, something larger and more suggestive: Johnson's belief, sincerely held and almost never articulated, that he had once had a supernatural encounter which went right to the heart of his very sense of himself as a writer. An encounter with his muse, no less.

It was clear from the halting, exploratory way he wrote about these things in his diary that they baffled him, made him fearful; and without doubt the lowness of his spirits would have contributed to this. And so it was here, paradoxically, despite the strangeness of the phenomena Johnson was describing, that he at last began to seem real to me. I was beginning to see that behind his protective wall of theoretical 'self-certainties', there were terrible doubts, terrible fears at work; for him as for everyone. Doubt and fear, after all, are the things that humanize us. He was no longer the literary superhero that my postgraduate imagination had made of him. *You're Human Like the Rest of Them.* Up until that point, the story of B. S. Johnson, as I saw it, had fit into a predetermined mould: embattled working-class modernist, with fiery temper and tunnel vision, pits himself against a complacent and reactionary literary establishment. Not a bad story, of its kind. But the role it gave to Johnson himself was two-dimensional. I don't actually like stories about superheroes, people without doubt: don't believe in them, as it happens. I began to sense that the story I was being led towards now was a better one – stranger, certainly, and a good deal more complicated, but also more truthful. At which point the book I had been writing (in my head) ground to a halt, paused for thought, turned in upon itself and metamorphosed into something else: into the very object you now hold in your hands.

One more unanswered question from that diary extract, by the way: the identity of 'Michael', whose meeting with Johnson in March 1955 is judged to have been so significant, and who is also mentioned, during these fragments, in the same breath as Morgan le Fay. His full name was Michael Bannard. He won't crop up very often in the story of B. S. Johnson. But when he does, he will certainly make his presence felt.

And now, bullets must be bitten, decencies must be observed, and it really is time to start at the beginning.

SOLITUDE

Here we go, then.

Bryan Stanley William Johnson was born in Hammersmith, west London, on 5 February 1933. His father Stanley worked as a stock-keeper at the SPCK Bookshop in Great Peter Street, Westminster, a job he would hold down, doggedly and uncomplainingly, for his entire working life. Johnson's mother Emily had been in service: first to a wealthy doctor and his family in Westminster, and then, briefly, to a family in Preston, Lancashire; after which she returned to London and worked in the 1920s as a waitress in the Cantref restaurant on Drury Lane, and at the Whitehall Luncheon Club, where she would have served lunches to most of the prominent politicians of the day. Stanley's parents were from Norfolk; Emily's family, on her mother's side, was from the Saffron Walden area of Essex. 'So we were really only one-quarter Londoner, if you go that far back,' Johnson would observe – with an air of disappointment – to his father in the last year of his life. That quarter was provided by Emily's father, Peter Lambird, who is described on Emily's marriage certificate as a 'master greengrocer'. He had two children – Emily (born in 1908) and Philip (born in 1912) – but shortly after the birth of Philip he abandoned his family and went to live in Canada for a couple of years. He seems to have made a no doubt shamefaced return to the fold, but after this he was almost immediately called up and sent out to the trenches, where he was killed in action on 12 March 1918. Stanley Johnson told his son, in 1973, that Lambird's wife Mary 'never quite believed he was dead, imagined that this might be instead just another way of leaving her to fend for the children on her own'.[1]

During the war Mary had worked at a munitions factory in White City; when it was over, widowed, she did her best to support the family by working as a cleaner. This meant that Emily, from the age of about ten or eleven, was often left at home alone and was forced to learn the skills of motherhood early, in order to look after her younger brother. Soon, however, Mary remarried. She married Charles William Savage, an ex-railway worker ten years her junior, and when he got a job as live-in caretaker at the

Wesleyan Teacher Training College for Men in Westminster the whole family moved to the college's lodge in Arneway Street, which happened to intersect with Medway Street, where Stanley's family lived. Stanley and Emily met in 1926: a date Johnson would later seize on hopefully, thinking that it might mean they had bonded as class warriors at some demonstration during the General Strike. But the truth was more banal: Stanley had simply introduced himself to Emily one evening as she passed by the street corner where he was loitering with some friends. As always, Johnson was forced to recognize that it was chance, randomness – chaos, as he preferred to call it – which determines the most crucial events in our lives.

When Charlie Savage – an inveterate boozer – was sacked from his job at the college, the family were forced to leave the lodge and rent a basement flat at 28 Mall Road, Hammersmith, London W14. They got it cheap because the Thames had just broken its banks and riverside basement flats were considered a liability: Johnson could always recall seeing the tidemarks halfway up the walls when he was a child. Emily, however, did not move with them; although not yet officially engaged to Stanley (that happened on her twenty-first birthday, in 1929) she moved in with his family and was given a back room of her own in their house in Westminster.

They were married on 7 June 1930. Forty-three years later, Johnson wrote about that day in his last, posthumously published novel.

2: EXTRACT FROM *SEE THE OLD LADY DECENTLY*

Stan's mother and father had had the dustmen and the Medway Street neighbours in for a drink that morning, and a friend of Father's* who ran a car hire firm had provided them with two Rolls or Rollses [...] In the basement at Mall Road Mary had made the meal and provided drinks for friends and relations: here her experience in giving parties must have stood her in good stead, of course. You can imagine what there was to eat, can you? Good workingclass meats and preserves, that kind of thing, and the ritual, symbolic, traditional cake in all its tiered, tiara'd pure white symmetry. I imagine they had a cake, I forgot to check with my father. But he did tell me that at this breakfast an old friend of Mary's at eighty or ninety took too much of the drink (the older you are the less you can take) and on a return from the outside lavatory was observed to have tucked her dress into her bloomers all round. Then Emily and Stanley left for King's Cross to catch a coach for their week at Withersfield.

---

* This refers to Stanley's father, Johnson's paternal grandfather. He was a corpulent, big-framed man. 'That's where you get your figure and that from, him,' the slightly built Stanley told his son in 1973. 'I take after my mother more.'

After their honeymoon, Stanley and Emily moved into the ground-floor flat at 28 Mall Road, so that they were now living one floor above her mother, brother and stepfather. The two flats shared a back garden, so it must have felt as though the whole family was living together. And it was here that the infant Bryan Johnson was brought after his successful delivery at Queen Charlotte's Hospital in the Goldhawk Road (he was given no cot to sleep in at home – just a specially padded orange-box), and where he would spend the first few years of his life.

Like many people (especially men, for some reason), Johnson felt a powerful urge to look back on his early years when he turned forty. In 1973, as an acclaimed (though never wealthy) novelist, married to a woman several steps up the social ladder, a semi-reluctant habitué of the middle-class world of book launches, literary cocktail parties and publishers' lunches, he began to spend more and more time both investigating his parents' history and revisiting the forgotten byways of his own working-class childhood. (Both activities would emphasize and increase, at a highly sensitive time, the distance between himself and his wife Virginia.) One of the manifestations of this process was a long article he wrote for the magazine *Education & Training* in the winter of 1972–3, in which he attempted (unsuccessfully) to retrieve some pattern from the 'chaos' that his fractured and episodic education seemed to represent. Read alongside some of his autobiographical novels – mainly *Trawl* and *See the Old Lady Decently* – and the short story 'Clean Living Is the Real Safeguard', it provides the clearest account of Johnson's development that we are likely to retrieve.

3: EXTRACT FROM ARTICLE FOR *EDUCATION & TRAINING* (*completed 14 January 1973*)

I started early. It seems that there was some distinction in being sent to Flora Gardens Primary, in Hammersmith, at the age of four, and that I was proud of it; most others went at five. That must have been 1937, presumably September. We had to lie down in the afternoons on canvas campbeds, I competed at whopeeshighestupthewall in the Boys', and was disappointingly too well-built to qualify for free codliveroil and malt. Of the learning process I remember nothing.

On the outbreak of war I was six, and was privately evacuated with my mother and the son of a Westminster publican to a farm that was really only a smallholding near Chobham, in Surrey. I went to the village school, St. Lawrence's I think it was called.

The pub in question was probably the Old Rose, at the corner of Medway Street, where Mary Lambird had once worked as a cleaner and her daughter

Emily had at various times helped behind the bar. At the outbreak of war, the landlord appears to have thought of this small farm in Surrey, owned by two friends of his, as a suitable refuge for his own son (aged four) and the six-year-old Bryan, with the maternally inclined Emily looking after them both. 'There,' Johnson wrote in *Trawl*, 'we would be out of danger. Why my father and grandparents were to remain in danger I do not know.' He remembered this episode quite fondly, all the same, and thought that the farm was 'a good place for a child to be growing'. His account in *Trawl* of the almost two years he spent there with his mother and Timmie (the landlord's son) is rich in the pungent, perversely nostalgic detail of wartime England: dogfights observed in the distant sky during the Battle of Britain, the awareness of a far-off London 'that often appeared as a fireglow lighting the sky to the east', nights spent in an ant-infested air-raid shelter, walks along the country road into the village with Timmie, 'the hedges all cow parsley, old man's beard and wild dogroses [. . .] our gasmask cases banging against our thighs'. Revealingly, Johnson remembers almost nothing about his father at this time: 'My father I hardly remember visiting us at all, though he must have done so quite a lot, perhaps even every weekend. Nor do I remember thinking that he must have been in danger.' He does not talk about missing him: his father, in short, is defined merely as an absence, while a powerful bond must have been developing between mother and son during these two years, which may account for the strength of Johnson's attachment to his mother for the rest of his life.

Later, he would say that there was only one episode of his life he would describe as 'idyllic' (the six months he spent as Gregynog Arts Fellow in Montgomeryshire, in 1970), but perhaps he would have used the same word about this period were it not for one thing: his keen awareness that his mother (who worked on the farm while she stayed there, although not as an official land girl) was treated with contempt both by the farmer's son, Jack, and by the parents of another evacuee who was staying there. 'They did not like my mother and the two children she looked after, Timmie and me, and I see now that this was something to do with class. We were working-class, my mother and I, and the boy Timmie, as the son of a publican, was scarcely better [. . .] Their dislike of us, their bare toleration of us, was certainly shared by Jack: my mother was in fact or virtually a servant.' It is therefore from this moment, as Johnson rather self-dramatizingly puts it in *Trawl*, that he became aware of the English class war being fought 'viciously and destructively of human spirit'. 'I was born on my side, and I cannot and will not desert: I became an enlisted man consciously but not voluntarily at the age of about seven.'[2]

For just a few months, during the so-called 'phoney war', Johnson returned to London, to the blanketing warmth of that extended family living in neighbouring flats at 28 Mall Road. The atmosphere there is strongly evoked in 'Clean Living Is the Real Safeguard'. The lone infant child being pampered by the women of the family ('she [Nannie – Mary Lambird] used to give me evaporated milk with porridge for my breakfast, and some out of her own ration'). The same child being drawn, meanwhile, into a parallel world of exclusive, conspiratorial maleness ('Still, I liked Dandy [Charles Savage] just as much. He used to give me sips out of his brown when Nannie wasn't looking, and he didn't used to talk so much as she did, and when he did he said interesting things, and he'd swear, and we'd both laugh about it, and Nannie would be very angry'). The routine but lovingly remembered details of pre-war, working-class family life ('He was sprawled asleep in an armchair, and there was half a glass of brown on the piano by him'). Notice, once again, that Johnson's father does not register very strongly as a presence: and it is also 'Dandy', Charles Savage, who is the beer-drinker – Stanley Johnson once told his son that he never touched alcohol until he was called up and went abroad later in the war – which suggests that the future novelist was taught his lifelong fondness for beer mainly by his maternal grandfather.

Here, in any case, are three different views of Johnson's parents, from those who met them:

Joyce Yates (who knew Johnson in the 1950s): 'His mother was a dazzling beauty. She was blonde and he once told me that she had been a barmaid – he never told me where or how long or when. I went to lunch at their house and his mother was one of these people who devoted her life to cooking and washing like on the telly ads; but the father was an absolutely quiet, unpretentious, totally working-class man. The kind who shuffled off to work at eight o'clock and worked for 60 years in a factory and came home at the same time every night. So his mother, I would say, is definitely the driving force.'

Julia Trevelyan Oman (who knew Johnson in the 1960s): 'I met his father and mother quite a number of times, because I would go to dinner with Bryan and Virginia in Myddelton Square, and the parents were often there, and since the parents lived in Barnes and I lived in Putney and had a car, I would often give them a lift home. And his father I thought was a charming man, he worked for the SPCK, and he was a typical bookseller of that sort of period: he was thin, and darkish, and had, you know, the typical type of maroon knitted waistcoat and rather badly fitting grey suit [...] well, you can imagine. But he struck one as an educated person, and he'd have to be if he was working for that sort of bookshop. This is why I was extremely suspicious about Bryan and his [claims about a working-class] background, because his father really did seem one of nature's gentlemen – he was polite, and civil and all the rest of it. And his mother was extremely nice, too, but she was what one would call big and blowsy. I think at one point she worked doing accounts or something, in a garage up by the Red Lion in Barnes: but you could easily imagine her behind a pub bar, pulling pints. Yes, big and blonde. Very nice and delightful and all the rest of it, but the father just didn't, sort of ... *fit* with the mother. It was very very strange.'

Marjorie Verney (Johnson's second cousin, twice removed): 'Oh, Stanley was extremely quiet, he never said hardly a word: yeah, very quiet. And Emily's family were all very noisy, weren't they? Yeah, very very noisy. When we first met Stan, we thought, Well they are almost complete opposites of each other, because Emmie loved a good laugh, that's why she got on with my mum and dad so much, they used to pull each other's legs all the time. But Bryan and his mum were so, so close: especially when it's an only child, when you've got an only child you're even closer aren't you? It must have been heartbreaking being taken away from his mother.'

It must have been heartbreaking being taken away from his mother. That complete and devastating rupture came when the official period of evacuation began, during the Blitz.

4: FURTHER EXTRACT FROM ARTICLE FOR *EDUCATION & TRAINING* (completed 14 January 1973)

In 1941, after a brief period spent in London during the bombing, I was officially evacuated on my own to High Wycombe. At some point and at no cost my 'name had been put down' for Latymer School, then in Hammersmith Road; I think going to Flora Gardens was a preliminary to this, and I would normally have gone to Latymer at perhaps seven. Latymer had earlier been evacuated as a school to a small village outside High Wycombe called Sands, and some administrative logic sent me there now I was of age. To accommodate the overflow, the village school had taken over a Presbyterian Church Hall opposite; the Latymer boys still wore their uniforms, were not assimilated. I wept at my first billet, was given another the London side of High Wycombe; and for the rest of the next three years I made the long bus journey there and back to Sands every schoolday.

At some point, perhaps after a year or so, Latymer returned as a school to London; for some reason two of us were left behind at Sands. Virtually the last link with London was gone; from then on my isolation grew, my whole life was dominated by the fact that I was away from everything I had known. I was wretchedly miserable, weepy at the slightest cause (or for no cause), bad company, a thoroughly unrewarding pupil for any teacher, even for the odd saint, I suspect.

Johnson writes about this period at great length in *Trawl*, and begins his account with a powerful (if, again, rather melodramatic) comparison. He contrasts two photographs of himself, one taken at Chobham, aged five, and one taken at High Wycombe, aged seven: 'The first [...] shows a bright, chubby, roughly fairhaired boy, his eyes burnished with interest. The other photograph is of barely recognisably the same boy two years later: anxious, narrowed, the eyes now look as though they have seen most disappointments, and expect the rest shortly, the hair is darker, combed and haircreamed back, parted, the mouth hard, compressed: in all, the face of a human being all too aware now of the worst of the human situation.'*³

And yet, reading his own memories of those years in High Wycombe, there is not much to suggest that Johnson was *really* experiencing 'the worst of the human situation'. Certainly he was isolated. His new school, as he says, was in a village called Sands (referred to as Brotton in *Trawl*, for some reason). At first he was billeted on a house in Gordon Road, in central High Wycombe, run by one Mrs Bailey (in *Trawl*, Mrs Davies). Then he was moved to a suburban semi but he kicked up such a fuss about this (his lifelong hatred of architectural mediocrity clearly well established by now) that he was allowed to move back to the house in Gordon Road, where he lived for the rest of his time there, at some distance from his fellow schoolboys. ('I instinctively preferred the life which I could sense went on in these old, even obsolete dwellings of the railway age, to life in the fletton boxes.'⁴) But otherwise he seems to have been a sociable boy, with plenty of friends, and many of the childhood reminiscences in *Trawl* are rueful and melancholic, rather than harrowing. One anecdote, however, certainly stands out:

5: EXTRACT FROM *TRAWL*

I had lost my Bible for one lesson: it had just disappeared from my desk: someone had obviously taken it: so I did the same, took someone else's, but was caught doing so. She – it seems she was a girl – complained to the teacher, who strode up to my desk, took the book away from me and returned it to the girl and then wrote in capital letters on the board the three words THIEF and LIAR and CHEAT. She turned, looked directly at me, and said Ugly words, aren't they? And repeated, Ugly words. No more. This time added to my embarrassment, humiliation, was also the injustice of it all: I had neither lied nor cheated, and the theft was only a nominal one, as schoolbooks were common property

---

* The second of these photographs can be seen on the opening page of the first plate section.

amongst children, not personal possessions like fountain pens or pencil boxes. She had no right: but she had the power, ah, the power!

I'm trying to avoid looking for 'defining moments' in Johnson's early life; but here, at the very least, we can see some of his most vehement grown-up attitudes in their infant form. The burning dislike of people who abuse their positions of authority; the sense of shame at being accused of *dishonesty* ('LIAR') which would translate itself, when Johnson began writing novels, into a self-destructive determination to avoid *fiction* at all costs.

The worst things about his evacuation, however, were without doubt Johnson's separation from his mother and the curious – even inexplicable – fact that it went on for so long. Why did only two of the Latymer boys stay on at Sands for almost the whole duration of the war, when all the others were sent back to be with their parents in London after only a year or so? Johnson himself never seems to have received a satisfactory explanation about this from his parents: if indeed he questioned them about it. (It would be odd if he didn't.) Stanley Johnson was away on active service in Europe. (One of the things he managed to do during that time was make a journey to the cemetery at Ypres, to establish beyond doubt that his father-in-law, Peter Lambird, had indeed died and was buried there.) Emily Johnson, Bryan's mother, was at home in the flat at Mall Road – presumably with her mother and stepfather still living in the basement flat downstairs. Why wasn't Bryan brought back to join them? It seems most peculiar. Instead he was stuck in Mrs Bailey's house in Gordon Road, High Wycombe, an object of ridicule to the other boys there because he was the only one who went to school wearing a uniform, and even more isolated when he failed the eleven-plus in 1944 and was separated from the only other Hammersmith boy left in town. He even missed out on the whole drama of his parents leaving Hammersmith to move across the river to a house in Meredyth Road, Barnes, towards the end of the war. Why? What were they trying to keep him from – or keep from him? I somehow feel that an obvious explanation must be staring me in the face. But I still can't see it.

6: FURTHER EXTRACT FROM ARTICLE FOR *EDUCATION & TRAINING* (completed 14 January 1973)

In 1944 I sat what I now know to be the eleven-plus. At the time I did not understand what it was about. By post came a promise from my parents (my father an RACC* private in Germany, my mother working as a shop assistant in London) of my first twowheeled bicycle if I passed;

---

* Royal Army Catering Corps.

so I knew it was important. Two of us took it, in the Headmaster's room; from this I presume it must have been a London paper, for the other candidate was the only other Latymer boy left. Afterwards the Headmaster called me back, pointed with his pipestem at my attempt at one of the questions:

'Couldn't you do even that one?' he said.

I had on a previous occasion been caught thieving fruit from an orchard in a mill; and humiliated when up before him by an offer of fruit from his own garden if that was what I needed. That was not what I needed, at all.

I do not remember being told I had failed; and they still gave me the bicycle, anyway.

The secondary modern they sent me to for the last year of the war and my evacuation was called Highfields, I think, but certainly the headmaster was called Perfect. Here my form-master was the teacher who meant most to me throughout the whole of my education; and his name, remarkably, was Proffitt. He took us eleven-plus rejects and shook us, restored our confidence, showed us we certainly mattered to someone, to him. He really worked us, worked himself: all my memories have him on his feet, usually marching about, delivering, cajoling, enlightening; a balding, greyhaired, springy little figure of about fifty-five. He really brought something out of me; but he could also be cruel, both physically and verbally. Principally, he made us compete: there were exams from the first week, placings, encouragements to do better, to go up the scale of Mr Proffitt's esteem.

At the end of the first term I ranked third in the class, which position was physically recognised by his placing me in the back row three from the window; the nearer you were to him, the less well you had done, the more he felt he had his eye on you. It all seems rather oldfashioned now, but it worked with me; I was now being stretched, for the first time in my life I think; no one had ever made me work before, had shown me what I could do, what I had in me.

Before the end of my first year at Highfields the war was over; I suspect they sent us home within weeks, whereas they could have waited till the end of term, July instead of June. But no. I remember saying to Mrs Bailey, my fostermother, that I would not have minded staying on in High Wycombe to finish my schooling. Whether this was an expression of dismay at the prospect of yet another change I do not know; but I cannot think I meant it.

Certain aspects of Johnson's life in High Wycombe are described in *Trawl* with a curious exactness. The conceit of the novel is that the narrator (Johnson himself) is on a deep-water trawler in the Barents Sea, lying on his bunk remembering his past life as completely as he can. In reality, although Johnson did make such a voyage, he wrote the novel in his flat in Myddelton Square, Islington, during the second half of 1965. Did he travel back to Gordon Road, at any point, to fill in the gaps where memory failed him? On 17 August 2002 I went there to follow in his wartime footsteps. They are still standing, those 'old, even obsolete dwellings of the railway age'. And you can still follow the route Johnson follows on page 58, past 'the coarse grass of the embankment narrowing and narrowing until it had swung through a right angle' down to the junction with the London Road. You go past the point where 'the River Wye to a child suddenly appeared on his left through a railing, going backwards through a grating into an arch-opening [...] swiftly and darkly'. You turn left across a footbridge over the river into the Rye, 'a rectangle of meadowland used as a public park', and make your way across its windy expanse until you reach the artificial waterway called The Dyke, drawing its water from the grounds of Wycombe Abbey. Here, everything is as he described it: the copse 'sole-deep in beechmast', the ornamental waterfall with its drop of 'perhaps thirty feet, no more, but mighty and impressive to us'. I walked past this, at the foot of Keep Hill, coming to the point where the Dyke turns into 'a tiny stream, very clear over a sandy, small-pebbled bed, with very bright green weeds, and I (I remember no one ever with me when I did this) I used to lie at length, bathe my face, drink the water, stare at the subtly-moving stream floor.' It was a bright, blazingly hot morning when I came to this spot, and it was easy to imagine the nine- or ten-year-old Bryan Johnson lying there, pensive, melancholy, abandoned, the cries of his schoolmates floating distantly across the Rye as they made mischief together, 'leaving me to my observant solitude'.* It was one of the few moments during the last few years when – even more than when I worked at Johnson's old house in Islington – I felt that I had come physically close to him: the intervening sixty years evaporating, reduced to nothing.

7: FURTHER EXTRACT FROM ARTICLE FOR *EDUCATION & TRAINING* (completed 14 January 1973)

During the war my parents had moved over the river from Hammersmith and London to Barnes and Surrey. Hence I could not go back to Latymer for administrative reasons, and I was sent to Barnes County Secondary Modern School [...]

At fourteen after passing some sort of simple examination I went to Kingston Day Commercial School, which was then at Hinchley Wood,

---

* To quote Johnson's poem 'Porth Ceiriad Bay'.

near Esher, and a long busride round the Kingston Bypass from Barnes. Doug White was the other of my contemporaries at Barnes CSMS to go with me, and we felt ourselves privileged; for by the standards of Surbiton and environs Barnes was then largely rough and workingclass. At KDCS they taught shorthand (Pitmans for the girls, Gregg for the boys), typing, commerce and book-keeping; besides the usual things. Ted Britton* was teaching maths there then. It was a two-year course designed to turn out shorthand-typists and clerks; those able and whose parents were willing could stay on an extra year and take School Certificate. I did; the Korean war broke out as we sat the papers; in the summer holidays I had a note from Ted Britton saying that he was pleased that White and I had gained Matric Exemption. I knew that this meant I had qualified for university, but no one had ever suggested that I stood any chance of actually going; no one had ever gone to university from Kingston Day Commercial School.

The B. S. Johnson who now starts to emerge, slowly, from written evidence and from the recollections of his friends is a strongly contradictory figure. To all outward appearances, he was an unremarkable teenager. Football had become not just a hobby but an obsession. In Barnes he played for an informal local team nicknamed 'Little Heathens F.C.', and for Johnson and his friends this team 'was for many years our passionate interest, a complete, self-sufficient interest: the week was one long irrelevance from Saturday night to Saturday morning, the summer hardly bearable with no match play and only desultory, overheated practice to be had.'[5]

When he wasn't playing football he was watching it, because his father Stanley would take him to see every Chelsea home game. This habit instilled in him a lifelong allegiance to Chelsea – which he passed on to his own son, Steve – and also seems to have been crucial in cementing whatever emotional bond there was between Johnson and his taciturn, undemonstrative father, who only ever seemed to come to life at Stamford Bridge.

8: EXTRACT FROM ARTICLE FOR THE *OBSERVER* (published 18 April 1965)

It was because my father used to swear there that interested me in the beginning. He never used to swear anywhere else when I was around. It became a bond between us, something we had together that my mother did not, unlike anything else, his swearing on alternate Saturday afternoons.

---

* Later Sir Edward Britton (1909–). Distinguished educationalist, who has been both president and general secretary of the National Union of Teachers.

This was just after the war ended, and as soon as he was out of the Kate* he started taking me and a Pratt's two-gallon petrol tin to Stamford Bridge. It was the team, of course, which made him (normally restrained to the point of near-inarticulateness) swear with a vigour and comprehensibility which surprised and delighted me: Chelsea [. . .]

In those days of huge crowds we used to get to the Bridge anything up to an hour and a half before the kick-off. That was the worst part, waiting. I came to know the roofline by the top of the main banking by heart: flats, acres of chimneys, a green copper dome, the asbestos whaleback of the Earl's Court Exhibition, and quaintly fretted decorations on the great grey and rusty gasometers over towards the river. In a gap at the back of the main stand steam occasionally fluffed as a train went along the single-track line, its pace oddly unrelated to that of the steam and smoke.

This enthusiasm for football did not always translate itself into skill as a player. Trev Leggett, a schoolfriend from Barnes County Modern, recalls that Johnson had two nicknames at this time: one was 'Orson Cart' (because he already resembled the rotund director of *Citizen Kane*) and the other was 'Pork and Beans' – an evocative but almost inexplicable piece of south London, Tony Hancock-like slang. 'We used to say he was "all pork and beans" because he was tremendously enthusiastic about sport, and always smashing the ball further than anybody else but seldom in the direction of the goalposts. To us, this was a slightly podgy bloke, all enthusiastic, who enjoyed kicking a ball about and cricket slightly less so. As for tennis, he swung a racket, but I think probably most of us could beat him at tennis. Any sense of his artistic nature didn't come through at all. I was probably being thick about that, as all of us were. I'm quite sure it was there, as it later transpired, and it was not deliberately hidden from his contemporaries but just unrecognized by them.'

Leggett remembers Johnson as a keen cyclist: they went on a cycling holiday together around France in 1950, and he once cycled to Brighton and back in a day – five hours each way. Also, he had a great enthusiasm for jazz; his heroes were Louis Armstrong, Jelly Roll Morton, King Joe Oliver, Earl Hines. 'It was Bryan who tried to introduce us to jazz, we would go around to his house, four or five of us, to listen to records and his mother would pour us a glass of milk and a biscuit. I don't remember his father much, he seemed to be very quiet, slightly shy. None of it seems very sophisticated, now – you know, I think all of us were fifteen going on five.' It's probably to these musical soirées that Johnson is referring in his 1949 diary when he

---

* The Royal Army Catering Corps.

writes, on 22 January: 'In the evening we had our usual pow-wow round my house.' About fifteen years later, in *Trawl*, he would write that, 'I saw through jazz, or rather through the lives the men lived who played it, what I had to be, an artist, in the broadest sense, though not a painter, not a jazzman'; he conceived of jazz, in other words, as 'an example of the sort of thing I must do, felt buried in me, something very small and quiescent to which I had to be loyal, could be disloyal to only at the utter expense of self.'[6]

Johnson's sense of himself as an artist was certainly 'small and quiescent' at this stage. His diary for the month of January 1949 (he gave up after that) is hardly indicative of a poet in the making:

9: EXTRACTS FROM DIARY *(January 1949)*

Tuesday, 4 January: Went to Bertram Mills Fun-Fair at Olympia in the afternoon with Trev, Don, George and Ted. It was not very good.

Wednesday, 5 January: Went up to see the Schoolboy's Exhibition in Westminster. It was not very good.

Thursday, 6 January: Went to pictures with Don and George to see 'Mother Wore Tights'. It wasn't particularly good.

Saturday, 8 January: Played for Barn Elms v. Twickenham Juniors at Twickenham. We lost 3–1. I hurt my right leg.

And an early girlfriend from Kingston Day Commercial School, Wendy Stacey, also describes a domestic world in which it would be hard for either poetry or romance to flourish. She first got talking to Johnson in the refectory at school: 'He and his friends were all very keen on football, so they spent most of their lunchtimes talking about that, but occasionally I got a word in about something else. I can remember thinking that he was rather fat: I don't think I ever discussed it with him but he was bigger than most of the other lads, and fatter. I went to his house for tea once, and his mother did strike me as being very young and very pretty, she seemed prettier than he did, she was fair and slight. I remember washing up with his mother and she was talking about Bryan and how she'd just taken a part-time job, and she said, "Well, anything I can do to help Bryan," and I remember that being quite a surprising thing for a mother to say to a friend of her son. We had kippers for tea and after that Bryan and I went for a walk on Barnes Common and he did sort of suggest that we sat down on the grass for a little while, and I remember him kissing me but I wasn't a bit responsive and I did hear later that he told someone that Wendy Stacey was as passionate as a fish. Which sounds funny now, but obviously I remembered that after fifty years.'

Junior football; Bertram Mills funfair; kippers for tea; 'pork and beans'.

What chance for a budding aesthete in that kind of atmosphere? And yet it's round about now that we encounter Johnson's first published work, in the *Chronicle*, 'The Magazine of the Commercial Department of the Hinchley Wood County Secondary School'. It's a translation of three stanzas of 'L'Isolement', the first of the *Méditations poétiques* of Alphonse de Lamartine.*

L'Isolement

Souvent sur la montagne, à l'ombre du vieux chêne,
Au coucher du soleil, tristement je m'assieds;
Je promène au hasard mes regards sur la plaine,
Dont le tableau changeant se déroule à mes pieds.

Ici, gronde le fleuve aux vagues écumantes,
Il serpente, et s'enforce en un lointain obscur;
Là, le lac immobile étend ses eaux dormantes
Où l'étoile du soir se lève dans l'azur.

Au sommet de ces monts courronés de bois sombres,
Le crépuscule encore jette un dernier rayon,
Et le char vaporeux de la reine des ombres
Monte, et blanchit déjà les bords de l'horizon.

This was rendered by the fifteen- or sixteen-year-old Johnson as follows:

10: TRANSLATION FROM THE FRENCH OF LAMARTINE *(1949)*

Solitude

On the mountain's slope, in an old oak's shade,
In mood melancholic I sit me down.
I pensively watch, while the sun doth fade,
The scene that from far unfolds at my feet.
The foaming waves of the river here
Merge there with the darkness on distant plains;
Here whisper the dreamy dark waves of the mere,
There, above, the bright star of the evening ascends.
O'er the brow of the mountain, crowned with firs,
The light from the west throws its parting glow;
Soon the queen of the shades in her cloudy hearse
Will ride through the sky and lighten its gloom.

BRYAN JOHNSON (U. VIA)

---

* Alphonse de Lamartine, 1790–1869. One of the key works of French Romantic literature, the *Méditations poétiques* occupy much the same place in the French canon – and had much the same impact – as the *Lyrical Ballads* of Wordsworth and Coleridge in English.

No masterpiece, maybe. But pretty good, for a teenager whose school reports show that French was one of his worst subjects, and who was labouring under the nickname 'Orson Cart' at the time. Presumably this translation was set as some kind of school exercise – Lamartine would be an odd writer for a young schoolboy to discover by himself – but it's still interesting to see Johnson responding so feelingly to these lines, with their overtones of introspection, melancholy and romantic disappointment. (The *Méditations poétiques* grew out of Lamartine's despair when he realized that he would never again see a young woman, Madame Julie Charles, with whom he had fallen in love at the spa resort of Aix-le-Bains.) Both this poetic fragment and the memory I mentioned earlier from *Trawl* – Johnson lying alone by the side of the Dyke in High Wycombe, staring for hours into the water – seem to evoke for me the same image: Narcissus at the pool.*

Clearly, then, Trev Leggett is right when he says that the darker, more sensitive side of Johnson was simply 'unrecognised' by his contemporaries, rather than being consciously hidden. A handwritten, barely decipherable note-sheet for some lecture Johnson gave in the 1960s refers briefly to his schooldays, mentioning an English teacher in his School Certificate year (1950) who gave a lesson about Christopher Marlowe: '*Marlowe stuck in my mind – later influence – v. important ... to that I date wanting to be a writer – possibly earlier, but this certainly directed what till then had been a sort of inner knowledge that I was going to be something – "remarkable". But v. lazy – knew I was a writer but hadn't actually written anything – very painful etc.*'

Something 'remarkable'. Where had this awareness come from? We find the same thing in heightened form a few years later, for his notes to *Christie Malry's Own Double-Entry*† reveal that when he was working as an accounts clerk at Fuller's bakery in Hammersmith he had the strong consciousness, whenever he signed a form, that his signature would one day be valuable. Such confidence – in one so unsure of himself, otherwise!

A curious belief seems to have taken hold of Johnson at some point during these years. His identification with Christopher Marlowe grew so strong that he became convinced he was going to die, like the playwright, at the age of twenty-nine. He only stopped believing this, in fact, when the relevant birthday (5 February 1963) had come and gone, and during the 1950s would tell many of his student friends about it – particularly the women. Why? Because it made him seem more interesting? (There was a streak of self-dramatization

---

* This copy of the school *Chronicle* was kindly lent to me by Marion Spicer. On the back page, her schoolfriends had scrawled typical messages of farewell. 'Best of luck', 'Be good!', 'Love and best wishes for the future', etc. etc. Only one of these inscriptions stands out – the one from Bryan Johnson, who wrote, '*Remember me, Marion.*'
† See Fragment 139 below, p. 316.

in Johnson, from the very beginning.) But where did it come from? What makes a healthy schoolboy – and, later, student – certain that he will die before his third decade is over?

I've come across several different answers to this question, none of them all that satisfactory. Possibly the belief was instilled in him by the mysterious Michael Bannard. Jean Nicholson, a casual girlfriend of Johnson's from the early 1960s, told me that it started after he was given a palm-reading by his first girlfriend, whose name was Betty. Or, possibly – just possibly – it had its origins in an encounter with a fortune teller during a family holiday on the Isle of Wight when Johnson was fifteen. That interpretation depends on how much autobiographical weight we attach to a poem he seems to have written a few years later, in the mid-1950s.

11: UNFINISHED POEM *(1955?)*

Twenty-nine

The full-leaved lanes are shrouded dark
Through southern Wight's cliff-bounded fields;
Across the vale a dog doth bark
And night her new-born sickle wields.

Atop a hill, faced out from shore,
A sandstone spire points at the sky;
Ghostly [seamews?] glide and soar
About its mitred crown on high.

Up to this spur, up through the lanes
A boy did stride, eager to know
Why ancient man did take such pains
To raise this stone 'gainst Nature's blow.

The summit gained, he walked across
A turfèd plot with bracken edge
Towards the foot, o'ergrown with moss,
Of that strange pin on Neptune's edge.

Within ten yards he 'proached, and then
Saw that which set him back a pace;
Among dark rags, nearly hidden
There crouched a hag, with weathered face.

A gipsy she, and as he stood
Half-frighted and half-curious,
She spoke, and said this meeting would
Beget no deed injurious.

His fears thus calmed he watched her face;
'This meeting was ordained above,'
Quoth she; 'Your hand in mine now place
To learn your future – and your love.'

She took his hand, palm upward turn'd,
And breath'd a sigh at what she saw;
'Thou art the boy, by Heaven spurned,
Who hath incurred the wrath of yore.'

'For twenty-nine thy number is,
At twenty-nine thou death shall meet,
When twenty-nine take one last kiss
Of this sweet life, and Heaven greet.

'Howe'er, before thou go to find
Kind Marlowe's shade in templed clouds,
Ten years and four thou hast, so bind
Thyself to beauty's cause, not shrouds.

'Three loves thou'lt have, it is decreed;
The first will love thee not and spurn
Thy proffered love; thou wilt not need
This fair young girl, but from her learn.

'The second, too, will have fair hair,
And she wilt love thee true and well
For twenty-nine full moons; but ere
The thirtieth rise, thy love's death knell

'Shall stricken be, when she deceive
Thee cruelly; therefore take care
To love not wholly, lest you grieve
And give your heart o'er much to bear.'

The poem tails off at this point: I don't think Johnson ever finished it.

I suppose we shall never know very much about this mysterious phase of Johnson's life. The early girlfriend called 'Betty' seems to have been one Betty Hilder. She is mentioned by her own (first) name in the story 'Clean Living Is the Real Safeguard' from *Statement Against Corpses*, where we are told that her parents 'kept this sweetshop in a Kingston back street, the corner shop in a workingclass area. When I first saw where she lived I said to Doug I thought she'd be easy, but she wasn't, she was extremely middleclass in all ways, the good and the bad.'[7] As a nine-year-old during the war she had been evacuated to Devon, where she had relatives, and her relationship with Johnson must have been fairly long lasting because he remembered that they went to stay with these relatives, in their 'farm-labourer's cottage' for three summers in a row. (I would say 1951, '52 and '53, at a guess.)

'Clean Living Is the Real Safeguard' records an episode from one of these summers in which Johnson accidentally shot a rabbit with his rook-rifle while out walking with Betty at dusk.* The bullet makes 'a bluish hole in its flank towards the tail', and there is a good deal of detail, rather morbidly dwelt upon, about how the rabbit's eyes are a 'seething mass of vermin [...] That was why the rabbit had sat there unmoving, waiting for death from disease, living death so patiently.' Johnson then kills the creature off with another bullet, and 'watched as the blood flushed over the edges of the smashed bone and across the mass of grey-white brain, welled over the soft fur down on to the grass'. The story was written in the mid- to late-1950s, and a much shorter version (in the third rather than the first person) appeared in the King's College magazine, *Lucifer*. It ends with a non-sequitur, but – in the light of what happened later – a suitably chilling one. 'Often I feel,' Johnson writes, 'that it has really only been the knowledge that I have the sure means to end it quickly that has made me put up with life.'

'Clean Living Is the Real Safeguard' also contains an account of how Johnson slit his wrists one day during a history lesson at Kingston Day Commercial School, over a failed relationship with a girl he calls 'Jo'. 'I would not actually commit suicide, I had thought, but I would just see what the pain was like, of a razorblade cutting my flesh. Whether it was worse than the pain of not having Jo.'[8] He claims that it was an almost involuntary gesture: 'when the mounting fears had reached high into my mind, the impulse could not be denied'. None of his contemporaries – nor Sir Edward (Ted) Britton, the only surviving staff member I could find – remembered this actually happening, which makes me wonder whether the episode should be treated as fiction: although everything else in the story appears real enough. However we explain it, in any case, it makes me suspect that Johnson, at times, may not have been the most easygoing of companions for the teenage daughter of a Kingston shopkeeper, so perhaps we can understand why Betty finally moved on to another boyfriend, whom she almost immediately married. In Johnson's eyes, this was a 'betrayal'. A few years later, in his first, never completed novel, *Not Counting the Savages*, he would fictionalize himself as a character called Henry, whose 'chief memory was of

---

* As a teenager, he belonged to a rifle club in Barnes, which was how he came to own a gun. Years later, in the course of their taped interview in 1973, his father Stanley would tell him that his paternal grandfather had been a keen marksman, and 'that's probably where you get your shooting from'.

a girl he had loved when he was sixteen, and who had betrayed him when he was nineteen; no day went by but that he thought of her.'

Thelma Fisher, an undergraduate friend of Johnson's at King's College London, was one of the few people in whom he confided this story. 'It was the sort of thing Virginia* and I talked about, whether he'd actually had a breakdown before he came to King's. My memory is that he talked about a girlfriend, and that he went to a farmhouse in Wales with her,† and something had gone wrong with that relationship and he'd been very hurt by it, and the White Goddess thing was around in those very early days. I don't know anything more than that. What's linked in my head over the years is the moon, the White Goddess, his mother and this girlfriend. Irrational though it may be, some sort of image like that does make sense to me somehow. And I can remember that it was a concession to me that I was learning all this, it was a big thing to tell me about.'

The White Goddess was published in 1948, and Johnson had certainly read it by early 1955; unfortunately I can't date his first reading of it any more exactly than that. But it is possible to identify some of his other most important early influences. 'I first learnt what literature was from Wilde,' he wrote in a letter to his friend Anthony Smith, 'and amassed about twenty books on him [...] when about 19.'[9] At this stage, he reiterates (in the *Education & Training* article), 'I already knew I was a writer, though I had not actually written anything. I was lazy, cocky, distracted by (in particular) sex, soccer and motorbikes.' He had left school by now, and after seven months working at the National and Provincial Bank was employed as an accounts clerk for a building firm in Barnes called Modern Builders, a job he held down from June 1951 to May 1952. The firm was located 'in an old coal barn just opposite Barnes pond,' according to Trev Leggett. In this unlikely environment, already enamoured of Wilde, Johnson first encountered the work of one of Wilde's earliest and most notorious biographers and, like many readers before and since, fell powerfully under its spell.

12: EXTRACT FROM ARTICLE WRITTEN FOR *20TH CENTURY STUDIES* (NO. 2) (manuscript dated 26 May 1969)‡

At the age of nineteen I was lent (by what I now know to have been a poodle-loving lesbian of indeterminate years and motive) the four limp volumes of Frank Harris's MY LIFE AND LOVES in the Obelisk Press

---

* Virginia Johnson, his wife from 1964 to 1973.
† This, I believe, must be a misremembering: it has to be Devon, not Wales.
‡ The published version of the article was much shorter and did not include this paragraph.

edition. It is to that library borrowing that I trace my interest in trying to write down everything, my whole truth: and I particularly remember his observation that one-third of anyone's life is passed in the bedroom but ignored by unbalanced novelists. That Harris was himself a great liar in print I discovered only much later, when I was both far too committed and had moved on anyway.*

In fact the observation about 'unbalanced novelists' ignoring their characters' sex lives was not made by Harris himself. He was quoting the prolific (but now forgotten) Walter Lionel George in his book *A Novelist on Novels* (1918): 'Our literary characters are lop-sided because their ordinary traits are fully portrayed while their sex-life is cloaked, minimized or left out [...] Therefore the characters in modern novels are all false.' Johnson was highly impressed by this determination never to be 'false', which implied, in his eyes, that it was morally wrong to omit graphic or potentially offensive details. In *Albert Angelo*, for instance – the book in which he first attempted to tell 'the truth' at all costs – he concedes it is a weakness that the hero 'defecates only once during the whole of this book: what sort of a paradigm of the truth is that?'

Harris, on the other hand, trumpeted his intention 'to tell the truth about my pilgrimage through this world, the whole truth and nothing but the truth, about myself and others.' In the foreword to *My Life and Loves*, he explained his aesthetic thus:

> There are two main traditions of English writing: the one of perfect liberty, that of Chaucer and Shakespeare, completely outspoken, with a certain liking for lascivious details and witty smut, a man's speech: the other emasculated more and more by Puritanism and since the French Revolution, gelded to tamest propriety; for that upheaval brought the illiterate middle-class to power and insured the domination of girl-readers. Under Victoria, English prose literature became half childish, as in stories of 'Little Mary', or at best provincial, as any one may see who cares to compare the influence of Dickens, Thackeray and Reade in the world with the influence of Balzac, Flaubert and Zola.

It's fascinating to know that Johnson read this passage when he was nineteen – just the sort of age when literary influences stamp themselves most indelibly on the emerging consciousness. For here, already, we have

---

* One of Johnson's notes made during the planning of his last project, 'The Matrix Trilogy', confirms this anecdote: 'The start of writing: Frank H – M L & L and the woman over Mod. Builders – lesbian? – a sort of mother figure? Seems that in retrospect.'

virtually the whole of his own philosophy of the novel in a nutshell: the 'liking for lascivious details and witty smut' which permeates all his writing; the outspoken contempt for the way 'middle-class' values have infiltrated literature; the hatred of Victorian fiction; the assumption that continental – especially French – novels are intrinsically superior to their English counterparts. Need we look any further?

A complex literary personality was already beginning to emerge here. Partly in thrall to the Frank Harris notion of truth, candour and sexual explicitness (and also strongly drawn, I suspect, to the colourful legend of Harris himself as a literary celebrity – drunken, brawling, hedonistic, profligate, lurching lovably from one romantic scrape to another); but then, on the other hand, captivated by the more mystical writings of Robert Graves, with their insistence that poetic inspiration comes from the Muse Goddess, a figure bound up with complicated myths of birth and death, the Moon and the all-providing Mother. Johnson has not yet discovered Beckett or Joyce, Burton or Sterne, writers who would become just as important to him. But the seeds are sown: the seeds of an aesthetic that would always be extremely conflicted, however hard he would later try to present it to the world as a watertight, cast-iron theory.

RATHER AN ELDERLY STUDENT

13: INVITATION CARD *(February 1954)*

Bryan Johnson has Great & Sincere Pleasure in Requefting the Prefence of his moft Esteemed and Well-loved Friend at a Convivial Gathering to be met at his abode upon the Sixth day of February in the Year of Our Lord Nineteen Hundred and Fifty-Four at Seven of the Clock, the Cause and Excuse of fuch Merriment and Airing of Bawdy Songs being the Celebration of His Majority.

So, Johnson is twenty-one at last. Only another nine years to go before his first novel is published. He knows that he wants to be a writer (although *we* do not know, and do not seem ever likely to know, how he came to feel this so surely), and yet the writing habit is not fully formed. His surviving diaries from this period yield up almost no information. His pocket 'Motorcycling Diary' for 1952 lives up to its name: 'Engine rebuilt with new main bearing & valve springs. Valves ground in and decoked', reads a typical entry (13 April – Easter Sunday – 1952). Only a few scraps written down on the final pages betray an emerging poetic sensibility: '*all covered oer with sweet sea-myrtle plucked from off the brow of Neptune's heady serving maids themselves* – orig. BSJ' is one such gem (if I've deciphered it correctly). Two years later, 'The Motorcycle Diary 1954' offers slightly richer pickings. True, we have 'Take bike to Putney Autos' (18 June) and 'Decarbonise Martin's bike' (19 July). But we also find evidence, now, of a serious film-, play- and concert-goer: Ken Colyer at the Royal Festival Hall, Eliot's *Cocktail Party* at the Richmond Theatre, René Clair's *Sous les Toits de Paris* at the NFT. A telling, but scarcely legible scrap mentions an entry 'on the Dr. side of my heavenly ledger', showing that he has already evolved something like Christie Malry's system of moral double-entry. And there are brief, enigmatic, scribbled memoranda which suggest – already – the beginnings of a more complex personality.

14: EXTRACTS FROM DIARY *(1954)*

Remember, my day is coming.

You now have the advantage of beauty to attract money; one day I shall have the money to attract beauty.

*

Once I saw an old man in a public lavatory his raincoat being buttoned up by a small boy. He was helpless. His useless arms swung from his shoulders and on his face was an expression of mingled sadness, regret, shame and pathos.

*

After all, what is the Bible but an embarrassment to the Church?

Who was accompanying Johnson to these concerts, I wonder? Had he already fallen in with a 'homosexual set', as a future girlfriend would later suppose?* Or would that come a few months later, when he met Michael Bannard for the first time? So much of this period is lost, lost beyond retrieval. If I were to write a novel about B. S. Johnson (and perhaps that's what I should have done instead, it sometimes occurs to me) this is the period I would home in on: so little is known, which leaves so much scope for the imagination. His own published recollections of these days are spare and unyielding, giving us the bare facts: that this was the time, for instance, he realized it was not too late to find his way into university:

15: FURTHER EXTRACT FROM ARTICLE FOR *EDUCATION & TRAINING* (completed 14 January 1973)

Gradually I saw that further education, perhaps even a degree in English, were there for the having, but the initiative had to come from me; no one was going to bring anything out. A friend at work showed me the Birkbeck prospectus, explaining the college was part of London University but held its lectures in the evenings for students with fulltime jobs. From it I saw that my Matric Exemption was nothing of the kind; I had, in particular, to pass O-Level Latin. The same West Indian friend told me about Davies's, the crammers in Addison Road. I did O-Level Latin from scratch in eight months with them, sitting three different Boards in the hope of passing one and actually getting all three. My tutor was an old man of seventy-odd who was gross, ugly, fat, slobbery; and he overindulged in Dr Rumney's Pure Mentholyptus Snuff. I loved him; he was a real master/teacher.

---

* See below, p. 427.

But there were other, more painful things going on in Johnson's life at the same time. We know from *Trawl*, for instance, that towards the end of 1954, when he was employed by the Fuller's bakery in Hammersmith, he had the latest in a bruising series of affairs, this time with a girl he calls 'Laura', who worked alongside him in the wages department. Johnson had already started his Latin evening classes by now (they began in September 1954), and he would call on 'Laura' every evening when these classes were over, on his way back from Holland Park. But soon, after a certain amount of casual, readily offered sex, she seems to have run scared of his emotional pressuring:

16: EXTRACT FROM *TRAWL*

I see now it was wholly physical, on my part too, and that she grew tired of it sooner than I: but at the time I wanted it to be a lot more, a lot more, and was hurt and bitter when it finished, for it was love, of a kind, and not to be rejected as I thought she had rejected it [...] Trite, the affair with Laura, casual sex, if anything ever deserved the cliché: but I wanted it to be more, I wanted it to be more! She made it that, kept it small, not me, she! I was even prepared to offer her, did offer her, that I would give up my Latin, abandon hopes of going to university to do an English degree, if she would stay with me, which meant marriage, and I swore I would become a successful accountant, as then I was a clever accounts clerk but contemptuous of everything to do with it [...]

All of which suggests that the diary note above ('one day I shall have the money to attract beauty') was inspired by this sorry episode. Johnson was so upset, in any case, that he decided he could not work at Fuller's any longer; and, feigning a cold, he took some days off in order to look for another job. Which he rapidly found; and shortly afterwards, on 21 March 1955, started work with the Standard-Vacuum Oil Company on Kingsway in Holborn – popularly known as Stanvac, although it has now mutated, after a number of mergers and acquisitions, into the company known as Exxon/Mobil.

How badly hurt had he been by the experience with 'Laura'? Very badly, I suspect. To any objective observer the situation is clear: here is a somewhat emotionally arrested young man, hungry for sex but unable to separate it from emotion, and so afraid of being abandoned by anyone who loves him that when a woman shows an interest in him – even when it's obviously just a physical interest – he clings to her and makes the most absurd promises (in this case offering to abandon his vocation and pursue a career he despises) in order to keep her. But it would also be perfectly in character for Johnson to be plunged, after receiving such a rejection, into a phase of serious depression: this is certainly what happened in 1958, in 1961 and – fatally – in 1973, when he and his wife Virginia reached a marital impasse. So my working hypothesis is that at this point in his life, during his first few weeks or months of working at Stanvac, Johnson was in a highly vulnerable state, and perhaps even clinically depressed.

This is worth remembering, because it was now, apparently, that two things happened. To quote from that 1961 diary again:

> (Jan 55) Physical manifestation of Goddess; indicates my servitude to her; death at 29; never able to have happy love/marriage as She was so jealous; but reward as writer; poetry really starts from then; NO BLACK MAGIC – BUT EQUALLY CERTAINLY NOT XTIAN. (Mar 55) Meeting with Michael; confirmation of all this [. . .]

The mystery of the 'physical manifestation of Goddess' will, I fear, never be cleared up. As far as I know, Johnson spoke about it only once, to Frank Lissauer, the librarian at King's College London. He is now dead, and I have not been able to locate any of Johnson's many letters to him. If the 'manifestation' took place in January 1955, then Johnson would still have been working at Fuller's, but this is contradicted by a note he made towards the end of his life, when he claimed it happened while he was working for Stanvac, which would place it at least two months later.* All we can say for certain is that Johnson must have read Graves's *The White Goddess* by now, and that from some time early in 1955 he must have laboured under the superstition that his destiny as a writer (or more precisely a poet) was conditional upon his servitude to some sort of supernatural being – his Muse, if you like – which he believed he had seen (and perhaps spoken to?) and that the allegiance he had sworn to this being precluded his ever having a satisfactory love-relationship with a woman.

Bizarre, but – apparently – true.

His 'meeting with Michael', however, can be discussed in rather more rational and specific terms. The Michael in question, as I mentioned some time earlier, was a man called Michael Bannard, but what, exactly, can have been so significant about this meeting, to make Johnson mention it again in that fragmentary journal six years later when he was confusedly trying to reorientate himself by noting down the landmark events of his life?

Michael Bannard – who died in a car accident in France more than fifteen years ago – was born in Banbury, Oxfordshire, in 1934: making him

---

* See Fragment 153 below, p. 366.

almost Johnson's contemporary. I know this, and other facts about him, because I have in front of me a CV he drew up himself in the 1980s. (Although I'm not convinced that I should be too trusting of a document composed by a man who was, by all accounts, a notorious fabulist and self-reinventor.) It tells me that from 1961 onwards he became a compulsive traveller, taking occasional teaching jobs in Egypt, Italy, Bulgaria, Algiers, Bangkok, the USSR, Scandinavia, Libya, India, Pakistan, Iran, Afghanistan, Bhutan and Nepal before finally settling in Tokyo, where he spent the last thirteen years of his life. Pretty different from Johnson, whose longest spell out of the country would be a three-month stay in Paris in 1967. Before that, however, Bannard's career was more settled and conventional. For a while, he read medicine at University College Hospital, London, and before that did National Service from 1952 to 1954 as a neurological unit radiographer.*

There was a physical resemblance to B. S. Johnson (Bannard was a big man – when playing Falstaff in a school production of *The Merry Wives of Windsor* the measurements for his costume had been 40–40–40) and also a similarity in their backgrounds: Michael Bannard's father, too, was working- or lower-middle class, quiet and uncommunicative; and although Bannard had half-sisters, he was the sole offspring of his father's second marriage, and his mother pampered and doted on her only son – while neither parent had the slightest comprehension of his wide-ranging cultural interests. In many respects, then, Johnson and Bannard could almost have been mirror images of one another. But there was one important difference. Johnson was still, at this stage, emotionally and intellectually unsure of himself; but Bannard was as openly gay as it was possible to be in the 1950s, and throughout his life he combined lasting (if turbulent) relationships with a vigorously pursued trail of one-night stands. He was a natural leader and teacher, with a vibrant, almost overpowering personality. Johnson – tentatively, at this point in his life, dipping his toe into cultural waters he longed to explore more thoroughly – was crying out to be led and taught.

'Bannard was the complete opposite of Johnson,' says the novelist Francis King, who knew them both (independently). 'He was jovial, superficial, rackety, unreliable, not markedly interested in literature, excellent company. He was also gay.'[1] Another man who knew him well was Peter Dunsmore – Michael Bannard's closest friend from 1964 to 1987 and the sole beneficiary of his will. He described him as 'larger than life. He was a

---

* Johnson's own National Service lasted for only three days. He entered the RAF but was discharged almost immediately because of a perforated eardrum, dating from the time he had scarlet fever at the age of three.

huge person. He became very big towards the end of his life, very grizzled – he was really an Orson Wellesian kind of presence. A very impressive person. But I think all this bluster and slightly bombastic exterior concealed some-one who was perhaps quite shy and private behind it all. He was a man of enormous appetites in everything – food, wine, sex I believe, and culture most of all. He couldn't sit still for a minute. On a typical day he would no sooner have come in than he'd be off somewhere, out to the theatre, he would meet someone for a meal, he'd then go to an all-night film show, some sort of fringe event. In the countryside when you drove around with him there'd be a relentless pursuit of country houses, Neolithic flint mines or long barrows, it was like this all the time, he would exhaust anybody. He lived life as if the hounds of hell were snapping at his heels.'

Among the few others who knew both Johnson and Bannard were the occupants of the house in Claremont Square, Islington, where both men lived for a while in the early 1960s: they included Doug Davies, Keith Andrews and Claire Andrews.* From them, I built up a picture of an extremely forceful personality, combining a passion for the arts (particularly music and architecture) with expertise in a daunting range of subjects, including esoterica and occultism. He would make pilgrimages to Lindis-farne, to Dublin to read the Book of Kells, to standing stones, barrows, numinous sites of every description. James Latham (Claire Andrews's brother) says that, 'There was a certain *pagan* side to Michael. He definitely wasn't a follower of any of the religions, but he did have a certain sympathy or rapport with pagan things. I went with him to visit the Rollright Stones just outside Banbury, and he would try to "pick up the vibes". He would stand there in the middle with his eyes shut, that sort of thing.' This is borne out by Michael Bakewell (Johnson's agent towards the end of his life), who says that he met Michael Bannard only once, in a London pub, and had a fierce argument with him over the mystical significance of the Rollright Stones. On that occasion he felt that Bannard had a 'whiff of sulphur' about him and exerted an unhealthy influence over Johnson. Some of Johnson's other literary friends have dim recollections of Michael Bannard turning up at parties wearing a Count Dracula-style cape and lurking, heavy and sinister, in the background. They called him 'the witchcraft man'. Johnson himself had a fairly well-developed interest in witchcraft and the super-natural,† and some of that might have come from Michael Bannard: in the

---

* Claire and Keith Andrews went on to anticipate the 'Nicci French' phenomenon by several decades, publishing a number of excellent collaborative novels (including *The Otherwise Child*) under the name 'Keith Claire'.

† See, for example, the short story 'Sheela-na-Gig'; references to witchcraft in *Trawl* (p. 62: 'once while reading something about witches I placed the performance of a potent female spell (dancing three times naked round a house while menstruating during a full moon) in this

autumn of 1961, for instance, he rather strangely invited himself to stay for a weekend with Bannard's parents in Banbury and, while there, spent an afternoon exploring the Rollright Stones.*

James Latham, while still speaking of Bannard with affection, recalled that he could be both overpowering and cruel: 'He could be tasteless, or prone to mockery, sending people up: people who in the end he didn't respect. He was a very dominant personality.' To which Doug Davies added, 'He might have tried to influence people but it couldn't have worked for me: I just wouldn't have taken him that seriously, because he was really not grown up. If anybody was going to be taken over by him I would have to say that the victim would have to be a willing victim, and would have had to have had plenty of insecurities of his own. You'd have to be fairly fragile.'

How did the two men meet in the first place? Well, we can answer that one straightforwardly enough by glancing at Michael Bannard's CV, which informs us that in the mid-1950s he was 'personnel clerk and later assistant personnel manager' at – you guessed it – 'the Stanvac Oil Co., London'. They met in that office, then, above the rumble of the traffic along Holborn Kingsway, just around the corner from the Covent Garden Opera House where Bannard was a habitué, and to which Johnson himself must have been no stranger, during this concert-going phase of his life. And what then? The Hammersmith boy, although slightly older than his new friend, fell under his spell, willingly submitted to his tutelage. He allowed himself to be swept along by Bannard's tidal enthusiasm for the arts, no doubt, but surely there was more to it than that. There must have been an undercurrent of intense, troubling emotion for Johnson to have written what he wrote next in that 1961 diary:

> (Mar 55) Meeting with Michael; confirmation of all this; unified concept of art and life; M on life, I on art – conflict; M wanted to go too deep and I was too scared to follow him; (Aug 55) break which freed me, broke him; real conflict [. . .]

No letters between Johnson and Bannard seem to have survived, rather mysteriously. Which leaves us with only one published source of information about their friendship – a poem written by Johnson early in 1958, and subsequently included in his collection *Poems* (1964), under the title 'An Eye for Situation'. (When first published, in the January 1959 issue of the King's College literary magazine, *Lucifer* – editor, B. S. Johnson – it was

---

meadow, though now I can remember no house there, nor what result the spell should achieve'); Henry's reading of a book on succubae in *Travelling People* (p. 265 etc.); the fortune teller's card reproduced in *Albert Angelo*; and the serio-comic references to Welsh witches and toenail cuttings in *Fat Man on a Beach*, among many others.
* See below, pp. 109–11.

called 'Poem for M. B.' Johnson's manuscript has the words 'for Michael Bannard' pencilled on it. And in the copy of *Poems* which he gave to Bannard himself, Johnson wrote alongside this particular poem the mysteriously inverted inscription, 'For Bryan, from Michael'.)

17: POEM (written 1–2 February 1958)

An Eye for Situation

Sometimes it is you who surprise me,
turning a corner, across the floor,
a sudden facing beyond a door;
at other times it is my preparation
that makes you start at what you see:
we both have an eye for situation.

I know just the concerts that you will attend,
and your comments upon them; your enthusiasm
somehow empty, provoking a spasm
of anger in me when I was with you;
these things I keep, and comprehend
my ignorance of what is true.

Recalling your intense obliqueness,
the unsaid things we knew together,
you would disapprove; whether
you are right I cannot say,
but you would call it treacherous weakness
that I thus take the normal way.

I have to admit that when I first read this poem, I gave it a fairly obvious interpretation. 'The normal way' I took to mean – in Johnson's terminology – heterosexuality, so that what he was recording here was a homosexual advance made to him by Michael Bannard, which he rejected. This would certainly fit in with his 1961 diary entry: 'M wanted to go too deep and I was too scared to follow him'. (To which he added the reflection, shortly afterwards, 'Homosexuality would be such an affront to the Goddess that I am tempted, merely to see if she would destroy me.') However, Peter Dunsmore was more guarded about this, saying simply, 'Well, that's one interpretation, yes. It's possible.' And Claire Andrews gave it a different reading altogether, taking it to refer to a deep-rooted temperamental difference and a dispute over different literary and artistic directions: 'Michael was all for the imagination; whereas Bryan stuck his toes in and said "No" to that. Michael wouldn't have gone along with Bryan's commitment to realism because it just wasn't the sort of art he liked. He was a Mervyn Peake and a Tolkien reader. Michael was always very full of Mervyn Peake. The thing is that they were both *totally* insecure when I met them, but they went in opposite ways: Bryan went back to what he thought were his roots and said very solidly, "You're not going to move me," whereas Michael never stopped for breath after that – as if on the basis that if you go on running, nobody will catch up with you. So he had this totally peripatetic life.'

Whatever the truth about Johnson's poem, one thing to note is that from this point onwards he was recurringly exercised by the notion of what constituted 'normality', both in art and in life. It's a subject that crops up often in his letters and also surfaces in the title and theme of his novel *House Mother Normal*: a novel conceived in the early 1960s, with early working papers being kept in a file labelled 'NOTES towards a novel investigating aspects of normality and abnormality [. . .]'*

After searching as hard as I could, then, all I can say with any certainty about this forgotten, intriguing period of Johnson's life is this: that early in 1955 – perhaps in January – he had, or believed himself to have had, a supernatural encounter with a figure he would later identify with Graves's 'White Goddess'; from this encounter he would date his belief that he would never have a successful relationship with a woman, because he was now in bondage to his poetic muse. And then, in March, he started work at Stanvac, where he met Michael Bannard, was drawn into a friendship with him which quickly became too intense and disturbing, and this led to some sort of rupture which meant that they saw nothing – or very little – of each other for the next few years. All of which took place in the wake of his rejection by 'Laura': the sort of rejection which was liable to plunge him into a state of depression and, I dare say, some emotional vulnerability.

Let's leave it at that, for the time being, and move on to more routine matters. And go back to Johnson's own words, as well, describing his year of part-time study at Birkbeck College, which would have started in the autumn of 1955.

18: FURTHER EXTRACT FROM ARTICLE FOR *EDUCATION & TRAINING* (completed 14 January 1973)

[My Latin tutor at Davies's] died not long after I started at Birkbeck. I worked for an oil company in Kingsway during the day, and at six most

---

* See also *Christie Malry's Own Double-Entry*, Chapter III, in which Christie's mother reminds him, with some pride: 'I have, husbandless, brought you up not to miss a father, without damaging what they would call your normality.' Clearly this is a reference to Christie's sexuality; although it is not so clear who 'they' are meant to be.

evenings went to Birkbeck for two or three hours. The course was an internal equivalent of A-Level called Intermediate BA; I did English, Latin and History. I became secretary of the Literary Society, arranged a visit to and a discussion on the first production of *Waiting for Godot*, made friends I still have. Of the staff, Barbara Hardy ravished me with her intellect, Geoffrey Tillotson bored me with his pompousness, and Arthur Johnston made sense of Chaucer by reading the *Prologue* in the original pronunciation.

Barbara Hardy may have 'ravished' Johnson with her intellect, but she, in turn, remembers being somewhat in awe of him when he arrived at Birkbeck: mainly because she, too, had ambitions to be a writer but did not have the rock-solid confidence in her own abilities or destiny that Johnson seemed to radiate. (As would anyone, I suppose, who was accustomed to personal visits from the White Goddess.)

'I don't have many memories of Bryan but certainly I thought of him as an extremely relaxed and funny and sociable person – though rather plain and plump, not strongly sexual, as I remember thinking. One of my strongest memories is probably rather personal to me, and that is that while he was still doing the degree he was totally, totally confident about his ambition [to write] and about the likelihood of realizing that ambition. I was very envious of this because I'd never been allowed to be creatively ambitious, only academically ambitious. And there was Bryan doing an English degree as I had done, but saying, "Yes, I'm going to be a novelist." And when he talked about Beckett, he clearly thought of himself as someone – not in that class, exactly, but he spoke of Beckett and his own ambitions as if they belonged naturally together. I found that really quite astonishing and admirable. In a way, I think, Bryan's deprivations were also his advantage – he came and did his degree late and he'd had time to knock about and mature and feel creatively ambitious. But I wouldn't say that he *stood out* as being mature, because all of the Birkbeck students were mature. That was the nature of the place.'

As soon as he arrives at Birkbeck, Johnson starts to re-emerge again as a concrete, recognizable figure. I feel that during his time at Stanvac, I have lost sight of him: which is why I find that period so fascinating. His friendship with Michael Bannard is over and done with in a matter of months; but it seems to have left a profound impression. Then, during the summer, Johnson appears to have gone to Rome (by himself?) to pursue his own 'art-course', but I can't find any trace of that episode either. It's not until he starts attending Birkbeck that we encounter a new, reliable witness to his development: a woman called Joyce Yates – a single working mother with two young sons, Stephen and Michael, to whom Johnson soon found himself acting as a kind of surrogate father when he began an affair with her.

Joyce Yates outlived B. S. Johnson by almost thirty years, and I was lucky enough to interview her towards the end of her life, in the small, book-lined terraced house in Leigh-on-Sea, Essex, where she was enjoying an active retirement. Few people that I talked to about Johnson for this book knew him so well, or indeed remembered him so clearly.

'When I got to know him he was about twenty-two and I was already in my forties. So I was really his second mother. I'm sure somebody's told you that he absolutely adored his mother – he worshipped his mother, actually, and she looked after him like you would look after a child: you know, she washed his shirts, admired him when they were white and was a typical working-class mother.

'Bryan wasn't in the slightest politically aware when I met him – not the remotest bit interested in politics or what was going on – he just said, "They're all the same." He wasn't interested, because he couldn't really remember the 1930s, so he never knew a world where there wasn't what we achieved: you know, a health service, and education and comprehensive schools. Of course, he was as leftish as everybody was in the universities then, and Birkbeck was full of people like us who mostly came from working-class backgrounds: we were the first generation who could move on from secondary school to university if we were good enough.

'My main impression was that he was very, very backward, in the sense that he was still a teenager in his mid-twenties, because he'd been babied by his mother. Also, most of the working-class women he would have met up until that point were drudges so it wasn't until he went to Birkbeck and met me that he moved into a completely new world. I was the first woman that he'd ever met who read books – he'd only known shopgirls up until then.*

'We were both madly interested in the arts: I was devoted to the theatre and the cinema and I'd been reading steadily since I was seven. His thing at that time was really music and he was mad on jazz. He was determined to learn to play the trumpet but of course it's a life's work. He used to play me this Louis Armstrong record round at his parents' place, and he used to desperately try to play the exact riff that Louis Armstrong did. I thought it was killingly funny. But he knew much more about music than I did and above all he changed my life by introducing me to Bach. We used to go regularly to the Festival Hall and sit in the cheap seats behind the platform. We saw Cocteau come over and give a reading, and marvellous things like Edith Sitwell coming into a concert in red velvet with a red velvet turban

---

* A reference to Betty, whose parents kept a corner shop in Kingston?

[...] London was absolutely seething with music then and I was only living two hundred yards from the Albert Hall so we went every year to concerts there. He was really the main musical education of my life.

'We had so much in common it was ridiculous really. We both loved sports so we would play tennis together at the Birkbeck fields. Bryan was a good sportsman. He was good at soccer, and he was a good tennis player, as was I. Soon after I knew him we went out to the sports ground and played tennis and I could stand up to him but he was very, very strong and he beat me and came off laughing, and said, "Well thank God I'm better at something than you are."

'I forget where I first met him. Probably in the refectory when we were all eating together. He wasn't particularly good looking – you know, he wouldn't have you thinking, "Ah! That's Robert Redford." He always tended to be overweight. At home I remember he was completely like a fish out of water. He had his own room and it was full of books, but once I went to lunch at his house and he'd decided that he wanted to put this great big statue up in his bedroom, and his mother was absolutely terrified when he took it upstairs that it would fall through the floor.

'When I met Bryan he'd decided that he was going to be a poet, but I think it came from this crowd of people – what I used to call his Auden–Isherwood gang – that he was still quite friendly with. These homosexual men that we would run into at the theatre and at concerts. I refused to read any poetry that he wrote. I just used to say to him, "You don't know enough about philosophy or the things that poetry is concerned with – these sorts of high-flown things – but what you do know about is working-class life, and your own life. So you should be writing about that." This was the fifties, when the first novels by Sillitoe and John Wain were coming out, and it was almost the first time that working-class life had been described in literature at all.

'So in a way I introduced him to the novel. One day he suddenly came up to my flat and said, "I've decided to be a novelist" – having decided to be a poet for years – and I said, "Oh yes, that's nice," because I knew he'd read scarcely any novels. I don't think he'd even read Lawrence. He'd read James Joyce but he certainly didn't know anything about the nineteenth century. So I said, "Have a go at nineteenth-century novels first," and a few days later he came back and said, "I've just read Emily Brontë and it's absolutely stunning." He liked it because of the form, I think – messing about with time, and so on. But after that ... I don't think he ever read Richardson, or any of those people. He never talked about George Eliot or Dickens. I remember he did go through one stage when he said Shakespeare was rubbish, but I think that was jealousy because all the plays in London at that time were by Shakespeare.

'My sons would have been five and twelve when I met Bryan, and he was in and out of the house for almost the whole of the children's young lives. Ironically, he was a little bit like a child himself in all sexual matters. He took himself very seriously and he once said to me, "You know, I'm madly in love with you, but I don't want to marry you," and I just answered back, "Well, let's be thankful for small mercies." I'd no more marry him than fly to the moon! He didn't find it hard to get women at all because he was so charming, despite not being very good-looking, but he could sometimes be very depressed. He did talk about suicide, and once told me that when he was at school he cut his wrists. He needed a warm, motherly love, you see – like a lot of writers get, I suppose: women who look after them. Which reminds me that he was a great admirer of Robert Graves. I was studying psychology at the time and Bryan used to come up with what was, to me, pseudo-rubbish that Robert Graves was writing about his "muse" – while I was probably scrubbing the floor. I used to just shrug it off, because I came down on the scientific side of psychology.

'And in fact the sexual side of our relationship had finished by the time he went to King's, but I didn't mind, because that had only been a small part of it, as far as I was concerned. Much more important than that, for a while we had one of those rare and marvellous things which was a friendship between a man and a woman.'*

Buoyed up by the emotional and intellectual support of Joyce Yates, Johnson did well at Birkbeck. When his results came through he was still working for the Standard-Vacuum Oil Company during the daytimes, and he wrote up the occasion in a jokey imitation of the firm's house journal, the *Stanvac Meridian*.

19: PARODY *(July 1956)*

Fair, stocky, blue-eyed Bryan Johnson, one of Stanvac's Marine Accounts personnel, was noticed one day recently to be even more cheerful than usual. Reason: requisition-checker Johnson had heard successful result of important examination at London's world-renowned Birkbeck College. Pausing during coding of immense financial transactions, twenty-three year old Johnson said, 'I owe it all to Stanvac. But for the quiet

---

* Joyce Yates died late in 2002, at the fine old age of eighty-five, some two years after sharing these memories with me. We had had to break midway through the interview, when her liquidized lunch arrived from Meals on Wheels: she was no longer able to digest solids, but in spite of this handicap, she was in excellent spirits and looked back on her relationship with Johnson with amused fondness. She was, in every way, a living refutation of his own frequently expressed horror of the ageing process. They kept in touch until 1968, and she may well have been the subject of one of his more brutal later poems, 'No, I've Not', included in *Poems Two*.

period of rest during the day, I would never have had enough energy to make the grade.'

Fellow employees at Stanvac's sunlit, happy, fifth floor office [in] Holborn's broad throughway, Kingsway, crowded round to congratulate the somewhat embarrassed and self-effacing Portage Account Auditor. Seated at his tidy, all steel $200 desk, smiling Johnson said, 'This is the happiest day of my life.'

20: FURTHER EXTRACT FROM ARTICLE FOR *EDUCATION & TRAINING* (completed 14 January 1973)

In the summer term I applied to go as a fulltime student to two London colleges, King's and University. Both required applicants to declare which they preferred; I was honest and put King's on both simply (and now it seems so asinine, so grossly irresponsible) because I liked the sound of the name better. I made no attempt to determine the respective qualities of the English departments, or to ask for any other help or guidance. I still wince at the naivety of that choice. Of course I was not even interviewed by University College; but I was promised a place at King's for September 1956, at the age of twenty-three. When I told the Birkbeck Registrar he tried to dissuade me:

'You'll be surrounded by eighteen-year-old girls,' he warned me.

The fact that they were girls worried me not at all, but what did make me apprehensive was that they were all bright enough to have come straight from grammar school, glowing with high achievement, and the roundabout way I had joined them after my failure at eleven led me to believe I should have to work very hard indeed merely to stay in their company, let alone compete with them. Not so. After only a few weeks I found very few to whom I might feel myself inferior; no doubt my five years' greater maturity made a big difference. I edited five issues of the college literary magazine *Lucifer*, I wrote, directed, and acted with the Drama Society in London and on two tours of German and Danish universities. I had a disastrously important love-affair. I read *Tristram Shandy* and *Gawain*.

But the three years were unhappy and painful for me. I think (though there were other personal and emotional factors involved) it was because the course I was following unexpectedly seemed insufficiently related to the reasons for which I was following it. That is, much of what I was obliged to read seemed, by any standards I had and was taught, bad, boring and irrelevant; and the London English degree is notorious for falling between the stools of language and literature. Perhaps it is too much to ask that English departments at least take into account the possibility that they may have young writers amongst their undergraduates [. . .]

I'm sure we can take this as a reliable account of how Johnson responded to King's: it chimes exactly with the memories of many of his contemporaries there. Two details seemed invariably to stand out whenever I talked to the people who had known him as a student: his imposing physical presence, and the sense of *seriousness* with which he by now conducted himself – a seriousness, too, about his vocation as a writer, which can only have come from the emotional and intellectual growth spurt he had been through as Joyce Yates's lover. The poet and translator Alan Marshfield, Johnson's predecessor as editor of the King's literary magazine, *Lucifer*, told me, 'He stood out from his generation, his year at King's, as anyone would who was into literature in a serious way. I think there were a group of us who did, in fact –Maureen Duffy being one of the others. I wouldn't say he was popular, exactly, but certainly he was respected. He wasn't a smiling sort of person, he had a kind of serious look, and one engaged him in conversation on serious topics. You wouldn't call him light-hearted.'

Not only did Johnson's demeanour seem more serious than any of his contemporaries', his whole presence and physical appearance was different. This was certainly the impression of Patrick Snaith, who went on to become a close friend and a fellow member of the *Lucifer* editorial board:

'He stood out because he wore a dark business suit, and had the portly build of a forty-year-old, and had light brown shoes, and carried a very heavy briefcase. A lot of chaps wore blazers and the King's scarf, which wasn't his style at all. He wore a tie and was dressing like an older person. And when you went to his parents' house in Barnes you were astonished to find how organized and clerk-ish he was, with all his personal correspondence in files and so on.'

And here is another of his friends from that era, Thelma Fisher: 'My memory of that English group was that there were quite a lot of us straight from school; but I'd had a year out, so I wasn't straight from school – I was nineteen. There weren't very many men: I should think about half a dozen. And into these classes at King's would come this figure. I'm amazed now when I see that he was born in 1933, because I thought he was a lot older, but he must have been only twenty-three at the time. But I think of him as a grown-up man and the rest of us weren't. And he used to come in wearing a pinstripe suit and a black overcoat and he didn't speak for a long time to anybody. He wasn't the sort of strange character we would laugh about. He was very solemn, frightening, silent: I don't even know whether he was interested, but he came in and sat on his own and I suppose that was what was interesting. We would all be saying, "Who's going to beard this character first and find out what he's like?"'

Like many of the female English students at King's, Thelma Fisher was asked out on a few dates by Johnson. ('We went out in the first year [...] A very uneasy relationship because I never knew what was going on, he was very hidden and shut in.') Another of his student girlfriends, Roma Crampin, remembers that there was never anything casual about these romances, however short-lived they might have been. 'He certainly did take relationships very seriously,' she recalls. 'It would be interesting to know how many women he actually proposed to. He proposed to me once and I simply took it as a joke, but if I'd said yes, I wonder if we'd have been up the aisle...? We often used to go to the cinema or the theatre together: this was at a film, when he turned to me and said, "Shall we get married?" and I just laughed and answered, "Oh well, maybe not this week." But as I say, if I'd said, "I thought you'd never ask..." – would that have been it? But then I don't flatter myself that it really meant anything much.' (At which point her husband, Johnson's good friend Stuart Crampin, chipped in with the comment: 'This sounds to me like somebody who'd actually never experienced women.')

Johnson seems to have had an uneventful first year at King's. His lecture notes show him to have been a conscientious student, doing his best to absorb everything, even on a course which placed such a heavy emphasis on Old Norse and Anglo-Saxon. This was part of his professional mentality: writing was like accountancy, you had to learn the rules, you had to acquire your professional qualification. 'When I got to talk to him,' Thelma Fisher says, 'I found that he simply believed if he was going to be a writer then he'd better learn about writing; and he'd chosen King's because there you were made to do everything, right from the very beginnings of the language, point by point, so he thought that he wouldn't miss anything and he'd be able to take it all in.' He didn't really start to come out of his shell until the summer of 1957, when, for ten days in July, he took part in a drama society tour of German cities, playing Edward Tappercoom in *The Lady's Not for Burning*. Stuart Crampin was also in the cast.

Perhaps it had taken Johnson this long to decide that most of what he was being taught was a waste of time and he would be better off immersing himself in extra-curricular activity: which is exactly what he now did. In the autumn of 1957 he took over the editorship of the King's literary magazine, *Lucifer*, from Alan Marshfield. Then, having got a taste for the theatre, he directed a production of Genet's *The Maids*, which was both performed at college and entered for a national student drama festival. It was Johnson's own choice of play, selected because he considered it 'an ideal introduction to Genet's work and ideas [...] The dialogue of the play is brilliant, and there are many effective minor climaxes.' Two important aspects of this production, however, had nothing to do with the play itself: it brought him into contact with Genet's London agent, Rosica Colin, and it enabled him to spend more time getting to know an imposing, slightly stand-offish fellow student called Muriel Starkey, who was cast as Solange. Thus began a relationship which would lead to one of his greatest ever emotional disasters.

Johnson's production of *The Maids* was well received (with Frank Fisher's set attracting particularly favourable comment) and he attributed this, in part, to the fact that it had been more generously subsidized by the King's College Student Union than previous efforts. 'A somewhat larger grant was allowed for this production,' he wrote in a report afterwards, 'and the result shows what the Drama Society can do when adequately financed.' A throwaway comment, for sure, but retrospectively significant: the question of how creative work should be 'adequately financed' would become, in a nutshell, one of the great dilemmas of his life. It also hung over his editorship of *Lucifer*. Typically, on taking over the magazine he had decided that the whole enterprise needed reorganizing from the bottom up and threw himself into the task with relentless energy and efficiency. (The kind of efficiency he would later expect, and in his view never receive, from his publishers.) He spent weeks drawing up business plans and writing to potential advertisers, trying to put the magazine on a secure financial footing. He began to learn the basics of page layout and typography, guided by the keen eye of his art editor, Stuart Crampin – one of whose unrealized ideas it was to cut holes through the pages of one issue, so that readers could 'see through' to a passage or illustration that came later. (Sound familiar?) In addition, this was when he made contact with students at Nottingham University, which he visited to watch their magazine being printed and to compare editorial policies: in this way, he first encountered a dedicated but convivial young scholar called Tony Tillinghast. A working knowledge of the methods of book production was beginning to take shape, and Johnson was starting to form the defining friendships of his adult life.

There is nothing too exceptional about the form or content of Johnson's issues of *Lucifer*, although for a student magazine its standards were pretty high. Some of his early poetry ('Natural Progress', 'An Eye for Situation') appeared here, as did 'The Rook Rifle', a short autobiographical fragment about a holiday with Betty in Devon, which later formed part of 'Clean Living is the Real Safeguard'. The review section at the back of the magazine reveals that he was already thoroughly immersed in the London theatre scene, writing knowledgeably about John Osborne, enthusiastically about Brendan Behan and Joan Littlewood and complaining at some length that 'There is comparatively little interest in this country in Bertolt Brecht, one of the great innovators in drama of this century.' (It sounds as though Johnson himself had been to see the Berliner Ensemble when they visited London in 1955.) A few pieces were written pseudonymously, under the name Henry Wriothesley, patron of Nashe and Shakespeare and possibly the 'fair youth' of the sonnets. Should we read anything into the fact that Johnson gave himself a homosexual alter ego? Probably not.

Lucifer rarely had much of a political edge under Johnson's editorship, but this may not have been his choice.

21: EDITORIAL *(May 1958)*

Editorial One

Let us add our still small voice.

In the name of humanity
Ban the hydrogen bomb
Begin unilateral disarmament *immediately.*
Let Britain lead in doing these things.

(Note by BSJ: This intended editorial for the May 1958 [issue] was vetoed by *all* other members of the staff – Kristin, Stuart, Muriel, Ted, Patrick – which hurt me not a little.)

If he was not always successful in getting his own way editorially, however, Johnson proved himself a good hustler, and a good advocate on behalf of *Lucifer* when the need arose. Early signs of his persuasiveness in obtaining public funding for his work appear in the college newspaper, *King's News*, of 14 November 1957, for which he wrote an article headed 'THE DAMNING OF "LUCIFER"'. His argument – that, since the magazine could be relied upon to lose money every year, it should be subsidized by union funds – would later come to be a leitmotif running throughout his literary career: for Johnson, financial insecurity always seemed to be a prerequisite of literary merit. 'If its standards are to be maintained,' he wrote, '*Lucifer* cannot avoid the risk of making a loss'; and he described the magazine as 'a platform for those who have something to say which is above the journalistic standards of *King's News*, and which provides interesting reading for those who have similar high standards.'

This unapologetic elitism won a good number of supporters, and in February 1958 a motion that the magazine should be subsidized was agreed at a general meeting of King's College Student Union, by a large majority. A happy state of affairs which lasted for only ten months, it being reported on 8 December that year that the union's executive committee had strong objections to the magazine on both financial and aesthetic grounds: 'Mr

Martin alleged that little of the contents were generally understood, but both Mr Bryan Johnson and the other editor, Miss Kristin Beaman, stated firmly that they would not lower their standards even if others regarded the result as esoteric.'* None of which would be worth recording at much length here, were it not for the fact that this little storm in a student teacup prompted the *King's News* profile writer to pen a fascinating portrait of Johnson, which eloquently suggests how he was perceived by the undergraduate population as a whole.

PROFILE – BRYAN JOHNSON

Bryan Johnson is not the sort of person one would expect to read about in a *King's News* profile. He is not popular, not even liked and, some would say, not likeable. Neither does he qualify for this honour as one who has 'got on' in the Union.

He left school at seventeen, without the usual honours, and learnt accountancy; then studied for 'A-level' at night school and eventually at Birkbeck College, while doing a full-time job with Standard-Vacuum Oil Company during the day. He entered the English Department at King's at the age of twenty-three, determined to pursue his particular interests – drama and creative writing – and to try all that King's had to offer him. Disappointed at finding how little this was, he concentrated on his two main interests.

In his second year, as treasurer of the Drama Society and editor of *Lucifer*, he soon found himself up against a Union financial policy which, to his disgust, could allow five-sixths of the Union's income to be spent on sport, but would not give adequate financial backing to either its Drama Group or its Literary Magazine.

As a result of his derogatory but constructive criticism, the Union financial system was investigated and revised. Both the Drama Society and *Lucifer* have been granted more money, but five-sixths of the Union income is still spent on sport. Bryan is not satisfied, but then he very rarely is.

Paradoxically, it is probably Bryan's experience and knowledge of Union procedure that prevent him from seeking any official position on the Executive Committee. He does not fancy himself as a public speaker, nor as a future politician; his criticisms are always based on a knowledge of the facts, and when he sees the need for reform he doesn't talk about it, he gets it done.

For the Drama Society he produced one-act plays for the L.U.D.S.

---

* A militant commitment to the esoteric, evoking philistine cries of outrage and incomprehension: here, in student microcosm, we have an exact rehearsal of Johnson's run-in with the *Daily Mail* twelve years later. (See below, pp. 290–2.)

and B.D.L. festivals, and *Much Ado about Nothing* for the European Tour last summer. But if you know Bryan at all, it will probably be in connection with *Lucifer*. As Editor it has been his aim to broaden the scope of the magazine while maintaining a high literary standard and publishing a proportion of purely creative writing. His purpose is to give a voice to student opinion – and not necessarily a majority opinion – on subjects which are of importance and interest to students.

Whether or not he has succeeded, you can judge only by reading *Lucifer*.

Certain Union officials who have met Bryan's opposition have come away with the impression that he makes trouble for trouble's sake. On the contrary, there is always some definite purpose behind his attacks, and he usually achieves it.

Most people dislike Bryan, even if they agree with his opinions, because he has no time for fools and is not afraid to show it. A few people like Bryan, even if they disagree with him, for the same reason. These are people who are not afraid to criticise and be criticised; who feel strongly about the things that matter and are prepared to justify their opinions in the face of opposition. If you are not one of these people, don't worry: the chances are he won't like you either!

It can hardly have been encouraging, for someone who was prone to insecurity in any case, to be publicly informed that 'most people' disliked him. Stuart and Roma Crampin also remember that, on the *Lady's Not for Burning* tour of Germany, Johnson was often 'derided': 'we tended to see him as the buffoon' and 'we poured scorn on him' for not knowing what a duvet was when they arrived at one guesthouse, and he asked for sheets and blankets instead. Another anecdote which tells us something about the social milieu from which Johnson had emerged – and the new one to which he was painfully trying to raise himself – concerns a party he threw at his parents' house in Barnes. (He lived at home with his mother and father throughout his time at King's – until he was twenty-eight, in fact. Even after that he continued to take his washing home every weekend until he got married in 1964.) Part of the midday preparation for this party, apparently, involved taking down the three flying ducks which adorned the wall of his parents' lounge, because these were such powerful signifiers of lower-middle or upper-working class bad taste. They left marks on the wall, however, and these were the subject of amused comment from his undergraduate guests.

If Johnson was an isolated figure at King's, regarded by some with awe and by others with derision, it made sense that he would meet his match in someone considered equally unapproachable. 'A very severe kind of woman,' is how Frank Fisher now remembers Muriel Starkey (he got to know her when he played the Archbishop to Muriel's St Joan in a college production of Shaw's play). His wife Thelma observes that 'I don't think anybody got very friendly with Muriel. There might well have been a kind of like-to-like attraction between her and Bryan, because both of them were obviously very complex, rather hidden characters and the rest of us weren't.' Remembering, vaguely, that she used to talk about some boyfriend from her past who had either died or otherwise been lost to her, she adds, 'Muriel had a sort of tragic air.' Roma Crampin, looking back on the time when Johnson's obsession with Muriel had reached overwhelming proportions, says simply, 'He got to the stage when he didn't know why it was. I think she just came at the right time to be this fetish thing. Even after it had all finished, he kept on and on about her.'

Readers already familiar with Johnson's work will know the extent to which he went 'on and on about her'. In poem after poem and novel after novel: *Albert Angelo, Trawl, The Unfortunates* – even, now I come to think of it, *Travelling People*, when Henry, having listened quite sympathetically to Kim's account of her boyfriend's death, suddenly spins off on a tangent of his own:

22: EXTRACT FROM *TRAVELLING PEOPLE*

'Look, you think you're so bloody tragic, your love having been killed. But there's much worse than that, love, much worse, much worse, much worse, when your love reveals herself to be utterly indifferent, to have betrayed you, to be nothing like the love she seemed; then it's just as final, just as definite, just as much a bereavement, as death, but still there's this physical *thing* that walks around, in the image of your love, reminding you of your lost love, tormenting you with what might have been. Believe me, that's worse than death, love, worse than the death of your love!'

It clearly got to the stage where his friends (never mind his wife!) got bored with hearing about it, and I have to confess that I, too, get bored reading Johnson when he insists on raking over the embers of this dead relationship again and again – especially now that I have come to believe that it wasn't even the most important relationship of his early life anyway. So I'm not going to write about it much. Readers who want the full account of how the affair began to go wrong on the second King's drama society tour of Germany, in the summer of 1958, when Johnson himself was directing *Much Ado About Nothing*, can refer themselves to the relevant pages of *Trawl*. (To which I have only one thing to add: a reminiscence by Patrick Snaith, who remembers helping Muriel put her suitcase in the luggage rack of a German train, only to find Johnson rounding on her in a jealous rage: 'He told her off for letting me do that. I was already quite a close chum of his, but his view was that men only do things like that if they want to get something in return. He was particularly watchful of her, to put it mildly.')

Anyway, Johnson and Muriel went out for a while, and then they split up: let's keep it as banal as that. She 'betrayed' him, in his parlance, and from then on he would usually refer to her in melodramatic phrases such as his 'dead love'. Even towards the end of his life, his tragic sense of abandonment would flare up sometimes, an immovable tumour of hurt lodged deep in his being, and in one of his last prose pieces, 'Everyone Knows Somebody Who's Dead', he was still clearly so wounded about Muriel's decision to leave him and return to her former boyfriend that he continued to refer to it in the most unforgiving terms.

The end of the affair plunged him into one of his worst-ever depressions, and for some time he considered giving up his degree and not taking his finals. It was Stuart Crampin who talked him out of this, and who allowed Johnson virtually to move into his room during their last few weeks of revision. Crampin, who read mathematics, had covered his walls with graphs and charts showing how many hours he intended to spend on each subject every day. Johnson was deeply impressed by this, and for the rest of his life would always draw up 'Stuart-style graphs' which showed, in two separate columns, the daily totals for how many words he had written and how many hours he had spent on each of his novels. (A useful biographical tool, I must say: but then Johnson always had his eye on posterity, and I reckon he was certain that someone like me would come along and write this book one day. I have the resigned sense of having been chosen to fulfil a confident prophecy.) Of course, there must have been a huge element of self-dramatization in all this: 'I think maybe he was enjoying feeling a bit suicidal about it,' Roma Crampin speculates, 'you know, wanting to give up everything – it was a drama.' Or perhaps he was simply trying to persuade himself, for some reason, that this affair with Muriel had been an emotional narrative of epic proportions, when in reality it was much less than that. Johnson's friendship with Joyce Yates, anyway, was still very much alive at this point (although it was no longer sexual) and as so often she recalled this whole episode with clear-eyed, rueful pragmatism: 'He got friendly with this girl [Muriel] but I never met her – I thought it was unwise, really – but he used to tell me about her. He was madly in love with her – exactly like everybody's first love, which absolutely transforms your life and is never repeated. He also told me that he was very jittery about it the whole time: he was nervous that she might break it off, you know how it is. Finally, he came in one day and said in a tragic tone, "She's betrayed me," or something. It took a long time for him to get over this and he was still talking about betrayal all the time. But the thing about Bryan, what I remember about him more than anything, is that everything he tried, he failed at for some reason or another.'

*

Johnson's formal education was now over. So before we leave it behind altogether, it seems worth recording his final words on the subject:

23: FINAL EXTRACT FROM ARTICLE FOR *EDUCATION & TRAINING* (completed 14 January 1973)

I came down with a 2:2. I thought it was very fair. I would have been pleased with any sort of degree at all, in fact. According to their rules, I was a lower-second-class of person; I accepted that, as long as it was clearly understood that it was according to their rules. For the next five years, until I could support myself wholly by writing, it counted (somewhat ironically) as a Good Honours Degree to increase my salary as a supply teacher through dozens of schools in west and north London. I will not say I necessarily knew which ones they were, but I think I saw many of my earlier selves going to waste, waste, in those five years.

All my life I have been underestimated by the educational system, I feel. Now when I win the odd literary or film award it is often against, in spite of those teachers and contemporaries who so misjudged me that I feel I have won them. Not that it matters, of course; no doubt none of them even remember me, and I now know none of them.

Do I sound paranoid and bitter? Yes, I am, that is indeed the way I feel about my educators, that is the way they made me. No doubt the war was not their fault; no doubt there are worse things than a fractured, fragmented education like mine (David Storey's novel *Pasmore* is about someone who has a breakdown at thirty after a long smooth progression on an educational conveyor-belt); perhaps the usual optimist is already contemplating a letter saying 'Ah, but you did win through in the end, you did get the university education for which your mind qualified you.'

Obviously I was university material, in the end; whether I was or not at sixteen seems doubtful. I tried hard to be an accountant, to be what my education had fitted me for. Even now I have the marginal benefit of being able to touch-type this article; my new novel *Christie Malry's Own Double-Entry* leans very heavily on knowledge I gained in learning book-keeping; and I could have annotated almost every paragraph of this account with page references from my books where I have made professional use of material related to my schooldays.

The point is that very few people are writers and thus able to make

some positive use of virtually everything that happens to them, including the disasters, the chaos; what do the others do?

This sour negativity about his education can be read, in part, as an indicator
of Johnson's state of mind early in 1973. But clearly he did not look back on
his time at King's with much satisfaction. All the same, he had at least
managed to get some writing done. Apart from the poems and short prose
pieces that found their way into *Lucifer*, he had also begun work on a novel,
Not Counting the Savages, which was later abandoned after a few thousand
words. The handwritten manuscript survives, and it turns out to be an
endearing piece of apprentice work, a serio-comic fictionalization of his
affair with Joyce Yates at Birkbeck and afterwards, which provides a few
useful insights into his young personality: superstition and romantic insecurity seem to be the main characteristics, with Joyce being thanked at one
point because 'she acted as an antidote to all my romantic pretentiousness'.
For the first time but not for the last, Johnson names his alter ego 'Henry',
and the few pages which he completed describe Henry and Joyce (who is
'17 years older than him, and seemed to him at that moment the fount of
all wisdom, honesty and maturity') walking near the Round Pond in Hyde
Park: a location which the narrator describes as 'Murphy country', thereby
telegraphing the book's clearest stylistic debt.

24: EXTRACT FROM THE UNCOMPLETED NOVEL
NOT COUNTING THE SAVAGES (1957-8)

Henry had a tremendous memory and affection for anniversaries; even
the smallest one would bring forth floods of nostalgia to his mind. Every
day in his life was memorable for something, and he regularly had a
moment's devotion to its memory sometime during the day. Henry's
chief memory was of a girl he had loved when he was sixteen, and who
had betrayed him when he was nineteen; no day went by but that he
thought of her, though it was now over four years since he had last
seen her. When his latest girl threw him over he would sink back, in his
anguish, into his great previous anguish, and lose himself in labyrinths
of self-pity. Yet all the time he realised that this first girl was a creation
of his own who did not really exist, a projection of his ideals and ideas
on to a girl who was hardly pretty and only of mediocre intelligence;
yet still he could not escape from her.

But enough of this, oh possibly unromantic reader; let us have:
action.

Henry was crossing Kensington High Street in the way that he
always crossed roads with three place-name elements in them: the left

foot first on to the road, eyes only performing the Kerb Drill (without turning the head) so that passers-by might not think him careful, then across the road finishing with a little run, and landing so that the sole of the right shoe touched the kerb whilst the back of the heel rested in the gutter; a quick contraction of the right hip abductors (the *gluteus medius* and the *gluteus minimus*) to raise the left ilium [?] slightly above the right, a considerable dorsiflexion of the right *tibia* at the ankle joint (the right leg being kept straight at the knee by contraction of the quadriceps muscle), the final contribution of the *gluteus maximus* (to say nothing of the action of the foot) and Henry was standing on the pavement.

These things, gentle reader, are most important; for how could one know just how Henry crossed the road without this detailed explanation? Not to put too fine a point on it, one cannot conceive how the circling spheres could continue to pursue their celestial orbits without this explanation. And so, reader, bear with me, and accept that these things are important.

The title *Not Counting the Savages* – which Johnson would use again, more than a decade later, for a completely unrelated television play – came, apparently, from 'a brilliant parody of Tennessee Williams by Richard Knight'.[2] Which brings us bang up against one of his most influential but, I'm afraid, seemingly untraceable friendships at King's. Richard Knight was a fellow English student who appears to have been instrumental in shaping Johnson's literary taste. When sending out the novel *Travelling People* to prospective agents a couple of years later, Johnson would write a letter locating himself in the minor but 'very virile and interesting' tradition of the novel represented by 'writers such as Petronius, Apuleius, Rabelais, Cervantes, Nashe, Sterne, and Samuel Beckett'. The very concept of this tradition might have been imparted to him by Richard Knight, whose particular enthusiasm was Burton's *The Anatomy of Melancholy* (on which he later wrote a thesis), and who was also an enthusiast for Elizabethan prose writers (he provided Johnson with the Elizabethan epigraphs that preface some of the chapters in *Travelling People*). Certainly, after Knight had left King's and taken up a research post at Washington University in St Louis, Missouri, they kept up a voluminous correspondence (some of it on reel-to-reel tape), although Johnson's half of it seems to be irrevocably lost. And Richard Knight was one of the companions who travelled with him to Dublin immediately after graduation in the summer of 1959 – the other being John Holden, a painter Johnson had known since his schooldays.

Johnson and Knight managed to find a rented flat together on the Lower Rathmines Road and proceeded to soak up the atmosphere of the city which had played host, at various times, to some of their greatest literary heroes including Swift, Joyce and Flann O'Brien. O'Brien's *At Swim-Two-Birds* had recently been rescued from obscurity by the London publishers MacGibbon & Kee, and Johnson had fallen in love with it – to the extent that one chapter of *Travelling People* (a clear evocation of this Dublin visit, albeit with a few name changes) would be written in close imitation of its style.* And meanwhile, although he was still ostensibly heartbroken over the collapse of his relationship with Muriel, he was also on the lookout for a replacement.

25: LETTER *(6 August 1959)*

To Stuart Crampin

[. . .] Now, I have met a girl here named Chris who lives in the flat below us, and who is My Sort in the natural way of things; we get on marvellously in everything except religion, and religion unfortunately affects sex from her point of view. In fact, it proves an insuperable barrier to everything except kissing and a little gentle ear-chewing: and even this latter is half regarded as devilish, and will no doubt be confessed in due time. The rot started the first time we went out; the morning after coming home from a dance at three in the morning (the dances here are civilized – they start at nine and end at two) I asked her how she had slept; she replied that she was so tired that she had fallen asleep in the middle of saying her prayers. I restrained myself, but with an effort, and I had to lean up against a wall to prevent myself from falling; I can't remember when I last knew a girl who said prayers – wait, yes I can, I was four at the time, and she was three; I think I had just seen through God, then, and was annoyed about Him for not existing. Anyway, I flatter myself that Chris is praying for my conversion; but conversion from what, I don't know, since I have no beliefs to be converted from. It's embarrassing, to say the least, as well, out in the streets, for whenever we pass a catholic church she crosses herself; not protestant ones, she says 'That one's yours' whenever I point one out to her that she has not crossed herself for; I, of course, hotly deny ownership. Ah, well. 'Tis enough to drive one to rape, or something.

The tone of the letter is fairly light-hearted; but Johnson, as always, took his relationship with Chris very seriously, making it the subject of what must count as his first major poem, 'A Dublin Unicorn'. A poem in which – as with *Travelling People* – you can't help noticing a mismatch between

---

* This chapter was deleted from the novel at his agent's suggestion; but was later included in both *Statement Against Corpses* and *Aren't You Rather Young To Be Writing Your Memoirs?* under the title 'Broad Thoughts from a Home'.

form and content. Casting himself as the noble, mythical beast, fatally wounded by the rejection of a woman who insists on preserving her virtue, Johnson writes:

> Proudly and humbly it laid its silver
> head and golden horn down in her lap, and
> looked upward to her face in trust and peace:
> and then the arrow juddered in its flank.
>
> Her horror made her wish the arrow had
> struck her instead, but it was unicorn's
> blood upon her thighs; her tears were too late
> now, and virginity was meaningless.

In Johnson's manuscript, there are several stanzas – later deleted – which make the point of the poem quite unambiguous:

> You are the virgin, I the unicorn,
> Your church, the hunters; and this city of
> Dublin represents the heavy forest
> To which I came from London solitude.
>
> The parallels will therefore seem to fit
> Quite easily; at least, enough for you
> To see the way I feel about your church
> And you, and being hunted down by both.

The language is high flown and romantic, the verse is carefully wrought, but is anything really being recorded here, apart from Johnson's frustration at not being allowed inside somebody's pants for several weeks? Well, I suppose the same could be said of 'To His Coy Mistress'. Which may indeed have been his inspiration.

Later in the same letter to Stuart Crampin, he describes a visit to a canal-side pub where 'one thing leading, as in the natural course of things, to another, [I] started drinking with the lock-keeper; this was about five, and we only stopped for a meal in his cottage before they shut at ten thirty. He is a wonderful man, and he had a friend over from England whom he knew at school; they are both old enough to have been here in the time of the Trouble, and they gave me some insight into the way The Black and Tans worked; we were right bastards to the Irish, you know, it was worse than Cyprus, and on our own doorstep, too.'

More than thirteen years later, on a winter's night in November 1972, Johnson was sitting at his desk writing – or rather, unable to write. By this stage, with his literary career beginning to feel like an uphill struggle, his beloved mother recently killed by cancer, and his marriage under increasing strain, he had more than enough reason to be depressed. That night, for some reason, he made a careful inventory of all the objects that were before him on his desk. (A desk which his good friend John Furse referred to as a 'shrine', so cluttered was it with semi-sacred objects.) Among the items he catalogued were a Byronic skull cup given to him by a former neighbour, Doug Bamford, and a candleholder 'given in Dublin by the lock-keeper at Portobello Bridge on the Rathmines Road'. Johnson made a note to this effect: 'Told him my son would have it. Do you have any, he asked. No, but I shall do. 1959, that was, Steven, six years before you.' Which makes me believe that his encounter with the lock-keeper must have impressed itself more than casually on his consciousness. There were some incidents in Johnson's life which he seemed to imbue with a talismanic significance, and this meeting feels like one of them. Johnson's trip to Dublin, like his 'vision' of the White Goddess, like his early friendship with Michael Bannard, is one of those things he never wrote about except in teasing fragments: and yet from those fragments it's clear that it was an episode of huge importance for him, full of portents and meaningful happenings; one of those peculiar times when he seemed to be living life with a sort of supra-natural, almost numinous intensity. While staying in Ireland he jotted down a brief, day-to-day account of his time there, which ends with a description of his saying goodbye to Chris, followed by the words, 'Amen. Please God I return soon.'*

He had travelled to Dublin by hitch-hiking all the way to the ferry point at Holyhead, in north Wales, and on this journey another extremely important encounter had taken place. Once again, he would look back on this encounter towards the end of his life, struggling to make sense of it, to find some sort of pattern. And this was how he remembered it, in October 1973, when he had little more than two weeks left to live:

26: EXTRACT FROM THE FILM FAT MAN ON A BEACH (1973)

How did I find this place in the first place. Well, I was hitch-hiking through north Wales. At the time I was rather an elderly student of twenty-six and I'd been reading English, which is a very bad thing for a writer to read – a quite stupid thing for a writer to read, actually, at university. And I'd been besotted by Irish writers like Sam Beckett, James Joyce and Flann O'Brien but I wanted to see the Dublin that they'd all written about. So I hitch-hiked from London on the Holyhead road through north Wales and was given a lift, not to say picked up, by

---

* Another curiosity which survives from this visit is a reel-to-reel tape recording of Johnson, Richard Knight and Christine reading extracts from Samuel Beckett's *Murphy* together. Johnson is the best reader, by some margin.

a man who owned a country club at Abersoch and he, during the course of perhaps three-quarters of an hour car journey along the A5, offered me a job as a barman; as I was a student I was obviously going to be cheap for him, at this country club he ran in Abersoch. I couldn't take the job then. I went on to Dublin, but after about a month my money ran out there, naturally, so I rang him up and said was the offer of a job still open, and I came here, and that's the way, one of those things [...] if I'd been sitting in a different place on that road, or if I'd in some way missed him by ten seconds, that man stopping at that point, the whole of my life would have been different subsequently. I shouldn't, for instance, have written the first novel I wrote, which was about the experiences of that summer, here in Lleyn. That was how I came to Lleyn. I remember leaving him on the junction of that road off the A5. He took me as far as, I think it is, Bettws-y-Coed, and he said: 'I am going down there' and I looked down there and it was a marvellously sunlit glacial valley. It looked like Eldorado. It looked absolutely marvellous. So this was probably one of the things which made me remember his offer of a job, made me want to go, because it looked like Eldorado. It looked like a very special place. Lleyn is a very special and a very curious and a very strange place.

The club where Johnson came to work in the summer of 1959 was called the Glyn Club, and it was run by a man called James Martland. It is now a pub which stands on Lon Garmon, leading up the hill west out of Abersoch towards Llangian. In those days it catered for wealthy business people from the Midlands and the north-west: being middle class, and largely uncultured, these were exactly the sort of people who were likely to raise Johnson's hackles. For the most part, however, he seems to have held his tongue, kept his head down, and got on with his work. He was to spend two consecutive summers at the Glyn (the second in the more exalted capacity of manager), but it was from the first that he drew most of the material for *Travelling People*. It seems strange, now, that he should have found the setting so exotic and the experience so eye-opening. But then Johnson had led a relatively circumscribed life up until that point, and the world was smaller then: nowadays the Lleyn peninsula is smothered by an almost unbroken coating of English caravans every summer, but in the late 1950s it was probably a better-kept secret. Certainly it would have been an unusual holiday destination for a Londoner.

There seems little point in dwelling on Johnson's time at the Glyn, because he wrote about it so faithfully and at such length in *Travelling People* – where the entire epistolary section, for instance, is pretty much a word-for-word reproduction of a long letter he wrote at the time to Joyce

Yates. Names were changed, of course (the Glyn becomes the Stromboli and Johnson himself becomes Henry Henry), but the vulgarity of the holiday-making guests and the petty sexual rivalries among the staff seem to have been drawn directly from life. The only serious piece of fictionalization (perhaps wish-fulfilment would be nearer the truth) comes in the climactic scenes of love-making, since Johnson's relationship with the co-worker he refers to as 'Kim' never appears to have reached that point.

One way or another, it had been an eventful summer: but now Johnson had to return to London to face an uncertain future. Outwardly, he was still maintaining a pose of absolute confidence that he would soon be making a living as a writer, but so far he was getting little official encouragement. A project over which he had laboured long and hard – a radio dramatization of Albrecht Goes's novel *Arrow to the Heart* – was summarily rejected by the BBC. (Sample comments from the rejection slip: 'This seems to me excessively gloomy [...] I should say it's a typical teutonic essay in pessimism: also the dialogue is terribly stiff and monotonous.' 'I entirely agree. Hopeless.' etc. etc.) On Boxing Day, 1959, he started work on *Travelling People*, a novel inspired by his few weeks' work at the Glyn Club, but progress was extremely slow and tentative. Later in his career, Johnson would refuse to show anyone – even his wife – the least sample of work-in-progress. But he sent off *Travelling People* almost chapter-by-chapter to several of his friends and hung on their criticisms and words of praise: depending, in particular, on the detailed and attentive comments of Tony Tillinghast whose hand-written notes are plastered all over the manuscript.

Meanwhile there was the small matter of supporting himself. For a few months he set himself up as a private tutor: but the money was poor, and besides, there was no satisfaction to be gained from teaching the children of the affluent. In January 1960 he applied, instead, to work as a supply teacher inside the state system, and within a matter of days found himself employed by Surrey County Council, teaching Maths and Religious Instruction, of all things, at a local secondary modern. This was to prove typical of the hand-to-mouth existence he had to cope with for the next three years or so: by March 1960, as he wrote to one correspondent, he had already taken 'English [...], Basket-making (at which I am rather good, and proud of it!) some Maths, lots of Library periods, Religious Knowledge, Current Affairs (I nearly got them to send a telegram to Macmillan over Nuclear Disarmament; but failed because sufficient money could not be raised [...]): I also take small groups for remedial writing and reading, which are quite rewarding. The other day I took a couple of music lessons, and played the piano (to my very limited ability) to them; before rendering Beethoven I asked them to name the piece; one boy guessed correctly: the Moonlight Sinatra. They are fascinated by the way I dress; the day I wore my purple sweater for a basketwork lesson one little boy came up to me and said: "Cor, Sir, you ent arf bashing up the old pullover today entyer?" And some new shoes came in for "Cor, dig them suedes!"'³

I have heard different verdicts on Johnson's skills as a teacher, but there seems little doubt that he had a rapport with children, and liked them. He was, after all, still helping Joyce Yates by looking after her children every weekend. Certainly an unpublished poem he wrote around this time, besides providing a good snapshot of his rather unhappy state of mind, suggests that his relationship with the pupils put into his temporary care was strong and affectionate:

27: POEM *(5 February 1960)*

> Twenty-seven today; and I have lived
> to be so much a different person from
> the one I hoped to be that only with
> the greatest difficulty can I think
> of myself then at all: the process of
> assimilation and acceptance does
> its work so well in superseding all
> my past ambitions and desires, forcing
> proof after proof upon me of the truth:
> freedom is not possible until the
> deadness of the past is acknowledged, and
> necessity granted recognition.
>
> And yet today the children bring small gifts
> for me, on this my birthday; although they
> have not known me long at all, a month in
> fact, our contact was immediate and true:
> thus emphasising the failure of my
> other relationships, where months and years
> pass and no-one seems to approach closer.
>
> Should I then take an option on the youth
> of these my children? Adopt their simple
> faith in the immediate? And does it help
> to remember a time of youth myself
> when I perhaps saw nothing further than
> the end of school today, play, and bedtime?

The convoluted, not to say incoherent, diction in the first stanza of this poem indicates that all was not entirely well in the Johnsonian consciousness at this point. He was still attempting to convince himself that, in Muriel, he had found and lost the love of his life, and he was still trying to find someone to replace her. He and Chris had seen each other a few times since his trip to Ireland, but their friendship had finally petered out. This was how he described their most recent meeting, over the Christmas period, 1959:

28: EXTRACT FROM LETTER *(11 January 1960)*

To Stuart Crampin

> Chris gave me to understand that things would be fine when I heard things from the man Up There; I replied that things would be fine when she heard things from men down here. So we parted Friends, the very lightest of brushed kisses being the only thing of a sensual nature that passed between us; except for Chris's congenital handholding. Not even an earnibble. I found myself very relieved, somewhat to my surprise, and feeling not much else. So, no doubt if I go to Ireland next year I shall see her, but nothing will ever come of it. Meanwhile I continue to enjoy Guinness.

Very soon after this, another of Johnson's tentative romances failed to blossom; but this one shows a rather different side to him. Just as Barbara Hardy had 'ravished him with her intellect' at Birkbeck, so he had been awestruck by one of his younger tutors at King's, Lucia Glanville. After his graduation – and her move to a lectureship at Oxford – they corresponded quite frequently, and his letters give the lie to any easy notion of Johnson the unreconstructed 1950s chauvinist: they are polite, thoughtful, consider-ate, even bordering on the reverential. Lucia Glanville (now Lucia Turner) told me that whenever she remembers Johnson – whom she described as 'an unforgettable person' – she always thinks in terms of Chaucerian qualities such as *gentilnesse* and *courteisie*. (Another of Johnson's King's contemporaries, Judy Cooke, remembers his gentlemanly treatment of Lucia Glanville: 'There was another teacher, who of course Bryan made a set at, a young girl, a redhead, a very nervous girl – it was her first job. We were really rather rude in one of her lectures and she just went pink, pinker, pinker, pinker! But it was Bryan who went up to apologize for our behaviour at the end of the lecture.')

Finally, on 20 January 1960, using tactics which would not have dis-graced an Elizabethan sonneteer, Johnson took the plunge and sent a poem he had written for her, accompanied by a long explanatory note. 'You must take it how you will,' he wrote, 'and never speak to me again if you wish.'

Struggling to express himself clearly, but not too crudely, he added that he was sending the poem because 'you are so bound by convention that (quite rightly – I am not saying this is wrong) the man must make the first move; and I am so aware that you are so good, too good for me, that I cannot make this first move; but perhaps I am, very clumsily, doing so now.'

I'm not sure why Johnson felt that Lucia Glanville was 'too good' for him: it might have been to do with her intellectualism, a quality he always found at once daunting and attractive in a woman, or with the fact that she was strongly committed to Christianity, a subject they discussed at length in their letters. In any case, having worked out (apparently with a certain amount of effort) what it was that Johnson was actually proposing, she gently turned him down. And for once – although it presumably didn't add to his joie de vivre – this rejection did not provoke him to bitterness:

29: EXTRACT FROM LETTER *(17 March 1960)*

To Lucia Glanville

> I'm sorry the 'difficult bit' was so hard to understand; but, as I said, our relationship seemed to me to be so subtle and almost intangible that I could not very well put it in any other way. And let me say at once that no one could have had a more sweet refusal than yours, and that I am immensely glad to have the prospect of you as a friend, but that I still feel that a combination of your sort of person and my sort of person would have been a successful one, and a rewarding one. [...] Yes, I thought, too, that we had disposed of the student/teacher relationship at Christmas; and hoped only at the end when the lights and the wind in your hair at Charing Cross hit me, that it might become something more. But, no, never think that you have misled me, nor that I have even misled myself; for I admire your honesty and freedom from deceit, and regard them above all things in anyone; and you don't *frighten* me – your brain may overawe me, but only in things in which I am quite happy to be overawed. And if you are "better off, by being ... a Christian", then I would agree, and say, yes, it would be wonderful for me if I could believe in the same way; how many problems it would solve! [...] I am glad that you are happy, and I hope to come and see you in your happiness at Oxford when circumstances permit; I have almost ceased to believe in happiness; the most which seems to be permitted me is a kind of uneasy content, or a numbness in which I am only half alive and in which I am unable to see my unhappiness. When I think about it, it seems so trite, so obviously self-pitying, so everything

condemnatory you can say about it, but nevertheless it's true, true, true, it exists, hurts, damns. But now I'm using religious language! But, as a friend of mine said a short while ago, who has been through the most awful experiences, "Life is just a series of clichés."*

This was the beginning of Johnson's time of struggle – emotional and literary. At this stage only two chapters of *Travelling People* were in a fit state to show people, but on the basis of these he had already got himself an agent. As he wrote to Stuart Crampin in May 1960: 'She is Rosica Colin, whom I met when I did *The Maids*, for she is Jean Genet's agent. I thought, if she's good enough for Genet, she's good enough for Johnson; and made an appointment to see her. Marvellous house just off Gloucester Road, tea and Fuller's walnut cake, unframed Giacometti over the mantelpiece, carpets on the walls (!) and a very pleasant chat for an hour and a half. She thinks the novel is funny, and intends to submit it to Fabers, with whom she works a lot, and who publish Genet. She is also going to act as agent for Mike Baker and I in collaboration [. . .] Rosica Colin is also agent for Alan Sillitoe, for whom, last year, she tells me she made ten thousand nicker; I gave her my permission to do the same for me next year.'

Mike Baker was a fellow graduate of King's, a mild-mannered, conservative law student who was rather surprised to find himself collaborating with the austerely radical Johnson. At King's he had written some humorous articles which had been accepted by *Lucifer* and done something to lighten its tone: the most celebrated of these was a facetious re-reading of A. A. Milne's Winnie-the-Pooh books as an allegory of the poet's role in a capitalist society. Johnson clearly felt that Baker was talented, and he had, at this point, ambitions to write comedy himself. So he proposed a collaboration, and for the next two or three years this unlikely twosome churned out an impressive number of scripts and proposals, most of which found their way onto the desk of some BBC producer or another, and were politely returned. Still preserved in Johnson's archive, they are richly evocative of the kind of high-spirited 1950s comedy which was on the point of dying out, with titles like *It May Be Just What We Need* and *In Case of Emergency*. Perhaps the

---

* This remark had impressed Johnson deeply. It was made to him by his friend from Birkbeck, Robin Purdue, while they were having coffee together in a Malet Street cafe, next to Dillons bookshop, in the summer of 1959. What Purdue is supposed to have said, in fact, is that 'Life is a series of clichés, each more banal than the last.' The 'awful experiences' he had been through involved the break-up of his marriage, an affair with a younger woman and a hastily arranged backstreet abortion. In the winter of 1967–8 he killed himself: Johnson, who was staying in Paris at the time, read of his death in a *Times* obituary – which was, ironically, how many of his friends learned about his own suicide six years later. (Source: 'Everyone Knows Somebody Who's Dead' from *Aren't You Rather Young To Be Writing Your Memoirs?*)

most interesting is a proposed *Goon Show* script, which went through several drafts before ending up as 'The Great Welsh Harp Abduction Mystery'. Showing, I would say, that Johnson was still at the level of imitating his heroes rather than being creatively influenced by them, the script is a sharp, workmanlike pastiche of a Spike Milligan original, full of Goonishly inventive touches (like the notion of an underwater steamroller, invented to supply the growing demand for flat fish). It's much less embarrassing to read than one would imagine, although light years away from anything we might have expected from the author of *Trawl* and *House Mother Normal*.

Maybe Johnson, with his deep-rooted temperamental insecurities, needed a collaborator at this stage as some sort of prop, someone whose encouragement and participation might confirm that he wasn't just striking out on some misguided path of his own. At the same time that he was co-writing his scripts with Michael Baker, he was also working jointly with Zulfikar Ghose on a satirical project called *Prepar-a-Tory*. Ghose was a graduate from Keele, who had taken over the task of editing a magazine (founded there a few years earlier by Bryan Reed) called *Universities Poetry*. It aimed to bring together the best student writing from throughout the country, and at this point Ghose had hand-picked an editorial team consisting of John Fuller (from Oxford), Anthony (A. C. H.) Smith (from Cambridge), and of course Johnson himself from King's College London. Most of the editorial business was done by post, but now that Ghose and Johnson had graduated and were both living back at home with their parents, they found themselves to be near neighbours in south-west London. Besides their continuing work together on the magazine, they would regularly meet at a pub called the Chelsea Potter on the King's Road to talk poetry and moan about the hardships of setting out on a literary career. The idea for their brief, jejeune satire on modern Conservatism had come from Johnson's experience of private tuition: attempting to get one of his pupils to write down the name of the kind of school he attended, Johnson had urged him: 'Look, spell it in sections ... like this: pre-par-a-tory, prepar-a-tory, prepar-a-tory, prepar-a-tory.' At which point he had found himself 'lost for a moment, a whole moment, for it had struck him with considerable force that this was exactly what such a school did do.' The book (which survives in a manuscript of only about fifty pages) tells of the birth, education and subsequent rise to power of one Ernest Highfly, and is divided into chapters with titles like 'Incubatory', 'Educatory' and 'Amatory'. The jokes are pretty obvious and, in its heavy-handed portrayal of a certain kind of upper-class Englishman, Johnson's and Ghose's satire was already out of date, particularly when you consider that *Beyond the Fringe* and *TW3* were just around the corner. A short sample should be enough to give the flavour:

30: EXTRACT FROM SATIRE *PREPAR-A-TORY* (1960)

Sir Duncan took great care over his son's upbringing right from the very first: being acutely aware of the need of his class for self-preservation and maintenance of power, he tried to foresee what sort of world in which his son would grow up [*sic*], and educate him accordingly; where he felt he could not prophesy accurately himself, he sought out the wisest counsellors from amongst his friends to advise him.

Thus it was that Ernest came to have the best of two worlds of education in his youth, the traditional and the modern: he was put down for Eden and Orthodoxford, and his father engaged one of the most famous psychologists of the period to give advice as to what toys and amusements the boy should have from birth. He was given, for instance, besides the usual military toys, all those aids that modern psychology could bring to bear upon the subconscious mind of a child who was to become a Tory: a small model birch, rows of small, mute, shareholders, dungareed workers with moronic faces, an exquisite quarter-size orb and sceptre, and many others.

Forty years on, Zulfikar Ghose has no great regard for his first collaborative work with Johnson. 'Of course, *Prepar-a-tory* is a piece of nonsense,' he wrote to me, 'though there are a few amusing moments in it.' He explained that, 'The way we worked on it was to come up with ideas when we sat drinking in the Chelsea Potter or some other pub. We would then go on to produce the episodes separately and exchange them: he would change mine and I would change his. Of course, whole chunks remain his and some remain mine and as such are quite recognisable.' (Among those which are recognizably Johnson's are those featuring a character called 'Mr Henry', making a cameo appearance from *Travelling People*.) It was during the time of this collaboration, all the same, that a bond of intense friendship grew up between Johnson and Ghose, cemented by their shared tastes in poetry and their burning youthful ambition for literary recognition. As Ghose himself remembered in his short memoir, 'Bryan':

> We walk and we walk. He in his charcoal grey coat. Barnes Common. Putney Heath. The silver birches ghostly. I in a long tweed coat, hands in pockets pressed against the suede lining. Winter evenings. 1959–60. Not half-a-crown between us. He says, 'We'll make it, mate.'[4]

*

I wonder what Johnson meant, exactly, by 'making it'. Had he 'made it' when his first book was published? Or during those – always temporary – periods later in his life when he was able (just about) to support his wife and children by writing? Or did he mean more than that: was he really counting on a kind of immortality, and has he in fact 'made it' now, now that someone has made it his business to retrace every one of his footsteps and memorialize him with a biography, a solid literary tombstone in 200,000 words? Most likely he won't have known what he meant. It's the kind of thing that every aspiring writer says, at the beginning, when things are tough. But Johnson, in any case, was already on his way, even if he didn't realize it yet. He had the talent, and in those days (which is probably not the case today) if you had the talent, it would soon be recognized. He had some poems accepted for a PEN anthology. A small provincial magazine called *Umbrella* employed him as their drama critic. The *Spectator* started to publish his poems and reviews. His friend Anthony Smith (the Cambridge member of the original *Universities Poetry* team) had moved to Bristol, established himself as the literary editor of the *Western Daily Press* and was regularly getting Johnson and Ghose to write for him. The young B. S. Johnson was slowly acquiring the beginnings of a reputation.

But still he was not happy during these lean years. The ghost of Muriel – or the ghost, rather, of what he had made her out to be – continued to haunt him. Zulfikar Ghose remembers this incident from the autumn of 1961:

> He had talked about her to me, but I had not thought of his experience of rejection as so deep a wound. One day I briefly met the woman at a party, and seeing Bryan a day later told him of the fact. His eyes stared at me with a terrible anger and a few days later I received a poem from him called 'Sonnet' and dedicated to me; after a touching description of our friendship, the sonnet concludes with
>
> > but when tonight you spoke my dead love's name
> > a hatred for you spat like a welding flame.[5]

Worse still, an unpublished poem from around this time suggests that his misery over the failed affair was even affecting his physical health:

31: POEM *(19 January 1961)*

So: I have these fainting attacks
dating from the time that I was
rejected in favour of an
epileptic.

So: at first I worried, but
then as months went by I laughed at
such childishness.

Then last week I had another,
fell hard and smashed my head and jaw:
I still feel pain.

I now believe I shall go mad
Unless I die.

Melodramatic language, to be sure: but I wonder how far from the truth this really was. As the year drew on, Johnson did begin to go a little bit 'mad', I believe. At King's, he had become very close to the college librarian, a man called Frank Lissauer who also happened to be a gifted poet. Throughout the early 1960s they wrote long, confiding letters to each other, and several times during 1961 Lissauer expressed concern for Johnson's mental well-being. Meanwhile, Johnson became violently attached to another woman – the young Irish folk singer called Kate, who has been mentioned before – and she, too, in writing to him, appeared worried that he might be experiencing some sort of breakdown. He began to read *The White Goddess* again, having been asked to review a reissued version for the *Western Daily Press*. Once again, it seemed to speak to him directly, referring explicitly to his own experience of personal visitation from the Muse Goddess, and reminding him of his superstition that his precious poetic gift was conditional upon a life of emotional isolation and unfulfilment. He tried to put this feeling into words but could only ever do so obliquely and mysteriously.

32: EXTRACT FROM LETTER *(? May/June 1961)*

To Stuart Crampin

Lots of things have happened to me since late January when I last saw you; possibly you will find me radically changed; accepting a lot more, particularly, less inclined towards change; but not, oh not, compromising; it's very difficult to say what I mean; just come and see; it's all connected with poetry, and the Muse, and love, and accepting the life that I can see now I must pursue but have always, stupidly, fought against: that is, being alone, perpetually; but even that is not really it. However; just don't expect me to be just as I was; though perhaps I have only not been to myself, and I shall seem the same to you.

This is going to be one of those incomprehensible letters.

And can it be coincidence that another name from the past suddenly resurfaces at this very time?

I refer, of course, to Michael Bannard.

The facts are few and far between, but this much is certain. Whether

Johnson had seen anything of Michael Bannard since leaving the Standard-Vacuum Oil Company in 1956 is not clear, but in April 1961 he finally left his parents' house in Barnes and moved into a large ground-floor flat in Claremont Square, London N1. This flat was just being vacated by Michael Bannard, who was about to begin his long years of travelling, and it was at his invitation that Johnson occupied it. (My source for this information is Doug Davies, then the tenant of the basement flat.) So it appears that they were still in touch. And indeed, Michael Bannard is mentioned, very fleetingly, in the opening pages of Johnson's second novel, *Albert Angelo*, which describe his first night at Claremont Square:

33: EXTRACT FROM *ALBERT ANGELO*

(Johnson, aka 'Albert', is making cocoa with Doug Davies, aka 'Joseph', in the company of an unidentified friend, 'Luke'. They refer to Michael Bannard as 'Graham'.)

Luke said: Did you know Graham then?

Albert said: Oh, yes, I knew Graham. Well.

Joseph said: Graham once called me a pathetic pseudo-disciple of Them.

[. . .]

Luke said: Y'know, I reckon that Graham was off his trolley. I mean, I've been here some evenings and you should have heard what was going on upstairs!

Joseph said: All through the bloody night, too.

Albert said: He was certainly unusual . . . eccentric . . .

Luke said: Eccentric! He was bleeding round the twist, mate, straight round the twist, no doubt about that!

Joseph said: I got used to it.

Luke said: Well, I wouldn't have got used to it. Bleeding groaning and saying his prayers with beads – and the music he used to play!

Joseph said: I liked it, I liked it. I didn't understand it, but I liked it.

Albert said: Well, I shan't make a lot of noise.

At this point, then, Michael Bannard has re-emerged – as a palpable, if not physical presence in Johnson's story. If their friendship during the Stanvac days had been so intense and disturbing that they had decided to stop seeing each other, was it really a good idea for Johnson, now (in his fragile and depressed state of mind) to take over a flat that Bannard used to occupy? He was still to some extent haunted by the memory of Muriel, but he would from now on also be haunted by the spirit of Michael Bannard, traces of whose domineering personality would surround him twenty-four hours a day. Concrete evidence of this is provided by some diary entries he made in the autumn of 1961.

Before then, however, he was to spend his third successive summer on the Lleyn peninsula. He had spent the summer of 1960 there as manager of the Glyn Club, but this had not been a successful experience and seems to have led to a falling-out with the club's owner, James Martland. Johnson took his revenge, on returning to London, by devising a conclusion to *Travelling People* in which Maurie Bunde – the character based on Martland – dies of a heart attack after trying to prove his continuing virility to his young lover, Kim. (Incidentally Johnson completed the novel in a fever of inspiration in the early months of 1961: '40,000 words in 23 days!' he wrote to Stuart Crampin. 'You should have seen the Stuart-type graphs I had on the walls!'[6])

His reason for going back to north Wales in the summer of 1961 was particularly bizarre. 'The third summer I spent down here was the strangest of all three in many ways,' he explained, in the film *Fat Man on a Beach.* 'I'd been asked to come down this time by a man I'd better call "Henry", who believed that the treasure ship of the Spanish Armada was somewhere out there.' 'Henry's' conviction on this point, Johnson claimed, amounted almost to a 'religious belief' that the treasure ship *Santa Cruz* had 'run for shelter in Abersoch here, and sunk in the bay and [. . .] was carrying all the treasure to pay the mercenaries in the Spanish fleet, the whole Spanish Army. So he got me here [. . .] for the whole summer with the promise of skin-diving down off Abersoch, with the promise of untold millions of gold doubloons and pieces of eight, and all those romantic things.'

Could this possibly be true? Apparently so. Zulfikar Ghose confirms that 'In the summer of 1961, he and I spent several days on the coast of North Wales interviewing people who spent their time looking for the *Santa Cruz*, a ship of the Spanish Armada that was reputed to carry bullion and to have sunk in that region. We wrote an interesting story together, but none of the magazines wanted it.'[7] (It survives in typescript, however, as 'Hunting the *Santa Cruz*', by Zulfikar Ghose and B. S. Johnson.) Ghose, it seems, was too level-headed to accept a follow-up invitation to come diving for the wreck himself, and so Johnson travelled to the peninsula alone later that summer. When he arrived, though, he was in for a disappointment: 'When I actually got here, I found that he hadn't got a boat; that he hadn't got any sort of skin-diving equipment. There was nothing we could do. It was a romantic story.' But Johnson decided to stay for the rest of the summer, all the same. 'This man, Henry, had a cottage, but it was very full up with his wife and children and things. So he put me in a sort of caravan at a field "called Dwylan". Now Dwylan is a very strange place. Dwylan was a place where you had to be very careful what you did with your toenail cuttings. Now I used to cut mine and keep them in a little pile and eventually I buried them in a stone wall. That seemed the safest thing to do.'

This reminiscence, delivered to camera with a straight face, sounds like the surreal invention of a mischief-maker who is deliberately trying to wind his audience up. But Johnson was being perfectly serious, if you ask me. He believed in witches, and more particularly he believed in Welsh witches, and of course it is a widespread superstition that if a witch gets possession of your toenail clippings, she is able to cast a spell on you. This is what Johnson believed, and what he was referring to in such a deadpan manner during the making of that last film. Which seems to imply that during his time in Lleyn in the summer of 1961 he was in an especially superstitious frame of mind. This may well have been because he felt himself, once again, to be on the edge of an emotional precipice: he had become seriously infatuated with Kate, but she seems to have gone home to Ireland for the summer, and he was left waiting for some sort of communication from her – a letter, perhaps, making it clear whether or not she returned his feelings. Meanwhile Johnson found employment helping out with the harvest on a local farm, and spent a good deal of time by himself in his caravan, re-reading *The White Goddess* and brooding fearfully on the implications it seemed to hold for his own literary and emotional future.

Through his father – who worked, as I said, as a stock-keeper for the Society for Promoting Christian Knowledge – Johnson used to obtain a ready supply of handsome, leather-bound parish logbooks, and it was in these that he would write his occasional diaries, scraps of poetry and, later, the first drafts of his novels. (Always in pencil – using pencils he had taken from the offices of Fuller's bakery in Hammersmith when he worked there in the early 1950s.) Here are some selected diary entries from the summer of 1961:

34: EXTRACTS FROM DIARY/NOTEBOOK *(August 1961)*

After living this almost anchoritic existence in peace and solitude at Llanengan, suddenly last night I was back in the life of last year.

Mos had asked me for a drink at the White House. Not there – Robert and Prue were – on fruit machine – Prue very glad to see me – says I have been avoiding her – partially true, for I have not sought her out as I could have done – looks slimmer – but makes her features sharper and less attractive, more bird-like – winning on machine – very well dressed – I am conscious I am wearing same suit as last year – have had my back to Mother Cook all this time – greet her – she seems pleased to see me too – my belief in my capacity to make and keep friends is returning after some weeks' atrophy – offer to get drinks, she insists Robert buy me one – talk – Prue is exactly in same relationship to me as last year – believes me gentle, organized, accomplished, placid: me, placid! – feel peculiarly towards Prue – sisterly but sexually – incestuously?! – Mos still not arrived – I buy drinks – the Cooks order dinner – Mrs Cook gives me one of those invitations meant to be politely declined – I dutifully do so – they'll give me dinner before I leave, I know, properly – say I must come and see them – agree to do so – with Ian and Gill, to sort out about their caravan – they go on to dinner [. . .]

Trevor comes in – Mos late – then two friends, Richard and Marlene – *very* pleasant – then Mos turns up – had been cutting a field of mixed oats and barley – Marlene very pleasant, intelligent – she and Richard run a boarding house in Abersoch though they come from Derby – just threw up everything 3½ years ago – they now apparently keep open house for the Mos set – invite me – I am now assured, talk very well and cleverly and diplomatically in a non-hypocritical way (oh, Johnson, you was very good last night!) – to Trevor as well about poetry – he has read *White Goddess* – must speak further with him about this – says Graves is wrong – promises to let me have Eng. Trans. of Cwm Pennant – Mos goes off to Glyn to ensure our drinking after 10 – follow a few minutes later – Glyn unpleasant, ruined by clutter of objects – Schofield very drunk – cut me – I wonder how long it will be before he tells me he would rather I didn't come? – good chicken sandwiches – further interesting talk with Richard and Marlene about education, politics – surprised at my own fluency and cogency – we are invited back to R & M's for coffee – a chap named Pete and I squeeze in front of Trevor's borrowed van – gear lever in my thigh – homosexual jokes – Trevor drives madly – more so than anyone I have ever known – goes from 1 to 3 down drive, straight out of gate in path of oncoming car – near accident [. . .]*

*

[Poem, inscribed '(for Kate)']

> I seem all my life to have been waiting:
> oh, I could give you many instances.
>
> Many instances. Specific instances.

---

* This entry is dated 19 August 1961. Students of coincidence will be interested to learn that, 150 miles away, Mrs Janet Coe, of the parish of Lickey on the outskirts of Birmingham, was labouring to give birth to a baby boy, Jonathan by name, who made his entry into the world on that very day. Furthermore, as for the White House hotel, in Abersoch, where this scene is laid, I know it well: the last time I was there was on 4 August 1998 at a dinner to celebrate my father's seventieth birthday. I am becoming almost as much of a believer in portents and time-loops as Johnson himself!

of periods of waiting for the loved one
To decide.

But always I am left waiting.
As though nothing were quite what is meant.
I seem all my life to have been waiting:

For you?

(To write a bad poem of this kind must be a sign of love! But the awful thing is that it is *true*!)

*

There are two ash-trees in Llanengan churchyard. One of them (the one nearer the road) has an elongated inverted pudenda at the intersection of two boles of similar girth.

*

Llanengan churchyard is the only place I have come upon cats copulating.

*

21/8/61

There being no baths here, I have to strip-wash; and the other day as I was so doing I was suddenly proud of my body, not for itself, but that it was something to offer to you, my lovely Kate, something that I could offer to no-one else; and which I have never offered to anyone, except perhaps Joyce. And I was pleased that my body had survived this long as being something I could take pride in, after all the neglect and shame. We have come through, I feel, but for this pause which may yet destroy us.

23/8/61

Oh, Kate, Kate, why no word from you? I find myself considering the possibilities: since this is now the sixth day on which I might technically have received a card, why have you not written? You may, at the worst, have been killed in an accident ... but perhaps this is not quite the worst, for for you to be maimed or disfigured, to be Kate yet not my Kate, seems even more terrible; or, nearly as bad, things may have crystallised between you and —, so that you cannot write from embarrassment/guilt; you may have received some other release which relieves you of need of me; at best, I suppose, you might be teasing or punishing me; or *she* may be punishing me for entertaining thoughts about Marlene; or for failing to worship Her.*

But, oh Kate, I am fighting hard! While I can only recall you in general detail, I hold the concept close of a love, fulfilled, total love, for

---

* i.e. the White Goddess, of course.

you, very tightly, very preciously, and see all my future in terms of love for and union with you.

I see us living now in Ireland, now in London: after an initial struggle I shall win through to literary dependence [*sic*], mainly through you, and our first child (I care not boy nor girl) will be the child of this struggle, and be dear to us, even dearer, because he will have shared it. And then quietly in Ireland, but oh so fruitfully and happily! Another child, conceived in the open air, born to us of a union so perfect in its completeness.

[Song, 26/8/61*]

> Oh, a short while ago I'd a pain in the head
> And my doctor advised me that soon I'd be dead
> So I drew out my savings and went on the spree
> With ten thousand pounds' worth of goods on H.P.
>
> *Chorus*
> For I knew I'd be dead in the summertime,
> I knew I'd be dead in July
> I knew I'd be dead when the roses were red
> And the leaves were beginning to die
> So hand in hand together they'll stand
> At the graveside with tears running free
> Ruined forever and ever
> My debtors for goods on H.P.
>
> I met with a girl who said she'd let me
> If only her husband I'd promise to be
> This bargain I struck with a dozen or more
> And said that I'd wed them at Christmas for sure
>
> *Chorus*
> For I knew I'd be dead in the summertime,
> I knew I'd be dead in July
> I knew I'd be dead when the roses were red
> And the leaves were beginning to die
> So hand in hand together they'll stand
> At the graveside with tears running free,
> Ruined forever and ever
> The women who said they'd let me.

---

* There's a note here which I can't quite decipher; I think it says, '(to the tune of "Nellie McNess")'.

Till the third week in June I'd the time of my life,
And seventeen women thought they'd be my wife;
Then my doctor dropped round for some tea and a cake
And gently informed me he'd made a mistake:

Chorus
I thought I'd be dead in the summertime
I thought I'd be dead in July:
I thought I'd be dead when the roses were red
And the leaves were beginning to die.
But hand in hand with wardens I stand
In the dock now with tears running free,
Ruined for ever and ever
By debtors and women – poor me!

Poem

> In the ember days of my last free summer,
> here I lie, outside myself, watching
> the gross body eating a poor curry:
> satisfied at what I have done, scared of what
> I have to do in my last free winter.*

Johnson was twenty-eight when he wrote this poem, and the song which precedes it. From the undercurrent of impending doom which seems to characterize both, I assume that he was starting to be preoccupied, again, with the notion that his thirtieth year was going to be his last. Altogether, he seems to have been in a pretty apprehensive frame of mind during this last summer at Abersoch: to say nothing of the fact that it was now, apparently, that he also had the frightening supernatural experience related in 'Sheela-na-Gig'.

And then, further misfortunes awaited him when he returned to London. His beloved friend Stuart Crampin was badly injured in a climbing accident, and it was even believed, for a while, that he might not survive. Kate, the woman in whom he had invested so many romantic hopes, rejected him by letter. All this happened in the space of a few days at the end of September ('Oh, that was such a bloody weekend!' he wrote in his diary). Rejected manuscripts of *Travelling People* and *Prepar-a-Tory* seemed to arrive by every post, and for a few days Johnson believed himself suicidal; he went back to Barnes to retrieve his boyhood shooting rifle from his parents' house. 'The only reason I go on living,' he wrote, 'is out of concern for how badly my parents would take my death.'

---

* Included in Johnson's first published collection, *Poems* (Constable, 1964).

But he did not shoot himself. Instead, he did a peculiar thing. He invited himself (at least, that's the only way I can interpret it) to Banbury, of all places, to spend a weekend with an elderly couple he had not seen for some five years and who barely remembered him. They were the parents of Michael Bannard.

Bannard himself was away, travelling somewhere in the Mediterranean – Italy, I think. But that seems to have made no difference. Johnson (who by now was living, you may remember, in Michael Bannard's old flat in Claremont Square) found himself compelled, as if by some irresistible inner force, to go and visit his family home.

This is the diary he kept of that visit.

35: DIARY *(October 1961)*

BANBURY – 13/10/61

The house larger than I thought it – Mrs B younger looking – again I think I am on a different time-plane to these people – I get older, and they get younger – Mr B just as I barely remember him – the picture of M – the room just the same – but now the meal different – luncheon meat for me where *we* had lobster ('It's good,' said M on that occasion, 'to have real lobster and not scampi posing as lobster') Mrs B very friendly – both seem to talk of little other than M – but perhaps because I am a link – Mr B's garden – good job I forgot to get flowers, as it happens, luckily – no hothouse overblooms in this unforced purity – his daughters (her daughters) come, tall and prim and older than the parents – sherry (poor) – Mrs B tells me of M's friend Raul – accident, embarrassing in hospital due to Raul's possessiveness and demonstrativeness.

M's room – *the* shell first thing to catch my eye – it seems to be central thing in room – did he ask her to put it there? Or is it intended to be the centre?

Disappointed by ordinariness of everything (again?) from moment I entered. Perhaps by thinking too much of E?*

Sleep.

14/10/61

After a splendid sleep – awoken to let the waters flow.

Not nice – M has left my present of *Tristram Shandy* here: it was

---

* I can't explain this reference.

intended to take with him. Strange that after breakfast Mr B should mention the night M & Dan walked back from Oxford (23 m) – this happened the weekend or so before I came down before – Neal mentioned M was going about with June – M does not tell parents anything – like me, and my parents, he *writes* more to them when he is away, tells them more by letter than by speech.

[Johnson now notes down some titles from Michael Bannard's bookshelves]

Letters to a lost Uncle – Mervyn Peake – E&S 1948
Pevsner's Guides to London
Witchcraft in England – Christina Hole – Batsford 1945
Nostradamus – James Laver – Penguin 1952 (f. pub. 42)

Mixed up time planes – a character without sense of time or TENSE 'You will be better if you had never met me'

Hook Norton, pm

Look up church in Pevsner

Eva first figure I saw on font as I entered. Church has nine pinnacles, each with a weathercock; late C16? A restored, mediocre C16 roof anyway; gargoyle spouts; Cotswold stone; pretty mediocre as a church, but well enough in its context.

Font exactly fits in with my progress; as M would know. As with Kilpeck, it looks older than Norman: not that I doubt it was made then, but the spirit behind it much older, *and* non-Xtian. Why should the sculptor need to *name* Adam & Eve boldly across their chests otherwise.

[He then copied the drawings on the font into his notebook]

The forces who control my life know my needs, whether I conjure them or not; and since I do not know their true identity, I might well be messing about with something dangerous and evil.

ROLLRIGHT STONES

Very weathered. First impression that they were fake – 100s but not 1000s of years old. Notice says 1500 BC. Only one over 6'. Mostly stumps. Badly pitted limestone made lovely with lichen. Ate 2 scones from Mrs B. Walked round. Noticed toadstools: are they the ones mentioned by Graves as having a narcotic effect? Nibbled one. Sat down. Nibbled longer but of another type of toadstool. Tastes like mushroom. Ate a Banbury cake. Nibbled third type. Evil taste, slightly. In *pine* on *fir* grove, as Graves says they should be.

———————

Freed a wasp stuck on a newly-painted Halt sign; in doing so disturbed a grasshopper with one leg; nothing I could do for him.

———————

Did Kate ring or come to N1 at 5.20? I felt she did, or wanted to think she did.

The account of his weekend in Banbury ends at this point, leaving a number of questions unanswered. For instance, I would love to know what Johnson meant by '*the* shell', which he found placed in the centre of Michael Bannard's bedroom ('did he ask her to put it there? Or is it intended to be the centre?'). And above all, I still don't understand exactly what feeling drew him back to this house, which he seems to have visited only once before, and whether he found whatever revelation, or consolation, he had been hoping to obtain there.

Well, it seems unlikely. He certainly wouldn't have been able to share much of his emotional turmoil with Bannard's parents. One of the many things he and his friend had in common was a relationship with their parents based on profound difference and lack of understanding. The Bannards no more comprehended their culturally omnivorous, homosexual son than Stanley and Emily Johnson would ever make head or tail of Bryan's writing. Nonetheless Johnson appears, out of gratitude, to have sent some of his poems to Mr and Mrs Bannard after returning to London. On 22 October 1961, Michael's mother replied:

> So many thanks for sending some of your poetry, it was indeed a pleasure to read, well written.
>
> I only hope that one day, in the near future, you will attain what you really hope to achieve regarding your writing, & I do not see it otherwise for you if, as you said 'some of your poems have been accepted', it will lead to bigger things for you, & you will then look back, (not in anger!!!), & say to yourself, time spent on it was worth while.

After this, Michael Bannard vanishes from our story. We will not glimpse him again for a good many years. Other, less turbulent friendships will intervene. But I'm convinced by one thing: that of the three major relationships I have touched upon in this chapter, Johnson's friendship with Michael Bannard was the most significant. The influence of Joyce Yates was of great intellectual importance, but I'm not sure that he felt for her very deeply. His affair with Muriel was a brief, doomed meeting of undergraduate incompatibles which he talked and wrote up obsessively until it assumed a disproportionate place in his emotional biography. But there is a certain quality to the way he writes about Michael Bannard – a mysterious intensity which creeps into his writing – that makes me certain that there was a strong and lasting bond between the two men, even after they had stopped seeing each other. What is the secret of all that shared iconography, I wonder? The carvings on the Hook Norton church? The Rollright Stones? The shell that Johnson found in Bannard's bedroom? A gift? From whom to whom?

Anyway. You'll be pleased to learn that now, at last, things are going to start looking up for our hero! For this time, at least, Johnson managed to pull himself out of his depression, and told himself, like Beckett's unnamable: '*You must go on, I can't go on, I'll go on.*' Perhaps it was humour that saw him through, on this occasion. After all, he recognized that 'because of the seriousness of all this, I have built up an enormous protection of laughter: there is nothing that I cannot laugh at [...] and people often hate me for it.' And again, he might here have been echoing Robert Graves, who wrote towards the end of *The White Goddess*:

> If he keeps his sense of humour [...] a poet can go mad gracefully, swallow his disappointments in love gracefully, reject the Establishment gracefully, die gracefully, and cause no upheaval in society. Nor need he indulge in self-pity, or cause distress to those who love him [...]

In his stronger, braver moments, Johnson would surely have agreed.

The last entry in this diary is a poem. Thus:

36: POEM *(of doubtful authorship; perhaps by Johnson)*

Life Presents a dismal picture
Dark and dreary as the tomb
Father has an anal stricture
Mother has a displaced womb
Uncle Herbert's been deported
For a homosexual crime
And the maid has been aborted
For the 42nd time
Little Albert in the corner
He has epileptic fits
Every time he coughs he vomits
Every time he farts he shits
Aunty Mabel's syphilitic
Aunty Ethel's up the spout
Poor old Grandpa's been and farted
Blown his arsehole inside out.

CLAREMONT SQUARE

37: REVIEW OF *THE WHITE GODDESS* BY ROBERT GRAVES

... it is to be hoped that a larger audience will now seriously consider the poetic thesis put forward in this complex (but never obscure) book.

It is an arrogant thesis, and has been attacked more for its arrogance than for its truth in the ten years since it first appeared. The function of poetry, Graves maintains quite simply and firmly, is ritual invocation of the Muse Goddess; true poetry is concerned with the relationship between men and women; since Christianity insisted on the worship of no other Gods than its own, it follows that there have been no true poets in English except by accident or through deliberate paganism.

Graves calls his book 'a historical grammar of the language of poetic myth.' It is very much more than that, for in his search for the Muse throughout history he finds that his central subject is life itself, the never-ceasing pattern of birth, consummation and death: *The White Goddess* as a result is a book which approaches the subject of Erich Neumann's Jungian *The Great Mother* from a poetic, supra-scientific angle.

This is not to say that supra-scientific methods, inexplicable as they may be, are in any way hidden from the reader: in a Postscript written for this edition Graves says:

> I am no mystic: I avoid participation in witchcraft, spiritualism, yoga, fortune-telling, automatic writing, and the like. I live a simple, normal, rustic life with my family and a wide circle of sane and intelligent friends. I belong to no religious cult, no secret society, no philosophical sect; nor do I trust my historical intuition any further than it can be factually checked.

Rather, these methods are of the poet's heightened perception, of which Eliot speaks and of which there are many examples in literary history. And if there is one thing that the Richards school of analytical criticism (and the Movement poets, too, for that matter) showed, it is that the factor which makes one line of verse poetry and another poetic cannot be isolated or even discussed by the scientific empirical study of vowel quantities, stress patterns or semantic splithairs; any more than it could be by Christian romanticism.

In speaking of the unspeakable in order to know the unknowable in poetry, Graves shows that pre-Christian poets were the possessors of infinitely more knowledge and experience than ourselves, and that their mystical and magical secrets survived, amongst Welsh and Irish bards, hidden from the clergy in riddles and gnomic poetry.

The result of Graves' historically-checked intuitive researches is a miraculous, fabulous book: adjectives that, for once, can be taken literally. Whether or not you agree with his theories and conclusions, you cannot but admire the man's enormous dianoetic capacity and wonder at the persistence with which he follows his quarry into branches of religion, sorcery, folklore, literature, mythology and history.

The White Goddess is unorthodox whether you are a Christian or a humanist: but challenging, impressive, and, to my mind, true. The paradox is that one does not necessarily have either to follow or agree with Graves' argument to be able to see quite clearly that he is making statements about the nature of poetry and poetic inspiration which are true, valid, and of the greatest importance not only to poets but to anyone who reads poetry. This in spite of the fact that, as Joyce himself could be the only real reader of *Finnegan's Wake* [sic], so only someone with Graves' own combination of specialised knowledge and intuitions could fully understand, and check, this book.

The White Goddess should be required reading for all who attempt to write poetry: then the attitude expressed in G. S. Fraser's remark, 'The writing of poems is perhaps becoming, as in Japan and China, a general social accomplishment of all educated and sensitive persons,' would be seen by them to be quite mistaken and almost meaningless.

This review was written on 16 October 1961, two days after Johnson had returned from his visit to the Bannards' house in Banbury. The two events cannot be unrelated: which is not to say that one precipitated the other, merely that we find, once again, that when he was at his most depressed and superstitious, Graves's book was never far from Johnson's mind. In fact his re-reading of *The White Goddess* must have dominated the whole of the summer of 1961. He was given a review copy of the book in April by Zulfikar Ghose, who did not want to review it himself.* It took him a long time to finish it (he later recalled), and he was certainly – according to another diary entry, for 19 August 1961 – still reading it in mid-August, when he was

---

* See Fragment 153 below, p. 366.

staying in Abersoch. It would be a further two months after that before the review was completed (and another five months before it appeared in the *Western Daily Press* – on 19 March 1962). All of the preoccupations which weighed so heavily on Johnson's troubled mind during this difficult period, therefore – primarily, his failure to form lasting relationships with women, and the way in which this failure seemed to be intimately connected with his poetic aspirations – were crystallized in the alluring but destructive figure of Graves's Goddess: a figure he believed (in his less lucid phases, at any rate) that he had once encountered in person. All of this was also bound up with the pre-Christian iconography to which Michael Bannard had introduced him and of which he had recently seen such a striking example at Kilpeck.

Somehow, as we have seen, the crisis passed. Johnson did not make use of his rifle, despite having fetched it over from his parents' house in Barnes to have it comfortingly close to his side in his room in Claremont Square, Islington. This time, it must still have been possible to believe that things would improve: that the next girlfriend would in fact turn out to be *the* one, the ideal woman; that if he sent his novel to enough people, and published the occasional poem or review, eventually his literary career would take wing.

For this reason, the *Western Daily Press*, where his old *Universities Poetry* colleague Anthony Smith was running a weekly arts page modelled very much on the *Observer*'s, proved a valuable outlet. Smith's pages were of a consistently high standard and featured regular contributions not just from Johnson himself (who wrote there about Brecht, Genet, Beckett and many others) but also Zulfikar Ghose and a young, Bristol-based freelance journalist called Tom Stoppard. Anthony Smith retains a 'very vivid' memory of introducing Stoppard to Johnson:

'Tom was quite impressed by Bryan's journalism because Bryan was fairly well up in areas that Tom didn't know that much about at the time, like Brecht. So Tom was disposed to be impressed by somebody like Bryan. It seemed like a good idea to introduce them so some time when Stoppard and I were in London together, and Zulf was there as well, I'd arranged that we go over to Claremont Square. And I introduced Tom to these two and I remember there was a gas fire burning, one of those old gas fires with its asbestos element, suggesting maybe that it was winter 1961. I introduced them and in absolutely no time at all, within no more than two minutes they were having a theoretical row: and like any theoretical row, a little bit of personality was entering into it, especially with Bryan who could be an absolutely dogmatic bastard. He was laying down his usual view that every subject will dictate its own form and every piece of fiction or drama – but fiction was probably what they were talking about – will be unique in that it will have a unique form dictated by the nature of the material. And Tom in effect was saying, that may or may not be true but it's not *interesting,* because what's interesting about theory? Instead he used this image of a children's join-the-dots picture: he said before you start writing you don't know what it's going to be, and then you start out and you think maybe it's going to be a hippopotamus and when you've finished you see it's actually a giraffe but you didn't *know* this, you find out as you do it. But Bryan was always much more theoretical and so therefore, as it were, prescriptive about how things work, and in his eyes I think Tom had presumed not just to disagree with him, but to be rather flippant.'*

Smith is almost certainly correct to date this anecdote to the winter of 1961. The notion of form organically dictating content was uppermost in Johnson's mind at this point because this was, in his view, the great strength of his novel *Travelling People.* In the light of Rosica Colin's fading enthusiasm for the book, he was now sending it out to other prospective agents.

38: LETTER *(18 October 1961)*

To George Greenfield

It has been suggested that I submit my novel TRAVELLING PEOPLE to you in the hope that you will act as agent for me in the placing of it.

I have the beginning of a reputation as a poet, my work having appeared in various literary and university magazines over the past four years. A group of three of my poems was recently accepted for the PEN anthology NEW POEMS 1962, and I am at present secretary of the Arts Council Committee of Universities' Poetry. I review books for the Western Daily Press, and theatre for the magazine Umbrella.

TRAVELLING PEOPLE is very approximately 100,000 words long, and was from the outset an experimental novel; the device of using a different style or literary technique for each chapter has succeeded well beyond my expectation, largely as a result of the unifying element of the central character's logical progression and development. Joyce used this device in ULYSSES, of course, but by allowing the nature of the subject matter of each particular series of events which form one chapter to determine organically the style chosen, I seem to have avoided the contrivance to which Joyce was sometimes reduced.

---

* According to his biographer, Stoppard wrote to Anthony Smith a couple of years later on the subject of *Tristram Shandy*, confessing that he could detect 'no connection between it and *Travelling People*, except that Sterne does certain things as marvellous, irrelevant and irreverent jokes (in 1728) [*sic*] which Johnson does in grim meaningful earnestness.' Quoted in Ira Nadel, *Double Act: A Life of Tom Stoppard* (London, Methuen, 2002), p. 134.

TRAVELLING PEOPLE is in the tradition represented by writers such as Petronius, Apuleius, Rabelais, Cervantes, Nashe, Sterne, and Samuel Beckett; not the main tradition of the novel, but a very virile and interesting one. More generally, my novel's affinities are with Elizabethan and eighteenth century conceptions of the form rather than with nineteenth century ones.

The novel has been seen and rejected by one publisher: Jonathan Cape.

I shall be pleased to hear from you when you have been able to consider my manuscript.

You could argue that an unpublished novelist would not be well advised, when submitting his unsolicited manuscript to an agent, to compare it to *Ulysses* at all, let alone say that his own novel was better because it was not so contrived. But at no point in his career did Johnson lack hubris. And in any case, his boldness paid off: subject to some revisions – which he agreed to undertake at once – Greenfield said that he would attempt to find a publisher for *Travelling People*. Thus began an unlikely literary partnership which lasted for the next three and a half years.

Novelist and agent must have made an odd combination. The two men had little in common, either socially or aesthetically. A product of King's School, Rochester, and Downing College, Cambridge, Greenfield had served as a staff major in the Western Desert during the war, and then for six years successfully ran the publishing house of T. Werner Laurie. From there he joined the John Farquharson literary agency and later became its sole owner. His clients included Enid Blyton, Sidney Sheldon, Edmund Hillary, Vivian Fuchs and – towards the end of his career – Jilly Cooper and Jeffrey Archer. Perhaps not an obvious person to take on the task of introducing the next James Joyce to the world, but he and Johnson at least shared an enthusiasm for squash and drinking, and, for the time being, their professional relationship seemed successful and friendly.

George Greenfield took the young writer on because he genuinely admired *Travelling People*; but he was rapidly to discover that there was more to B. S. Johnson than his novels. It was to become one of Johnson's recurring complaints that he could never find an agent who would promote his writing in all its different aspects – the plays, the poetry, the journalism and (later) the television work. Midway through *Albert Angelo*, lamenting the fact that a woman has declined to sleep with him, Albert complains: 'I hate these women who only want bits of me. I offer her the enormous totality of me, and she says, yes, I'll have the conversation bit, and the company bit, but not the bed bit, nor even the handsonmybigtits bit. I hate the partial livers. I'm an allornothinger.'[1] And it was just the same with agents. Instead of wanting the 'enormous totality' of Johnson's talent, they usually just wanted the novel-writing bit, and not the drama bit, or the poetry bit, or the screenwriting bit.

At first, then, Greenfield's job was to interest a publisher in *Travelling People* while Rosica Colin, with diminishing enthusiasm, did her best to find a home at the BBC for Johnson's television and radio collaborations with Michael Baker. But Johnson no longer had any faith in his first agent, and soon it was Greenfield alone that he was bombarding with proposals and samples of finished work: a number of the short stories that would eventually find their way into the collection *Statement Against Corpses*, sketches for *That Was the Week That Was*, articles for *Private Eye*, an outline for a schools' edition of Sidney's *Astrophel and Stella*, proposals for a television sitcom called *And All That Jazz* and several drafts of the collection that was eventually to become *Poems* in 1964. Greenfield submitted to this torrent of ideas gracefully, commented upon most of them generously, but was never able to place anything other than the more 'literary' productions. Generally speaking, Johnson was lacking in the popular touch. He was at heart an aesthetic elitist whose amused contempt for the tastes of the mass audience (see, for example, his sarcastic asides on this subject in *Fat Man on a Beach*) usually showed through whenever he tried to write for it.

In any case, if there had, over the last few years, been a half-hearted battle going on within Johnson between the populist and more rarefied sides of his artistic personality, the balance began to tip decisively towards the latter during the next few months. In December, responding to an advertisement in the *Spectator*, he put himself forward for a Gregory Award, enclosing the manuscripts of *Travelling People* and *Selected Poems* as evidence of his talent. These awards had been set up by the late Eric Gregory (formerly director of *Burlington Magazine* and honorary treasurer of the ICA) as a means of encouraging young writers: the amount of money made available varied from year to year; candidates had to be under thirty and British by birth.

39: APPLICATION FORM FOR GREGORY AWARD *(submitted 9 December 1961)*

My career has not followed any usual pattern; I went to University late after studying Latin and taking Intermediate B.A. in my spare time, desiring to learn more about writing and particularly about poetry. To do so I had to overcome many obstacles inherent in my working-class background, not the least of which was the deadening weight of the cosy indifference of my parents.

All my writing has been done under some kind of economic restriction, often almost crippling; as a result, I find myself in my late twenties with a body of work smaller than that of many graduates of twenty-three or so. A Gregory Award would enable me for the first time in my life to devote myself solely to my vocation. At this stage in my life, I believe that complete freedom from economic shackles, even if only for a period of weeks, would be of great importance in my development as a writer.

Results were announced at the end of March, with awards being made to four young writers: Johnson was ranked joint third. The money (£100) was more than useful – it was the equivalent of about eight weeks' supply teaching at the junior school on the Balls Pond Road where he was currently working five afternoons and one morning a week.[2] But it was even more important to feel that his work had been appreciated by such a distinguished set of judges, to whom he was then presented personally: 'Naturally, I'm delighted,' he wrote, 'not least because I've actually shaken hands and conversed with T. S. Eliot, Herbert Read, and Henry Moore; hardly to mention Bonamy [Dobrée] and Howard [Sergeant], and the lawyer Wade. My right hand has not been washed since Tuesday in celebration or reverence or something'.[3] It was to be the first of several gratifying nods of encouragement from the literary establishment that Johnson was to receive over the next few years.

At this point Michael Baker, now articled to a firm of solicitors in Holborn, could see the direction that Johnson's career was taking. He also had little faith in their latest collaboration, yet another TV comedy pilot, this one called *Rolling Stone*. 'It was becoming increasingly clear to me that his and my interests were far apart,' he says. 'I wasn't prepared to spend time – I couldn't afford to – writing pot-boiling scripts that I couldn't believe in. My recollection is that I contributed nothing to the final script. When I saw it, I thought it was feeble and that Bryan was wasting his time (and, I think, talents) writing this sort of thing. I can't remember now if we met (I don't believe we did), or if I spoke to him on the telephone; but in any case, I said that we ought to call a halt to the collaboration. I fear I must have hurt him but think it was right, because we were never going to go anywhere together.'

Johnson, as we know, never took rejection – any kind of rejection – kindly, and it's no surprise that his friendship with Michael Baker fizzled out fairly soon after this. But forty years on, Baker still remembers him with a certain rueful fondness:

'I liked Bryan; I realized in a way that he was vulnerable, though he always seemed much more assured in the literary world than I was. I was, in fact, very grateful to him for giving me some sort of entrée to his circles. Heaven knows what he can have seen in me – perhaps it was because I was no kind of threat to him that we rubbed along together without any real friction. He may have needed me as a sounding-board for his ideas; if so, I wasn't as much help to him as I might have been, because I was too much in awe of him to tell him outright when I thought an idea stank, and perhaps he didn't realize that quickly enough. I sometimes wonder whether, after Bryan left Kings, he had many friends. I had a feeling that he was clinging to our collaboration (which came to be in name only) rather desperately in the face of the facts.' As for the 'enormous protection of laughter' with which Johnson considered himself able to ward off life's hurts, Baker himself saw little sign of it. 'He did take himself far too seriously for his own good and seemed unable to laugh at himself, which I have always found to be a good defence mechanism.'

Meanwhile, not content with revolutionizing the novel at his first attempt, Johnson had also been attracted by an academic vacancy at Bristol which looked as though it might give him the opportunity to perform a similar service for the theatre.

40: LETTER CONTAINING DETAILS OF AN APPLICATION FOR FELLOWSHIP IN THEATRE STUDIES AT BRISTOL UNIVERSITY *(July 1962)*

To Anthony Smith

Basically, I see the fellowship as the only opportunity in the country to do deep research into what the theatre is to become; at present it seems to me (in London certainly) to be kept alive by (a) social aunt ednas (b) the fashionable cult-audience, sustaining respectively pop and art theatre. Both of which lifesaving acts are artificial – they do not spring out of the theatre and *attract* an audience, but the other way round. Wesker, Delaney et al have revolutionised material, subject matter only – useful, but not now (five years later) very important. The really import-ant change must come in *technique*, to attract an audience specifically to the theatre to see something they can't see anywhere else: this break-through in technique I would attempt to achieve (I already have ideas about it that I don't propose to reveal until I am prepared to do so) within the fellowship, ideally in a form that would enable other playwrights to work in the renewed medium, i.e. by publication and example. I do not expect to invent; rather to rediscover through action and the application of deep exploration. This seems to me the highest function of this fellow-ship. I should, of course, also hope to produce at least one bloody good play as well, and probably many shorter pieces written to explore certain techniques. Re-thinking form, as I believe I have done in my novel. Such work as I have in mind could not be done in the context of the com-mercial theatre; only in this Bristol fellowship, as far as I am aware.

As you can see, I'm aiming high; but feel I must.

This application seems to have come to nothing, but no matter: one week later would come the best possible piece of news. After only three more rejections (from Macmillan, Secker and The Bodley Head) *Travelling People* had found a publisher. It was bought by Richard Sadler at Constable, who made his offer to George Greenfield on 24 July, met Johnson a few days later to discuss some cuts and amendments and then, by 31 July, already found himself in receipt of a newly revised manuscript. Under the terms of the contract dated 13 August 1962, Johnson was to receive an advance of £150 against royalties. George Greenfield wrote to congratulate him:

'When I first read *Travelling People*, I recall telling you that I was enormously impressed with it and, although there has been a certain slump in fiction sales during the past few years with a result that it is all the more difficult to launch a new novelist, I felt pretty confident that we should have success in your case. The fact that a first-class publishing house has now come forward with an offer endorses my opinion, I feel, and I do want to congratulate you on this auspicious start.'

Johnson's letters to his agent from this period are equally warm: here, with the prospect of literary success beckoning and thoughts of romantic failure temporarily banished from his mind, we can catch occasional glimpses of another B. S. Johnson – the high-spirited bon viveur many of his friends and family vividly remember him to be. Shortly after signing his contract with Constable, for instance, Johnson wrote to George Greenfield playfully bragging that 'I shall be away from August 22nd to September 4th in Provence, staying apparently with some mad woman who keeps open château for writers, painters and general layabouts.' But the reality of this holiday, like so much else in his life, seemed beset with frustration.

The chateau in question was at Blauvac, in Vaucluse, Provence. It was owned by a painter and designer of tapestries called Marie Bonheur whose pleasure it was, every summer, to allow creative friends to stay there in order to work, relax and, if necessary, be fed in a sunny and restful atmosphere. Anthony Smith, who had stayed there as a guest before, invited Johnson to join him this time but remembers the occasion as marking a cooling-off point in their friendship:

'This whole story really is a way of trying to give you a take on that very easily nettled side of Bryan's character, something short of paranoia, but sort of the 3rd division south of paranoia, a minor version of it: his sense that when things went wrong, people were doing it in order to get at him and upset what should be an otherwise untroubled life.

'We went to France for just over two weeks and I'd got a brand new car, a Beetle, and I'd only just collected it. I'd hardly driven it when I drove to London to pick up Bryan. There was some arrangement, which he didn't know about, whereby I would meet this woman called Sandra from New York at Bryan's parents' place in Barnes. She was supposed to meet us there and the three of us would go on to France. Well, she never appeared and that kind of held us up and Bryan was already, you know, he was probably a bit pissed off with me for having said that she could have a lift anyway, and then she doesn't turn up and we're running late because we've been waiting for her. So, we got off on a bad foot.

'In those days it was a service called Silvercity where you went to Lydd in Kent and drove onto a plane and flew over to Le Touquet in France and drove off again. So we arrived at Le Touquet in the late afternoon. It would be about an eight- to ten-hour drive to Provence, so we started driving and we'd hardly got out of Le Touquet before I went into a ditch. The driver's side headlight had gone so I'd got very little illumination and there'd been no indication of where the road stopped and the ditch started. We weren't hurt or anything but the car was, and we somehow limped back into Le Touquet, got it to a garage and then had to wait the best part of 48 hours while the thing was mended. Bryan certainly took this as a personal affront, a personal betrayal of his trust in me to give him a good holiday. First I'd kept him waiting with this woman who never showed up and now I'd driven into a ditch. How much more could I let him down?

'He never really forgave me, certainly not throughout the holiday, and I've got an idea for the rest of his life he sort of vaguely held it against me. And when we made it down to Blauvac, there were two girls there who I didn't know – I think they were from Keele, there was some connection through Zulf, and Bryan must have known that they were going to be there. They got there before us because we'd been held up for two days in Le Touquet, and then I got lucky and Bryan didn't. Everything had gone wrong and it was all my fault and yet I was the one who wound up with a nice girl and the other one didn't work out for Bryan. So I think that compounded the most horrific holiday he could have had.'

Returning to London, Johnson attended to the more gratifying business of beginning to prepare *Travelling People* for publication. His early, hand-written draft blurbs for the novel reveal a shift in his conception of its lineage. Originally Henry Henry was described as 'a rich comic creation in the tradition of Fielding and Sterne'. Later, in the first of many bows to the writer Johnson considered 'of all living [...] the man I consider most worth reading and listening to',[4] this became 'a rich comic creation in the tradition of Sterne and the early Beckett.' As for Johnson's own assessment of his achievement at this stage ('it seems likely that B. S. Johnson will develop into one of the most original writers of this century') this was quietly dropped by Constable before it got as far as the dust jacket. (On which, incidentally, the author requested that there should appear 'no photograph at all of me [. . . and] unless you have strong objections, I would also prefer that no biographical details be given either.')

Constable were soon to find out, in fact, that they had an unusual author on their hands. Johnson wished to be involved in every stage of the production of *Travelling People*, and even asked for a meeting with the Garden City Press, the book's printers, so that he could discuss the various typographical challenges it posed. Letters between Johnson and the firm's proprietor, Harvey Warren, show a cordial but rather wary relationship developing. But Johnson was not impressed when Richard Sadler informed him that these same printers were suddenly jittery about the sex scenes towards the end of the book – which, although incredibly mild by today's standards, might still have been considered strong meat in a country still recovering from the aftershock of the *Lady Chatterley* trial.

41: DRAFT OF LETTER *(16? September 1962)*

To Richard Sadler

> I understand that the law under which they assume a prosecution might be brought requires that the book *as a whole* tends to deprave or corrupt. For the printers to talk of 'some passages' requiring modification, there-fore, is beside the point. They must decide whether or not to accept the job on the basis of the book taken as a whole. Myself, I am quite sure that it is extremely moral in totality. As you know, evidence of literary merit can in any case be used, and the printers can refer to the judges of the Gregory Award (T. S. Eliot, Herbert Read, Bonamy Dobrée & Henry Moore) if they are not satisfied with our assurance. Professor Dobrée, in particular, as a university teacher of Eng. Lit for over forty years, should be able to give them an opinion in which they could trust.

> I am very surprised at their attitude, which (in spite of their disingenu-ous disclaimer) does strike me as censorship, and on the basis of a superseded law seems to me, if it is not a genuine mistake, a deliberate attempt at censorship.

When Johnson wrote to Professor Dobrée about this, however, he found him less supportive than he had been anticipating. He was told, 'I am prepared to say that your book has literary merit, but I do not think that those vivid descriptions of copulation [. . .] are part of its merit. Even D.H.L. didn't go into quite such detail.' Dobrée's concluding advice was to 'think again, my dear Bryan, and don't let irritation sway you, or obstinacy take charge.'

Never a stranger either to irritation or obstinacy, Johnson unsurprisingly disregarded the professor's advice.

42: LETTER *(27 September 1962)*

To Bonamy Dobrée

First of all, thank you very much for caring enough to write to me about my novel; I am sincerely grateful, although I fear I must disagree with you.

I consider the Kim–Henry love scenes to be most important: there are so many instances of sex-in-bad-faith in the earlier part of the book, that to restore a proper balance there must be a thoroughly convincing example of love-in-good-faith. I did not feel it enough merely 'to indicate successful copulation': by example I hope it is obvious why the Kim–Henry relationship is 'good', and the others 'bad'. It is interesting that you should mention DHL: I consciously tried to better his love scenes, which I think are very unsatisfactory and often unintentionally comic.

I rang Constable immediately after I had spoken to you, and when I told Richard Sadler that my first reaction was to refuse to change a word he said 'Good for you.' I met him a couple of days later to make a final decision, and we agreed to leave the book as it stands. He thinks an action very unlikely, and I am very pleased that he is backing me up [. . .]

I would like to thank you once more for the Gregory Award, the second instalment of which I received the other day. I shall be writing formally to you and Mr. Wade as trustees in a day or so, but I'd like to say to you personally that the Award seems to have marked the beginning of my establishment as a writer and therefore has been of far more than financial importance to me.

With kind thoughts

Yours

The fuss blew over, in any case; but Johnson would run into similar problems with *Albert Angelo*, by which time his rhetoric would have changed slightly.*

43: LETTER *(8 November 1962)*

To George Greenfield

I enclose another collection of poems, *Too Many Flesh Suppers*, slightly larger than the last one but still providing a classic illustration of Dylan Thomas's remark about 'fat poets with slim volumes', for submission to Constable as we discussed.

---

* See below, pp. 151–2.

Over half of the poems are written in syllabic metres – unusual in English poetry, which usually uses stress metre, as you know. (George Macbeth at the BBC assures me that I shall have my footnote in future literary histories as a forerunner of the Syllabic Movement – ha-ha.) I use such metres because they enable me to adapt colloquial, immediate speech to verse forms. That there is an inherent tendency towards flatness worries some people; but not Bryan, who is deeply suspicious of the rhetorical and the high-flown, consciously 'poetical': hence the quotation from Rabelais at the beginning.*

The title (taken from one of the poems) is rather precious, and so may have to be changed later. It attempts to convey that sort of calculated remorse made bearable only by wit, by a refusal to take it seriously, which is the tone of many of the poems.

Here again we find Johnson stressing his belief that painful feelings can be kept at bay through a resilient sense of humour – a coping mechanism which was still necessary for him, since even the prospect of imminent publication seems only occasionally to have shifted his mood of settled melancholy. He persisted in regarding his split with Muriel as a devastating blow, and was soon to start work on his second novel, *Albert Angelo*, in which the doomed progress of that short-lived love affair was to be commemorated at considerable length. Claire Andrews, whose mother was the landlady at Claremont Square, was studying sculpture in those days and had a little studio in the basement of the house, with French windows looking out over the garden: this gave her regular contact with the tenants, and she had many opportunities to gauge Johnson's state of mind during this period.

'I think Bryan was clinically depressed, for the years we knew him. He spoke a lot of a girlfriend that he'd parted from. And the unfortunate thing was that Keith and I were getting married, and nothing's worse if your love affair's broken up than being surrounded by youngsters who are getting married. My brother was getting married too. And I remember that Bryan kept asking me, But how do you *know*? How do you know this is the right one?'

What Claire Andrews didn't realize, of course, was that this already urgent question was bound up, in Johnson's mind, with a sense of his impending mortality: although this too was a subject which he was now prepared to discuss openly:

'I remember that my course involved doing letter-cutting, and for my finals exam I was set a text to carve: and the text I was set was, "Webster

---

* This was dropped from the published version.

was much possessed by death". And I talked about this with Bryan: I can see him now in that basement room, drinking tea out of his mother's tea service (which was so incongruous because it was all red roses and gold edge) – this large, blond *maudlin* man, at the time, talking about death and saying that he was sure he was going to die young, when he was 29. He identified strongly with Christopher Marlowe. I think my reaction was just to say, "Come off it". But he was *very* serious about it.'

For those readers who, like me, have always been slightly puzzled by the 'future event' (which then turns out not to have been a future event) revealed by the holes cut through the pages of *Albert Angelo*, here at least is a partial explanation. It seems to have been intended as a cryptic reference to Johnson's identification with Marlowe (who was killed at the age of twenty-nine in a tavern brawl) and belief in his own imminent death. The complex of bewildered feelings which seem to have overwhelmed him during the autumn of 1961 – the sense, in particular, that his destiny had been predetermined and was outside his own control – had not altogether left him, even now. (Remember, too, that he was still living in a flat that had once been occupied by Michael Bannard, so whatever anxieties were associated with that friendship would never be far away.)

'Life in general is pretty miserable,' he wrote to Stuart Crampin on 23 December 1962, 'but working hard seems to help.' Sometimes – as in *Albert Angelo*, which he was just beginning to write – Johnson could transform his gloomier feelings into something more energetic and meaningful. At other times they just lie there on the page, flat and motionless, leaving the reader to feel inexpressibly dampened. This is true, for instance, of another work which appears to date from this time, a curious, unperformed and unpublished play called *The Proper End*.

This was written, bizarrely enough, for Roy Hart, a singer whose amazing vocal range inspired works by many of the greatest modern composers, including Stockhausen, Henze and Peter Maxwell Davies. Hart had been a pupil of Alfred Wolfsohn (1896–1962), a singing teacher from Berlin and 'pioneer in the realms of voice research', who had served in the trenches of World War I and been forced, upon hearing the cry of a dying soldier, 'to re-question the significance and potential of the human voice'. Wolfsohn's methods are still used today in the field of vocal therapy, and there is a Roy Hart International Voice Centre in Thoiras, France.[5]

Johnson decided to take advantage of the unusually wide range of Hart's voice by writing a monologue in which the unnamed speaker's age would range from eight years old to sixty.* Described as 'largely autobiographical',

---

* In which respect the play is a forerunner of Johnson's second film as director, *Paradigm*. (See below, pp. 260–5.)

the play centres on the reminiscences of an embittered sexagenarian who is still brooding on the 'treachery' of a woman called 'Margaret' with whom he had an unhappy love affair forty years earlier. 'For years afterwards,' he says, 'perhaps even now, everything I did was with her as an audience, for her, and I would try to succeed, for her sake, and do nothing wrong, for her sake.'* Just before this, his forty-five-year-old self voices another Johnsonian sentiment: 'I have discovered that I lack forgiveness completely. I could never, can never, forgive anyone for anything they do to me. My feelings towards them are changed, and remain changed.' The play also contains a detail which would recur in *Christie Malry's Own Double-Entry*: a small child who feels so rejected by his mother that he takes a spiteful revenge, putting a bottle on the railway line to make ground glass to put in her sugar. (And indeed the play ends with a statement of 'the double-entry theory of love: love automatically creates a force of hatred which is its opposite, its equal, its complement, its corollary.')

44: EXTRACT FROM RADIO PLAY *THE PROPER END*, WRITTEN FOR ROY HART

(The figure in brackets represents the age of the character at the time of speaking.)

(20) R: Look, Margaret, you do *understand* what I mean when I say I can't do without you? Don't you? Please! All you can do is offer people love, and hope that they won't throw it back at you. All you can do is hope. All you can do is . . .

(60) R: But I never did do it. But I did buy the bullets, and the pistol. And wrapped them in an oily duster, comfortingly in the drawer these forty years. That's the only thing that makes life livable, the knowledge that you have handy the means to end it. Kept me alive all these rotten years, these . . . Brass. Dull. Smeared with oil.

(20) R: But you just don't *stop* loving someone just like that! Margaret! I've got a . . . I'll . . . Never mind. No. That would be to prey upon your pity. To prey . . . Look, you promised, all those promises! You meant them! But only when you said them. Even though some committed you to the future, to the forever! No matter then. Refuge in bitterness, relief in the not having to give, not having to love. But a part of me destroyed.

---

*   Echoed in a note Johnson wrote to himself shortly afterwards. See Fragment 51 below, p. 135.

> The end of love is to destroy. The *proper* end, perhaps, to destroy, a quality, a condition of, the loving.

The Proper End therefore acts as a kind of compendium of some of Johnson's most typical themes, as well as providing another insight into his state of mind during the second half of 1962. It is not, however, a successful play, and it was never produced because Roy Hart himself disliked it, writing to tell Johnson that 'failure and suicide are so far removed from the essential aims of the Wolfsohn singer [. . .] that I wonder if you could try another angle'.

Needless to say, he could not 'try another angle' on this material or any other. Johnson's view of the human condition would always tend to be bleak, even when – as now – on the surface everything appeared to be going well for him. For in spite of the continuing barrenness of his emotional life, his literary career seemed to be gathering pace nicely in the run-up to the publication of *Travelling People*. Two chapters of the novel had been bought for publication in the *Transatlantic Review* by Joe McCrindle, its American editor, thus beginning a friendship which was to be one of the most important of Johnson's professional life. Francis Hitching, the editor of the new and highly fashionable culture magazine *Scene*, had heard talk of this intriguing new novelist and was anxious for him to contribute to his pages as often as possible. And Johnson had already struck up a good working relationship with the *Spectator*, which was regularly publishing his poems as well as his reviews. He had quickly established himself, for instance, as their resident Beckett expert, and on 23 November 1962 was to be found making this entirely characteristic point:

'A lot of the trouble [in understanding him] begins with a failure to place Samuel Beckett in his tradition: in spirit, he belongs with Petronius, Rabelais, Cervantes, Nashe, Burton, and Sterne. As with the latter, admiration or loathing of him is an indication of whether the reader is really interested in the novel as a form, or merely in being told a story. Thus to try to understand or discuss Beckett in terms of the 'great tradition' or of a main contemporary one which would include Graham Greene, Iris Murdoch, and Elias Canetti, for example, is as useless as to try to compare *Tristram Shandy* with *Clarissa Harlowe*.'

Note the unmistakable implication of this: that the 'great tradition' of the English novel, as defined by F. R. Leavis and as inaugurated by Samuel Richardson, is inferior to the alternative tradition with which Johnson claimed kinship – a tradition for those who are 'really interested in the novel as a form', as opposed to being 'told a story'. The following note is also to be found among his papers at this point:

45: SCRAP OF PAPER *(? 1962)*

A note to my Masters
Petronius
Rabelais
Burton
Nashe
Sterne
Beckett

(Only the last two of these, incidentally, are 'novelists' in any meaningful sense. And both of them interrogated and deconstructed the form so ruthlessly that they ended up being unable to use it any more.)

The second half of December 1962 found Johnson staying by himself in a cottage owned by Joe McCrindle at Winchelsea on the south coast. Here he wrote up his strange Welsh out-of-body experience in the story 'Sheela-na-Gig', began the writing of *Albert Angelo* in earnest ('4,000 words of my new novel on Friday', he trumpeted to Stuart Crampin)⁶ and produced a few fragments of poetry.

47: UNPUBLISHED POEM, WRITTEN IN WINCHELSEA *(2 January 1963)*

Nineteen hundred and sixty-three –
A year I hardly thought to see.
But since it's here I won't complain –
Just hope it won't come back again.*

Round about this time, he also wrote an outspoken article (published on 26 January 1963) for *Scene* magazine, expressing his contempt for the sitcom *Steptoe and Son* and extolling, instead, the virtues of the now almost forgotten comedian Arthur Haynes. *Steptoe and Son*, he argued, was an insult to the working class: 'the material, the characters, the writing I think objectionable almost to the point of disgust [. . .] Many people say the show is so "natural" and "realistic", but how many totters† do they know?' Haynes, on the other hand, he considered a 'real comic', part of the 'dying music hall tradition', who was 'truly vulgar in that he is in touch with and appeals to the common people'. The article illustrates, I think, one of the intriguing

---

* Intimations of mortality once more. You will notice, by the way, that Fragment 46 is missing. This is because it was almost the last thing that I found while going through Johnson's archive, so I think you should read it at the end of the book. (No flicking forward, by the way: this is a bound object, a work of 'enforced consecutiveness', not some box full of loose sections to be shuffled and read in any order that you choose!)

† Cockney slang for rag-and-bone men.

paradoxes about B. S. Johnson. It appeared in a magazine which prided itself in being at the cutting edge, and in the byline caption deliberate attention was drawn to the fact that its author had also written an 'unusual and exciting' novel. Yet not only does it display a somewhat strait-laced and puritanical sensibility, but it is mired in loyalty to a dying tradition – the British music hall, whose (working-class) practitioners were rapidly being pushed aside to make way for a new generation of (middle-class and Oxbridge-educated) comedians. Johnson is nearly always discussed as a champion of the avant-garde, but in many ways he was an intensely conservative writer and thinker. The explosion of pop culture which began round about now (and of which *Steptoe and Son* was part – Wilfrid Brambell, of course, soon went on to appear in the first Beatles film, *A Hard Day's Night*) would pass him by almost completely. His loyalties would remain firmly with the jazz musicians and music-hall comedians he had discovered in adolescence, during the 1940s and 50s. As he would write to Christine Brooke-Rose a couple of years later: 'I know nothing of pop art, nor is my own work aimed at or read by a mass audience.'[7]

A related point was made by George Greenfield in a letter written to Johnson in January 1963. Greenfield had been sent the manuscript of *Prepar-a-Tory*, which he now returned, saying that it was simply not 'a publishable proposition, commercially speaking'. He continued: 'Publications like *Private Eye* and, in the TV medium, *That Was The Week That Was* are so much more savage about real, live politicians that satire about an imaginary character sounds comparatively gentle.' It wasn't always the case, then, that British culture needed to run to keep up with B. S. Johnson: sometimes it was the other way around.

Greenfield also rejected Johnson's proposal for a monograph on Samuel Beckett, and shortly afterwards the latest of his dramatic ventures also came to nothing. In November 1962 Johnson had written enthusiastically for *Scene* about the Boundary Theatre Group, an experimental theatre group run by Peter Bridgmont and based in a Balham meeting hall which had until recently been used mainly for seances. Bridgmont had been a member of Joan Littlewood's Theatre Workshop, whose work Johnson much admired: his enthusiastic article about the new, young company led first to a meeting and then to a commission to write something for them. The result was another of Johnson's unperformed dramatic oddities, *Scenes from the Last Day in the Pathetic Old Age of George Offord Murrain*.

As you might guess from the title, this was a play about old age – not a subject, on the whole, about which Johnson had very positive feelings. His central character is essentially the twin brother of Maurie Bunde in *Travelling People*: instead of running an exclusive country club and surrounding himself with young staff to make himself feel more youthful, he makes himself feel more youthful by running a hairdressing salon and surrounding himself with young staff. The action proceeds in a series of discrete and disconnected episodes, one of which is set on the steps leading down to the river by the Embankment, where Murrain has a richly symbolic encounter with a talkative tramp.

48: EXTRACT FROM THE PLAY *SCENES FROM THE LAST DAY IN THE PATHETIC OLD AGE OF GEORGE OFFORD MURRAIN* (January 1963)

Tra: Sad when you think of it, isn't it, the Fleet. I mean, can you imagine it – originally it must have been a lovely little brook coming bouncing down from Hampstead Heath, pure and clean and beautiful like, and you could drink from it. Now what's happened to the Fleet? No sooner does it bubble up from the Heath than they stick it in pipes and shoot it out at Barking Creek with all the shit.

GOM looks distastefully at him.

Tra: Oh, have I offended you then? (offhandedly) With all the sewage, then. (pause) The poor bloody little Fleet. Don't you feel sorry for it? (pause) Still we couldn't be sitting here if it did still have its estuary here, could we? (pause) And why are we sitting here? (pause) We couldn't be thinking of jumping in, could we? Ha. Ha! *Felo de se*. Suicide. Man shall not take arms unto himself. Sounds like the bible, but I made it up. Sounds like it, I know. But no, you wouldn't commit suicide. Not you. And certainly not down here, in the river. You've got money enough to choose an easier way. Barbiturates from bent chemists. Or spirits of salts, obtainable from any reputable oldfashioned ironmonger. No, never for you in the old Thames. Water's bloody cold. Always, water's bloody cold in England. Even in summer. And filthy, too, think of it, oil and driftwood and french letters and cork and leaves and rubbish and sh ... I mean sewage. (smiles) Our lovely Thames. She still is our lovely Thames, you know, the most wonderful river in the world. She eases her way through this city like a woman of forty, dirty, past her best, but still infinitely more mysterious and attractive than women half her age, a Cleopatra among rivers. (pause) [...] Let's see why you're thinking of suicide – but not so much as to actually do it. You've got enough money, I should think, by your clothes. Not that clothes mean anything. (pause) Of course, I suppose you could be in some sort of financial trouble ... but I don't think so. (pause) Love? No, the thought is comic at your age! (laughs)

GOM's face contorts savagely, but he conceals it from Tra.

Tra: But you take a lot of trouble with your appearance, I can tell that. Why? (pauses, then aggressively) Why? What are you wearing clothes like that for? What have you got to hide, that you so much want to hide, eh? Now I look at you, you're not your clothes, there's a vast difference between the you of your clothes and the you of your face.

GOM conceals face by turning it away from Tra.

Tra: That's it — you don't want to be *you* — you probably don't even know you, know yourself! So you have this elaborate refuge behind clothes! That's it — you don't want to be your age! You're older than the man those clothes would suit! Let's have a look, then . . . . .

He tries to look at GOM's face, but he turns further away.

Tra: Yes, yes. . . . . you're older than I am, and I'll be fifty-seven in the Spring. . . . Look at my face, beaten and creased and smudged by the weather — but I'm proud of that face — it's an honest face, an acknowledged face, acknowledged for what it is, in its fifty-seventh year. Not like yours — you want to hide yours. Ha! I bet you sunlamp yourself! To smooth out the wrinkles — but everybody can see it's false — it's an act — like the clothes, a refuge! And the hair must be false, too, a wig . . . . .

GOM turns to him with a sort of smile; for the hair at least is not false.

Tra: Ah well, I can't tell in this light. (pause) Poor audience reaction tonight. That's the trouble — you never know which of their illusions they want you to pander to.

49: EXTRACT FROM LETTER *(18 January 1963)*

To Anthony Smith

My dissatisfaction with them [the *Spectator*] is only part of a larger dissatisfaction. And since they're currently my only source of income (I work for *Scene*, but they haven't paid for stuff I did at the beginning of November yet) I shouldn't complain. It's like I'm bored, man, for the first time in my life, looking for something to be interested in. Perhaps the real answer is that I'm dissatisfied with collaborating in any way: the stageplay I'm doing for the Boundary group is being got in the way of by actors, and so is a radio play I've done. I'm getting really bloody about it: look, I say, I want to say *this*, and if you want to say anything else then you should be writing your own material. (This doesn't mean dialogue, of course, but theme.) So I'm urging myself to go on with the novel, where I can say what I want to without it going vicariously through actors. Perhaps it's just as bloody well I didn't get the Bristol fellowship!

'The play for the Boundary group was a total failure, disaster,' he wrote two months later, to Roma Williams (soon to be Roma Crampin). But again, he put the blame less on the play itself than on his own shortcomings as a collaborator. 'Mainly my fault for I just can't get on with anyone else. Looks as though I shall never be able to do anything in the theatre until I have the same setup Brecht had.' In the same letter, he described his current financial circumstances: 'I'm at the in-between stage: in all sorts of ways. One day I'm feeling myself very lucky to have two bobs' worth of f&c for lunch, and the next some publisher or agent is buying me two or three pounds worth. *TP* has had quite a lot of advance publicity, which I am assured is quite unusual for a novel. Constable are going to publish my poems next Jan or Feb.'[8]

The contract for *Poems* (still at this stage called *Too Many Flesh Suppers*) had only just been signed, in fact, and had already been the subject of a misunderstanding which had given George Greenfield the chance to observe – perhaps for the first time – his client's insecurity and short temper. In Johnson's opinion, neither Greenfield nor Richard Sadler at Constable had been showing enough enthusiasm for this first collection; they seemed to be committing the cardinal sin of not wanting the 'enormous totality' of him, just the novel-writing bit. Sadler had suggested that they wait a little longer before accepting the poems for publication, purely in order to give Johnson time to write some more and bolster what was currently a rather slight collection. But he had interpreted this as an out-and-out rejection and wrote to Greenfield making it clear that he was deeply upset: 'I had had little sleep the night before, and you try explaining to a rozzer that you are wandering abroad up the Liverpool Road with no visible means of support at three in the morning because Constable haven't accepted your poems, mate. [...] Let me tell you why I was angry [...] You don't seem to have taken as much interest in selling the poems as you did the novel – and obviously I was wrong to think you would. Mr Sadler seemed to know nothing of why poetry was so important to me (and I was surprised to have to explain it to you again) [...] I don't think my anger was unreasonable.'

Poetry continued to occupy him during these weeks, with readings at the house of Edward Lucie-Smith (where the Group poets used to meet, although Johnson was only ever loosely affiliated with this movement) and at the Contemporary Poetry and Music Circle, Kensington, with George Buchanan and Nathaniel Tarn. Poems from his first collection dating from this period include 'Preconception' and 'For a Girl in a Book', inspired by the central female character in *Travelling People*:

50: POEM *(19 March 1963)*

Kim, composite of all my loves,
less real than most, more real than all;
of my making, all the good and
some of the bad, yet of yourself;
sole, unique, strong, alone,
whole, independent, one: yet mine
in that you cannot be unfaithful.

And now the publication date of *Travelling People* beckoned. The novel had already been reviewed in the trade press, with *Smith's Trade News* concluding on 6 April that 'This title can be recommended, with confidence, to your customers who enjoy experimental originality in novel writing. This brilliant bow to the world of books is emphatically for adults only.' Publication itself was on 18 April: Johnson celebrated with a drinks party at Claremont Square.

There were two significant absentees from this party: Tony and June Tillinghast. Tony had had to go into hospital for a 'minor operation' that spring, but Johnson had thought this 'did not sound very serious': 'It seemed so trivial, he had been ill before, I knew that he was prone to illnesses.'[9] But Tony's failure to make the trip down to London in April made his friend think again. 'That it was serious, the first thing that brought it home to me, was that he was too ill to come down to London for the publication party of my novel, in my flat, the novel which was so much better for his work on it, for his attention to it. It was dedicated to them! This shocked me, I was annoyed, angry even, that he, that both of them, should find any excuse whatsoever for missing something so important.'[10] What Johnson did not know, at this point, was that Tony had been diagnosed with cancer, that doctors had found a tumour on his collarbone and 'cut him open to remove it but had found that its feelers or fingers or tentacles had grasped right round the collarbone and that therefore surgery would not be effective.'[11] He would have to undergo a course of radiotherapy instead.

Temporarily unaware of the life-threatening condition that was afflicting one of his closest friends, Johnson travelled that weekend (20–21 April) to Ruthin in Denbighshire, north Wales, for the wedding of another of his King's College friends, Anne Bufton. On Sunday morning, two reviews of his novel appeared. It had already been praised (unsurprisingly) in the *Western Daily Press* by Zulfikar Ghose, but this was a far more important test. What would the two heavyweight Sundays make of it? Would they even notice it at all? In the event, both pieces were favourable: the *Sunday Times* called it 'clever and funny', picked up on its affinities with Rabelais and Thomas

Nashe and said that the author showed 'no small talent'; Simon Raven in the *Observer* wrote that 'his scene [...] is both comically and decoratively rendered; his language is incisive; his thought is paradoxical and often disquieting'. Most remarkably of all, at a time when it was common practice to group several novels together in the same review, *Travelling People* was given pride of place in both papers, even ahead of the latest Daphne du Maurier.

'Went up to Wales last weekend,' Johnson wrote to Roma Crampin, 'for the nuptials of Anne Bufton; where I read the Sundays; and executed a short dance round Ruthin Market Square on the morning, early, when I had got up and gone out and bought them and perused them in very decent solitude. To the astonishment of several natives and bleary eyed wedding guests.'[12] One of these guests was Patrick Snaith, who asked Johnson what he would have done if the reviews had been unfavourable. To which he received the simple answer: 'I would have killed myself.'

'I didn't believe him at the time,' Snaith recalls. 'In retrospect, it's the sort of thing you give extra weight to.'

Indeed.

GINNIE AND ALBERT

51: NOTE *(probably from May 1963)*

All my 'success' (the novel, the money, the other women) means nothing: I have been, and still am, incapable of loving anyone else but you: it means nothing if I cannot lay it at your feet; for all I have done has been for you, for your memory.

I still love you.
I have been unable to love anyone else since you. I have tried. I feel I shall never love anyone else, having given it every chance.
This is what life, poetry is about.
This is what my life, my poetry is about anyway.

So even now, it seems, he was still hankering after Muriel. Johnson was a romantic at heart, and we know that he had been presented by his 'Muse Goddess' (whether her 'manifestation' had really been physical or was some kind of hallucination) with a stark choice between two kinds of fulfilment: artistic or emotional. It wasn't possible, apparently, to have both. ('Never able to have happy love/marriage as She was so jealous.') And so, for the whole of the period from the 'betrayal' of Muriel in 1958 to the summer of 1963 he had been celibate, finding compensation, as best he could, in the act of writing. But it had been cold comfort, on the whole. Hence the fundamental theme of *Albert Angelo*, as revealed in the 'Disintegration' section: 'the writing and nothing being an answer to the loneliness to the lack of loving'.

Actually, Johnson did not strictly regard himself as having been 'celibate' throughout this time. In 1970 he wrote a short prose piece called 'Instructions for the Use of Women', which recalls – with a degree of rancour that leaves a bitter taste in the reader's mouth (this reader's, anyway) – another failed relationship from the early weeks of 1963. 'I was not (like any of us) as young as I used to be,' he writes there. 'I was, indeed, as late in the twenties as it was possible to be in those days, and I had been, moreover (and this may come as a shock), in an unblessed state as regards actual penetration of a female for something approaching four years. Not that, you must understand, I considered myself celibate: like an athlete I had kept the appropriate muscles in fine fettle by regular (for periods, indeed, nightly) exercise.'[1]

An admission which falls into the category of 'too much information', perhaps. (Except that Johnson, of course, would not have recognized that such a category exists.) Nonetheless, he went out with a number of women during these years, one of them being Jean Nicholson, a friend and flatmate of Roma Crampin's. (Who described her in a recent email to me as 'one of the tall, blonde "posh birds" that Bryan seemed to like'. Intriguingly, Johnson's class loyalties, about which he was always so vocal, did not extend into his romantic life.) Now a successful painter and printmaker, she remembers her relationship with Johnson as being somewhat prickly, because she preferred to keep things platonic whereas he – the self-confessed 'allornothinger' – naturally wanted more:

'Yes, he did get a bit keen on me, but I just didn't see it that way. Very sadly, I never fancied him, he just wasn't my type. We went to lots of films together, and that sort of thing: I was between serious boyfriends, and he was around and he was interesting, so I just thought, Why not? And I don't think I realized at the time that this could be hurtful to him at all. His main grouse about me was that I wasn't prepared to commit, but the other thing was that Bryan didn't see me as *me*: he saw me as the person he would like me to be, or as the person he could make me into. That was one of the reasons it didn't work.'

Despite the fact that the relationship never became physical, it was still close enough for Johnson to suggest, shortly after the publication of *Travelling People*, that they hire a car and spend a week in Wales together: which might have been, in its way (and certainly from his point of view) an equally momentous step. Jean Nicholson had already read the novel, and had also been presented with a typewritten copy of 'Cwm Pennant', the verse sequence which was the first of Johnson's several attempts to express the depth and complexity of his love for north Wales. In the course of their week together (during which they slept in separate rooms in a succession of guest houses), he took her to all of the places mentioned in these works.

'That whole week,' she remembers now, 'was full of bizarre incidents. I think it was very significant for him because we were reviewing lots of important bits of his life. He gave me a copy of "Cwm Pennant", and we drove past the tower which is mentioned in the poem, and which really was where he said he would love to live and write.'

> I could see a tower flagstaff about a mile away,
> as, swinging left at Dolbenmaen and holding the long car

onehanded against a gracile curve, its uncapped sliver
completed a crenellated outline above the trees.

Poems, p. 46

'And as we drove up to Wales he talked a lot about how life is always too long, just as it says at the end of the poem.'

> However propitious the scenery,
> the dull charade is much the same: the same
> problems demand solution, but any
> one is never solved, just superseded
> in urgency by one of the others;
> and solitude is not the same as peace.
> Who would wish extension of such pain, since, in
> particular, a shepherd's life is never short?

Poems, p. 51

They also revisited the location of *Travelling People*: 'I do remember that we went into the Glyn Club and Bryan was playing the fruit machine and he won the jackpot, and we both thought that was marvellous, just so appropriate.'

Most interestingly of all, however, it was on this visit to Wales that Johnson underwent a curious experience, one which he did not talk about publicly until the making of *Fat Man on a Beach* ten years later. There, towards the very end of the film, he recounts the episode in hushed tones, with his own and the camera crew's mirrored faces in shot as if purposely to put some reassuring distance between himself and the substance of his anecdote.

52: EXTRACT FROM THE FILM *FAT MAN ON A BEACH* (1973)

Some things can only be said indirectly. One can only reflect the truth of what they were. I am not quite sure that I know the truth about this particular thing I want to talk about indirectly. There's a mountain called Card Fadrun on Lleyn. It's the last mountain towards the tip of the peninsula which can be called a mountain, that is it's over 1,000 feet tall. I found myself one morning at dawn on top of that mountain, almost not of my own volition and stripping off all my clothes and making what I can only think of as religious gestures – worshipping some sort of female deity. Now I am not a religious person. I can't explain how that happened or why I felt the need to do it. That's the sort of place Lleyn is. I feel nowhere else on earth here, in Lleyn, doing that sort of thing, that Jung calls the archetype. Something that we do despite the last 2–3,000 years of civilisation. There is a much longer period with archetypal patterns of behaviour inside us that we respond to sometimes in certain places, and Carn Fadrun must have been the same way for hundreds of thousands of years. Lleyn, in many ways, has been that sort of place for many hundreds of thousands of years.

Jean Nicholson remembers this incident well, although her telling of it is slightly more prosaic:

'Bryan had this rayonny artificial silk dressing gown, sort of mustard yellow, and he came into my room one night wearing this thing and said that he was going to get up terribly early. He was mad about Robert Graves at the time, and we'd been talking about *The White Goddess* all week, and he was going to go up the mountain early in the morning, about six o'clock. Well, when he came back he looked rather pleased with himself, and I said, "Ah, you've been dancing naked with the Goddess, haven't you?" and he looked at me and said, in a shocked voice, "*How did you know?*" But I just knew that if he was going to go up there at 6 a.m. all by himself, he was going to dance naked with the Goddess. It seemed so typical and appropriate.'

Finally they stopped off at the hospital in Chester where Tony Tillinghast was undergoing the initial stages of treatment for cancer. 'I wandered off so that they could have a proper talk and I remember seeing all these patients with holes in their faces and thinking, "This is just terrible."'* A stark end to an excursion which – although Jean Nicholson still remembers it with affection, as a very special episode in her life – does appear to emphasize Johnson's unshakeable preoccupations with death, decay and futility.

On the subject of which, see this letter from around the same period, written to the luckless subject of 'Instructions for the Use of Women':

53: LETTER *(? early summer 1963)*

As for my 'dark night of the soul' or 'gloomy nature' – you are far too facile: I must be the supreme optimist that I go on living *in spite of this* – don't you see? I *will* not *can*not live by means of illusion, escapism: I try to perceive the reality in everything – that this reality is often tragic and depressing is not my fault; but it is no reason to delude myself it doesn't exist, as you do, as almost everyone does. That I teeter between despair and suicide doesn't mean that I don't see the good things as well; and that I stay alive is the most amazing thing about me:

---

* For Johnson's own account of this visit, see *The Unfortunates* (Picador, 1999), 'Just as it seemed things were going his way', pp. 4–8.

O the mind, mind has mountains; cliffs of fall
Frightful, shee, no-man-fathomed. Hold them cheap
May who ne'er hung there.

To quote Hopkins back at you.* (Incidentally, it was nice to be quoted myself!) What I want is someone who will recognise the same things as myself: someone able to face *our* human condition and stay alive in spite of it, not by pretending it doesn't exist. And when you can learn to sacrifice, then you might well be beginning to understand.

I don't much care, if that's the same as forgiveness.

And in what black hell I do live, I don't think you can even guess at.

How much of this 'black hell' derived from his seemingly never-ending preoccupation with Muriel is not clear; but in any case, two things were about to happen which might make it possible for her spell to be finally broken. First of all, Johnson was given a stern talking-to on this subject by Tony and June Tillinghast, two of the friends whose opinion he most respected. Tony had survived his initial course of radiotherapy in Chester and was now recuperating – along with June and their six-month-old son, Kelvin – at his parents' house in Brighton. It was here that Johnson visited them at some point in the early summer and was told that he could no longer continue to obsess over the failed affair.

54: EXTRACT FROM *THE UNFORTUNATES*

(The setting of this passage seems to be May or June 1963)

I was still then troubled, burdening them with my troubles, which were Wendy,† still Wendy, or rather the failure to find anyone to replace her, be as good as she was, or as I had thought she was, had made her out to be, for my own purposes, no doubt, and no doubt I was boring these two, as I remember they were rather sharp about it, by then they had had three or more years of my lamenting the loss of Wendy, on and off, my failure, her defection, and this I think was the occasion when they said so, but gently, and it did me a lot of good, helped me to understand that it was the loss I wanted, the self-suffering, not her, or I would surely have gone out and found her again and made it work. And this helped, they made me realize it was true, yes, and paradoxically it freed me from her, Wendy, or rather from the suffering, and that and the

---

* These lines are from Hopkins's sonnet, 'No worst, there is none'. Incidentally, I can hear an echo of these lines in the phrase 'The mind has fuses', from *The Unfortunates* ('Then they had moved to a house', p. 5).

† i.e. Muriel.

coincidence of Ginnie, later, and the new novel, marriage, freed me from her and what she had done, for good, for good, finally.

Then, in July 1963, something more momentous happened. At a party given in Soho by an old friend from King's, Simon Evans, Johnson's eye lighted upon a tall, beautiful, unmistakably well-heeled female (a work colleague of Evans's girlfriend, as it happened), and he made a move towards her. Catching an earful of her cut-glass accent, he addressed her thus: 'Did you go to Roedean, then?' A few seconds later he was quizzing her about her views on James Joyce and she cheerfully confessed that she had never heard of him. In this way Johnson first met his future wife.

With a father who had been the civilian administrator of Chatham Docks, and later a chairman of Rothschild, Virginia Kimpton seems an unlikely match for the aggressively proletarian B. S. Johnson, who continued to insist that 'the class war is being fought as viciously and destructively of human spirit as it has ever been in England'. At the time she was working as a production manager on a project developing 'programmed learning' (a sort of early proto-computer), but after marrying Johnson she would give this up. (He was insistent that his wife should not work and 'I was very happy complying with his dictums in those days.') Looking back on her own state of mind when the relationship began, she recalls a prevailing sense of being adrift and angry, particularly at the loss of her father (who had died at the age of seventy-one, when she was only eleven) and more recently her brother John. She was looking, perhaps, for a strong, confident man (a father figure – or is that too simple?) to give her some direction in life, and Johnson seemed to fit the bill, as well as being delightfully down-to-earth and 'not at all bookish or fusty'. He appealed to her sense of rebellion, as well, whereas she appealed – among other things – to his unacknowledged but very real aspirations towards social mobility. Doug Davies, then the tenant of the basement flat at Claremont Square, witnessed the early stages of their relationship and remembers Virginia as a 'very charming young lady who, it did strike me at the time, epitomized all that he wanted to be. She came across as this typically English-looking, very beautiful South Kensington type. I don't mean "Sloaney" in the nasty way, but she could easily have been an army officer's wife – the English beauty, with all the good things about it. I would think that she represented everything that he aspired to.'

The new affair certainly worked a transformation on his mood, and an unaccustomed note of perkiness enters his correspondence at this point. Here he is writing to George Greenfield on 9 July 1963: 'Things are going well: new novel nearly done, two new poems written since I saw Glazebrook, very enthusiastic about the children's photos, and a girlfriend who can type. What more can I ask?'

Virginia, of course, is the woman romantically designated as 'a girlfriend who can type', while 'Glazebrook' is Ben Glazebrook, Johnson's new editor at Constable. In one of the minor upheavals which were, even then, a routine feature of British publishing, Richard Sadler had been edged out of the company in difficult circumstances after many years' service: a small but significant blow for Johnson, who had thereby lost the advocate whose enthusiasm had first brought him to the company, and would now be looked after by someone who – while never less than a vigorous supporter – would not bring quite the same quality of passion and loyalty to his relationship with the difficult author.

As for the 'children's photos', these were the work of the designer and photographer Julia Trevelyan Oman. Oman, in those days, was beginning to make a name for herself as a set designer for television, but she recalls that 'that period at the BBC was extremely boring, because you weren't given things that you would necessarily enjoy or be interested in. I was quite artistically frustrated, and being interested in cameras I did a lot of walking around Clapham Junction and those sorts of areas, and built up a folder of photographs of children playing in the street. Eventually I became aware that these could be put into a book, but I didn't know anybody who could do the text. They were shown to Richard Sadler at Constable and he was fascinated by them, and I think he could see that casting Bryan and myself together workwise might be interesting.'

Thus began the partnership that was to result in *Street Children*, published in 1964. Again, on the surface of things, it seemed an unlikely collaboration. Oman's striking photographs were of 'working-class and immigrant children [...] seen in relation to the conditions which helped to create them', but this was scarcely her own background: she was directly descended from two great families of historians (the Macaulays and the Trevelyans) and her father had been keeper of the department of metalwork at the Victoria and Albert Museum. Johnson, meanwhile, was adamant that he could empathize with the children in these photographs completely, because he knew exactly what it was like to grow up in streets like this. (Shortly before publication an argument raged over whether the book should be called *Pavement Children* – the title preferred both by Oman and the publishers – or the more gritty *Street Children*, as Johnson insisted. He won the day, in the end, by being – in Oman's words – 'very difficult' about it.) Certainly he had no hesitation in projecting his own thoughts and feelings onto the children caught so vividly by Oman's camera. The very first caption in the book – alongside a picture of a small boy with a dummy in his mouth, staring moodily into the middle distance – could stand as a classic expression of the Johnsonian philosophy, circa 1963:

55: EXTRACT FROM *STREET CHILDREN*

They don't have to tell me about this human condition: I'm in it. They don't have to tell me what life's about, because I know already, and it's about hardness. Hardness and being on my own, quite on my own. You understand that much right from the beginning, from the first time the pavement comes up and hits you, from the first time you look round for someone you expected to be there and they aren't. Oh, I know you can get close to people, but that's not the same. In the end you're just on your own.

But that's not the point. The point is that you have to go on living in it, life, and not only just put up with it, either, but let it see that it doesn't matter to you. That you're going to go on living however many times things come up and knock you flat, however many people aren't there when you expected them to be.

So they don't have to tell me about it: I'm in it, right in it. You just have to go on.

Some time after their collaboration on *Street Children*, Julia Trevelyan Oman was also commissioned by the *Observer* to take some photographs of Johnson in the classroom with his pupils. This is how she recalls the occasion:

'I went with Bryan to Newington Green Junior Modern School, or something like that, where he taught once a week. I was to take photographs. I don't know what the class that he taught was called, it was something like creative plane making. The photographs I've got, there are about two children doing anything active. The rest are lying down bored stiff, just absolutely, utterly bored. The children must have been about seven or eight or nine, that sort of age. The only time Bryan intervened was when the tough boys were getting a bit too rough with each other and then he intervened. Otherwise he sat in the background looking morose.'

This would have been at the very end of his time as a supply teacher, when disillusionment might have set in pretty thoroughly. Certainly the self-portrait Johnson draws of himself in *Albert Angelo* shows something very different: a highly motivated – if frustrated – teacher doing his best to instil enthusiasm into some impossibly recalcitrant pupils. And the hilarious sequence of children's essays included in that novel – all of them, as I discovered from my trawl through his archives, verbatim transcripts of essays set by Johnson himself and written by his own pupils – certainly suggests that there was plenty of vitality among the children he taught. The portrait that they reflect back at *him* through those essays also shows a memorable, larger-than-life figure who is not lacking in his own peculiar brand of dynamism:

56: EXTRACTS FROM *ALBERT ANGELO*

Mr Albert is alright sometimes, but he gets very anoyed at us and shouts and calls us peasants and he goes round hitting people for nothing he only hits the boys so I'm glad I am not a boy.

He is very morbid and gross and he thinks that everybody is seducing him.

I think Mr. Albert is horrible sometimes because he is allways morneing you can never say any think without get told of or getting moved somewhere elese. Mr Albert is fat and has fair hair, he allways has a joke with the boys but never with the girls because he's to morney. He is not a bit moden he wears old fashion round toe shoes baggy trouser and a dirty looking tie. His hair is always over the place, any body would think he has't got a comb. I think he is a bit spitefull to the boys just because they say something silly but some do need hiting but not on the head.

He is orable for one thing for a nother he is a nosens
　　His face is like a back of a bus.
　　He is to big for his boots.
　　He is a bit of a film Star he acted the part of Garula.
　　He walks like a firy elephant.*

The central character of *Albert Angelo*, incidentally, went through two changes of name. First of all he was going to be called 'Henry', presumably to provide continuity with *Travelling People*. This idea was soon abandoned and he was called Samuel instead: a name which lasted almost until the very moment the novel was completed.

57: LETTER *(30 July 1963)*

To Zulfikar Ghose

Hurrah Hurray finished SA: only it's not SA any longer but AA = ALBERT ANGELO because I wanted a quotation from Sam at the beginning and it would look as though I was writing about Beckett, or might do, so I chose Albert, which is only slightly worse. However. RAH RAH RAH
　　Mind you, I've got bloodywell to revise it, let alone type it yet.

---

*　Johnson himself always read this phrase as 'like a fiery elephant', but the more common expression, of course, is 'like a fairy elephant'.

58: LETTER *(30 July 1963)*

To George Greenfield

Just a note to say that I finished my new novel *ALBERT ANGELO* about fifteen minutes ago, and that I shall start revising it this afternoon and typing (I hope) at the weekend.

So you should have it before your holiday.

As ever, but relieved,

Bryan.

Travelling People, at this stage, had been out for about three months and was faring moderately well. Reviews had been for the most part both prominent and favourable, although Johnson – like every author before and since – had been disappointed by their superficiality. ('Having now had time to reflect on the reviews of my novel,' he wrote to one correspondent, 'I am more than a little disappointed that no one has made any attempt to examine the validity of my reasons for a new approach, for the necessity of experiment.'[2]) In July he had signed a contract with Mondadori for an Italian edition, which was certainly gratifying as well as bringing him an extra 200,000 lira (£114 13s 5d in the currency of the time). But in fact this was the only foreign sale to date, and over the next few years this failure to spread his reputation abroad would come to gall him considerably. He was especially annoyed that he was never published in France – birthplace of the nouveau roman with which he felt such an affinity – nor (until 1973) in America.

Indeed, despite George Greenfield's best efforts, a steady stream of dispiriting rejections was already trickling in from the US, couched in those terms of regretfulness and *faux*-enthusiasm which are often so irritating to authors who would rather be told straight out that their books stink. 'Johnson's basic talents are undeniable, but I don't think that this is a successful novel,' wrote one editor. 'I sat up late one night unable to put down *Travelling People* [...] At the end, though I'm afraid I found it just too gimmicky, and I just don't think we could do very well with it here.' 'For a while we felt this would be in the tradition of *Catch-22* and *V*, but I think Johnson bites off more than he can chew.' 'Every single reader responded to the brilliance and exceptional talent manifest in this first novel. We did feel, however, that there were many excesses of style and attempts at cleverness which tended to impair the book's overall accomplishment.' 'It is original – and funny – in spots, but it seems to us also to be extremely self-conscious and very derivative. We don't think it comes off, but it is the work of a gifted young man.' 'Although Mr Johnson is an imaginative and talented writer [...] I thought some of his humor a little "British" for the American market.' And so on and so on.

Most authors have to put up with these brush-offs at some point or another, but it is worth noticing, at this point, that there is already the seed of something potentially destructive being planted here. Doug Davies, Johnson's friend as well as neighbour, discussed theories of literature with him several times and has this comment to make:

'He had this conviction that you could only write from personal experience: if you hadn't personally experienced it you couldn't write about it. And it seemed to me at the time that that would give any reasonable person at most a five-year writing career, because none of us is that interesting – you don't have time to live the life to get the experience to write about it. I think I said to him, then, that this was a cul-de-sac, and not a very long one, and to base your whole philosophy of writing on that was going to lead to heartaches.* And I imagine – well, by this time we weren't seeing each other, but I imagine that that is exactly what happened. Certainly that particular cul-de-sac didn't strike me as being one which was likely to give an awful lot of money, which he wanted, because he wanted to be recognized and the way you know you're recognized is when you're being paid a lot of money for it: apart from which he wanted the things that money could buy. So all of this seemed to me to be not *thought through*, not realistic – and bound to lead to unhappiness. There were agonizing moments being stored up within those attitudes.'

Davies may well be right. It was to become one of Johnson's recurring complaints that his work was not translated as often as he felt it should have been and that it generally did not reach a wide enough audience. At the same time, however, from *Albert Angelo* onwards he was set upon an aesthetic course which would give his books a narrower and narrower focus and make them progressively less attractive to a commercially driven international literary market. Stark evidence of this was provided in October 1963 when Michael Legat, the editor at Corgi paperbacks who had bought rights in *Travelling People*, read *Albert Angelo* and rejected it in no uncertain terms. 'Quite apart from the gimmicks,' he wrote (to George Greenfield), 'I am bitterly disappointed in the book. As I think you know, we bought *Travelling People* with considerable enthusiasm – it seemed to me to combine exciting quality with a good sales potential. *Albert Angelo*, however, seems to me a complete nothing of a book.'

Thus we can already see Johnson cruising towards a head-on collision not so much with the *literary* establishment – which tended, throughout his career, to allow him at least a certain grudging respect – but with the commercial arm of the publishing industry. Which might not have mattered,

---

* Other people expressed a similar concern to him, over the years. For Johnson's response, see his letter to Edward Lucie-Smith below: Fragment 99, pp. 216–17.

had he been content (like Samuel Beckett, say) to allow his work to have been published by small independent firms, without a thought for sales figures, but his determination never to compromise his artistic vision went hand in hand with a belief that his work also deserved to reach a wide audience, and if it didn't the fault lay with the incompetence of his publishers. In retrospect it seems obvious that reconciling those two impulses was always going to be difficult.

Meanwhile Johnson was already preparing to move on, already thinking of a new book, and his publishers were not going to find it a very saleable one. He had in mind something that would follow on from the conclusions he had reached in *Albert Angelo*: the complete abandonment of fictional pretences, and a new concentration on actuality, on documentary realism. This was his literal-minded interpretation of Beckett's position in *The Unnamable*: that from now on he should write about 'nothing else but what happens to me'. What he had to write, then, would by definition be autobiographical. But it would not be *an autobiography*. Tony Tillinghast had written his doctoral thesis on Boswell, and Johnson had been deeply impressed by the way his friend had argued – or proved, even – that a journal could itself be a work of art, with all the formal patterning and aesthetic satisfaction that these words implied. As for the novel, it had become obvious to Johnson (but not, apparently, to anybody else) that to deploy the words 'novel' and 'fiction' as if they were synonymous was a corrupt use of language. Intrinsically, the two words had nothing to do with each other. 'The novel is a form in the same sense that a sonnet is a form,' he would write later. 'Within that form, one may write truth or fiction. I choose to write truth in the form of a novel.'[3]

The novel that was now beginning to take shape in his mind involved two levels, and two voyages. One was a voyage of rediscovery, a process of remembering; the other would be a real voyage, taking place in the present – a voyage across water. The unifying image that would draw the two levels together would be the fisherman's net, trawling up fish and trawling up memories from the 'vasty deep' of the ocean and the subconscious. But Johnson had never been on a deep-sea trawler, and he could not allow himself to imagine what it would be like. That would be dishonest. If he was going to write about it, he would have to live it first.*

---

* How original was Johnson's image, incidentally? Gordon Bowker first met him in 1965 (when Johnson was writing *Trawl*) and later became the acclaimed biographer of Malcolm Lowry and George Orwell. On 5 March 2002 he emailed me to say: 'One other thought [...] In 1962 Malcolm Lowry's "Selected Poems" were published by the City Lights Press in Los Angeles, and his novels and stories were published here by Penguin. I was then greatly in thrall to Lowry and must have talked about him to Bryan at boring length – I did to most others. I was struck on reading "Trawl" again about a year ago how like it was to Lowry's first novel, "Ultramarine" [...]

He contacted Barbara Hardy, who had taught him at Birkbeck. Her husband Ernest worked in the government department with responsibility for the fishing industry, and he was able to put Johnson in touch with the secretary of the British Trawlers' Federation.

59: LETTER *(13 September 1963)*

To J H Ray, Esq.

> Mr Hardy has very kindly given me your name, and suggested that you might be able to help me to make a trip on a trawler.
>
> I am a writer: my first novel was published earlier this year, and a book of poems and another novel will come out in the Spring of next year. I wish to go to sea for one voyage in a trawler, as soon as it can be arranged, to obtain background material for my next novel, and I would be most grateful if you were able to help me to do this.
>
> I understand from Mr Hardy that I should not be allowed to work on a trawler, and that it would be advisable to undertake a medium- or near-water voyage. If you require references, I shall be pleased to supply them.

It would be unfair to present this rage for authenticity as being little more than a quirk in Johnson's artistic personality. As Claire Andrews reminded me when I spoke to her about her days with Johnson in Claremont Square, when she had only recently left art school: 'This was again part of the Zeitgeist. It was the same with all my contemporaries: we came away from art school with this belief that you would not work from photographs, you were not to work from imagination, you were to work from the *actual thing*, which was also Bryan's belief. And indeed he didn't say that he couldn't write about something he hadn't experienced, he said that he *oughtn't* to.'

When Constable heard of the trip Johnson was planning to make, they wondered if it could be used to generate media interest. This was how he (partially) explained his motivation to the head of their publicity department:

Lowry, of course, came from a more Classical background (The Leys School and St Catharine's, Cambridge) and in writing the novel was under the tutelage of the American poet Conrad Aiken, who at the time was himself heavily influenced by Joyce and Freud. However, they seem to have shared the idea of going on a voyage in the hope of getting a book out of it and then writing a stream-of-consciousness novel. There are strong parallels and interesting differences between these books.'

60: LETTER *(13 October 1963)*

To Miles Huddleston

I've found it pretty difficult to think of any angle for the S. Times. Briefly, I'm going as supernumerary on the *Northern Jewel* from Grimsby 2.30 a.m. Monday [14 October] to distant-water fishing grounds: which might be Iceland, Greenland, North Russia, Bear Island, Labrador or Newfoundland – it depends where the skipper thinks he can best catch fish at this time of year.

I'm making the trip to get first-hand material for a new novel, the theme of which is deliberate isolation in order to solve a problem mechanistically. The trip will last at least three weeks.

That's about all there is to say: apart from things like I'll have three books out next year,* and general plugging.

See you when I return.

'Deliberate isolation in order to solve a problem mechanistically': is that really the theme of *Trawl*? The novel's blurb – written by Johnson himself, as always – would later use similar wording: 'A man who has deliberately isolated himself in this way from everything connected with the life he has previously known in order to try to discover why he has felt himself to be isolated all his life: an attempt to resolve his problems which is desperate in its seriousness'. But if someone really wanted to isolate himself in order to think long and hard about his emotional problems, a much simpler course of action might present itself: renting a distant cottage, for instance, on some Scottish island, going away for a few weeks, taking no radio with him, sitting in an empty room looking at fields and recollecting to his heart's content. Whereas, a voyage on a deep-sea trawler? This would mean putting yourself in a distractingly new situation, surrounding yourself with fresh stimuli, subjecting yourself to new physical sensations and putting yourself in very close physical proximity to other people. As an aid to tranquil contemplation of the past, it's hard to think of anything more unsuitable.

Barbara Hardy remembers that, 'Certainly Bryan talked about why he wanted to go on a trawler, but when I went back to look at *Trawl* I was quite surprised to find the reasons given in the novel weren't the reasons he actually gave to us. He told us that he wanted very much to bring in the now, the immediacy of living – I'm certainly putting words into his mouth but not, I think, ideas. He wanted an exotic environment and therefore its physical presentness would be very clearly defined. It wasn't that he wanted to know lots about fishing, it was that he wanted to provide himself with a

---

* Actually there would be four: *Albert Angelo, Poems, Street Children* and the short story collection *Statement Against Corpses*, written with Zulfikar Ghose.

sort of arbitrary present-tense reality. I think he was doing it both for himself – so that he would perhaps come to understand his own familial isolation – but also for the book, for this other, literary reason that it was a kind of ready-made symbol.'

With these mixed motives, anyway, Johnson set off for Grimsby in mid-October: but shortly before departing, he had some further pressing business to attend to. He proposed marriage to Virginia. Bewildered, and thinking that it was too early in their relationship to make such a serious commitment, she turned him down. Patrick Snaith, who was staying with him in Claremont Square at the time – prior to travelling to Norway the next day to take up a teaching job – remembers that this was the second time in a few months he had seen his friend appear suicidal. A year later, when he and Virginia were happily married, Johnson would claim that the only thing that had stopped him from killing himself that night was the fact that Snaith had been staying with him: 'He thought it wouldn't have been very nice for me to clear up the mess the next day, particularly as I had a boat train to catch at nine o'clock in the morning.'

61: EXTRACT FROM *TRAWL*

The ship grates slightly on the starboard side. Now we are through and can see our berth, first on the far side of the fish market, open buildings, long, low. And a small group of people waiting where we shall berth, women from the colours of their coats, fawn, red, blue. Mick comes forward with his duffelcoat and suitcase, ready to land. Duff's wife and sister-in-law, says the Skipper, drawing my attention again to the quay by where we shall berth. It is too far to see faces: he must tell by their coats: fawn, blue, red, another blue, the red just like the coat that Ginnie has – – Ginnie? Can it be her? She could not know what time I was due in, nor even which ship I was on, for I would not tell her. But she could have found out, if she had tried hard enough, of her own accord she might have tried to break my isolation in the only way it could be broken. Ginnie! But is it she? My eyes narrow, strain to see through the early-morning light, the mist, the shadows on the quay, to the face of that figure in red. It must be of her own accord, to contain, to accept the knowledge, the certainty· · · · · · I, always with I · · · one always starts with I· · · · · · · · And ends with I.

62: LETTER *(21 November 1963)*

To Patrick Snaith

My trawler trip actually took me nowhere near you. Norway, I thought, as though it were Bootle, Patrick's there. Actually, probably the nearest

I got to you was Grimsby. We went straight north up the North Sea to Swino, turned half right, and finally went through the western fjords. This was marvellous – if you get a chance to go there, particularly in the summer, do – fabulous scenery for 300 miles in sheltered water. I was seasick a hell of a lot – about a third of the time, and not all at once, but on and on. It was as though I lost my immunity as soon as the ship calmed down, even for a couple of hours, and then I was sick again. Me shipmates laughed like drains. We went up to the Barents Sea, off the coast of Russia. We saw a red cruiser, which fired a few shots four or five miles away: I was pretty sure it was practice, but I had the crew mustered aft and we all sang God Save Mr. Kruschev [*sic*], just in case, rather loudly. Our skipper called the Norwegians lots of very rude names: potty little two-man boats would lay lines straight across where we were trawling, and they've extended the fishing limits, and then they sell the bloody fish to us as well.

[. . .] Thanks very much indeed for the invitation to Oslo, but I'm afraid I'm so desperately hard up and in debt that I doubt if I could come: I'd love to though, and if something is sold between now and Xmas I'll certainly let you know. As it is, I've had to go back to teaching this last week, which is hell, and so low.

Stopped in Northern Norway on the way back for water – 20 minutes in a place called Honnigsvåg, where there's a warning station like Fylingdales – big silver Balls perched on mountain tops. Rushed ashore and bought fresh fruit and a present for Virginia.

There was this cook, in the galley, and I found him one day crimping a jam tart or pie thing with his false teeth. So I said, haven't you got a proper tool? And he said, yes, but I use that for making holes in the doughnuts.

I'm sorry, but as things have turned out, far from being in a position to give you reviewing, I'm finding it very hard to find enough for myself. But if I ever do, I will, if you see what I mean: things have a habit of changing suddenly in the litworld.

Johnson spent twenty-three days aboard the *Northern Jewel*. He made notes, he sketched diagrams of the ship (one of three triple-deckers – the others being the *Northern Crown* and *Northern Sceptre* – built and delivered to Grimsby in 1954), he bonded with the skipper, Jack Douglas, and the mate, Tiny Harris, and – perhaps most of all – he lay on his bunk feeling seasick. ('When one asked him about the trip afterwards,' Julia Trevelyan Oman remembers, 'he just hardly wanted to talk about it. I think he'd been really sick, and he had thought that he was a big tough chap and I don't think he'd been through such physical agony in all his life. It was the most terrible

Right. The infant novelist.

Below, left. A youthful photograph in which Johnson, as an adult, thought that he could see 'the face of a human being all too aware now of the worst of the human situation'.

Below, right. Schooldays at Kingston Day Commercial School.

Left. Johnson was a keen tennis player but soon learnt (according to the poem 'Love-All') that 'love was merely another means / of saying nil'.

Below. 'I was lazy, cocky, distracted by (in particular) sex, soccer and motorbikes.'

Right. 'He was determined to learn to play the trumpet but of course it's a life's work.'

Below. With Joyce Yates and her son Stephen. (Her other son, Michael, took the picture.)

Above. In his late teens, perhaps at Brighton.

Left. In fancy dress (rather than authentic graduate's robes) at the Chelsea Arts Ball. Companion unidentified.

Right. The unveiling of a statue at the Glyn Club in Abersoch, 1959: an episode incorporated into *Travelling People.*

Below. With Tony Tillinghast.

Above. At a Dulwich
Group poetry reading. The
evenings were organised
by Howard Sergeant,
editor of *Outposts*
magazine.

Left. Aged thirty:
a publicity photograph
for *Albert Angelo*.

With Virginia, who is pregnant with their first child. In the background is the statue Johnson's mother was convinced would fall through the floor of his bedroom.

With Virginia and the newborn Steve, outside their flat in Myddelton Square, north London.

Left. On the beach with Steve at Estepona, southern Spain. The Johnsons were on holiday with Zulfikar and Helena Ghose.

Below. With his infant daughter Kate.

shock. He was grossly ill, poor thing. Somewhat naive.') As for how much time Johnson actually spent during the voyage looking back on his years as an evacuee or his several failed romances, and how much of that recollection would be done in the relative comfort of his flat in Islington when he finally came to write the novel in late 1965, we simply cannot know.

The breezy familiarity with the vagaries of the 'litworld' which he shows in his letter to Patrick Snaith suggests that he now considered himself entirely at home there. Back in London, he had a series of parallel projects to attend to. Ben Glazebrook had not inherited his predecessor's enthusiasm for the *Street Children* project, so Johnson and Julia Trevelyan Oman were now looking for a new publisher. Through George Greenfield he had been introduced to Clifford Makins, editor of the *Observer* sports pages, and taken on as a soccer reporter: his first contribution – a report of a cup tie between Kettering and Millwall in which he got the names of both goal scorers wrong – appeared on 16 September. The blurb for *Poems* had been written and the contract for *Albert Angelo* finally signed. Once again, however, the new novel was running into censorship problems: not over any explicit sex scenes, this time, but over the use of what the printer considered to be obscene language. Johnson, naturally, was not impressed.

63: DRAFT OF LETTER *(mid-November 1963)*

To —, printers of ALBERT ANGELO

To the Directors:

I understand that you have refused to print my novel ALBERT ANGELO because of the use, perhaps a dozen times, of certain four-letter words.

I write to make known to you my opinion that your refusal is an act of moral cowardice: the *Lady Chatterley's Lover* case gave serious writers a freedom to express the truth as they found it in life which you, sirs, seem determined to limit by imposing a form of censorship of your own.

My use of these words, in their various contexts, is justified by its truth to life: your refusal to print them allies you with the forces of hypocrisy and ignorance.

Furthermore, your action is a gross insult to me (and to Constable as well, I think: though that is not my concern) in that you imply by your decision that evidence as to the literary merit of ALBERT ANGELO could not successfully be brought. My literary reputation is such that many expert witnesses would maintain the seriousness of my work; so much so that the DPP must consider my work extremely unlikely to provide a case to clarify the position.

You may of course choose, sirs, what you will or will not print: you may also be very sure that whenever the printing history of ALBERT ANGELO is discussed your pusillanimity will not go unremarked.

Ben Glazebrook returned this letter to Johnson on 21 November, saying that although he thought 'you were right to get it off your chest', it was better that it remained unforwarded. The same day Johnson wrote to Patrick Snaith, telling him that a new printer had now been found: 'I wrote a nasty piece of invective to the first one, but did not send it,' he added. 'There are some letters one writes but does not send. It'll go in me memoirs.' As indeed it has.

That month Johnson also signed another contract with Constable, for the volume of short stories entitled *Statement Against Corpses*. His collaborator on this project was to be Zulfikar Ghose, who has given this wry description of its genesis: 'I had to report some sporting event at Wembley for the *Observer* and, having two press tickets, Bryan came along with me. In the tube to Wembley, we talked about the short-story form, lamented its wretched state in England at the time, and came to the thrilling conclusion that it was our destiny to revive the form. Some six months later, we had written our stories for the book – a book that I have regretted publishing, for my own stories in it are a miserable lot.'[4] And it's true, the book would not receive a very favourable reception: but that was in the future. For the moment the two authors were content to pocket their advance, which came to a princely fifty pounds each.

At this level of remuneration, Johnson was never likely to be made rich by his writing: a fact of which he was becoming daily more aware.

64: LETTER *(22 January 1964)*

To Patrick Snaith

[. . .] All I really want to do is get on with another novel. I began one at Xmas (as yet untitled). The poems have been held up: all printers are bastards.

I was amused at your surmise that you thought TP 'made' me: here beginneth a sermon on facts of Literary Life. Most first novelists are lucky to clear £150 on a novel – and on later ones, too. I made about £500, due mainly to £250 from paperback rights and £100 from Italian translation rights. Considering it took me 2½ years to write (or was written over that time) it's byourlady awful. But the really bad thing was that society, having praised the first one so much, was not interested in paying me enough to keep me alive to write another.* That is

---

* The advance on *Albert Angelo* had been £200.

diabolical, as I probably told you before. You're probably right to be writing plays: the rewards are certainly greater.

As it is, writers are exploited (as all primary producers – agricultural labourers, factory workers – are) because publishers know they will write without expectation of reward. Everybody else concerned in the production of books can earn a living from it – publishers, booksellers, papermakers, printers, every silly little typist in their pools – but not writers.

I've thought of an answer, too. A classic Marxist one: start a writers' co-operative. You'd pay every writer say 90% of everything made after production costs had been covered. All we want is half-a-dozen established writers who would be prepared to chuck in their next books to float the company.

American publication of *Travelling People* would certainly have helped his financial situation, but it continued to prove elusive. Instead, Johnson had to content himself with the pleasing (and surprising) news that a new, independent New York house, the Chilmark Press, had agreed to take on *Poems*. A fair amount of correspondence was fired off during the winter of 1963–4 attempting to persuade its director, Louis Cowan, to publish the novel as well; but this long, typographically complex book was more than the fledgling imprint could cope with at this stage, and he reluctantly declined. Meanwhile Johnson was busy correcting the galleys of the British edition of *Poems*. He had decided to conclude the book with a self-justifying 'Note on Metre', rationalizing the fact that many of the poems were written in syllabic metres. What we find here is an early, mild version of 'the polemical, belligerent tone [...] the posture of deliberately provoking offence and the suggestion that the writer is in exclusive possession of the truth' which Zulfikar Ghose remembers as being characteristic of Johnson's way of arguing. 'It is as legitimate to use syllables as the element from which to form metrical units as it is to use elements like stress or quantity,' he wrote. To put the statement into context, it should be remembered that a minor debate on this subject was taking place at the time, in the pages of the *London Magazine* and the *TLS*, involving figures such as Zulfikar Ghose, George Macbeth, Ian Hamilton and Johnson himself (who fired off a letter to Hamilton, for instance, telling him that by opposing the use of syllabics 'you have abandoned good sense' and 'not thought deeply enough about versification').

Nothing feels more dusty than a forty-year-old literary spat. And yet it is one of the paradoxes of the writer's world that arguments like this, once you find yourself drawn into them, can feel like matters of life and death and assume an importance which, in the parallel universe of the creative mind, is equal to anything that might be going on in your daily life. We would never guess, from the enthusiasm with which Johnson allowed himself to become 'locked in mortal combat with various trogs and nignogs over syllabic verse in the TIMES LITSUP'[5] that he was also on the verge – seemingly – of solving the great conundrum of his existence, and finding the essential, stabilizing, domestic and emotional harmony that had eluded him ever since the disaster with Muriel. 'Myself, I had the best Xmas for years,' he wrote, in the same letter. 'Mainly because of Virginia; the *sturm und drang* with whom is all over, leaving a nicely settled relationship.'

By now the relationship had, in fact, become rather more than 'nicely settled'. Towards the end of March 1964, Johnson invited Julia Trevelyan Oman over to the flat at Claremont Square. 'It was a real sort of uncivilized bachelor's room,' she remembers. 'Piles of clothes and things like that. The text of *Street Children* was finished by then and he was handing it over to me, and I think that in passing, he just literally announced to me, "Oh, I'm getting married on Saturday to a woman called Virginia Kimpton" – it was just like that. I hadn't heard *anything* about her before – it was *very* odd.'

Johnson married Virginia on 31 March 1964. There was a small civil ceremony at the register office in Islington, attended only by Virginia's mother and Johnson's parents, Stanley and Emily, after which this party of five travelled to South Kensington for lunch in a restaurant with Zulfikar Ghose and his wife-to-be, Helena. It was 'a fine lunch', according to Ghose, and 'the conversation was what the occasion demanded, which is to say the usual frivolous nonsense'.[6]

This was to be the start of Johnson's annus mirabilis. Quite apart from his marriage, 1964 would be a year in which four books were published bearing his name as author or collaborator: *Poems, Albert Angelo, Street Children* and *Statement Against Corpses*. Two years ago, he had still had nothing at all accepted for publication apart from a few poems in literary magazines. True, three of these books would have only a muted impact: but *Albert Angelo* would be a watershed in several different ways.

For one thing, the 'almighty aposiopesis' contained in the novel's 'Disintegration' section – 'Oh, fuck all this LYING' – was not an empty piece of authorial rhetoric. It really did announce Johnson's conversion to the view that the confessional mode was the only acceptable one in novel-writing as well as in poetry. Using the novel to 'tell a story', he had decided, was both immoral and artistically contemptible. Samuel Beckett knew this, even if no other living novelist did.

65: EXTRACTS FROM REVIEW OF *HOW IT IS* BY SAMUEL BECKETT FOR THE *SPECTATOR* (published 26 June 1964)

As in *The Unnamable* the first person narrator merges with the author (although not until a much later point in the new novel) and breaks the fiction of storytelling:

that wasn't how it was no not at all no how then no answer how
was it then no answer HOW WAS IT screams good

there was something yes but nothing of all that no all balls from
start to finish yes this voice quaqua yes all balls yes only one voice
here yes mine yes when the panting stops yes

[...] Beckett seems to me to be exploring a cul-de-sac, and while I
cannot help admiring both his integrity and his dedication in breaking
new ground therein, I deeply regret at the same time that he has
abandoned on the way those incidental qualities of language and
intellectual exuberance and wit which so magnificently characterise his
first two novels, *Murphy* and *Watt*. But let us be very sure of one thing:
Samuel Beckett is out there in front, this is certainly the way the novel
is going. No writer need cover this particular ground again, but it is his
example (towards truth and away from storytelling) which makes it
clear that almost all novelists today are anachronistically working in a
clapped-out and moribund tradition.

This sense of himself (and Beckett, of course) being out on a limb, being 'in
exclusive possession of the truth', of the vast majority of novelists unthink-
ingly pacing the same well-worn ground while Johnson boldly set out to
explore a new path (except that Beckett had already proved this path to be
a 'cul-de-sac' – could he not see the contradiction there?) – all of this would
give him, paradoxically, a deep insecurity. At heart, Johnson did not *trust*
the literary establishment to understand his work from now on: which he
would no doubt have rationalized as well-founded scepticism about that
establishment's competence and intelligence, but which might, at some
deeper level, have come from a fear of personal failure, an anxiety that *the
work wasn't strong enough to speak for itself.*
    This was certainly Anthony Smith's view: 'Whenever I read anything of
his, I got the feeling that there was a sense of having proved a case, a
proposition, which is not quite what we want in a novel: you don't *mind*
having that but you want other things as well. And I may be being a bit
simple-minded here, but it's partly as though his insecurity when writing
meant that he needed more theoretical underpinning or clothing to protect
himself than most people. Or perhaps, just as my contemporaries at
Cambridge who were reading English all found it rather difficult to write
anything themselves, because they were constantly being told about great
writers, it may have been that Bryan had a version of that: in his case it
would have been not English writers but Beckett above all – that because
he was so impressed by Beckett, he felt he had to prove something in his
writing, because there's always that sense in a Johnson book that he's trying

to prove something instead of simply enjoying the beast for whatever it is. There's always a sense of QED at the end of Bryan's books, which does limit him as a writer.'

Smith's view is supported, I feel, by the fact that three of Johnson's four books in 1964 were sent out into the world with accompanying notes for the reader: instructions, basically, on how they should be read. In *Poems* it was the argument for syllabics contained in the 'Note on Metre'. In *Statement Against Corpses* it was the jointly signed introduction claiming that the short story was in decline, that it 'deserves, but seldom receives, the same precise attention to language as that given normally only to a poem', and that Johnson and Ghose between them were about to attempt, 'through demonstration of the form's wide technical range, to draw attention to a literary form which is quite undeservedly neglected'. And for *Albert Angelo*, most provocatively of all, Johnson provided his publishers with several pages of notes to be sent out to all prospective reviewers in case they were too dim to grasp what he was aiming at.

66: NOTES ON *ALBERT ANGELO* (May 1964)

In technique, ALBERT ANGELO is a logical progression in the direction taken by my first novel, TRAVELLING PEOPLE: that is, subject-matter and function are allowed organically to determine form and style. But this is the only resemblance between the two novels: since their respective subject-matter differs so much (to use a crude distinction, TRAVELLING PEOPLE is a comedy whereas ALBERT ANGELO is a tragedy), then their respective forms are correspondingly dissimilar.

I take the end to which the means of all literary technique is dedicated to be the communication as nearly as possible of some truth believed in by the author: and on one level ALBERT ANGELO is a dramatisation of the problem of the near impossibility of conveying truth in a vehicle of fiction. The problem, and its solution or avoidance, are epitomised by the quotation from Beckett which forms the epigraph: why 'invent' characters when you know of yourself so much better.

It is no accident that my hero, Albert, is an architect, for I believe that my aims have much in common with those of many modern architects. The following quotations from Louis Sullivan and Mies van der Rohe, for instance, seem to me completely relevant, *mutatis mutandi*, to literature:

Form follows function

To create form out of the nature of our tasks with the methods of our time – this is our task.

We must make clear, step by step, what things are possible, necessary, and significant.

Only an architecture honestly arrived at by the explicit use of available building materials can be justified in moral terms.

... the road of discipline from materials, through function, to creative work.

And Mies' four principles (though I have reversed the order) seem to me equally those of the serious writer: truth, clarity, order, discipline.*

Various unconventional devices are used in ALBERT ANGELO for effects which I felt I could not satisfactorily achieve by any other means. Thus a specially-designed typecharacter draws attention to physical descriptions which I believe tend to be skipped, do not usually penetrate sufficiently; to convey what a particular lesson is like, the thoughts of a teacher are given on the right-hand side of a page in italic, with his and his pupils' speech on the left in roman, so that, though the reader obviously cannot read both at once, when he has read both he will have *seen* that they are simultaneous and *enacted for himself* that they are simultaneous; when Albert finds a fortuneteller's card in the street, it is further from the truth to describe it than simply to reproduce it; and when a future event must be revealed, I can think of no way nearer the truth than to cut a section through those pages intervening so that the event may be read in its place but before the reader reaches that place.

To quote from ALBERT ANGELO:

– A page is an area on which I may place any signs I consider to communicate most nearly what I have to convey: therefore I employ, within the pocket of my publisher and the patience of my printer, typographical techniques beyond the arbitrary and con-stricting limits of the conventional novel. To dismiss such tech-niques as gimmicks, or to refuse to take them seriously, is crassly to miss the point.

I am not saying that all novels should be written like ALBERT ANGELO, or that all those which use conventional techniques are bad: but rather that I find the conventional novel unsuitable for what I have to say and have therefore had to solve my problems unconventionally.

Predictably enough, when the novel was published on 23 July (the cutting of holes through two pages having caused many logistical headaches

---

* Johnson kept these quotations from Sullivan and van der Rohe pinned above his desk whenever he wrote.

and printers' delays), several reviewers' backs were put up by this little lecture. 'If an author has to explain himself, I think he has to that extent failed,' wrote the *Glasgow Herald*. The *Daily Mail* called the novel a 'pretentious kaleidoscope of a teacher's reactions to a tough London school' and found the innovations 'solemnly sterile and imitative'. *The Times* concluded that Johnson's 'departures from the orthodox are not so radical as they first appear' and wondered, 'Is there such a thing as a timid experiment?' Even a sympathetic reviewer, David Lodge in the *Spectator*, was disturbed by the paradoxes inherent in the author's climactic revelation of 'the true facts on which the preceding narrative has been based': shrewdly enough, he posed the question, 'are these facts "true" (i.e., autobiographical) or is the appeal to them merely a rhetorical device? Either way, it is a Pyrrhic victory in the writer's struggle for sincerity, since the inevitable effect is to diminish the imagined life of the novel.'

Given that Johnson had convinced himself, by this stage, of the entirely circular argument that 'To dismiss such techniques as gimmicks, or to refuse to take them seriously, is crassly to miss the point', it was not to be expected that he would be put out by these verdicts. Rather, they would simply have confirmed his thinking. He was far more excited by two reviews which appeared the weekend after publication. The first was in the *Irish Times*, where Val Mulkerns wrote:

> Mr. Johnson's talent is a very special one indeed, the talent of a poet exploding through the confines of a novel and making magic out of the wreckage. Without Joyce and Beckett, whose cadences drift like a summer breeze through these pages, it is of course unlikely that 'Albert Angelo' would have happened in just this way, but if a man is not a match for the best of his masters he can achieve nothing but a pretty obvious pastiche or fake. Mr. Johnson is more than a match for his starry company. [...] Using something very like the French methods, including all sorts of dazzling typographical devices, Mr. Johnson has achieved, to my mind, (and why baulk?) a masterpiece, serious, salacious, rumbustious, lyrical, full of the very stuff of life in our time.

Meanwhile, in the *Sunday Times*, Johnson's fellow poet and novelist Adrian Mitchell was just as enthusiastic:

> Anyone who read B. S. Johnson's first novel *Travelling People* will know that he is one of the best writers we've got. Some people called it promise, but that was a fulfilled and mature book.
>
> His new novel, *Albert Angelo*, is just as good and just as exciting, a beauty. Mr Johnson is a fine poet and he writes the prose of a fine poet. Every word is weighed for its rhythmic effect as well as for its sense, sound – and even, I suspect, its shape on the page. So every word tells

and the book flows quickly and delightfully. As Nathaniel West proved, the long poem is far from dead if you disguise it as a short novel.

'Value this man,' Mitchell concluded, resoundingly. 'His writing sings. He walks like a fiery elephant.'

'VALUE THIS MAN'

To Louis Cowan, Chilmark Press NY

Thank you very much for sending me the ad from *Partisan Review*: it was most kind of you.

Please note that I have moved: perhaps you could send the complimentaries of my POEMS to the new address? But if you have already sent them, they will be forwarded.

My new novel, ALBERT ANGELO, has just come out and I am most pleased with the reviews. The *Sunday Times* said that I 'was one of the best writers we've got', and the *Irish Times* called it a masterpiece and said I was in the same class as Joyce and Beckett.

Yours sincerely

For two weeks in August 1964, Johnson returned to the chateau at Blauvac, accompanied this time by Virginia, Zulfikar Ghose and his wife Helena. He and Ghose were planning to write a critical survey of contemporary poetry, and they took a portable tape recorder to France with them, with the idea of recording some of their discussions on this subject. The tape survives, although the sound quality is poor and much of the conversation is hard to decipher. But here at least we can catch a flavour of Johnson talking: the voice quiet, modulated (most quiet of all, in fact, when he is being aggressive or threatening), the distinctive flattened west London vowels very different from most of the other speakers on the tape, who mainly deploy the impossibly starchy (to modern ears) received pronunciation that was current among the educated classes at the time. Here we find him identifying his three favourite living poets (Graves, Causley and R. S. Thomas), and having a conversation in which he wrestles with his own 'vulgar curiosity' about Graves's love poetry and the autobiographical truth that might lie behind it.

At one point Ghose speculates that this poetry might not be strictly autobiographical at all. 'You are always stressing the importance of honesty,' he says, 'and I suppose one can be honest in the abstract, as it were.'

Johnson insists: 'The poems *are* honest – I'm just intrigued to know whether the experience they spring from, their source, is memory or contemporary experience.'

'Suppose it's neither,' Ghose replies. 'Suppose it's something abstract and something within him. Would it bother you?'

'No, it wouldn't bother me. It wouldn't at all. I'd regard this as being the distilled essence of all his experience. He would say himself that this is the White Goddess working through him. I don't think *that*. I think the White Goddess is a metaphor – for me, at least.'

The assertion that the White Goddess is merely a 'metaphor' suggests that, at this point in his life, Johnson must have been on a pretty even keel, temperamentally. But a further discussion, at which other guests (including Virginia) were present, finds him in a rather more confrontational frame of mind.

68: TRANSCRIPT OF TAPE-RECORDED DISCUSSION AT CHÂTEAU DE BLAUVAC, VAUCLUSE, PROVENCE *(18? August 1964)*

The speakers: BSJ, Virginia Johnson (VJ), Zulfikar Ghose (ZG), Ted Lambton (TL), other female voice (FV).*

> *The tape begins with Zulfikar Ghose reading a new poem called 'Blauvac'. It describes the grounds of the chateau and the surrounding countryside as a 'sophisticated wilderness', and this phrase provokes a spirited discussion.*

> ZG: You cannot judge a piece of work simply because its ingredients seem to contradict your own experience.

> BSJ: Again and again you come across this problem. If I know that you're telling the truth, am I therefore going to say [. . .]

> *Microphone is knocked off table while women distribute food and wine. Raucous female laughter*

> BSJ: We should really have these conversations alone. I mean [. . .]

> *Chaos*

---

* Ted Lambton had graduated in philosophy from Keele a couple of years after Zulfikar Ghose; Ghose believes that the other female voice belongs to Lambton's girlfriend Jenny.

BSJ: Before you defend this attitude I should like to know that your untouchable truth – your spiritual truth – in this poem is better than the literal truth. I want to know why you did it, why you departed – why did you depart from the literal truth? I want to know this.

ZG: Well I'm not sure that I did.

Agreement from the others

BSJ: Yes, you did. Blauvac isn't a wilderness.

ZG: When I look out of the window, Bryan—

BSJ: Ah, but then you should say Provence, not Blauvac.

TL: For goodness sake, Bryan, you're talking to a poet, you're not supposed to be demanding that he write—

BSJ: Look, mate, the *first* thing that poets do is tell the truth.

Uproar: everybody is talking at once, indecipherably

BSJ: [. . .] this is *not* a wilderness – to me this is one of the most productive and farmed areas in the world. What he's written is not *literally* true. When you think of a wilderness, what do you think of? A wilderness. Something completely untouched by man, surely.

FV: A field is a 'sophisticated wilderness'. And if you came here from a town you would call this a wilderness.

BSJ: No, I wouldn't at all.

VJ: Well, you're not the author of the poem.

BSJ: No, I know, but I'm being asked to judge whether this is true or not.

TL: Surely, Bryan, it depends whether you're reading poetry or not. In poetry a large amount of the object is not to use a concept in its normal way but to develop it, into a different point of view . . .

BSJ: No, I dispute this absolutely. The best poets have spoken the truth about the things they have faced.

TL: What sort of truths have they spoken?

BSJ: Something that seems true to *them*, whether it seemed true to anyone else or not: there's no such thing as—

Everyone (drowning him out): Well there you are, you see! (*etc.*)

BSJ: We can talk about things – if the word 'chair' means the same to Zulf as it means to me, then the word 'wilderness' – we can talk about this and say, Does this mean the same to you as it means to me? This is what we're disputing and *it does not*. We're trying to get to a position where we can say, What does it mean? Right?

Long pause

VJ (gently, sadly): No. No.

BSJ: Well, you know, this is putting it on a very low level. That's how it started.

TL: What does what mean?

BSJ: 'Wilderness'. What does wilderness mean to you?

TL: It means what we choose to make it mean, in poetry.

BSJ: But you're not telling me what it means to you, you're telling me what it means to Zulf.

TL: He could have used it to describe somebody's mind and you wouldn't have said he was using the wrong word – you would say he was using an analogy, wouldn't you?

BSJ: I would say he was saying to everyone, 'You know what a wilderness is, it's an area untouched by man, completely wild. This man's mind is completely wild' – a very good image. Fine. But when he says it of land that's been cultivated for three thousand years – you know, this isn't literally true, first of all.

TL: If he's using language literally here then he's wrong, but if he's using an image it's a very fine one.

BSJ: If he fails to take account of the literal meaning of the word then it's a failure of language.

VJ: What of the fact that he qualifies it with an adjective?

TL: But, Bryan, the thesis you seem to be trying to defend is that one should use language inflexibly, and this just wouldn't do for poetry. Surely it's because language is flexible and you want to extend it from its normal use and give it new meaning–

BSJ: It seems to me a poet must at least know what he means absolutely and use that inflexibly, there must be one meaning to him, he must know what he's doing. If he doesn't communicate that meaning then he's failed, unless he writes poems solely for himself.

TL: I think what he tries to do is—

BSJ: No, this is getting terribly general.

TL: All right, let it be terribly general, there's no reason why—

BSJ: Well, what do you understand by 'sophisticated wilderness', then? Hm?

TL: 'Sophisticated wilderness'? I really don't know what it is.

BSJ: It's using the landscape as an image of his own mental state, surely – isn't that it? Or trying to seek through the landscape some parallel to your own experience and what you want to say.

TL: All I want to say is that one of the principle objectives of the poet is to try to express thoughts for which there has not yet been any adequate language developed.

BSJ: No, I wouldn't agree with that at all.

TL: You wouldn't. Well I think that's what poetry *is* to a large extent.

BSJ: Poetry is the expression of the poet's feelings however many times they've been felt before, however many times they've been said before.

TL: But the whole point really is that language is most inadeqate when it has to deal with mental states. Consequently—

BSJ: Surely as a philosopher you would argue that all states are mental states.

TL: No, I wouldn't. I'm not a phenomenalist. I wouldn't argue that all states are mental states. Well, I don't know what I would understand by that statement.

BSJ is silenced, temporarily

TL: But that is a phenomenalist view, actually. It's a view which is not very widely held. There aren't many British philosophers nowadays that hold it.

BSJ: The point isn't whether there are or not. What state is a poet describing if not a mental state?

TL: I agree that he's trying to describe a mental state and it's my view that language is most inadequate in trying to describe mental states, and—

BSJ: Of course it is, it's second hand. Language is the straitjacket in which thoughts have to be communicated.

TL: Yes, and there are various concepts in language which can be regarded as fairly fundamental. They tend to be material object concepts – solid-type concepts like table and chair. This is possibly philosophically old hat, but it is this sort of language that we have to develop and to extend to deal with mental states. And language is therefore at its most cumbersome, its–

BSJ (quietly, accusingly): Would you therefore say that poetry should be used to deal with mental states? Used as therapy, in effect?

TL: No, I'm not suggesting it's used as therapy, I think it's trying to do what language is always trying to do, which is to communicate. This is the object.

BSJ: Yes, of course. But to communicate what – lies or truth? It can be used for either. This is the trouble. This is dodging the question.

TL: To communicate lies or truth . . .?

BSJ: I could say to you, 'This table is black,' and I've communicated with you, but I'm telling a lie.

TL: You're not necessarily telling me a lie. The statement could be interpreted in several ways. It could be interpreted to mean your vision was defective.

BSJ: Well, nevertheless, whatever it was, it would be a *lie*, because–

FV: No, it wouldn't, because if you *felt* that that table was black–

TL: It might be a mistake. And I think people do make mistakes about their feelings, especially when they talk about them.

BSJ: But let's accept that I *am* telling a lie.

TL: No, you're–

BSJ: No, you're moving away from it.

FV: Well, that's because he can't tell whether it *is* a lie.

BSJ (quietly, contemptuously): Of course he can, he can look at it himself and check for himself.

TL (genuinely indignant): Now I think you're being facetious. I think in this context, no.

BSJ: Well, so what? I'm telling a lie, it's still a lie, whether it's a facetious lie or not.

TL: It's not a *lie*. It's not a lie.

FV: In your state of mind this table's—

BSJ: Wouldn't you accept that—

Disorder, many voices joining in. ZG intervenes

ZG: What he's saying is that language is used as propaganda sometimes.

BSJ: Of course it is. Communication is not the test of whether it's true or false.

TL: Uh?

BSJ: 'Communication' is not the test of whether it's true or false.

TL (seriously fed up now): Whether *what's* true or false? For goodness—

BSJ: A statement. The poem. Merely because it's in communicative language—

TL: From what you say it sounds as though you want to classify any statement as being either true or false. Well, I don't see—

BSJ: There are some in between, of course there are.

TL: But you don't seem prepared to recognize them.

BSJ: Of course I do. Of course I do. Some poems are more true than others. Some truths—

ZG: Why are they more true than others?

BSJ: Because they contain parts of the truth. Falsified in some particular, you know. Some queer poets have transposed their emotions into heterosexual . . . situations.

TL: You really need to produce examples of this, don't you?

BSJ: Well, I can. Walter Savage Landor wrote lots of love poems and all the time it was a chap called Arthur . . . There's a funny story about that, because—

Slightly despairing noises all round

BSJ: Because in one poem he said, 'Nature loved I first, and next to nature, Art.' *(Silence)* That's what he called Arthur, you see.

Silence

TL *(solemnly):* Yes.

BSJ: You've heard it?

TL: No, I hadn't heard it, actually.

Long pause

BSJ: Some people think it's a funny story.

Laughter

TL: That was Walter Savage Landor?

BSJ: Yes.

TL: Was he a very great poet?

BSJ: No, he's *not* a very great poet, and this is one of the reasons why he's not. The job of the poet is to take his own emotional problems and put them into verse. But he *hadn't* got the courage to do it and say, 'I am a queer and I love a boy,' you know?

TL: When did he live?

BSJ: Late Victorian.

TL: Well, then . . .

BSJ: Oh yes, there are *excuses*, there are reasons.

TL: But that wasn't *why* he wasn't a very great poet.

BSJ: Wasn't it? What was the other reason?

TL: I don't—

BSJ: Well, then, how can you make a statement that that wasn't the reason? Hm?

TL: How can you make a statement that it was the reason?

BSJ: Because I happen to have read him. *(voice rising)* And know something about his life.

TL: And you're maintaining that the reason he wasn't a great poet was because he was a queer and didn't have the courage to admit it?

BSJ: That's one of the reasons. Because he couldn't face the truth and write about it.

TL (repeats to himself, wonderingly): Because he couldn't face the truth . . .

BSJ: He couldn't write about the truth.

TL: Socially he was not permitted to face the truth.

BSJ: Yes, he could have written them in a book and put it away in a drawer to be found after his death, because maybe after his death—

TL: Maybe he did but they haven't found it.

VJ gasps in horror

BSJ: What's wrong?

VJ (pointing to tape recorder): That bloody thing is on.

BSJ: Didn't you know that?

VJ: No, I didn't! My God, what did Bryan tape, for Christ's sake?

BSJ: Well, this is the great advantage of tape recordings, they can be rubbed off.

While staying at Blauvac, Johnson received a letter from Ben Glazebrook informing him that *Albert Angelo* had now sold 'just under the 1,400 mark'. (Although there was some confusion over this, because many booksellers had sent the novel back, thinking that they had been supplied with damaged copies.) It was not especially promising news, given that *Travelling People* had sold rather more during a comparable period. He also heard from Anthony Smith – who had not been able to join them in France this year – writing to express enthusiasm for the book, tempered by certain serious reservations: he questioned the need for such a fragmentary form and for the holes cut through the pages; he thought that the book's theme had been made too explicit; that it was too derivative of Beckett; that the 'Disintegration' section was superfluous and that here, as in *Travelling People*, the female characters tended to be idealized. Johnson replied, as always, with a robust defence:

69: LETTER *(20 August 1964)*

To Anthony Smith

[. . .] About *AA*: first of all, thanks for taking so much trouble over it – to write and tell me, especially, I'm very pleased you did; secondly, I'm so much exposed to talking and thinking about it when I don't want to (after all, I finished my bit of it over a year ago – I've passed on since then – it's merely a printers' delay which makes me have to go back to what I was thinking then) that I can hardly talk about it at all: but for you will certainly try. And, again, the more I think the more I become convinced of the utter *uselessness* of lit crit, and begin to think like: 'AA just *is*, and it's that way because it is that way, and it's no other way because I rejected all the alternatives as being worse, and no one, but no one, can think themselves into the position of the writer and consider those alternatives'. However.

Neither Tom nor Hemingway nor myself invented the fragmentary method, of course: if I got it from anywhere it was from the SATYRICON, which I think extremely funny, and which is of course in fragments because that's how the ms. has come down to us. Not to deny chapters absolutely: I can see some subjects which would require exactly their formal shape and counterpointing. But as a convention, no, I agree, in most cases in our time they're out. Yes, I feel that there's too much self-indulgence in TP, too much is expendable, as you say: and when I think that I cut 15,000 words from it at the request of Constable! [. . .]

As for my women, I must protest you are wrong: Kim has protruding teeth and slack breasts and I reject absolutely that she is idealized or abstract. Jenny too has an ugly hooked nose:* but in any case most of the time Albert is remembering her (and, it is stated in the disintegration section, remembering only the good things, the things he wants to) and deluding himself about her by idealizing [. . .]

For anyone to ask if the Breakoff works seems to me impertinent: what I was saying at the beginning, no one can know how worse the alternatives were. I *know* the book could not have been written any other way, I *know* that my failure to assimilate the experience, to fictionalise the experience, must have resulted in this breakdown, off, up. That is arrogant: but, I insist, no one else is in a position to *know*. It is a Brechtian device, if you like: it poses this question, which I keep asking, but no one answers, least of all reviewers and critics, if you accept that serious literature is about some telling of truth believed in by the author, how does he convey that truth in a vehicle of fiction? The two terms are diametrically opposed.

Why is there no need to make the theme of the book explicit?

Who has done split-column before, which you say is not completely original?

I have asked around, and there are people (the majority of those I have asked) who say they did not cheat over the holes. What evidence have you for saying that everyone without exception will? [. . .] Suggest

---

* Just like Graves's White Goddess.

a better way of making the point about Marlowe being killed in the east end, and Albert (this is a hint he is a poet) also coming near a violent end in the same east. In other words, work from the author's point of view: and this again is where all criticism is useless: it always works from the outside.

'I *know* the book could not have been written any other way, I *know* that my failure to assimilate the experience, to fictionalise the experience, must have resulted in this breakdown, off, up. That is arrogant: but, I insist, no one else is in a position to *know*'; 'this again is where all criticism is useless: it always works from the outside.' By taking up these positions Johnson had built an entirely impermeable wall, through which no criticism could ever reach him: the only person, he seemed to be maintaining, whose opinion about a book could carry any authority was the person who had written it. (Which does not explain why he continued to review other people's books for a living.) It was because of positions like this that Anthony Smith always found arguing with Johnson to be a fruitless experience: 'I could never understand it really, but in so far as I tried then and still to this day occasionally try to understand what was going on in Bryan's head, it must have been a kind of insecurity because at root Bryan was a very insecure man. That's why he needed theories and rules, and why he was so dogmatic and not a good arguer because he wouldn't leave from any position he took up.'

The development of this side of Johnson's personality was also, in Smith's view, a continuing process and one which went hand in hand with his increasing literary profile. 'When I left London, I remained in touch with Zulf and still do: Bryan I saw less often. When I did see him or hear from him, it was apparent to me that conceit had consumed him, a self-protective arrogance asserting his own gift as a writer in excess of his achievement.'

Shortly after returning from Blauvac, annoyed that *Albert Angelo* was yet to find a British paperback publisher, Johnson sent this letter (without, it appears, consulting his agent George Greenfield) to Allen Lane, the founder and then joint managing director of Penguin Books:

70: LETTER *(27 August 1964)*

Dear Allen Lane:

In reviewing my novel ALBERT ANGELO, the *Sunday Times* described me as 'one of the best writers we've got', and the *Irish Times* called the book 'a masterpiece' and put me in the same class as Joyce and Beckett.

You have refused to buy the paperback rights of ALBERT ANGELO. Why?

    Yours sincerely,
      B. S. Johnson.

A courteous enough reply was sent off on 10 September – signed by Allen Lane but actually written by a junior editor called Peter Buckman. 'I have talked with my editorial colleagues,' it said, 'and their feeling is that while this was a novel of some promise they feel that your next book might be such that it would be an advantage to bring it out first to be followed by ALBERT ANGELO and they have already spoken to Constable on these lines.' Johnson replied a fortnight later.

71: LETTER *(25 September 1964)*

Dear Allen Lane:

    Thank you for your reply of 10th September to my rude letter.

    Who the hell are you and your editorial colleagues to determine the order in which my work reaches the paperback public? And what makes you so sure you're even going to be offered my next book?

    The word had gone round that Penguin were not in touch any longer, and if your editorial colleagues think that ALBERT ANGELO is merely a 'novel of some promise', then it's certainly true. 'Anyone who read B. S. Johnson's first novel TRAVELLING PEOPLE will know that he is one of the best writers we've got' (the *Sunday Times* said, and I quote again to you, but this time more fully) 'Some people called it promise, but that was a fulfilled and mature book. His new novel, ALBERT ANGELO, is just as good and just as exciting, a beauty.'

    May I suggest that you find yourself some new editorial colleagues, some who know what direction fiction in 1964 is taking?

    Today Corgi published TRAVELLING PEOPLE.

    Yours sincerely,
      B. S. Johnson.*

It seems to be from around now that a pattern starts to develop: a refusal to turn the other cheek, a belligerent and contemptuous overreaction to any kind of rejection or slight. Was it because these two ecstatic reviews had been enough to convince Johnson that he was already one of the very

---

* Shortly afterwards Johnson met Peter Buckman at one of Joe McCrindle's famously lavish and decadent parties, and magnanimously forgave him for having written the offending letter. Buckman and his wife Rosemarie became close family friends, and their home would even provide a refuge for Virginia during the last, traumatic days of their marriage, when Johnson had become violent towards her.

greatest of contemporary writers and that anyone who failed to agree must be blind or ignorant? Or did it have something to do with the fact that he was newly married, and that freedom from emotional insecurity meant that he had nothing to distract him from the progress of his literary career? (Remember, too, that he would not allow Virginia to work: he was now attempting to support two people – and soon there would be a baby – so the pressure to make a financial success of his writing was getting stronger all the time.)

Virginia had been given her first glimpse of her husband's temper a few months earlier, when the married couple had moved from Claremont Square to a larger flat in neighbouring Myddelton Square. (What Johnson called 'a pawnlike move from one square to another'.[1]) She suggested that the smaller but sunnier back room should be used as Johnson's study, with the big front room as their shared bedroom. This led to an extraordinary eruption on his part, a tirade about the centrality of writing to his life and its overriding importance in any domestic arrangement, which left Virginia feeling 'utterly amazed. I'd never seen anything like it before.' Sure enough, the front room became the study; although soon Johnson would find himself sharing it with his son's cot.

When Claire Andrews re-read *Albert Angelo* prior to my meeting her, it vividly reawakened her memories of Johnson when she knew him in Claremont Square, and one of the first things she said to me was, 'My goodness, that temper's in it. Suddenly you realize that this author is very depressed, and has a vile temper: that was what came over from the book. Which in a way I was too blind to recognize at the time, because he put on a very polite, very gentle front. Or more often just a surly one, in my case.'

Julia Trevelyan Oman had been warned about Johnson's temper so she always trod warily around him: 'I knew that he was liable to go purple in the face and burst into a sweat and start screaming and all the rest of it. I did see that happen, but not to me: it was either with Hodders [the ultimate publishers of *Street Children*] or at one of Joe McCrindle's parties, with someone who provoked him. It was weird; he sort of got bigger and bigger – it was rather terrifying. He would argue with people the whole time: it was almost as if he was out to pick a quarrel. Very strange. George Greenfield had the patience of a saint, he really did. What he took from Bryan must have been quite unbelievable, because Bryan wasn't really making money; but I suppose George Greenfield's money came from Enid Blyton: her rights brought a perpetual income to the agency. Bryan was sheer charity: as I was, too. He was an enormously fatherlike, avuncular figure to us both.' In October 1964, she remembers, the *Sun* newspaper bought the rights to one photograph from *Street Children* and asked for a new caption to go with it: they requested that it should consist of factual description, adding – rather facetiously – 'Plus of course, Mr Johnson's own lyricism'. 'But then, he was so rude to the newspaper,' Oman recalls, 'that they used the photograph but they didn't use his text. That was a typical example. George had set that whole thing up, and repeatedly you would get these agents and other people setting things up and then they just didn't work, simply because Bryan would start telling these people their business and being abusive.'

In that suggestive phrase 'telling these people their business' we perhaps have a clue to the exasperation which lay behind Johnson's outbursts. He believed himself to be surrounded by incompetents: incompetent reviewers, incompetent publishers, incompetent publicists, incompetent newspaper editors. From one point of view this was arrogance: from another, it was a reflection of his own enormous energy and curiosity about the ways in which all aspects of the publishing and newspaper businesses worked. He was a tremendously *dynamic* man, and if a cause was worth working for, he would work for it, unstintingly. Often, that cause was merely the furtherance of his own literary reputation. But there were other causes, too: and his devotion to them, at times, could be heroically unselfish.

One of these causes – in 1964, at least, before his disillusionment with Harold Wilson's government set in* – was the Labour Party. Johnson was a passionate socialist ('socialism not given a chance' is the offence that creates the biggest debit in Christie Malry's account book), and it always gnawed at his conscience that novel-writing was not an especially useful means of political intervention (in the same book, Christie Malry tells the narrator, 'You shouldn't be bloody writing novels about it, you should be out there bloody doing something about it'). And so he was very impressed when he heard that his friend and fellow poet Alan Brownjohn was standing as the Labour candidate for Richmond and Barnes in the general election of October 1964.

'I think what attracted him,' Brownjohn recalls, 'was the thought that a writer, a poet, was going out on a limb, getting involved in politics and actually getting himself selected to stand for parliament. Also it happened to be in the constituency where his parents lived, and so he said, "Well, can I come down and help you do some canvassing?" and I said I'd be delighted.'

A secondary motive for offering support, perhaps, was the opportunity it provided Johnson to have lunch with his beloved mother every day for two weeks. Alan Brownjohn, a softly spoken, still prolific and regularly published survivor of the sixties poetry scene, has always looked back on that fortnight with wonder. 'He was *so* exceptionally generous,' he says. 'Every day he would drive the car hired by the Richmond and Barnes Labour party, which was quite a large Vauxhall Victor, about 1800 cc, with red

---

* See Fragment 138 below, p. 313.

streamers on it. He would come down at about ten o'clock and say, "Right, where do we go today?" and generally in the daytime we went to the more affluent areas. I seem to remember him coming every day, and driving me around for two hours before lunch, then having lunch with his mother, then another two hours with me. We went around the wealthier areas just to try and find where there were pockets of Labour voting, and we often found that the daily help would answer the door, and so if *they* came from nearby in the constituency we felt we were doing a useful job. On a couple of occasions Bryan stayed on in the evenings and knocked on doors in the working-class areas, and he would say to this same woman, "Oh, hello – we met this morning in East Sheen, or something. Can we rely on your husband's vote as well?"'

It was not as if Johnson could drop his literary work completely while doing this. Brownjohn recalls that every morning, on arriving at the local Labour Party office, the first thing he would do would be to ask to use the telephone, and make a number of calls to publishers, editors and agents. It was as if he was afraid that his literary career might wither and die if he relaxed his own vigilance even for a moment. George Greenfield's representatives abroad, for instance, had to be prodded into action:

72: LETTER *(16 October 1964)*

To Erich Linder

> Can you tell me when Mondadori are publishing my novel TRAVELLING PEOPLE, please? I'd be grateful if you would let me know.
>
> Please note that I have changed my address to the above.
>
> Have Mondadori made a decision on their 90-day option on my second novel ALBERT ANGELO yet? As you probably know, this book got tremendous reviews here. The *Sunday Times* called me 'one of the best writers we've got', and the *Irish Times* called the book a masterpiece and put me in the same class as James Joyce and Samuel Beckett.
>
> I assume you will also be dealing with two other books of mine, STATEMENT AGAINST CORPSES (short stories with Zulfikar Ghose) and STREET CHILDREN (with photos by Julia Trevelyan Oman).
>
> I trust you are well, and I hope that we will be able to meet in the not-too-distant future.

Johnson had not done any supply teaching since July, and no doubt this was a relief. All the same, even though it had been physically and mentally draining work, the teaching had at least fed his writing in certain ways: helping to solve the conundrum that Doug Davies has identified – how the writer finds 'time to live the life to get the experience to write about it'. The following poem, for instance (according to a discussion between Johnson and Zulfikar Ghose on the Blauvac tape), arose out of a day spent in the classroom teaching children how to draw a basic landscape, followed by a train journey to report a football match during which Johnson, looking out of the train window, realized how crude his instructions had been when he considered the ever-shifting complexity of the real world around him.

73: POEM *(late 1964)*

Basic Landscape

Teaching elements, I quickly washed earth
and sky on to the pinned sugarpaper
(soft as talc) and ran an unlikely range
of smooth black mountains right across my rough
horizon: I placed a full moon low left
and told them they might, reaching this stage, add
such objects as they chose: trees, woods, houses,
animals, cars, roads: or even people.

Silently today I stare through rainpocked
glass as sulphur drifts through brown broadcloth woods
silverthreaded with gaunt leaning birches,
as damp outlines the random crack-patterns
of a grey limestone syncline, stare at the
complexity of this northern landscape;
then turn for relief to station roofs and
names: Ambergate, Whatstandwell, Matlock Bath.

All teaching must be simplification,
and to simplify is to falsify:
how teach the landscape of the complex heart
to those who have no wish to learn: and why?

Some of the most characteristic features of Johnson's mindset are to be found in this poem: notably the tendency to agonize over whether he is being faithful to reality and, in the last two words, the movement beyond even this degree of nervous self-interrogation to a more generalized existential despair about the futility of all human activity. Clearly, for someone who was so intensely concerned only to see 'the reality in everything', and who usually found this reality to be 'tragic and depressing', the public platform which the classroom provided was always going to inspire a crisis of conscience over what he should be telling his pupils. And this, too, was the state of affairs that would inspire one of his most important works outside the novel form: a work which would rapidly begin to take shape at this very time.

It began with an unexpected letter from Jeremy Brooks, literary manager of the Royal Shakespeare Company (and himself a successful novelist). Brooks wrote on 24 September 1964 to say that 'Peter Hall and I are both admirers of your novels', and invited Johnson to submit a play of between ten and thirty minutes for an evening of experimental drama at the Aldwych Theatre to be called 'Expeditions III'. ('Expeditions II', mounted in June, had contained a piece by Beckett.)

74: LETTER *(20 October 1964)*

To Jeremy Brooks

> Your letter was one of the most marvellous things ever to happen to me: thanks.
>
> For years I've wanted to write a play, but the prospect has always seemed to me terrifying: just length alone, besides the difficulty. Now, your letter provided just the stimulus I needed: I *can* write a play between ten and thirty minutes long! Even though it'll probably be nearer ten than thirty.
>
> The problem of verse in the theatre has worried me for a long time: the failure of Eliot, Fry and Duncan to convince that there is an *organic* reason for using verse. I don't know if you know my poetry, but I write a lot in syllabics, which I think is more suited to 1964 than clapped-out stress metres. Anyway, I've thought up a new (?) idea for using verse in this play I'm writing: whether it works or not is impossible to tell until it's been staged – that's part of its experimental nature. I think it will take intelligent acting to put it across.
>
> The form is loose – better explain that: three (perhaps four) scenes merging into one another; the single set you mention suits it; only chairs, tables, a screen (small), odds and ends of props; two/three main characters, six/ten others (could be done by offstage voices). The material is the human condition, not at all generalised, but in a specific group of situations concerning one character. I hope it will seem funny to people, as well.
>
> Now the election's over, it's my first job [. . .]
>
> The title is provisionally YOU'RE HUMAN LIKE THE REST OF THEM.

Johnson's short verse play, written in lines of ten syllables, concerns a schoolteacher called Haakon who is suddenly confronted, after a visit to hospital to get his back treated, with his own terrifying mortality. He returns to his school and finds that the staff are blithely indifferent to his revelation: 'We rot and there's nothing that can stop it / Can't you feel the shaking horror of that? / You just can't ignore these things, you just can't!' In the classroom, he presents his young pupils with what might – at the very least – be charitably described as an unorthodox lesson, and finds them similarly indifferent:

75: EXTRACT FROM THE PLAY *YOU'RE HUMAN LIKE THE REST OF THEM*
(written 19–29 October 1964)

HAAKON:
> Shut up you little bastards, just shut up!/
> I'm trying to teach you something real, real!/
> Something that I've learnt for myself this time/
> Something that has to do with all of you/
> You're all going to die but before then/
> You're going to decay, rot, for years, rot/
> Slowly your bodies are going to rot/
> Slowly, mind, just slowly, for years, slowly/
> And painfully, your bodies just give up/
> They just stop working, function by function/
> I saw old men this morning with their skin/
> Cross-wrinkled like the neck of a tortoise/
> Skin lined and loose like a flaccid penis/
> Then, after pain, comes death, you are cut off/
> Like a city street-end by the railway/
> > [*Long pause*]

HAAKON:
> Only one cheer for good old God.

CAPON: Hooray!

CHILD ONE: He's off his quiff

CHILD TWO: Mad, mad

CAPON: Straight round the twist/

HAAKON:
> Already you cover up like adults/
> Know you can live only by illusion/
> You must choose to believe that I am mad.

Johnson delivered the play to Jeremy Brooks on 29 October 1964. When it was published by Penguin Books in 1970 (in *New English Dramatists 14*), Edwin Morgan described it in his introduction as 'autobiographically emerging from the shock of a close friend's early death from cancer' – but this cannot be literally true (to use a regular Johnsonism) because Tony Tillinghast did not die for another two weeks after the play was finished. But this is beside the point, probably. Certainly Tony's condition had deteriorated terribly, by this stage, and Johnson's recent visits to see him (he had tape-recorded a conversation with him in Brighton on 27 September) are without doubt the major influences on this bitterly dark and comfortless play.*

76: EXTRACT FROM *THE UNFORTUNATES*

Just in the few weeks since we had last seen him he was grossly altered, distressingly, his face had shrunken, lost much of its flabbiness, rotund-ness, life, the skin was now tighter so that it was shocking, yes, to recognize him, now, from what he had been, then. This diminution made features stand out more, which were not that noticeable before, his eyes stood out, stared, fixed you, I slip into the second person, in defence, stared for longer moments than you wanted, than I did want, yes. And his teeth, I never remember seeing Tony's teeth before, they were there, of course, in that fleshy mouth, but now the mouth was not fleshy, the flesh was gone, not gone, but tautened, disfigured, and the teeth were there, their roots showing, the ones at the sides, molars, incisors, gaps visible between them which were unexpected, not that any were missing, as I remember, but there were gaps between, perhaps the gums were shrinking, too, withdrawing, perhaps it was affecting the gums, that the teeth should appear so unnaturally, I do not know, but it was affecting him everywhere, I seemed to think, now, from the way he looked, his skin was too yellow, where it had been white before, a pallid, unhealthy colour, then, when he was healthy, now it was as in jaundice, I imagine, the kidneys affected, is it, I don't know, or the liver, how little I know about medicine, the body, anything, ah.

It is extraordinary to contrast the mood of high spirits in which Johnson began writing the play (if he ever penned a more joyous sentence than, 'Your letter was one of the most marvellous things ever to happen to me', then I have yet to read it) with the overwhelming pessimism of what he actually put into it. It's as if he was so unaccustomed himself to 'cover up'

---

* Johnson's hope that audiences would find it funny probably hinged upon the inclusion of an old music-hall joke about a girl called Helen Hunt, and an ingenious pun involving the radio soap opera *The Archers*. In the second scene, Haakon switches off the radio just as this programme is being announced 'as an everyday story of count–', and remarks, 'Yes, quite.' *You're Human Like the Rest of Them* was later filmed and shown on BBC television, and it was always one of Johnson's proudest boasts that he was the first person ever to smuggle the word 'cunt' onto British TV.

and 'live only by illusion' that he could not remember or imagine what it must be like to do so: i.e. what it must be like to live life as most of us do, in the full knowledge that our bodies are decaying but without finding that knowledge unbearable. Consequently, he was baffled when people didn't like the play, or were not prepared to recognize its essential truth. Gordon Bowker recalls encountering Johnson in the foyer of the National Film Theatre in 1967, immediately after the film version of *You're Human Like The Rest of Them* had had its premiere. He found it 'a very black (even pathologically morbid) comedy about a teacher experiencing intimations of mortality while being treated for a slipped disc in a London hospital [...] The grim truth, which the teacher then conveys to his bewildered class, is that from the very moment of birth we begin to decay and die. All we can hope to do is die awkwardly, like a locust being consumed by a lizard. There was, it seemed, no thought of going gently into that good night for Johnson. After the film's premier I met him in the cinema foyer, surrounded by admirers. "Is that how you really feel?" I asked him sceptically, expecting to be laughed at for too closely identifying an author with his work. But he answered coldly and emphatically, "Yes, that's exactly how I feel." And it was a strangely grim and melancholic Johnson who then drifted off with his friends into the night.'[2]

'Pathologically morbid' is probably a fair description of *You're Human Like the Rest of Them* – at least from the 'normal' perspective that Johnson did, admittedly, spend much of his writing life questioning. It conveys a strong sense of the 'QED' that Anthony Smith has identified as being typical of Johnson's work, but the audience might well feel, when they reach the end of the play, that the proposition that has been demonstrated is an obvious one, one which they understood perfectly well beforehand. This seems to have been Jeremy Brooks's point when he rejected the play, nineteen days after receiving it: he admitted that he 'felt dissatisfied with the play, without being able to pin down very accurately exactly where the cause of the dissatisfaction lay. It is at least in part the sensation that great strength is being put out to lift an enormous dumb-bell, which turns out to be made of balsa wood.'

Johnson would not give up on this play, one of his most cherished achievements, as easily as all that. But for the time being, its moment had passed. Its abrupt rejection, so soon after it had been commissioned, was one of many disappointments, small and great, to be visited upon him in the closing weeks of 1964.

Of these, undoubtedly the greatest was the death of Tony Tillinghast, who had finally lost his short, brutal battle with cancer on 14 November 1964. The Johnsons had been planning to visit him in Brighton again the next day. For three days before dying he had been vigorous and lucid, 'for which she had been grateful, June, it had seemed like a miracle [...] and they had talked very seriously about everything, for the first time had talked about death.'³ He was just twenty-nine years old. Gordon Bowker – who knew them both, indeed met Johnson through Tony Tillinghast – has written that, 'Over those last months [...] he'd had to watch his friend slowly wither as the cancer advanced, the jovial Falstaff shrinking by degrees to a barely recognizable skeleton. To say he was deeply moved by this experience would be an understatement. He was utterly possessed and completely devastated by memories of Tony's agonizing death.'⁴

In addition to this, two trivial, irritating setbacks: *Statement Against Corpses* and *Street Children* were published within a few weeks of one another, and neither of them seemed to get much attention. *Street Children* received notices rather than reviews, and small ones at that. What's more, the warmest praise was reserved for Julia Trevelyan Oman's photographs, which were universally acclaimed: as for Johnson's text, the *Times Literary Supplement* found it 'ingeniously done' but 'sometimes pretentious', the *Daily Telegraph* found it 'sometimes apt, often rather pretentious', the *Manchester Evening News* said it was 'too out of tune with the pictures and the lay-out too pretentious by far', while the *Daily Worker* opined that Johnson's contribution 'introduces an alien and rather sordid element that could well have been left out'.

Statement Against Corpses fared rather better: in fact, it got off pretty lightly, considering that it contained some of Johnson's weakest ever pieces ('Perhaps it's these Hormones', 'Only the Stones') and that it had a general air of reheated juvenilia and rejectamenta. In one or two places, Johnson's contributions attracted such plaudits as 'brilliant' (*Daily Telegraph*) and 'a pleasure to read' (*Spectator*). But there were some loud dissenting voices, most of them stung into protest by the tone of the book's introduction. 'The book has a pretentious, and erroneous, introduction on its efforts to bring poetical precision to an "undeservedly neglected literary form," and this should be ignored,' said the *Sunday Telegraph*. The *Times Literary Supplement* recognized that 'both writers have some reputation as poets, and Mr. Johnson has been noticed as an "experimental" novelist; but it was surely a mistake to launch this volume as if it were some sort of high-class demonstration kit for inspiring faith in either a "literary form" or the talents of Mr. Johnson and Mr. Ghose'. Brigid Brophy in the *New Statesman* was scathing:

Statement Against Corpses is a bizarre object consisting of nine stories by B. S. Johnson, five by Zulfikar Ghose and a preliminary manifesto signed by both to the effect that the short story is in decline, but deserves 'the same precise attention to language as that given normally only to a poem', and is now to be rescued from undeserved neglect by the two authors' demonstration of its 'wide technical range'. In a week when Mr [Francis] King is publishing his stories and a year in which Hortense Calisher and Shirley Hazzard have published theirs, the statement that the form is in decline, if it means artistic decline, is patently untrue. From the start the rescue attempt looks as officious as an offer to administer artificial respiration to a man walking soundly on dry land: when you read the actual samples by which the resuscitation is to be performed, it looks more like an assault. Most of Mr Johnson's prose is of a banality, verging on bathos, which makes me conclude he has given it the same precise attention as that usually given only to a poem by Patience Strong, but he occasionally takes off into a facetiousness which would sound jejune in a sixth form debate.

In *Books and Bookmen*, Alex Hamilton was more succinct: '*Statement Against Corpses* is an embarrassment. B. S. Johnson and Zulfikar Ghose have collaborated expressly to rescue the short story, and produced 14 nails for the coffin.'

Hamilton's funereal imagery cannot have been very welcome for Johnson, coming in the month when Tony Tillinghast died and his mind – 'much possessed by death' at the best of times – would have been of an even more morbid cast than usual. However, attuned as he was to the 'the never-ceasing pattern of birth, consummation and death' which he considered to be the main theme of Graves's *The White Goddess*, he would have taken great comfort in the fact that Virginia was now pregnant and he could look forward to the new experience of fatherhood in July. (Hence the opening lines of his poem 'Change is the only Constant', written in the winter of 1964: 'Unpleasurably I remark the coming / of the winter of my last childless year'.)

There is no let-up, at any rate, in his correspondence with printers and publishers during these weeks. Even in the midst of the most profoundly life-affecting experiences, Johnson always found time to monitor the public progress of his own work, and its treatment at the hands of those entrusted with it, with an extraordinary attention to detail.

77: LETTER *(25 November 1964)*

To Harvey Warren, The Garden City Press Ltd, Printers and Bookbinders

I understand that Constable are to do a reprint of my POEMS, and I would be grateful if you would give particular attention to the following points:

VERSO TITLE PAGE   The last line of your imprint *Letchworth, Hertfordshire* is not centred. Constable may also wish to add my later books under 'by the same author'.

CONTENTS PAGE   in no. 40, *Myddleton* should be corrected to *Myddelton*. And there should be no space between nos. 40 and 41.

PAGE 49   The number-title *FOUR* should be closer to the poem below (as the other number-titles are) than to the one above, as it is now.

CREASE   There is, in all the copies I have seen, a bad crease in the paper at the centre of each section, pp. 16–17, 32–33, and 48–49. Please do your best to avoid this.

CASE   The overhang of the case was intended to be 1/16" and not 1/8" right from our first meeting about the design of the book, and I am at a loss to understand how it never came to be carried out. I trust you will see that it is done correctly on the reprint.

Thank you for your work on this book, rather belatedly, and also for binding (if not printing) ALBERT ANGELO. I hope you are well, and your family.

Best wishes,
Yours sincerely

Johnson sent a copy of this letter to Ben Glazebrook at Constable, adding: 'I hope you are also trying for a paperback edition of the short stories. I have been bitterly disappointed by the reviews of the latter, incidentally: things are worse for the short story than we imagined.' But Glazebrook, understandably enough, did not altogether share the view that the mixed reception for *Statement Against Corpses* indicated a wholesale disparagement of the entire short story form on the part of literary critics: 'I think that on the whole the reviewers have been very much on your side,' he wrote, 'but undoubtedly their backs were put up by the Authors' Note in the Prelims. I blame myself, as I ought to have been much more vehement in dissuading you and Zulfi from putting this in.' Johnson was having none of this. 'I can free you from blame over the note at the beginning of STATEMENT,' he answered, on 4 December. 'I assure you that the book would not have been published without it, and I must say that I am surprised that you can see no further than reviewers'.

Here we can sense a new, tetchy note entering the relationship between Johnson and his editor. It continues over their next few letters, which concern authors' copies, how many Johnson has been buying and when he should be billed for them. Glazebrook's letters remain polite, and Johnson's respectful, but one can feel a growing irritation on both sides. And there is another new development: when Panther, who are putting in an offer for the paperback rights to *Albert Angelo,* say that they can only pay £250 and won't be able to cut holes through the pages, it is Johnson himself who telephones them and tells them to reconsider. Shouldn't this, strictly speaking, have been George Greenfield's job?

With the prospect of a family of three to support and a slightly larger flat to maintain, Johnson was looking for a steady source of income which would not involve going back to the dreaded supply teaching. To this end he had engaged a second agent, Robin Dalton: her job was to find him screenwriting work for film or television, and Johnson's first commission was to write an adaptation of *The Savage Canary* by David Lampe, a book about the German occupation of Denmark. Writing to Patrick Snaith in February 1965, he explained how he had written the first draft of the script but had then been contacted by the film company and 'told it would have to be scrapped as they'd thought of a better idea'. This, he concluded, was madness: but at least it was 'well-paid madness'. He added that, 'I'm learning a lot, though it's nothing to do with *writing*'. Very true: nor – though he did not mention this in the letter – was it ever likely to provide material for a novel, as supply teaching had done. Doug Davies would have had something to say about that.

Johnson at least had the satisfaction, on 13 January 1965, of hearing some of his drama performed on the radio at long last. That night the Third Programme, as it was then called, finally broadcast *Entry*, a radio play he had submitted to the producer John Wilson almost a year earlier. It is a short piece, running less than fifteen minutes, and shows Johnson even more in thrall to Beckett than he appears in his novels. The model here is *Krapp's Last Tape*, but instead of listening to tape recordings and sifting through his memories, the old man at the centre of Johnson's play is listening to a scratchy old seventy-eight of Handel's 'Arrival of the Queen of Sheba' and wondering whether the first word of the title should in fact be 'Entry' rather than 'Arrival'. There is the hint of a sexual pun here, but it doesn't seem to lead anywhere, and the whole play is enigmatic to the point of incomprehensibility. The Beckett link was underlined further by the casting of Patrick Magee as the old man (by which Johnson himself was delighted). But even Magee's performance was not enough to impress those few critics who noticed the play: On 16 January 1965, Anne Duchene in the *Guardian* wrote that 'Mr Johnson is a writer of some potential virtue; but this doesn't mean we must yet dote upon his doodles and he does seem perversely bent on making "experiments" of no conclusive, or even incidental interest. This private mumble suffered further, of course, from having Patrick Magee eating the air, promise-starved, in its monologue, and probably wishing as much as his hearers that he was back with some Beckett.'

It's hard to avoid the impression, looking back over this period, that Johnson's work was beginning to lack focus: he was dabbling in so many different genres, setting out in so many different directions at once, that the results were either inferior (*Statement Against Corpses*), miniaturist (*Street Children, You're Human Like the Rest of Them*) or both (*Entry*). No doubt this was the result of his own diffuse energy and enthusiasm and fecundity of ideas: but the fact remained that he had not done any serious novel-writing since the completion of *Albert Angelo* eighteen months ago, and the material he had gleaned from his trawler voyage in the early winter of 1963 was still gathering dust, unused. It was surely time to begin work on another major project: if only those nagging fears of financial insecurity could be resolved.

By now he had thought of a solution: a characteristic one, based on his concept of social justice, his sense that writers were the 'primary producers' in the book business and as such deserved to be paid a living wage. Emboldened by the fact that Panther seemed to have responded to his direct approach (they had raised their paperback offer for *Albert Angelo* to £300, and their production department had reluctantly conceded that it would be possible to cut the required holes through the pages), and following an informal conversation with another publisher (probably Secker & Warburg), he wrote to Constable as follows:

78: LETTER *(19 January 1965)*

To Ben Glazebrook

> Recently I was offered a three-year contract for novels. Naturally, I said I was not thinking of changing publishers, but the idea of such a contract interested me. Would you be prepared to consider a five-year contract with me to write three novels in return for an annual salary? From your point of view, it would give you security and protect your investment in me for the next three books; from mine, it would give me an assurance that I need not go back to teaching for perhaps the crucial period of my career. Anyway, think about it, and let me know what you think.

Again, the unwritten protocol of the author–agent relationship would dictate that George Greenfield should have made this approach. But Johnson no longer had any patience with literary red tape, and merely did his agent the courtesy of writing to him the same day with details of his proposal. Greenfield discussed the matter with Glazebrook on the telephone, and mentioned a figure of £750 per book (a fairly dramatic increase on what Johnson had been paid so far), or – in annual salary terms – £450 per year. Glazebrook seemed quite happy about this and offered, as a goodwill gesture, to backdate the salary to 1 January 1965. He wrote to Johnson saying that 'it is heartwarming to know that you are so loyal to us'.

Everything seemed to be proceeding splendidly: except that Johnson and his agent had misunderstood each other, and George Greenfield had asked for the wrong amount of money.

79: LETTER *(25 January 1965)*

To George Greenfield

> The point of this contract is that it should free me from the necessity of teaching for the next five years. When I left last July, I was doing three days a week for approximately £15. If I had taught for a full week it would have been £25. Any contract should, therefore, replace the former sum at least, if it is to be of the use intended: i.e. £750 a year. Preferably a thousand, since teachers are just about to receive an increase (call that illogical if you like) and the cost of living five years hence will have increased as well. I don't think I could have mentioned £450 to you (ask yourself whether anyone could live on it) and I don't know how you arrived at it.
>
> Two other points to be incorporated in a possible contract: 1) the standard of production not to be less than Constable's of TRAVELLING PEOPLE in hardback. 2) Author's complimentaries to be increased to a maximum of not more than fifty.

One thousand pounds a year would mean £1,666 per book: more than twice what Glazebrook had so far agreed to pay. George Greenfield believed that this was a tall order in Johnson's case and wrote back somewhat warily the next day, warning that 'the guarantee per book must bear some relation to the earning capacity of the book'. He had a point, in that the latest sales figures for *Albert Angelo* showed just 1,769 copies sold in hardback. On the other hand, Johnson also believed that *he* had a point, because Corgi had by now managed to sell an impressive 23,687 paperback copies of *Travelling People*, confirming his opinion that there *was* a large audience for his work out there and it was Constable's incompetence that was preventing him from reaching it. Of course, *Travelling People* was the more commercial book; and *Trawl* would be even less commercial than *Albert Angelo*. But these novels, although narrower and more introverted, were getting more *truthful*, in Johnson's view, and were therefore better works of literature. In his eyes this meant that their author deserved greater financial rewards. A head-on collision between art and commerce was looming just around the corner. His two closest relationships in the publishing business would be destroyed as a result.

But then, wasn't this a pattern that repeated itself throughout Johnson's life? 'The proper end of love is to destroy', he had once written, and all of his own relationships were ultimately destructive: his relationships with publishers and women, at any rate. Johnson demanded uncritical, unconditional devotion and commitment from both. Anything else he regarded as a betrayal. And when this 'betrayal' was visited upon him, the hurt he suffered was limitless. Even art could not console him – because he was committed to a form of art which reflected reality as closely as possible, reproducing its mess and untidiness, rather than shaping, rearranging and containing it as most artists do. Did he recognize this fact in himself, realize that its implications were not just destructive but potentially fatal? He certainly recognized it in other writers:

80: EXTRACT FROM REVIEW OF SYLVIA PLATH'S *ARIEL*, PUBLISHED IN *AMBIT*, 24 *(1965)*

Sylvia Plath was an embodiment of the loving/destructive goddess/ witch that Graves has tried to delineate. One of her poems, 'Lady Lazarus', ends

> Out of the ash
> I rise with my read hair
> And I eat men like air

Any review of her posthumous volume *Ariel* must be irrelevant, unimportant, and useless: the book simply *is*. That she was a fine poet was acknowledged after her first volume, *The Colossus*, and that these later poems sprang largely from an ultimately disastrous personal crisis is widely known. Many misleading and unnecessary claims have been made for her [...] which have made true assessment impossible for years yet: but the important thing is that she should be read.

Much in *Ariel* remains private, and it seems likely that most of the poems were not intended in any sense primarily to communicate with others but to make an emotion external in order to try to come to terms with it. (The lack of any attention to form, apart from regular grouping of lines, would seem to confirm this.) Even so, the effect on me of some of the poems ('Daddy', for instance) was overwhelmingly moving.

But while to read Sylvia Plath's book is a remarkable experience, and one which (the only real function of this review) should be recommended to others, I must yet question the *value* of these poems to me and to them: after all, they did not save her, did they?

So many of Johnson's reviews and occasional writings seem poignant in retrospect: the recurring themes are all there, and it's hard not to look for prophetic implications. In just over eight years' time he would be consumed by his own 'ultimately disastrous personal crisis', and already we can see the seeds being sown. On the personal front, however, everything seemed placid and satisfactory at the moment. He had been happily married to Virginia for more than a year. 'Little Albert', as they had tentatively christened their child, was due to make his appearance in a few months. A fishing holiday in Ireland had been relaxing and successful, besides providing Johnson with material for a piece of short prose to which he would shortly give one of his most celebrated titles, 'Aren't You Rather Young To Be Writing Your Memoirs?'. And back in London, thanks to George Greenfield, he was about to obtain almost the contract – and the financial security – that he wanted.

Not with Constable, however. It was Secker & Warburg, spurred on by the enthusiasm of the editor David Farrer, who would eventually offer Johnson a two-book commitment at an annual salary of £800 over three years. It was to become a famous deal, the subject of newspaper stories and much comment within the trade – despite being nothing less, in Johnson's opinion, than what he deserved and indeed any author deserved. And the fact that Ben Glazebrook had failed to see it that way meant, effectively, the end of their friendship.

81: LETTER *(21 May 1965)*

To Ben Glazebrook

My dear Ben

'*Value this man...*' Who would have thought the Constable estimate of that value to be not even enough to keep him alive to write his next three novels, not even as much as Constable quite happily pay a *secretary*?

I shall not here discuss the naïve concept of socialism which you mistakenly impute to me in your letter of 19th February since the views I do hold are about to be published:* but I am surprised that even according to your own capitalist lights you are not prepared to pay for my work what has been established as the market price.

No doubt it will come as a surprise to you to learn that more than one other publisher assumed (on the basis of reviews and publicity) that the sales of my novels must have been at least four to five thou-

---

* In an article called 'Writing and Publishing: or, Wickedness Reveal'd' for *Socialist Commentary*, June 1965. Glazebrook had, in fact, represented Johnson's 'naïve concept of socialism' thus: 'You take the view,' he wrote, 'that as serious writers are perhaps the most important interpreters of the society in which they live, they should be supported and made secure by that society, and specifically by their publishers'.

sand each. I hope you will be able to understand, therefore, that (quite apart from the lost sales) it makes me particularly bitter that you base your refusal to pay me a living wage on the efforts of *your* sales department. The surprise of these publishers at the actual figures confirmed the suspicion of your sales inefficiency (as compared with your excellent production and publicity departments) which had resulted from my own observation, from talking to booksellers and to other writers, and from various people who had great difficulty in buying my books.

Naturally, Constable and the editors who accepted my early work must always have a special place in my affections, and I am both very surprised and very sorry that Constable will not be the publishers of my future work. But how can a system be defended which rewards the writer (without whom none of you would make a living from books) with £180 out of the £2,000 paid by the reading public? It is clearly inequitable, it cannot be defended, and I am greatly disappointed that Constable were unwilling to be as courageous in making the initial disavowal of such an iniquitous system as they were in their editorial support of my books.

It would be very sad if this example of Constable surrendering the initiative were to represent a halt in the progress of rescuing a fine imprint from its conservative past, and I sincerely hope that it does not do so.

With best wishes for the future,
Yours sincerely

Retelling the story of those turbulent months, almost forty years on, Ben Glazebrook recalls:

'He had come to see to me and said, "I am getting less through my royalties than you pay to your secretaries, and I want a three-book contract for *x* thousand per book regardless of what I write and how commercial it is." Now, one did do that sort of thing in those days (for instance, I remember we guaranteed a mortgage for Julian Mitchell), but I didn't think we could really do this for Bryan because the books were not bringing in enough money. He was always going to be a writer with a minority readership. He *was* one of the writers we wanted to support – we all thought he was something very special – but, well, I'm afraid one can't run a business like that.

'So anyway, he went completely over the top about this: within about forty-eight hours he'd gone off me in a big way. And he came round to our offices in Orange Street and he wanted to collect every single copy of his books, including *Statement Against Corpses*. He didn't want a single copy of his work to remain in our offices – I think it was a symbolic as well as a practical thing.'

I hate the partial livers. I'm an allornothinger.

The new contract with Secker was signed by the beginning of June.

82: LETTER *(2 June 1965)*

To George Greenfield

> I am delighted to enclose the contract with Secker, which I have duly signed and initialled. The letter which explains clause thirteen is also enclosed, signed.
>
> The contract is exactly what I wanted, and I couldn't be more pleased that the months of negotiation and worry have ended so well: I shall certainly do my best to produce two novels which exceed anything I've done so far. The contract itself is a work of art for which you should take credit! David Farrer is everything, as far as I can see, that you've claimed for him as an editor, and it is a great relief to me that there is now someone I can trust with my work. I feel, as I have not been able to feel (this is a terrible sentence) since the death last year of Tony Tillinghast (to whom TP was dedicated, as you remember) [...]
>
> Thanks for all you've done: for bearing with me: Jane [Greenfield] once said (it seems very long ago) that I was a model author: how things have changed!
>
> Ever,

George Greenfield replied, warmly, the next day: 'Model authors can be terribly dull and I am far more interested in really good authors. So don't let us have any anxieties on that score!' But his own relationship with Johnson had only a few more weeks to run.

That Johnson did not feel, even now, sufficiently valued by the Farquharson agency was revealed when Innes Rose, its co-director, sent him his first payment under the new contract accompanied by a form letter.

83: LETTER *(7 July 1965)*

To Innes Rose

> Thank you for your letter of 5th July, enclosing your cheque for £180.
>
> I was rather surprised that you did not comment on the fact that this was the first payment on a contract of a kind which is extremely rare: that is, a publisher acknowledging that a writer is worth keeping alive by paying him a living wage.

This contract may well start a great many other things and lead to a general acknowledgement that writers should be paid a living like everyone else in publishing: I know that the idea of such a contract had to come from me and not from John Farquharson, but I should have thought that in this case our interests coincided in that the more authors are paid, the larger your share: and that it was worth you mentioning, not to say congratulating me, in your letter.

However, I hope that you will now press for all you're worth for similar contracts for all your other writers: after all, writers and agents are on the same side, aren't they?

Best wishes

Furthermore, there remained a massive sticking point: the failure of the Farquharson agency to sell foreign rights in any of Johnson's books to date. Yes, there had been an Italian sale of *Travelling People*, but no translation was ever produced and the book never appeared: suddenly, and capriciously, Mondadori announced that they were terminating the contract. A new American firm, Stein & Day, finally put in a bid for the novel, but Johnson considered their offer of $300 to be so insulting that he turned them down. Visibly exasperated, George Greenfield pointed out to him that the novel had now been seen by 'close on two dozen New York publishers', and they were in no position to be choosy. But the author was not to be swayed. As for *Albert Angelo*, there had recently been four rejections from Germany, and more continued to dribble in from the United States. 'Less impressive than *Travelling People*, although everyone continues to feel he is an author of promise and vitality.' 'I continue to think that he is a gifted man, but it just doesn't seem to me that this experiment in collage technique works effectively. The point against the book is not that it's experimental; the point is that the total effect of the various experiments isn't particularly impressive.' 'I am afraid that *Albert Angelo* by B. S. Johnson is just too way out for me. Johnson seems to bury his characters in the story under a mass of literary techniques* – I'm not sure that they are all successful.' 'My doubts were confirmed by my colleagues and we all agreed that the humor and attitude are far too intrinsically British to make their full point in this country. We felt, too, that *Albert Angelo* was something of a let-down after the other.'

There was only so much of this sort of stuff that Johnson could take. When, on 8 June 1965, Thomas Wallace of Holt, Rinehart and Winston, Inc. wrote to Farquharson's American sub-agent declining *Travelling People*, he made several mistakes. The biggest was describing it as 'a far better novel than his last one'. Another was admitting that he liked Johnson's more

---

* Literary techniques? In a novel? Outrageous!

conventional passages, but thought that 'when he is experimenting, he is not quite as good'. When the letter was passed over to Johnson (to whom it had not been addressed), it ignited his short fuse.

84: LETTER *(28 June 1965)*

To Thomas Wallace

You ignorant unliterary Americans make me puke.

I don't know how you came to read my novels in the opposite order to that in which they were intended to be read, but, for your information, ALBERT ANGELO was reviewed by the *Sunday Times* here as by 'one of the best writers we've got', and the *Irish Times* called the book a masterpiece and put me in the same class as Joyce and Beckett. And TRAVELLING PEOPLE, my first novel, won a Gregory Award: the judges for which were Herbert Read, Henry Moore, Bonamy Dobrée and TS Eliot: what did you say *your* name was, mate?

Since I am 'experimenting' (your word: I said I was using the best technique available: if you imagine you know a better one for any section, I'll be pleased to hear of it) throughout the whole work, how can you make statements as crassly irrelevant and un-understanding as the 3rd and 4th sentences of your letter? Eh? Did you give the book the same attention as I did in writing it?

Your letter makes clearer to me why it is that America has never produced a great writer: and you won't recognise him even when he comes.

Secker and Warburg have just given me a contract for two novels in the next three years at £800 a year. You will not see these novels, my third and fourth; or if inadvertently you do, despite my wishes, you will certainly not be able to buy them.

On 19 July he wrote to William Miller at Panther paperbacks, who were contracted to publish *Albert Angelo* and a new edition of *Travelling People*: 'As you will no doubt have seen, Secker and Warburg have taken me on on a salary basis for the next three years and two novels. I'm sure you were interested in this [...] as it is almost the first time a publisher has acknowledged that a writer is worth a living like everyone else in the book trade.' This was but a preamble to the main point of the letter, however, which was to confront Miller with the deadly 'enormous totality' question: 'I would like some indication within the next month as to whether you are interested in me as a writer, or only in those books which happen to be more saleable than others.' He asked him (bypassing George Greenfield again) to make or decline to make offers for *Poems, Statement Against Corpses* and *Street Children.**

The next morning, Johnson asked for a meeting with Greenfield to discuss the agency's continuing failure to sell any foreign rights. We can assume that it did not go well. By the afternoon he was back at Myddelton Square typing out a brief letter.

85: LETTER *(20 July 1965)*

To George Greenfield

Dear George:

This letter is to confirm that from the above date you are no longer representing me as my agent.

Please withdraw all copies of all my books at present with your representatives abroad, and return them to me.

Best of luck for the future.

Yours sincerely,

B.S. Johnson.

After that, for the next three years, Johnson would represent himself.

As a short postscript to this episode, in the spring of 2000, realizing how important it was to hear George Greenfield's side of the story, I called him on the telephone. I explained my business and he did not sound especially pleased to hear that somebody was writing a biography of B. S. Johnson. But he also sounded tired and ill, and perhaps I was mistaking frailty for lack of enthusiasm. He said that he was not well at the moment, but would call me back soon and we could meet when he had made a full recovery. I waited for a few weeks and then, on 21 April, I read his obituary in one of the national newspapers. After that the only thing I could do was to read his autobiography: but in a book devoted to colourful stories and affectionate reminiscences of the many authors with whom he had been associated, he made no mention of B. S. Johnson at all.

---

* Miller, a huge enthusiast for Johnson's novels, replied on 11 August: 'We do, of course, take you seriously as a writer but this does not mean that we should do anything with you which would be a publishing disaster.' He declined all three.

THE PLEASURETRIPPER

Anyone would think I was writing for the PUBLIC

B. S. Johnson's wife, Virginia, once described him to me as 'the most superstitious man I ever met'. Quite apart from his obsessional habit of picking up and storing every paper clip that he saw, even when walking down the street, even in mid-conversation (something that Samuel Beckett himself remarked on, when they finally got to know each other), this avowed atheist and rationalist had a number of rituals that he was careful to observe when engaged upon a novel. There was the candlestick he had been given by the lock-keeper in Dublin: a candle always had to be burning in this while he was writing – a symbol of hope? memory? inspiration? There was also the Byronic skull cup which sat on top of the Edwardian bank clerk's sloping desk at which he always wrote in pencil (and those pencils themselves came from Fuller's bakery – he had hoarded them since the early 1950s). And, perhaps most importantly of all, there was the superstition that every novel had to be started on Boxing Day, in one of the parish log books his father supplied to him, while sitting in his old back bedroom at his parents' house, 8 Meredyth Road, in Barnes.

This meant that the commencement of writing a particular novel was, for Johnson, often a symbolic or gestural event, rather than an indication that he was ready to begin work on it in earnest. Thus, although he had 'started' *Trawl* in this way on 26 December 1963, it was not until the early summer of 1965 that he began to make any real progress with it. How can I be so sure, the sceptical reader wishes to know? Simple: because, throughout his working life, Johnson never lost the habit of drawing up 'Stuart [Crampin]-style graphs', with which he meticulously recorded the number of hours spent writing every day, and the number of words written. They looked like this:

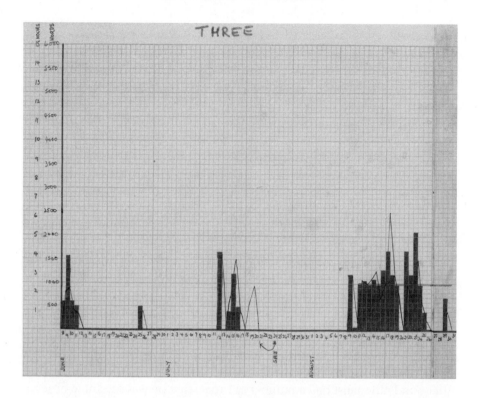

And here we come up against the chief problem with literary biography: the thing that makes me, essentially, mistrust the genre just as much as Milan Kundera does. Take 17 August 1965, for instance. Johnson got involved in no literary bust-ups that day, wrote no fiery letters for me to quote. He did not go out and get hilariously drunk with a fellow author, to provide me with a spiky anecdote. He did not have a secret tryst with a beautiful journalist, leading to a torrid but eminently disclosable affair. (He was not, you will have gathered by now, the sort of person who had affairs.) No, he sat at his desk for six and a quarter hours, and wrote 1,700 words of *Trawl.* Boring, or what? *But this is what writers do.* Not only is it what they do, but it is what they do best, it is when they are happiest, it is when they are most themselves. If they did not do it, none of the other, superficial, gossipy stuff that fills up books like this would matter in the slightest. It is the essence of the thing. But it is the one thing I cannot write about, that I cannot make interesting. It shows up the whole process I am engaged upon for the potentially dishonest enterprise that it is. (Dishonest, Bryan, in a way that novels never are!)

All I can say is this. I know – from my own experience of writing – that 17 August 1965 would have been a great day in B. S. Johnson's life. At the end of those six and a quarter hours, he would have felt exhilarated. He would have felt a degree and a quality of satisfaction that he felt in his short life only very rarely. He would have left his desk with a proud, contented sigh, put away his pencils, blown out the candle and then he would have spent the evening with Virginia and been kind and generous and attentive to her. He would have played with his son, relishing the time spent with him, not resenting it at all. (By the way, Bryan, how did you do it? Six and a quarter uninterrupted hours at home, just four weeks after your son was born?) And even though there would be nothing for us, as spectators (voyeurs would be a better word), to see while he sat at that desk, inside his head there would have been the most tremendous, miraculous activity taking place: memories, reflections, observations, even (yes!) inventions, all competing for space, all jostling with each other and fusing together into strange shapes and compounds, all being turned over and examined and sifted through and then alchemized into words; made permanent, for readers to savour and enjoy even now, thirty-nine years or more since he wrote them down. *Trawl* is one of B. S. Johnson's very best books: purely as a writer of prose, he was then probably at the height of his powers, and to spend a whole day exercising those powers would have seemed an incomparable privilege and luxury. If only he (if only all of us!) were able to spend more days the way that B. S. Johnson spent 17 August 1965.

We cannot know what he wrote that day, exactly. But perhaps – purely for the sake of example – it was this.

87: EXTRACT FROM *TRAWL*

They hose the deck clear of the accumulated guts, debris, starfish, ginnies, dabs, rejectamenta. All disappears in foul surges, through the scuppers, doors wide open, and then the gulls descend like white harpies, have been following us like white-winged erinnys, scream in their hundreds as they drop and fall, plunge and plummet, into the gut-lightened sea, squawk and fight over the stream of offal, flap and settle and hit the sea and air to raise themselves with some intestinal particle draped from their beaks, scavenge and hawk and eye each others' lots for chances to improve their own. The anthropomorphic fallacy. The gulls are wild, wary, no tame Thames visitors these: they will not land upon the deck to take their fill of the tumbled guts, far less will they snatch the liver from the deckie's hand as he selects it from the slimy living guts to keep it for its special value, no: but perhaps they are more daring when food is scarcer.

The several absences and lacunae in Johnson's graph are intriguing, of course. What was he doing on the days when he wrote nothing? Sometimes we can say. If he wrote almost nothing between 20 June and 3 July, this was because he was at Wimbledon every day, reporting on the tennis tournament for the *Times of India* (his other main outlet for sports reporting, besides the *Observer*). And if he wrote nothing on 21 July, this was because his son was born that day: Steven Anthony Johnson (the second name given in memory of Tony Tillinghast). Johnson had not been allowed to attend the birth – it was fairly rare for fathers to do this in the mid-1960s – even though he had put in an eloquent request.

88: LETTER *(14 July 1965)*

To the Chief Obstetrician, St Bartholomew's Hospital

Dear Sir:

I enclose a copy of my novel TRAVELLING PEOPLE for you. On the publication of my second, ALBERT ANGELO, the *Sunday Times* called me 'one of the best writers we've got', and the *Irish Times* called the book a masterpiece, and compared me with Joyce and Beckett. If you have already read these books, you will know that they are based upon a relatively new technique of truth to all experience.

However, it seems that I am to be denied the opportunity of a most profound and important experience: of being present with my wife Virginia when our first child is born at your hospital on or about July 24th.

May I respectfully ask you for allow me [*sic*] to be present at all stages of the birth? I have recently seen films of labour and delivery at the National Childbirth Trust (where my wife has attended classes) and have read appropriately: I am therefore prepared for what should normally happen.

Hoping you will grant this reasonable request,

I am,

Yours sincerely,

B. S. Johnson.

Steven was born the day after Johnson's explosive argument with George Greenfield. Interesting to see that on that day (20 July) he had still been composed enough to credit himself with two and a quarter hours' work on *Trawl*, even though no words were written as a result. In any case, something appeared in the *Times Literary Supplement* two weeks later which no doubt reinforced the feeling that his actions had been justified. The journal printed a roll-call of the most significant works to have appeared in Britain in the first half of the 1960s: and there they were, *Travelling People* and *Albert Angelo*, both listed. To a writer less burdened with personal and class insecurities, this might have been cause, say, for a few moments' private self-satisfaction. After all, such lists are arbitrary: the personal, often whimsical, outcome of a few people swapping opinions in a room. But Johnson – as when he won a Gregory Award, as when he was praised to the skies in the *Sunday Times* and the *Irish Times* – saw it as rather more than that.

89: LETTER *(15 August 1965)*

*To Ruth Liepman**

I am sorry that you must have been very surprised to learn that Farquharson are no longer representing me. I have been very disappointed with the way Farquharson have handled me abroad (with the exception of yourself and Erich Linder in Italy) and when I suggested (not very tactfully) to George Greenfield that more effort ought to be made, then he decided not to represent me any longer.

My point is this, and was confirmed by the TIMES LITERARY SUPPLEMENT a fortnight ago (the issue which consisted of a survey of the first five years of the sixties): I am one of the two or three important novelists to have emerged in this country in the last five years and to have established a considerable reputation. It is high time this reputation was extended outside England, and the net result of Farquharson's efforts was one novel sold in Italy: and Mondadori have just relinquished rights to that, by the way. I do not consider that my attitude towards Farquharson (with whom I have no quarrel as to the way they have handled my English rights) is an unreasonable one, and I am surprised at Greenfield's reaction to it.

Secker and Warburg, who are my new publishers (you may have heard that they are paying me a salary of £800 a year for the next three years in return for two novels: an almost unheard-of thing for English publishers) have expressed a desire to handle my agency work as well, and I have agreed. I have asked them if they would continue the contact with you, and, though they will have to clear it with their usual agent, they foresee no objection. I too would be very happy to continue with you: but if you disagree in any way with my estimate of my work (and that of the TLS), or would feel any embarrassment in presenting me as a very important English writer to German-language publishers, then it would be better if we went our separate ways.

I am sorry if this letter seems boastful: but there comes a time when it is necessary to present one's claims against those of far lesser writers who get sold all over Europe. I hope that you will understand, and that

---

* German sub-agent for John Farquharson.

a relationship that has begun warmly and well will continue to be so: and that it will shortly be successful in selling my books in German-language countries, as well.

Johnson had signed his contract with Secker & Warburg two months earlier, and he and his new publishers were still enjoying their honeymoon period. The chairman of the firm in those days was its founder, Frederic Warburg, the descendant of a wealthy and prestigious Westphalian Jewish family. He had bought the insolvent firm of Martin Secker for £3,100 in 1936, when his chief publishing rival was Victor Gollancz. Warburg was solidly left wing, but thought that Gollancz's Left Book Club was blind to the evils of Stalinism: in this he agreed with George Orwell, whose publisher he became, on a list which also included Colette, Moravia, Robert Musil, Thomas Mann and Gunter Grass. Warburg was the friend as well as the publisher of most of these writers, and, a cigarette holder permanently clamped between his teeth, he carried himself with the bearing and presence of someone who belonged naturally in such circles. 'His is an almost classical countenance,' wrote his colleague David Farrer some years later, 'with its long face, straight nose, crinkly, close-cropped hair. In moments of anger or frustration he looks like an arrogant Assyrian preparing to attack a sheep-fold.'[1]

How many of those 'moments of anger or frustration' did Johnson give him? Quite a few, I suspect. But at first his letters to the young writer are characterized by a mixture of exasperation and warm affection, always ironically expressed. On 19 August 1965, for instance, he wrote:

> My dear Johnson, I have now read your *Albert Angelo* with considerable admiration and some slight increase in my knowledge of London architecture. It is an interesting book in which you try to do something very difficult by typographical methods and it is a moot point whether you have wholly succeeded [...] However, one cannot but be amazed at the technical skill of your work and your intricate handling of the English language. These put you into a very small category of writers.

'Interesting', one cannot help feeling, is a little lukewarm compared to the sort of thing (i.e. being put in the same class as Joyce and Beckett) that Johnson was by now beginning to regard as his due. And Warburg seems to be coming dangerously close here to the hated position of telling Johnson that he could be a good mainstream writer if he would only drop all this experimental stuff. With that delectable hindsight afforded by the writing of biography, I can already see the storm clouds gathering in the distance.

Meanwhile a rather depressing royalty statement from Hodder & Stoughton showed 1,158 copies of *Street Children* sent to the shops but only 586 sold. Johnson and Julia Trevelyan Oman had enjoyed their collaboration and were planning another book together – a photographic celebration of South-end – but they were not finding it easy to generate enthusiasm for the idea.

90: LETTER *(7 October 1965)*

To Robin Denniston, Hodder & Stoughton

Dear Denniston:

I understand from Miss Trevelyan Oman that you have decided not to take up the option on the next work we have decided jointly to do. I would like your confirmation in writing that this is so in order that we may offer this and subsequent works elsewhere.

Since I have heard vaguely that STREET CHILDREN was chosen as one of the best 100 books of the year or something, I would like confirmation of this from you: I know I am only an author, but many of the typographical ideas in the book were mine and if it has won some sort of distinction partly because of these, I feel the least a publisher could have done was to have told me about it.

Your marketing policy on STREET CHILDREN, as revealed in your last letter to me, I thought abysmal, and I am bitterly disappointed that as a result the book has made nothing like as much as it cost me to write it.

Yours truly

As we can see, an alarming number of Johnson's professional relationships were by now beginning to fracture. Another that would only have a few more months to run would be his association with the *Observer* sports pages. Throughout 1965 he continued to report on matches for them most Saturdays, but Zulfikar Ghose (another poet–novelist–sports reporter, whose unavailability to report Wimbledon for the *Times of India* that year had led to Johnson getting the job) could tell that there were deep resentments brewing: 'He was always anxious that his words appear in the paper as he had dictated them and was always furious when he found that some of his phrases and sometimes, of course, whole paragraphs had been edited out. I tried to console him by saying that that was the nature of journalism, but he would not accept that, for he believed that he ought to be respected as a writer whose every word was important and that to cut out a phrase was to emasculate his style. He would complain about this bitterly to [Clifford] Makins, but he received no satisfaction.'[2] Sure enough, the pages of the lever-arch file into which he pasted his cuttings are full of irritated scrawls: 'cut', 'hideously cut', 'made nonsense of', and so on. Nonetheless, his football reporting was at this time a valued sideline, giving him the opportunity to keep up with the game which he loved passionately, above all others, and offering a welcome social dimension to offset the prevailing solitariness of the writer's life. 'He enjoyed the Fleet Street ambience,' Ghose remembers. 'There was a time when he was regularly at El Vinos with Makins, John Arlott and Hugh McIlvanney (I was there a couple of times and have a vivid recollection of this) drinking Moët et Chandon before lunch.'[3]

Indirectly, too, his sports writing now led to another important commission. The World Cup was looming, and in 1966 it was going to be held in England. One Octavio Senoret, a Chilean film producer living in Paris, had been commissioned by FIFA to make a film of the event for cinema release: a highly ambitious project, which would involve hiring eight separate camera crews to film the action at each of the different grounds. What was also needed, of course, was a writer: a writer who loved and understood the game but also had some kind of reputation as an artist, to add prestige to the whole enterprise. Step forward, inevitably, B. S. Johnson. With a writer of his calibre on board, Senoret hoped to surpass even the achievement of Kon Ichikawa in his acclaimed (and commercially successful) film of the 1964 Olympic Games. Or, as Johnson himself was quoted in a magazine interview: 'Our ambition is to make something even better than the Japs did of the Tokyo Olympiad.'[4]

Johnson wrote a three-page treatment – with which Senoret seemed, at first, perfectly happy – and was paid fifty pounds for it. Later in the year the two men attended an international match together at Wembley (England v. Northern Ireland, on 10 November), so that they could share their enthusiasm for the game. They got on well, and, like so many of Johnson's projects, this one was begun in a spirit of optimism and goodwill. Senoret would be one of the people he would phone in the New Year with the news that he had completed *Trawl*.

His graph reveals that work on the novel continued solidly for the rest of the year. The only substantial interruption was when Johnson flew to Barcelona with Steven and Virginia to report on the Davis Cup interzone final for the *Times of India* at the beginning of November. 'Good tennis today,' he wrote to Zulfikar Ghose, 'but getting copy out is so difficult – the Spanish services are impossible: I haven't been issued with some bureaucratic pass or other so I can't send cables: telex is said to be highly subject to delay [. . .] So I phone London – or rather, they phone me at set times.'[5] Steve, by now, was 'taking more and more notice of what goes on around him, and he even attempts to make noises back at whoever speaks to him'.[6] Journalism and fatherhood must have been providing Johnson with a vivid, consuming present-tense reality; meanwhile, at the back of his mind, always, was the novel which was now nearing completion, a sustained feat of memory and personal excavation. Negotiating between these two levels must have required considerable writerly dexterity: but Johnson was currently on top form, and it's from this period that we can date not only one of his best novels but also some of his best journalism.

In late October, for instance, he published a lengthy profile of Peter and Alison Smithson for *London Life*. The Smithsons were a husband-and-wife team of New Brutalist architects who had met as students at Durham University and later married. Founder members of the ICA's Independent Group and closely associated with Team 10, they were (like Johnson) never lacking in the outward appearances of self-belief: when their school at Hunstanton in Norfolk was completed in 1954, Alison Smithson had bluntly told the *Architects' Journal*, 'We are the best architects in the country.' Over the years, very few of their designs actually got built, but certainly their most famous work, at this time, was the *Economist* building in St James's Street, London SW1, of which Johnson was a huge admirer. Frank Fisher recalls that 'he had a very definite, and quite a good knowledge about architecture. That's one memory that's very clear, that he was excited by the *Economist* building in London, and I remember him taking us there and looking at it, some time after we had graduated from King's. He had a great admiration for that pair, the Smithsons, and there was something about the way they'd designed the building so that all the muck washed off, he was very appreciative of the whole design, and I remember now going there with him and him pointing out several things about the detailing.'

The Smithsons by now were personal friends of Johnson's, and he also felt a strong aesthetic affinity with their work: in countless articles and radio interviews throughout his life he stressed the relationship between writing and architecture, and particularly between his own work and that of the New Brutalists. (The narrator of *Christie Malry* epigrammatizes that the modern novel should be 'nasty, Brutalist and short'.) From the *London Life* article we can sense what at least three of these affinities might have been. First, there is the need not just to *practise* one's art but to back it up with a manifesto, a solid foundation of theory (Johnson writes approvingly of the amount of time the Smithsons have spent 'evolving theories' and credits them with 'much theoretical work of obvious validity and importance done over the decade and more since their manifesto' [*15 Criteria for Mass Housing*]). Then there is the essential insistence on *honesty* in their architecture, the concern to put structural materials such as concrete on show, not to hide them, just as Johnson himself always liked to make the mechanics of novel-writing visible to the reader. Lastly – and this was perhaps the main reason for their closeness – we have the sense of noble embattlement, of being the sole harbingers of progress and innovation in a world full of reactionaries: 'Only in painting, sculpture and (to a lesser extent) music,' Johnson wrote, 'have the pioneers of the Modern Movement become the establishment in their respective arts.

In literature and in architecture the reactionaries who use the techniques of Dickens and put up Shell Centres are still not only in the majority but even represent these arts to many people. Thus Alison and Peter Smithson are faced with a multiple problem: not only to overcome the opposition of reactionaries to a previous generation, but also to have ideas accepted which are an extension and development of those of that generation.' The words could, of course, apply exactly to his own position (as he saw it) in the British literary culture of the mid-1960s.

Johnson had few allies in that culture, and several of those that he had he was busy alienating. One of the people with whom he still remained on good terms – despite his unenthusiastic response to *You're Human Like the Rest of Them* – was Jeremy Brooks at the Royal Shakespeare Company. Brooks continued to believe that Johnson had it in him to be a good playwright and that this first attempt had been merely a false start. When he heard that he was working on a new idea for a play – a violent, large-scale assault on the established Church and its abrogation of moral power – he was immediately interested, and offered to put up half the fee for commissioning it (the other half to come from an Arts Council grant which had already been awarded). His suggestion was that they should meet to talk about it in the new year, and in the meantime Johnson should get on with the more urgent business of completing his third novel.

A novel, incidentally, which still had no definite title. The manuscript of *Trawl* reveals that *All's Well That Ends* had been one possibility; more ingeniously – for a book about the therapeutic externalization of emotion, and which also happens to describe the effects of seasickness in some detail – Johnson had thought of calling it *Better Out Than In*. But at the moment his preferred title was *The Pleasuretripper*: a reference to the disdainful nickname which the crew members of the *Northern Jewel* had given him, and which Johnson saw as bitterly ironical, since in his view the personal situation which had driven him to write this book and therefore to take this voyage was – in the words of his own blurb – 'desperate in its seriousness'.

Under the terms of his Secker contract – a contract which he held to be almost sacred – the novel was due for delivery on 31 December 1965. Such dates are usually taken with a pinch of salt by both publisher and author.* But Johnson, perhaps because of his early background in the business world, was a fanatical deadline keeper: it was a matter of professional pride. (The same professional pride and efficiency which he looked for in return from his publishers and seldom seemed to find.) And he met his target. 'I was working like mad just before Xmas,' he wrote to Patrick Snaith in late January 1966, 'and got this novel (TRAWL) in on the deadline – even with

---

* At the time of writing I am three years and 254 days late delivering this biography.

eleven hours to spare. Secker were surprised – I was almost the first author to meet such a deadline: the day before they'd just received a book commissioned in 1938.'*

Johnson was writing to Patrick Snaith, on this occasion, for a specific reason: 'How do you feel about making a Guest Appearance in my new novel?' Snaith crops up a few times in the long section about the King's College drama tour of Germany and Denmark, and is portrayed under his own name: but Muriel, this time around, is referred to as 'Gwen'. Johnson had wised up to the fact that, if he was going to write 'truth in the form of a novel' from now on, he was going to have watch out for the libel laws. Also, when *Albert Angelo* had been published, Muriel had been personally identified not just in the novel itself but also in the *Observer*'s review. Shortly afterwards, he had received a furious and anguished letter from her mother, reprimanding him for betraying confidences and pleading with him not to write about the affair again. Johnson's reply had been to sit down and pen the poem 'Bad News for Her Mother', later published in *Poems Two*:

91: POEM *(1964)*

Bad News for Her Mother

Yes, I shall write it all down, you old cow,
all: the first time, the last time, all the times
in between, and then all the times I should
have liked there to have been. I shall go on
writing it down even out of habit,
till there is nothing left to exorcise.

You may judge from that the emotional
debt I feel your lovely daughter owes me.

Not his most noble moment, I feel. And the fact that he was always careful to change her name from then on hardly seems to make much difference.

Both David Farrer and Fred Warburg read *The Pleasuretripper*, as it was still called, within a week of delivery. Warburg wrote to the author at once with an ominous response: 'it raises some very acute problems and we ought to discuss these early next week'. What did this mean, exactly? I imagine (although Johnson would not of course have approved of that), or speculate (which is not much better, but what else can I do?), that this was the

---

* In the same letter he added, 'Had a row with the *Observer* – they subbed my copy so badly for the umpteenth time that I had to say I'd not write except under a pseudonym [. . .]: and they wouldn't wear that.' He wrote no more sports journalism for that newspaper.

occasion on which he and Frederic Warburg had their argument about generic definitions: had he actually written a *novel*, this time, or was it just a very particular kind of autobiography? In fact, while I am speculating, let me go even further: I believe, or at least I have a strong *hunch* (half of this book is composed of hunches – had you not realized this by now?) that at this meeting Warburg must have posed, in that friendly, joshing, slightly provocative way of his, the impertinent question 'Aren't you rather young to be writing your memoirs?', which lodged so firmly in Johnson's indignant memory that he would later use it as the title for the last book he saw published in his lifetime, the collection in which he made his most emphatic and irritated statement of what seemed to him an obvious fact: that a serious novel must not be a work of *fiction*, it must tell the *truth*.

In every polemical or discursive article that he wrote, Johnson gnawed away at the terms *novel, truth, fiction, lies* and *stories* relentlessly. But he rarely used the word *imagination,* I now realize. One rare exception was a letter he wrote from Spain a few months later, in April 1966, in response (apparently) to a direct question about the relationship, as he saw it, between imagination and reality in poetry.

92: LETTER *(14 April 1966)*

*To Barry Cole**

I say this. I act as though there is no difference between reality and imagination: [...] as far as I'm concerned nothing a writer produces comes from nowhere, everything he does comes from somewhere: you can't push anything out that hasn't gone in some way or another. What most people come back at me with when I say this is that the ten-headed monsters of Sf couldn't have been experienced or gone in the writer: but this is simple to counter: a tenheaded monster consists of the concept of ten + the concept of head + the concept of monster: the *act of combining them is what many people consider to be 'imagination'.* For myself, I think this to be a useless concept: for others who do not possess it (ie the ability to combine in this way) it may be interesting,

---

* Then a poet, novelist and civil servant working in the Central Office of Information. He recalls meeting Johnson for the first time while innocently walking along the pavement in Myddelton Square, and being hailed with the accusing words 'You're Barry Cole!' by a portly stranger yelling at him from the window of a van. (Johnson's vehicle of choice in those days was a white transit van, for reasons which have never been made plain to me.) Johnson had recently been sent some of Cole's poems for the *Transatlantic Review* (of which he was poetry editor) and had been hoping to meet him. They became close friends. A few years later it would be Cole who broke into Johnson's home with a local policeman to discover that he had committed suicide.

either because they want to possess it and 'wonder how it is done' or for other reasons. It is sufficient for me that I do possess it: but I beware of it, because it leads to telling lies, of which I've certainly spoken ad infinitum, even though you don't watch the telly.*

More particularly, tied to this poem,† *seeing* is well established by psychology and now by op art painters as being capable of lying: and if you haven't seen it for yourself how your eyes can mislead you then you must be metaphorically blind; and *remembering* even more so: how many times have you remembered something you thought accurately only to find it was not so when you had it checked by some independent means?

So, answer to an as if simple lad, there is no *practical* difference between reality and imagination in my opinion, life, practice, work: but why do you want that opinion, etc? You must decide for yourself.

This letter was written during a three-week holiday on the Costa del Sol with Zulfikar and Helena Ghose. Ghose wrote about this holiday at length in his memoir 'Bryan' (although he mistakenly gave the date as spring 1965), capturing in particular the splendid moment when Johnson drove out of Spain into France, shrugging off the political unease which had clouded his holiday ('as a confirmed socialist, he could not escape a measure of guilt enjoying himself there'), and the two of them shouted out 'Balls to Franco!' from the open-topped car as soon as they had crossed the border. An anecdote which can't help but raise the question of how Johnson, the perennially underpaid 'primary producer' on the literary shop floor, who had to shout and stamp his feet before his publishers would pay him a 'living wage', had nonetheless by now traded in his van for a smart two-seater convertible Sunbeam Alpine: hardly the vehicle you would normally associate with a struggling hack with a family to support.

Ghose also recalled that 'I had anticipated that much of the two weeks we were to spend in Estepona would be passed sitting in bars talking literature. We did indeed spend a good deal of time in bars, but Bryan always made for the pinball or the soccer machines, finding a great delight in them.' Perhaps the Spanish machines were not as modish and hi-tech as the new ones which were, in Johnson's view, infiltrating the London pubs and cafes and spoiling one of his favourite recreations. An article he published shortly

---

* Ten minutes of the BBC programme *New Release* had been devoted to Johnson's novels on 22 December 1965. All the points he had made on the programme resurface in the *Aren't You Rather Young To Be Writing Your Memoirs?* introduction, and indeed in all his other articles on the subject. Rather optimistically, Johnson had written to the sales managers of his various publishers in advance of the programme, telling them when it would be broadcast and saying 'you may think it worth while to see that my books are readily available in bookshops for the month or so after that date'.

† 'Living By', *Poems Two* (Trigram Press, 1972), p. 13.

after returning from Spain[7] waxes nostalgic for several paragraphs about the simple pin-tables of his youth, and the hours he whiled away playing them in pubs and amusement arcades, before lamenting that 'all this has passed away in the last few years'. He berates the garish new machines which come equipped with 'all sorts of solenoids and electronic cantrips', and are decorated with naked women instead of modestly attired bathing beauties. Writing as though the very manufacture of these machines is a personal affront, Johnson even complains that 'no space is provided for beer or crisps, of course', and concludes by describing the new versions as 'modern trash'. But behind the seemingly frivolous nature of the piece, we can hear him lamenting the loss of a simple, authentic working-class culture, trampled underfoot by the forces of commercialism and modernity. Even in scraps of occasional journalism like this, his nostalgic melancholy can be noticeable.

And as with pinball machines, so with football: Johnson could not separate these recreations from the culture which had introduced him to them and in which they were richly embedded. This was why the forthcoming World Cup was going to be so important: he envisaged a country and, more specifically, a capital city transformed, galvanized, by the celebration of an event which for a few weeks would colour and vivify every aspect of British life.

93: EXTRACT FROM SCREENPLAY FOR FILM OF WORLD CUP *(1966)*

23) Coach, from inside, with one of teams. Leaving airport, out through tunnel on to M4. In the distance the London skyline, with PO Tower prominent.

Series of London shots, many of which can be seen as if from the players' coach. Many can be tied in with PO Tower, from near and far off.
Locations suggested:

24) St James's Street: 18th Century Boodle's Club next door to excellent modern Economist buildings (architects: Alison and Peter Smithson). Fine example of combining old and new.

modern link to: 25) City tower blocks (Barbican, off Aldersgate) still being built: shoot across bombed sites, cellars, purple weeds: stainless steel and glass.

glass link to: 26) Hothouse by Decimus Burton at Kew Gardens: magnificent flowers, colour.

grass link to: 27) Regent's Park: Cumberland Terrace (Nash) pan down to pretty girls in striped shirts and mini-skirts.

clothes link to: 28) Carnaby Street (if you must) clothes shop windows, stripes, possibly World Cup special displays, snob junk.

junk link to: 29) Real junk in Club Row Sunday morning market, football items (early photos, piles of old football boots, new boots, balls). Many of the alleys in this area have a group of posts (iron, cast like upright cannon): pan from a group or one to PO Tower.

tower link to: 30)   Pan from tower in semi circle over Waterloo Bridge (camera on Shell House, south bank) to recently cleaned St Paul's: down to River Thames.

cathedral link to: 31)   St Paul's in foreground, PO Tower in background.

tower link to: 32)   Centre-Point building, Charing X Road. Very near PO Tower. 'Pop' architecture, includes pub at southern base.

pub link to: 33)   Football game in London pub, colours as 2 actual teams if possible.

ball link to: 34)   Father teaching small son to kick football in tiny back garden

child link to: 35)   A London school playground: game on asphalt with plimsolls, master joining in.

ball link to: 36)   Street game: goal marked out in chalk on wall covered in graffiti . . .

Only B. S. Johnson, I feel, could have incorporated a plug for the Smithsons in a film about the World Cup. Which is not to accuse him of predictability, merely to emphasize the contiguity of the Johnsonian universe, how everything in it always connected up. Even in this script we can see all the familiar preoccupations: the pressing awareness of how football can forge an emotional bond between fathers and sons, the impulse to celebrate London architecture and more especially to get behind a touristy London of 'snob junk' and penetrate to the real thing. Elsewhere in the script Johnson pursued the same themes but cast his net even further afield: he proposed to show how the different teams might occupy themselves between games (Argentinians attending music concerts in Birmingham town hall and going to the theatre in Stratford; Brazilians in Liverpool attending 'beat group performances in cellars or cinemas', Russians in Sunderland and Middlesbrough having visits down coal mines and attending an Industrial Eisteddfod). Finally there would be extracts from matches, vox pop interviews, interviews with referees and match organizers, even groundsmen: 'Build this and other material to give a picture of a London dominated by one thing: football.'

Unfortunately – but perhaps not surprisingly – this was not what Octavio Senoret had in mind at all. Johnson was supposed to be paid £500 for the script: £250 on commencement, and £250 on delivery. (This was a substantial sum of money, when you consider that Secker were only paying him £800 a year. It would have gone some way towards the running costs of that Sunbeam Alpine.) He did deliver the script at the beginning of July, just before the tournament started (the first match was on 11 July) and then set about preparing detailed briefing notes for the cameramen. Besides his work on the film, he was going to be reporting matches for the *Times of India* as well, so would be attending most of the games in a dual capacity. Or so he thought. But abruptly, on 19 July, he was sacked from the film. The agency that handled his film work received this letter from Senoret's solicitor: 'My Client has asked me to tell you that he considers that the script delivered has not been competently prepared and is quite unsuitable for the purpose for which it is required [. . .] In the circumstances my Client cannot make any use whatsoever of the script submitted by your Client and indeed further he has been put to considerable inconvenience by reason of having to arrange for the preparation of a further script at very short notice.' Senoret even asked for the return of his initial £250 commencement fee.

94: LETTER *(24 July 1966)*

To Douglas Rae of GAC Redway Ltd

   re: World Cup film

Thank you for your letter, and copies of [the solicitor's] letter to you and your reply.

I of course deny the allegations made by Senoret, which are at once unspecific and so ludicrous that I can only assume that he is seeking dishonest pretexts to avoid paying the second half of my fee.

When the World Cup is over I shall consider whether or not to refer the matter to the Television and Screen Writers Guild. At the moment I feel relieved that my name will not be associated with a film which through Senoret's inexperience and incompetence looks like being nothing more than a lengthy newsreel cum corny travelogue, and in no way as good as *Tokyo Olympiad*, as it was intended it should be when I was engaged.

Thank you for your work on my behalf.*

This nasty dispute cast a pall over what should have been some of the best few journalistic weeks of Johnson's life. He spent much of July either in football stadiums or on trains, shuttling between Hillsborough in Sheffield,

---

* Johnson was right, in that *Goal!*, Octavio Senoret's film of the 1966 World Cup, directed by Ross Devenish, was poorly received on its release in October. The *Sunday Times* said 'It all rather puts you in mind of those Walt Disney nature films where they lay it on not so much with a trowel as with a mallet.'

Goodison Park in Liverpool and of course Wembley Stadium itself. He was so busy that it even took him three weeks to sign the contract Jeremy Brooks sent him for the (as yet untitled) anti-Church play to be written for the RSC. Even this – certainly one of the most important and deeply felt projects in the whole of his career – seemed temporarily of little importance besides the gathering momentum of the World Cup and the slowly dawning, incredible realization that England themselves were heading towards the final. And if one sample has to be taken from Johnson's prolific body of sports journalism, it should surely be this: his lengthy, spontaneous response to the match which even non-enthusiasts remember with pride and astonishment as a defining moment in the social history of post-war Britain.

95: FOOTBALL REPORT FOR THE *TIMES OF INDIA* (31 July 1966)

ENGLAND PREVAIL IN EXTRA TIME
Hurst ensures World Cup Stays In Home of Soccer
England ... 4. West Germany ... 2.
By B. S. Johnson
Special to 'The Times of India'

In the shortest of times, it is impossible to do justice to the World Cup final, a match that must surely stand with the greatest ever played, a match that had as many changes of fortune and direction as a gypsy's life, a match even better than the semi-final in which England beat Portugal.

This afternoon, at Wembley, England won the 1966 World Cup by beating West Germany, 4–2. The scores were level, 2–2, after 90 minutes, West Germany equalising in the last minute, and so half an hour of extra time had to be played.

Geoff Hurst scored two more goals to complete his hat-trick and England were home and Alf Ramsey's prophesy [*sic*] of three years ago that England would win had come true. For the first time in these championships, the crowd chanted his name.

England won the toss and chose to kick towards the players' tunnel, though there was little sun. The pitch was damp from rain half an hour before the kick-off, and the air was humid.

Hurst was heavily tackled by Schultz in the first minute, and Peters had a chance, but did not catch the ball right. At the other end, Held had a chance, but was ruled off-side. Both West Germany and England were attacking fast from the start.

HUNT TOO SLOW

Hunt was too slow on a difficult chance after excellent approach work by Stiles and Ball with just on five minutes played. In the eighth minute a great centre from Stiles went over Tilkowski's head, but Hunt could not reach it. Bobby Charlton lobbed the ball back and Hurst only just failed to beat Tilkowski to it. The German goalkeeper appeared to be knocked out in the collision, though the referee did not give a free kick.

Peters had a lovely shot deflected round the post, showing that Tilkowski suffered no real harm, but from the corner Hurst mishit a wonderful chance. Schnellinger twice failed to get the ball in tackles on Ball and from his final pass Peters again shot wide.

CRUCIAL FIRST GOAL

A bad clearance in the thirteenth minute led to West Germany gaining the crucial first goal. Wilson very badly misjudged a ball, hitting it straight to Haller, who moved a step and shot quickly under Banks's dive. Thus a situation had arisen which England had not so far faced in this World Cup: they were behind, and it now remained to be seen whether they could fight back from such a position. The goal was all the more disheartening for them, since, until then, they had been well on top.

The answer came within six minutes. Overath was pulled up for the second time for a foul, being warned by the referee, and Moore very quickly took the free kick. It was directly to the head of Hurst, running in, and the West Ham player easily beat Tilkowski with his header. So it was one-all, and England were again attacking with all their old confidence.

Peters was warned for a foul on Overath, and from that free kick Seeler headed into Banks's safe arms. Cohen had a blinder at a loose ball, but it went straight over in the traditional manner of full-back's free kicks.

West Germany were showing few imaginative ideas in attacks as at 25 minutes the sun came drizzlingly out. They relied on the forcefulness of Seeler through the middle, the short man getting up to a staggering height for his headers. Charlton had a shot going for the corner along the ground, but Tilkowski got down to it.

Both Moore and Wilson appealed to the referee for fouls against them, but they were not allowed. Yet when Jackie Charlton made a fine tackle the referee was so impressed by Emmerich's nose dive that he gave the West Germans a free kick. Allegations of unnecessary histrionics on the part of the West Germans appear not to be without foundation. Moore was playing a great game in the English defence, but his shooting was not in the same class, as he shot over just on half-time.

WONDERFUL ATTACK

A wonderful England attack, composed of 20 moves without a West German touching the ball, ended with Hurst heading a ball Tilkowski could not hold, Hunt cutting it back but the German defence desperately clearing for a throw-in. It was a great movement, full of grace and power, and it deserved a better fate.

BANKS BRILLIANT

Cohen caused symptoms of heart failure amongst the English supporters as he dallied too long with the ball, lost it, regained it and finally lost it for Jack Charlton to save the day with a slide for a corner. But from the corner Held sent in a great shot that Banks did well to see, let alone punch away, and then Emmerich smashed in the rebound only to see Banks make yet another great save and hold the ball this time.

A magnificent tackle by Moore took the ball away from Emmerich in the 42nd minute when the German was clean through. Hunt had a marvellous chance to put England up shortly afterwards, but shot straight at the goalkeeper from four yards. Seeler had a fine long shot well saved by Banks and the match boiled towards half-time with both teams attacking and counterattacking.

Already it had been a great final on the strength of the first half alone. Surely the second could not live up to it, surely one team must crack first at this cracking pace?

As the teams came out for the second half umbrellas were up round the narrow band of the pitch exposed to the light rain. From the kick-off England went surging through, and with a little more luck in the run of the ball Bobby Charlton would have had another goal. The only thing that seemed likely to spoil the spectacle now was the state of the pitch, which was becoming muddy. England were attacking three times for Germany's one, and both Wilson and Cohen were making dangerous thrusts down the wings. But still England lacked fire power in the middle through the weakness of Hurst and Hunt.

Jack Charlton was tackling well, and the defence in general containing the Germans. Beckenbauer had a shot but the English snuffed all the power and direction out of it.

But it was noticeable that both sides were not playing now as fast as in the first half, both pacing themselves now.

Both Tilkowski and Banks saved high shots safely, and Moore made one superb aerial interception to relieve his defence. Peters had two following-up shots, and good chances they were, too, but each was off-target.

Jack Charlton just failed to carbon copy the first England goal from Moore's free-kick, after Hunt had been fouled, but with three-quarters of the match gone it was Germany who were now doing slightly more of the attacking.

STILES CAUTIONED

Stiles was cautioned for a tackle on Haller after 69 minutes, but protested his innocence strongly.

There were more theatricals from the Germans three minutes later when Tilkowski again starred in a goalline drama, but again the referee was not interested in awarding a foul.

England came back and Bobby Charlton missed a fine chance to give England the lead. Yet another high cross was nodded on but from a narrow angle Charlton shot just wide with the goalkeeper beaten. Hunt put Hurst through, but Hurst let the ball run too far and Hottges gained possession. Schultz charged down Bobby Charlton's first left foot special of the match, and Held hit Banks' side-netting. The German defence was the first to crack, so it resolved itself in the 32nd minute. A cross by Moore was confusedly dealt with by Schultz, the ball glancing up off his head into the middle, where a group of three England players stood unmarked. But it was to Peters that the ball ran naturally and it was Peters who hit it unstoppably past Tilkowski from just five or six yards out. England were in the lead with only 13 minutes between them and winning the World Cup for the first time ever.

West Germany had a chance to draw level five minutes from time when a free kick was given against Stiles. But Emmerich glanced the subtle chip well wide of Banks's goal anticlimactically.

Beckenbauer, who has scored four goals in this World Cup, started a great run to try to bring his side on equal terms again, but Moore stopped him beautifully and started an attack which ended up with Charlton shooting wide, after being slightly impeded. Overath took his time about a shot and Ball rushed in to rob him, and then it happened.

A free kick was given against Jack Charlton for heading and leaning over a German. From this the ball bobbed about in the English goal-mouth and finally Weber put it in from close range to bring Germany level two-all. This happened in the very last minute. Germany thereby won the right to half an hour's extra time. England could legitimately claim that the free kick decision was a harsh one, but nothing can excuse them not clearing the ball after it had been taken.

So, after five minutes' rest, the match was on again and Wembley buzzed with the excitement of it all. Ball made a fine run and ended with a long shot that Tilkowski did well to push over the bar. Charlton had a shot saved just on the line, almost stealing into the net until Tilkowski went down full length for it. Hunt bored determinedly into the German penalty area and shot just wide from 20 yards. All this in the first four minutes of extra time!

Haller cut one back across the English goal with the defence beaten, but England counterattacked strongly. In the tenth minute of extra time fine approach work gave England a chance, but yet again the ball ended up with Hurst apparently about to waste the chance. But no, he beat his man, turned and shot to beat Tilkowski. The shot hit the bar, bounced down over the line and out again due to its spin and a German defender kicked it clear. At first it seemed as though the referee was waving play on, but he was persuaded to consult the linesman and then ruled that the ball had indeed crossed the line and that England were back in the lead, 3–2.

When the players broke at half-time in extra time after 15 minutes (105 minutes played) Wilson was seen to be receiving attention for an injury. But this did not affect the English defence, which covered and cleared with as great efficiency as ever.

Could this incredible (the word for once is justified) match take yet another dramatic turn? The Germans attacked sullenly now, Schultz coming up from defence to make a manoeuvre. The English kept them at a distance, and when shots did not go over they were safely gathered into the hands of Banks.

Seeler was reduced to operating on the periphery, a tubby lone figure out on the right wing. Haller gave Emmerich a difficult chance, but the ball went for a goal kick with four minutes of the match left. The Germans did not look like getting the goal that would mean a replayed match next Tuesday, but then they did not look like getting the goal they got to give them extra time, either.

A last Held shot held by Banks easily, the police cordon forming itself round the pitch against God knows what excesses, a last corner for Germany punched away by Banks and then a last attack by England in which Hurst completed his hat-trick to make the score 4–2 with the last kick of the match, the final miraculous twist of a great World Cup final.

There is also a short, poignant, undated and unpublished poem from this period which nicely conveys Johnson's sense of football as a paradigm of (to use his own favourite terminology) 'the human condition'.

96: POEM (1966)

World Cup shot

I must have seen it forty times:
Taking the ball past one, another,
Stumbling, recovering, scoring

Always I want the defeated full back
to stop him

Ah, the chances let slip!

Did he see his work on the World Cup film as a 'chance let slip', or as yet one more instance of other people's treachery and inability to recognize his talents? Certainly his first two brushes with the film world – on Senoret's film and on Irving Allen's *The Savage Canary* – had been frustrating. But any novelist who has tried his hand at screenwriting would have similar stories to tell. Johnson and the commercial film world simply didn't understand each other, and (as seems perfectly obvious in retrospect) never would. At around this time he drafted a letter to John Osborne (in his capacity as a director of Woodfall Films). 'I write in despair,' it began. 'My novel *Travelling People* would make a great film (it says something relevant about the stupid, unscrupulous affluent, for crissake, at the very least) and no one has even made an offer for it in the 3 years since it was published. You're the only man/Woodfall are the only company [...]' The draft tails off at this point, and it's not clear whether Johnson ever finished the letter and sent it. But he did make another approach a few days after the World Cup final, this time one that would bear fruit: an approach (significantly) to a different sector of the film business – the publicly funded sector – where he found himself dealing at last with people who were roughly on his own wavelength.

97: LETTER *(9 August 1966)*

To Stanley Reed [Director, British Film Institute]

> – I was delighted to hear that the Experimental Film Fund has been revived.
> – I'm an experimental novelist whose work has been very highly praised: see the sample review attached.
> – I've had two very nasty (for a writer) experiences of working in commercial films.
> – I long to have the chance to do real work in the cinema, on however small a scale, as like Robbe-Grillet I feel the medium to be potentially more satisfactory than the novel.
> – Can the Experimental Film Fund help me?
> – Very succinctly put!
> Yours sincerely

Things moved on very quickly after this. Johnson was immediately invited to the BFI for a screening of some recent experimental shorts and to meet Bruce Beresford, then the head of the production board. Beresford, like Johnson, was a robust intellectual with a down-to-earth sense of humour: in a few years' time he would begin to make his own reputation as a director with that lovably filthy celebration of Ocker culture, *The Adventures of Barry MacKenzie*. The two men hit it off at once. Johnson went away to try to come up with an idea for a short film, and soon saw an opportunity for a little bit of creative recycling.

98: LETTER *(21 August 1966)*

To Bruce Beresford

Got it! Why didn't I think of it before?

The words/images bit in Don Levy's short film reminded me that I'd eighteen months ago tried to use verse legitimately, for our time, in the theatre: in YOU'RE HUMAN LIKE THE REST OF THEM.

This short (15–20 minutes) play was written for the Royal Shakespeare Company's programme EXPEDITIONS III (were you here when they put on I and II, evenings made up of short experimental pieces by various writers?). One of the greatest things ever to happen to me was when they (Peter Hall and Jeremy Brooks) wrote and said they liked my novels and would I write them a short stage play. YOU'RE HUMAN was the result: they liked it, bought a year's option, and then EXPEDITIONS III was cancelled through lack of money.

This isn't the time to talk about the play's technique (I think you have to like or dislike it for what it says, rather) but I will just say that the stroke at the end of each line indicates a pause: the line unit is ten syllables spoken regularly, with no break even if two or more speakers share the line.

When I remembered this piece (the evening after seeing you) I became very excited: I think it will make a far better film than a stage play, and I've already thought of various ways of doing things. Of course the whole thing will have to be re-interpreted, but as printed it forms a workable basis, I feel.

I hope you'll be as excited about it as I am: in any case, could you let me have your initial reaction as soon as possible?

The initial reaction was good. The BFI production board met on 28 September and agreed to stump up fifty pounds for Johnson to make a test sequence, which would have to be ready for them to view on 15 December. If they liked it, he could then have the money to make the whole film. And so Johnson looked set to add yet another string to his bow: a new sideline as a film director beckoned.

Meanwhile *Trawl* was about to be published, and Frederic Warburg was beginning to feel a growing frustration (expressed, as always, in a good-natured way) with his troublesome author, whose inflexible literary theories did not appear to sit comfortably with any profit-led concept of publishing. The paperback rights had been sold to Panther, but not for the £750 that Johnson had in mind. Why not? he wanted to know. Warburg replied:

You ask why James Price wants to accept a low paperback advance. The answer is that he does not want to accept a low paperback advance but that so far he has not succeeded in getting a high paperback advance. Nothing has yet been accepted. It appears that Penguin do not love you overmuch because they feel you were very rude to them in the past. I know nothing of this but no doubt you will have a memory. The advance offered of £350 is at least better than the advance you got on your previous book. *Trawl* would appear to be an extremely difficult book to sell, either in hard or soft covers, and this is the reason for the advance. Literary merit is not a good test for paperback sales. Nor for hardcover sales in the ordinary course of events. Your ideas about how novels should be written are, if not unique, at least held by a tiny, but tiny minority. Novels often described as fiction are usually fiction, but you are horrified at the idea of incorporating what you call 'lies' in your novels which tends to make them equivalent to a slightly unusual form of autobiography.

We shall all have to wait and see what happens when we publish *Trawl* and maybe it will be a big success, financially I mean. If not, maybe your second novel under the contract will be a great financial success. That obviously depends on what kind of autobiography you propose for the next novel, about which I have no knowledge.* If, however, at the end of our contract we are in the red to a substantial extent, as I think not improbable, I shall (of course!) remind you of your promise to write us a brilliant bunch of lies which we shall describe as fiction, which it will be, and you will consider presumably a vulgar pandering to an ill-informed public.

Devotedly, Fred.

Proof copies of *Trawl* had by now arrived, and the author busied himself sending out copies to friends. One of the first people to write back was Edward Lucie-Smith, at whose Chelsea house Johnson had, a few years ago, attended some of the Group poetry readings. Lucie-Smith was highly enthusiastic about the book – he thought it was the best thing Johnson had done so far – but did express doubts about how much longer he could continue drawing on his own experience without resorting to fictional invention at all.

99: LETTER *(23 September 1966)*

To Edward Lucie-Smith

Dear Teddy:

Thanks very much for your kind letter and generous praise for TRAWL: it came just when I needed it. As for your question as to

---

* Johnson marked this sentence in green ink.

how long I can write this sort of novel ... it's one I've asked myself long ago, of course. And in a practical sense I've never had to answer it because I've always had at least two novels ahead: and at the moment have three. The trouble is I don't like writing *fiction*: I like writing the truth. I had a disagreement with Fred Warburg when I delivered this novel, over terminology: he thinks fiction and novel are synonymous terms. While to me the novel is a form in which I may write truth or fiction. I really do believe that everything is in a sense autobiographical: one can't push anything out that hasn't gone in some way or another. And so called inventions (i.e. that which I haven't experienced) are just impossible for me to believe in when I write them down: though other people may not be able to tell the difference, I certainly can, and am unwilling to write in that way. It may be that one day I shall reach a position where I have to invent: but I can't see it. With TRAWL, I had the reverie bit: the idea for the novel, if you like, was the seagoing bit which, in 1962, when the idea came, I didn't have. So I went and did it, went on a distant-water trawler for three weeks in order to be able to write about it as convincingly as I could. Perhaps this represents an intermediate stage away from pure autobiography: deliberately exposing myself to an experience in order to write about it, rather than having the experience and having to write about it to expiate or evacuate it. So the answer to your question comes in two parts (1) As far as I can tell at the moment, with three more I want very much to write, I'm not boxed in for at least the next three years: even if I had the money to devote myself entirely to novels, which looks most unlikely: so for the next five years I have material, possibly longer, that I can actually see. (2) If ever I am out of material, I shall just go and find it (as Hemingway did – to his loss, I feel): as I have partially done with TRAWL. And (thought of a third) (3) There is always an extension of Beckett I've always thought I'd like to try: say more or less on the first page "I'm going to write a novel – don't know what's going to be on the next page, let alone in the middle, the end: but fear not gentle reader, I have written novels before, you're in fairly safe hands." And just go on, and after 250 pages stop, and see if it *is* a novel. If it is, leave it exactly as it is; if not, chuck it.

But (paragraph at last!) anything could happen disastrously to upset the next few years: this is just how I feel *now*.

[...]

Thanks again for your kindness: and your sureness that I will be successful comforted me at a time when I had recently (over the world cup film) fallen amongst thieves: if I hadn't had the Secker contract, I would have been back teaching this term.

It wasn't the first (or the last) time that someone had written to Johnson upon publication of a novel, expressing admiration but also a sort of friendly concern for his literary well-being, a well-meaning anxiety about the extremism of his theories and where they might lead him. Johnson inspired great affection in most of those who knew him, and you get the sense that even those friends he had left behind were still watching over him: every new novel was keenly anticipated, not just for itself but because it would serve as the latest bulletin on an aesthetic (and personal) progress which was regarded by many as fraught with danger and frustration. People were troubled by his growing entrenchment.

And his theories, although they had not changed (Johnson's thinking never seemed to *evolve*, there was no organic growth, just a final, inflexible position), were reaching a wider and wider public. A lecture he had originally delivered in Belfast in 1964 – and which itself incorporated most of his 'Notes' on *Albert Angelo* – had been expanded into a radio talk called 'Holes, Syllabics and the Succussations of the Intercostal and Abdominal Muscles'. (Well, he always did have a penchant for long titles – although this is perhaps the least catchy of the lot.) Much to his annoyance, the BBC had declined to broadcast it, and it had finally appeared in the second number of a small Belfast literary magazine called the *Northern Review*. Apart from the space it devotes to a justification of syllabics in poetry, it reads very much like a dry run for the introduction to *Aren't You Rather Young To Be Writing Your Memoirs?*. And an article which appeared in the October 1966 edition of *Vogue* is even closer to that legendary polemic. Published, presumably, to coincide with the appearance of *Trawl*, it rams home all of the usual points: Joyce is the Einstein of the novel, 'telling stories is telling lies', the curiosity of the reader to know what happens next is 'primitive, vulgar and idle' and the author who relies on it is no different from 'the stranger who tells you the story of his troubles in a pub'; here, too, is the story of the Australian customs officer who impounded copies of *Albert Angelo*, believing that obscenities had been cut out, and the black-paged review copy of *Travelling People* being returned as faulty by a national newspaper – 'admittedly one known for its reactionary opinions'. The version published in *Aren't You Rather Young To Be Writing Your Memoirs?* is longer, and contains more specific discussion of Johnson's novels. But the *Vogue* article shows that, both in substance and in his manner of arguing them, Johnson's ideas would not shift even slightly in the intervening seven years.

In response to this article, Johnson received a letter. It was a formidable, challenging letter: so much so, in fact, that I thought it worthwhile to obtain its author's permission to quote it in full. It was from Gordon Williams, the author of two novels for Secker & Warburg, *The Last Day of Lincoln Charles* (1965) and *The Camp* (1966). Soon, Williams would go on to write *From*

Scenes Like These (shortlisted for the first Booker prize in 1969) and *The Siege of Trencher's Farm* (filmed by Sam Peckinpah as the notorious *Straw Dogs*). A hardworking journalist and a working-class Scot with solid socialist principles, he had plenty in common with Johnson: but he was no 'experimentalist'. Taking issue, first of all, with the article's championship of James Joyce as a contemporary role model, this was the letter he wrote on 18 October 1966:

Dear BS,

I found your books 'impressive' but I don't see why you have to formalise your own defensive nature into a Vogue philosophy on the "novel".

There is nothing *modern* about a writer of forty years ago. If language means anything at all this is an impossibility. What you seem to be doing is putting up a spirited justification for an increasing tendency among contemporary writers to shrug off real problems and bury their heads in a desert of introspection and narcissism. For a man who put black pages (the ultimate, I suppose, in anti-language) in his novels it is surely a bit much for you to claim that you are on the side of Joyce, of all people?

A novel is no more a specific category than, say, a 'television programme'. It depends on what your talent and inclination leads to – and in turn those depend on what it is you are trying to say. Words must say something, otherwise they are wallpaper.

Personally I am inclined to a commitment on the side of humanity. In a starving world riddled with wars and torture and the frustration of human life (let alone happiness) I see no justification *for me at least* to write books that merely prove what a fine writer I am. Even if I was a fine writer, which I am not, but I have no desire to work at it.

Has it occurred to you that your attitude (as expressed in the Vogue article – which is a different attitude from your books) is sure to lead us to a state of affairs where art is in the hands of esoteric coteries – the very thing that's suffocated most English writing in the past?

If there is any hope for writing and/or the writer it is to stop seeing life as a battleground of techniques and for writers to get back into the mainstream of life as it is lived by people. I agree that our mainstream novelists are a sad and dreary lot but for a different reason – they cling to the techniques of Dickens without realising that his technique sprang from his contact with life.

If I may remain on this somewhat knockabout level (prompted, I may add, by a sincere belief that you are one of the few contemporary novelists who *might* free yourself from all this technical twaddle) what you are setting yourself up as in this article is a glorified school-of-writing instructor.

You are *not* saying let us break up the dusty edifice of rules. You seem to be advocating a new set of rules. Only bad art follows preconceived patterns. Your rules may have the attraction of an experimental gloss, but the dust will settle on them sooner or later.

We're all in this for different reasons but the common denominator would seem to be a desire (or compulsion) to write. I would like to write books that communicate criticisms of life, criticisms that can perhaps be crystallised only in a novel form, crystallised, that is, for the reader. One may use tricks of narrative to keep the reader interested, but this is to make sure he gets the message. And having brought in that dirty word may I put it to you that the 'message' inherent in your arguments is purely one of self-proclamation? Is this, the process of proving that you are a real artist, any more high or low-minded than being David Jacobs?

Mind you, I don't really think that the Vogue article represents the spectrum of your own attitudes as shown in your books. I hope not anyway. There is a weight of incomprehension and prejudice facing anybody who tries something new in the novel. Your article would seem to me, to be merely substituting a new face of prejudice.

Yours fraternally,

Gordon Williams.

P.S. This is meant to be a friendly letter.

100: LETTER *(21 October 1966)*

To Gordon Williams

Your letter is so full of inconsistencies and apparent misreadings of the piece in VOGUE that I hardly know where to start to answer you. But had better say as well that this is a friendly letter, too, and I'm not trying to prove I'm right but to find out whether I am.

I nowhere said or even implied Joyce was a modern writer: indeed towards the end of the article I made it clear that there were writing problems today which did not exist even in Joyce's time. I did say he was revolutionary/modern forty years ago, but that the revolution he caused had been largely ignored by subsequent writers: why don't you read more carefully?

As for the *real problem* bit – what for crissake *is* a 'real' problem? One you have yourself? Or Vietnam? or what? Are not introspection and narcissism real problems for those suffering from them? Merely because you don't (apparently) suffer them doesn't make them any the less real for those who do. And you can't accuse me of either: TP is about old age, illusion and reality: AA is about truth and the human condition: TRAWL is about the philosophical problem of everyone's basic isolation (man is a windowless monad – Liebniz). So what are you on about, buster?

It seems strange to have to explain (I disdain to defend) the black pages in TP. You just haven't understood the problem, which is what I was complaining about in the article. The section in question is taking place in interior monologue, in the man's mind, right? So how in words can you convey he's dead? He can't *say* after the event I'm dead, now can he? How would you have dealt with this problem? Is not this simple device the best solution to the problem? You can't even see the problem as far as I can see. Every device I use has an organic, empirical justification.

This phrase 'commitment on the side of humanity' trots out so often. Can't you see it is meaningless? Everyone living is committed to humanity, being human: and that includes everyone you and I hate, disagree with, the bad writers, the lot. They're all *human* for crissake: you must be using 'humanity' in some special sense: why don't you make yourself clear? Which special bit of humanity are you talking about, on the side of?

I do not write books 'merely to prove what a fine writer I am'. I write books to say the things I mentioned above, and I do so to the best of my ability: that this ability makes me in your eyes a 'fine writer' I take as a compliment, and understand your envy. Apart from that, why shouldn't a book both say something and be well written, eh?

As for coteries, they usually just exist in the minds of poor or failed writers. I know of no coteries in London writing, that I'd call by that name. I belong to none of them: I have been a failure at every group action I've ever tried to join, from the boy scouts onwards. That's inconsistent: what you call coteries exist: but where's your evidence of the harm, except that you're not (apparently) in one?

For crissake, I *live* my life as it is lived by people – can't you see this again is as meaningless a statement as the other one? Which people are you talking about? The working class? I see my parents every week, am still working class myself in most of reactions. Anyone living is 'in contact with life': again, you must be using 'life' in a special sense: why don't you make yourself clear? Which particular bit of life are you committed to, which bit don't you approve of?

Very good crack about 'glorified school-of-writing instructor': partly deserved: I am didactic: if one says anything with any force one risks being called a teacher.

But you really do misread. I'm not advocating a new set of rules – wherever did you get that? I said that 'it is a matter of realising that the novel is an evolving form, that it is simply not worth writing (let alone publishing) anything which has been done before: of accepting that for practical purposes where Joyce left off is a starting point.' What's that, if not advocating change, a fresh look? Where do I set up new rules? You seem in a fair old state, projecting your pet hates on to me as if I held them.

Of course I shall become outdated in my turn. But now I am of my time, in both material and technique: and there are very few novelists of whom you can say the same.

Is it not an enormous act of self-proclamation to set yourself up as a critic of life? Who are you, for crissake? God? Look, every act of writing which is shown to someone else is the greatest act of conceit I know: and that includes your letter and my article. All writing is self-proclamation, and you bloody know it: to accuse me of it as though it did not apply to you as well is grossest hypocrisy. And I don't have 'to prove I am a real artist' by writing in Vogue: my novels, poetry, short stories, plays do that for me or they do nothing. It doesn't worry me, anyway: it was settled for me a long while ago, and if it's not settled for others, well, tough bananas, ignorance is rife.

Almost finally, perhaps you will consider this if you think my ideas are wrong. Do you think there is anything *new* to be said about being human? My reading of past and present literature inclines me to the view that there is not: there is no new material, therefore. It follows logically that therefore the only way to do something new in writing is in finding better ways of saying the same things: in this, my position is that of Pope and the Augustans:

What oft was thought, but ne'er so well expressed.

I may be wrong: you may think you know something which no one has ever thought of before: but even if you do, does that excuse you from expressing it at the very highest level?

In mitigation, the way I wrote for VOGUE is not the way I wrote about my ideas in a little magazine called NORTHERN REVIEW. When the writers I mentioned, and the ideas, become accepted in the same way as the establishment as your Greenes and Amises, then I think you could legitimately accuse us of substituting a 'new face of prejudice': as things are at the moment, the charge is just a cheap jibe and shows yet further you have not read the article properly.

After which.

Are you the Gordon Williams I used to know on SCENE? And whose novel THE CAMP I keep picking up when waiting the pleasure of Secker and Warburg in the waiting alley? I'm sure you must be, and a Scot, to boot. Let's have a drink some time? If you're not too furious at the above. I've just wasted the whole of my sodding writing morning on you, anyway.

Yours

Well, it's clear from Johnson's diction ('buster', 'eh?' and no fewer than four usages of 'for crissake') that he was seriously riled. More correspondence ensued, including this from Gordon Williams about a month later, on 24 November:

Dear Brian [*sic*]

I have not been in touch because I wanted to read *Trawl* and be suitably briefed for any skirmishing that might take place. I am about halfway through and I must say that your trumpet blast on behalf of experimentalism seems, now, to have been the last despairing howl of a sinking radical. By this I mean that *Trawl* – unless the latter stages are different – is getting as near the fringes of mainstream novel writing as makes little difference.

Some guy wrote recently that some of our *best* novelists cannot write. I'm sure this doesn't bear analysis, yet there is a suggestion in this statement of the very problem you aired in *Vogue* (I think it was the placing of your argument in that magazine which excited me to attack). I cannot remember ever reading such a true description of what it is like to be a boy as in *Trawl* (Brotton); the same applies to the shagging campaign in your first flashback. In fact, I would, without facetiousness, say that your writing, when you give it a fair chance, is about the only real (as opposed to stylised) stuff I've read from a 'contemporary British novelist'.

I think that *Trawl* is some justification for my irritable criticisms of your *Vogue* argument. For the first time you seem to be giving yourself a chance – perhaps the first time you've taken yourself seriously. *Albert Angelo*, to my mind, was spoiled by intellectualism, and that self-destructive ending came across as an admission of this. For a working-class protagonist you certainly revealed a strong leaning towards the flippant, self-deprecating attitude which marks the style of the *other* class. In your first book I was continually irritated by what appeared to me to be wilful obscurantism. Whether you agree or not, these 'experimental' devices give me the impression of having been grafted on artificially – almost as though your contact with the culture market made you think that you had to put up a display of avant-gardism. [...]

When I say that *Trawl* is not experimental, I am sticking out my tongue and cackling ya-ya I told you so. Experiment that means anything comes from inside. Attempts to formalise it into didactic public addresses must necessarily *look* either like bandwagon jumping (fashion being the art of labelling tomorrow's stray impulses as a trend) or slightly desperate efforts to convince oneself that one is doing the right thing. My view is that any writer with a conscience is entitled to wrestle publicly with his attitudes *in his books*. I think one might even be allowed two or three books in which one's internal arguments about the nature of books themselves dominated other considerations. Sooner or later, however, you have to get onto questions of a more serious nature: What are you saying? Does your writing prove you have any right to say it? To whom are you addressing yourself?

Somewhere in this area arise such stray thoughts as the subject of *Albert Angelo*. An artist (and for a devoted experimentalist I thought your choice of a frustrated *architect* might be significant) in a bad period? Do I sound like a pamphleteer when I say that your glimpses of our educational system made that individual's personal problems seem of small importance? We've had many books about the state of London schools – but not, I think, from a writer. Do I sound like the CND lobby when I say that this is a case where self seems criminally narcissistic? Who is going to speak out for these children if not you? Isn't this the crux of our original argument – of course your problems are human and important, but in this context they do have a strong let-them-eat-cake flavour.

Artists are already far enough separated from humanity as a whole without taking their art to that remote and exclusive pinnacle where the only problems that matter are those of being an artist [. . .]

I have quoted this correspondence at such length because here, at last, we get to the crux of Williams's argument and to the strongest possible statement of the case against B. S. Johnson. It has nothing to do with whether or not his 'experimentalism' is justified: anyone can see, I would have thought, that his ceaseless quest for new forms and devices was an intrinsic part of his artistic temperament and that to require him to write 'conventional' novels would have been as pointless as asking him to write them in Serbo-Croat. It's to do, rather, with the subject matter of his books and whether they say anything meaningful or not. Is it not self-indulgent, as Williams argues, to set your novel in a tough London school and concentrate on the emotional hardships of a well-educated teacher? Or to set it on a deep-sea trawler – in one of the most gruelling and dangerous industries in the country – and focus almost entirely on the romantic disappointments of a protagonist who has a comfortable intellectual life in London to return to in three weeks' time? Were not the crew of the *Northern Jewel* entirely justified, in other words, in referring to Johnson as a 'pleasuretripper'?

Johnson's responses would have been – in fact they *were* – that 'introspection and narcissism [are] real problems for those suffering from them', and that, on a deeper level, the theme of his books was 'the human condition': a condition which he believed to be predicated on isolation and the fickleness of other human beings, the human body and the physical world generally, and which was therefore as much of a problem for a semi-illiterate Cypriot schoolboy or the skipper of a Grimsby trawler as it was for himself. But I wonder how satisfied he was, at heart, with his own position. Of all the many memorable passages in his books, one that haunts me with peculiar intensity is the moment when Christie Malry tells his narrator/creator, 'You shouldn't be bloody writing novels about it, you should be out there bloody doing something about it'. It reminds me of Thomas Hardy sitting at his desk being watched over by the accusing moon, which tells him, 'I am curious to look / Into the blinkered mind / Of one who wants to write a book / In a world of such a kind.' In a world riddled with misery and injustice, is writing novels a responsible act? Johnson's consciousness that we live in such a world was acute; at the same time, he absorbed that consciousness and subsumed it into a more solipsistic, personalized sense of his *own* victimization and misfortune. The general shittiness of the world became just one more burdensome problem that he, as an individual, had to recognize and cope with. I believe it was only in *Christie Malry's Own Double-Entry* – a novel about 'doubleness' in many different senses – that he started to confront, as an artist, this duality, this *simultaneous* awareness of injustice as both a social and a personal phenomenon, and his attempt in that novel to forge a relationship between the two results merely in disintegration and breakdown. *Christie Malry* poses the question: should a man be condemned for killing 20,000 innocent Londoners because 'socialism has not been given a chance' and he feels this as keenly as any personal insult? Johnson doesn't say that he should. (Nor does he describe these Londoners as 'innocent'. In fact he implies that they are complicit with a corrupt social system.)

If we finally encounter, in *Christie Malry*, a clear expression of the political philosophy towards which Johnson's senses of personal and global injustice had for years been driving him, it turns out to be an impossibly extreme one, and one which presented him with unenviable alternatives: terrorism or madness, basically. By the time Gordon Williams threw down his gauntlet in response to *Trawl*, Johnson hadn't yet arrived at this point, but we can tell, from the way he thrashes and writhes under Williams's questioning that deep down he feels the insufficiency of the position he has reached in those first three novels. It is dangerous, I can't help feeling, for a writer to question his own motives and procedures quite so ruthlessly: but also courageous, and therefore (in Johnson's case) entirely typical. As for Gordon Williams's observation that *Trawl* was getting 'as near the fringes of mainstream novel writing as makes little difference', that would have galled him, too. It was true that there was nothing especially original about the mode of interior monologue with which he currently felt comfortable: but something could easily be done about that. It was time to upset the apple cart again, and go for his most radical experiment yet.

THE LAUREATE OF SCUNTHORPE-ON-LOIRE

Trawl was published on 7 November 1966, and, more than either of Johnson's previous novels, it split reviewers down the middle. The *Guardian* named it their 'Fiction [*sic!*] of the Month' and announced that 'Mr Johnson has grown up as a writer, and is getting down to business [. . .] What he has learned from the rhythms of Beckett's prose has put muscle into his own.' The anonymous *Times* reviewer found it 'both entertaining and artistically satisfying'. The *Evening Standard* thought the maritime scenes 'vividly-described in semi-blank verse' and admired the courage of the narrator, 'while watching the gutting, wrestling with sea-sickness and piles'. (Someone should really do a thesis on haemorrhoids in the work of B. S. Johnson. In fact, someone probably already has.) Perhaps appropriately for a book that collapses the distinction between novel and autobiography, what some of the most perceptive reviewers found themselves writing was not literary criticism but character analysis of Johnson himself: Phyllis Bentley in the *Yorkshire Post* wrote that 'The chip on his shoulder is as large as the ship; he can extract humiliation from the most unlikely sources'; while Montague Haltrecht in the *Sunday Times* concluded that Johnson was essentially a sentimentalist: 'I wonder [. . .] if the heart of the matter is not something simpler, if it does not lie, in fact, in the hero's quest for an ideal, romantic love-relationship, rather than in his earnest obsession with the problem of isolation.'

The loudest dissenting voices came from Hilary Corke in the *Listener* (who considered the portrait of the narrator 'dragging up memories from his deeps while the nets drag up fish' to be 'a crude bit of off-the-peg tickle-the-customer symbolism if ever I saw one') and from one of Johnson's most inveterate critical enemies, Martin Seymour-Smith in the *Oxford Mail*, who accused the book of 'pointless straining after a spurious technical original-ity', and added – in an admittedly clever bit of phrase-making – 'the effect is one of Dorothy Richardson writing about merchant seamen'.

Well, as someone who could 'extract humiliation from the most unlikely sources', Johnson probably smarted a good deal when he read some of this.

At the same time, however, he would soon be provided with a great (and long hoped-for) piece of comfort: namely, the knowledge that the great Samuel Beckett himself – a man, in his view, who made the weekly novel reviewers look like moral and intellectual pygmies – was no longer just a literary hero to him, but a personal acquaintance. After years of sending him copies of all his books, and writing fan letters, Johnson had finally persuaded Beckett to meet him in Paris. He and Virginia travelled over there in early December 1966 – hoping to meet Alain Resnais on the same trip, although I don't believe this ever happened.* To Johnson this became an enormously important friendship; how important it was to Beckett himself is, of course, difficult to gauge, since he was notoriously guarded in his personal relationships. Certainly he and Johnson met many more times in Paris over the next five years, to drink whiskey and play billiards together. His letters and postcards to Johnson are brief and functionally worded, but again, that was in the nature of the man. He wrote enthusiastically on Johnson's behalf in support of an Arts Council grant application,† and, when he learned in the early 1970s that Johnson was so hard up that he was considering putting his letters from Beckett up for auction at Sotheby's, he told him not to and sent him a cheque instead.‡ And his letter of consolation to Virginia when Johnson killed himself was quick to come, and deeply felt. Personally I think there was more to the friendship, on Beckett's part, than writerly courtesy. A Hungarian friend, István Bart, once observed them together: 'I met Beckett in Paris once, for twenty-five minutes, through Bryan. Beckett was playing pool and he was very taciturn and didn't talk much, but Bryan was at ease with him. He talked to him like you would talk to an older uncle.' And after their second meeting, Johnson wrote to Zulfikar Ghose to say that 'When I opened the door to him, I was not prepared for his appearance though I'd of course met him before: he is a weird, startling man – not in a frightening sense, but just his intensity is so ... tense. I can't really describe him: I hope if you manage to come over I can arrange for you to meet him. Yet at the same time I don't think I've ever met anyone who is so humble.'[1]

The friendship of Beckett, his unfailing kindness and supportiveness, would become one of the cornerstones of Johnson's life. Another, even more

---

*   Virginia had drafted a letter on her monoglot husband's behalf, in which he described himself as 'partie du trop petit nombre d'écrivains "avant-garde" de ce pays', and proposed to Resnais 'une possible collaboration dans la domaine du cinéma.' It never led to anything. In 1971 he made a similar overture to Ken Russell; that never led to anything either.

†   See below, p. 328.

‡   This incident has been distorted, in Anthony Cronin's biography of Beckett, into the following myth: 'One of the recipients of his generosity was the experimental novelist B S Johnson, whose sports car was said to have been bought with Beckett's Nobel money.' Virginia strenuously denies this, insisting that the modest amount that Beckett donated was spent on supporting the family. In any case, Johnson had traded in his sports car for a family saloon by then.

important, was the fulfilment he continued to find in his marriage to Virginia. Of course, he was a difficult person to be married to, at times: but her most powerful memories, now, are not of a moody or temperamental person. 'He was a loyal and affectionate husband,' she says. 'He drew me into his life, taking me to places that held special importance for him. We had long talks about writing, and art, and architecture, and France, and Beckett, and politics, and ... everything, though the exception to this was that he would never talk about something he was working on, for fear of "talking out" the experiences he needed to keep for the book. I learned endlessly from him. He even made a book for me, *The Discovery of Virginia*, writing a special piece each year to put in it on our anniversary.'

On 26 November, before he and Virginia made their short trip to Paris together, Johnson had shot a brief test sequence for *You're Human Like the Rest of Them* at Hugh Myddelton School, Sans Walk, London EC1. The pupils used in the sequence were brought over from Ealing Mead School in west London, under the supervision of their English teacher – Zulfikar Ghose, as it happened. To add to the convivial, amateur atmosphere, when the test sequence had been approved and the complete film was shot in January, Johnson's good friends Barry Cole, Gordon Gridley and Gianni Zambardi-Mall would also be included in the cast. There would only be one professional actor in the whole film, in fact – a rising star from the Royal Court called William Hoyland, who would take the pivotal role of Haakon.

Hoyland remembers being slightly disconcerted when he saw the script, and discovered that it was written in blank verse. This was not, in his experience, what experimental 1960s theatre was supposed to be about: 'When Bryan said "It's in iambic pentameters", I thought – well I was, I have to say, very anti-iambic pentameters at that point in my career! We were the kind of actors who weren't interested in speaking received pronunciation in the way we'd been taught to. And then when he told me that he was planning to cut the film to the rhythm of the verse, and then always with a cut at the end of the line, and when the drama heightened every foot, and then every syllable, I thought, "This is madness, but it could be interesting".' Once again, we find that Johnson, despite thinking of himself as an avant-garde writer, could equally be perceived as a crusty old formalist by those who were more thoroughly caught up in the sixties counterculture.

'We shot the rest of the film the first week in January,' Johnson wrote, 'and it went perfectly except that on the second day we were told the lab had ruined the whole of the first day's shooting by scratching the negative – a great white line down the whole bloody thing [...] We had to work very much harder to get five days' shooting into the remaining four, but we did it. Got some great old men for the hospital scene – all over seventy-five, and dropping on their feet practically. One of them had arthritis and we had to move him from time to time as he got set in one position and that was that. I thought of a rather macabre credit for them: With the Assistance of the Late Messrs ... And if you think that's in bad taste (all the crew did) then You Just Don't Think About These Things Hard Enough. Bill Hoyland was rather upset by the old men, poor old sods, but, as I said to him, that's what the bloody play is all about.'[2]

Johnson's inexperience behind the camera created few problems because he had excellent back-up in the persons of David Muir (director of photography) and John Furse (art director), among others; also, Bruce Beresford and Stanley Reed were on the set most days to make sure that nothing went wrong. Bill Hoyland remembers: 'There was a bit of resistance to Bryan at first, because he hadn't made any films at all before, but Bruce was always around to interpret for him. Whenever the cameraman said something like, "Oh, you can't do that," Bryan would say, "Well, why can't you?" and they would talk it through and sure enough in fact he could do it, it was just that he'd never done it that way before. Apart from that, Bryan was ebullient, really enjoying it, and he gave good direction to me, certainly. The whole thing was great fun, as I remember it.'

How does *You're Human Like the Rest of Them* stand up, when viewed today? It sounds odd for William Hoyland to describe the shooting of it as 'great fun', when what survives from the experience is fifteen minutes of the most downbeat material ever committed to celluloid. (I wonder what the punters made of it when it ran for six weeks in the West End as support to Richard Lester's *Petulia*.) It's hard to detach yourself from what the film is saying and judge it on its technical merits. The editing – with a cut coming at every line-end (Johnson wanted it to be every syllable, but this proved unwatchable) – does create a strange, hypnotic rhythm, but this one-off experiment doesn't give much sense of how Johnson might have developed if he had been given, as he wished, further commissions to direct his own work at greater length. The film comes most *alive* when it breaks out of its formal constraints and Hoyland's performance is allowed to take wing, or in the occasional shots of schoolkids nattering to each other in conspiratorial, pre-class huddles. At moments like this, you begin to get a sense that Johnson might well have had a film-maker's instinct for capturing the spontaneous, organic texture of everyday life when he wasn't wrapped up in proving his cinematic and philosophical theses. The climax is powerful, but my own overwhelming response is to regard it as a case study in the depressive mindset, and to agree with Gordon Bowker in finding it far too 'pathologically morbid' to enjoy on any aesthetic level.

This morbidity is also one of the main characteristics of the novel Johnson was finally beginning to write at this time, after brooding on it for so long: *The Unfortunates*, his memorial to the life and death of Tony Tillinghast. I assume that the decision to write this book must have come only a few weeks after Tony's death in November 1964. Johnson always maintained that he had been inspired, first of all, by the random decision of the *Observer* sports editor to send him to report on a football match in Nottingham, the city he had come to know while visiting Tony and June there in the late 1950s. The only time I'm aware of his reporting on a Nottingham Forest home game was on Boxing Day, 1964, when he was sent up to cover Notts versus Spurs, which means that two years must have passed between getting the idea for the book and starting to write it: but that makes sense, because roughly the same time had elapsed between his voyage on the *Northern Jewel* and the writing of *Trawl*.

Whether the radical idea for the *form* of the novel came at the same time is not clear. Zulfikar Ghose remembers Johnson enthusing to him about the notion of unbound sections contained in a box as a tangible metaphor for randomness at a party given by Joe McCrindle, but he cannot date the incident.[3] When Johnson took the idea to Secker & Warburg some time in 1966, at any rate, it was not received with wild enthusiasm; David Farrer would later write to him to say that 'I personally think it is the wrong form',[4] and no doubt at the back of his mind (and the front of Fred Warburg's) was the certainty that it was going to be hellishly expensive to put into practice. Nonetheless, Johnson was not to be deterred. Unlike him, his editors had simply not thought the matter through: otherwise they would have seen – as he did – that the marriage between form and content in *The Unfortunates* had an inexorable logic. As Ghose puts it:

> He had been assigned that game by chance. He thought nothing about it until he stepped out of the railway station when he was over-whelmed by a personal emotion [...] Before he wrote [the novel], and while he was writing it, he discussed with me the form he had chosen. It was based on randomness, because that was the nature of cancer. The randomness that had led the author to write this novel had begun with the random decision on the part of the sports editor to assign him a game in Nottingham, and the game itself is a series of random moves where chance either makes the ball hit the crossbar or enter the net, and that led to his decision to insist on the shuffled pages of the text.[5]

The form of *The Unfortunates*, all the same, was not entirely original. Just as Malcolm Lowry's *Ultramarine* is a shadowy presence behind *Trawl*, and Philip Toynbee's *Tea with Mrs Goodman* anticipates some aspects of *House Mother Normal*, *The Unfortunates* finds Johnson not so much innovating as adapting somebody else's idea for his own ends. There can be no doubt that

he already knew of the existence of *Composition No. 1*, by Marc Saporta.*
This novel – featuring the stream of consciousness recollections of a car-
crash victim – had been published in Paris in the early 1960s, and translated
into English by Richard Howard in 1963. Although Howard's translation was
only ever published in America, by Simon & Schuster, the book's reputation
had extended to Britain: as early as October 1962, *Scene* magazine had
contained references to it in a piece by William G. Smith called 'Shuffle the
pages as You Will'; and since Johnson himself had an article about Beckett
published in the very same issue, he must surely have seen this, and been
aware, when he began work on *The Unfortunates* several years later, that his
boxed format was by no means unprecedented.

'The other fiction pioneer,' Smith had written (after discussing Burroughs's cut-up techniques), 'is the French Marc Saporta whose idea is that
the pages of a novel should be issued in an unbound stack which the
readers will be invited to shuffle around in any order they please.'⁶ The main
difference between *Composition No. 1* and *The Unfortunates*, in fact, is that
Saporta's novel is *entirely* loose-leaved, and every single page runs on to
every single other page, no matter what order you arrange them into.
Technically, this makes it a far more remarkable achievement than *The
Unfortunates*: but Johnson maintained – unsurprisingly – that his version
was superior. In August 1967, an academic from Warwick University called
Bernard Bergonzi wrote to him, enclosing a transcript of his talk for the
Third Programme, 'The New Novel and the Old Book'.⁷ It contained a
glancing reference to Saporta's novel, prompting Johnson – then in the very
midst of writing *The Unfortunates* – to reply on 21 August asking, rather
desperately, 'Have you read his book? where can I?'. In describing the *modus
operandi* of *The Unfortunates* he now found himself obliged to refer to it as
'a modified form of Saporta's technique'. But he had already worked out why
his own experiment would be the more successful: because the Frenchman's
device of 'separate, unbound pages to be arranged or re-arranged by the
reader . . . seems to me to impose another arbitrary unit – the page and what
type can be fitted on it – on the material', whereas the 'separate *signatures*'
which Johnson preferred, could extend to 'whatever length the material
dictates'. In other words, content could still be allowed organically to
dermine form – the same feature which, as he had boldly argued a few years
ago, gave *Travelling People* the edge over *Ulysses*.

Johnson had always known that writing the book was going to be a
gruelling experience, which would involve dragging up some of his most
horribly painful recent memories. He wrote to Tony's widow, June, early in

---

* Marc Saporta (1923–), author of *La Quête* (1961), *La Distribution* (1961) and *Les Invités*
(1964). Also the French translator of Kerouac and Hemingway among others.

1967, informing her of his intention and asking if she could send him copies of all his correspondence with her late husband, which she did. He took a special trip up to Nottingham to watch another Saturday game, to remind himself of the atmosphere of the city and how it had felt to arrive there, at that railway station, more than two years ago. Good financial news started to come in: the Arts Council agreed to pay him another £800, to match Secker's 'salary', 'so I won't have to do any journalism, which is a blessed relief';[8] and at the end of March it was announced that *Trawl* had won a prestigious Somerset Maugham Award: another £500 in the bank (with the stipulation that it was to be spent on foreign travel) and further confirmation of his literary eminence. He had everything that he needed now to get on with the book: time, financial security, a brilliant formal idea ... Except that ...

Except that he could never resist a good commission, and could never settle to anything when there was the option of firing on several different cylinders at once. For one thing, there was the small matter of a full-length play on the subject of religion to be delivered to Jeremy Brooks at the RSC by July. And then, 'out of the blue', came a sudden request from William Gaskill of the English Stage Society to write something for the Royal Court: specifically, he wanted a writer to take Georg Buchner's uncompleted anti-military satire *Woyzeck* and come up with 'the two-thirds [...] that he didn't (being dead) finish'.[9] Johnson agreed immediately – despite the fact that he was still spending every day in the BFI cutting room, learning the art of editing on the hoof while he tried to get *You're Human Like the Rest of Them* into shape – and he dashed off *One Sodding Thing after Another* (as he chose to call his Buchner adaptation) in a frenzy of productivity in the middle of March. In a letter to Zulfikar Ghose he claimed to have written ninety minutes' worth of stage material in one week.[10]

The consequence of this was hardly surprising: the play doesn't work. But this was only partly to do with the haste in which it was written: the plain fact of the matter is that Johnson was not a natural dramatist. The influence of Brecht hangs over everything he wrote for the stage just as louringly as Beckett's shadow hangs over his novels, but in *One Sodding Thing after Another* it feels so oppressive that the play hardly rises above the level of pastiche. 'The Brecht influence is intentional,' he wrote to Ghose defensively; ' – indeed, it makes the wheel come full circle: the fragments of Buchner's *Woyzeck* very much influenced Brecht, and in writing it I had in mind *The Threepenny Opera* and Piscator's *Schweik* which Joan Littlewood did about 1955.'[11] He even wrote some astringently comic songs to break up the stage action and specified in his production notes that 'The music for the songs should be nearer Weill than Berg.' But Johnson's gift (as all of his novels show – with the possible exception of *House Mother Normal*) was not for taking imaginary characters and breathing autonomous life into them, which is what a dramatist must do; instead he was a creator of puppets, to be deployed avowedly (and honestly) at the service of an authorial thesis, and while he knew how to do this with some agility in a novel, the same technique transferred to the theatre – allied with an overfamiliar repertoire of Brechtian alienation effects – always seemed to produce something lumbering and stilted. *One Sodding Thing after Another* was turned down by the Royal Court: and indeed, one year later, Johnson would ask his then-agent Deborah Rogers to return all extant copies to him, whereupon he gave up on any attempt to get it staged.

The correspondence files for April and May 1967 show that, despite the relative financial comfort in which he was now able to sit down and start *The Unfortunates*, Johnson was busily writing to three different publishers with suggestions for poetry anthologies and architectural textbooks. And then finally, on 31 May, he began work on his commission for the RSC, an anti-clerical polemic called *Whose Dog Are You?*, which was due for delivery at the beginning of July.

He had, of course, strong but deeply conflicting feelings about religion. Just as Johnson's writing about sex is often blunted by an apparent desire to leave the reader in no doubt as to his voracious red-blooded hetero-sexuality, so his most insistent expressions of atheism seem to betray, at heart, something more ambiguous: a yearning for some possibility of belief, the closest he had ever found being (as we have seen) in the Mother-worshipping rituals of the pre-Christian church. But he could never allow any of this ambiguity to show up in his writing (not at this point, anyway: it starts to rise to the surface in *See the Old Lady Decently*), and so *Whose Dog Are You?* is at once one of his most belligerent and unsatisfying works. All the faults of preachiness, dogmatism and overemphasis which had disfig-ured *One Sodding Thing after Another* are to be found here in spades. More of a series of revue sketches than a play, it makes no attempt to disguise its didactic intentions, consisting as it does largely of a series of lectures delivered by a master of ceremonies in front of a blackboard. These are broken up by parodic television interviews in the manner of a (below par) Peter Cook and Dudley Moore routine, and schematic dialogues between corrupt, blustering churchmen and a sincerely (but rather smugly) sceptical 'Young Man'. Only a few passages give isolated glimpses into the darker, more complicated and fearful currents of half-belief that might bring us closer to Johnson's real position. At which point we also encounter some familiar landmarks: oblique references to the figure of Christopher Marlowe and to the magical age of twenty-nine.

101: EXTRACT FROM THE PLAY *WHOSE DOG ARE YOU?* (1967)

The MC – and the audience – look towards DEREK expectantly. A long pause, then DEREK slowly stands, his face impassive, stares out at audience. Another long pause. Crown of thorns.

MC: Aha, he's finished his discoveries!

Blackout on Derek.

MC: What he had discovered after all these years was something that many had suspected but no one had been able to prove. This young man did it by synthesis, that is by combining theological chapter, verse, and precedent, with interpretation and a modicum of personal intuition and revelation, with study in depth of science, divination, prophecy and what used to be known as the black arts. He published his findings in a small-circulation magazine run by a fairly loosely-knit order of monks, and it was there picked up by a religious television producer: with the result that our young divine was invited to appear on the Bishop of Bromley's Sunday evening programme 'God Now' . . .

Quick fade down on MC.
    Bring up lights on scene representing a television studio: DEREK and the BISHOP OF BROMLEY (about forty-five, balding, well-fed, sportsjacket and dogcollar) sit in armchairs facing one another.

BISHOP: Good evening. (*professional smile*). God be with you. Christopher Marlowe once said that 'Hell hath no limits, nor is circumscribed in one self place, for where we are is hell, and where hell is there must we ever be.' For where we are is hell. You know, we modern churchmen have been rather embarrassed by Hell, all that fire and brimstone stuff, and we've tended to play it down a bit this century, or at least to say it's really only a metaphor, you know, for what we can't explain in ordinary words, and so on, and so forth. But at various times throughout the glorious history of Christianity certain men have come up with the idea that perhaps this earth *is* in fact Hell, and so forth and so on. It's a very attractive idea, from some points of view, but it appeared to run right against the scriptures and many of the men who dared to suggest the idea ended up being put to death rather unpleasantly, one way or another, as heretics. (*Smiles*) We don't do that now, of course, but nevertheless we don't in our modern church look kindly on heretics. However, we would do well to remember that heresies are really experiments, experiments in finding out the truth, if I may be permitted to put it that way. Recently, this young theologian of twenty-nine has been experimenting, and has come up with exciting new evidence which does indeed seem to suggest a *prima facie* case for supposing that Earth might well be ... Hell. Now, I won't bore you with the exact theological nature of this evidence – though I would urge you to read again the fourth chapter of Revelations – but you can take it from me that this is the genuine article, that there has been a theological breakthrough, that we have crashed the sound-barrier of religious thought, as a result of this young man's work.

Setting aside the obvious limitations of this passage as a piece of drama, there is certainly a strong temptation to identify Johnson with the figure of Derek here. What were his own novels, after all, but 'experiments in finding out the truth'? And doesn't this extract give us an even better label than the loaded word 'experiment' to describe them? Wasn't Johnson really, throughout his career, engaged in producing a series of 'heresies' against the established faiths of the traditional English novel? To say nothing of his insistence, during his worst moments of depression, that he was living his life in 'black hells' of which those around him had no intimation whatsoever.

On 17 July, anyway – a fortnight after *You're Human Like The Rest of Them* had been shown to the press (who singled it out as by far the best of the BFI's latest experimental production slate) – Johnson delivered the typescript of *Whose Dog Are You?* to the RSC, with a covering letter that was by his own standards positively defensive. As someone who prided himself so highly on his professionalism, he felt obliged to apologize for being a week late delivering, but explained that 'part of the last-minute lateness has been due to the problem of writing a play on this particular subject'. Nonetheless, 'I am convinced', he wrote, 'that my approach is not only the best one, but the only practical one. My execution may be faulted, of course, but I don't think the approach can. And I am sure that this is theatre: WHOSE DOG ARE YOU? could not be done in any other medium.' Finally, he added, 'this is [...] to be regarded as the first draft, to be modified in rehearsal as experience shows'.[12]

This was all profoundly out of character. Johnson, as we have seen, was not much given to qualifications or second thoughts when it came to evangelizing about his own work, and yet over the next few days he was besieged by them. First of all he wrote to Jeremy Brooks again on the 18th, offering some casting ideas for the lead roles. Apart from a gesture in the direction of popular comedy, his suggestions showed the familiar influence of Beckett and the usual fierce loyalty to former collaborators: 'The Master of Ceremonies I saw as a comedian of the calibre of Frankie Howerd; Belcon and the Priest in the confessional scene were both written with Patrick Magee in mind; and I see William Hoyland, who played the lead in my film, as the Young Man'.[13] And the next day he wrote to Peter Hall, again in a manner which seemed designed to forestall criticisms he was already anticipating:

102: LETTER *(19 July 1967)*

To Peter Hall

Thanks very much for your letter, and I'm sorry you couldn't come to YOU'RE HUMAN LIKE THE REST OF THEM. I hope you're now quite recovered, and that nothing further disastrous will happen to your MACBETH.

My film had far more notices than I'd expected, all of them very favourable apart from the *Guardian*. I'm now hoping to be able to find enough support for a film of ALBERT ANGELO.

Last Monday I delivered the play commissioned by you, WHOSE DOG ARE YOU? As you may know from Jeremy Brooks, its subject is religion and it questions the basis of the moral authority of churches. It's the result of several years' thinking about the subject, and the approach I finally chose (sending it up, playing for laughs, exploiting the fact of the stage/audience relationship) seemed to me the only one for such a vast subject: to have treated it seriously would have been death: and yet it cannot be other than basically serious. If my treatment of it is faulty in any way, however, I hope that you will point it out to me and that we can work on it together.

It seems to me that, though many maintain that the real power of the churches was broken in the twenties and thirties, this is the crucial moment at which to make sure that no one need remain ignorant of the basis on which they claim authority: it is one of the demolition jobs of our time which has to be done: and balls to those who ask what we'll put in its place – one doesn't have to decide what to build before clearing slums – and in any case there *are* people who don't feel the need to believe in anything, to whom belief is a meaningless term.

I've probably said too much, and sounded too serious about this: but your reputation is such that I know you'll give very serious attention to WHOSE DOG ARE YOU? [...]

Perhaps Johnson was overanxious about the play's merits because he had already received less-than-encouraging feedback from one of his most trusted friends. Zulfikar Ghose had written to him by now, expressing serious reservations; Johnson's reply continued to show a curious mixture of self-doubt and his more typical bullish aggressiveness: 'I did not, as I told you, enjoy the DOG thing. Perhaps that's why it's not as good as I'd hoped. There are lots of reasons/excuses: I ought to have written it two or three years ago when it meant more to me: I don't trust the judgment of Brooks/ Hall since their treatment of YOU'RE HUMAN was rather off-handed [...]. But in several points I think you do it less than justice.'[14] He went on to defend the humour of the play (maintaining again that 'the MC is intended to be played by a comedian of the stature of Frankie Howerd'), to stress the extra comedy and inventiveness that performers would bring to it, to justify the repetitions from *Albert Angelo*, and so on. But he admitted that 'I do feel it's intellectually less than satisfactory, as you say: but if it makes people laugh, then that's enough, that's all I was trying to do, or the first thing I was trying to do. The church on its side is TOTALLY intellectually unsatisfactory, so all you can do is bloody laugh at it'. But one of Ghose's criticisms, it seems, particularly hit home: 'the main thing that upset me was your pointing out that the language wasn't up to my usual standards'.

How much should we read into the fact that, of all his major works, the only one about which Johnson ever expressed clear reservations, or palpable self-doubt, was the one in which he attempted to tackle, head-on, the subject of religion? His own feelings of spirituality were profoundly conflicting. Immovable hatred of the Christian Church coexisted, in his case, with something much more troubling and ambiguous: a consciousness – which itself ebbed and flowed according to his changing moods – of some kind of commitment, some kind of devotion to a hazily conceived 'Goddess' who was herself bound up with the problematic, competing demands of womanhood and poetry. In *Whose Dog Are You?* he did not even begin the attempt to address these contradictions. The result was one of his least palatable pieces of work and the rejection which he already half anticipated would not be long coming.

But, as always with Johnson, a combination of his own boundless energy and fluctuating state of financial security drove him on to other projects and allowed no leisure for much-needed self-examination. Work continued intensively on *The Unfortunates* throughout the summer before being interrupted in August by an unforeseen problem: 'a monstrously enlarged right bollock'.[15] To Zulfikar Ghose, he passed on the news of its 'subsiding at last after being got at with penicillin and tetracyclin', but confessed, 'My novel's been plagued by all this bollocking around, which has fair turned me over one way and another'.*[16]

Nonetheless he managed to get the completed manuscript out to his editor, David Farrer of Secker & Warburg, on 29 September 1967. The accompanying letter, on this occasion, was noticeably more upbeat than when he had submitted *Whose Dog Are You?* to the RSC. 'I think the idea has succeeded well beyond my expectations,' he announced. 'To me, at least, it really does reflect the random way in which past and present interact in

---

* On 29 November 2001, over lunch at the Gay Hussar in London WC1, and admittedly under the influence of an excess of Tokai, Virginia Johnson was unable to remember any significant engorgement of the Johnsonian testicle during the period in question. Its cause must remain a mystery.

the mind: it is an enactment of randomness which the bound book simply cannot achieve.' He further congratulated himself that 'the book has a noticeable confidence about it', and attributed this confidence, in part, to David Farrer's advice and encouragement at an early stage of the writing: it was Farrer's idea, this letter reveals, that the first and last sections of the novel should be indicated as such. Only one possible area of conflict was identified. In his 'Author's Production Notes', submitted both to the publisher and the printers, Johnson added this caveat: 'NB While the production of TRAWL was in every other respect excellent, the quality of the paper used was not: item 6 of my contract with you provides that the production standards of my books with you shall not fall below the standard set by my previously published novels, and I hope you will be able to find a more suitable paper for THE UNFORTUNATES.'

Even without taking into account Johnson's demands for a particular kind of paper, *The Unfortunates* presented a formidable technical challenge not just for his publishers but for the book trade in general. True, the unusual format might have some unforeseen advantages: two people could now read the book at the same time, passing the sections over to each other, and it would also be possible for readers to choose a long or a short section, depending on how much time they had available to read. Johnson had not thought of either of these benefits before, but when they were pointed out to him he resolved to use them 'at the Grilling I will get from Fred [Warburg] within the next couple of weeks'.[17] However, as Bergonzi had already remarked in his radio talk when mentioning Marc Saporta, the prospect of loose leaves presented unbound in a box 'would not be very popular with librarians' – a criticism that unleashed one of Johnson's fiercest tirades.

103: EXTRACT FROM LETTER *(16 October 1967)*

To Zulfikar Ghose

> As for loss of sections, or damage of sections, this book may be more
> *prone* to these: but in principle no more so than any bound book (qv
> the case of Joe Orton and homicidal mate,* various scribblers in margins,
> tit-drawers on HM QE, etc.): one simply can't control what happens to a
> book after it's been sold, indeed, has no right to: when I occasionally
> look at my books in public libraries, it is only to see whether anyone

---

* In 1962, Joe Orton and his lover Kenneth Halliwell had been found guilty of stealing and defacing seventy-two books from public libraries in Islington and Hampstead. They were sentenced to six months' imprisonment and ordered to pay £450 damages. Orton lived in Noel Road, London N1, which made him Johnson's near-neighbour, but as far as I know they never met, and I have the sense that despite their class affinities, the essentially fastidious Johnson would have given the theatrical enfant terrible a wide berth.

has been inspired to write comments like BALLS! at any point – and they never have, as far as I've seen. And bollocks to librarians, too, – of all the ponces who feast off the dead body of Literature, the carrion who feed on the dead corpses of good men, writers, pay us fuckall and go out to lunch every day of the working week, etc, you know the syndrome, my predilections, hatreds, etc, of all these, I SAY, the bleeding (though they have no lifeblood) librarians are the worst, and I shall be very interested to see how they take this book: there are, of course, the librara (I'll misspell the cunts) suppliers, who buy sheets and bind up their own special copies: they'll be buggered, ha ha! I think – they might buy sheets and bind my book up like a Proper Book, the sods, but there ought to be a law against that, and I'll try to find it.

He never did, of course. Several libraries were known to have lent out bound copies of *The Unfortunates*, and such copies are now prized collectors' items.

Still, it's clear that Johnson was on fighting form at this time, and was in no mood to take his latest insult – the RSC's decision not to proceed with *Whose Dog Are You?* – lying down. Jeremy Brooks had written to him with this news on 14 September, just when he was in midflow on the last stretch of *The Unfortunates*. As you might anticipate from this source, it was a thoughtful, generous-minded, articulate rejection: but a rejection all the same. Brooks had delayed writing, he said, because 'one inevitably puts off unpleasant duties'. And while he found that *Whose Dog Are You?* contained 'great moments, plenty of laughs, more ideas per square inch than most plays have per square mile, and, as I had expected from you, some really first-class dialogue', there was a problem: 'I don't think you've written a play at all. It is a tract.' Brooks put the matter as simply as he could: 'Just as Forster glumly admitted "the story – oh yes, the novel tells a story", so we have reluctantly to admit that until we have "drama" we have no play. Drama means conflict.'

Perhaps on the principle that one should never reply to letters in anger by return of post, or – more likely – because he wanted to get the novel finished first, Johnson delayed replying for almost three weeks. This interval, in any case, did nothing to allay his feelings of resentment.

104: LETTER *(5 October 1967)*

To Jeremy Brooks

Dear Jeremy:

Your rejection of WHOSE DOG ARE YOU? was not altogether unexpected, but both your reasons for doing so and your contempt for the intelligence of the Aldwych audience did surprise me.

Perhaps you have by now seen the irony of quoting Forster to a novelist like me. A novel *may* tell a story, but it does not *have* to: or haven't you noticed what's been happening in the last twenty years? This I find difficult to believe, of course, and there is perhaps more excuse for quoting that old stuff about Conflict and Drama: you weren't to know I specialised in drama at university and know all that theoretical crap.

My play is certainly a *piece of theatre*: in the sense you use the terms, I am quite happy to believe that to you it is not a play, or drama. You admit it has plenty of laughs, and what better way is there of keeping an audience interested? Make them laugh well just once at the beginning of a piece, and they'll sit there for a long time in the hope (fulfilled, in my play) that it will happen again. There are, after all, many kinds of theatre, many ways of keeping an audience's attention through two hours, besides Drama and Conflict. That is why I suggested casting a comedian of the calibre of Frankie Howerd as the MC, and, far from presenting you with 'experiment and untried forms' I thought I was working within well-defined and proved conventions, those of music-hall and revue and Brecht.

I suspect that because I am (for want of a better term) an experimental novelist, you have subconsciously or consciously thought that my play must be *a* experimental and *b* novelistic. Ah well, you theatre people are always type-casting, and the dogma that novelists can't write plays must be maintained, of course.

Don't think this is an unfriendly letter: it's all a matter of opinion, and to anyone unbiassed yours and Peter Hall's must obviously be worth more. But I believe (and hope one day to prove) that while WHOSE DOG ARE YOU? is not the best piece of work I've ever done, it will make a better evening in the theatre than anything new you've put on at the Aldwych this past year.

Best wishes for your own writing,*
Yours ever,

To Peter Hall, who had written on 20 September backing up his literary manager's assessment of the play ('I do not think it can really be classed as a piece of *dramatic* art – a piece to which performances in a theatre would add'), he replied on the same day:

---

* Brooks was also the author of the novels *The Water Carnival*, *Henry's War*, *Jampot Smith* and *Smith, as Hero*. The latter two had been bestsellers.

105: LETTER *(5 October 1967)*

To Peter Hall

Thanks for your letter endorsing all that Jeremy Brooks had to say about my play WHOSE DOG ARE YOU?: but I hope you don't really believe that a novel must tell a story, and I enclose a copy of my own reply to him.

I think it may be that I have failed in this play to communicate my conception of what I want to see on the stage: that my way of putting down in words what I want to see is simply not your way of receiving it.

Thank you for your expression of continued admiration for me as a writer. I shall not, however, write for the theatre again unless there is a much greater chance of seeing my work performed: a play does not exist until it is on the stage, and I'm sure you will understand that I prefer to use my energy on things in which the satisfaction is completely in the writing. I had thought that your commission for WHOSE DOG ARE YOU? would be enough to see that it would be at least tried in some way or another; but not so.

Let me say in conclusion that I would still rather have my work directed by you, as Beckett's first director in this country, than anyone else.

Best wishes for your work.

Yours sincerely,

This was not quite the end of Johnson's career as a dramatist: there would be more pieces for television, and one for the stage. But it would be more or less the end of *Whose Dog Are You?.* Eventually, a couple of extracts were staged by Michael Bakewell at the Soho Basement Theatre in 1971, along with *You're Human Like the Rest of Them* (another RSC/Jeremy Brooks reject), under the umbrella title *B.S. Johnson vs God.* But the play was destined never to be performed in full. For all his bluster to Jeremy Brooks, it would appear that Johnson himself had limited faith in it. One week after firing off his letters to Brooks and Hall, he heard from another plain-spoken friend, Bruce Beresford, who admitted, 'I didn't like the play very much at all. It struck me as little more than a spoken anti-church pamphlet [...] I had heard all the arguments before so never felt I was being told anything. The presentation is so much on one level that the play reads a bit like one of those articles written by people who believe there are international conspiracies behind everything.' Which must have put the final nail in the coffin. After that, it was into the bottom drawer for *Whose Dog Are You?.*

Beresford was writing to Johnson not primarily about the play, on this occasion, but about his nascent screenplay for *Albert Angelo*. At the end of July the BFI production board had approved a subsistence grant of £300 to enable him to start work on this, and as soon as *The Unfortunates* had been delivered he began in earnest. (This meant that he would produce four full-length works that year, in three different media.) Besides Beresford, to whom Johnson would send individual scenes for close analysis as they were written, the project was being overseen by both Stanley Reed and Sir Michael Balcon at the British Film Institute. Sadly – but as is often the case with feature film development – it would prove difficult to satisfy all of these individuals at once.

Balcon, for instance, seems to have been hoping for a solidly commercial screenplay with a minimum of 'experimental' overtones. At the beginning of September he asked Johnson to provide a story outline and was rewarded with a single sheet of double-spaced typing which did little other than to offer a bald, 150-word summary of the original novel's milieu. Clearly, Johnson's feeling was that since the novel already existed, it could speak for itself, and indeed as adaptor he considered his task as being simply to translate the action, setting and formal devices of the book onto the screen with absolute and rigorous fidelity. This he proceeded to do. The screenplay opens with an almost complete transcription of the Luke/Joseph/Albert dialogue which begins the novel; then a credit sequence over shots of Percy Circus, for which Johnson's directions are also taken directly from the novel (including the detail of the houses 'leaning upright against the slope like a practised seaman'); then voice-over narration from Albert reproducing the first-person narration from the novel's 'Exposition', and so on.

Later on, the book's parallel columns juxtaposing classroom dialogue with Albert's private thoughts[18] are replicated by subtitles: 'During the whole of the following scene [Johnson writes in the screenplay], SUBTITLES are used to represent ALBERT's thoughts: thus the further dimension of thought is added to the action represented by images, and the speech represented by sounds. At first it may be thought necessary to show physically that these subtitles are ALBERT's thoughts by placing them as if issuing from his head rather than in the normal position at the bottom of the frame: but perhaps this is to underestimate the sophistication of audiences which now accept subtitles in many films.' Ten years later, Woody Allen would use the same device to famously comic effect in *Annie Hall*: the difference being that Allen's scene with Diane Keaton lasts a punchy two or three minutes; Johnson's largely static classroom episode sprawls – again, with his manic fidelity to the published text – over twenty-six pages of screenplay, which represents exactly twenty-six minutes of screen time.

Voice-over was suggested again for the schoolkids' essays towards the end of the book. And for the 'almighty aposiopesis' which concludes it, the actor playing Albert was to step out of character, and Johnson himself, as director, was to come before the camera to engage him in dialogue. Once again, it's a device which was picked up by a more high-profile film-maker a few years later: Lindsay Anderson ends the surreal, picaresque *O Lucky Man!* with a similar confrontation between himself and his leading actor, Malcolm McDowell. But Johnson's version is blunter and more explicit:

106: EXTRACT FROM SCREENPLAY FOR *ALBERT ANGELO* (1967)

> ALBERT
>
> I'm sorry to bore you, mate, but you seem to understand better than anyone else – which is more than I bloody do. Look, I just can't feel it, I'm just not convinced by it!
>
> B.S.J. (V.O.)
>
> Well, *I* felt it. It *did* happen like it's written. It happened to me.
>
> ACTOR PLAYING ALBERT
>
> But I'm not you, am I?
>
> B.S.J. (coming into
> SHOT, back to CAMERA)
>
> No, you're not me – that's the whole thing, I'm trying to say something through *you* about what happened to *me*. You stand for me ...
>
> ACTOR PLAYING ALBERT
>
> There's a limit to what I'll stand for!
>
> MONTAGE
>
> A MONTAGE of some of the tail-ends of scenes throughout the whole of the film until this point.
>
> In some of these the ACTOR PLAYING ALBERT is seen vee-signing at the CAMERA as a gag after *cut* has been called; in others B.S.J. and other technicians wander into SHOT; once B.S.J. in SHOT gestures *cut* to the CAMERA as though he had forgotten while going to direct an actor for the next take.
>
> Incidents like this will be SHOT at the end of most scenes, and an element of improvisation and chance will be involved: only the most relevant to be used.

> The effect will be to expose those unguarded moments
> which the audience does not normally see: the intention
> being subtly to expose the mechanics of film-making in
> the interests of honesty and truth.

Of course, if these 'unguarded moments' were to be purposely 'SHOT' at the end of most scenes, then one could argue that they would not be unguarded at all, and all that Johnson would have accomplished would be to insert an *extra* layer of dishonesty into the film-making process. Leaving this reflection aside, however, we can see why the film adaptation of *Albert Angelo* was so close to his heart. He was writing this screenplay on the assumption that he would be allowed to direct it; in this way he hoped to achieve what he had been too inexperienced and too constrained by time to achieve in *You're Human Like the Rest of Them*: a demonstration of the fundamental untruthfulness of mainstream narrative cinema, just as he believed that he had already demonstrated the untruthfulness of fiction in *Albert Angelo*.

In any case, he would not be allowed to get that far, or anywhere near it. When the completed screenplay was delivered – bang on time, of course, on 1 November 1967 – the letters that accompanied it were upbeat. To Michael Balcon he wrote, 'I am very excited by the possibility of directing a film of ALBERT ANGELO, and am most grateful to you for your interest in my work'. To Stanley Reed he was even more breezily confident about his adaptation: 'I think I've solved all the problems,' he wrote, before adding, rather enigmatically, 'though whether I have done so completely satisfactorily or not remains to be seen.'

Neither Reed nor Balcon had any doubts on that score, as it turned out. Stanley Reed's memo to Bruce Beresford, dated 20 December 1967, admitted that 'the original idea of bridging the gap between the experimental film and the popular audience cannot be solved with a film of the sort Bryan proposes'. There was a lot of agonizing about the requirements of this 'popular audience' – which he also referred to as the 'Odeon audience' – before he reached the conclusion that 'it is asking a lot of them to accept all these [experimental] devices, along with a story they will find frustrating *and* a defeat ending'. His general tone was one of disappointment, suggesting that Johnson had set himself an almost impossible task and failed to bring it off. Michael Balcon, on the other hand, who got his memo in first (on 14 November), took a more robust line. 'It is very distasteful to me to have to be completely condemnatory of the work of any creative person,' he began, but then he set his distaste aside and allowed himself to be completely condemnatory. 'All I think that Johnson has succeeded in doing is to demonstrate that ALBERT ANGELO is entirely unsuitable source material for a film [...] I would not even submit the present script to any people I know concerned with the finance and distribution of films [...] There appears to me to be no definite story line, no dramatic conflicts, very little detailed characterisation and a mixture of devices which are confusing and unacceptable [...] It is quite true that our conversations with Bryan Johnson when we met at luncheon were fairly tentative but all of us gave him advice on certain basic principles [...] and it is my opinion that he has taken very little notice of any of the advice then given to him.'

'Frankly, Sir Michael Balcon's comments made me despair,' Johnson would write, a couple of months later. For the time being, however, he remained in ignorance of them, and had happier projects to keep him busy. He had so far failed to find a publisher for a proposed layman's introduction to architecture, to be co-written with John Furse (the art director on *You're Human Like the Rest of Them*, who had since become a close friend), but far more importantly, *The Unfortunates* had been delivered to Secker & Warburg (how much they actually liked it was not clear at this stage), and the BBC had already been sufficiently intrigued by the rumours surrounding this unusual novel that they wanted to make a short film about it for their arts strand *Release*. Better still, they had agreed that Johnson himself could direct. And he had been commissioned by Gollancz to edit *The Evacuees*, an anthology of reminiscences by writers and celebrities who, like himself, had been traumatised by the experience of wartime evacuation. Restless as always, he was driven to accept all of these challenges and move further and further into other media – the novel never seemed to be enough for him. (And even when some of them might have looked like hackwork, the kind of thing an acclaimed but struggling novelist had to take on to keep body and soul together, consider how he was always coming back to the same subjects – that unforgivable wartime betrayal, the horrific, inexorable decay of Tony's body. Even in what might, for other writers, have been minor, negligible work, Johnson was always personally engaged, could never stop scratching the same sores.)

There was also the question of what he should do with his money from the Somerset Maugham Award. Then, as now, the terms of the award stipulated that the prize money be spent on travel. Not for Johnson, however, a trip to Borneo or three months backpacking in the Andean foothills: he set his sights no further than the other side of the English Channel. He had made the first of his literary pilgrimages at the end of his university years, when he had travelled to Dublin (and made a fateful detour to north Wales). Now it was time to immerse himself in Joyce's other spiritual home, with the added bonus that Joyce's heir, and Johnson's personal mentor, Samuel Beckett, would be living just around the corner. It was time to do what you clearly *had* to do, at some point in your career, if you were going to be a great modernist writer. It was time for a sojourn in Paris.

The plan was for the whole family to spend two months (December 1967 and January 1968) in the French capital, before driving south, along the French and Italian rivieras until they reached Turin, where they would visit Gianni Zambardi-Mall.* The trip began less than smoothly when their flight was prevented from landing at Orly because of fog and re-routed to Tours, which Johnson rather cruelly dubbed 'Scunthorpe-on-Loire'.¹⁹ (He would soon have cause to be grateful to Scunthorpe-on-Loire, all the same.) Anxious that their passports had not been stamped ('Xst knows how we're going to get out of the country, since it can be demonstrably shown that *we never came in*'), Johnson checked the family into a cheap hotel while he looked for a suitable apartment. 'Impossible to stay here more than a week,' he wrote, from this hotel, 'without feeling suicidal'. Far from feeling excited on the threshold of this modest adventure, Johnson revealed that 'I feel doom-ridden anyway at the moment – but there, I thought I would die at 29 anyway.'²⁰

His premonitions of doom came true in a minor way a few days later when he woke up in the middle of the night to find a burglar rifling through their possessions: 'I was awoken by the wardrobe door creaking, and sat up, thinking it was Steven out of bed – he [had] awoken us the previous morning, shouting at lorries: but it wasn't – it was a man. I shouted GET OUT! and luckily he did – there was me all starkers, what the hell could I have done? There was a bottle of water (yes!) by the bed, but I didn't think about throwing that until the next morning. He'd been across the room to Ginnie's handbag, taken it to the door and emptied it, and then was getting at my wallet in the wardrobe door when the door creaked.'²¹

Within a week, however, they had found themselves a large, top-floor apartment at 146 Boulevard Montparnasse, an art deco block not far from the Observatoire and the Jardin du Luxembourg. 'This flat is big, modern, on the seventh floor – great view out over greyblue roofs to the Observatoire, own terrace, big sliding doorwindows. Bloody expensive, but it was so dreary, looking [...] and probably nothing would be cheap.'²² They would stay here until early February, much of the time being spent on the sort of routine administrative work that could more easily have been done back in London (most of the contributions to *The Evacuees* arrived during these months and had to be revised, edited and commented upon) and some of it being spent either entertaining a stream of visitors or simply getting the most out of the Parisian good life:

---

* Johnson's old friend from supply-teaching days, and the original of Terry in *Albert Angelo*.

107: EXTRACT FROM LETTER *(16 January 1968)*

To Zulfikar Ghose

Dawn comes about 8.30. It does not often happen that we see it. We (that is, I) tend to wake about half past nine, or be woken by Steven thundering into our bedroom full of le sport, as they say. About ten minutes later I get up and shave, watched and imitated by Steven. By this time it is ten. I wander out to the street and buy marvellous bread and croissants and pate and quiche lorraine and Figaro or Le MONDE. By the time I have got back it is half past ten, and with luck (women need an extra hour's sleep) Virginia is up. By the time we have finished breakfast it is half past eleven. This is not a good start to the day, but it is our start, day after day [...] Within a couple of hours of finishing breakfast it is lunchtime – note, we do not feel like lunch, but, for crissake, it is lunchtime, so we have lunch. I am strictly doing like the natives, which means wine or booze for lunch, which means I tend to fall asleep in the afternoon.

Altogether Johnson seems to have done little writing in Paris, apart from one short, breezily phallocentric poem, which was to become one of his own favourites.

108: POEM *(December 1967)*

The Poet Holds His Future in His Hand

Tonight I looked at it: I don't often

it performs its two functions well enough
in return I keep it reasonably clean

but quite by chance I looked at it tonight
and there were several dirty marks on it

I of course looked harder: and they were veins
underneath the skin, bloody great black veins!

they weren't there last time I happened to look
certainly the light was bad in that place

but there's no doubt that the pressure is on

He did, on the other hand, write a good many letters during this time, from which with some accuracy we can gauge his mood. As when he had written to George Greenfield about his impending trip to Blauvac ('staying apparently with some mad woman who keeps open château for writers, painters and general layabouts'), he never sounded more high-spirited than when enjoying the lifestyle of the expatriate writer. Sometimes he seems overexcited by nothing ('Had oysters for lunch today!' he exclaims, triumphantly, in a letter to Zulfikar Ghose), but often he had good reason to feel pleased with the way things were going: 'Heard yesterday that You're Human is almost certain to be accepted for competition in the Tours Short Film Festival at the end of Jan. This is the most important short film thing, so it's quite an honour.' At moments like this, when he was away from London, the constant financial worries, the sense of artistic embattlement, the struggle to find a place for himself in a fundamentally unwelcoming literary culture, Johnson's tone becomes positively upbeat and at last we encounter the naive, boyish, bubblingly cheerful figure many of his friends remember. And yet it only takes a downbeat letter from Zulfikar Ghose, for instance, for his burning sense of literary and personal victimization to re-emerge.

109: FURTHER EXTRACTS FROM LETTERS WRITTEN IN PARIS
(December 1967–January 1968)

Have just counted, and find I have thirteen bottles of booze in the place. This sounds unlucky, so I shall have to drink one. Or buy another and drink two. Or buy two and drink three. Or something. Have run the gamut – Irish whiskey on plane, Scotch, [. . .] Vodka (cheap here), Green Carthorse, Cointreau, Marc (ever had it? – brandy made from what's left after they pressed the wine out – cross between petrol, meths, and stewed football boots: you have to be a real hard man to take this: I've given it to Ginnie for cooking, so now we have everything flambé and flavoured with dubbin) and today I just graduated to the drink that killed Oscar Wilde, Verlaine, Dowson, and various others of that ilk – Pernod, the polite name for absinthe.[23]

On John Furse's contribution to *The Evacuees*:

I've tidied up the punctuation a little (may I introduce you to the colon – or is that too evacuative in context for you – a very useful punctuation mark – enables you to do without all these little dashes – which tend to leave you up in midair – have a few to be going on with ::::::::::::::::::::: ::::::::::: Let me know if you need any more.[24]

On James Jones, author of *From Here to Eternity*:

Met the fabulous James Jones, who is considerably less than his wife, who is a right gorgon. Had them round for dinner, and it was a disaster: he and his wife, who are a team (she says she does the writing and he edits) are opinionated, boorish caricatures of the American abroad. I believe he really thinks it's Shakespeare and him, but not in that order.

Ignorant. Furthermore, he thinks every writer he meets is looking for a handout (or, rather, she does) and I must therefore have the distinction of being the ONLY WRITER WHOM JAMES JONES OWES A DINNER TO!!!!!!! Within an hour of meeting them the wife told me they were worth a million dollars; How much is that in real money? I riposted; rather well, I feel.[25]

On a new volume of poetry published by Zulfikar Ghose:

It must be nearly heartbreaking that your poems have had such little attention: it hurts me, too. The bastards. All I can offer is the experience of the Smithsons, who had years of neglect, knowing they were good, knowing they were far better than the people who got attention and money: live through it, most particularly OUTLIVE YOUR ENEMIES. We are going to live (give or take accidents) longer than Lambert and Kilmartin and that crap. The thing not to do is give up, to let it stop one: just live, do, and outlive. In ten years' time things will be very different. Just write for your own reasons.[26]

While in Paris, he also received the bad news of Stanley Reed's and Michael Balcon's responses to the *Albert Angelo* screenplay. It was a serious blow. Not just because, as usual, he felt that what he had written was good, and original, and unusual, and that its brilliance had simply not been understood by these narrow-minded readers. This was just par for the course, in Johnson's experience. It was a more devastating setback than that, because he was determined to prove himself in the film world, just as he had already – in his own opinion – demonstrated to the literary world that he was the most gifted novelist of his generation, and *Albert Angelo* was to have been the crucial opening salvo in this campaign. He replied to Stanley Reed in the New Year, and it was a difficult letter to write, because he liked and respected him. Nonetheless he felt, as always, that a major injustice had been done.

110: LETTER *(4 January 1968)*

To Stanley Reed

I shall try to put down my feelings as they are now, but please excuse the form being rather chaotic due to various emotions.

First of all, I think there must have been some sort of misunderstanding: I came late to the idea that ALBERT ANGELO was supposed to be a 'bridge between the experimental film and the popular audience': I had supposed you wanted me to make a feature as good (better?) than YOU'RE HUMAN was a short. (Parenthesis here: I think my film could make it with the popular audience, but obviously this cannot be proved without the film being made, that is without someone putting up the money.) The one thing I am sure of is that I could not make a film which would be either an art-house one or a commercial one without it being *my* film: that is to say, being done my way. I'm not interested in making ordinary films (there are plenty of people who can't make anything else) and regard this (all right, I'm arrogant) as a waste of my time and particular abilities. It does not matter to me whether I just clear my living expenses or make ten thousand pounds; I simply want to make permanent (within the limitations of your archives department!) a vision I have, and to be able to feed myself and my family while I do it. Just as I don't want to write (say) John Braine's type of novel (it is, forgive the immodesty, too easy and irrelevant) nor do I want to remake CARRY ON TEACHER (though that, I admit, exaggerates the commercial position).

So: I've always thought of ALBERT ANGELO as an art-house film which, if it didn't break through to mass audiences, would merely reflect on their crassness (which is none of our fault).

I would like to make an audience (the mass audience?) think about WHY they demand a story from films (art?) and not from life. I am quite certain that this direction is the way things are going: non-representational painting is accepted now far more than in other arts, literature and films, for instance: though even here literature is in advance of film – Duras, Joyce, Beckett, and so on – and is not the history of the cinema one of *following* other media in such respects? EG censorship? It is simply a matter of time before the 'advances' that ALBERT ANGELO seems to represent will in fact be accepted as normal practice.

Which brings me to another point. At the moment I very much (even desperately) want to make ALBERT into a film: it is simply the biggest thing in my life, in my future. The immediate future. But my fear is that if the money is not raised within the next year or so..... One moves on. I have seen it in my writing. I shall not have the same sort of enthusiasm, it will not be the film I want to make when I have the opportunity to make it. If I have the opportunity to make it.

And I feel guilty about the misunderstanding. I must therefore, since we appear not to have been talking about the same film, offer you the return of your £300 [...]

Whether Stanley Reed accepted the repayment of the BFI's development money remains unknown: but it seems unlikely. Reed must have known Johnson well enough to see that the offer was made gesturally, by a wounded man. A man who ended his letter by confessing, 'the other day I read that the Beatles are supposed to be setting up some fund to promote

experimental films like their own: in vague hope I am writing to them [...]
See, to what depths I descend: applying to the Beatles!'

This, remember, was in the days before postmodernism had persuaded
us all that there was no real evaluative distinction to be drawn between high
and popular culture. One or two music critics had by now popped up to
suggest that Lennon and McCartney were the greatest songwriters since
Schubert, or some such claim. But to an unapologetic elitist such as Johnson
(in artistic rather than class terms, of course), who believed that if his work
'didn't break through to mass audiences, [it] would merely reflect on their
crassness', going cap in hand to a writer of pop songs really did represent
some sort of nadir. And being unable to spell his name probably didn't help
much either.

111: LETTER *(4 January 1968)*

Dear Paul MacCartney:

I read in the SUNDAY TIMES recently that you were setting up a
fund to help experimental film-makers.

My first film YOU'RE HUMAN LIKE THE REST OF THEM, lasting 16
minutes, was made with the backing of the British Film Institute and
was the first film ever to use poetry: that is, making the images reflect
the metre of the verse as well as the sound.* It was first seen at the
National Film Theatre on July 4th 1967, and received generally excellent
reviews. It has now been chosen for competition in the Tours Short Film
Festival later this month [...]

The BFI is trying to set up my second novel ALBERT ANGELO as a
feature. It is the kind of proposition that will not attract commercial
backing, though there is no reason (to me) why it should not appeal to
a large audience. Why not back it? Or is that too direct? It's low-budget:
they estimate less than £50,000.

I am also a novelist: I am here in Paris at present on the Somerset
Maugham Award for my third novel TRAWL. And a poet. Besides being
a film director. But if you want to know all that sort of crap you can
find it out easily enough.

Look forward to hearing from you.

If Sir Paul, as he would later become, ever replied to this letter, Johnson did
not keep a copy in his files. The film version of *Albert Angelo*, like the play
Whose Dog are You?, was destined never to be realized. Over the next four

---

* An extravagant claim. A strong case could be made, for instance, that *Night Mail* (directed by
Harry Watt and Basil Wright in 1936, with verse by W. H. Auden) integrates poetry and image
just as interestingly as *You're Human Like the Rest of Them*.

years Johnson would write further drafts of the screenplay, and make further attempts to secure funding – usually under an independent banner, although still in association with Bruce Beresford – but to no avail. His ambition to direct a feature film would always remain unfulfilled, thwarted (as Johnson himself would no doubt have seen it) by the same backward-looking, middlebrow mentality – personified in this case by Michael Balcon, the force behind Ealing Studios – that pervaded and calcified the literary establishment.

Whereas the French – ah, yes, the French! – didn't have hang-ups like this. They were no longer in thrall to the hated 'story' as the engine of all literary and cinematic art. The French would understand what Johnson was trying to do: and sure enough, when he and Virginia travelled down to the much-maligned 'Scunthorpe-on-Loire' at the end of January, a pleasant surprise was waiting for them. On Monday 22nd he had met Beckett again in Paris, and privately screened for him a 16mm print of *You're Human Like the Rest of Them*. The next day, the Tours Short Film Festival began: *Vous êtes des hommes commes les autres* was shown in competition on the evening of Wednesday 24th, and was enthusiastically received, not just by the press but – rather more importantly – by the jury (which included Volker Schlondorff, who would go on to direct *The Tin Drum* and *Swann in Love*, among other films). On Saturday, the last day of the festival, it was announced that Johnson's first foray into cinema had won the Grand Prix.

For the next few days the young laureate ('jeune poète et romancier britannique passé au cinéma') was courted, fêted and interviewed. He told again and again the story of how he had shot the film in sixteen days with only one camera, and announced again and again (unbowed, temporarily, by the responses of Balcon and Reed) that his next project would be a full-colour, feature-length, all-singing, all-dancing version of *Albert Angelo*. His novels at this time were unknown in France, but journalists soon seized on his apparent affinity with the nouveau roman. *Le Nouvel Observateur* asked him whether his literary output belonged to any particular movement, to which Johnson was quick to reply, 'Aucun. Ou, à la rigueur, disons que ce n'est pas le nouveau roman, mais la voie anglaise du nouveau roman. – Et votre film? – Ce n'est pas du Godard. C'est la voie anglaise de Godard.'* At the black tie reception which closed the festival – for which Johnson had to hire a dinner suit, the despised uniform of the ruling class – he was presented with his trophy, a magnificently weighty bronze sculpture by Jean Arp, and was then seated for dinner next to the festival's guest of honour,

---

* 'None. Or, at a pinch, let's say it is not the "nouveau roman", but the "nouveau roman" with an English slant. – And what about your film? – It's not Godard. It's Godard with an English slant.' Johnson would have spoken to the interviewer in English, of course.

Jacques Tati. He later described the occasion to Zulfikar Ghose: 'Had a great evening afterwards, at the Prefecture, where there was a reception in a 14th century palace that was as sparkling and grand as you could expect a french occasion to be: and where Jacques Tati, here to boost his latest film,* kept hitting me hard behind the ear with his open hand and saying "You are 'appy?!" Three times he did that, it's my one coherent memory of the evening, perhaps because it hurt each time.'[27]

Johnson did not record his answer to Tati's question. Perhaps we can assume, if Tati felt compelled to hit him three times, that his countenance wasn't betraying the required exhilaration; but he must have been feeling it. How very satisfying, after all, to come to France – where radical, modernist narrative art seemed to be actively encouraged – and to receive this kind of recognition. Had the jury really understood his film? Perhaps not. 'The aesthetic experiment side escaped us,' one journalist confessed. 'It appears the visual rhythm follows the decasyllabic verse of the text; but one is "captured" by the absolute predominance of the dialogue, or to be more exact the monologue, over the visuals [. . . and] there is a strange underlying humour, peculiar to B. S. Johnson.' Another writer, besides describing the film as 'original, intelligent and deeply human', found it 'typically British' – which Johnson himself might have regarded as a dubious compliment.[28] But this was still better praise than he was ever likely to squeeze out of his own benighted literary culture. Was he 'appy? In Tours, on the evening of 27 January 1968, he probably was.

---

* The ill-fated *Playtime* – a genuine attempt to build 'a bridge between the experimental film and the popular audience', if ever there was one.

HUNGARY AND WALES

112: JOKE *(19 February 1968)*

In a letter to Zulfikar Ghose

> Heaven is getting a bad press, so God, Jesus, and the Holy Ghost have a top-level meeting about it. Lots of holy hot air is expended which boils down to JC being reluctantly persuaded that the time for the Second Coming is Now. Approaches are discussed. JC suggests the Loaves and Fishes bit, but the HG ousts this one by pointing out that with supermarkets, packaged fishfingers, Oxfam airlifts, etc., people just wouldn't be impressed. When the HG suggests a second Lazarus, JC just laughs and points out that with kidney machines, heartgrafts, and so on, people have already seen that one. Eventually they settle for the Walking-On-The-Water, which no one has done since. JC duly reincarnates, announces his intention to a credulous world, the press boys hire launches, the tv boys a helicopter, JC steps over the side – and sinks like the proverbial stone. Back in Heaven, a post-mortem: HG says Next time send me, God says What happened, son? JC says, Okay, so last time I didn't have holes in me feet . . .

After his triumph at Tours, Johnson returned to Paris with Virginia to pack up their flat. The Parisian interlude was over, all too quickly. Early in February 1968 he flew briefly back to London to deliver the completed manuscript of *The Evacuees* to Gollancz in person, after which he and Virginia struck out for the south of France to dispose of the remainder of his Somerset Maugham prize money.

One of their first stops was Aix-en-Provence, where they visited Ruth Fainlight and Alan Sillitoe. Eight years earlier, unknown and unpublished, Johnson had approached Sillitoe's agent and asked to be represented by her – impressed, among other things, by the rumour that she had been making him £10,000 a year. Now the two writers, equally well established (but still not equally remunerated, as Johnson would have been all too well aware) maintained a cordial, occasionally wary friendship.

'We've been staying with the Sillitoes a couple of days,' he wrote to Zulfikar Ghose. 'Very pleasant – they have (rented) a big home, a girl to do their typing and look after their son (6). I must say I think he's unaffected by success – which I remember thinking when you and I first met him at Dulwich [...] But what he and I are doing is completely opposed – he *makes up* everything for god's sake! And his carelessness about language appals me. However, he's easy and entertaining to get along with.'[1]

When his horror at Sillitoe's carelessness with language became unendurable, perhaps, the Johnsons resumed their journey south. From La Grave in Les Hautes Alpes, he sent John Furse a jokey postcard: 'Greetings from beyond La Grave,' it said. 'No sign of Him here either.'* A week later they were staying with Gianni Zambardi-Mall in Chieri, outside Turin. Here, Johnson wrote the poem 'Nothing More', another of his attempts to 'exorcise' the by now ten-year-old memory of Muriel, later included in *Poems Two*. We can see where the inspiration for this one came from: he was still brooding over Stanley Reed's and Michael Balcon's comments on the *Albert Angelo* screenplay, in which they had told him, among other things, that the character of Jenny was insufficiently developed. Johnson's response to this suggestion, if the poem is anything to go by, was half-resigned and half-defiant:

113: POEM *(26 February 1968)*

Nothing More

fill out her character more
they said
rightly
so I worked hard remembering

and the sad thing perhaps was
all had
been said
there was really nothing more

These twenty-eight words, however, are about the sum total of his creative output from this period. As he wrote to John Furse, the best thing about this trip was that 'I'm doing no work and loving it – no mail because I don't have an address.'[2]

On the day the Johnsons finally returned to England, their car broke

---

* But what's interesting about this postcard is the handwriting. The 'H' on 'Him' is scribbled over twice – Johnson couldn't decide whether to capitalise it or not. Reverence, or irreverence, when referring to the deity? Religion always brought out the most conflicting feelings in him.

down on the M2 and they had to be towed into Faversham before taking the train back to London without their baggage: it was the first problem they had encountered after a month's trouble-free driving in continental Europe. Too easy to read an omen into this, I suppose. But even if we don't believe in omens, we're allowed symbols, aren't we? Good – so it was symbolic, then, of something that was to become a pattern in the rest of Johnson's life: the sense that whenever he left London – whether it was for France, or (later) Wales or Hungary – everything suddenly seemed easier, everything fell into place, and he no longer felt the sensation of embattlement, of continually struggling against daunting odds, that always overcame him in his home town and in his native culture. There seems to have been a strong sense, upon returning home, of sinking almost at once into a familiar cycle of frustrations and obstacles: and the breakdown of a previously reliable family car midway between Dover and Faversham seems, to me, as good a symbol of this as any other.

Anyway.

Johnson had now got a taste for the film world and most of his activities for the next two years would relate to the screen in one way or another. On the one hand, in the wake of *You're Human Like the Rest of Them,* he would start to be offered a number of directing jobs which – although invariably small – would at least allow him to hone his craft and, in one or two cases, express something close to a personal vision. (The chimera of a feature version of *Albert Angelo,* however, remained tantalizingly out of reach.) On the other, still finding that his income from novels was not sufficient to support his growing household, he continued to look for commercial screenwriting work, with the help of his film agent Robin Dalton. In fact he had written to her from the Auvergne on 15 February to say that 'as far as I can see I'll be free during April and May and would therefore like to do some film writing as well paid as possible: could you please try to arrange this?'

What Mrs Dalton arranged, it seems, was for him to start work on a screenplay called *The Perfect Tickle,* from a story by C. Scott Forbes* under the title *The Perfect Friday.* It was hardly promising BSJ material, being an entirely generic and typical late 1960s caper/heist movie, about an elaborate bank robbery that goes predictably wrong: a feeble stab at recreating *Rififi* among the stylishly decadent upper-middle classes of swinging London. Johnson's only personal point of contact with the milieu was that it allowed him to draw on his brief experience as a bank clerk (one of his first complaints about the story was that the banking background seemed unconvincing and insufficiently researched). It was reasonably well-paid

---

* Remembered (if at all) as a prolific writer for ITC adventure series during the 1960s and early '70s, such as *The Saint* and *Special Branch.*

hackwork: he was paid £250 on signature, and there was the usual structure of incremental payments, with a proviso for £500 to be paid if the producers did not like his first draft and wished to try another writer immediately. Sure enough, this was exactly what happened. In the end the screenplay was credited to Scott Forbes and Anthony Greville-Bell and the film – starring David Warner, Ursula Andress and Stanley Baker, directed by Peter Hall and reverting to the title *The Perfect Friday* – was released in 1970, quickly disappearing into the morass of similar product clogging up the West End screens. For a while Johnson pursued his claim to a shared screen credit through his professional union, the Association of Cinematograph Television and Allied Technicians (ACTT): such a credit would, after all, have earned him more than £10,000. But when he saw the completed screenplay, he dropped this claim with a sniffy letter. ('Just for the record, I've seen what calls itself the final screenplay of THE PERFECT FRIDAY, and I do not wish to pursue any claim to a credit further.'[3]) The whole experience merely confirmed his contempt for Britain's commercial film producers, which he would express in a steamingly vitriolic essay for the ACTT journal a few years later.*

No, if Johnson was going to make any headway with film, it would be in the more rarefied, closeted atmosphere that he found most conducive: publicly subsidized art movies and licence-fee funded work for the BBC. At this time his first piece for the BBC was already beginning to take shape. In response to enthusiastic lobbying from Carmen Callil, a young Australian then working in the publicity department at Panther Books, a BBC producer called Lorna Pegram had decided that a short film about the conception and writing of *The Unfortunates* would make a good item for the BBC Two arts strand *Release*. Johnson wrote a fifteen-minute script on this subject while he was in Paris, and it was immediately accepted as the basis for the film. (How easy life could be when people were on his own wavelength!) Recording took place at his flat on 16 April 1968 and in Nottingham during May. By the end of that month, the film was all but finished. This was a rare case of television production proving to be less problematic than book publishing, because the Secker and Panther production departments were still floundering with *The Unfortunates* and publication, once scheduled for spring 1968, was now postponed until the autumn. The book eventually made it into the shops in February 1969, which meant that Johnson's film, always designed to accompany publication, had to sit on a BBC shelf for eight months. (And if you look at the sequence shot in his flat in April, you

---

* See Fragment 135 below, pp. 307–9. Later in 1968 he would also work on an adaptation of Brian Aldiss's novel *Greybeard*: a slightly more fulfilling project, but, again, one which was fated not to lead anywhere.

can see that the box he is holding is a primitive mock-up which bears little resemblance to the final appearance of *The Unfortunates*.)

Viewed more than twenty years later, this little film is a powerful, unsettling piece of work. The extracts from the novel are not read by Johnson himself, in his gentle baritone, but by (of course) William Hoyland, who barks them out in a peculiarly aggressive version of received pronunciation, so that the melancholy undertow of the prose disappears and we are left with a furious, in-your-face rant against the cruel randomness of cancer. Visually this effect is compounded by a controversial device by which photographs of both Johnson's and Tony Tillinghast's likeably chubby faces distort and decay in fast-motion until they have transformed themselves into withered death-masks.

According to Gordon Bowker, this aspect of the film brought accusations of bad taste from some viewers,[4] but Lorna Pegram had nothing but praise for Johnson and his direction. In point of fact, owing to an embargo on the employment of directors from outside the BBC, the credit for direction had gone to David Cheshire (although it had previously been agreed that he would 'accommodate all your [Johnson's] ideas about how the film should be made'),[5] but when this embargo ceased to operate for a few months, Lorna Pegram seized the opportunity to employ Johnson behind the camera again. And this time he made a short film which at first seems to bear little relation to the rest of his work, but on closer reflection turns out to be absolutely central.

It was called *Charlie Whildon Talking, Singing and Playing* and consisted of exactly that: a record of Charlie Whildon, one of Johnson's favourite north London pub pianists, reminiscing about his life and performing for customers. This entertainer was by now very elderly, and Johnson had been his admirer for almost a decade. He is mentioned in *Albert Angelo* as 'Georgie': 'Pity Georgie isn't here lunchtimes, for the piano. Great he is, so in control, found his way in this way, playing the songs of forty years ago with such dedication, interest, sheer interest.' But his enthusiasm for Whildon's playing went beyond mere admiration for the skills of a consummate professional. He felt a strong personal bond with the pianist, whose life had parallels with his own (Johnson had heard somewhere that Whildon had been devastated by his first marriage to a woman who had subsequently abandoned and 'betrayed' him), and who had been one of the consoling presences in his life during the miserable Claremont Square years of 1961–3: in those days Whildon had come to recognise the depressed-looking young writer and would even launch into a rendition of 'Who's Sorry Now?' whenever he came into the pub.

Following an afternoon of camera rehearsals in the Benyon Arms pub in De Beauvoir Road, N1, on Thursday, 13 June 1968, there were two days of filming. From what I can tell, it must have been a perfectly straightforward, formally unadventurous little documentary portrait of Whildon, capturing his memories and his music as well as something of the pub culture of Johnson's beloved north London. Given his powerful attachment to a disappearing ideal of working-class community, however, and to the musical heritage of the 1920s and '30s, I think we can assume it was one of his most personal and deeply felt films. He felt an urgent need to preserve and memorialize this vanishing world – of which Charlie Whildon was, for him, the epitome.

114: NOTE *(June 1968)*

All is shoring up against decay
   I really want to record Charlie so that I can see him for*ever*

It is ironic, then – and finally symbolic of the impossibility of Johnson's project – that this is the only film of his which seems to have been lost, irretrievably. Furthermore, there is no record in the BBC archives of its ever having been broadcast in the *Release* slot for which it was intended. All that survives are a number of reel-to-reel audio tapes containing some of the musical numbers and some fragments of dialogue recorded on location. The process of 'decay' against which Johnson wanted to protect himself has proved too strong, in the end.

Four more short films followed during the next year. *Up Yours Too, Guillaume Apollinaire* was a weightless two-minute 'filmed poem' in which words such as 'breast', 'tit' and 'eyeball' floated around the screen before arranging themselves in suitable positions on the animated bodies of a naked man and woman. Johnson was commissioned to make it by the ICA, to mark the fiftieth anniversary of Apollinaire's death: 'The ICA's idea', he wrote to John Furse, 'is that if GA were working today, he'd be doing his verbal calligrammes on film: so they've asked a dozen or so people (including Godard, Brook, Marker, Resnais, Varda et moi)!!!! to make 16mm silent bits.'[6] In the event, of course, none of these distinguished individuals agreed to take part, and Johnson's little cartoon – entirely shot in one day, 5 October 1968 – ended up adding little to his prestige as a film-maker. Also that autumn, he shot a short selection of interviews with contributors to *The Evacuees*, including Michael Aspel, John Furse and Gloria Cigman, all filmed revisiting the scenes of their evacuation. It was broadcast first as an item on the BBC's *Release*, and then as a half-hour programme in its own right. Gloria Cigman – then a young academic based, like Bernard Bergonzi, at Warwick University – recalls that Johnson was an inflexible director, impatient with her own inexperience in front of the camera. One of the stories she had told in her piece for the book concerned a conker tree. 'The whole TV crew took me back to my village, but it was a nonsense. You know, having been a scruffy kid in that village during the war, I turned up as a Lady Lecturer in a Jaeger suit and first of all I was asked to reproduce the scene where I sat in the farmyard with all the pigs snorting around, and I couldn't do it. But Bryan also liked the story about conkers and said, "Go back to the conker tree." So there was me again in my Jaeger suit sitting in the grass under the conker tree and there was the camera on the other side of the field, and I was expected to reminisce, and again I simply couldn't do it. He didn't even ask me questions behind the camera, he just kept saying, "Talk about it. Talk about the conkers . . ."'

A few months later, wearing his architectural expert's hat, he made another documentary for the BBC, this time about redevelopments taking place in the city centre at Bath (broadcast on BBC Two on 14 June 1969). For the time being, his work behind the camera seemed to be completely taking over from writing. Partly it was a question of needing the money – his 'salary' arrangement with Secker having by now run its course – but also he found that he enjoyed this work, the relief it offered from the isolation of the writer's life: the camaraderie of the location shoot and the editing suite. How highly he *rated* his own television work is difficult to say. Viewed today, few of these TV films can be seen as an important part of his output. Julia Trevelyan Oman, with whom Johnson was still in occasional contact, remembers watching his early television efforts and thinking they were 'Not very good. In fact, they're very amateurish. I watched one or two of them at the time and was incredibly embarrassed by them. In order to make good TV programmes at that period you really had to go through the corporation's training so that you learned the grammar, and I don't think he would have been prepared to do that: he wouldn't have been accepted, anyhow.' (In fact Johnson did apply to go on a BBC director's course in 1972 but was brushed off with the information that there was a three-year waiting list.) 'But I imagine', Oman surmises (correctly), 'what happened was that at first they brought him in and appointed a director over him or something of that sort, because that's what they would do to bring him in as a name. Technically it was a medium that he just didn't understand.'

The fourth and final film from this period, however, is better and more interesting. This was *Paradigm*, an eight-minute short in full colour which he wrote and eventually directed himself, with the ever faithful William Hoyland taking the leading role. The initial treatment for the film had been written in Paris, either in December 1967 or January 1968.

115: PROPOSAL FOR *PARADIGM*, SUBMITTED TO THE BFI PRODUCTION BOARD

This film is a paradigm (exemplar, demonstrative example) of one view of the writer's condition: the older you get, the less you have to say and the more difficulty you have in saying it. By extension, it is also a paradigm of the human condition.

The statement is reduced to very simple (though not the simplest) terms; it is also very short. Both these facts reflect what the statement is about.

Running time will probably be between two and four minutes, depending on how well the actor can sustain interest at each stage [...]

116: EXTRACTS FROM SCREENPLAY FOR *PARADIGM* (1967-8)

An arrangement of rostra providing five stages or steps.

Cyclorama with fast-moving clouds at back: the pattern of movement may be a quickly-repeated one: the clouds may be stylized ...

STAGE ONE

Long shot: full set.

A MAN aged twenty sitting one stage up off floor.

Cut straight after title into the middle of a very fast, almost fevered speech: lucid, eloquent, emotional but under control: it is, however, in no known language: *not* gibberish in the sense that it does not appear to be nonsense, but rather a very foreign language: the same non-language to be used throughout film ...

STAGE TWO

Medium long shot.

MAN up one stage farther: same man, but now aged thirty: his discourse is now noticeably less copious, but still flowing: more reasoned, but with flashes of aggression and cunning: didactic, proselytising, persuading, absolutely sure of the rightness of what he is advocating, saying ...

STAGE THREE

Medium shot.

MAN now aged forty: sitting on third level: he has some little difficulty in beginning to speak: several false starts, hesitancies: when he does speak, however, it is one perfectly-formed and modulated sentence, at the end of which he permits himself a quiet smile . . .

STAGE FOUR

Medium closeup.

MAN up one further (ie on penultimate) stage: now aged fifty: he is looking very tired, worn: at first he makes no attempt to speak: then appears to summon strength, courage: many hesitancies, lapses, but he still struggles to speak: eventually he bursts out with one monosyllabic non-word . . .

STAGE FIVE

Big closeup.

MAN on top stage . . .: now aged sixty: head in profile, bowed: long pause: head slowly raised: slightly less long pause: head turns slowly to full face: mouth shut, eyes stare into camera for as long as actor can hold it without blinking.

BLACKOUT

Johnson assumed that the British Film Institute would want to finance *Paradigm*, since they were so pleased with his success at Tours (and indeed the Melbourne Short Film festival, where in the summer of 1968 *You're Human Like the Rest of Them* picked up another Grand Prix). However, he was turned down on a technicality: the Experimental Film Fund could only finance the production of first films. Disappointed, he let the project fall into abeyance for a while and then, while in Poland for one week in early June, 1968, reporting for the *Guardian* on another short film festival in Cracow, he ran into a Belgian-Polish producer called Bronka Ricquier. She had a production company based in Brussels called Elisabeth Films and expressed her willingness to finance *Paradigm*, which Johnson himself had modestly budgeted at £1,400.

With the money apparently in place, he began more detailed work on the script, collaborating as always with his actor of choice, William Hoyland. 'Because we invented a whole language,' Hoyland remembers, 'there were weeks and weeks of preparation. I used to go round to Myddelton Square every working day for two or three hours. Bryan's knowledge of language was much greater than mine, but I had to learn the bloody thing, so we were both working hard. And there is a written script, the language trans- lates perfectly. Bryan wrote the script in English and then we invented the language and he translated it. It was great fun.'

Rather than writing a script, in fact, Johnson took three pre-existing texts and used them as the basis for the speeches in Stages One, Two and Three. Although it does indeed sound as though Hoyland is speaking gibberish at the beginning of the film, he has actually memorized an elaborate speech which concludes like this:

> *Raw quen, Goddor ut trustram zambard leeson art heathcolity, of fedmor-nicher lit, trustranshub shub shub shub che valna don darve ot tar mulst dersend knacker ludba, quol ut pullsty tar chingrom woxes fo am oopen mezaf day ter drailmerong woxes for em knackner Dinmah day ut hanose sayform woxes for veeve … Lere, clom, glods tad rack hoshn op taraw em lemascs gel?*

Perhaps only the true B. S. Johnson enthusiast – or fanatic – would be able to recognize this passage as the end of the long (indeed, interminable) joke in the 'Disintegration' section of *Albert Angelo*, with its dreadful punchline, 'Here, mate, what's that you're doing up against my camel's leg?' It's a very personal in-joke – like the hidden references to his friends Gianni Zambardi-Mall and Heathcote Williams in the above extract – of a sort Johnson often practised in his writing: suggesting, perhaps, that he was sometimes more wrapped up in the private meanings of his work than in the task of communicating with his audience.

Certainly it's the case that *Paradigm*, for the first-time viewer, is one of the most impenetrable and peculiar of all his works. One of the strangest things about it is the soundtrack, which features a sustained electronic whine rising higher and higher in pitch as the Stages progress from one to five. (A projectionist who showed the film for me assumed this was a technical fault and spent several minutes trying to put it right.) It did not fare well with the public. Shooting finally took place over three days in January 1969 at Eyeline Studios, 77 Dean Street, Soho: the art director was again John Furse and the editor David Muir. Mme Ricquier saw a rough-cut of the film and did not seem very happy with it, which was ominous, but it was soon selected for a short film festival in Oberhausen in March 1969 and Johnson travelled over for the occasion with Virginia – fondly hoping, one imagines, for a re-run of their triumph at Tours. It was not to be. The film was shown to a young, highly politicized audience, in the aftermath of the wave of student unrest which had swept through Europe. These people were in no mood to be sympathetic to an overtly Beckettian meditation on the communication problems of an ageing artist, however 'paradigmatic' of 'the human condition' it was intended to be. The film was greeted with boos and catcalls. None of the distributors present was interested in picking it up.

117: POSTCARD, FROM OBERHAUSEN, GERMANY *(31 March 1969)*

To John Furse

> *Paradigm* had a very hostile reception – apparently, we weren't actually there – from an audience largely of students and hippies – won no prize, Bronka despairs of selling it, all is gloom and despair. But at least we beat them in the World Cup!

(Incidentally, this would not be the last time the word 'hippies' appeared in the Johnsonian vocabulary with an undertone of dislike.)

This screening seems to have sounded the death knell for *Paradigm.* Bronka Ricquier wrote to Johnson a month later to say that she wished to dissociate herself from the film. Reminding him that she had not liked it even at the first screening, she mentioned to him 'the conversations I had with some fifty of the best reporters and film-makers assembled at Oberhausen. I am sorry to say that their opinion was more unfavourable than mine, [Walerian] Borowczyk's being the most severe of all.' She added that she did not want to take the film to any other festivals: 'If you wish to present it, I have no objection; I would simply ask you, if you do so, to cut out the last cartoon, bearing my name.'

Johnson's reply was untypically subdued.

118: EXTRACT FROM LETTER *(6 May 1969)*

To Bronka Ricquier

[...] What I simply don't understand is how you find the finished PARADIGM so different from the script you read and were so enthusiastic about. The only differences I see are ones you surely approve of – the camera mobile instead of stationary throughout, for instance, and the extended length. The film turned out very much (apart from the makeup) as I had always envisaged it, and, as I say, I can't understand how you thought it would be otherwise.

But of course I accept the fact that you are so bitterly disappointed, and I am as sorry as you are that you cannot sell the film. As for opinion, the ludicrously wide differences and lack of real standards I find more prevalent and damaging in the film world than in any other art [...]

I am still very grateful to you for giving me the chance to make PARADIGM, and, like you, the pleasure I had in working with you and our friendship remain unaltered. If this friendship gives me licence to say so, I think that you must direct films yourself if you want to see *your* concept on the screen: others' visions can never exactly be your own, and only disappointment can result.

Paradigm never found a British distributor and was never sold to British television. As far as I know, apart from perhaps two or three screenings at the ICA in London, it has not been shown publicly since its failure at Oberhausen in 1969.

So much for film, for the time being: what of literature? How were relations, in the meantime, with his current publishers, Secker & Warburg? Not too good, predictably enough. Disappointing sales of *Trawl* and muted editorial enthusiasm for *The Unfortunates* meant that the firm was not prepared to repeat its celebrated offer of 1965. Instead, David Farrer wrote to Johnson on 25 April 1968, saying that they could only pay £400 a year for four years (in the expectation of two novels) or an advance of £800 for the next novel, with an option to publish the following one 'on fair and reasonable terms'. Johnson's reply was succinct.

119: LETTER *(29 April 1968)*

To David Farrer

Dear David:
 The offers contained in your letter of 25th April are not only quite unacceptable, but insulting as well.
 Yours,
 B. S. Johnson.

He also drafted a longer letter on this subject, but I don't believe he ever sent it. However, the surviving fragments hint at his characteristic themes of injustice, institutionalized incompetence and missed opportunity.

120: FRAGMENTS OF A DRAFT LETTER TO SECKER & WARBURG *(? late April 1968)*

(1) Was promised better sales
    in fact *worse* with easier book

good reviews, wide other coverage
you didn't sell
second bite with SM [Somerset Maugham] award
didn't take it

If you're down, at least take part of the blame
it's your business to sell books.

(2) Novs. of 60s – no other Secker author*
    First SM.

(3) Don't owe you anything
        Press coverage)
        TV programme)† added up in adv. terms

This contract has given you
    (a) Yr first SM winner
    (b) The most original, novel, exploitable for novelty book since the war.‡

What more do you want?
What are you complaining about?

———

Furthermore, the amounts you pay to American novelists of doubtful value either as literature or bestsellers

———

Second book not out yet – nor even first in paperback – not moment to draw accounts or conclusions

———

Given your image a boost

———

Will not sell the products of my maturity for less – put them at the mercy of your sales department

———

Technically broken with both on time–
    Trawl 10 months
    TU by 30th June§

———

Why not take on my other books from Constable?

———

Why not take on ALL my books?
    You turned down EVACUEES
    Anthology
    2 plays

———

———

* Johnson is arguing that no other Secker author appeared in the TLS's 1965 list of significant books of the decade.
† A reference to the BBC's *New Release* item in December 1965.
‡ i.e. *The Unfortunates*.
§ He is pointing out here that Secker broke the terms of their contract by publishing both books late.

Standard of production lower in Trawl: see Clause 6

Option clause 1: not less favourable than this

Both novels dead on time – you will agree that I have fulfilled my side of this agreement impeccably?

By mid-May, in any case, relations with the firm seem to have been severed.

121: LETTER *(19 May 1968)*

To David Farrer, Esq

For nearly three years now you have been acting as agents for my books abroad. I wish to end this arrangement, and give notice herewith.

Please return to me all the copies of ALBERT ANGELO, TRAVELLING PEOPLE and STATEMENT AGAINST CORPSES which I gave you at the beginning of this arrangement.

This meant that Johnson now required a new agent to handle his overseas publications, and perhaps to find him a new deal at home. After a brief, unsuccessful association with Jan Davies, the wife of his journalist friend Stan Gebler Davies, he took the advice of another friend, Peter Buckman, and agreed to be represented by the highly regarded Deborah Rogers. He wrote to her warmly on 5 November 1968, welcoming their new association and mentioning the names of some possible future publishers – although, interestingly, he advised her not to bother with Gollancz (publishers of the *Evacuees* anthology) because they may 'have had enough of my bullying, interfering ways'. In any case, Rogers got onto the case quickly enough, and Johnson had a new contract with Collins signed by March 1969. This story was even thought worthy of an item in the *Evening News*, which reported (on 25 March) that 'B. S. Johnson, the novelist, has just secured his future until 1972 [...] The deal is a triumph for Collins, to secure a writer of increasing importance, and a loss for Secker and Warburg, who had him under contract up to the middle of last year. Secker's contract had given him £1,200 a book; the first of them, *Trawl*, had won a Somerset Maugham Award. On the strength of this Mr Johnson thought he was justified in asking for a higher figure. In the end the publishers offered to renew the agreement at £800 per book. "I wrote and said this was an insult and they knew I wouldn't take it," he says. "Then I asked my agent to start looking around for someone else."[*]

Collins, in fact, were giving him a two-book deal at £1,500 per book. His editor there was Philip Ziegler. Naturally, the relationship would end in tears, but at this point, as always, there was nothing but goodwill and jubilation on both sides. The money would have been badly needed at this point, because the family continued to grow: on 12 December 1968 Johnson's daughter Kate was born. And to accommodate the new addition, they had finally moved out of the flat in Myddelton Square and into a four-storey terraced house about half a mile away, just north of Islington Green. Now Johnson had two rooms in which to work: a back bedroom on the second floor, which he used for typing and administrative work, and a tiny attic room just big enough for his bookcase and desk – cluttered with all the various icons and symbolic objects which inspired him to creativity – at which he proposed to write in longhand.

The new house was largely paid for by Virginia's mother, who sporadically, over the next few years, would take up residence in the self-contained flat in the basement: not a good arrangement, from Johnson's point of view, since he was wary of his mother-in-law (and vice versa), and it no doubt did little for his masculine pride to reflect that he had not been able to house his family satisfactorily without her financial help. If he seems to have written little during the winter of 1968–9, the explanation could lie with the birth of Kate and the domestic turmoil that followed the house move. There were builders on site for the first six months after the family had moved there, and living conditions sound chaotic: 'There's a lot that needs to be done to it,' Johnson wrote to Stuart and Roma Crampin on 7 February 1969, 'not least because of a council sewer which collapsed and flooded our basement a couple of weeks ago'.

In the thick of all this, the long-awaited publication of *The Unfortunates* on 20 February 1969 might have seemed a little anticlimactic. Johnson was by now in the slightly unusual position of having broken off relations with the people who were nominally publishing his book. But despite having been written under the Secker contract, *The Unfortunates* had become more of a Panther project anyway. Since 1962, this excellent imprint had been steered by two young editors, William Miller and John Boothe, who made no secret of their desire to challenge the dominance of Penguin over the paperback market: to this end they were publishing writers like Nabokov, Genet, Norman Mailer and John Barth, and they had also, of course, snapped

---

[*]   Also in this interview he referred to the way hardback publishers would retain fifty per cent of paperback rights, describing this practice, in a wonderfully Hancockian turn of phrase, as a 'diabolical liberty'.

up paperback rights to *Travelling People* and *Albert Angelo* after Penguin had so enraged Johnson by turning them down. Their enterprising production department was run by David Larkin, and it was here that Johnson came with his proposal for the unbound sections, Secker having shown themselves to be completely nonplussed by the daunting practicalities of the idea. The final publishing credit on *The Unfortunates* reads, 'Panther Books in association with Secker and Warburg', which reflects the secondary role that the hardback publisher took in this exercise.

Despite his reputation for being difficult to deal with, Carmen Callil, the publicist who worked on *The Unfortunates*, has nothing but good memories of Johnson, perhaps because, temperamentally, they were quite similar. 'I have always cared far too much about everything,' she says, 'and Bryan did too. So when I worked on his book – and it was a special thing, a book in a box – I did what he wanted, which was to care about his work. That's what most writers want anyway: but Bryan *was* needy, I could sense that.'

A 'needy' writer was hardly going to be satisfied with the kind of notices *The Unfortunates* attracted. Even in the more sympathetic reviews, the same reservations kept recurring. Richard Holmes in *The Times* lamented the lack of solidity in the way that Johnson had reported (not created, of course) his characters: 'this technical self-absorption – for both author and reader – is finally at the expense of the reality of other lives: Tony and June, Wendy and Ginnie, blow away like loose leaves in the wind.' Julian Jebb in the *Financial Times* made an almost identical point: 'Tony, June and Wendy have peculiarly little concrete life. They seem more like visitors to a consciousness than individuals encountered, observed and described.' In the *Observer* Stephen Wall called the book a 'little experiment' with 'a mild logic of its own' and said that 'A comparison with novelists like Robbe-Grillet or Nathalie Sarraute, who really have done their theoretical homework, can only be to Mr Johnson's disadvantage.' He concluded with the deadliest insult of all, describing *The Unfortunates* not as 'an important fictional experiment' but 'a modest, sincere, small-scale novel'.

A couple of weeks later Hugh Hebert in the *Guardian* gave Johnson a platform in which to respond to these comments. The interview captures him pacing the floor of the new house while licking his wounds. Recalling his feelings upon delivering the manuscript back in September 1967, he said, 'I had known then what the critics' reactions would be, but I'd forgotten – it took 17 months for the book to come out – so it did come as a shock, the hostility: it did upset me for a couple of days.' But in fact, most of the reviews of *The Unfortunates* had been fair. John Boothe, one of Johnson's editors at Panther and for many years one of his most loyal supporters, remembers that during the whole of the novel's editorial and production process, 'there was a certain amount of debate about *The Unfortunates* – about whether the novel itself was a good enough vehicle for the idea. We believed that it was, and I still believe it was. But there was a good deal of discussion about that.' In the light of which, all the reviewers had done, really, was to continue this discussion in public. By and large, they saw the point of Johnson's experiment and had simply looked beyond it in order to judge whether the end justified the means. Nonetheless, the novel's critical reception would do little to alter Johnson's opinion about the reactionary philistinism of British literary culture, which remained a strong preoccupation of his own reviews during this period. Discussing *Terra Amata* by J. M. G. Le Clézio for the BBC World Service's *Bookcase* programme, he repeated his by now familiar quotation from Nathalie Sarraute about literary relay races, and added 'I can only envy French writers the literary climate in which a book like *Terra Amata* can be written and taken seriously'.[7] And reviewing Elizabeth Bowen's *Eva Trout* for the same programme three weeks earlier, he had lamented the book's old-fashioned methods and concluded, despairingly: 'That so many people won't agree but buy *Eva Trout* in thousands, makes me feel that the real trouble with the modern English novel is the standards of its readers.'[8]

This perverse appetite on the part of British readers for plot, characterization, narrative, authorial invention and all the other things Johnson despised in the traditional novel meant that the sales of his books would never be large and he would always run into the same problem with his publishers: if they paid him anything like the 'living wage' which he insisted was his due, there would eventually be a large unearned advance on the balance sheet. There was an alternative source of income, however: public subsidy. On 8 March 1969 the *Bookseller* announced that Johnson had been awarded a £2,000 Arts Council bursary, the second he had received in just over two years. Alan Brownjohn remembers that Johnson was on good terms, at the time, with Eric White who was then the Arts Council's literary director and assistant general secretary:

'Eric was a most splendid figure, but an absolutely establishment man on the face of it: yet he liked Bryan very much, and they got on well together. He once referred to him as a *bonny* applicant, which was absolutely the case, because Bryan had the knack of applying for things and getting them, convincing people that he was worthy. Also, I think, he played a little bit on their feeling that they would be very mistaken and rather unkind not to give so earnest and committed a writer a grant – that they'd be missing an opportunity. But equally, when *he* served on committees like that he would spend endless time trying to advance the cause of particular writers, and especially trying to get the ones he liked onto the committees, or into the fellowships, or to get the grants for them. He was very, very loyal, very devoted to helping certain writers in this way: people like Eva Figes, Alan Burns, Ann Quin, Giles Gordon.'

Johnson's knack for obtaining grants and impressing interview panels was, to put it bluntly, an absolute necessity if he was to survive in the cultural marketplace. Bitter experience was beginning to show that neither he nor his allies were going to make a living from writing alone. Zulfikar Ghose, for instance, had been offered a teaching post at the University of Austin, Texas, and had decided to opt out of the London literary rat race altogether. No doubt Johnson was pleased for him: but it was a severe personal and professional blow, to lose one of his closest friends like this. For his own part, in the autumn of 1969 – after a summer of more domestic chaos in which he admitted '[I] haven't written a word (except furious letters to dilatory builders)'[9] – he applied (at Ghose's suggestion) for a job as arts fellow at the University of Wales. This would involve taking up residence for six months at Gregynog, the university's house in rural Montgomeryshire where students came to attend residential conferences. There were to be no specific duties: the arts fellow was simply to be a presence, free to concentrate on his or her own work for most of the time, but also available to stimulate discussion and conversation among the visiting students by any means that seemed appropriate. The warden of Gregynog, Glyn Tegai Hughes, explains the thinking behind the fellowship:

'We had two or three student groups coming every week and this was the general idea: let's say, at the beginning of the week, the history departments would come with forty students and ten staff, drawn from the various colleges, and they might be followed by microbiology and they might be followed by English. So that would go on for two, or a maximum of three nights. And they might vary in their attitudes and interests towards the arts fellow. They might want a poetry reading, or readings from somebody's prose work, or if it was an artist, to visit his or her studio, and so on. It might be best if the fellow was a performer, but it was intended to be very free in that kind of way.'

122: LETTER OF APPLICATION FOR GREGYNOG ARTS FELLOWSHIP
(10 September 1969)

I wish to apply for the Fellowship tenable at Gregynog during the Spring of 1970.

I am perhaps best known as a novelist (Somerset Maugham Award 1967) but I have also published short stories, poems, and articles; been commissioned by both the Royal Court and the Royal Shakespeare for full-length stage plays; and written/directed both short films and television. An up-to-date list of my work, and awards it has won, is attached.

My first novel, TRAVELLING PEOPLE, was set in North Wales, and for the last ten years I have had a great affection for that area of your country. The part I know best is the far end of the Lleyn Peninsula, particularly around Llanengan, and this area has featured in several of my short stories and poems. I would therefore welcome the opportunity to make an extended stay in Wales: hitherto my visits have not lasted longer than a couple of months.

Graves' THE WHITE GODDESS, for all its faults, has had a great effect upon me and upon my work: part of what attracts me about your Fellowship is that I would be able to attempt to learn some Welsh and to be able to follow Graves' sources much more closely with undoubted benefit to my own work.

Yours sincerely,

B.S. Johnson.

Glyn Tegai Hughes's first meeting with Johnson was during the selection process in October 1969. He recalls that, 'He didn't know much about interviews. He told me afterwards he was absolutely thrown by the last thing we said, "Well Mr Johnson, have you any questions you'd like to ask us?" and he wondered what the hidden thrust of that was! He simply came across to us as interesting and we reckoned that students would find him interesting, too. In Bryan's case we were pretty sure that he would make an impression on a student group.'

Despite (apparently) not knowing much about interviews, Johnson was chosen from the shortlist of six.

123: LETTER *(17 October 1969)*

To Zulfikar and Helena Ghose

I got the Welsh job! You know, the Gregynog one you sent me the application form for. Went there for an interview last weekend with five others (Peter Porter, Richard Hughes who wrote HIGH WIND IN JAMAICA, FOX IN THE ATTIC, etc., two sculptors called Jonas Jones and Michael Pennie, and a painter called Gillian Ayres) and heard a couple of days later that they wanted me. The place is marvellous – a huge estate with a great Victorian house (not that the house is very good – mock Tudor, but after all they did invent Tudor) in some very unspoilt country – that area's being de-populated. We'll live in a three-bedroom 'cottage' about half a mile from the main house (that is, if Virginia likes it when we go down this weekend) which they'll furnish, heat and light for us for nothing as part of the deal. So as they're giving £1,000 plus a hundred expenses as well, we should make a little profit on it: that is, we've got to live there for 4–6 months and will have only food to buy, more or less. The cottage has a great view across a classic English/Welsh valley, cows and horses. Will send you a Mamiya photo of it in due course. Have been reading the WHITE GODDESS again, hope to write some poems down there. And to finish the next novel. All I've got to do is to be available to talk to students: they come to this place in groups of fifty or so each weekend for courses in various subjects. And I'll have to go to Aberystwyth once a week to talk to students, if they want. While students are at Gregynog I have to take most lunches and all dinners with them in the big house, which is one of the drawbacks as far as I'm concerned. But I'm delighted about it, and thanks for ringing me up about it that day – I'd probably have not thought very much about applying but for you seeing it would suit me excellently – being at that time still suffering from the trauma of removal once and not keen to do it again. [. . .]

Hope the Lotus has arrived by now. I'm still fed up with the 1300 – keep toying with idea of buying a 5–6 year old Jensen, the CV8 or 541. But V's got to learn first – she's driving us to Wales this weekend, and says she'll take her test in Wales, where it will be (she imagines) easier.

Am off to Hungary in a couple of weeks. Have just read a very stern Foreign Office pamphlet called SECURITY ADVICE ABOUT VISITS TO COMMUNIST COUNTRIES, which advises me that homosexuals may be *trailed before* me, or women, or if I get drunk I may be compromised, all the hotel rooms are bugged or under surveillance by infra-red cameras or both. Perhaps they're scared I might do a Kuznetsov in reverse, as well.

124: EXTRACTS FROM REPORT TO THE BRITISH COUNCIL ON A VISIT TO HUNGARY

Thursday, 6th November 1969
At Budapest airport I was waved through customs without a search, and in the main hall was met by the Cultural Attaché, Mr Hewer, who shortly introduced me to Professor LÁSZLÓ KÉRY, Mr. MIKLÓS VAJDA and Miss JULIE SZÉKRENYÉSY. The latter two drove me from the airport, and on the way through the city I remarked on the amount of neon advertising to be seen: after my visit to Poland I had not expected this, had indeed, as a writer, looked forward to a rest from visual bombardment by words, and wondered what advertising had to do with socialism. The two answers I was to receive from numerous people I questioned about this were never really satisfactory: one was that it was part of the 'new economic measures' introduced a year or so before, and the other was that they wished Budapest to *look* like a 'great European capital'.*

---

* Johnson wrote a poem on this subject: '7 11 69', included in *Poems Two*.

Miss Székrenyésy and Mr Vajda took me to the Hotel Szabadság, near the main railway station, where I was shown into a pleasant, warm, international-style room with its own bathroom. The room, and the hotel in general, were to prove excellent.

I had dinner in the hotel soon after arrival with Mr Vajda (an editor on NEW HUNGARIAN QUARTERLY, and also the translator of various plays) and Miss Székrenyésy (who is to be my interpreter) and rapidly felt at home with them and with the hotel. Miss Székrenyésy read a suggested programme to me, but mentioned that there would be more time in the morning for discussion. The three of us discussed literature and many other topics in great ease and informality until after midnight.

Friday, 7th November 1969
At 10 the next morning in the hotel lobby I met Professor Kéry and Miss Székrenyésy again, together with a Miss Judit POLGÁR from the Institute for Cultural Relations. We discussed my programme, a copy of which was given me. I felt that three Shakespeare plays in Hungarian was two too many, and had no interest in opera; on the other hand, I wished to meet Hungarian film-makers (particularly Miklós Jancsó) and go to a soccer match. These changes were readily accepted. [...]

Miss Polgár gave me the sum of 1,890 forints, explaining that it was made up as follows: 160 forints per day for 14 days, less 25 forints per day for the breakfast included in the hotel bill. The money was intended for subsistence during the stay, and proved just about adequate for the purpose.

Professor Kéry then took me sightseeing round Budapest. The day happened to be the anniversary of the October Revolution, and the city had a Sunday air about it. Professor Kéry was an excellent guide, and I was impressed with this first view of the city, the Danube, and so on. He is professor of English at Budapest university and (like myself) an ex-student of Professor Geoffrey Bullough, who curiously enough is also here on a visit and came over on the same plane as I did. He (Prof K) is also head of Hungarian PEN. In Hero Square we went to see the Vasarely op-art exhibition, which was very crowded on this public holiday. We had lunch very enjoyably in the Gundel restaurant next to the zoo, and talked a great deal about literature in general and Lawrence in particular, in whom Prof. Kéry is most interested. After a walk through the city, I returned to the hotel. [...]

Saturday, 8th November 1969
Met Miss Székrenyésy in the foyer of the hotel at 5.45 in the morning in order to catch a train from Budapest to PÉCS, a city in the south of Hungary, for a two-day visit. Very cold, and it began snowing in the taxi on the way to the station: and at the station, dawn just breaking, steam

trains, it was just as romantic a feeling of Middle-European foreignness as one could wish.

The train comfortable enough: we travel first class, another surprise, that they have classes at all; at every station the stationmaster stands to attention as we depart, at every signalbox the signalman does the same, and I imagine this to be one of the few obvious signs of the Austro-Hungarian empire days.

Arrived mid-morning in Pécs, where it was raining heavily, and booked in at Hotel Nador. Went sightseeing in afternoon: much Turkish influence, mosque in main square now a church, another mosque much smaller and with a minaret from which there was an excellent view. A C19 cathedral on medieval foundations; two museums which proved to be shut, since this Saturday was a public holiday. Mid-afternoon went to restaurant in the middle of its own hillside vineyard, very pleasant light white wine: until early evening. Back to the hotel, rather depressed by the Sunday atmosphere and the rain: think in retrospect it was not a good idea to be rushed off to Pécs before I had really had a chance to settle in Budapest – like experiencing the same sudden shift twice in rapid succession. Dinner in an interesting place combining the functions of restaurant, pub, and dance-hall: customers mainly miners.

Sunday, 9th November 1969
Although this day was normally a holiday, because the two previous days had been free this Sunday was declared a working day, and the shops were open and many people were about. My depression lifted.

At eleven we came to what I presume was the main purpose of my visit to Pécs, a meeting with the group of writers centred round the local magazine JELENKOR. Pécs, I was told in Budapest, was one of the most lively and independent centres of provincial culture. The magazine's office was in a fine late C18 building on the same side of the main square as our hotel, and about eight to ten writers had gathered to meet me. Through Miss Székrenyésy we talked for about an hour and a half: about their magazine (of which two copies were given me, and which I was later to see on news stalls throughout Budapest), my work, Beckett, Updike, Salinger, Auden. They were most friendly and interested and interesting. The inevitable question of freedom to publish without political censorship came up, and I was able to explain that in England writers were free to publish whatever they like because no one takes any notice of what writers think, they are not a threat in political terms; indeed, I suggested that I could come to envy a system in which writers were thought important enough to want to suppress. I found the meeting with these writers very stimulating, and Miss Székrenyésy thought it went very well: she said it was important that such writers should get answers directly from me.

On our return to Budapest early that evening, I asked for treatment to remove a foreign body from my right eye. Miss Székrenyésy arranged at once for me to go to a large hospital near the hotel. On production of my passport treatment was promptly given which cleared up the trouble within 24 hours.

Monday, 10th November 1969

In the evening Professor Bullough and I are to address the PEN club in the House of the Writers' Association. Professor Kéry introduces me, gives resumés after both of us have spoken. My own talk seemed to interest a number of people who came up to discuss my work afterwards. GÁBOR MIHÁLYI, an editor of *Nagy Világ* the foreign-language magazine, asked me to lunch the next day; and ZOLTAN KENYERES, a lecturer in English to whom I had already had an introduction in England through Barry Cole, was very friendly and asked me to dinner later in the week. [...] The meeting was to prove important for the contacts it gave me.

After the meeting I went for dinner to the house of ISTVÁN BART and his wife MARTA, two Hungarians I had already met in England through the British Council. Felt very much at home with them, and had a most enjoyable evening. István took copies of my books when he returned from England, and he says there is a chance Europa Publishing House may publish one of them, THE UNFORTUNATES, which he is keen to translate himself. But a decision will take time. István tells me that my novel TRAWL is considered obscene by Hungarian standards, which surprises me.

Tuesday, 11th November 1969

I give a talk to fourth year students of English at the Eötvös Loránd University in the morning: three-quarters of an hour talking, with another three-quarters for questions. Good, intelligent audience, mainly of women: it is explained to me that men tend to do science subjects. The chairman is MR. SZABU, who has spent some time in England doing a thesis on the English social realist novel. I felt afterwards that the talk was very successful: certainly from my point of view.

Lunch with GÁBOR MIHÁLYI of *Nagy Világ*, to whom I gave a copy of my short stories STATEMENT AGAINST CORPSES for consideration for his magazine. Afterwards he drove me to the building shared by PEN and Hungarofilm and together we saw Jancsó's latest film THE CONFRONTATION. This excellent film was made all the more interesting to me in that Mihályi had taken part in the events just after the war with which the film was dealing, and I therefore had the benefit not only of his translation but also of his commentary. The viewing of THE CONFRONTATION was one of the most worthwhile events of my visit, and I learned something of immediate relevance to my stay: something of why Hungary is as it is. At the same session they also ran for me Sandor Sara's THE UPTHROWN STONE, a very moving and honest film which also impressed me and in technique (especially the ending) was very relevant to my own work.

In the evening I gave a long interview to Mihályi SZEGEDY-MASZÁK, a lecturer in English at the University of Szeged, who was another of those I had met the previous evening at PEN. He seemed very interested in my work though he had read only ALBERT ANGELO, and that since the previous evening, and he obviously had grasped what I am trying to do. Gave him copies of the other books, and before I left Hungary we had several more discussions for an article on my work he had decided to write. I have since corresponded with him on the same subject, and he has asked one of his students to write a thesis on my work.[*]

Wednesday, 12th November 1969
Another film at Hungarofilm in the afternoon. WALLS, directed by Kovács, is almost all talk, and while the subject (freedom to leave the country, responsibility to return despite the attractions of other countries) is obviously of key relevance to Hungarians, I could not identify with it myself sufficiently; and technically I learnt nothing from it since Kovács hardly used the medium of film at all.

In the evening to a cellar restaurant under the castle with ISTVÁN and MARTA BART. Much wine and talk: especially about the films I had seen and the views they represent. I learnt much about Hungary, art and the political situation, and found the Barts and I have much in common.

Thursday, 13th November 1969
To the office of *Nagy Világ* with Miss POLGÁR for meeting with Gábor MIHÁLYI and other editorial staff. Scruffy old offices just like English publishers. Gábor Mihályi tells me they wish to print my story *Broad Thoughts from a Home* from the book: I am pleased, not least at the very quick decision. General discussion followed about various literary topics.

Lunch with Gábor Mihályi and Julia Székrenyésy. Again discuss THE CONFRONTATION, and its reception in Hungary (it caused great controversies) and find it all more complicated than it seemed last night with the Barts.

---

[*] The student in question was György Novák, then a secondary school teacher in Baja; now Associate Professor of American Studies at the University of Szeged (where he runs a B. S. Johnson website). See also below, pp. 346–7.

Friday, 14th November 1969

To the Petöfi Literary Museum with Miss Polgár, who is an enthusiastic and informative guide on Hungarian literary history, particularly poetry, and seems pleased that I am not bored out of my mind. Particularly interested in the later poets Attila Joszef and Radnöti.

In the afternoon a visit to the MAFILM Film Studios, and the first hitch in my arrangements on this visit. I was to have shown my own films and to have seen some of their shorts: but some mix-up in the bookings on the part of Miss Karda of PEN has occurred. Eventually I see by mistake part of a rough-cut of an C18 nudie film, am introduced to the charming senior producer LÁZÁR GYÖRGY, and finally see two rather mediocre shorts called TUESDAY and ENCHANTED. But an invitation to show my films to the studio's experimental club next Tuesday is extended.

I entertain the Barts and Miss Székrenyésy to dinner in my hotel: much talk, exchanges of views. Give István Bart the novels of Alan Burns and Ann Quin, with the highest recommendations.

Saturday, 15th November 1969

Up at 5.45 to meet István Bart at the (genuine) Turkish baths below the Gellert Hill: an invigorating and architecturally remarkable experience.

At 10 with Miss Polgár to the main television studios, which are situated in what was the Stock Exchange building. Studios fairly makeshift by English standards, equipment, too, oldfashioned, only three cameras per studio. Go to largest studio where JANOS HERSKÓ (head of the film college, director of THE IRON FLOWER) is directing a film scene set in a TV studio: I was told the plot and theme (should academics seek popular reputations through appearing on television?) and this and later experience led me towards the opinion that Hungarian television is at the Gilbert Harding stage of development. The filming techniques I saw (which were the purpose of my visit) were in no way out of the ordinary, though Herskó looked to be a dedicated professional.

Also met television director KARPATI working on a Saturday night comedy programme: seemed a talented man doing hack work.

Lunch with Miss Polgár in the Gresham, once a famous literary restaurant with some nominal English connection. But a poor lunch by Hungarian standards.

Through the suburbs to an industrial section of Budapest ('do you know the term *lumpenproletariat?*' asked Miss Polgár) to go to football match UJPEST DOCSA versus MTK. Fortunate to see the great Hungarian player BENE add three to the greatest number of goals he has ever scored in a season in helping Ujpest win 6–1. Miss Polgár said she quite enjoyed her first football match.

To formal dinner in the evening with the Barts, and to meet ISTVÁN GÉHER and his wife, she a teacher and he head of the foreign language sections of Europa Publishing House and the man to whom István Bart had already given my books for consideration. Since I have a formal meeting with Géher on Monday, we talk only in the most general way about my books on what is primarily a social occasion; but useful contact is made.

Monday, 17th November 1969
With Miss Polgár to the Europa Publishing House to discuss with ISTVÁN GÉHER the possibility of publishing my work in Hungarian translation. István Bart was also there. I was shown some very well-produced books, and was impressed with the range of translating carried out in Hungary. Géher said the decision whether or not to publish my work would take a long time: four or five readers' reports, offer to wholesalers who turn everything new down on principle then accept the next offer because they've vaguely heard the name somewhere before: so it may take 2–3 years from first consideration to publication, if at all. But he is hopeful of publishing perhaps ALBERT ANGELO and THE UNFORTUNATES. TRAVELLING PEOPLE is not well thought of, and TRAWL is thought obscene.

Lunch at Hungaria restaurant, famous literary meeting-place, with Professor KÉRY and Miss Székrenyésy and to meet SHURKA (phonetic spelling, as I never saw his name written down) a young-ish playwright who was said to be avant-garde in Hungarian terms. Pleasant conversation, exchange of pleasantries.

Tuesday, 18th November 1969
Show my two films YOU'RE HUMAN LIKE THE REST OF THEM and PARADIGM to an audience of about thirty film-makers at the Film Club of the Film Artists Association, and give a talk about them with Miss Székrenyésy translating. Discussion follows, interested but not very lively.

Wednesday, 19th November 1969
The Cultural Attaché rang at 8.15 a.m. to apologise for having neglected me during my visit: we can have exchanged no more than twenty words since I arrived. But I told him not to feel guilty about this as I came here to meet Hungarians and not my fellow countrymen. I was unfortunately unable to accept his offer of lunch that day as I was already committed to a full programme.

ISTVÁN BART and I had further discussions, regarding points of translation in my novels, over lunch at the Apostolok and during the morning. I am very happy that he wishes to translate me, as he very clearly understands the intentions of my work.

Miss Székrenyésy arranged for me to meet the avant-garde writer GYULA HERNÁDI in the afternoon at the Astoria Hotel. Besides being a novelist Hernádi is also the scriptwriter of all Jancsó's films, and I was surprised and delighted to find that MIKLÓS JANCSÓ himself was also there. Through Miss Székrenyésy we chatted for about an hour and a half: about writing and making films, the difficulties of setting up art movies, THE CONFRONTATION, and many other things that made this one of the best things about my visit. Jancsó promised to get in touch with me when he next comes to London, and I intend to write an account both of our meeting and THE CONFRONTATION.

In the evening a farewell dinner given by Professor Kéry, with the Barts, Professor Bullough and one or two others.

Thursday, 20th November 1969
Returned to London at midday.

SUMMARY of Talks/Readings and Reactions to them
At both PEN Club and the University I attempted to set my novels in particular and my writing as a whole in the context of English writing today. I stated my firm belief that James Joyce's ULYSSES was a revolution in the novel but that most English novelists choose to write as if it had never happened; that Samuel Beckett's novels were of equal importance, and continued in the direction Joyce had indicated; and that I myself and a handful of others (Alan Burns, Ann Quin, in particular) were also, however humbly, at least going in the same direction. From this generalised statement I proceeded to talk about my own novels, how they came to be written, why I have adopted unconventional typographical devices to solve certain problems, what my intention was, and so on; and because the books had not been generally available in Hungary before my visit, I read from each one to demonstrate some of the points I made. At the University there was a very lively discussion after my talk.

On a more personal level, I talked about my work with many of the people I met in the literary and film worlds, and distributed the copies of my books I had brought: four copies of each of six titles.

Reactions were almost universally of interest, ranging from mild to greatly enthusiastic. It was apparent that this was a new concept of the English novel to them; indeed, Mr Szegedy-Maszák told me that two previous literary visitors had left the impression that Joyce was rubbish and that Beckett was meaningless. This at least I did my best to set straight: but ULYSSES is available only in what they told me was a bad Hungarian translation, and Beckett is really only known for a production of WAITING FOR GODOT done very belatedly at an experimental theatre a couple of years ago. I urged that Beckett's novels (which are certainly more important than his plays) should be published; there was at the time a certain amount of interest in Beckett since he had just been awarded the Nobel prize.

Conclusions and Suggestions

I very much enjoyed my visit to Hungary, apart from feeling unexpectedly homesick for my wife and children. It certainly gave me considerable insights into another way of living, and I made at least two good friends (the Barts) and several contacts (Géher, Szegedy-Maszák, Prof. Kéry, and others) who may well prove valuable to my work. I was most stimulated by an atmosphere in which *avant-garde* and *intellectual* were not considered words of abuse, as in England. And I found no subject which anyone was unwilling to discuss freely. At the time of writing, three months later, I am sure the visit was of much benefit to me and I certainly intend to return.

On the whole the administration of the visit was efficient. I am still not sure whether the subsistence allowance was too small, or I was too extravagant: certainly I spent all the money (£35) I had brought from England as well, but brought home a number of presents.

I found that the advice given in the pamphlet *Security Advice about visits to Communist Countries* had a severe inhibiting effect on me, and hampered me in making friendships with, for instance, my interpreter Miss Székrenyésy: that is to say, it proved impossible to be ordinarily friendly with her for fear that she was a member of the security services warned about so seriously by the Foreign Office. I understand that it was essential that I be warned; but I suggest that the way it is done should be less melodramatic, and that some idea of the statistical probability of it happening to any one visitor should be given.

The only other (and very minor) way in which I think arrangements might be improved is that English visitors could be provided with a short glossary for menus: in all but the international restaurants there was no way of telling whether one was ordering pork or beef, for instance, and the excitement of that uncertainty can wear off in a few days.

As a follow-up to my visit I suggest that another English writer representative of what I have explained as the direction the novel is going be sent on a similar visit: Alan Burns, for example, Rayner Heppenstall, or Ann Quin. Furthermore, I think it would be useful for an academic like Bernard Bergonzi (an expert in the really contemporary novel, of Warwick University) and/or Professor Christopher Ricks (authority on Beckett, Bristol University) to visit Hungary.

B.S. Johnson
London, 9th February 1970

Johnson's language in this official report is guarded, and formal. It gives us only an oblique sense of how profoundly affected he was by what he found in Hungary, on this visit and – even more importantly – on the several further trips he was to make there during the last four years of his life. It was not simply that he at last found himself dealing with a culture that felt perfectly at home with the notion of an avant-garde: the sense of *belonging* that struck him more and more forcibly whenever he returned derived from the fact that in Hungary, during this period of its history, the literary, cultural and educational establishments were entirely and unequivocally committed to an oppositional point of view – his own point of view, in other words. When dealing with a figure like Philip Ziegler, his new editor at Collins, for instance – a charming and good-natured man, but strikingly posh and patrician – Johnson would find himself running up against the exact opposite of his own beliefs and attitudes at every turn. And this was entirely typical of the British literary culture of the 1960s and early 1970s. At Europa, on the other hand, where István Bart worked and where *The Unfortunates* would eventually be published, opposition to the political and cultural status quo was not even discussed: it would simply be taken for granted. Opposition was the very oxygen which everybody in that milieu breathed, so that even the permanent sense of *anger* which Johnson carried with him in the suffocating cultural climate of England would evaporate whenever he went to Hungary, where resistance and good living – two of the principles to which he was most seriously committed – seemed to go easily and delightfully hand-in-hand.

Such, at any rate, is the memory of two of Johnson's best Hungarian friends, István Bart and Ferenc Takács.*

Takács: 'These Hungarians were much more open, it was easier to get close to them, and I think he appreciated that very much. He suddenly found a few people who spoke English, who were intelligent, who knew what he was talking about, and were living a life of carnivalesque dissipation, which he always wanted to live but stuffed-shirt Britain never quite allowed him to do.'

Bart: 'He liked the talk, the food, the booze, and the unstuffiness. I think

---

* As director of the Europa and Corvina publishing houses, István Bart has had wide experience of publishing British writers in Hungarian translation. Takács was then a teaching assistant at the English Department of ELTE University in Budapest, where he is now Associate Professor.

he found the un-Britishness of it exhilarating. Part of this was to do with socialism, which *we*, of course, utterly hated – but that didn't matter – the country lived a life apart from that, in which there was a lot of equality, nobody was rich and nobody was poor, it was a very brotherly existence. We didn't care about money because there was no money. Money wasn't important. Wine was important, and friendship was important: money didn't matter. It was something you spent on wine anyway. Looking back we had a wonderful life, and Bryan was looking with envy at that kind of existence, which was not constrained by money or success or anything like that. Success didn't exist – and who cared about success anyway? You cared about your friends, and about acceptance by your friends. And not acceptance by some outside powers, which were always so hateful to Bryan.'

Was Johnson naive, then, to be seduced by the cultural atmosphere of a country in the grip of such an oppressive regime? Gordon Williams thought so, and still does, mentioning somewhat disdainfully in a letter to me 'Bryan's enthusiasm for Hungary's treatment of writers in general and himself in particular. The rights and wrongs of the Stalinist system didn't come into it.'[10] Bart, too, remembers Johnson as an old-fashioned 'English socialist' who never really got to grips with the real situation in Hungary: recalling their dinner with István Géher (head of the Europa foreign-language section, who later described Johnson as 'the last and only true angry young man'), Bart says that 'Géher's attitudes were, and still are the opposite of Bryan's.' (*Takacs*: 'Back in those days he was a kind of self-styled Christian conservative, and despite that he was visibly won over by Bryan's charm.') 'Bryan was provoked by him into overstating his views and he proclaimed himself to be a communist over that dinner, which he certainly was not: he had no idea what a communist was. But the point was that we were, all of us, very much together: there were no political division lines at the time, this was a unified *cultural* opposition – not a political opposition, because that wasn't possible. It was spread all over the country, but we all knew each other and were watching each other and lived in a democratic society of our own, which was quite separate from real life. The most anarchistic ones of us made their money outside the structures; most of us *worked* within the structures, but we did not *live* within the structures. We lived outside the social structures. And it was wonderful, a very good life, very satisfying. You weren't motivated by money or success, there was absolutely no competition, and general acceptance. And I think this is what Bryan found so attractive. He felt very much at home in a place where art and politics mixed so wonderfully: this was the charm of those times, and he understood this and enjoyed it tremendously. Looking back, that was the best part of our lives, when art and politics mixed so well.'

Having made his first contact with this alluring culture, anyway,

Johnson returned to Britain with the appealing prospect of six well-paid months in Wales to look forward to. Before that, he had two small projects to pursue, both of which should have been satisfying, and both of which went wrong. At the request of the Mermaid Theatre, he agreed to direct a one-off performance of two short experimental plays by a former East End docker by the name of Johnnie Quarrell. Both plays – *Backwards* and *The Ramp* – might have had a superficial appeal for him, being full of Beckettian non-sequiturs, imbued with a sort of poetic semi-realism characteristic of both Beckett and Pinter, and written in a lively working-class demotic for a cast of tramps, down-and-outs and meths drinkers. But they were poorly structured, thin and repetitious pieces. Produced on a shoestring (the cast, including the inevitable William Hoyland, were asked to provide their own costumes), the evening did not find favour with critics. Nicholas de Jongh, writing in the *Guardian* the next day (Monday, 5 January 1970) remarked on 'the oppressive boredom of the evening' and complained that *The Ramp* 'desperately needed more pace, point and less of the sprawling inconsequence that intermitted the author's attempt at jerking us into honest, old-fashioned tears'. In the *Listener* later that week, D. A. N. Jones complained of the same play that 'Johnson has directed this lengthy piece at a crawling pace' and wondered whether these 'two prole-weirdo one-acters' represented an early attempt by Johnson and Quarrell to win 'the award for the most boring production of 1970'. Even the director himself seems to have regarded the production as a mistake. A couple of years later, when Philip O'Connor approached him hoping that he might be interested in directing one of his film scripts, he replied, 'I've once tried to direct other people's work and it didn't work. I have enough trouble trying to direct my own, without added complications.'[11]

Shortly before this disappointing brush with theatrical direction, Johnson had also been able to realize a long-held ambition to make a television documentary about his two great architectural heroes, Peter and Alison Smithson. *The Smithsons on Housing* was to feature location reports from the building site at Robin Hood Gardens in Poplar – where they had designed an enormous housing estate, one of their biggest ever commissions – intercut with straight-to-camera interviews with both of the Smithsons, in which they would have plenty of opportunity to air their theoretical ideas. The original idea was to do a fifty-minute programme, although this was then scaled down first to thirty minutes and then to twenty-five.

Of all the films Johnson made for the BBC (of which this was, perhaps significantly, the last) none is more 'amateurish' – to use Julia Trevelyan Oman's damaging word – and none has dated more noticeably. Watching it today is a positively eerie experience. This is not just a question of hindsight – of knowing that the brave new housing project which these two theorists discuss with such daunting intellectual fervour would come to be regarded, by many, as a social and architectural disaster – but of the whole *atmosphere* of the film, an atmosphere dictated by the screen presence of Peter and Alison Smithson themselves. Never can late '60s fashions have looked so eccentric, for one thing. Sitting upright at what seems to be a kitchen table in extreme close-up, reading from cue cards with all the expressive variety of a dalek with a PhD, Alison Smithson appears to be wearing a child's spacesuit impro-vised out of tin foil for much of the film. The effect is frankly terrifying, and it's frequently hard to concentrate on what either of them is saying. Johnson's surviving production notes hint at his own frustration during the making of the film, his sense that the Smithsons were doing themselves no favours at all by presenting themselves in such a forbidding light.

125: EXTRACTS FROM SCRIBBLED NOTES FOR A CONVERSATION WITH ALISON AND PETER SMITHSON

Not what you are saying – but way you are saying it
You are *NOT* talking to yr architectural mates
But to a lay audience – don't complain if they smash yr building up
     because you
haven't explained it in terms *they* understand

either you discipline yourselves or I do in the cutting
And *persuade* the audience – as we talked of – by personality

When the programme was broadcast in 1970, John Drummond – who had commissioned it for the BBC Arts Features department – wrote to Johnson as tactfully as he could. 'I would be wrong if I didn't let you know that your film aroused extremely strong feelings both in this build-ing and in Television Centre,' he said. 'There was a fairly high-powered attack on it by the Controller who felt that one had simply not solved the problems of presenting sympathetically the opinions of people who are basically unsympathetic.[. . .] There was then a lively debate which is still continuing in the corridors about how best one copes with this kind of problem. In my view to ignore people whose views are important simply because they are not "very nice" is ducking our responsibility. But, never-theless, it is also important that they should be presented in a way that holds the audience, and what has personally depressed me is the number of my colleagues who told me they didn't stay with the programme to the end.'

126: LETTER *(26 July 1970)*

To John Drummond

Thanks for your honest letter.

No one knows better than I do that THE SMITHSONS ON HOUSING was boring to anyone without a special interest in architecture: I must (and do) take full responsibility for that. At the same time, I am quite sure that it was the only film that could have been made at the moment with the Smithsons appearing in it. The alternative would have been a film about their work and ideas, but without them.

That the film disappointed me was almost solely due to not getting the full cooperation the Smithsons promised me at the beginning: and my friendship with them has suffered severely as a result.

Of course the ideas put over are important, despite the fact that the people themselves are unsympathetic, and I am grateful to you [...] for supporting this view.

On 20 December 2001, shortly after viewing *The Smithsons on Housing* for the first time, I spoke to the late Peter Smithson – then aged seventy-eight – at his not at all New Brutalist South Kensington home. It wasn't one of my more successful interviews. I began by telling him that the film seemed, in technique, quite different from Johnson's other television work: the static camera, the tedious emphasis on talking heads in close-up, the depressing resemblance to a late-night Open University programme, a general drabness and absence of vitality. Could he explain this, I asked? He could: it was because Johnson had handed over complete creative control of the programme to the Smithsons themselves. After that, the interview proceeded rather awkwardly. Peter Smithson could remember almost nothing about B. S. Johnson, not even how they had first met.* The only revealing piece of information he let slip was to hint that Johnson had 'fallen' for Alison, and that this BBC programme was his gift to her. 'A pretty nice gift,' he added. Alison Smithson herself died in 1983, so her side of the story must remain untold. I can only say that if there was any simmering sexual tension between the three people involved in the making of this film, it doesn't translate onto the screen.

---

* According to John Furse, they had met as fellow campaigners in the (unsuccessful) fight to save the Euston arch in the early 1960s. Shortly afterwards, Johnson had approached the Smithsons by letter, suggesting he write a profile of them for the *Observer*. (It never appeared, although he did of course eventually write a long article on them for *London Life*. See above, pp. 201–2.) Initially they refused, prompting him to write a follow-up letter on 21 October 1964: 'Enclosed is a copy of my second novel ALBERT ANGELO [...] in which architecture is used as an objective correlative for poetry. I send this to assure you that the standards of the article would not be merely journalistic ones: I think it is fair (though probably conceited) to say that my position in the avant-garde of my profession resembles that of yours in architecture'.

Johnson remained, at least, on good enough terms with the Smithsons to write them a letter in February 1970, giving them news on his family's departure for Gregynog in Wales. 'We had a difficult journey here through the snow, only just making it, but we've settled in well. Steven has a marvellous polythene sledge with levers for braking and turning, and since it's snowed every day there's been plenty of opportunity. The first course of students last weekend were okay, didn't tear me to shreds, that is, so were a reasonably soft baptism. And I've discovered the joys of working in a library again.'[12]

This letter was written on University of Wales headed notepaper and signed 'B. S. Johnson, Fellow in Art', reflecting the pride Johnson was taking in his newfound role as member of a welcoming cultural establishment. Within days of arriving, he seems to have felt thoroughly at home at Gregynog. 'The snow is great here,' he wrote to John Furse. 'Makes the scenery even more marvellous than it already is. Am working well, too: have typed a piece of short prose* (note the avoidance of the word *story*) and drafted a poem (new) [. . .] Feel like a writer again, too, after messing about with all that visual crap. People are very welcoming, feel for about the first time in my life that I am actually being encouraged to write! Strange [. . .] Chopping logs is all the go, remarkable how quickly they burn – I reckon I spend half an hour a day chopping them. Is this how they lived in the olden days, Daddy?'[13] The same cheerfulness is apparent in a letter to Peter Buckman and his wife Rosmarie (who had by now become two of his best friends): 'I'm doing some trout fishing for only the second time in my life – the class overtones of this apply only in England. Am also learning some Welsh: difficult. Very pleased with myself in general, work going well, no financial worries, lovely family.'[14]

Meic Stephens, a friend of Johnson's going back to *Universities Poetry* days, has kept in touch with the warden of Gregynog, Glyn Tegai Hughes, and they still reminisce about that fellowship. 'Glyn Tegai told me that when Bryan was at Gregynog, he would get on extremely well with the gardening staff and would disappear for days on end: he would be out in the woods with the head gardener learning the names of plants and that kind of thing. They all liked him immensely and even the serving ladies in the refectory, they all thought he was wonderful.' (In a number of letters from this period, in fact, Johnson writes that he feels himself 'in great danger of becoming a nature poet'; and poems from this time include the *Three Gregynog Englynion* entitled 'Fern', 'Broom' and 'Beech'.) Hughes himself has the fondest memories of Johnson as a presence at Gregynog and recalls too the sense of contentment he seemed to radiate during his six months' fellowship:

---

* Probably 'Instructions for the Use of Women', later included in *Aren't You Rather Young To Be Writing Your Memoirs?*.

'He was terribly good at joining in at mealtimes and starting up arguments in a way that we had felt some of the other candidates wouldn't have been.' (Of course, 'starting up arguments' was more or less second nature to Johnson.) 'It worked very well and got the fellowship off to a terribly good start. He was liked all round: I have someone who comes in once a week to clean for me – she's been coming to us for getting on for thirty-five years – and he's about the only one of the fellows she actually remembers. He took part very vigorously in anything that went on. When the Welsh Literary Group met six times a year, he would come in and one of the things I remember very well was after one such meeting where the speaker was Kate Roberts.* Kate was probably the major Welsh short-story writer of the interwar years. Her stories are very, very good indeed – they really are of a European standard. Anyway, we all knew about her work and a lot of us knew her personally. And I remember Bryan saying to her, "Here I am, I've been writing for ten years and I get practically no feedback, my readers don't know me. And here are *you* in a group which not only knows the background to your work, and the work itself but they actually know *you* as well." That was one of the things that appealed to him most strongly: there was a feeling that the writer here had a community, a background.

'He wrote a lot while he was here. He wrote quite a bit in the hall itself, in the small library. There were two library rooms, and the smaller one was more secluded than the other. I suspect he found it easier to write not surrounded by two small children, and indeed we didn't see a tremendous lot of Virginia. The fellow and his wife could dine in at night, if they wanted. But with the two children Virginia couldn't do that most of the time while Bryan did, just about every night I'd say. There's only so much talking to students that you can put up with so I used to arrange quite often to be on the same table as him; and the other thing I remember him saying to me one night was that during those six months, when there was a monthly cheque coming in, he felt a sense of solidity in his life, almost for the first time.'

Not everything, of course, went as smoothly as these recollections make out. There were a number of clouds on the horizon, one of them provided by Collins, who were about to commit what constituted, within the Johnsonian moral framework, one of the cardinal sins of publishing: that of wishing to concern themselves only with his novels, not the 'enormous totality' of his talent. One of his first tasks after arriving at Gregynog was to assemble

---

* Kate Roberts (1891–1985), Welsh novelist and short-story writer. Her major works include the novel *Traed Mewn Cyffion* (1936) and the collections *O Gors y Bryniau* (1925) and *Prynu Dol a Storïau Eraill* (1969).

the collection called *Aren't You Rather Young To Be Writing Your Memoirs?: Selected Shorter Prose, 1960–70*, consisting not only of – what would he have allowed me to call them: short stories? creative pieces? works of the imagination? – anyway, not just these, but articles, book reviews, plays, even football reports: writings culled from the entire range, in other words, of the Johnson canon. Philip Ziegler came all the way to Gregynog himself to pick up the manuscript on 11 May 1970 – an encouraging sign of commitment, surely – but there was no immediate, enthusiastic response from London in the next few days, or even weeks. Some time in June, Johnson wrote to John Furse expressing his forebodings: 'I don't think Collins are going to take my SELECTED SHORTER PROSE,' he said, 'in which case they'll take a belting (verbal) instead.' At the end of the month, there was still no decision, but 'if they turn it down,' Johnson wrote to Zulfikar Ghose, 'I'm demanding an interview with the Chairman to sort him out.'[15] Whether this interview took place or not, I'm not entirely sure. Certainly by September a firm rejection had come through, and Johnson had confronted Ziegler about it. 'Irresponsible publishing, I called it,' he told Ghose, 'and he got very annoyed. They did not even bother to discuss the book with me – just turned it down. Relations got very strained because of this [...] They're very autocratic and commercial, unlike any publishers I've dealt with before.'[16]

In the same letter, Johnson claimed of Philip Ziegler that 'the two occasions on which I've tested his judgment [...] he's failed'. The other had been in 1969, when Ziegler, in his own words, had 'tried to get Bryan to do a sort of travelogue, a non-fiction book, to move around England and write his own experience of places. He did a piece about Bournemouth, but I couldn't see it working for us at all.' The proposal collapsed, as so often, in a tetchy exchange of letters, and the piece – of which Johnson was particularly proud – eventually appeared in *Aren't You Rather Young To Be Writing Your Memoirs?* as 'What Did You Say the Name of this Place Was?'

More than thirty years on, Philip Ziegler is still concerned to emphasize that 'I was genuinely fond of Bryan. He was the only person ever to persuade me to go to a football match, I remember – he dragged me off to watch Chelsea a couple of times.' All the same, it's clear that this was not an editorial marriage made in heaven. Ziegler had thought that the boxed format of *The Unfortunates*, far from being a courageous near-replication of the mind's randomness, had been 'rather a silly idea', and he was hardly likely to be seduced by the polemical fierceness of Johnson's *Selected Shorter Prose*, given that 'I could not take his theoretical thing particularly seriously. For me Bryan was a writer of great gifts, he had in fact got a remarkable narrative capacity but he did his best to conceal it, and the really annoying thing about him was that he could certainly have written, without sacrificing his standards, very successful books. And I kept hoping he would.' (The full meaning here, of course, is 'commercially successful'.) As for that confrontation in which he was accused of 'irresponsible publishing', Ziegler has no clear memory, but Johnson's highly specific promise of not just a 'belting' but a 'belting (verbal)' rings a definite bell: 'Yes, there always seemed to be a potential violence, with Bryan, but it was usually worked out on paper. I never felt entirely sure that he wouldn't throw a major tantrum in one's office, and start throwing things around, but on the whole he was rather like Malcolm Muggeridge or Auberon Waugh, he was much more violent on paper than he was face to face. I can't remember ever having a serious row with him face to face.'

The other conflict in which Johnson found himself embroiled while at Gregynog involved a newspaper: none other, in fact, than that doughty, lovable conduit for the bigotries and neuroses of Middle England, the *Daily Mail*. For a couple of years now the *Mail* had had the Arts Council in its sights, and on 16 March 1970 it ran a prominent article giving full vent to its paranoid loathing of this benign organization. The headline for this fine piece of investigative journalism on the part of the paper's 'Newsight' team read, *'They're giving away YOUR money to spoonfeed hippy "art"'*. Shocked readers throughout suburbia and the Home Counties must have choked on their cornflakes as they read that 'The Arts Council is making some astonishing decisions about the way it shares out its £9-million-a-year budget'. The Arts Council, they learned, was 'now established as a patron of the underground-anarchist-drugs world'. As an example of this sinister abuse of taxpayers' resources, it was reported that one recent Arts Council grant had been used to pay off back rent by the Midlands Arts Lab, a cinema and theatre complex 'housed in a ramshackle building in New Town, Birmingham', where – wait for it – 'girl members often paint their faces and bodies and simply sit around'.*

Most of the article, however, was concerned with grants being made to writers, some of whom, it was claimed, 'make it their life's work to live off cash hand-outs from the Arts Council. Each year familiar faces figure in the lists of awards winners.' There followed two parallel columns, headed by photographs of Johnson and Alexander Trocchi. Trocchi was described as a 'former pornographer and self-confessed heroin addict', while Johnson was profiled as follows:

---

* The present author must come clean and confess that he was himself a patron of this louche establishment in the late 1970s. Things must have changed in the intervening years because I remember it as a rather quiet place where sensitive souls like myself could repair for a cup of coffee, a slice of fruitcake and – if we were feeling racy – perhaps a Werner Herzog or Howard Hawks film. To be honest I never saw any 'girl members' at all, let alone ones with their bodies and faces painted, 'sitting around' in (for such is the *Mail*'s clear implication) nude and provocative poses. Too late, as usual: to quote Johnson himself – 'Ah, the chances let slip!'

291 / HUNGARY AND WALES

BRYAN JOHNSON

A 'very bonny applicant' who is 'usually able to make out a very good case for financial assistance,' says Mr White.*

In less than three years, Mr Johnson got £3,200 from the Arts Council – sums of £800, £400 and finally £2,000.

But for the current financial year, the council at last said 'no'. So Mr Johnson moved on – to the Welsh Arts Council.

Last month he clinched the newly created Gregynog Arts Fellowship, jointly sponsored by the Welsh Arts Council and the University of Wales.

In return for talking to students about his work, Mr Johnson gets for himself, his wife and two children, a rent-free house, £1,000 in cash and £100 expenses.

What sort of books does he write? One contained blank pages covered in grey or black to signify unconsciousness and death; another had holes cut in pages so readers could glimpse through to see what was going to happen.

Eight days after the article appeared, Johnson wrote to John Furse to say that 'a furious letter I wrote to the MAIL, demanding a printed apology and damages, brought nothing but a smooth reply saying no liability.' So instead he contacted his friend Alan Burns, who put him in touch with a solicitor, and the affair dragged on for two more months:

127: LETTER *(28 May 1970)*

To Zulfikar Ghose

As for the DAILY MAIL. In March they published an article about the Arts Council and how it was giving money away to hippies. And there were photographs of Trocchi and me. Me a hippy!† But it also implied that I got this job at Gregynog and my other Arts Council money corruptly, that by association I was a drugtaker and pornographer, and that TP consisted of nothing but blank pages. The sub-head above the photos said TWO 'WRITERS' IN THE AWARD LIST.‡ All rather upsetting – I spoke to Alan Burns (who used to be a libel lawyer on the Express) about it, and he thought I ought to go to law – mainly because the cutting would go into every paper's file on me and they

---

* Eric White, the Arts Council's literary director. See above, p. 270.
† Alan Brownjohn remembers asking Johnson exactly what the *Mail* had said, and being told, in a tone of high-pitched indignation, 'They were associating me with a lot of ne'er-do-wells, hippies and berks!' (It's 'berks' that somehow conveys his real sense of insult and injury.)
‡ This was in the *Mail*'s Welsh edition, rather than the London one.

would therefore think I was an easy mark if I didn't do something about it. So I went first to Lord Goodman's outfit (the only lawyers I knew, since I gave evidence in the LAST EXIT case) but he wouldn't take it because the Arts Council were involved; but recommended Rubinstein, Nash. The present state of play is that the DAILY MAIL are offering to print a really fulsome apology, pay my costs, and £250 damages: I'm trying to get at least £100 more damages. It should all be settled in the next few days. But it's been very worrying: to go to law at all I am very shy of, and was told that if it went to court (which would take two years anyway) and I lost (as I might – nothing is certain in law) then the costs to me would be perhaps £5,000. Obviously I could not risk that much (not having even got it) and the MAIL would know this and exploit their strength. [...] They offered to settle out of court, without our even having to issue a writ, at once: though only apology and costs: it's like a game – now we've moved on to the damages stage. Trouble is I'm not sure of the rules and (with my natural paranoia) that my solicitor is wholly on my side. However, it seems to be nearly over. The MAIL did a similar piece, knocking the AC, two years ago: I never saw it, and perhaps it was because I never complained about that that they felt encouraged to do the second piece. A bastard called Bob Hitchcock rang me here: the first thing I said was that the last time the MAIL mentioned my name it was in connection with knocking the AC: Oh, I wouldn't know anything about that, he said, I'm doing an article on the Arts Tomorrow and we're interested in you as an innovator. So I talked to him – on that basis. Just like the stories you hear about popular journalists, ain't it? Ginnie wants to buy a freezer with the damages. Freezer jolly good fellow, I said.

The 'really fulsome apology' appeared on 1 June.

Mr B. S. Johnson

It has been represented to the Daily Mail that an article on March 16 linked Mr B. S. Johnson, the award-winning author, with drugtakers, pornographers, and hippies, and implied that his Arts Council grants were obtained corruptly.

No such implications were intended and we apologise to Mr Johnson for any misunderstanding or embarrassment which the article may inadvertently have caused.

Dr Glyn Tegai Hughes, warden of Gregynog Hall, University of Wales, where Mr Johnson won the arts fellowship, in open competition, has described him as 'one of the most serious and promising writers in English', and has paid tribute to the intellectual quality of his lectures.

The purple-faced *Mail* readers of Middle England could relax, or preferably turn the page to find some other provocation to apoplexy. And Johnson could relax, too: he could devote his energies to writing again. Which seems to have been what he did, because June 1970 was an exceptionally productive month in the writing of his new novel – so much so that by the end of the month *House Mother Normal* was almost completed.

Perhaps it should be enshrined, as a general rule of writing, that the tone and content of a novel will invariably bear an inverse relationship to the circumstances in which it was written.* In other words, we probably shouldn't be surprised that this book – one of Johnson's bleakest, in the grim thoroughness with which it explores the indignities of old age – should have been written during the longest period of sustained happiness he seems ever to have enjoyed in his personal and professional life. How else could he have been emboldened to apply the word 'comedy' to a novel in which the main character – a nurse – is shown to treat her helpless and dependent charges with sadistic contempt, and in which these charges are portrayed as increasingly infirm and pitiful, some of them being completely senile and one of them dying (unnoticed) in the middle of the book? I wonder whether at any other time in his life Johnson might have found either the courage or the freedom from external distraction to present his vision of human bodily and spiritual fallibility with such harrowing clear-sightedness.

Nonetheless, *House Mother Normal* had not begun life as a novel about old age. It had been started, as usual, on Boxing Day: Boxing Day 1968, to be precise, in one of Johnson's father's parish logbooks. But this, as we know, was never the *real* beginning of the writing process. In the case of *House Mother Normal*, that process had started almost ten years earlier, when Johnson had first spoken to Tony Tillinghast about his idea for a novel in which the same event would be told from several different perspectives, each one presenting the scene to the reader with a different degree of 'normality'. Shortly afterwards he began to make notes on the novel and keep them in a blue folder headed 'NOTES towards a novel investigating aspects of normality and abnormality provisionally titled *Whose Dog Are You?*' (This title was later crossed out and replaced with *The Unfortunates*, which was itself crossed out and finally replaced with *House Mother Normal*.) Gradually this focus started to shift, and old age itself became the central preoccupation: as Johnson wrote to Philip Ziegler when delivering the novel, 'the normal/abnormal theme became more and more oblique in the writing

---

* The dreariest parts of my own novel *The Rotters' Club* – an attempt to evoke the rain-sodden milieu of south-west Birmingham in the 1970s – were written during a few sunny weeks in a comically palatial villa, overlooking Lake Garda, owned by my Italian publisher.

– to the good, I think'. But when writing the introduction to *Aren't You Rather Young To Be Writing Your Memoirs?* three years later, Johnson showed that this aspect of the novel was still important to him. He alludes to the technical challenge of making the same events seem interesting nine times over and describes his intention like this: 'Due to the various deformities and deficiencies of the inmates, these events would seem to be progressively "abnormal" to the reader. At the end, there would be the viewpoint of the House Mother, an apparently "normal" person, and the events themselves would then be seen to be so bizarre that everything that had come before would seem "normal" by comparison. The idea was to say something about the things we call "normal" and "abnormal" [. . .]'[17]

And so there's an unresolved tension at the heart of *House Mother Normal*, which tries at once to be a novel about old age *and* a novel about 'normality', without facing up to the fact that these themes never quite mesh. As a result, I've always considered the novel – which is a firm favourite among diehard Johnson fans – a very qualified success. And what this unresolved tension throws up, I think, is a plausibility problem, when it turns out that what the inmates have been witnessing over dinner (and describing, in the two most alert cases, as 'disgusting' and 'filth') is an outrageous sexual floor show performed by the House Mother, culminating in her receiving oral sex from a giant Borzoi dog.

Now it's true, of course, that strange and disturbing stories of staff behaviour in old people's homes – including sexual abuse of inmates – have been reported in the newspapers. Broadly speaking, the climax Johnson devised for *House Mother Normal* is possible, but this does not, within the context of a novel, make it believable. Nor does it really prove his thesis about normality and abnormality. For one thing, most forms of human behaviour would look 'normal' besides the spectacle of a dog and a woman engaged in an act of cunnilingus in front of nine decrepit onlookers. Johnson overstated his case so drastically – made his example of 'abnormal' behaviour so outlandishly weird and freakish – that his intended thesis carries very little weight. And in any case, no real link is ever established in the novel between abnormality and the infirmities of old age. What is supposed to be so 'abnormal' about senility and incontinence in the first place? Most people, even before reading the book, would presumably regard these as among the perfectly 'normal' (if undesirable) consequences of ageing. The nine inmates of this old people's home may seem progressively more sad, pitiable and even brave, on occasion: but at no point do any of them appear to be 'abnormal'. Our sympathies are already with these characters as they struggle movingly to cope with the loss of their mental and bodily faculties: we don't need a live display of on-stage bestiality to 'normalize' them.

Anyway: back to the blue file in which Johnson kept his working papers relating to this book. The file's contents are various, but mainly it consists of clippings from magazines and newspapers: some of these are concerned with the form of the novel, others with its subject. There are, for instance, a number of reviews of Kurosawa's film *Rashomon* – the urtext, if you like, for the notion of reporting the same events from several different points of view. There is a list of possible titles, too, including:

> *We've all got it coming!*
> *The Old Maids*
> *Almoners*
> *A Most Efficient Almoner*
> *Our Normative Almoners*
> *St Joseph's Hospice for the Dying*
> *(Our) House Mother*
> *House Mother to play*
> *House Mother Decides*
> *House Mother Defines*
> *House Mother Defaults*
> *House Mother Presides*
> *House Mother, Normal (A Geriatric Comedy)*
> *Orphans in Reverse*

There are many clippings from magazines and newspapers relating to conditions in old people's homes and mental hospitals. An undated review by Dan Jacobson of *And Yet We Are Human* by Finn Carling (published by Chatto & Windus in 1962) is of particular interest. The title of Carling's book is the probable inspiration for Johnson's own title *You're Human Like the Rest of Them*, while its subject seems to have had a strong influence on his early thinking about *House Mother Normal*. It's not clear that he actually read the book (as opposed to the review), but this short memoir by Carling, a Swedish writer who suffered from cerebral palsy, contains accounts – in Dan Jacobson's words – of 'a number of encounters he has had with other cripples and with people who thought of themselves as "normal" – normal, at any rate, in comparison with himself.'[*]

An even more direct influence seems to come from Keith Pople's review (in *Peace News*, 25 August 1967) of *Sans Everything: A Case to Answer*, an anthology of shocking revelations by former nurses in mental hospitals, edited by Barbara Robb and published by Nelson. This book

---

[*] Of course, what is shocking to contemporary readers is the use of the word 'cripple' in this context. It's even more shocking in the book itself, and in Angus Wilson's short introduction, where it recurs about fifty times, each instance slapping the reader in the face as if it was the word 'nigger' that was being bandied about with such cruel abandon.

(although it's possible, again, that Johnson read only the review) explicitly raises the question of 'sado-masochistic behaviour on the part of the nursing profession', and some of the detail in the House Mother's closing monologue (geriatric wards where 'confused patients ate each other's puke. Where I have seen a nurse spray a patient's privates with an aerosol lavatory deodorant', and psychiatric nurses who have been known 'to scatter the ward's pills for everyone to scramble for, and to put Largactil in the tea unmeasured') are certainly extracted directly from this review. Finally there is an article from the *Islington Gazetteer* (Friday, 21 January 1966) which may have sown the seeds of the novel's closing scene. It describes – in a wholly celebratory manner – a social evening held for thirty elderly people by the Lower Holloway Branch of the British Legion. "After the meal – a turkey dinner with all the trimmings – everyone joined in the community singing [... the party] was so successful that even Sally the guide dog joined in'. And there is Sally herself, pictured with her tongue hanging out, blissfully ignorant that she might be about to provide the model for Ralphie the sexually voracious Borzoi at the climax of Johnson's book.

There is another, shadowy literary presence lying behind *House Mother Normal*: a novel by Philip Toynbee called *Tea with Mrs Goodman*, published by the Horizon Press in 1947. Toynbee's short, almost plotless novel is set during a tea party in which the events are narrated by seven different characters – including a dog – who enter the room at different times. The action is divided into twelve 'time-units', each one lasting about a page and a half, with the same descriptive details and the same fragments of dialogue occurring at roughly (not exactly, as in Johnson's book) the same point on each page. The methodology, in other words, is strikingly similar to *House Mother Normal*, as is the way each section is introduced with the narrator's name – 'Daisy Tillett', 'Tom Ford', 'Charley Parsley', etc. This was how Toynbee explained his system at the start of the novel:

NOTATION OF THE BOOK
The pages are numbered both according to the periods and events described (by the number itself), and according to the narrator (by the letter attached to the number). Thus page A7 covers the same period as pages B7, C7 and so on, but each is the experience of a different person. A narrator always begins at the point of his entry into the room, and concludes at his departure from it. Thus narrator F's account opens on a page marked F6 (and not F1) because it is not until time-unit 6 that she enters the room. Thus narrator B's account is numbered from B1 to B12, because he is present throughout the whole twelve pages covered by the book.

The following plan should make the notation clear:

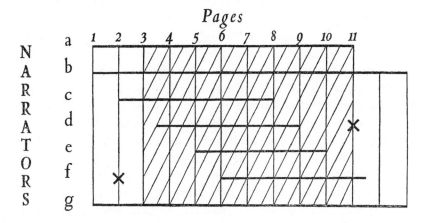

The book progresses along the horizontal lines from left to right and downwards, as in reading. Pages A1 to A10 are followed by pages B1 to B12, followed by pages C2 to C7, and so on. The faint vertical lines represent simultaneous moments of time. There is no page F2 (point crossed above) because narrator F is not yet in the room at page 2. Similarly there is no page D11 because narrator D has left the room by time-unit 11. The meaning of the shaded portion should become apparent in the course of the book.

Philip Toynbee (the father of journalist Polly Toynbee) was a well-known novelist and, for a long time, the chief book reviewer for the *Observer*. Johnson was certainly familiar with his work, including this book: reviewing Toynbee's *Pantaloon* for the *Western Daily Press* on 11 December 1961, he had written, 'Gone are the mathematical permutations and re-reading intricacies of *Tea with Mrs Goodman*'. So it's inconceivable that *House Mother Normal* was not to some extent inspired by the earlier novel, and just as Johnson had earlier found himself obliged to describe the box of *The Unfortunates* as 'a modified form of Saporta's technique', so we should probably refer to the page layout of *House Mother Normal* as 'a modified form of Toynbee's technique'. None of which is to imply, of course, that Johnson *stole* anything from Toynbee's novel without acknowledgment, or to detract from the power of *House Mother Normal*, which, even if it turns out not to be completely original in form, is a much more impressive novel than Toynbee's. Johnson's book is rich in human sympathy where *Tea with Mrs Goodman* is arch, fey and chillingly remote. (As a sample of the dialogue: 'I believe that your breasts are nothing but two dear little snakes, curled up under your bust-bodice.')

What the contrast between the two books demonstrates, in fact, is precisely why Johnson is such a remarkable writer. Everything that is sterile and academic in Toynbee's novel he humanizes: formal experiment becomes not a substitute for emotion and sympathetic involvement but the very means by which these things are brought about. *House Mother Normal* was the novel to which Johnson was referring when he wrote in *The Unfortunates* about a future book he had discussed with Tony Tillinghast in the winter of 1961: 'Perhaps we talked about the next one, an idea I had had, was very enthusiastic about, but was aware that I was not big enough to write it, yet, that the idea was bigger than I was and I would not have the techniques to handle it, would have to grow towards it. I do not remember what he said – no, now I think about it, we discussed that on a building site at the university, he was showing me around. I am still not big enough for that one.' That passage was written in 1967. Three years later, Johnson was 'big enough' to write *House Mother Normal*: big enough, before consigning her to the silence of those blank pages, to grant Rosetta Stanton her fragment of sudden, terrible honesty ('I am a prisoner in my self. It is terrible ... Let me out, or I shall die'): what he called, in a scribbled note to himself preserved in his files, her *'moment of lucidity before death (cf. Tony)'*. Big enough, too, to allow her a triumphant, subversive dignity: because the words strewn across her pages in what might seem, at first, to be a realistic notation of senile mumblings turn out to be Welsh words indicative of strength and lucidity: *digrif* ('delightful'), *gwron* ('hero'), *iachus* ('healthy') and so on. Big enough to realize that this 'geriatric comedy' was a necessary consolation for him, a desperate attempt to convince himself of his own great good fortune in having Virginia and Steve and Katie: *'writing about the sadness,'* he reminded himself in those scattered notes, *'the old, the more to appreciate what I have now.'*

And let us remember that the nurturing context in which this courageous novel took shape was provided not just by Gregynog, but by an entire culture of 'Welshness' that Johnson discovered for himself: a culture he may well have idealized, but which was nonetheless premised on reality. Jeremy Hooker, an English poet and academic who got to know Johnson pretty well during his time at Gregynog, remembers his growing empathy with that culture and with the Nationalist movement (including the rise of the Free Wales Army) that went with it:

'Bryan would have seen Welsh Nationalism simply as the defence of a different culture, even a different civilisation: a defence against the tremendously powerful forces that undermine it. I mean the forces associated with Englishness – it's not just a matter of language, it's a matter of history and a whole spread of uniformity and of things identified with an Anglo-American, materialistic way of life. The Welsh way of life is based on certain ideals – religious, communal, fraternal, which it hasn't always lived up to, but it is a culture that has very deep roots in history and pre-history, and throughout that, the tribal, communal element has been very strong. If you go back 1,500 years then you have got a tribal situation and the poet is the bard of the tribe. Culture changes, the society changes as the centuries pass and you have the rise of nonconformity which takes the place of the earlier Catholic religion, and nonconformity has its centre at the chapel and the community that centres upon that. So in a way the tribal spirit translates into the chapel spirit, which in turn translates into the socialist movement which was so powerful here in the nineteenth and twentieth centuries. So you really can talk about a poetic tradition that is 1,500 years old: it's not just romantic nonsense, there's something at the core of that and it's an idea of the *poet* relating to a people who are part of a culture that stands against the more powerful English and latterly American capitalist-imperialist forces and so on. And that in a nutshell, I think, is why Bryan was sympathetic towards Welsh nationalism.'

While staying at Gregynog, Johnson had also struck up a friendship with Philip Pacey, a young academic from Aberystwyth University who had written a short appreciation of his work for the literary magazine *Stand*. It was with Pacey's help that he spent several days towards the end of his time there attempting to print up a limited edition of his three *Englynion* on Gregynog's famous Albion Press. It was a comical, frustrating process but one which eventually gave him great satisfaction: later he wrote an amusing account of it in an untypically light-hearted piece for *The Private Library*.[18] Pacey recalls that, 'What I saw of Bryan during that time was very much the best of him, I think. As a younger writer of poetry I looked up to him and was pretty much in awe of him, and his encouraging of me and sharing of friendship with me was very generous; more than I had earned with that first essay about him in *Stand*. Much the longest period of time I spent with him was when my wife and I stayed with Bryan and Virginia at Gregynog, and clearly we were very lucky to share a portion of one of the best times of his whole life. The qualities I knew in Bryan were his generosity and kindness, his wonderful sense of humour, the quality of his writing and his engagement with the process of writing – I was attracted to his work precisely because he was a "writer's writer", whose every book made me want to write and helped me to write. And his feel for books and printed matter as made things, capable of providing physical and aesthetic satisfaction.'

In that essay for *The Private Library*, Johnson even went so far as to describe his six months at Gregynog as 'idyllic', adding, reflectively and parenthetically, '(not a word I have ever used seriously before, I believe)'. And although, as a convinced New Brutalist who believed that construction materials should always be 'honestly' on show in the finished building, he could not approve the hall's mock-Tudor, he said that 'it was possible very early on to forgive the house its deceit, and I shortly became very fond of it; and later, as a sort of compliment it would never be able to appreciate, I included a description of it in the novel I wrote in its small library.' With which we shall now conclude this chapter:

128: EXTRACT FROM SIONED BOWEN'S MONOLOGUE IN *HOUSE MOTHER NORMAL*, DESCRIBING THE HALL AT GREGYNOG

The house itself I loved from the first moment I
saw it, though it meant servitude to me, it was
the people who made me a servant
walking from the village with Megan Williams along
the galloping drive, miles of rhododendrons,
suddenly you could see a top corner of the house,
black-and-white, but big, bigger than any other
black-and-white I'd seen, though when you were
nearer you could see it wasn't wood, it was a black-
and-white pattern in plaster or something like
that   but it was a lovely house, I forgave
it that   cheating.

BLOODY DOING SOMETHING ABOUT IT

129: EXTRACT FROM POSTCARD *(17 March 1970)*

To John Furse

Am too happy, contented: something must go wrong soon.

130: EXTRACT FROM LETTER *(5 April 1970)*

To John Furse

We'll be up the weekend after next almost certainly. My mother is about to undergo a hysterectomy for what appears to be a non-malignant growth: but you never know with these lying doctors, it may be cancer.

131: EXTRACT FROM LETTER *(25 May 1970)*

To John Furse

Mothers are no joking matter: what can I say about yours? Mine had a terrible time – when we went to see her a couple of days after the operation she was very bad – is better now, a little. Went to see her last Thursday (came up for the day as the wife of my Hungarian translator turned up) when she'd had umpteen stitches out. As far as I can see, they have removed all the equipment that brought little BSJ into the world, on my mother's side, that is, I haven't been informed of my father's condition: sell that to an American library, I've just thought, though they're not interested in my mss. let alone my old mum's innards. But it's no joking matter, really, as I said, except that's all there is to do. Ovaries, too, and appendix while they were about it, just for the hell of it. Wonder what they left? Ironies, she's in Bart's where Steven and Katie were born.

132: EXTRACT FROM LETTER *(28 May 1970)*

To Zulfikar Ghose

My mother's illness was sudden and unexpected, and has got progressively worse – at least in the way it's been communicated to us and, I think, her. The latest thing today is that she's got to stay in another five weeks for radiotherapy – so it must be malignant, despite what they told us before and after the operation.

133: EXTRACT FROM LETTER *(25 September 1970)*

To Zulfikar Ghose

My mother is home now, and pronounced cured: but who believes doctors? We can only wait and see. After cutting out everything in sight, they then declared she had to have five weeks' radiotherapy. So they couldn't have cured it by surgery. Anyway, she's been home three months now and goes next week for a big examination to see whether or not.

After Johnson's return from Gregynog, he suffered a number of blows. His mother's illness weighed heavily upon him – raising the ghastly possibility that his terrible experience with Tony, bearing witness to his slow decay, might have to be relived, only this time with someone he loved even more. An opportunity to realize what had now become a cherished dream, and to buy a permanent base in Wales, had been defeated by 'conniving, swindling estate agents', who were all 'rapacious liars'.[1] A major Penguin anthology of *British Poetry since 1945*, edited by his one-time friend Edward Lucie-Smith, had failed to include either Johnson or Zulfikar Ghose. ('Sod Lucie-Smith. I can understand him not having me but I am both disgusted and surprised at him not putting you in [. . .] I shouldn't let these things annoy me: but it's impossible not to feel something.'.)[2] England had been knocked out of the World Cup. A Tory government had been elected. Things were going from bad to worse.

Philip Ziegler, at least, had responded to *House Mother Normal* with unqualified enthusiasm, much to Johnson's surprise. But he was still finding it impossible to live off the advances he was paid by Collins and had become more and more dependent on his secondary career as a television director to support his family; now this in turn was about to fizzle out. Having spent some weeks before going to Wales working on a BBC script about one of his biggest literary idols, Flann O'Brien, he returned to find that the project had been cancelled and his work was to be unrewarded. (Fallout, perhaps, from the frosty reception given to *The Smithsons on Housing*?) As a result, 'I shall be coming back to London with no visible means of support. But I expect something will turn up: it always has done so far.'[3]

This was the beginning of a phase in which Alan Brownjohn remembers work and money, the nuts and bolts of surviving in the literary marketplace, always being the primary topic of conversation. 'When you asked him "How's it going?" he would say, "It's going pretty well at the moment, I'm going to be OK until next March," – this being say in October. Meaning financially, with work to do, with things coming out – he could see himself surviving, I think, that was the primary note of the usage, that he was OK financially to keep on going as a writer for the next nine months or whatever. And then there would be occasions when he'd say, "It's awful" or "It's terrible", and this would crop up again and again, and you'd see him the next time after one of those and he'd say, "Oh, it's looking up a bit, I'm OK for a certain period".'

The relationship between writing and financial security is foregrounded in the script of a short television programme Johnson made at around this time for LWT. *On Reflection: Samuel Johnson* was made for the channel's educational wing and contains thirty minutes or so of Johnson (B. S.) standing next to statues of Johnson (Samuel) and speaking to camera, presenting a biographical sketch which is brief and workmanlike. We get a strong sense of Johnson's hero worship of his eighteenth-century namesake and an even stronger sense that he identifies with him personally. Countless details in the script could apply to the corpulent, beleaguered, prolific twentieth-century experimental writer as much as to the ostensible subject of the programme. Like Samuel, B. S. Johnson had an early and significant relationship with an older woman who already had children; he considered himself, like Samuel, to be enslaved to 'publishers who think the miserable percentages they allow authors can in some way be excused by taking an author out to lunch'; like Samuel, he undertook a lot of hack-writing but found it 'more difficult to do than a piece of writing one is really interested in, for the self-disgust at undertaking rubbish makes it all the more difficult to bring oneself actually to get on with it'. He talks of Dr Johnson's 'deep-seated melancholia' and describes with glee the occasion on which he knocked over an 'impertinent' publisher with a folio and 'held him down with a foot on the wretched publisher's neck' (although B. S. Johnson, as we know, confined himself to 'beltings (verbal)' on such occasions). In his portrait of this garrulous, combative, heroic, much loved figure, Johnson is clearly indulging in some wish-fulfilment. Explaining how his hero 'overcame [...] great physical and personal diffi-culties to become the object of enormous respect and affection not only to his own generation but to every later one as well', he seems to be reaching out towards a fantasy of how his own literary personality might come to be perceived.

The latest person to have received a belting (verbal) at his hands was his current agent Deborah Rogers.

134: EXTRACTS FROM LETTERS *(12 May 1970 and 21 June 1970)*

To Deborah Rogers

> It's now two years since you became my agent, and so far you have not managed to sell even one of my books to one single foreign country [. . .] I enclose an up-to-date list of my credits, and am sure you will agree that there are only one or two other writers of my generation who have achieved or published as much. How is it you do not present my work in such a way that sales are made abroad? I would like to read your comments on your past failure and what you intend to do to ensure future success [. . .]
>
> It would be a little different if you found me work in this country: but I do not think there has been a single piece of work in the two years that has originated from you. Why is this? Do you not have publishers and magazines asking you to provide writers for projects? If you don't, then there's something wrong with your business: if you do, then why doesn't a fair share come my way? [. . .]
>
> Please try to understand my position. I now find myself worse off than when I had no agent at all: still no foreign sales, and paying you commission on work I find for myself [. . .]

And then, after Rogers had replied by saying that the format of *The Unfortunates* was deterring potential overseas publishers:

> The originality of the format is *not* an excuse, and I hope you will be honest enough to admit it. Incidentally, there is every prospect of the Hungarians *starting* to publish my work with THE UNFORTUNATES! The interest and concern I found there is directly at variance with what you say you find with foreign publishers: I am of the opinion that I am not being properly represented by you, and I must ask you again what you intend in future to remedy this: to say, as you do, that you will do what you have done in the past is to say nothing [. . .]
>
> As for work originating from you: I was absolutely staggered that, after two years as my agent, you should have to ask me what subjects I'm interested in! And rather insulted, as well.[. . .]
>
> I think it would be best from both our points of view if we regarded the next six months as the period in which you justify yourself in terms of actual results.

Well, not surprisingly, at the end of those six months, Deborah Rogers had signally failed to 'justify herself' in Johnson's eyes, and so he moved on to the third agency of his seven-year career (the fourth if you count his brief representation by Jan Davies; the fifth if you count the attempts of Secker & Warburg themselves to sell his novels abroad). MBA was a new agency set up by Michael Bakewell, a former producer of BBC radio drama and a friend of Johnson's since the early 1960s. (He had worked extensively with Beckett on the Third Programme and of course this meant, as far as Johnson was concerned, that he was touched with greatness.) Significantly, the agency began by representing film and television writers, and only later branched out into the book world. This meant that Johnson was at last dealing with people who were committed to the 'enormous totality' of him, not just the novel-writing bit. In the words of Diana Tyler, Michael Bakewell's colleague (who still represents the Johnson estate today): 'Bryan could see that what he wanted was something that was more encompassing: he clearly wanted to do more directing and he wanted to write more for television. He had this vision of himself as doing lots of different things, and had maybe felt neglected in that area because of his wide interests and was hoping that we could help it all along. And Michael was able to set things up, his influence got Bryan into new places and I think that was very satisfactory for him.' It would evolve, in fact, over the next two years into a unique author–agency relationship. Michael Bakewell and Diana Tyler would not just negotiate contracts for him, they would set up poetry readings, *take part* in the poetry readings, perform in radio adaptations of Johnson's novels, produce and direct stage productions and generally act in every respect as *collaborators* rather than agents. Certainly no agent or publisher had ever taken so many aspects of his work so seriously before.*

'It was a fairly clean break with Deborah in terms of publishing contracts,' Diana Tyler remembers. Johnson, in a letter to Zulfikar Ghose, put it slightly more colourfully: 'Various things may happen since I have given delicious Deborah, toast of the publishers, a well-earned boot. Michael Bakewell has set up as an agent-producer [...] and is really getting things moving – has some sort of an offer from France, where Beckett apparently gave me a reference without my knowing,† and is producing YHLTROT and extracts from WHOSE DOG ARE YOU? in a basement lunchtime theatre in Greek Street next month.'[4]

---

* Another of the affinities between the two Johnsons: Samuel, according to Bryan, 'attempted virtually every literary form, always with professional competence, sometimes with brilliance. This very versatility has of course led him to be undervalued as (say) a poet.'
† Nothing came of this.

This was the production known as *B. S. Johnson vs God*, which ran at the Basement Theatre, at 49 Greek Street, Soho, from 18 January until 29 January 1971. It consisted of the stage version of *You're Human Like the Rest of Them* sandwiched between two 'lessons' from *Whose Dog Are You?* and was directed by Michael Bakewell himself. The cast included the ever faithful William Hoyland. It was one of several scraps of work with which Johnson filled up the 'dead time' between finishing *House Mother Normal* and its publication in May 1971.

Having just written that sentence, though, I realize that it's wrong. There was never any 'dead time' for Johnson: he crammed an amazing amount into his ten- or twelve-year writing career. It's easy to forget, for instance, that all the time he was writing his novels or planning his films, he was also working as poetry editor for the *Transatlantic Review*, and we would be wrong to think that this in itself was anything resembling a part-time job. The *Transatlantic* in those days was a major literary magazine with the largest European circulation of any English-language quarterly, and 'It is simply a fact,' wrote George Garrett (its American poetry editor, Johnson's US counterpart), 'that poems came in from poets of all kinds all over the English-speaking world – by the thousand.' As a result, Garrett believed that Johnson 'was closely in touch with what was happening in English-language poetry; more so, probably, than any other poet in England or America at the time.' Garrett himself had been co-founder of the magazine with Joe McCrindle in 1958: 'When McCrindle moved to London in the 1960s, taking the *Transatlantic* with him, he hired Bryan Johnson because, as McCrindle allowed, only in part facetiously, Johnson was "the closest facsimile I could find" to George Garrett. Both were about the same size and coloring. Both wrote novels and poetry. Both were editorially open-minded'. Throughout the whole of the 1960s and early '70s, Johnson was intimately bound up with the magazine and its fortunes; if a poem or short story or play of his could not find another home (as frequently happened) it would invariably be published by Joe McCrindle, with whom he maintained a loyal friendship. As George Garrett has touchingly recorded: 'By the end, he [Johnson] had become so much the leading, shaping *character* of the *Transatlantic* that after his death McCrindle was unable to imagine continuing the magazine without him and so closed it down.'[5]

And yet even while fulfilling this sustained, long-term commitment, Johnson was still making time for a disorientating variety of other jobs. These included directing (but not writing) another educational programme for LWT, *On Reflection: Alexander Herzen*, presented by Alan Brien; beginning work as a member of the Literature Panel of the Greater London Arts Association, his first job being to co-edit, with Margaret Drabble, a serial novel called *London Consequences*, each chapter to be written by a different novelist (including Paul Ableman, Melvyn Bragg, Wilson Harris, Adrian Mitchell and Alan Burns);* and forming a company called Filmfront with Bruce Beresford, Don Levy, David Muir, Richard Saunders and Barry Tomblin with the aim of moving into independent feature production.

Johnson wrote on behalf of this company in February 1971 to John Terry of the National Film Finance Corporation, asking him to finance the shooting of *Albert Angelo*. He had prepared a detailed budget which put the cost of the film at £54,000. The application was rejected on 16 March. A few months later there seems to have been an attempt to revive the project as some sort of co-production with a Canadian producer called Kevin Francis, but this also came to nothing. After which, there was no choice but to relinquish the dream. The film which, in Johnson's opinion, could have done for British cinema what he had already done for the English novel had been stifled at birth by ignorant, short-sighted, money-obsessed producers; and he would never forgive this breed. His resentment festered for months and then broke out, in the autumn of 1971, in what was – even for Johnson – an exceptionally bitter and bilious polemic:

135: ARTICLE FOR *FILM & TELEVISION TECHNICIAN*, THE JOURNAL OF THE ACTT *(published August 1971)*

One day very soon (next Wednesday?) it will become possible for the definitive history of British cinema to be written. It will become possible because British cinema will have ceased to exist in any meaningful sense.

And the first question to be asked will be whether it ever did exist in any meaningful sense, the sense of leaving a lasting impression, of having produced films which have stood the test of time.

Look at what it must be compared with the other arts during the same period (say roughly from the end of the first world war and thus mercifully exclude the infantilia). During that time Britain has produced Henry Moore and Barbara Hepworth in sculpture; Robert Graves, W.H. Auden and Ted Hughes in poetry; Benjamin Britten and Peter Maxwell Davies in music; Samuel Beckett and Graham Greene in the novel; British acting has produced Gielgud and Olivier; British painting has produced Francis Bacon, Ben Nicholson and David Hockney; and British theatre has produced Samuel Beckett (again) and Harold Pinter.

And what has British cinema produced in the same period? *Oh! Mr. Porter* and *Carry on Puking.* There is not one British film which could scrape into the world's top hundred, judged from an artistic point of

---

* Burns was the one British writer of whose intellect, seriousness and literary and political commitment Johnson remained permanently in awe. Inviting Burns to take part in the novel by form letter, he added a handwritten note: 'I fear your contempt – but it's *not* a gimmick.'

view, unless the judges were grossly chauvinistic. You know which film the French generally believe to be the only British one worth considering? *Brief Encounter*! That comically distorted view of what it was like to be here and at war: indeed, the French must like it exactly because it represents a cardboard cut-out of what they think Britain and the British are like.

No, there is not one British film which can compare with our high achievements in all the other arts. And the very selective list I have jotted down is only a sample of the top of the cream. These are all world figures, they command respect everywhere for their contributions to international art. It seems probable that British art in general has never been at a higher peak: we have never before had a sculptor of the stature of Henry Moore, for instance, nor a painter like Bacon.

But why has cinema been so poor in this country? Obviously it is not because the acting and writing talent has not been available. Nor is it because British technicians have been inferior to those of other countries, for they have not. But their contribution to a film is one of craft, not art: most British films are full of beautifully lit and shot rubbish. The fault lies with the moneymen, the producers (in the widest sense) who have treated writers, actors and technicians with a disregard amounting to contempt. As a result, none of them have taken the medium seriously enough: writers have accepted large fees for scripts (which were sometimes not even properly read, and often not used for the most arbitrary reasons), and with the money subsidised other more important and more properly appreciated work in the novel and so on; actors took even larger sums for the trivial performances demanded by ignorant producers, while reserving their real work for the theatre; and technicians equally responded to a moneysick situation by laughing or crying, according to their insight, all the way to the piggy bank with as much as they could squeeze out of the conmen.

It was a failure of artistic nerve on a really disastrous scale. After all, artists know more about art than anyone else: and not to give them freedom to exercise their skill and instinct but to make it subject to the barbarism of the counting-house (the anachronistic term is used deliberately) is crass philistinism. Indeed, it might be possible to formulate a Law of Increasing Philistinism: the more money involved in an art, the more it is adulterated, and the less real art is produced. At least such a law would explain why as a nation we're so good at poetry.

And now on television we see the last throw, the final deal of the gold-lichened moneylovers: there the British film industry is really shown up (not quite in all its dishonour, for someone in television has had the bright idea of chopping them up slotwise and thus making them better, since it is impossible to make them worse), shown up for the stinking crap it is. Displayed are fatuous stories about sexless lovers, quaint old trains, action pictures which move the stomach to retch and not the heart to feel, the class-riddled setpieces of a dead culture, desperately unfunny double-entendre comedies, all forming a Victoria Falls of cesspool effluent. Only the purer water of the British documentary tradition prevents complete pollution of the environment.

Whoever does sit down next Wednesday to write this definitive history of British cinema should name these men, the barren producers, describe their criminal irresponsibility (where they have not cunningly covered their webfooted tracks), attempt to discover why it happened, to prevent anything similar happening again. For these men have denied us the opportunity of being able to say, 'This is our cinematic equivalent of a Moore, a Bacon, a Beckett.'

They have thus diminished and impoverished us all, the bastards.*

As for his own ambitions as a director, Johnson would do no more work behind the camera after spring 1971. On his last two short films, he worked anonymously. They were his most politically unambiguous works, being a direct response to the new anti-union legislation which Edward Heath's Conservative government had pledged to introduce after their election victory in June 1970.

136: EXTRACT FROM LETTER *(21 December 1970)*

To Zulfikar Ghose

Things are going to the dogs here. You may have read about all the things Heath is doing – and to think only a year ago we were complaining that there didn't seem to be any difference between Labour and Tory! The way things are going we'll have something very like a Fascist government within the next five years. I'm particularly incensed about the trade union legislation they're bringing in: it could not be more

---

* Even this piece did not seem to lance the boil of his resentment. Four months later, the same magazine published 'Uncle Tom's Cobblers', Johnson's scabrous, lavatorial profile of Aloysius K., an invented British film mogul who was supposed to have produced a film called *I Was Linkman for Goebbels* in the 1950s. In this little squib, the producer is portrayed as a greedy, criminal recluse, heartlessly indifferent to the well-being of his former employees. E.g. 'Since we were talking about technicians, I took the opportunity of bringing Aloysius up-to-date on the doings of some old friends. The lighting cameraman on GOEBBELS he was sorry to hear had had only three days' work in the last year, and I could see those sloe-green eyes were troubled when I gave him the news that the sound man had only just last week committed suicide as a result of being out of work so long that his esteemed building society had foreclosed on his mortgage. And generous, indeed, was his response: "I'll have a word with the holding company I sold the property to all those years ago," he said, pulling with infinite compassion on a *corona corona*, "and see if something can't be done."'

serious if they were trying to abolish unions altogether – in some sense it would be better if they were. I know there's a lot wrong with the unions, but not enough to warrant throwing people into gaol if they strike, which is what is proposed. It's stirred me out of my lethargy (political, that is) enough to involve me in making some propaganda films against the bill.

The much-hated Industrial Relations Bill, overseen by the new Tory employment minister Robert Carr, had been published on 3 December and given its second reading in parliament just six days before Johnson wrote this letter. It sought to impose, among other things, the necessity for pre-strike ballots and 'cooling-off periods' before strike action was taken, and most controversially of all it aimed to impose fines and possibly gaol sentences on unions and individuals who took part in industrial action which was deemed to be 'unfair'. The definition of what did or didn't constitute 'unfair' behaviour was to be decided by the courts.

Johnson was, at this time, a paid-up member of the ACTT, a film-makers' union with offices in Soho Square. Its general secretary, Alan Sapper, was a close friend, and it seemed logical that someone with proven – if limited – film-making experience and vigorous pro-union sympathies should help out with the making of propaganda films to alert workers to the insidious dangers of the bill. The idea behind these films, made under the banner of a group called Freeprop, was that prints would be driven round the country and projected on makeshift screens set up against factory walls during lunch- and tea-breaks. Johnson's contribution was a ten-minute black-and-white short called *Unfair!*, a series of sketches in which three actors represented workers, management and the judiciary. (The worker was played by Bill Owen, aka Compo of *Last of the Summer Wine* fame.) Co-written with Alan Burns, it's an effective, if crude, piece of agitprop: the level of argument is summed up by a final close-up of the Industrial Relations Bill itself with a loud raspberry being blown on the soundtrack. The best you could say about it is that it probably served its purpose. The worst is that its attack on Edward Heath displays a crass homophobia which does Johnson, as an artist, no credit at all. (Off-camera, we hear him ask one of the actors, 'How soon do you think we'll see a woman as prime minister?' The actor – *sans* shirt – pouts and simpers and answers: 'Oh, I thought we had one already, dear.')

On 21 February 1971 the TUC organized a mass rally in Hyde Park, followed by a march to Trafalgar Square where 140,000 trade unionists gathered to hear their leaders rail against the bill. It was one of the biggest political demonstrations ever seen in London. Johnson was there, and made a short colour film of the event entitled *March!* which, even though it shows no sign at all of his own directorial personality, preserves a valuable record of a landmark day in the political history of the early 1970s. It was well received by the TUC and led to a further commission, this time to make a film commemorating the golden jubilee of the Transport and General Workers' Union. Johnson chose the Joycean title *Here Comes Everybody!* and spent much of late spring 1971 preparing a detailed treatment. His idea was to reflect the breadth of representation the TGWU had achieved, by travelling around the country and filming workers in many different industries: he went to Coventry to visit the Standard-Triumph car factory, he visited a Guinness brewery, a GEC electrical plant and a Walls meat-processing factory (where his expenses claim showed '£2.75 for shoes ruined by blood' – decimalization having been introduced a few weeks earlier). Everything proceeded smoothly until late June 1971 when something – I don't know exactly what – seems to have gone wrong with the film. Probably someone saw his treatment, didn't like it, and appointed another writer/director over his head. In any case, a letter to Ralph Bond of the ACTT, dated 16 July 1971, states that, 'This is also to confirm our telephone conversation of 25th June, when I made it clear to you that I do not want my name further associated with this film. My name must not appear in any credit on the film or be used in any other way in connection with it, and I shall immediately take legal action if you attempt to ignore my express wishes in this matter.' He was ultimately paid £40 'as a gesture of good-will, and [...] as an additional and final payment for the treatment-script you wrote'. The day after that telephone conversation he wrote a letter to Barry Cole, describing himself as 'furious at being cheated out of a film job; and very broke as a result. As always, it seems.' Even his brothers in the trade union movement, apparently, were not above swindling him.

The Industrial Relations Act passed into law on 6 August 1971 despite the bitterness of the protests it had provoked, both inside and outside parliament. In any case, it had been poorly drafted and turned out to be unworkable. According to one historian, 'the trade unions were largely able to ignore its provisions simply by refusing to register under the act, a development which the government seems not to have foreseen.'[6] Its passage was symptomatic, all the same, of an exceptionally troubled and confrontational era in British politics, in which the rhetoric on both sides became hysterically divisive. Those on the right thought that the country was in danger of being overrun by communists and anarchists; those on the left (including Johnson) were happy to describe the Heath government as fascistic.* Underlying all this, the wave of radical unrest which had emanated from Paris in 1968 had

---

* One of the protestors' banners captured by Johnson's camera on 21 February reads, 'Heath Carr & Co Ltd: Their Mothers Wer'nt [*sic*] Married: Remember the Thirtys in Germany. Don't Let it Happen Here.' The slogans were flanked by two swastikas.

created a mood of paranoia among the political establishment. MI5 surveillance of potential troublemakers was routine, and Britain currently had its
own, home-grown, somewhat unfocused terrorist movement in the form
of the Angry Brigade. This loose-knit assembly of malcontents, twelve of
whom were brought to trial for offences relating to explosives in late 1972,
had become specifically identified with the protests against the Industrial
Relations Bill when they planted a bomb outside Robert Carr's home on
12 January 1971 and almost succeeded in killing him. They also had tangen-
tial links with the avant-garde literary circles in which Johnson moved. His
friend and fellow experimentalist Alan Burns published a novel about them,*
and Johnson himself regularly went down to the Old Bailey to observe their
trial in the last few weeks of 1972. Writing about it shortly afterwards, he
gives a vivid sense of the paranoiac atmosphere of those times:

137: EXTRACT FROM ARTICLE FOR *FILM AND TELEVISION TECHNICIAN* (published January 1973) †

On January 12th, 1971, Robert Carr's house was the subject of a bomb
attack. It was also the day massive protests were taking place against
the then proposed Industrial Relations Bill. At the time I was among
those who were working anonymously on Freeprop Films as part of
ACTT's protest. I say 'anonymously', but a week before some generous-
hearted brother had blown a number of our names to *The Times*:
immediately after the Carr bombing my telephone was (I am as certain
as I can be) tapped.

After the first amused and flattered surprise (they think *me* worthy
of surveillance?) I became annoyed, not because anything I said on the
telephone could get me into trouble, but because my telephone service
became appalling. Crossed lines three times out of four, wrong numbers,
silence with the sound perspective of a huge hall with occasionally a
whistling phantom, no dialling tone.

Several times I rang up my telephone manager and complained
about the poor service. At length I suggested to him that the cause
might be that my phone was being tapped. The conversation then went
something like this:

'We do not tap telephones in this country, sir,' he said.

'But it came out in court recently that Rudi Dutschke's‡ phone was
constantly tapped. We know that from the papers.'

---

*   *The Angry Brigade: A Documentary Novel* (Allison & Busby, 1973).
†   Incidentally, the typescripts of the articles Johnson wrote for this magazine were cordoned
off into a special section of his lever-arch file labelled 'Strictly Anonymous'. Beneath which he
typed the words 'codename: Bombay Potatoes'.
‡   German leader of radical student protest.

'It can only be done with a Home Office order, sir.'

'And is there such an order on my number?'

'No, sir.'

'That's just what you'd say anyway, isn't it? But I've just caught you out in one barefaced lie.'

A lot of people reading this must know from similar personal experience that the Carr bombing (which was only one of a series: news of the earlier ones had been suppressed by the media) sparked off a massive police hunt which covered anyone who had anything to do with opposition to the Industrial Relations Bill. It was (of course) denied at the trial that this had happened at all, let alone that someone at Cabinet level had ordered it. What it now seems to me must have happened is that the police just did not know where to look, so there was blanket surveillance of everyone connected in the slightest with opposition to the Bill. Panic in the copshops, in fact.

Was Johnson himself an anarchist? A communist, as he liked provocatively to describe himself when visiting Hungary? Almost certainly not. His friendships and allegiances were with the hard left, or – as it might now more usefully be called – the old left. (István Bart recalls him holding up Michael Foot as a political and intellectual role model.) Without doubt, disillusionment with Harold Wilson's government had set in pretty firmly with many thinkers on the left (and times haven't changed that much – a parallel with Tony Blair springs inevitably to mind). There was a strong feeling that the democratic process had failed British socialists, and that alternative – not necessarily peaceful – forms of protest would have to be tried. An article on this subject by the jazz musician Humphrey Lyttelton (published in the *Morning Star* in 1968) had already warned of 'a direct relationship between the increase in violence in demonstrations and the failure to provide an outlet and inspiration for the kind of support which the Labour Party had two or three years ago', prompting Johnson to write the following:

138: LETTER *(18 April 1968)*

To the Editor of the Morning Star

Dear Sir,

Humphrey Lyttelton has certainly expressed for me, as for others, the discontent and disappointment I have felt for the last two years about the Wilson government.

What I simply do not understand is how the man can have gone back on so much. What has forced him to abandon nearly all the principles and programme for which we voted? If he does not have the power (and I have sufficient residue of respect for Wilson to assume that this is more likely to be true than that he is deliberately refusing to exercise it) then where does it lie? Who *does* run this country, or allow it to be run by its elected representatives only within very narrow limits and inexorably in the same direction?

I think it is to finding the answer to this question that all those similarly disillusioned should seriously apply themselves: *now*.

All the same, whatever his privately held views (which rarely find direct expression in the novels – avant-gardism itself being, as far as Johnson was concerned, an explicitly *political* position), my sense is that Johnson did not much enjoy (and why should he?) being in the political firing line once the Tories came to power. I make this point simply to suggest that from early 1971 onwards, one of the factors feeding his growing sense of persecution and paranoia might have been the belief that unnamed forces – identified, partly, with the security services – were starting to keep an eye on him. I put this suggestion to Bill Holdsworth, one of Johnson's closest friends from this period, and he agreed.* But Holdsworth himself was – and remains – entirely laid back about the fact that MI5 probably had a thick file on him, whereas he recalls Johnson being profoundly disturbed by the thought, in a way that seems somehow typical of his general hypersensitivity. As a member of such anarcho-socialist movements as the Committee of 100 and Spies for Peace, Holdsworth was used to having his house raided and to being taken out to the Reform Club for shepherd's pie lunches ('you know, all that public school food') at the end of which his mysterious host would hint to him that it really might be a good idea to resign membership of *this* organization, or not to publish any more articles along *those* lines. 'And Bryan knew about all this – so when he told me he thought his phone was being tapped, I told him, "Of course it is, you silly sod." It was happening to all of us. But Bryan for some reason found this terribly difficult to deal with. You know, I just had the attitude that "all coppers were bastards" – that was where I came from. But Bryan never had that. He always described himself as working class, but he was a little bit up the ladder from me, I would have said, coming from Barnes, and so on. He was always very intrigued by my

---

* At my request, Holdsworth supplied me with this potted self-description: 'In 1973 he was a professional engineer at the leading edge of alternative energy technologies and applications. A renaissance man who created an international consultancy in parallel with politics, theatre, writing and the arts, now thirty years later he is still at technology's "sharp-end", but spending more time as a successful journalist, author, lecturer and world-wide traveller.' (Among other things, Holdsworth designed and supervised the building works at the Johnsons' new house in Islington, and was invited over for dinner to celebrate when they were completed – an evening which ended with Johnson dropping his trousers and demonstrating how to light your own farts, much to Virginia's horror.)

world, because my world was more at street level. I was a street boy. Bryan in a way was much more – well, I used to look up to him as this man of letters, this personality; and yet *he* always wanted to bring himself down, socially. And he didn't have that "street" sense of humour that I had, to get him through some of those tough times.'

The making of his trade union films, the activities of the Angry Brigade and their subsequent trial, the sense that Britain was drifting inexorably in the direction of 'fascism' and that anyone who spoke out against this was likely to be persecuted by unelected powers – all of these factors weighed heavily on Johnson's mind as he began to think about his sixth novel. Moreover, he seems at this point to have wavered in his conviction that the writing of novels – even militantly avant-garde novels – was a valid contribution to the political struggle.* Suddenly, in the light of what seemed to Johnson to be increasingly urgent political circumstances, the value of his own role as an oppositional artist started to look highly questionable. This was one element in the crisis of confidence that was starting to take shape within him. The other was more personal. The continuing deterioration of his mother's health (her cancer was advancing slowly but unstoppably) and the first signs of tension within his marriage to Virginia were beginning to weaken the support structures upon which his working, creative life was founded. Johnson was now thirty-eight, married with two children; his parents were elderly and their health was failing. It would hardly be uncommon if he were to begin experiencing something akin to a midlife crisis at this point. And one of the classic symptoms of such a crisis is a reaching back into the past, an attempt to relive one's adolescence, perhaps even to get back in touch with one's former lovers and partners.† This, too, is a process we can see at work in the planning of the novel that was to become *Christie Malry's Own Double-Entry*.

One of Johnson's earliest diary entries shows that the idea for this book had been in his head since the mid-fifties.‡ Also, shortly before she died, Joyce Yates told me that during their time at Birkbeck she and Johnson had once discussed the concept of a *moral* double-entry system, in which every act of insult or oppression had to be balanced out by some sort of recompense. On top of which, even though it's never specified when the novel is set, exactly, it reeks of the austere, sexually repressed 1950s rather than the

---

* John Furse, after reading a first draft of this book, alerted me to another of Johnson's more hands-on political activities: he worked as an occasional speechwriter, apparently, for the Labour mayor of Islington.

† The highly successful website friendsreunited.co.uk has built its entire existence around this phenomenon. And B. S. Johnson would soon (in 1973) begin work on an anthology of his own and his friends' earliest sexual reminiscences, under the title *You Always Remember the First Time*.

‡ See above, p. 63.

early 1970s. The large file of notes Johnson left behind him shows how these different threads – personal resentment and frustration (as experienced by his younger self as an accountant at Fuller's in the early 1950s), and political anger and frustration (as epitomized by the Angry Brigade and other contemporary terrorist movements) – coalesced into the story of Christie and his one-man cycle of revenge.

139: SELECTION OF NOTES FOR
CHRISTIE MALRY'S OWN DOUBLE-ENTRY (1970-1)

– One is deliberately annoying the reader in order to punish him for daring to like rubbish! That's your rubbish, one is saying, what you like so much!

– An old-fashioned CONTENTS page (+ old-fashioned rubrics à la Fielding?)

– 'And I'm very fond of you, too, by now, Xtie. You remind me of myself when young."

– It is not *possible* to write long novels today, in this situation!

So much so that we should not be *writing* about the revolution [*crossed out, replaced with:*] change, but making it!

– Angry Brigade: unexpected target is the *CHURCH*: property + power/ influence

– Fullers: researchers seeking my signatures on receipts. I *felt* that as I was signing them.*

– working class with money doesn't make you anything else but working class

– Xtie's mates can be the Barn Elms

      lot

      if necessary

– Motives are never as easy as 'he never had a chance'.

Lots of people (millions) 'never had a chance' and do not become revolutionaries. Indeed, they love it and vote tory.

Motives do not help us.

But this is Xtie's young life.

(then invent (my) happy young life in working-class Hammersmith/ Barnes/Mortlake)

so all is chaos: *act on that*

– *(cf. Fuller's incident when I went back as a student: & they sacked me for not wearing a tie!)*

– *the key is Fuller's*: H'Smith Bdy comes into my mind as the key situation, place, location for this frustration.

---

* An early intimation of literary immortality?

– Xtie also had an older woman. This one had to earn her keep by her superior conversation, her greater Experience of the World. She did it admirably, more than compensating for the slackness of her vagina (if that is the word). She would never, however, give Xtie a shine on those days in the month when the painters metaphorically took up the slackness (somewhat). In this she was a stickler for some sort of Freudian purity, even slapped Xtie's (I nearly said Henry's) wrist when he suggested there were other ways for her to give him an orgasm. He(nry) accepted this, and made do with only conversation at such times.

– Xtie would go to his Latin lesson.

Daphne's room. A girl's room. Xtie loved it, it was so much unlike his own.

– Is this a moral tale? It's a bit difficult to see what else it is if it isn't.

– care to make it as *timeless* as possible

– The urban guerilla is a man who fights the military dictatorship with arms, *using unconventional methods*

His principle duty is *to attack and to survive*

He must possess initiative, mobility and flexibility – esp. *initiative: it is better to err acting than to do nothing for fear of erring*

Without initiative there is no urban guerilla warfare

Urban g. warfare is a pledge the guerilla makes to himself

The UG must be careful not to appear strange and separated from ordinary city life.

The UG must live by his work or professional activity.

The UG must be very searching and knowledgeable about the area in which he lives or operates.

The UG should kill police chiefs and expropriate capitalist funds.

Surprise compensates for the UG's inferiority to his enemy, who has no way to fight surprise.

– the time is no longer to write novels; or to write at all?

– BUT if the right were not in power, then would I/Xtie be carrying out similar UG against a left establishment? Is this merely man's need for war? ANYWAY? Are the people involved merely the FIGHTERS (whatever the cause?) This must be *faced* (? no – why do the devil's work?!)

– *novel six*

(end?)

he resolves to commit one really serious act of sabotage

– bombing

then he promises himself he will sit down and get back to writing!

OR   I am about a personal revolution

when I have proved to my personal satisfaction that it works
then I shall write it all down!

– *Ending*

He is perfectly, superbly successful
– but *on his own*:
how does he communicate his success, ideas, technique to others?
the thought finishes him.
– Nulla fides unquam miseros elegit amicos
   Nobody ever chooses the already unfortunate as objects of loyal friendship
          trans. Graves

The graphs of Johnson's progress show that he didn't make much headway with *Christie Malry's Own Double-Entry* during 1971, despite the fact that he had undertaken to deliver it to Philip Ziegler at Collins in February 1972 and there was no way he would allow himself to miss that deadline. Instead, driven as always by the need to find sources of income other than his publishing advances, he had sought and obtained commissions to write – but not, this time, direct – two television plays: *Not Counting the Savages* (for BBC Two's *Thirty Minute Theatre*) and *What Is the Right Thing and Am I Doing It?* (for ATV's *Armchair Theatre*): both of which make interesting companion-pieces to *Christie Malry*.

Not Counting the Savages (which bears no relation to his unfinished novel of the same title) is virtually the only thing Johnson ever wrote with a domestic setting: an examination of the dynamics of a family and, more specifically, a marriage. At its centre is a surgeon called Dr Noone: fifty years old, boorish, gluttonous, callous towards his children (he has cheated his son out of an inheritance) and indifferent towards his wife. When the play opens, this wife (never named) is describing her encounter earlier in the day with a flasher in a graveyard, still in a state of great agitation to which her husband responds with silent contempt. Instead of listening to her story with sympathy, he wolfs down his dinner, gorging himself on a whole Camembert and 'coarsely feeding, finishing what remains of a huge main course [...] he is gross, getting down to his food piggishly'. The thesis of the play (because it conveys, as Anthony Smith pointed out about so much of Johnson's writing, a strong sense of 'QED') is that a man who behaves like a pig at home and like a brute to his family can, nevertheless, be a saint and a genius in his professional life. The closing scene shows Dr Noone in the operating theatre, performing surgery on a patient who is suffering from (of course) cancer, at which point his character is transformed: his voice is 'infinitely concerned, compassionate, reassuring: in as many ways as possible his manner is diametrically different from his earlier behaviour'. A tight close-up on his face as he operates shows 'concentration, compassion', while the closing image of the play is '*BCU NOONE's eyes: the concern, the care*'.[7]

It could be that Noone was based on one of the many doctors with whom Johnson must have had dealings during these stressful months as his dying mother was shunted in and out of hospital. Or it could be that he was trying to draw a distorted, unflattering self-portrait, and the play should be read as a distillation of anxieties about his own role as husband and father. The parallels between Johnson himself and Noone are too close to ignore: not just the caricatured overeating, but the succession of anecdotes the doctor tells about his visit to Russia (where all possibility of friendship with his interpreter was scuppered by paranoid warnings from the Foreign Office, and he suffered from a painful irritation in his eye) which are drawn directly from Johnson's own recent experiences in Hungary. Given that Johnson was prone to moments of self-disgust, there seems, here, to be a certain amount of gloomy speculation going on about his looks and his behaviour ten years down the line – in the midst of which he also raises the compensating possibility that he might still cling onto a certain grace and dignity as long as he remains faithful to his art.

Not Counting the Savages, then, can be read (albeit obliquely) in just as personal and self-questioning terms as any of Johnson's more explicitly confessional writings. The second of the television plays he wrote in 1971, *What Is the Right Thing and am I Doing It?,* is intriguing for a different reason: because it is one of his most overtly political works, and tackles – in a less supple, inventive way – exactly the same theme as *Christie Malry's Own Double-Entry:* the relationship between writing and terrorism; the validity of literature as an expression of political protest.

The main character, Ghent, is a distinguished poet of about fifty who has just finished serving a long prison term for his (alleged) part in a pub bombing which went badly wrong, killing one of his colleagues. Ghent is 'part of the core of a dedicated minority nationalist movement' at large in the British Isles, although it is never specified which one. (Here, as in *Paradigm,* Johnson invents his own language for them.) Again the character seems, in part, to be a projection of the author's own anxieties about what sort of figure he might cut in ten years' time: to his own generation Ghent is a hero and a martyr; to the younger supporters of his cause he is an embarrassing anachronism. Like Johnson (in the last, paranoid stages of his life), he is tortured by the thought that his wife may have been unfaithful to him. Like Johnson, he is fond of wine, has started drinking too much for his own good and is prone to belligerence when drunk.

140: EXTRACT FROM THE TELEVISION PLAY *WHAT IS THE RIGHT THING AND AM I DOING IT?* (1971-2)

GIRL TWO

I mean, everyone's entitled to an opinion ...

GHENT is by now very drunk, almost falling around.

GHENT

Opinion! Entitled! I've decided to give up opinion! What use is opinion! What does it matter? I didn't go to prison for being entitled to opinions, but for holding them so strongly that I was prepared to back them up with action! With violence! (*pause*) Without it, mere opinion is useless — (*mimics childishly*) he holds this, someone else holds that — what does it mean! (*pause*) I had a long while to get used to mere opinion! (*pause*) The 'intellectual support' is about as useful as a truss with perished elastic! Ha!

GHENT's voice has been raised so much that everyone in the room has fallen silent: a certain amount of embarrassment is evident at his drunkenness, but it is mingled with realisation that, having been deprived of alcohol for so long, it was virtually bound to happen; and, in any case, the occasion entitles him to a certain amount of licence.

GHENT (*cont.*)

What use are these intellectual theorists without action in support of their ideas? None at all! (*pause*) None! (*pause*) I judge people by what they do, not by what they say! Ha!

He is now totally dominating those present; and knows it.

GHENT (*cont.*)

Why are you all here tonight? (*pause*) No answer. You're here because of what I did all those long years ago, eight years, it seems a lifetime, eh? I am your conscience, I was the one who did what you all wished you had the nerve to do, the courage, the guts! (*pause*) There are people here tonight who should have been there instead of me, there are others (*pause*) who should be here tonight who cannot be. (*pause*)

He is lost as to how to go on. Anti-climax. To cover up, he searches around for yet another drink; and fortunately finds one to hand; drinks; end on BCU GHENT drinking.

The play (which was written to fill an hour-long ITV slot – fifty minutes with commercials) ends with what amounts, by Johnson's non-conformist standards, to a fairly traditional moment of climactic suspense. A newspaper editor and his chief journalist (both of them described in the cast list as 'Americanised') have been trying to dig up some dirt on Ghent since his release from prison. Eventually he confronts the editor in his office, taking with him a suitcase which the editor (and the viewers) assume to be full of gelignite. The editor seizes the case and throws it out of the window – at which point it comes open, and hundreds of pieces of paper flutter to the ground. And so, after all, it is not gelignite, Johnson seems to be implying, but literature – Ghent's poetic output – which is the real incendiary device. This is, for him, an unusually confident statement of the case that writing can be a more powerful political act than terrorism; and indeed, this is an unusually confident play, with easy, naturalistic dialogue and not too many schematic situations. His dramatic art had made considerable advances since the sledgehammer polemic of *Whose Dog Are You?*.

While Johnson was writing *What Is the Right Thing and Am I Doing It?*, his mother's health deteriorated. Virginia knew that her death, when it came, would hit him badly. There had always been a strong bond between mother and son – although never, Virginia insists, a 'fierce or over-dependent' one. 'Bryan's relationship with his mother was loyal, affectionate, ironic. There was none of that close childhood bond you sometimes see, where neither mother nor son can let go. Definitely he needed her – needed both his parents – but he was resigned to the fact that they weren't able to understand him, that he would never remake the past. He was always slightly wistful for the early nurturing he felt he lacked.' On the sitting-room wall downstairs, he had hung a portrait of the great Welsh poet David James Jones ('Gwenallt'), whom he had come to revere for his pacifism, socialism and commitment to the Welsh nationalist cause.* In a subsequent note he would write of his mother's last summer in that sitting room, with the 'accusing, painracked face of Gwenallt looking down on her'. She had come there to be with the younger members of her family during what were obviously her final days. Meanwhile, in the tiny study upstairs, at his cluttered Victorian clerk's writing desk, Johnson did his best to press on with the script. Graphs for the months of November and December show good progress being made: and then, abruptly, the writing stopped. Against the line representing 14 December 1971, he wrote simply 'My Mum died.' And the columns for the rest of that year are blank.

---

* After growing up in the industrial Swansea valley Gwenallt (1899–1968) was a conscientious objector during the First World War and won the Bard's Chair at the National Eisteddfod in 1926 and 1931. Subsequent volumes of poetry included *Ysgubau'r Awen* ('Sheaves of the Muse'), *Eples* ('Leaven'), *Gwreiddiau* ('Roots') and *Coed* ('Wood'). In the last year of his life, Johnson was working on a series of translations of Gwenallt's poems, in collaboration with Ned Thomas, editor of *Planet*. At least five poems were translated: none was published.

DISINTEGRATION

141: EXTRACT FROM LETTER *(26 December 1971)*

To Zulfikar Ghose

This Xmas has been made very drear by the death of my mother on 14th Dec, after a most distressing final illness of three weeks at Bart's. It was just like Tony all over again, but this time I was much nearer, and saw her rot day by day, hour by hour some days. She was 63, and I always assumed my father would go first for some arbitrary reason. But neither of them before 70. It's such a waste (again) for she had so much to give the kids as they grew up. What they did and tried to do to her at the hospital (them, not the kids) is indescribable, though (as we said about Tony) all one can try to do is to describe it. I had known she was seriously ill, probably had the same as Tony, since eighteen months ago, of course, but her death upset me more than I could have suspected: I wept at her bedside, at the funeral, tears I did not suspect I had.

*

They don't have to tell me what life's about, because I know already, and it's about hardness. Hardness and being on my own, quite on my own. You understand that much right from the beginning, from the first time the pavement comes up and hits you, from the first time you look round for someone you expected to be there and they aren't. Oh, I know you can get close to people, but that's not the same. In the end you're just on your own.

*

'Yes, she was a lovely lady. There is a picture, oh yes, oh yes. She had a heart of gold. Oh yes, she was a very generous woman, wasn't she? She would help anybody, she wouldn't say, Oh I can't do that, I can't do that, it would just be, "Of course I will." She was that type wasn't she? Yes, that is right. We did because when she died we said at the time, didn't we, I wonder how Bryan is going to cope with this?'

(Marjorie Verney, interviewed by the author, 12 September 2001)

*

There was still literature, of course. But his mother's death had brought Johnson the kind of pain that literature is rarely able to assuage. ('"Unassuageable" is the word that comes to mind, when I think of Bryan,' one of his friends said to me.) *House Mother Normal* had been published several months earlier, in May 1971: as well as the Collins version there had been a handsome limited edition from Trigram Press, a small firm run by Johnson's friend Asa Benveniste. It was his fifth novel, and publication by now had become largely a matter of routine, each time with the same predictable outcome: 'The press for it was good, sales are lousy,' as he wrote to Barry Cole on 26 June. For every reviewer (most notably, this time, Gavin Ewart in the *Evening Standard*) who praised him to the skies, there was always someone who shot him down: and besides, getting a generally favourable press and selling 1,200 copies in hardback was not what Johnson wanted, or believed he deserved. Where were the critics proclaiming him the Beckett and Joyce *de nos jours*, as when *Albert Angelo* had appeared?

More and more he looked back with longing on his idyllic stay at Gregynog, and the respect that he had been given there, the sense of belonging to a close-knit, supportive community. He spent much of September 1971 writing a long poem about the experience for Ned Thomas's magazine, *Planet*. At the same time, he was gathering together the whole of his last eight years' poetic output for a second collection, called *Poems Two*, also to be published by Asa Benveniste. But for some reason his celebration of Welshness, 'Hafod a Hendref' ('Summer dwelling and winter dwelling') was never included, and it remains one of his least-known but most substantial and important poems.

142: EXTRACT FROM THE POEM 'HAFOD A HENDREF' *(September 1971)*

Once at Gregynog, not long after
arriving, we walked across a field
maculate with snow and lambing blood

and amongst the scattered animals
came upon a lamb so newly born
it had not yet laid eyes on its dam:

some instinct set it unsteadily
towards us as though we must have caused
the monstrous expulse it had suffered

were the womb to which it could return —

I should not stretch the image too far
for my purposes; but certainly
it parallels the raw helplessness

> I feel in moving towards your so
> much benigner and more properly
> valued older civilisation:
>
> a feeling I have hardly had since
> bribing glass in hand outside a pub
> I was a child, waiting for parents.

This is one of the poem's more lyrical sections. Elsewhere, Johnson's diction becomes highly colloquial and he almost seems to be writing prose as he expresses, with even more than his usual forthrightness, his embittered sense of the difference between the Welsh and English literary cultures: 'In London,' he writes, 'if you should (unwary) / call yourself a writer they mostly / say: *Yes, but what do you really do?* / In Welsh society, however, / the writer has always had his place, / accepted for himself: so was I. /For once in my life I felt secure, / could work at my limits; physical /stress symptoms subsided, disappeared.' And perhaps the bitterest note of all is sounded in his curt, unexpected self-description – imagining how he must have appeared to the locals – as 'a fat obscure writer from London'.

Unless I'm mistaken, this is the first time that Johnson referred to himself, bluntly and unambiguously, as 'fat'. A gloomy preoccupation with weight would also be evident in the plays *Not Counting the Savages* and *Down Red Lane*, but it's the use of this particular word that indicates when his mood was blackest: in the title of his valedictory film, of course, it sounds ironical and almost appealing, but even there, there seems to be an under-current of genuine self-dislike. Virginia used to reproach him about this, tell him that it didn't matter. 'It was Bryan himself who was weight-conscious, critical of his appearance,' she says. 'I liked him as he was.'

In any case, for a few weeks after 14 December 1971 this 'fat obscure writer from London' did not even do much writing, so flattened was he by grief. The vast majority of *Christie Malry's Own Double-Entry* (a novel, as the author himself reminds us in the text, of only 20,000 words) was written in a burst of willed, manic energy starting on 31 January 1972 in order to meet his publisher's deadline of 31 March. (In fact, with his usual consummate professionalism, he delivered it a few hours early, at 12.20 p.m. on 30 March.) But the month of January itself was barren.

On 6 January, Johnson's mother's ashes were interred and placed along-side those of 'Nanny', his beloved grandmother Mary.* Three days before this, at 10.10 p.m., *Not Counting the Savages* had been broadcast in BBC

---

* She had died in the mid-1950s, and this death, too, had left Johnson inconsolable, according to Joyce Yates. 'She was still a charlady at eighty!' she remembered, marvellingly.

Two's *Thirty Minute Theatre* slot. This, surely, must have given him some cause for satisfaction: but no. Quite the reverse, as it happened. The whole production had been a disaster, and a most upsetting one for Johnson personally.

143: EXTRACT FROM LETTER *(26 December 1971)*

To Zulfikar Ghose

It was recorded on Dec 5, and was a very curious experience. The chief actor (Hugh Burden) decided an hour before the recording to wear his youthful wig: thus making him into a forty year old despite the script calling for a fifty-five year old. In the crunch which followed, the director and the producer backed him (for fear of putting the darling off his stroke in the performance) rather than me, the writer. Since he was a monumental miscasting in the first place, being thin instead of fat, etc., it was the final straw [. . .] I was very pleased with the writing of this play, think it as good as most other things I've done, so it was all the harder.

In the memory of William Hoyland, who played the part of the young son, this whole episode was even more traumatic.

'There was something about a wig [. . .] The actor was bald, and he insisted on wearing a wig that made him look more charming, and that was the point at which it all went wrong, and Bryan said, "Look, this is ridiculous." He was trying to turn him into a middle-aged charmer when he was meant to be a ghastly autocrat.

'There was a terrible terrible row between Bryan and the lead actor, and the whole experience was just awful. The play itself didn't work because the actor just refused to be unpleasant. He wanted to be charming, he wasn't interested in what the writer had written. In those days it was all done on videotape, and you rehearsed in a church hall or something and then you went to the TV centre for two days to do camera rehearsals and then you'd tape the whole thing, usually in one session from 7.30 until 10 in the evening. And during this it just became an absolutely head-on collision, and Bryan really did become furious, quite furious, and at the end of it he just came to the actor and said, "You have ruined my work, this is a pointless waste of time, you have ruined the whole thing, thank you and good night!"

'We didn't even go for a drink afterwards – he was so furious that he couldn't speak to anyone. Then we met up later on and he was still angry and was saying things like, "Your bloody profession."'

The director was Mike Newell (of *Four Weddings and a Funeral* and *Donnie Brasco* fame), then at the very beginning of his career. William

Hoyland was fairly sure that 'Mike Newell was on Bryan's side', but Johnson never forgave him for allowing Hugh Burden to sabotage the play. I thought about contacting Mike Newell to find out more about their working relationship. However, having gone through the file on *Not Counting the Savages*, and found a scrap of paper in Johnson's handwriting on which he had written down Newell's phone number and added the note 'CUNT OF A DIRECTOR', I felt that perhaps I already knew everything I needed to know.

'I think that it sort of put him back a bit about actors,' William Hoyland adds. 'He'd always directed his own stuff before and that absolutely convinced him never ever again to hand over control of his work to anyone else. Which was sad because at the time I just remember feeling pleased that some of Bryan's work was getting more into the mainstream, and then of course it all went horribly wrong.'

In fact, Johnson did continue to hand over control of his work to other people, but only those in whom he had complete confidence. Foremost among these was his agent, Michael Bakewell, who also had a good deal of experience directing films for BBC television. When HTV expressed an interest in turning 'Hafod a Hendref' into a fifteen-minute film, Johnson readily seized the chance both to collaborate with Bakewell and to spend a few days back at his beloved Gregynog.

Filming took place in the last days of January 1972. 'It was a very simple film,' Bakewell remembers. 'Essentially a setting of that little group of poems, and my main function was just to record him reading them. A lot of it was very abstract – images built up from the actual black and white surface of the exterior of the house at Gregynog, just black and white squares. We also had a sequence about a new-born lamb which we had endless trouble getting hold of. Bryan spent a number of evenings at a pub in the village chatting up this shepherd who just wanted to play dominoes all the time, so we used to play endless games of dominoes or cribbage or one of those country pub games with this shepherd, who finally found us a young lamb for that sequence. I seem to remember he had to sit on the lamb's mother and hold her down while we played about with the lamb! But the whole film was effective simply because of its simplicity.

'That was when I really got to know Bryan, I think, because we shared a room then. And Bryan used to put his head out of the window and hoot at the owls, who hooted back, which he was very enthusiastic about. He loved the countryside, the open air, the birds [...] Part of the town boy's wonder I suppose. But this was also when I began to realize that there was something slightly tormented about him: he was terribly restless during the night – he would cry and shout and moan and all that kind of thing. A much more deeply tormented character than I'd ever thought.'

With Steve while shooting *You're Human Like the Rest of Them* at
Myddelton School, late 1966, and, *below*, with Bruce Beresford (just visible)
and cameraman David Muir.

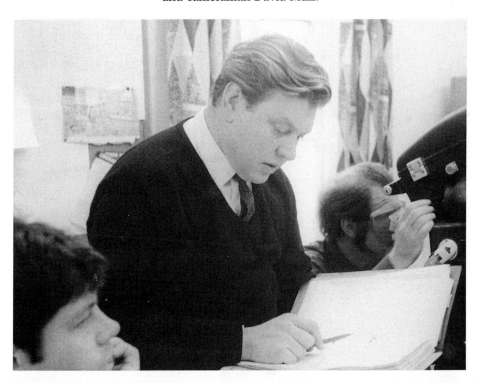

Left. With Virginia and unidentified guest at a short film festival in Cracow, June 1968. Virginia is pregnant again.

Below. Shooting *The Evacuees* for the BBC.

Above. Publicity photo for *The Unfortunates*, taken in 1968.

Right. With Glyn Tegai Hughes, warden of Gregynog House, next to the Albion Press on which Johnson printed his *Three Gregynog Englynion*.

Left. With Kate and Virginia at Gregynog.

Below. Gregynog again: teaching his children to fish, in the company of poet, publisher and good friend Asa Benveniste.

On the set of *Unfair!*, Johnson's propaganda film against the
1970 Industrial Relations Bill.

Above. With agent and collaborator Michael Bakewell during rehearsals for
B. S. Johnson vs God (January 1971).

Opposite, top. In his tiny upstairs study, at the antique writing desk where
he always wrote – Byronic skull cup in hand.

Opposite, bottom. Reading for György Novák's students in Szentlõrinc, Hungary,
during the summer of 1973.

At home with Steve.

The film of *Hafod a Hendref* was a happy and satisfying experience for Johnson, but it was hardly going to propel him through to a wider audience. If it was only on Welsh television that he was allowed to do what he wanted, then he was being marginalized. On 7 February 1972 he wrote to the BBC proposing television documentaries on Oscar Wilde (with Frankie Howerd as Wilde), A. E. Housman, Sterne's *Sentimental Journey* and the tenth anniversary of the abolition of National Service. At around the same time he wrote to Jeremy Isaacs at Thames Television, enquiring about his forthcoming series, *The World at War*, and asking if he could direct the episode about evacuation. None of these proposals came to anything (although the National Service idea was to have serious repercussions). At this point, as far as his screen work was concerned, he was still being represented by Robin Dalton of the International Famous Agency, but on 16 April (five days after the launch party for *Poems Two*) he wrote to her announcing that he wanted to terminate the relationship. 'I haven't received any offers of work from IFA during the seven months since I signed a contract with you,' he wrote, crossly, and reminded her of the prizes which *You're Human Like the Rest of Them* had picked up four years ago. A few days later she wrote back to say, 'I should have been stronger with my warnings that work would be difficult [...] I am afraid that your awards don't hold much water in a market where there are many screenwriters with impressive credits out of work'. But this was not going to satisfy a man who lived permanently (in Anthony Smith's phrase) in 'the foothills of paranoia'. 'The last three months', he complained to Zulfikar Ghose, 'have been full of work for next to no money.' And to the catalogue of the maltreatments, injustices and broken promises Johnson had recently received at the hands of publishers and producers, Ghose replied, 'I do feel more and more that the London literary-cultural-etc set has let you down. You're in the strange situation of being praised and neglected at the same time. I suppose there's something curiously British about that; I have no doubt that an American with your reputation would be in the lap of luxury licking up the pussy hairs of ultimate bliss.'[1] Johnson would certainly have agreed. His sense of having been treated unfairly was mounting all the time.

Coupled with this was his seemingly permanent state of financial insecurity. When it came to money, Johnson was generous rather than prudent: generous with himself and with other people. He enjoyed celebrations, he enjoyed big lunches and he enjoyed getting drunk: the signing of any contract, or the receipt of any advance, was usually an excuse for such an occasion with close friends like Bill Holdsworth, John Furse, Peter Buckman or (best of all, on his rare return visits from Texas) Zulfikar Ghose. Favourite venues were Rules restaurant in Covent Garden, Wheeler's and the Gay Hussar in Soho. Often, therefore, he gave the impression of being prosperous when this was hardly ever the case. Even his most intimate friends would have been surprised, I suspect, to learn that in 1972 and 1973, while he was often to be found entertaining lavishly at these establishments, he was also applying for jobs as assistant secretary (Editor/Information Officer) at the Royal Town Planning Institute ('I can offer writing skill of the highest kind [...] excellent publicity contacts [...] and a capacity for hard work'),[2] and as publishing editor with Routledge & Kegan Paul. Johnson simply continued to find that he could not live – in the style to which he had become accustomed – on the advances he was being paid on his novels (none of which, however modest, ever seemed to earn out). The nadir had been reached in August 1971 when he had been so broke that he had taken his letters from Beckett and offered them to Sotheby's for auction. (They had been valued at around £500.) He wrote to Beckett asking for his consent, which he received by return of post, along with a cheque for a hundred pounds. Johnson 'nearly wept' when he discovered this, and then withdrew the letters from sale when he received ATV's commission to write *What Is the Right Thing and Am I Doing It?* in October that year.

Beckett came to his rescue again more than once in 1972. Shortly after Johnson had visited him in Paris and given vent to doubts about his current publishers, Collins, and whether they had any faith in him, Beckett wrote personally to Sir William Collins expressing his warm opinion of Johnson as 'a most gifted writer and deserving of far more attention than he has received up to now'. And in March 1972 he agreed to be his sponsor for another Arts Council grant. By now Johnson had conceived his most ambitious project yet: a trilogy of novels to be called *Aspects of the Death of My Mother*, the first volume of which (provisionally entitled *I Consider You*) was already taking shape in his mind. In his words of support on Johnson's Arts Council form, Beckett recognized that it promised to be a technically and emotionally draining task; he also wrote that he had been impressed by the younger writer's work ever since the publication of *Travelling People* and believed that his latest novel promised to be a very significant one.* Beckett had noticed, however, that the application form included a CV upon which all of Johnson's novels were listed alongside a selection of critical encomia – 'one of the best writers we've got', 'his most accomplished tour de force so far', and so on. His advice, in a letter dated 18 March, was: 'I think it would be better to give the list of publications without any critical appreciations. In fact far better.' Johnson replied a few days later:

---

* I am paraphrasing, because permission to quote from the form itelf was denied by the Beckett estate.

144: LETTER *(24 March 1972)*

To Samuel Beckett

Dear Sam

Thanks for the very generous remarks you were so kind as to make on my Arts Council form: there is no one whose opinion and sponsorship I could value more highly. Now it's up to the Arts Council, in whom I have no faith whatsoever – it's all chaos, who has what.

I hope I shall never have to trouble you in this way again.

I did, by the way, re-type the list of my books without the critical bits – I'm sure you're right about this.

I'm just typing the final version of my new novel – due next week, Good Friday as it happens, when the publisher is shut! XTIE MALRY'S OWN DOUBLE-ENTRY it's called, and it's short: about 23,000 words – long by your standards, though!

Hope to see you in May,

as ever,

Bryan.

And so Johnson was to embark, now, on his final work: a work which might well have turned out to be the last of his novels even if he had not curtailed his own life while it was still in progress. 'I have a trilogy in mind,' he wrote to Zulfikar Ghose on 16 April 1972, and added, with a valedictory air, 'Then I suspect my contribution to the novel form will be at an end; Promises, Promises!' Of course, Johnson was prone to self-dramatization, at times, but on this occasion I think he might have meant it. In the closing dialogues of *Christie Malry's Own Double-Entry*, after all, we already have the sense of an author taking stock, looking back over the broad outlines of an oeuvre which he already seems to believe might be nearing completion. ('"Your work has been a continuous dialogue with form?" "If you like," I replied diffidently.')

See the Old Lady Decently, then, as the first book in the trilogy was soon to be retitled, was going to be a difficult book to write: partly because it was a book about, and inspired by, grief, but also for the more practical reason that a good deal of research into Johnson's family history would be required if he was going to memorialize his mother more faithfully and more completely even than he had memorialized Tony in *The Unfortunates*. The precondition for writing such a book, really, was an uncluttered life: Johnson needed plenty of space for this novel – mental, emotional, physical. Unfortunately he had none of these. He was contracted to produce a kind of follow-up to *The Evacuees*, a book of reminiscences about National Service called *All Bull*, and would spend much of 1972 soliciting, receiving and editing a series of typescripts from his twenty-four contributors. He took another trip to Hungary in May, as part of a fact-finding delegation from the ACTT, investigating conditions in the Hungarian film and television industries: a chance, too, to renew his friendships with István and Marta Bart (later Marta Szabados), and with György Novák, the bright young teacher who had just completed a thesis on Johnson's novels. He wrote a short television play called *Compressor*, the action centred on a squash court. He accepted a job as presenter on a weekly programme, *The World of Books*, for the BBC World Service, which involved reading several novels every week and preparing interview questions for their authors. He was overstretching himself. This was no way to limber up for the most ambitious and demanding novel of his career.

Johnson had always liked to keep himself busy, to present himself as a highly professional writer with something to contribute to every medium. There was a difference, now, though: where once he had played this part with gusto, now it seemed to be more a question of habit (partly) and also of keeping his head above water financially. 'I noticed he seemed to be tired,' William Hoyland remembers, 'which was a word you would never associate with him before. He'd always been full of energy, at any time of the day or night, the ideas would keep coming. He was very up when he got the job in Wales because he thought this was just the sort of thing he should be getting – being paid to have ideas – and indeed we all thought he should be getting. But after he'd come back from Gregynog he seemed to have lost a bit of zip. He didn't seem quite as lively or resilient.'

Doubtless there were several factors at work here: the sense that his literary career, which had begun so glitteringly in 1963–4, was turning into an uphill struggle, and the immortality which he was convinced was his due was threatening to elude him; his increasing sense of literary isolation – especially now that Zulfikar Ghose, who had done so much to talk up his ambitions during those early years, was thousands of miles away across the Atlantic; and his drinking, which was getting heavier and heavier. All of these things can be seen coming to a head in an uncharacteristically sour letter he fired off to Ghose at this time: prompted, it would seem, by lukewarm praise for the collection *Poems Two*, which he had sent to his friend in Austin, Texas.

145: LETTER *(13 July 1972)*

To Zulfikar Ghose

Dear Zulf .

   As usual, apologies for not being as good a correspondent as you are. I just don't have any energy left from being a good anything else. In fact, I am not a good anything else, except perhaps drinker.

   Thanks for being kind to my poems. I realise they're not very good and that they do stand up better next to one another, leaning on one another. But there, I think that no one is much good anyway, what's the point, etc.? Eh? WHAT IS THE FUCKING POINT? And don't give me all the old cock. There is *no point*: it is understanding this that is the point. You can (anyone can, the academics can) verbiage on about what's in it: but what's in it is DEATH, nothing more, and they can't admit to that because that would cost them their *living*.

Tasteful, indeed, where did you learn that bloody word?

No doubt the point is simply to live as well as we can while we can, i.e. coin as much money as possible. What a fucking object! Do you realise that is simply what your father is trying to do, has done? If that's the *point*, leave me out!

Chameleon Zulf, unrecognisable in the violent west, doing violence to his talent. What are you trying to prove? Forever forsaking, never committing absolutely. And, incidentally, what an appalling production they gave [your] book! Why do you not control these things? Who do you think they are?

I've passed on the short stories to Joe, after receiving them from your agent. There is simply not enough time to get on with the important things; as (after a moment's thought) you must know.

As for The Writing Centre of Great Britain, I shall be pleased to be made its head at £50,000 a year, since I am best qualified. But I shall give one lecture a year, if I think so, on a subject of my own choosing, to last no longer than three seconds. I'm a writer, not a teacher. The two activities (as Joyce, Hamburger, et al have pointed out for centuries) are opposed. How dare you suggest I should turncoat for money? Should I not rather die? Put your idea to the macduffs of this world. They'll make it make money for you. I'm glad you admit it's a dream: I forgive you.

as ever,

[*handwritten*] Bryan.

As for physical space, that was turning into a problem as well. Johnson was a big man (as we know) and the upstairs workroom in his Islington home was tiny: just big enough to accommodate his bank clerk's desk and a small glass-fronted bookcase containing his most precious volumes (first editions of his own books, a handful of novels by Beckett and Joyce, and *The White Goddess*, of course). The roof was low and slanted: there would scarcely have been room for him to stand up or turn around. It was really just a little attic, and from downstairs the distracting din of his growing family would rise up to make concentration even more difficult. Nonetheless, this attic had become his refuge. Late in the evening he would climb up the stairs with a bottle of red wine and attempt to write.

One thing he wrote during this time, the autumn of 1972, is surprising: a lengthy report on his three months in France in the winter of 1967–8. It had been a condition of receiving the Somerset Maugham Award money, in fact, that he write an account for the Society of Authors describing how he had spent it. Some years back, on 8 January 1969, Johnson had written to Miss Julia Wootten, then the society's secretary for awards, apologizing for his delay in sending her this document. He explained then that 'It has been on my mind for some time now, and I can only think that I have not written it because the experience itself upset me in many ways (as Maugham no doubt intended) and it is taking some time for me to come to terms with what happened.'

What could this mean, exactly? Johnson did write his report, in the end, but I don't believe he ever submitted it. Nonetheless, a badly typed draft has survived in his files. Since his typing was usually excellent, we can probably conclude that he was the worse for drink when he wrote this one, as well.

146: DRAFT OF REPORT TO THE SOCIETY OF AUTHORS CONCERNING JOHNSON'S THREE MONTHS IN PARIS UNDER THE SOMERSET MAUGHAM AWARD

(Spelling and punctuation have, where possible, been regularized.)

It is now as I write (October 1972) some four and a half years since I embarked on the Somerset Maugham Award I had won in March 1967. This represents the report I gladly undertook to write for THE AUTHOR as part of the conditions of accepting the Award.

Why has it taken so long? There are several reasons: I ought to explain that I have never missed a deadline before, of which I am as proud as any journalist; but this article has been very difficult to write; I have put it off and off again, absorbing the experience; for Somerset Maugham was right, believe it or not.

Why did I go to Paris? in 67/68 the most expensive city in Europe? One should be more modest in this sort of place. But there is an anecdote which will figleaf my pretensions to grandeur.

Next door to us in the Bd Montparnasse there lived a great friend of Beckett's, by chance, the retired and enlightened academic A J Leventhal, 'Con' to his friends from Dublin days. Talking to Con one day, no doubt over a drink, I asked him why he had left Dublin, where he had taken over Beckett's job in (1931) [in] the French department at Trinity College and had been ever since; particularly to live in Paris, I no doubt could not have forbore from mentioning, where his nickname could not but help to make him a subject of occasional bawdy ribaldry?

Well, you see, he replied, no doubt making allowances for me, I've always thought of Paris as home.

There was also the money. £500 and the obligation to stay away for three months implies, with a wife and child, that as little as possible be spent on the fares.

So Paris seemed good, especially as my wife had lived there for a couple of years and knew the language fluently. I had stopped at ordinary level.

The literary reasons for going to Paris are obvious to me; having learnt from bitter experience that most people know of my work only through reviews, I cannot say, I dare not say that if you know my work the reasons should be obvious to you, too. But there was nowhere else that was within the range of £500 which could possibly have meant so much, historically and emotionally, personally and influentially.

So it was Paris.

The thing that surprised me was that Somerset Maugham had been right. So diametrically opposed to him was I as a writer, as a class-member, as a heterosexual, that it had not occurred to me he could be right in anything. Had he not described state-aided students as scum, had he not written as though Joyce had not existed, had he not stood for class privilege and wealth in its most craven form?

But about the insularity of young English writers he was undoubtedly right in my case. The first two months were shattering. My poor French actually became worse, and I was reduced to pointing in shops and proffering an enormous note and not counting the change in order to escape conversation of any kind. Mostly I sent my wife out shopping. In restaurants together I would take cover behind her. Once a veal kidney I had ordered was presented streaming with blood: through my wife I rejected it: 'Bien cuire?' enquired the waiter; Bloody queer, I said, and the macaronicism pleased me more than eating the kidney.

For the third month we left Paris and drifted around France as we pleased; a month I look back on with infinite nostalgia, pleasure, for its relaxation. In the Auvergne Jean-Claude Killy won the winter Olympics at Grenoble; by the time we reached Grenoble by way of the Vaucluse, Nice, Turin, La Grave (from just beyond which I sent postcards saying 'No sign of Him here, either') and the Benedictine of Green Chartreuse there was nothing to see; nor had we wanted to see anything special, just what there was. And there were all these odd things. Like when a television programme on Tours was shown, the film festival at which my film *You're Human Like the Rest of Them* had won the Grand Prix the month before, we were in a *pension* in La Grave, watching in the kitchen with the madame and her trusty lover; precious little there was to see however; the picture kept doubling and trebling; 'Ah,' says madame, or the henchman, 'the picture keeps bouncing off the glaciers.' By which the observant amongst you must have noticed that my French was improving, or my wife was translating the *mots sals*. It was improving, I could understand a lot; given another £500 of Somerset Maugham's money I might have done him even prouder.

In the Gorges of the Tarn our second (and last) child was conceived; we think, though like in everything else there can be no certainty; it felt as though it ought to have been, though ...

To return to the money, the constant preoccupation of writers. I calculate that it cost me another £500 to spend Somerset Maugham's £500. Obviously, I did choose an expensive country to visit. Equally clearly, I did go to the expense of a wife and child, which Somerset Maugham clearly did not allow for. But I would have been very unwise to have gone without them; I doubt if I could have lasted a fortnight without them in fact. I have heard of people going without their wife and child, but I should have thought it most unwise, if not fatal.

So, in Paris for the last tidying up before going, staying with friends we had met there, we in duty felt we should take them to La Coupole for the last final evening in France, leaving for the coast next day. This foursome escalated into a sixsome with the addition of our friends' agent; and then into a reeling eightsome with another of this agent's clients, the film actor George Segal. Whom I admired, as it happened. The first course took me over the level of the money I had left to get back to England, oyster cocktails and all. Ah, I thought, fatalistically, I shall bounce a cheque, as my last act, off that nasty bank manager (devaluation had taken place the week I arranged to transfer Mr Maugham's £500 from here to there; and he was appropriately supercilious, and I had a protracted fight as to which exchange rate it had to be transferred at); thus I resigned myself to eating as expensively as possible. George Segal sat at the far end, our friends in between, the nice agent, George Segal's nice girl or wife, too. I ate very well indeed, like the financially condemned. Since then I have learned that in France it is a criminal (as against a civil) offence to bounce a cheque. No doubt I should have been stopped at the boat and made to disgorge. Towards the end of the meal I was too frightened to be drunk, even. I kept expecting the waiter. But when I nervously asked the agent, he passed it off with one hand, would not talk about it. It was some time later, to my embarrassment almost as much as the bouncing, that I realised that the blessed George Segal had in fact picked up the tab, as I was only too pleased to agree to call it, had (really quite surreptitiously and nobly) actually paid for us all, the eightsome, and I had money not only to buy a meal and petrol on the way back to Boulogne but also, if I chose, to indulge my duty free allowances.

I have never been able to look at a George Segal movie without giving thanks, since.

Coming back from Dover on the M2 the car which had given us not a moment's trouble during 3,000 miles through France and Italy stripped its distributor drive. Ignominiously we were towed into Faversham, thought of staying the night, but came by train into London, anticlimactically, sans duty-free allowances, sans baggage, sans.

But Con was right: I too now think of Paris as home, hope to retire there as soon as possible, get on to the mainland as Alan Sillitoe calls it, where the writer has some sort of status and is not thought of as part-time, 'But what do you really do?'

'I would have been very unwise to have gone without them; I doubt if I could have lasted a fortnight without them in fact. I have heard of people going without their wife and child, but I should have thought it most unwise, if not fatal.' Tipsy though he may have been, there is a new quality to Johnson's prose, as he writes these words. At once tender and facetious, a little self-mocking. It's almost as though he has acquired (at long last) a lightness of touch! And there is a genuine depth of feeling there, however ironically expressed. No one could doubt, reading those words, that Johnson's family meant everything to him.

This is confirmed by countless stories from Virginia and Steven, whose most vivid memories of Johnson portray a contented family man, even when his professional life was full of frustration. 'Bryan was an enthusiastic and devoted father, building intricate models with Steve; taking him to the pub where they would sit in the late afternoon, Bryan with a pint and the evening paper, Steve with his Coke and the *Beano* – at times buried so deep in the cartoons that he put his glass back on the table without watching, where it would crash to the floor and there would be a moment's wait to see if the barman would throw them out (as Steve was well below the permitted age). Bryan would carry Kate round on his shoulders, or lie on the floor to play with her. She would carefully climb the seven stairs to the tiny study where he wrote, and he would put aside his work to talk or give her paper to draw and write on.'

As any writer with children will tell you, all the same, there invariably comes a point where you crave freedom from these distractions. At around this time Gordon Williams was renting a small office in Dryden Chambers, off Oxford Street to the north of Soho.* He invited his old sparring partner – with whom he had maintained a spasmodic, prickly and combative friendship – to come and share it with him, at a rent of about five pounds a week.

---

* Used as a location in Hitchcock's *Frenzy* as the home of the killer, played by Barry Foster.

The arrangement lasted for several months, starting in the winter of 1972, and gave Williams the opportunity to observe Johnson at close hand. Thirty years later, his stark conclusion (not shared by everyone, it must be said) is that, 'He was in a desperate state.' Williams added that Johnson at this stage had 'no friends' (within the publishing industry, that is) and that 'people were not taking his phone calls – many of whom I know were at his funeral a few months later'.

Gordon Williams never did buy – and never has bought – into the notion of Johnson as the natural heir to Joyce and Beckett. To him, he was simply a gifted writer with a somewhat inflated opinion of himself and a baffling compulsion to insult and offend the very people who were most in a position to help him. How could he expect publishers to work with him when he made it perfectly clear to them that he held their values and their literary judgments in absolute contempt? As an instance of his tactlessness, he remembers beginning to collaborate with Johnson on a potboiling thriller about a bank heist, which could be written in a couple of weeks and would earn them both some much needed cash. They got no further than planning the first couple of chapters when Johnson announced that the book, when completed, would have to be published under Williams's name, with his own contribution remaining strictly anonymous. 'He was quite specific about this: it would go under my name but we'd split the money – because he couldn't afford, with his reputation, to be seen writing a cheap detective story. I said "Oh, great, Bryan: I have no reputation, then?"' This was a fair question – it was Williams, after all, who had been shortlisted for the very first Booker Prize with his autobiographical novel *From Scenes Like These* in 1969. 'Well, yes – but that would just show you what creeps they all were, in his eyes.'

With his cheerfully resigned philosophy that 'Life's a merry hell', Williams was Johnson's opposite, as a man and as a writer. He wrote the books he wanted to write when he could find the time, and was otherwise prepared to churn out genre novels, ghostwritten memoirs and unlikely collaborations (most notably with Terry Venables on the *Hazell* series) to pay the rent. He was breezily cynical about the publishing and newspaper businesses, accepting that they were run by fools and charlatans and that this was how the world worked. He was thick-skinned. Johnson's skin, however, was painfully thin. His work was a continuing, urgent attempt – 'desperate in its seriousness', to quote the self-penned blurb for *Trawl* – to exorcise lifelong personal demons. His working routine was composed of rituals and superstitions. There was no way, for instance, that he could begin work on *See the Old Lady Decently* in the anonymous atmosphere of Dryden Chambers. At the same time, with his mother no longer there, he could not bring himself to resume the habit of starting each novel on Boxing Day in his old bedroom at the house in Barnes. So instead, the day after Christmas, he climbed up to his attic study in Islington and wrote this:

147: NOTE *(26 December 1972)*

Written in parish logbook intended for See the Old Lady Decently:

> Here with my yellow Fuller's pencil I begin the longest haul of all, self-consciously this Boxing Day; and this is the first I have begun in *a different place*. Always before it has been in my parents' back upstairs room at 8 Meredyth Road, latterly even more self-consciously than this, going over there specially: *Xtie* was the last, two years ago, 1970, my mother's last Xmas, too. So this time I have made the commitment to this place, too, am committed to my own home, here, ours, as I now have no nearer mother than my wife, all is committed to these rocks. I am pleased about it, reassured, perhaps this is health.

Johnson wrote no more of the novel that day, however – the rest of this logbook is empty, except for a scrap of paper which reads:

> *Let us embrace – ha! – the mindless (?) chaos.*

The logbook also reveals the other titles he rejected for the novel: 'I Consider You', 'What Else Do I Have?' and 'Taking the Words for an Airing'. But the graphs he kept of the novel's progress show that he wrote nothing more – apart from some 'odds and ends' – until 9 July 1973. One of the graphs, for the months March–June, is entirely blank. Across its white expanse Johnson later scribbled the single word, 'Ha!'.

*

Gordon Williams is wrong, in fact, to say that Johnson had 'no friends' in the publishing business at this time. He certainly had Michael Bakewell and Diana Tyler of the MBA Literary Agency: they continued to work for him unstintingly, and he continued to repay their faith in him with acts of generosity and kindness. It was not, I think, that Johnson always demanded to see *results* from his agents and publishers: on the contrary, he could be very forgiving, provided that he was certain they were doing their professional best for him. (Which, in his view, had rarely been the case in the past.) Diana Tyler, for instance, remembers him taking her out for a drink on the eve of her first visit to the Frankfurt Book Fair, where she would be attempting to sell foreign rights in his books. 'I remember Bryan took me out the night before, and we had a drink and he said, "Now I don't want you to worry." And I said, "Worry? What about?" And he said, "About Frankfurt

– you don't have to come back, you know, having done anything for me." And I thought that was very sweet and very thoughtful, that he might have thought perhaps that there was a pressure on me. To me that was a clear example that he could be very caring. I've always remembered that.'

The first few weeks of 1973 saw MBA playing, as before, a dual role on Johnson's behalf. On the one hand they were busy trying to find a new publisher, and the best possible deal, for what was now referred to as 'The Matrix Trilogy'. 'There was a real rapport between Bryan and Philip Ziegler,' Diana Tyler recalls, 'despite them being such different people. But I don't think the sales had been very good – you know, the usual things that weren't right. And so Collins's offer on the next books was not what we would have wanted. The trilogy was quite a big thing to sell – we had to find someone who was really prepared to take that on, and as I remember the outline and synopsis were not really received with open arms by Collins at the time.' So instead Johnson was moved to Hutchinson – who also agreed, crucially, to publish a slimmed-down version of his volume of 'Selected Shorter Prose', *Aren't You Rather Young To Be Writing Your Memoirs?*. (He had never really forgiven Collins for turning that down.) And so, for his seventh novel, he signed up with his fourth publisher. 'The day he signed that contract he felt very happy about it, and secure,' Diana Tyler insists. 'The intention was there, and the commitment.'

Meanwhile, both Diana Tyler and Michael Bakewell took performing parts in an innovative radio production of *Christie Malry's Own Double-Entry*. 'For the first time on British radio,' announced the London edition of the *Radio Times*, 'a new novel read in full by the author, B. S. JOHNSON, with the voices of MICHAEL BAKEWELL, VIRGINIA JOHNSON and DIANA TYLER. Also all sorts of other noises including the sounds of the LITTLE VERMIFUGE. Producer TOM VERNON.' Broadcast by BBC Radio London on 30 January and repeated on 4 February 1973, it was one of Johnson's finest moments, and a brilliant piece of publicity for the novel itself, which was to be published on 5 February – the author's fortieth birthday. He was a fine, supple, expressive reader of his own prose, and got spirited and surprisingly accomplished support from Diana Tyler (as Christie's mother) and Virginia (as the Shrike). Sparing but inventive use of music and sound effects even recalled one of his most beloved early influences, *The Goon Show*: when it came to Chapter XVI of the novel, for instance, which explains in some detail how to make a Molotov cocktail (Johnson seems to have possessed a copy of *The Anarchist's Cookbook*), Michael Bakewell's narrator explains – truthfully – that the passage has been banned by the BBC, and instead we get a recording of Johnson reading the chapter, but speeded up more and more until it becomes an incomprehensible stream of high-pitched noise. Good-quality tapes of the broadcast survive: it ran for just under three hours and someone should really put it out as an audiobook.*

At this point, early in 1973, you might almost have been forgiven for thinking that Johnson was on a roll. *Christie* was published, and was welcomed as his funniest, blackest, most compelling novel yet. With a couple of notable exceptions (Anthony Thwaite in the *Observer*, the *TLS* which 'read me its usual little lecture about being a naughty unconventional boy and why did I waste my talent not writing in the way they would have me write'[3]) the novel received wildly enthusiastic reviews. Auberon Waugh in the *Spectator* said that it was 'undoubtedly a masterpiece' and 'if I had any say in the matter it would probably win the Nobel Prize for Literature'. As always, of course, his tongue was planted firmly in his cheek when he said it, but if there was any irony intended, Johnson – who almost certainly did believe that he was worthy of the Nobel Prize – probably never spotted it. The quote duly went onto the cover of his next book, in any case. And at last, the Holy Grail of publishing – the American edition which Johnson, for all his anti-Americanism, so eagerly craved – turned out to be within his grasp. On Beckett's recommendation (again), Richard Seaver of Grove Press made an offer for the novel and proposed to publish it in the autumn, with the possibility of a lecture tour to promote it.

Surely, this could only mean that things were looking up, at last?

What went wrong?

Even now, after seven years of living alongside Johnson, reading everything, published and unpublished, that he ever wrote, talking to the friends who were closest to him, talking to Virginia, I'm not sure that I can answer that question. To answer it properly would mean seeing inside his head, and that's the one place that I – that any of us – will never be able to go. Of course, Johnson regarded each of his novels as 'a diagram of certain aspects of the inside of his skull'; but those 'certain aspects', I've come to believe, were carefully, if subconsciously, chosen. Some years after his suicide, his friend and fellow experimentalist Eva Figes reminisced about his theory of the novel, his commitment to literal truth, and said, 'It might have worked for him, both as a person and a writer, if he had been more in touch with his inner problems, and had really explored them in his writing. Instead he tried to seal off the seething cauldron, truth became a lie, and the result was destructive.'[4] This, I think, is very perceptive – especially in its stress on Johnson 'both as a person and a writer'. The imminent crisis would not just be too big for him to handle, emotionally: it would also be too painful ever to write about. It would make

---

* The producer, Tom Vernon, was so impressed by the experience of working on this programme that he subsequently named his own quirky series of TV documentaries – starting with *Fat Man on a Bicycle* – as a sort of homage to Johnson.

the prospect of writing any more novels or poems so daunting that it would probably have felt, at the time, almost inconceivable.

*

A short play which Johnson finished in the first half of 1973 illustrates both the strengths and weaknesses of his autobiographical approach. This was *Down Red Lane*, a lunchtime theatre piece written for (but rejected by) Walter Hall of the Basement Theatre in Soho. Its central conceit is funny enough. The setting is a gastronomic restaurant, and there are three characters: a waiter, a diner, and the diner's belly – a disembodied voice to be provided by an actor concealed beneath the dining table throughout the play. Most of the comedy comes from the belly's horror-struck reactions as the diner threatens to order ever spicier and more acidic items from the menu, washed down with challenging quantities of alcohol. At times it seems to foreshadow Monty Python's famous 'Mr Creosote' sketch, in which Terry Jones played an obese gourmet in the film *The Meaning of Life*.

It appears to have been written shortly after Johnson's return from Czechoslovakia, which he had visited on a two-week British Council tour in April 1973. As with his Hungarian visit, he wrote this one up in a long report for the Council. Here he is, for instance, recording his encounter with one of the most eminent Czech writers:

148: EXTRACT FROM REPORT TO THE BRITISH COUNCIL
(completed 15 May 1973)

Wednesday 4th April
At nine I returned to the hotel to meet Miroslav Holub. I did not know whether it would do him any good to be seen talking in public with a western writer, so suggested my hotel room; or did he suggest it? Anyway, he talked quite openly and freely despite presumably knowing that the room would be bugged if we are to believe the Foreign Office. And indeed what we talked about could not have been considered subversive by anyone; he was chiefly interested to know what was going on in the literary world in England, of news of friends like Ted Hughes. We had a most friendly and wideranging discussion on these subjects, and I asked him whether he would let me have some poems for TRANSATLANTIC REVIEW, of which I am poetry editor. [. . .] He was not, he said, though forbidden to publish, as badly off as many writers since he still had his job as a research scientist and did not have to resort to taxi-driving and so on as many writers in disfavour did. A day or two later I told Miss Kožnarová* that I found it difficult to understand

---

* Miss Eva Kožnarová was Johnson's interpreter for the first week of his visit.

how the works of a writer like Holub could possibly be seen as a political threat; she replied that I would have to live in the country a long while before I could understand [...]

Also on that Wednesday, Johnson had given a lecture at the English department of the State Library – the first Western writer to do so since Margaret Drabble in 1969. The night before, the head of the English department, Dr E. Strnadová, had begged him 'in a state of noticeable emotion' not to say anything too controversial as 'this was the first of a series, and [...] if my one was in any way controversial then the whole series could be cancelled'. Johnson confessed himself completely unable to judge what might be considered controversial or not. In the event I would guess that he delivered a version of the only lecture he ever delivered in his life: viz. a polemic about how the novel must evolve and how it was no good writing Dickensian fiction in the age of Beckett, etc. 'There was seating for 150 people, but the audience must have been twice that size and I was told more failed to get in. Throughout an hour's lecture on a hot afternoon they sat and stood perfectly quietly, apparently held. After an interval, my film *You're Human Like the Rest of Them* was shown (a copy had been provided by the British Council from its own library). The audience was for some reason smaller by then [...]' Self-deprecating irony, creeping untypically into his discourse, again? It's difficult to tell.

The report is for the most part terse and factual and bears out William Hoyland's observation about Johnson seeming 'tired' and having lost his 'zip'. 'Sightseeing to the Red Castle; Marie Antoinette's sledge and much other priceless junk,' reads one day's entry (Sunday 15 April) in its entirety. Altogether, it gives the impression that Johnson felt nothing here like the coup de foudre that struck him on entering Hungary in 1969. And yet, reading *Down Red Lane*, it's hard not to imagine that something significant must have happened to him in Czechoslovakia, because the play is full of references to it – even though they are obscure, sometimes to the point of incomprehensibility.

It is an unmistakably self-referential piece, which is what gives it such a hard core of melancholy, despite its light-hearted premise. Johnson's identification with his central character seems, on this occasion, to be unambiguous and absolute. At one point this character (called simply 'The Diner') reminisces about a dinner in Paris with 'Ginnie' and 'Sam' (Beckett), and later recalls eating oysters in Nantes 'with Zulf, late at night'. Who could he be, in that case, other than an imagined future version of B. S. Johnson himself? Taking that on board, his description in the opening stage direction is revealing: 'He is gross, fat, enormous, but likeable; aged anything between fifty and seventy; dressed in dinner suit, but it is carelessly maintained; yet he has a certain dignity, even when he behaves grossly; he still has a human dignity.'

The play finds Johnson meditating – sorrowfully, for the most part – on a number of highly personal topics. Foremost among these is his relationship with food. 'I don't know why I was born with an appetite,' the Diner says. 'Or, if you like, I don't know why I was conditioned to think that my appetite was the most important thing in my life. I do know I have suffered from my appetite, my grossness, my peculiarity.' He is plunged into sudden depressions and does his best to talk himself gamely out of them. 'Look on the bright side,' he exclaims. 'Don't forget the good times ... There are always enough good times to make it worthwhile! That's the secret! No doubt. The reason why one does not actually (*pause*) do it.' And along with reflections on his own 'grossness' comes a pervasive nostalgia for a lost world of sexual activity. The Diner refers to his penis as 'Winkle', and when challenged by his belly to remember, 'When did you last see your Winkle in the flesh?' replies, defensively: 'He still performs one of his two functions.' 'But when did you last see him?' the belly insists, and the diner answers, 'Bratislava? No? Zvolen?' And to this he enigmatically adds: 'Zvolen was when they started, where the idea came from.'

What 'idea'? Who or what are 'they'?

We probably cannot know. Zvolen lies some 120 miles north-east of Bratislava, and Johnson had visited it on Saturday,14th April: not alone, apparently, although his British Council report does not specify in whose company. 'Up very early,' he wrote, 'for a three-hour drive in snow, then rain, to Zvolen, where the resistance against the Nazis began and where there is a very impressive national memorial to the fact. This building has a permanent exhibition aided by those audio-visual techniques of presentation that had impressed me in Prague. [...] Back fairly late after a puncture had delayed us.'

The town is mentioned again in the last moments of *Down Red Lane*. We are told once more that Zvolen was 'where it started', and left to ponder a final speech from the Diner even more cryptic than what has gone before:

149: EXTRACT FROM THE PLAY *DOWN RED LANE* (1973)

DINER: There was the baby, sitting up, with that unbelievably stupid look of *hope* upon his stupid face! (*pause*) There was Mahler on at the time, *Das Lied von der Erde* if I remember rightly, I objected to that, too. And the baby with this look of expectancy, the baby expectorant, ha! (*pause*) And she said, she said as though she could not have meant it to mean more, (*pause*) sincerely, she said, I shall dry out without you. (*pause*) I shall dry out without you.

What on earth is being alluded to, here? Nobody I questioned was able to enlighten me, and the ending of this play can only lead one to concur with the observation implied by Eva Figes: that for all his protestations about authorial honesty and literal truth, Johnson was as willing as any other writer, sometimes, to cloak his meanings behind multiple layers of obliqueness, obscurantism and even evasion.

*

Nobody could make that criticism, admittedly, about his journalistic writings. Throughout the first half of 1973 Johnson had continued to write journalism; not literary journalism as such, but polemical and politically engaged journalism on literary subjects. He wrote for the *Film & Television Technician* (April 1973) complaining about the lowly status of the writer in the film industry. For *Education & Training* (March 1973), he wrote the article I have already quoted, at some length,* about his unsatisfactory education. And for *Tribune* (15 June 1973) he wrote a piece lamenting the political feebleness of the Society of Authors and urging writers to form themselves into a real union.

There is a noticeable grumpiness about all of these writings – even more so than in his previous journalism. Perhaps he was already beginning to leave the 'foothills of paranoia' behind and set out onto the main slopes. ('Do I sound paranoid and bitter?' he asks, at the end of the *Education & Training* article.) But still, they are coherent, rational, well-argued pieces. It was only when he made his views known in person that Johnson was starting to get out of control. Zulfikar Ghose recalls how he boasted of giving someone a 'dressing down' at a party of Edward Lucie-Smith's at around this time.[5] The luckless recipient was, in fact, Anthony Thwaite, who four weeks earlier had given *Christie Malry* a 'vicious, meanminded little attack' in the *Observer*. 'I saw him last week at ELS's 40th birthday party,' Johnson wrote, 'and gave him a public roasting'.[6]

In May and June Johnson took his whole family on an extended trip to Eastern Europe. *The Unfortunates* was about to be published in Hungary,† and he decided to use this as the occasion for an ambitious family holiday. It also gave him an excuse to buy a new car: a Citroën GS Estate 1220, registration number PGU 409L. ('Tons of room, does 95 mph cruising, very

---

* See the chapters entitled 'Solitude' and 'The Student', *passim*.
† Not, however, in a box: the economics of Hungarian publishing would not allow that. It was published as a regular, bound paperback, with each chapter prefaced by a different printer's symbol. These same symbols were reproduced on a page at the end of the book: Johnson then invited Hungarian readers to tear this page out, cut around each symbol, throw them all in a hat and bring them out one by one – randomly. I wonder how many of the novel's 9,000 readers (far more than it ever sold in Britain!) ever bothered to follow these instructions through.

Frenchie sexy.'[7]) The purchase of this car gave rise to some puzzlement among his friends, who began to assume that Johnson must be wealthier than he was letting on. Here, maybe, we have an explanation for that rumour about 'Beckett's Nobel Prize money' being given to the struggling writer and subsequently spent on a sports car; although, as we have seen, Beckett sent him only one hundred pounds, and the car was bought almost two years later. Still, one can imagine how the two stories might have been conflated.

The family set off on 26 May, stopping at a motel in Beaune after their channel crossing and then staying a couple of nights with John Berger at his flat in Geneva ('interesting for me if not for the others').[8] They drove on through Switzerland and Austria and made it to Hungary in two more days: Steven (by now almost eight) and Katie (four and a half) behaved themselves well during the long drives. (Steven, in fact, retains a vivid memory of being detained for some hours at the Hungarian border: the main reason being his father's insistence on listing his occupation as 'poet' on his passport.) Once in Hungary they spent only one day in Budapest before travelling on to Siófok on Lake Balaton, where István Bart had a country house. They stayed for a fortnight on the Balaton, with Johnson making a brief trip back to Budapest halfway through to conduct some press and radio interviews about *The Unfortunates*.

This time, besides meeting István Bart, Johnson also became friendly with the Hungarian academic Ferenc Takács and his then wife, Annamária. And somehow – though the details of this have never been made clear to me – they all managed to meet up with Bill Holdsworth in Budapest as well. Takács remembers, at any rate, that he, Bart, Johnson, Holdsworth and an unnamed friend of Holdsworth's ('one of the navvies in his building operation – I remember him, his whole hand was covered by a tattoo, he had two gold rings joined by a chain, and he was full of songs') went to a cellar bar in the castle district of Budapest and got incredibly drunk. 'Bryan immobilized himself by drink,' Takács recalls, with some relish. 'It was one of these deep-cellar drink places, and I had to help carry him upstairs. We were all very very drunk.' István Bart adds, 'Do you remember the song Old Harry Pollitt? Surely you remember his name – he was a British Communist Party man. Bill and his builder friend were Communist-leaning, and Harry Pollitt was a frequently mentioned name.'

The song exists in several versions. One of them goes like this:

Harry Pollitt was a worker; one of Lenin's lads
He was foully murdered by those counter-revolutionary cads
Counter-revolutionary cads, counter-revolutionary cads
He was foully murdered by those counter-revolutionary cads!

Old Harry went to heaven. He reached the Gates with ease,
Said, "May I speak with Comrade God, I am Harry Pollitt please
I'm Harry Pollitt please, I'm Harry Pollitt please
May I speak with Comrade God, I am Harry Pollitt please.'

'Who are you?' said Saint Peter, 'Are you humble and contrite?'
'I'm a friend of Lady Astor's.' 'Well, OK. that's quite all right.
OK, that's quite all right, well OK, that's quite all right
You're a friend of Lady Astor, well OK, that's quite all right.'

They put him in the choir, but the hymns he did not like
So he organized the angels and he led them out on strike
Led them out on strike, led them out on strike
He organized the angels and he led them out on strike!

One day when God was walking around heaven to meditate,
Who should he see but Harry chalkin' slogans on the gate?
Chalkin' slogans on the gate, slogans on the gate
Who should he see but Harry chalkin' slogans on the gate?

Well, they brought him up for trial before the Holy Ghost
For spreadin' disaffection amongst the heavenly host
Amongst the heavenly host, amongst the heavenly host
For spreadin' disaffection amongst the heavenly host.

Well, the verdict it was guilty, Harry said, 'Ah, well'
And he tucked his nightie round his knees and he drifted down to hell
Yes, he drifted down to hell, he drifted down to hell
He tucked his nightie round his knees and he drifted down to hell.

Now seven long years have passed, Harry's doing swell
He's just been made the first people's commissar for soviet hell
Commissar of soviet hell, commissar of soviet hell
He's just been made the first people's commissar of soviet hell!

Well the moral of this story is easy for to tell,
If you want to be a Bolshevik, you'll have to go to hell,
You'll have to go to hell, yes, you'll have to go to hell,
If you want to be a Bolshevik, you'll have to go to hell!

That's one way to remember Bryan Johnson, I suppose. Immobilized by drink, a contented smile on his face, being carried out of a bar by two Hungarians while his British friends sang drunken revolutionary songs beneath a starlit Budapest sky. That was another night, I'm sure, when he must have been 'appy.

Where were Virginia and the children in all this?

Back in Siófok, presumably. And that was where they stayed, as well, on

Monday, 11 June 1973, when Johnson drove down by himself to the small village of Szentlõrinc (about 20 kilometres from Pécs) to see György Novák. The meeting was fraught with misunderstandings: Novák had written to ask if Johnson would mind talking to his students, but the letter had arrived in London too late for him to read it; they were supposed to have met in Baja, not Szentlõrinc, and Virginia and the children were meant to have come as well. Novák was surprised when Johnson arrived alone: 'We expected him to come with the family, as planned, but apparently there had been a quarrel in the family so he came alone in his white Citroën.'

For his own part, Johnson was taken aback to have turned up on what he assumed was a social visit and found an audience of some twenty-five students, aged about fifteen or sixteen, who had camped overnight in the back yard of Novák's parents' house and were now eagerly expecting to sit at the feet of a great English poet and novelist. But as usual, he took it in his stride:

'He arrived in the morning, around ten or eleven and he stayed until five or six in the afternoon. We had a meal, and then he talked to us all in the garden and then we went into a room. Then he sat down and he made this recording – ' (on a reel-to-reel tape recorder) ' – and he took his two volumes of poems and went through them, reading them and then commentating. He started with the ones about his great love [Muriel], then "Good News . . ." and "Bad News for Her Mother", and he took the poems one by one, explaining them.' (Novák still has the recording: he also shot some cine-film of the day, which is now lost.)

'He'd left his family in a summerhouse on the Balaton. I'd met them all before, just for one day, at Gregynog in Wales, and he seemed happier then, everything was OK then. The lack of the family, and then the fact we had expected them and they didn't turn up, suggested that something was wrong, but he didn't discuss it. He just said that they couldn't come and there had been some kind of unpleasantness. But he wasn't preoccupied, at least I couldn't see, he took in everything, he appeared to take in everything and he was listening to us and responding, pleasing us and being at our service, and all that.'

A couple of days later Johnson and his family drove home, through Czechoslovakia where he tried to follow up on some of the publishing contacts he had made in April. Nothing ever came of these attempts. 'We arrived back exhausted,' he wrote to Zulfikar Ghose. 'Perhaps including Czechoslovakia wasn't such a good idea.'[9]

Some months later, on 15 October, he would write to György Novák to say, 'We get nostalgic about Hungary', and he would admit to thinking, often, of that strange, still, unexpected summer afternoon when he had held an audience of young students enraptured with a reading of his poems, in an unfamiliar foreign village: the poet as spokesman, the centre of the community. Novák sent him some photographs as a memento. On Sunday, 4 November, with his marriage in crisis and nine days left to live, sitting alone in his upstairs study, Johnson wrote back, with the photographs on the desk in front of him: 'I sit here,' he wrote, 'in the same shirt staring at such visions of a fat foolish man [. . .]'

*

Eva Figes, in a brief memoir of her friendship with Johnson published almost twenty years ago, recalls 'sitting next to him at a very rowdy and enjoyable Annual General Meeting of the Society of Authors where he called for the instant resignation of the entire Committee of Management'.[10] This meeting took place not long after his return from Hungary in 1973. Gordon Williams also remembers the meeting as being rowdy, but less enjoyable. Johnson despised the Society of Authors, thinking it toothless and effete compared to Equity, the Writers' Guild or the ACTT, and would sarcastically refer to its offices in Drayton Gardens, SW10, as 'the powerhouse of the literary trade union movement'.[11] He had recently been appalled by a survey in the society's own magazine, *The Author*, which revealed that writers' earnings had, on average, dropped substantially since the mid-1960s, and it was for this reason that he decided to propose his radical motion. Gordon Williams, also a strong union man, agreed that the society was 'a fucking awful organization', and agreed to second the motion, but recalling the meeting afterwards he said, 'I was sick about that, really sick.' Johnson had not told him in advance what he was going to say, and Williams had not been prepared for the violence of his tone, or for the attacks on individual Committee members to be so personal. This, in any case, was the text of the speech:

150: SPEECH TO THE SOCIETY OF AUTHORS AGM *(26 July 1973)*

'In view of the facts revealed by the latest survey of authors' earnings (which are now at a lower level than in 1965 when the last survey was taken) this AGM questions whether the administration and leadership have been effective in promoting the objects of the Society of Authors; and recommends that all those responsible for such administration and leadership should resign forthwith.'

Proposed by B. S. JOHNSON   Seconded by GORDON WILLIAMS

Proposer's Speech

It's not in fact necessary for me to prove the evidence in this proposal; it's been proved for us by the Society's own survey into writers' earnings.

I take it that every member in this room has read the results of that survey in the winter issue of *The Author*.

It shows a disastrous state of affairs. Book writers were very badly off in 1966; they are even worse off in 1973. Writers actually receive less, pound for pound, than they did in 1966 – and without taking inflation into account. Inflation from January 1966 to June 1973 has amounted to 63.4%. In real terms, therefore, writers will still be earning in 1973 something like a third or a quarter of what they earned in 1966.

That is a disaster for book writers; no one can dispute that. What one can ask is: who is responsible for it, for not at least seeing that writers' earnings kept up with inflation? What one can ask is: if the Society of Authors is not responsible, then who is? What other organisation is there which is supposed to protect the interests of book writers?

The objects of the Society listed first read as follows: 'To represent, further, aid and assist the objects and protect the rights of Authors.' The present administration and leadership of the Society have failed in their duty to carry out those objects. What clearer example of failure could there be than incomes reduced to a third of their value in seven years? They have failed, and the only honourable course for them is to resign.

In view of the facts of the survey, is there anything that can be said in favour of the Committee of Management and the Secretariat? What have they done recently? They've been fighting (if that's the word) for Public Lending Right for twenty years, of course, and have now dedicated themselves to the sellout of Purchase Right and caused the greatest split in the membership since television writers went off and formed themselves in a trade union, the Writers' Guild. But the PLR issue is dealt with elsewhere in this AGM.

What else have they done recently? It's easier to ask what they haven't done. The administration has said nothing about Midway editions, for just one example.* Since they appear to know nothing about them, I had better explain that Midway editions are paperbacks published simultaneously with the hardback edition, but at about half the price. They are not to be confused with the cheap mass paperback published two years or so later than the hardback. Publishers of course wish to pay a paperback royalty of 7½% on Midways; those of us who have been approached with contracts for Midway editions have argued that the sales will hit the hardback, and that therefore a royalty of

---

* Why was Johnson so exercised about this particular subject? Because he had just signed a contract with Hutchinson for *Aren't You Rather Young To Be Writing Your Memoirs?* to be published in this format, which turned out in any case to be a short-lived experiment.

12½% should be paid. But what does the Society of Authors think about this new development in publishing? It doesn't think. It has no policy as far as members are concerned. Not a word about Midways has been published in *The Author.*

Midways are another example of the present administration of the Society simply not doing its duty; meanwhile, authors are picked off one by one because there is no support by their professional organisation. Unless something is done soon about Midways, then we'll end up with another disaster: we'll find ourselves in a situation similar to the mass paperback one, where the hardback publisher takes half of the author's money.

One is entitled to ask some questions about how it always seems to happen that the Society of Authors is outflanked by publishers, book-sellers, librarians and everyone else connected with the book trade. It's when one looks at the composition of the Committee of Management that one may begin to understand why the Society's performance over the last seven years has been so appalling, how they have failed to carry out the very objects of the Society.

There's been the odd university professor on the Committee, for instance. He does write books, of course, but only part-time, by defini-tion. If he were committed to full-time professional writing he would be defrauding his employers, the university. How then can he be commit-ted to the cause of the professional writer? How, indeed, can he know anything of the problems and circumstances of the professional writer? Yet someone thought him a fit and proper person to be nominated for the Committee of Management, and to help make decisions which vitally affect professional writers.

Then there's another member of the Committee whose father is a publisher. A publisher! How total can her commitment be to the cause of writers, to the objects of the Society of Authors? There must be a conflict of loyalties for the daughter of a publisher. Am I alone in thinking that that relationship is too close for someone on the Com-mittee of Management, someone who should be totally concerned with representing writers' interests?

Then there's been another member of the Committee for the last three years who owns and runs a bookshop. He's a bookseller! A bookseller! Again, am I alone in finding it improper that there should be a bookseller on the Committee of Management of the Society of Authors? How is it possible for a bookseller to act wholeheartedly in the interests of authors? Surely his loyalties must be divided?

Now don't misunderstand me. I'm not saying these people shouldn't be members of the Society: they've all written books, all qualify for mem-bership. But should they be members of the Committee of Management, the highest authority in the Society of Authors? I question whether it is in the best interests of authors that decisions should be made on their behalf by (amongst others) part-time writers, the daughter of a publisher, and a bookseller. I could go on to other members and ex-members of the Committee of Management; but my point is made – the distinction between committed writers and those on the other side of the fence is blurred. I submit it should not be.

But now who is it who has thought that these people with close associations with publishing and bookselling should be suitable leaders of our Society? Almost always they have been nominated by the existing committee, which therefore becomes self-perpetuating; but the constant element over the seven years of disaster have been the Secretary and the Secretariat. They must take perhaps the largest share of responsibility for the reduction in writers' earnings and the failure to promote the objects of the Society successfully. And so must the editor of *The Author*. It seems to me that he has too close a relationship with publishers, newspaper publishers in his case. For as a Features Editor of the *Observer* he employs writers, he has hire and fire power over writers. His employers dictate that he pay as little as possible to writers for economic reasons; whereas his editorship of *The Author* surely implies that he do the opposite. His loyalties are divided, his position is equivocal; and as an honourable man he should resolve it one way or the other.

Now the close connections with publishing and bookselling that I've described may seem improper, but one might not be shocked by them. And in view of the revelations of the rottenness of public life over the last couple of years one would hesitate to use the word corrupt.

But I was very properly shocked, and I hope you will be too, to learn that a member of the Secretariat, Victor Bonham-Carter, is in fact a publisher. That seems to me deeply shocking; it means, for instance, that authors were represented on the PLR Working Party by a publisher. The publishers and librarians and booksellers must be laughing their heads off that authors are soft enough to let a man with interests in publishing be their representative on such a vital matter. No doubt he'll tell you in a moment that he's only a publisher in a small way, he's only a partner in the Exmoor Press; but the principle is the thing that matters, and on the certificate of registration of the Exmoor Press he and his partner's business is described as that of publishers. As a man of principle, Victor Bonham-Carter should see that no administrator of a writers' organisation should be a publisher, in however small a way. It is a matter of principle, and as a man of principle he should resign at once, together with the rest of the Secretariat, the editor of *The Author*, and the Committee of Management: resign at this meeting, now.

Winding up: Proposer's Speech

I want, if I may, to ask all of you here to try to understand the purposes behind this proposal, which must seem extreme. The sole aim is to improve the lot of writers. The administration has behaved with great arrogance towards any form of criticism; it has refused to change to meet genuine grievances. This meeting is the only chance ordinary members have of trying to influence those who make decisions on their behalf.

No doubt some of you are put off by the manner in which I have expressed my own dissatisfaction with the present state of affairs. But adult, intelligent people should be able to see beyond that. Think for yourselves; and remember that if you vote against this action, or if you abstain, you are endorsing failure, a known, admitted and demonstrated failure by the administration over the last seven years. Do you want another seven years of failure? Something must be done to make the Society of Authors into a positive force for success on behalf of writers; and the first thing to do is to clear away the known failures, those who have consistently let us down in the past. Demonstrate now that you can think for yourselves, and that you have no intention of allowing the next seven years to be like the last seven years of failure and impropriety. Now is the time to show just how serious you are about the future of the Society of Authors. Vote *for* this proposal; anything less is a vote for complacency, arrogance, impropriety, inefficiency, and failure. Vote *for* the proposal.

The delivery of this speech is mentioned in the text of *See the Old Lady Decently*, which Johnson was attempting to write at the same time. It's an extremely revealing passage:

151: EXTRACT FROM *SEE THE OLD LADY DECENTLY*

There has been a terrible gap since I last wrote about Virrels. Four days. The reason is that I was preparing what I was to say at the AGM of a Society of which I am a member. It was on a subject which is very important to me. This novel trilogy is also very important to me. I was going to put in my speech as a document, the speech, what I had to say, but I realise it is probably not very important to you. In any case, my motion failed by twenty votes to fifty-eight. Those who did not support me are corrupt. It has taken me two days to settle down to this novel again. Such activity is a direct drain on the same source of energy that is used in writing. Is it worth it? I often ask myself; and I remember Leonard Woolf's remark, at the end of his long life, that all the years of political and humanitarian activity he had undertaken had been ultimately useless.

Yet I cannot be uninvolved.

So here I sit, just about able to write, just about able to put something down, looking for the excuse to be able to be interrupted again, surrounded by Larousse and Escoffier in search of clues as to how a restaurant Kitchen may have looked in the late 1920s when my mother began to work in one.

Does it matter? Does anything matter? The thing is that all seems very similar. Nothing seems capable of being new, I feel as old as the whole of history, knowing everything that mankind can. Except the details.

It must be an illusion. My mind may be going.

That was all I could manage yesterday.

Here we can see definite signs of paranoia ('Those who did not support me are corrupt') and increasing weariness and despair about the essential futility of his vocation ('Does it matter? Does anything matter?'). As for his speculation that 'My mind may be going': could there have been any truth in it?

'I don't know what the propensity or susceptibility for paranoia is, how you gauge that,' Gordon Williams told me, 'but events did contribute. Once it started going wrong, nothing seemed to go right for him.' True, the publication of *Christie Malry* had been more than usually successful, and it had been sold to America; but how heavily did this weigh in Johnson's scheme of things, when he seemed otherwise to be continually confronted by setbacks? He had been devastated to learn, for instance, that without consulting him, Secker had pulped all the remaining unsold copies of *The Unfortunates*, the novel that was, as a physical object, by far the most dear to him – 'The most original, novel, exploitable for novelty book since the war' as he had called it. Gone. All destroyed. And another cherished hope had been dashed earlier in the year: 'I still hold you [...] in most affectionate memory, have no one I can talk to as we used to talk', he had written to Zulfikar Ghose. He keenly missed that writerly solidarity, the shared values, the waspish amusement against the literary establishment that had marked their 'tidal friendship' in the dog days of the early 1960s. For months, letters had been flying backwards and forwards between London and Austin, Texas, as Ghose tried to arrange for his friend to come out for a few months as a visiting lecturer: it promised a change of scene, a generous salary, another respite from the London battleground, a revival of that precious friendship. But eventually, and suddenly: 'No, they said no. In a telegram.' It wasn't going to happen. Another escape route cut off.*

---

* 'Had I succeeded,' Ghose now says, with quiet understatement, 'he would have been here in 1973 and possibly history would have been different.' (Email to the author, 21 January 2003.)

Minor disasters continued to pile up. For a while Johnson even fell out with Beckett, whose enthusiastic remarks about his work ('a most gifted writer', etc.) had always been intended as part of a private correspondence with his then publishers, Collins; but Johnson had assured them that it would be acceptable to use this endorsement on the dust jacket of *Christie Malry's Own Double-Entry*. 'A blast of rage from Beckett followed,' Philip Ziegler recalls. 'He said he'd never given a quote in his life for publication and he was extremely indignant about it, that he'd been tricked in this way. He didn't deny that he'd said it – we had it in writing – but he was extremely cross about our using it without permission. Bryan was slightly shamefaced about it, I think. Beckett wrote him a letter of reproof and it may have been one of the few letters he destroyed.'

And in the meantime, Johnson may have been the proud owner of an expensive car (bought on hire purchase), but to his best friends he put up no pretence of financial well-being. Alan Brownjohn recalls that 'The last occasion I spoke to him was at a GLAA gathering or party or something, and I said, "How are you doing, Bryan?" and he just said, "It's terrible, terrible." So I asked, "Well, have you got things coming up?" and he said, "No, it's terrible, awful," and that was the last thing I remember him saying to me. I took it then as just another phase, assuming that after another month I'd say, "How's it going, Bryan?" and he would say, "Ah, you know, not too bad, it's getting better, I can carry on for three months," or something like that, because that had happened so regularly. But that last time it clearly was for real, he really did think things were over for him.'

At this point the only paid work Johnson had on the horizon, in fact, was a series of scripts for schools' television, commissioned by Lester Clark at Thames and called *You and the World*. Gordon Bowker (who helped him secure the commission) remembers that it was to be 'about a Secondary Modern class of "C" stream school-leavers. It took him back to the dreaded classroom of *Albert Angelo*, but as a writer not as an impoverished supply teacher.'[12] All the same, returning to that milieu must in some sense have felt like a retrograde step, and it was hardly the most prestigious commission for someone of Johnson's reputation. When Bowker himself inherited the project some months later, he looked over Johnson's notes and was chilled to discover the opening plot device: a supply teacher arrives in a new secondary modern class and 'The kids want to know what happened to their previous teacher. The answer is – he has committed suicide. It was shocking and uncanny to read these lines, which only hinted at what must have already been playing on his mind when he wrote them – composing, as it were, his own final scenario.'[13]

Otherwise, as far as the worlds of film, television and journalism were concerned, doors continued to close in his face. A request to the *Observer* for work as a book reviewer was declined with frosty politeness. And in July 1973 – just two months after the publication of *All Bull* – Johnson learned something which he could scarcely believe. As long ago as February 1972 he had suggested to the BBC that they allow him to make a programme to tie in with the book, in celebration of the tenth anniversary of the end of National Service. They had turned him down and he had then spent months in negotiation with ATV, who also rejected the proposal, but only after a much longer and more agonizing delay ('it makes me sick even to think of it – they told me it was 90% certain and kept the idea so long that I cannot now set it up with any other company').[14] It all seemed so different to the days when he had published *The Evacuees* and the BBC had leapt at the chance to have a tie-in programme directed by the acclaimed and prize-winning young film-maker. And then, from a notice published in the *Radio Times* on 12 July, Johnson learned that another programme maker, Tony Cash, had won a commission from the BBC to make a documentary on exactly the same subject. Clearly it was not the *idea* they had disliked: it was the very notion of *him making it*! And now the idea – the very same idea – had been stolen! His paranoia whirring into overdrive, he immediately contacted legal representatives at the ACTT and started proceedings against the corporation.

*

I was also told some more peculiar stories about this period of Johnson's life. I don't quite know what to make of them. But they came from a number of different sources, so are probably worth repeating.

Like several of his closest friends, John Furse attempted to make sense of his feelings of grief and anger after Johnson's death by writing something about him. In 1975 he began (but never finished) a fragmentary memoir of their relationship, in which his friend was fictionalized – appropriately enough – under the name of 'Albert'. It was never published, but Furse gave me a copy of the typescript and it paints a vivid, evocative picture of Johnson in his late thirties, probably the best that I've ever read. Here he is, sitting in his favourite wine bars (the Bottle-Screw in Hatton Garden, the Boot and Flogger in Southwark Street) or pubs (Dirty Dick's in Amwell Street), drinking a couple of bottles of wine a night ('in the last years ... it really got a hold on him and there was never a day when he was strictly sober'), gorging himself on pâté fingers with anchovies or sardines, finishing with a glass of champagne and then stopping off to eat salt-beef sandwiches on his way home through Clerkenwell. Furse recalls fragments of conversation ('he often said that he had only one subject – that he called "young love" and that his job was to put what he had to say into a formal framework so that – quite simply – the young love could be well seen'), and even provides an explanation – unexpected, but obvious when you think about it – for the crew-cut hairstyle which so shocked Johnson's friends when he returned from Paris in 1968: 'an imitation of Beckett', of course, even though it was 'a thin man's cut and it didn't look right above all that flesh [...] Earlier photographs show him to have been much less knowing – schoolboyish almost but then only in his early thirties before he'd eaten into himself. So self-destructive in the end.'*

One of the curious features of this fragment is its title: *Memoirs of a Porcine Lout,* and when I asked John Furse to elaborate upon this, he gave me an interesting explanation. Towards the end of his life, Johnson had told Furse the following story, which had been repeated to him by a contact at the British Council. An unnamed writer or academic, it seems (nobody appears to know who), had been lecturing in Bangkok and talking about contemporary British poetry to the usual audience of artistically inclined ex-pats. He had mentioned the name B. S. Johnson, describing him as a 'sensitive' poet; whereupon a heckler at the back of the audience – apparently acquainted with Johnson – had risen from his seat and shouted at the speaker – 'B. S. Johnson is not sensitive: B. S. Johnson is a *porcine lout*!'

And Johnson regarded this, I asked John Furse, as a funny story? A story he told against himself?

Yes and no, Furse answered. He seemed to know who the heckler must have been, and he regarded him as sinister, somehow. The whole anecdote seemed to make him strangely fearful. And it ties in, in Furse's hazy memory of this time, with other things Johnson was saying in his last few weeks: about a man who was following Johnson, persecuting him, controlling him. 'He was trying to persuade him to do something: to do something evil.'

I spoke to Johnson's university friends Frank and Thelma Fisher about this subject. This is a transcript of that part of our conversation:

TF: Then there's that awful story of Ginnie's about that bloke following them in his later years . . .

FF: The idea of it has come back now, but I wouldn't be able to say whether Ginnie had seen this man, whether he actually called or whether it was something in Bryan's mind.

JC: He felt that he was being stalked, that kind of thing?

FF: And like people hear voices.

---

* John Furse added to me in a letter (1 June 2003): 'The only time I felt in any danger when drinking with Bryan was an evening in Hennekey's when Stan Davies smashed a beer glass on the counter and threatened the barman. We got out just before the police arrived. My then wife was not amused.'

TF: This was a kind of evil, dark kind of character and Bryan had walked a lot just before he killed himself. We weren't in touch closely enough to know what was going on.

JC: Do you know if this man was phoning Bryan, sending letters? Physically following him?

TF: Physically around but I don't now know where I got that from.

FF: And something threatening about him, too, somehow. What I have a vague recollection of, is it was as if this guy was trying to persuade Bryan to do something, and that in a sense was what was haunting him, but that's just the vague memory of it.

JC: What might he have been persuading him to do?

TF: I don't think he would have said, anyway.

FF: No. I think again it must have been something that Ginnie told me, that he'd developed this fixation with the moon, it might even have been a full moon when he died or something . . .

(*See the Old Lady Decently*, rather strangely, is dedicated to the moon – albeit in the guise of a quotation from *Tristram Shandy*: ' – The rest I dedicate to the MOON, who, by the bye, of all the PATRONS or MATRONS I can think of, has most power to set my book a-going, and make the world run mad after it.' Virginia also told me that on the night of the Apollo landings Johnson couldn't bear to watch the television and just went up to bed in a fury, incensed – I suppose – at the American violation of something that should have stayed virginal, symbolic, sacred. Later he wrote to John Furse claiming that it was all a fake anyway, all done in a TV studio.)

One more story, told in Gordon Bowker's article about B. S. Johnson:

I heard later that, in his last months, Bryan had fallen in with an occultist, who seemed to exercise a strange power over him. He might jump up in the middle of a family meal and leave the house saying that he 'knew' this man wanted him. His behaviour had become increasingly bizarre . . .[15]

Virginia gives no credence to this at all ('Family meal? No – not one Steve or I were present at'). But she does recall that in the last few weeks Johnson became very preoccupied with security: constantly checking to see whether the doors of the house were locked, or the doors of his beloved white Citroën GS 1220. In her anxiety she phoned Helen Sapper (wife of Alan, the ACTT's general secretary), then working as a GP, who remembers: 'Virginia was enormously worried about him. He sounded pretty sick, actually, from what she was saying. There are certain things that ring alarm bells when people start talking about them. He was very isolated, not wanting to talk, but this was *peculiar* behaviour, beyond the realms of someone just wanting to get on with their work. He was very suspicious all the time, and having lots of paranoid ideas about Virginia's relationships. Jealous delusions that were well over the top. As a lot of people are when they're that depressed, he was very reluctant to get help, and he really did need help: I'm quite sure he was sectionable, actually, towards the end of his life.'

Part of the problem, without doubt, was to do with Johnson's drinking. Frustrated by Britain's draconian licensing laws (pubs couldn't open in the afternoons in the 1970s), he had recently made it his business to seek out places where he could drink all day: Alan Marshfield, a friend from King's days, met him that year at a drinking club in Soho and recalls that, 'He seemed to be pretty proud of the fact of belonging to that kind of circle of writers who inhabited or frequented places like that. I wasn't mad about that sort of thing, but he seemed to be impressed by it.' This might be the same establishment to which he once invited Gordon Bowker: 'a drinking club off Leicester Square called Death in the Afternoon, where cheap booze was available at all hours, and where I found myself in a riotous company of celebrity alcoholics. The actor Ronald Fraser I remember, holding forth in his inimitably expansive fashion, and a famous singer making an operatic exit bound for an anticipated afternoon seduction to cries of "He just can't have enough, can he!" In this artistic underworld, Johnson was at home, one of the joint's most popular habitués.'[16] Bowker seems to have relished the spectacle of Johnson in this milieu, whereas his old schoolfriend, Trev Leggett, was rather shocked and saddened by his last meeting with him in those months. They met in central London to discuss Leggett's contribution to *All Bull* and 'I think we opened three bottles of wine, and I was just drinking a glass or two, which was my standard rate. But we were well into the third when we pushed off so he must have drunk a good two bottles of wine himself – and the other thing was his language! I mean, I thought he was a writer with a wide vocabulary and a real interest in language and the f-word was about every third word, as far as I could see.' Leggett thought that his friend's behaviour had changed over the years – for the worse.

There must be more to this than alcohol, however. Johnson's last period of serious depression had been in Claremont Square, back in the early 1960s, and the root cause of that had been the failure of his romantic relationships. Fearfully, he had to confront the possibility that something like this was happening now. Virginia had always meant everything to him. Since the death of his mother, the burden of emotional expectation on her was even heavier ('as I now have no nearer mother than my wife, all is committed to these rocks'). But cracks were beginning to open up in the marriage.

Virginia herself put it like this: 'From the beginning our marriage was a fairly traditional one, arranged around work for Bryan and looking after the children as my priority. Bryan had to juggle the writing he really wanted to do with journalism and whatever else would make a living – made more of a burden for him because he wanted to be the one who provided for his family rather than sharing the wage earning. Early on this was a happy arrangement, good for both of us, but as time went on I felt we needed to make changes, without being clear what that might mean. My thoughts about what I wanted from marriage were changing; both of us felt awkward and wordless when it came to talking about ourselves and each other; and for a while there was an impasse, both of us confused, stressed and generally at a loss to know how to go on.'

Michael Bakewell remembers Johnson believing, at least, 'that Virginia was no longer physically attracted to him – he took this very, very badly because of his basic nature. This was something with which he could not cope at all.' It might not even have been as much as that: it might have been little more than the inevitable physical growing apart which affects many married couples in middle age, especially when one of them is preoccupied by work all the time and there are two demanding children to be kept happy. It certainly seemed to most of their closest friends that the couple were beginning to move in different directions. Michael Bakewell, again, recalls that, 'There were a lot of tensions because they were developing completely different lifestyles: Bryan was becoming more and more devoted to his work, particularly while writing *See the Old Lady Decently*: he'd given himself rather an impossible deadline on that book [30 September 1973], which contributed to him isolating himself a great deal. Meanwhile Virginia wanted to live more of a commune-type existence, she wanted to open herself out and open the house out. And the kind of people who came round were the kind of people Bryan didn't particularly want to be in the house – people with whom she found freedom and fulfilment, which I don't think he did. As far he was concerned they made an awful lot of noise and were a bit of nuisance.'

That summer, Ferenc Takács and his then wife, Annamária Róna, came to visit them from Hungary and stayed in the house for a few days. Takács remembers one day, in particular, when 'Virginia came back from town in the afternoon – their relationship must have been quite tense by that time – and she went into a kind of spiel about what a wonderful afternoon she'd had, going into town, and she'd met a couple of Hare Krishna people and made a donation, and bought a pair of trousers for Bryan which he tried on: they were quite tight, and Virginia said Bryan didn't like tight trousers.' News of the Hare Krishna movement had not reached Budapest, so Takács asked Johnson who these people were. The scathing reply he received was clearly intended to show Johnson's dislike for Virginia's burgeoning hippie values: 'He just told me: Frank, they're people who like to cheat you out of your money.'

Although the space shared by Johnson and his wife at the house in Islington was not large, there was, already, a sense that the growing separation between them was physical as much as emotional or intellectual. 'The house was existing on two levels,' says Michael Bakewell. 'One was Virginia's level, and then when you got upstairs to his study, that was where it all changed: "I begin here," Bryan used to say. Here it was terribly neat, terribly precise and everything in its place which was very, very different from the chaotic world that Virginia was enjoying downstairs.' Alan Sapper, too, clearly remembers the almost obsessive orderliness in Johnson's study: 'it was totally neat, and dusted'. (And, in fact, there were really three strata to the house, because Virginia's mother had recently moved in to the self-contained flat in the basement. That could hardly have helped matters, either.)

On the one hand, then, we have a woman who is anxious to experience, at last, something of the late sixties/early seventies counterculture which has so far been resolutely kept locked out on her doorstep; on the other we have a writer who is more and more in thrall to a world of vanishing working-class values: more than that, in fact, someone who is attempting actually to *reinhabit* that world imaginatively, for the purposes of his new novel which takes him right back to the calcified moral assumptions and antique courting rituals of a bookshop stock-keeper and a servant girl in 1920s west London. A situation which reminds me of what Claire Andrews said about Johnson in the early 1960s: that he was '*totally* insecure', and in order to cope with this insecurity, went 'back to what he thought were his roots, and said very solidly, "You're not going to move me".'* All at once, therefore, Britain's great champion of the literary avant-garde is beginning to look anchorless and adrift, stranded in a sea of values to which he cannot relate at all. The times have moved too fast for him and the moment for his particular brand of working-class high modernism has already passed. (When *See the Old Lady Decently* was published in 1975, Peter Ackroyd's review would complain about its 'lamentably archaic "experimentation"', and describe it as 'an anachronism masquerading as something different and new'.)[17]

In several respects, then, Johnson was becoming an isolated figure. Against the background hum of a growing marital crisis, he was also limbering up to embark bravely and effortfully upon 'the longest haul of all', a complex trilogy which would involve even more raking over the past – including, in the (never written) second and third volumes, periods of his

---

* See above, pp. 70–1.

own life which he had already mined pretty thoroughly for material in *Trawl*. This much we can deduce from the thick bundle of notes which he made, but never used, for the trilogy as a whole.

152: NOTES FOR 'THE MATRIX TRILOGY' *(? winter–summer 1973)*

This must be a novel of the most intensely poetic I can manage
Mankind cannot stand too much of the poetic
A man writes what he can!

(1)	Her life up to my birth	FICTION
(2)	My life as I knew her up to early manhood	HALF TRUTH HALF FICTION
(3)	My adult life/to her death	ALL TRUTH pointing out the fiction

the conviction – *people who advocate a way which to them is* right *and* only right – *in the face of people equally convinced*
the absurdity of that conviction in the face of chaos is what interests me

in a way

Notes for *overall* plan of (3) novels

they must *shimmer* in relation to each other

they may *distort* and *amend* each other (e.g. by disputing what was said earlier, giving another version
= tension

Vol. 1   creates a fiction – popular
Vol. 2   sheds doubt on that fiction
Vol. 3   tells the truth

I mean, what I really want to be writing about is now, how I made a commitment to my wife, and how I still want that to be my commitment, after ten years, how that is the most important thing.

My mother's new teeth changed her: all that pain for what turned out to be such a short while

In the beginning, we do not know. In the end, we know we do not know, if we are lucky.

Few of us are lucky.

Phil* boiling pudding in nappie

Phil's tremendous sense of phun

All this ordinariness: people putting up with it in the expectation, the hope of something better coming of it, that it will be justified. Or do they even hope?

I am all that has come out of it, this is the only justification of the ordinariness. What a hope! For this is nothing more.

The mother is she who makes all things possible (even when those things seem to be done against her; even when at least some of those things must necessarily have been done against what she stood for).

When I'm gone you'll understand —

ah —

The debt one owes to one's parents, which I had thought one paid by having children oneself, I now see is more heavily paid in having to watch those parents die.

In particular, watching the mother die.

Always the brave right get trampled under. It is not enough to be right it is not enough to be even right for oneself.

They hold the power, often through inertia.

To change everything is like trying to uproot a forest of Douglas Firs with one's bare hands in an afternoon.

The uncommitted are perhaps the true enemy, the uncomplaining uncommitted.

(make it more political in Jiri's† sense, what I learnt)

but not his hopelessness?

The snowball fight at Mall Rd as a kid I remember: do it really well, exceed in description, fire.

Is it important that she tried so few (if any, let us decide upon) the positions in the Kama Sutra? Knew so little in other ways?

---

* Johnson's Uncle Phil – his mother's brother, who I believe had died of a brain tumour some years earlier. Nobody seems to remember much about this figure, and yet from what Johnson says about him here – the emphasis on his sense of 'fun', together with his reported comment about suicide (see below) – it's possible that uncle and nephew had a good deal in common, temperamentally.

† Jiří Menzel, Czech film director, to whom Johnson had been introduced in Prague earlier in 1973.

How important is that, are those?

Nannie finding contraceptives sewn in my jacket – sewing up holes –
not telling Mum – saying, Enjoy yourself while you can

MATRIX   *Must* be as *funny* as Xtie, in the 'invented' bits, at least:

                then the 'hard' bits will have the maximum impact

                And I do enjoy doing the Xtie bits, after all

How one gets defined *by a child*
   - a chance remark, & one is forever that?

YPRES (seeing the death of Empire starting there)
(M1)   death
(M2)   Dad's visit in war
(M3)   a special visit by me (& Dad? V?)

    M 2/3
- The snowball fight at Mall Rd one Xmas
- My saying of Nell Gwyn's cottage by the river, 'I've seen her there.'
- The enormous ice cream cone – my mother licked it as a joke – I repeated
that joke every other time I saw it
- The heavily hooded old shopping women, side to side like ancient black
scales, motherly
- At the Windmill Hotel at St David's – Oct – as she was really bad also
describe the state of having no work – those *bastards*

My father, working all those years in books like these: I found out what
work was like, realised it must be similar for him.
Is what I am doing now that much different?
Working at an Edwardian bank clerk's sloping desk, in looseleaf journals
he passed on to me? It seems close, the working habits.
What I am writing is so very different though, and at least I have more
choice in the times I do it, and the places.

I am fortunate, I tell myself, in some ways. A lot of people think, and
they find it a pity.

(M2) Attempt some earliest-possible interior monologue myself; if
necessary, go for hypnosis à la Heathcote*

---

*   Heathcote Williams – poet, actor and artist (now, perhaps, most famous for the poems *Whale
Nation* and *Sacred Elephant*) – was then art editor of the *Transatlantic Review*. A few letters from
him are to be found in Johnson's files. Some of them were written in hospital, where he was
being treated for burns to the inside of his mouth. He had been trying to teach himself fire-
eating.

I was a terrible man to my mother, I was short with her, a — bastard, I had almost written.　　　Sometimes

Walking to Granny's through Scrutton [?] Ground as a child: the shiny streets, the long bus journey by No. 11, the landmarks. Sleepy.
A later journey, middle 50s: 'stuffed marrow' hilarity on tube.

––––––––

Xmas morning motorbike trip along embankment

Uncle Bert's account of PL's death for third vol?
Casually, just as I heard it
of tremendous importance in Vol 1.
of hardly any in Vol 3?

Third book
Lyricism re own marriage – early on

incorporate reviews/crits of 1st volume in 2nd? of 1 & 2 in 3rd?

Bannard – letters

Curiously, my family was very secretive, or uncommunicative, abt its past (Granny)
– 'Best forgotten'
– Mum telling stories about *her* Mum/Nannie
– the ancestor worship of her photograph.

Welcome coloured brothers now you force yourselves on us
We forced ourselves on you for long enough and on the bus
(Graffito?)

the organism decides to die

Just before Xmas (it must have been 1960) I had to go back to state teaching. From when I left the Glyn Club (early Sept) to about mid-Nov. I had stayed alive (ah – that means I lived on my parents) by private coaching (elaborate on private coaching) but for some reason, financial I have little doubt, but why then? I needed more. £17 more seemed extravagant for what I did, then. They sent me to Barnes CSM, the school I had attended for 2 years (12–14) as a boy (elaborate). No one there was a teacher when I was a boy. The Asst Head I missed by six months, I think he told me. Johnson, said the then Head, Wilkinson, was it, do you play any musical instruments? Only the gramophone, I said, as they then were called by some of us. And still by the magazine titled The Gramophone.
　　　Soon I will get round to the quote from Sam.
　　　Ah!

There are so many things worth writing about, for me, sod the others, a reason to be going on, for me, for others past, & for others to come, sod those now! Except Ginnie, the Kids, Dad, perhaps one or two more.

Where was I? 9th Oct 1972, about 20 to 12 at night, soon be 10/10.

At any rate, I had to go back to teaching for regular money. And the man whose job I took over was a retired teacher I knew by sight, he wandered around that part of Barnes the immigrés knew as the Village. I must have met him drinking, in the Sun or the Red Lion, and he had shown me photographs (perhaps that was later) of his African students, large-muscled athletes suspended with toothy rictus(es) over 4 foot highjumps.

I knew him, that is.

When I went on supply I did not know it was he I was replacing.

But it was.

They told me he had (lumbered me – it must be an English expression) me: [*sic*]: that the reason he had gone sick, or just gone, was that the exams were coming up, & he did not want the toil of setting, invigilating & marking them. This came up later. To their surprise, I did not mind: I had not done it before.

I set Beckett (the quote – look up the whole paper – it's at Dad's).

The way my mother defended my 'Leda & the swans' postcard – Dad said it was obscene – she said he did not understand (she did!)

Let us talk about the failed mothers – Muriel
US? who is doing the *father* writing?

V is in this too of course: v much

    - early things: viz:
        making the cushion
        *typing SAC**

All the words for *mother* in all languages I can find

'Barnes is much the same, but much poorer with the loss of your dear mother's cheery face one was so pleased to see. She was very proud of you Bryan and you gave her great happiness.'
[Letter from family friend ('Alan') living in Barnes, dated 30 January 1973]

The start of writing: Frank H – M L & L† and the woman over Mod. Builders – lesbian? – a sort of mother figure? Seems that in retrospect

---

*   *Statement Against Corpses.*
†   Frank Harris, *My Life and Loves.* See above, Fragment 12, pp. 60–1.

earlier: the poem at school*

later: going to drama classes – through Noel (what?)

Whole section on that school:

    e.g. (1) the head – deathly
          (2) the sports master – the last match I played – rehearsing in
          the school – 'think of that coming at you!' – drafting in the
          training college students
          (3) apologising for New Left Review
          (4) the building master – my old sheds and wanking
          whatsisname

NLR – the interview – girl I met with Robin Purdue [?] – no word for weeks – when I rang, 'oh, didn't they tell you?'

Fuck them.

Asked 'What do you see yourself doing in 5 yrs?' And answered: 'earning a living as a writer'. Their disbelief was tangible.

I was!

There was an occasion at college (my first real success) when in a competition set at the end of the first year a poem of mine won not a prize but some sort of distinction

And (Strindberg said 'What is success unless one offers it at the feet of a woman') I told her [Muriel] first about it, at W——'s† house, having no one else, at that time

And she rejected it, not interested, went on talking about
Nothing
to W——.

\-\-\-\-\-\-\-\-\-\-\-\-\-\-\-\-\-\-\-

think ahead
to when you're dead

Woman of 80+ next to Mum in hospital – 'Nurse I'm ever so worried, I haven't come on this month!'
Thought I was Albert – Edie's Albert

of course! Sam is not talking about
    <u>*bicycles*</u>
        but
        <u>*cycles*</u>

---

* Presumably his schoolboy translation of Lamartine.
† The name is illegible.

- birth, copulation, death etc.

Mum saying: Goes on top of bus to smoke?
   – doesn't like back, get everyone's germs.
____

Also on top of No. 9
(1) – she'd been faithful to Dad all war (now he had to be good to her?)
(2) – what did passing my Latin mean?

Some academic cunt will produce a study on it.

Also bundled into this file – presumably because he considered it of direct relevance to the trilogy – is a fragment labelled 'Gregynog, 17/3/70', followed by a reminiscence of his time at Stanvac in the mid-1950s. Both items refer to *The White Goddess*.

153: FURTHER NOTES FOR 'THE MATRIX TRILOGY'

Z gave me *The White Goddess*: I think it was spring – it seems so, though this may be a later imposition (no – date inside is 1/4/61). He did not want (or have time) to review it for *Western Daily Press* where ACHS was then running an Arts Page. Remember being in the old and very special Armstrong-Siddeley he had at that time: his father in the back puzzled at the worn leather, which he convinced himself was rust. Z was just going abroad somewhere? I had just a few days before moved to the Angel. It took me a long while to read – or, rather, I took a long while to finish it. Review date given is 16/10/61.

*

That heavy, statuesque Jewess at SVT — very attractive in her heavy way — took her out once, more, in motorbike & sidecar borrowed from Martin the Irishman — she was scathing about that sidecar, said it was not what she was used to: I deliberately misunderstood, said did she normally go solo: she did not reply: we both knew it was *cars* she was used to
that was the evening, when I came home, that I had the White Goddess experience (see notebook) and certainly with her I was (but that evening?) walking down Northumberland Ave. near the Playhouse Theatre and I made some slighting remark about the Jews: I'm a Jew she said! I was embarrassed, young, ignorant.
or was I?

Johnson never showed work-in-progress to anyone, by the way – not even Virginia. The only exception had been during the writing of *Travelling People*, when he had shared some of the early chapters with graduate friends from King's, and then encouraged Tony Tillinghast to read and comment upon the complete manuscript. This arguably paranoid fragment mentions that fact:

> *Never shown anything – except Tony – tell*
> *besides* – they *cd pinch*

Who are '*they*'?

There is another issue Johnson dwells on in these notes: the fact that he was a rhesus negative baby. This condition – easily treatable with an injection by the 1960s – used to mean that antibodies carried by the firstborn child would fatally damage any subsequent fetus while still in the womb. Put dramatically, it could be said that the first child, in effect, becomes the killer of his unborn brothers and sisters. Three times Johnson mentions it here:

> – What age was I when M had the miscarriage, my sister was undone? (Ask Dad) – v. important

> *(Long?) description of rhesus neg. condition.*
> *then at end: my mother was rhesus neg*
> *I was the only one she could have*

> - The Rhesus negative factor: not discovered at my birth – I seemed a normal birth. But at that time, to be RhN meant that the first must also be the last, the only. (for (M2))

This thought – the notion that he had somehow condemned himself to be an only child – seems to have tormented Johnson for many years. Alan Burns's ex-wife Carol Burns (a writer and artist) has a distinct memory of this, and wrote to me as follows:

B S Johnson

We were playing dream games at supper. He said he'd dreamed a recurrent dream of something about to explode. I asked if his mother had ever had a miscarriage. He replied, 'No!' We went on playing and eating. Suddenly, B. hit the table with his fist and shouted, 'How did you know? How did you know?' He said that when he was very young his mother had conceived and lost a baby. He'd forgotten this until now. I explained that when I was two my mother was pregnant with my brother. As her stomach swelled, I had been frightened she would explode.

Years later, he said he never dreamed the same dream again. I have always wondered how much guilt at survival played on his mind and contributed to his suicide when faced with the loss of Virginia.

Most of all, however, Johnson's notes for 'The Matrix Trilogy' find him dwelling on his mother's death: the agony of watching her 'rot day by day, hour by hour', and his feelings of forlornness and abandonment since she had gone.

154: FURTHER NOTES FOR 'THE MATRIX TRILOGY'

that feeling – M&D were secure, my basic security, all I could ultimately bank on

I had been to see B* in Paris

I had plenty of brandy

I drank half a bottle
still felt sober
that Sunday evening I talked to the doctor

Did she know?
I never knew

No more than this I have to offer than my yellow pencil — I was lucky that December/Nov whichever, had brought back more than they allowed of brandy, drank a half-bottle that evening after returning from the hospital the night I spoke with a doctor who told me the worst (cliché)

Traitorous thought: now she is dead I am free of it happening at some inconvenient time in the future,
a dearly paid for freedom
a dear — freedom

twice (possibly thrice)
    I have felt presences of HER
    in the study
    as I was working on MT.

We (I) am (are) able to act
    because of our (my) mother's (s')
    continued existence

('When I'm gone you'll understand'
    [– understand? I doubt it
    – know? perhaps])

Because of her continued existence
    I was able to go on,

---

* Beckett.

behave as though all were possible
(because she was there to fall back on)

For me

Now I know it is not
Never was
Cannot be

Except thus?
(in writing)

it smells too much like human decay, my watchstrap – like my mother smelt

When she was staying here, that late summer: the accusing, painracked face of Gwenallt looking down on her, in the sitting room, as she lay on the sofa (her own room, we thought of this, too dismal, dark) and the kit plastic skeleton bought for Steven's sixth birthday, Bony Man, grinning at her from the side.
(remember the 1st floor was two, then: 1971, her last summer)

Writing NCTS* & talking to her in hospital about it (June 71?) – the way she added the flashing torch story – from the war.

all those times she must have known,
    been protecting us (by absence)
    while longing for us to come,
        to be with her while there was still time

(But did she know? whole section)

The last lunch: she broke down and cried before
we tried to be normal (as she seemed to want)
Not embarrassed

Perfumes my mother wore
    Apple blossom
    I (gasped) at the price
    She gave it back . . .

    Goya sandalwood soap . . .

all to keep out the stench of death

JUST DEAD
(an epigraph on a tomb)

---

*   *Not Counting the Savages.*

Mum – too much away from as an evacuee
    now about to be an evac. for ever.

When she wrote me that cheque: her hands trembling, her writing barely recognisable

-----

My Shakespeare from her, on my 21st.
I take it down, notice with concern it is damp

the sight
looking at her
tubes from most of her
sweet orifices
once sweet

how much more than
now
the simple visual statement
of her agony

last

The notes also contain some scattered references to suicide. Johnson remembers a remark made by his mother's brother:

Uncle Phil saying very forcibly one Xmas (was V there?) 'If we all knew what was coming, then we'd commit suicide tomorrow'

He remembers the image of a family pet – driven mad (he imagines, anthropomorphically) by his never-ending confinement.

Suicide – the goldfish – not to feed – but he came up mouthing – was he trying to commit suicide?

And then he records his own feelings: his anxiety that he does not himself have the *means* to commit suicide, and an experiment he has conceived to find out whether it could be done.

I am now thinking of this myself

I once had a gun (ref. SAC)*

Now I have an air pistol, the cheapest

Buy a leg of lamb, say, belly of pork, see how far the pellet can penetrate

---

*   A reference to the story 'Clean Living is the Real Safeguard' in *Statement Against Corpses*.

Sharpen a dart, cut off the marking spreading (vane?)

(a whole suicide section – the agony, what I did to V)

*

Another item of 'Matrix Trilogy' source material which survives is a taped interview Johnson made with his father in 1973. It makes uncomfortable listening. Stanley Johnson is meant to be telling his son about how he courted Emily, back in the 1920s. But his anecdotes are sparse, they are punctuated by long silences, and Johnson is audibly impatient with his father for being able to divulge so little. Stanley spends much of the tape talking about the family's various cats and dogs, which he seems to remember far more vividly than he does any of his human relatives. (From *Albert Angelo*: 'In this house, in my parents' house, my parents' home, all affection is channelled through the dog. No one is affectionate to anyone else except through the dog.') He sounds quiet and lost and desolate: clearly, Bryan was not the only one to have been flattened by Emily's death. Father and son have little to say to each other. 'I never asked anything about that, Bryan, I didn't pry, well, you know what I am, I don't bother about anything,' Stanley says, when asked about Peter Lambird's (Emily's father's) desertion of the family and disappearance to Canada. 'I don't poke my nose in anybody's business, if they want to tell me they tell me, if not then I'm not worried.' At the end of the tape, Stanley suggests that they travel together to Ypres to visit Peter Lambird's grave. 'Yes, we'll do that one year,' Johnson agrees quietly, but you can hear in his voice that he doesn't really mean it. Possibly he has already made up his mind that he won't be around by then.

155: NOTE AT END OF *SEE THE OLD LADY DECENTLY* MANUSCRIPT

Finished ready for typing 8.12 pm, 22/9/73.

*

The ACTT Joint Shops Committee ruled that there was nothing Johnson could do to stop Tony Cash and the BBC making a documentary about National Service without reference to *All Bull*. 'They' – whoever 'they' were, in his paranoid frame of mind – had defeated him again. One of the committee members, Adèle Winston, wrote to me about the discussions they had tried to conduct with him: 'My strongest impression of him was his lack of responsiveness – we all were totally in sympathy with him but he seemed to be somewhere else. I think it can't have been very long after that he killed himself . . .'[18]

*

'Everyone Knows Somebody Who's Dead' is the title of one of Johnson's last prose pieces. It wasn't just that he knew people who were dead, however. These days, he seemed to know an uncommon number of people who had taken their own lives. 'I have recently become aware that an uncomfortable number of my contemporaries are dying before what I had imagined to be their times, simply jacking it all in, for one reason or another,' he wrote in that piece. The latest was Ann Quin, the troubled, talented author of *Berg, Passages* and *Tripticks*, a writer whose work he respected a great deal, even though he had never felt at ease with her personally. She had drowned herself by walking out to sea off Brighton beach. He admired the courage of the act. Quin – like him – refused to 'live by illusion'. Better to end your life altogether than to live it dishonestly, pretending everything is hunky-dory. He could see the logic of it.

*

What is so remarkable – and heroic, for that matter – is that Johnson continued to function, and to put such a brave face on things for his friends and colleagues. He finished the first volume of 'The Matrix Trilogy', meeting (as always) his publisher's deadline, after spending between six and eight hours every day typing the novel between 24–30 September. He continued to work on the *You and the World* scripts for Thames TV. His poetic output, admittedly, seemed to have more or less dried up since 'Hafod a Hendref', but he did write some short poems for inclusion in *See the Old Lady Decently*, and another fragment survives from this period – a last, adamant celebration of continuing sexual activity:

156: POEM, 'BEYOND CONCORDE' *(1973)*

> she strokes my variable
> geometry into the
> takeoff position and we
> fly, go through the barrier,
> sink to rest.

Nagging away at the sexual theme, he also began to send out cheery commissioning letters for a new anthology, to be called *You Always Remember the First Time*, in which writers were invited to recall the first time they had had sex. Aiming high at first, Johnson targeted celebrities such as Sean Connery, Ingrid Pitt, Sybil Thorndike and even Malcolm Muggeridge. One letter came back to inform him, with magnificent indignation, that 'Lulu has no interest whatsoever in recounting her earlier sexual experiences'. (Only B. S. Johnson could have thought that Lulu was hip, in 1973!) All of which sounds a good laugh: but such activities are time-consuming ('a direct drain on the same source of energy that is used in writing', as Johnson put it himself) and he was being paid only £300 for his trouble.

And, meanwhile, there was another television script to be written.

*

Aled Vaughan, controller of programmes at HTV (and a novelist in his own right), had been impressed by the Johnson/Bakewell collaboration on *Hafod a Hendref* and wanted the same team to work together on something more ambitious. A simple but audacious idea was proposed: Johnson should revisit his beloved Lleyn peninsula, scene of his strange experiences at the Glyn Club and the setting for *Travelling People* (looking backwards again!), and he should make a film about it. The format would be quite straight-forward: forty minutes of Johnson sitting on his favourite beach, Porth Ceiriad, and talking directly to camera about anything that happened to come into his head. Poems, anecdotes, corny jokes, visual gags, rants of every description. Chances were that he would find time, somewhere or other, to share his belief that 'telling stories is telling lies' and that life consisted purely of chaos.

Filming was scheduled to take place from 19 to 27 October 1973. The charge sheet prepared for the ACTT reveals that on Friday the nineteenth, Johnson and Michael Bakewell drove up to north Wales in time for a 'script conference' (actually the first in a succession of drunken get-togethers) at the Sun Inn in Llanengan. This was a place charged with memories for Johnson, memories of a strange, emotionally unsettled, superstitious phase of his life ('Llanengan churchyard is the only place I have come upon cats copulating'). And these 'script conferences' involved meeting up again, for the first time in years, with friends from that period – specifically, one Trefor Owen, whose disembodied voice was even supposed to feature in the programme itself.*

'The dimension of the film which never happened was the Welsh Nationalist dimension,' Bakewell recalls, 'because after Bryan's death I just couldn't find a way of making it work. There was supposed to be a sequence in the film where he suddenly looks up into the sky and says, "I hear voices," and at this point he wanted to introduce the voices of some of his friends talking about their aspirations for Welsh identity. Well, I'd met these chaps with Bryan in a pub, and they were all slightly astonished by his commit-ment to their cause. They couldn't understand why an Englishman should be this way. Some of them were writers and one ran the Welsh-language

---

* This, I believe, was the 'Trevor' mentioned in Johnson's diary entry of 19 August 1961. Sadly I have not been able to trace him.

bookshop in Pwllehli and some of them I think Bryan had known for quite a while. But although I did some tape-recorded interviews with these people afterwards, it turned out that their voices didn't sound convincing enough, really, shoved across the extra bits of film. I felt very guilty about this because I felt it was an area of Bryan's work that I hadn't managed to reproduce, and I knew it was important to him.'

The Saturday, Sunday and Monday were taken up with more reconnoitring of the peninsula and the beach itself. Shooting began on Tuesday the twenty-third, and lasted until the Friday.

Bakewell's memory is that 'It was a very, very happy film, and one of the most spontaneous things I've ever been involved with, even though it involved a vast amount of Bryan's past. There were sections that he would simply write overnight: he'd take a bottle of red wine up to his room and kind of sit there writing it and then come down with it the following day. The PA was a little Welsh girl who he said looked like a primitive mother goddess. Everybody entered into the spirit of it.'

I formulated a rule, in an earlier chapter, to the effect that the bleaker and gloomier any novel appears to be, the happier will have been its circumstances of composition. The same seems to hold true for films. Billy Wilder always said that *Sunset Boulevard,* one of his darkest films, was the most fun to make, whereas *Some Like it Hot* – one of the most joyful comedies ever made – was an endless nightmare of setbacks and personality clashes. Similarly with *Fat Man on a Beach* – a 'very, very happy film' which, despite one or two (truly dreadful) dirty jokes and a handful of surreally clever sight gags seems as much possessed by death as anything in Johnson's work. There is, for instance, the long, horrible anecdote about a motorcyclist being thrown from his bike and landing on a wire fence which cuts through his body 'like a cheese cutter cutting through cheese'. I've screened the film for people sometimes, when giving lectures about Johnson, and this sequence always gets a strange reaction from the audience. Nervous laughter sets in – and always at the same point: the point where Johnson loses his thread and starts talking about how cheese comes in packages, so we never see the cutting process by which the squares are produced, and he adds, feelingly, 'Thank God.' For a moment he has forgotten that he is talking about cheese, not about the human body. Suddenly, he has 'no access to metaphor' – a common symptom (for what this is worth) of people with delusional disorders.

And then there is the notorious sequence at the very end of the film, where he says goodbye to Wales, goodbye to his audience, and walks, fully clothed, out to sea, as the camera spirals into the sky until he is just a tiny dot in the ocean, lost to view.

'I think that must have been entirely a reference to Ann Quin, some sort of *hommage*,' Bakewell says. 'I don't believe it was a foreshadowing of what happened afterwards. I do remember that Bryan was enormously concerned that he shouldn't unduly suffer from this, while in extremis, and we had bottles of brandy and hot towels standing by for the moment it was over. In any case the sequence never came off in the way that Bryan intended, because no helicopter could do what he had in mind – lifting off vertically and going up to a shot of the whole of Llŷn, rather in the way that earlier in the film he holds out his hand to show you the shape of it all. We would have needed a rocket!'

It's curious to discover that while making such a personal film, one so fixated on the figure and personality of Johnson himself, the crew were not alone on this beach at all – even in October. They were sharing it, in fact, with some of his longest-standing enemies.

'In order to do the helicopter shot we had to clear the beach, and the mother goddess PA had to persuade a group of hippies to leave. What I hadn't realised when I went up in the thing was that they'd written "Good Riddance to Fat Trendies" in enormous letters all along the beach. So we had to come down and clear it all up before we took the shot.'

Not those bloody hippies again! Here was another reason for Johnson to resent everything about the burgeoning counterculture that the rest of the world – including his wife – seemed to be embracing so eagerly.

*

And now, a short digression, if I may.

I signed the contract for this book in 1995. Eight years ago, more or less. Yes, I know it sounds a long time, but I have not been exactly idle in the interim. I've written two novels, and I've played a role (a supporting role, I suppose it must be said) in the parenting of two children. But now, at last, it's time for me to begin my own 'longest haul of all', and write the section which I've been putting off for so long. To write the narrative of a man's death, in a few pages. A death which to me now, having come to know Johnson's family, and his closest friends, having seen what it did to them, seems so futile and wasteful and aggressive an act that I have even started to feel – obliquely, vicariously, at thirty years' distance – some of the same anger and bewilderment that they felt at the time.

How can this be done? How can these pages be written?

When Johnson delivered the manuscript of *See the Old Lady Decently* to Hutchinson, his editor (and the firm's then chairman) Charles Clark had reservations about it. He felt, according to Michael Bakewell, that 'the three main strands of the work had not been satisfactorily woven together' and suggested 'reconstructing the book as a "visual novel"'. Johnson drafted a reply – which he doesn't seem to have sent – insisting that 'I am *not* trying to set a puzzle – but randomness, chaos, is not neat and tidy'. He also justified some of the more personal, discursive elements in the book – the passages about being interrupted by his children, for instance – on the grounds (as usual) of honesty: 'to be absolutely honest, the process of writing must enter into it, for that is the actual thing one is doing – the basic true thing.'

Perhaps I can take my cue from this.

So:

I am writing these words in a tiny octagonal eighteenth-century building called the Bath House, which I have rented for this very purpose, for three days only, from the Landmark Trust. It stands a few miles from Stratford-upon-Avon and as I write I have a fine view over Warwickshire fields. Somehow it seems an appropriate place: various lines appear to converge at this point. It was built in 1748, the year of publication of Fielding's *Tom Jones*, my favourite novel. A few miles to the north lies Warwick University, where I wrote my thesis on *Tom Jones* in the 1980s and where I discovered Johnson's work. A few miles to the south are the Rollright Stones, where Johnson sat one Sunday afternoon in October 1961 and nibbled some toadstools and ate two scones which had been baked for him by Michael Bannard's mother. A mile or two to the east of those stones lies the village of Little Tew, which is where Virginia found refuge when she fled the marital home with the two children, in November 1973.

And something else: as I lay in the bath this morning thinking about what I was going to write, I tried to work out how old Johnson would have been were he still alive. And realized (although I sort of knew this, in the same way that Johnson must have really known it was Nottingham – Tony's town – he was travelling to when he went to report on that football match) that today is 5 February 2003. This would have been his seventieth birthday.

I took a break just then for a cup of coffee. Snow has started to fall, thinly, outside the windows.

I shall keep it brief; perhaps that is the best way. And really I have no choice in the matter, because after talking to all these people I still know so little. Nobody remembers these last days very clearly. Accounts contradict each other. I suppose when you are caught up in events of such emotional intensity – ferocity would be a better word, yes, that's right, ferocity – then chronology just goes to pieces. 'I do get confused about time. If one loses one's emotional focus [...] that's what happens. Aeons – split seconds – they interchange. One gets outside the usual way of counting.' Rosamond Lehmann wrote that, in her novel *The Echoing Grove*. It's one of my favourite quotations. It has come in handy more than once before now.

*

B. S. Johnson returned from filming in Wales on Saturday, 27 October 1973. Virginia remembers, or thinks she remembers, that they had a huge confrontation almost as soon as he walked through the door. She was being visited by a (female) friend and the presence of this person seemed to enrage him.

That night they must have quarrelled violently, and the next day Virginia left – temporarily. Johnson woke up to find himself alone in the house with Steven and Kate. He drove them round to Diana Tyler's house and left them with her husband Bill while he and Diana went out for a long talk.

'He hadn't really talked about suicide before,' she remembers, 'but he was certainly talking about it after *Fat Man*. That was terribly hard, that was a very strange few weeks. I remember him bringing the children to my home, it was a Sunday morning and he phoned at eight o'clock and he said, I think Virginia is going to leave me – you know, he basically said, Get out of bed, get dressed, I'm on my way. That was a day when he was deeply, deeply upset. I think I'm talking about three weeks before he died,* they had just finished the shooting and they had come back, and clearly they had all spent a very memorable time on that shoot, and even the camera crew, they were worried about Bryan a bit, they were concerned about his mood in the making of that film. When he came back he was clearly disturbed by whatever was concerning him in his own personal life, and on that first Sunday he suddenly came out with the children and Bill looked after the children – who were still very young – and he said to me, "I think Virginia is going to leave me". That was his fear. And I said, "Don't be so ridiculous" – I actually said that. I thought, What on earth is the man talking about? but there was something in him, whatever it was, that made him feel this, and then he started talking to me about getting in the car and going up the motorway and just crashing the car ... He would say, That is what I feel, I feel desperate.'

... You must go on, I can't go on, I'll go on ...

'We were all concerned that perhaps something which was a minor matrimonial thing was becoming to Bryan something much bigger. Whereas somebody else would go out and have a couple of glasses of wine, you see for Bryan it would be more than that, it would be a major thing. That was really the start of not a good period at all.'

How long was Virginia gone? Nobody can be certain any more. I assume it was only for a few days (although 'split seconds' can feel like 'aeons' in these circumstances, as we know). And this must have been the time when John Furse and Barry Cole – so the story has it – were taking it in turns to 'watch over' Johnson, visiting his house in shifts, day and night, to make

---

* Sixteen days, in fact.

sure that he was never alone. Both men now say that the arrangement was never as formalized as that, exactly, but Cole certainly remembers meeting John Furse on the steps of the house and taking over from him: 'I can remember John at the door, and I can remember us sort of exchanging some hopeless glance: as if to say, "Best of luck", that sort of thing.'

In his *Memoirs of a Porcine Lout*, Furse recalls a defiant attempt Johnson made to throw a dinner party in Virginia's absence:

> Then when she left him he cooked the meal and that didn't work either and the children were always around and the guests weren't sure what it was all about and when they'd gone he changed all the pictures on the wall around as a sort of gesture she'd immediately notice when she came home. He knew she would – and it was rather like scribbling naughty words on the lavatory wall just to show her – and them – that he was the important one he had written the words to prove it she was just a woman who apparently needed someone else [...] It never occurred to him that there might be something else – something that he couldn't give her – affection – friendship even something that she knew must be though she couldn't easily find it with him.

If this dinner ever did take place, it must have been a morose occasion. The clearest memory most people have of Johnson during those days is that it was difficult to get a word out of him. Depression and his mounting sense of panic made him silent and inert. One morning he went round to the house of his friend the writer (and – some years later – highly successful agent) Giles Gordon, and simply sat at the kitchen table, his head in his hands, saying nothing. 'Daddy,' Gordon's children asked him, 'why is that man asleep?' Diana Tyler recalls that 'When he was very disturbed about something, he used to sit very silently, he used to go into his shell.' And Barry Cole remembers their last conversation: 'It was difficult to get any response from him, you know. When I would try and buck him up by saying how much he was admired, and how much we all loved him, he just said things like: "There is no point, there is no point."'

Another factor to take into account: Virginia says that during those last two weeks, Johnson never ate. But he did drink – constantly and methodically.

Diana Tyler says: 'He was in touch with us every day, on a professional and a personal basis. Some days you thought it was all right and other days you didn't, but then I think Bryan and Virginia began to talk to each other again, about the whole thing, whatever it was.'

For most of that time, in any case, Virginia had not been very far away: she had been staying with her mother, in the self-contained flat in the basement of the house. It seems that towards the end of the week she moved back upstairs. 'I sat down with Bryan,' she says, 'and we decided to seek professional help with a marriage guidance therapist.' They had one such meeting, but it wasn't a success. Johnson had always felt wary of any kind of therapy: whenever anyone suggested that he try it, he would always retort, 'My *books* are my therapy.' He took little notice of what the therapist said; afterwards, this woman (an experienced psychoanalyst) told Virginia that her husband 'had the most *hurt* eyes of anyone she had ever seen'.

The weekend of 3 and 4 November 1973 the Johnson family went to Little Tew in Oxfordshire, to stay with their friends Peter and Rosemarie Buckman. The Buckmans remember no loud arguments, just a quiet, shared sadness between Bryan and Virginia. The women stayed at home to play with the children while Johnson and Peter Buckman went for a long walk, taking in the Falklands Arms pub in Great Tew. Johnson confessed that he was feeling suicidal and described a conversation he had recently had with his father, in which he had tried to get him to see how desperate his unhappiness was. 'Dad,' he had told him, 'I'm thinking of doing myself in.' His father had reacted blankly, uncomprehendingly. These things were outside his emotional frame of reference. He didn't know what his son was talking about.

When they returned home to Islington on the Sunday, Johnson sent the Buckmans a copy of the newly published *Aren't You Rather Young To Be Writing Your Memoirs?*. He inscribed it, 'For Peter and Rosemarie, with much love and such thanks, on this unhappiest of days – Bryan, 4.11.73.'

The same night, he sat and typed a letter to György Novák in Hungary: the letter in which he referred to himself as a 'fat foolish man'. Much of the letter is businesslike, written in answer to Novák who wondered about the title of *Christie Malry's Own Double-Entry*, and why Johnson had allowed the hero's name to be changed from 'Xtie'.

157: EXTRACT FROM LETTER *(4 November 1973)*

To György Novák

I changed XTIE to CHRISTIE at the urgent insistence of the publishers; they thought the book difficult enough without an impossible title [...] in order to get through certain other things (which you may well understand) I agreed to this (surely fairly minor) change in order to deflect them from making major changes inside the book. But it is (I agree and am ashamed of it) a concession, an unforgivable deviation from what I wanted to do, say. But who do you think I am, god? Or, rather, the white goddess?

The story you tell me about the map with your students' place for me on it flatters me very much, and moves me, too; I have the happiest memories of you and that place, and was not prepared for it, to do it justice; perhaps next time I shall be.

[...]

Now the sad news. My wife left me last weekend; she's back in the house again, but the marriage is no longer a marriage. I am totally shattered, and am trying to pick up the pieces. What happens now?

I hope I shall survive to come to Hungary again, and that it will not be too long in the future; I have the happiest memories of your country, and you, and hope that the future contains further visits to both.

As ever,

Bryan.

Johnson's drinking continued. So did the work. That week he was still managing to attend meetings and keep appointments, but he developed a strange habit of phoning Diana Tyler several times a day to tell her exactly where he was and on which telephone number he could be reached. 'He was continuing working and he used to ring to say I'm going here, I'm going there, and that was odd, at first, but to me it became quite normal. I did think, Why is he doing this, why is he always saying, "I just want you to know this is the number I'm going to be at, should you need me." Well, perhaps he was really saying, "Should I need to be rescued..." It was almost as if you had to know where he was every second.'

As far as work was concerned, Johnson was still wildly overstretched. He had the Thames TV scripts to finish, the letters to be sent out for *You Always Remember the First Time,* and yet most days he had to be in the editing suite with Michael Bakewell, looking at *Fat Man on a Beach.* He also had journalistic commitments to fulfil. Barry Cole remembers that 'a day or two before he died, I can't remember which day, I was there and Bryan was writing a review in his little study room at the top of the house, and Steven was there and Steven took a photograph of his father, seated at his desk. It's taken from a child's point of view, Stephen sitting on the floor and looking up, looking up at Bryan at his desk. I don't know what the review was, I can't remember, it was something he had to finish. That would have been a couple of days before, it was obviously when Virginia and the children were there.'

And then there was *See the Old Lady Decently.* Charles Clark had read the manuscript and expressed strong reservations. He and Johnson had had what Diana Tyler called a 'harsh meeting', but 'Bryan was actually very sensible about it. We had a meeting and talked about it, and he didn't take it that badly. I think Bryan knew – and Michael persuaded him, too – that there was a lot more work to do on that novel. I also think it was a very difficult undertaking. We'd always thought as agents that this was going to be a very difficult one to see through to its conclusion. But I don't remember he was particularly angry about it. I personally think that was such a difficult book to write. I think it took a lot out of him. I think it was a very emotional book to write, and at the end he was very tired.'

Clearly, Charles Clark had done nothing but express a responsible editorial opinion – an opinion with which, as a matter of fact, many people would agree. But the thought that he had yet another mountain to climb on this project must have been another severe blow for Johnson. None of his novels written under contract had ever been turned down in this way before – and this was meant to be the most important one of all. If even his writing was starting to fail, what else did he have?

Friends, maybe: but he was even beginning to antagonize those. The last time Bill Holdsworth saw Johnson was at the Gay Hussar, where they went for what was supposed to be a convivial dinner with their wives. This Soho institution was one of Johnson's favourite places, especially since his conversion to all things Hungarian: he was always recognized by the staff there, his books were proudly displayed on the bookshelves, and normally a meal at the Gay Hussar was a riotous occasion. But this evening, eating little and drinking lots, his mood curdled and the dreaded subject of the BBC's forthcoming National Service documentary came up. He insisted again that 'they' had 'stolen' the idea from him; Holdsworth (one of his best friends), shrugged his shoulders and said something along the lines of 'What can you do, Bryan? Nothing's changed.' Johnson's response to these stoical words of comfort was an outpouring of vicious abuse, aimed first at Holdsworth and then at Virginia, who tried to defend him. The meal ended in angry silence.

Methodical to the last, Johnson stuck to his habit of ending every working week at 5 p.m. on Friday by meeting up with Michael Bakewell, Diana Tyler, John Boothe and others at a pub in Fitzrovia which they called the 'Quartet pub', because it was just around the corner from his paperback publisher. After the drink on the evening of Friday, 10 November, he stopped off at a florist's. 'All that previous week,' says Diana Tyler, 'he had been hoping everything with Virginia was fine, and that evening he got a dozen red roses, and he rang me and said he'd got these roses to take home.'

The roses had been intended as the prelude to a reconciliation; but it never took place. Instead, things got badly out of control. That night, Johnson found himself 'rejected' again, and responded – according to Michael Bakewell – 'in a fairly heavy-handed way.'

'It was during this very stressful period,' Virginia says, 'when Bryan was gradually drinking more and more and eating less and less, that one day, out of the blue, he attacked me physically, something that was totally uncharacteristic of him, a danger signal that could not be ignored.'

'Whatever happened on the Friday evening didn't turn out right,' says Diana Tyler, 'and Virginia fled. Clearly she must have been very frightened.'

*

The next day was a Saturday. So, obviously, Johnson went to see Chelsea playing at home. With John Furse who recorded that day in his *Memoirs of a Porcine Lout*:

> They parted – funnily enough on a corner of Upper Berkeley Street so it was then ... later and that was the last time he saw him. Balzac? No a fat man lost without his mum with his father who had no idea – after football on a Saturday evening sometime in ... the past. Why remember that?
> Chelsea it was – against – that he couldn't remember but he knew that Baldwin scored. He turned to Albert and said – clearly he remembered the words 'one thing about Baldwin you can always rely on him to do the obvious' – whereupon the centre-forward – number nine – Baldwin T. put the ball over the centre-half's head – I suppose it was – Everton if I had to say – turned around him and hit it into the back of the net. Albert leaped to his feet pounding his hands together jumping up and down between the packed seats and shouted triumphantly – The fuckin' obvious – and chuckled wide eyed and delighted for a full three minutes.

After the match he went back with John Furse to the door of his flat in Upper Berkeley Street where they said goodbye for the last time. Meanwhile – or perhaps some hours earlier – Virginia had packed and had fled to the Buckmans' house in Oxfordshire with the children.

'Next day [Saturday], after Bryan had gone out, I called our GP who advised that I should leave a note for Bryan explaining that I was taking the children away to the country for safety's sake, and that Bryan should contact the GP as soon as possible as he needed medical attention. However Bryan, reading the note at a time when he was totally unable to think straight, must have believed he was being abandoned outright. I was far from planning to leave the marriage – Bryan and I were still seeing the couple therapist as an ongoing commitment at the time.'

*

> ... and then suddenly [*wrote John Furse*] while he was out in Upper Berkeley Street she had taken his children – their children – and run for it leaving him nothing but an old man without a wife and without his mother.
> She said they'd barred their doors against him when he went

looking but that he couldn't really believe because he wasn't a frightening man in spite of his size just like a hurt animal – hippo floundering around the streets of Islington behind the puppet-theatre trying to find his kids to take them to the pub and to tell them how Baldwin did the obvious and so had she . . .

*

The house must have seemed eerily quiet without them. On Sunday morning Johnson phoned Diana Tyler and asked her to come over.

'I had no idea where Virginia had gone, hadn't a clue. I didn't know for nearly a year later that she had gone to the Buckmans'.

'Nobody was around, it felt very odd and the house was obviously very quiet to him and he was confused. But at the same time he was very systematic about some things, he was talking about his work and he was showing me where everything was – you might think that makes me naive but he didn't say anything about suicide. He was deep in thought a lot of the time. The way I saw it, whatever was at the root of the marriage problem was to him unacceptable, because he was such a loyal person and that was the kind of thing that would never happen to Bryan, it would just be outside Bryan's rules. But he just really wanted someone to sit with him, he wanted somebody to be there, because he couldn't come to terms with what had happened, he didn't understand what he had done. Quite clearly what he had done was not acceptable but I didn't know that at that time. Quite clearly he was in a state of shock.

'Then we went to his pub and of course I realized afterwards that we'd gone to his pub for the last drink.

'He was indicating at that time that he really wished he could start all over again, maybe with somebody else: he wanted to start his life again in order to get right whatever he felt he'd got wrong – because he was a perfectionist, and that's very hard. Then he went back and he had a sleep and I sat reading. It was the most extraordinary experience.

'After that I drove him: he was going out to dinner and there was this great discussion about whether he should leave the lights on or off, and he said I want to feel that the house is lived in and that people are here, so we went around the house and we put the lights on, so the house was safe and he was much, much calmer. I drove him to his dinner party. He was going out with a friend to dinner and it was in Holland Park and I dropped him off. He was dining with somebody from Paris, a man I didn't know, somebody from Paris that Bryan had become friendly with. I just dropped him at the bottom of the road, I don't even know what house it was.

'All that Sunday he hadn't spoken to anybody else. He kept trying to phone Samuel Beckett, that was the only call he made.

'He did say, "I shall be much more famous when I'm dead." I remember him saying that.'

Diana Tyler could not identify the 'friend from Paris' Johnson dined with that Sunday evening: presumably the last person to see him alive. His remaining movements are unaccounted for. But she is fairly certain that he phoned her later that evening, to say that he was all right.

Some time on Monday, 12 November, he was driving through Islington – going somewhere? coming back? – when his car broke down. His precious Citroën GS 1220. This car represented so much to him: his family life, his material success, his glorious Hungarian adventure. He had to pull into a cul-de-sac off Upper Street in Islington and leave it there. It was not discovered for weeks afterwards. Was this breakdown, this simple mechanical failure, the last straw? One symbol too many?

Something else occurs to me: I wonder if he ever really got over the death of Tony Tillinghast. He had died on 14 November 1964. It's almost as if Johnson were marking an anniversary.

Back in the empty house, he must have been very drunk. Floundering, he smashed a painting by John Furse – 'a symbolic representation of womanhood', Furse remembers, all too ironically. Johnson scrawled a note, almost but not quite the last thing he ever wrote.

158: NOTE *(12/13 November 1973)*

John – the painting was damaged by accident – *not as any sort of a gesture.*

As ever, Bryan

Michael Bakewell says, 'Although what had happened was fairly horrifying, I think we all thought it would eventually find its own level. But Bryan wasn't prepared to let anything find its own level. He was working himself up into this tremendous state of vengeance, apart from anything else, I think. And his death was a kind of attack on all the rest of us as much as on himself.'

Did he continue trying to contact Beckett?

Late on that Monday night, the telephone rang at István Bart's flat in Budapest. 'Bryan called, on the night of his suicide. He was sort of telling me that he was going to commit suicide. It was a desperate telephone call, I didn't know what to say, I couldn't say anything, so I sat down to write a letter, because the communication at that time was ... Well, after that the telephone did not answer, there was no other way but writing a letter. I wrote a quick letter. I remember going to the post office that was open till midnight – all night – to mail the letter for the morning. It was certainly not quick enough. But I didn't think that he would do it, actually. I felt that he was in a very bad mood, but I didn't think that he would be committing suicide. I was telling him to get on the plane and get out to Hungary fast, as fast as possible, and we were going to take care of him. But that letter was read by Virginia only.

Even as István Bart was writing it, Johnson was running a warm bath. He had decided to do it the Roman way, like Petronius. Perhaps even his death can be seen as a kind of tribute to one of his literary masters. He knew who would be the one to find him, as well. He left a bottle of brandy by the side of the bath, with a message attached:

159: NOTE *(13 November 1973)*

Barry – finish this

Then he wrote the last thing of all: five words only. Not so much a suicide note as a kind of concrete poem.

160: CARD *(13 November 1973)*

This is my last

word

*

The body was discovered on Tuesday, 13 November, when Virginia returned from Little Tew after receiving no answers to her telephone calls, and asked Barry Cole to look inside the house for her. Johnson's father, Stanley, was told the news that night. He died one month later.

A LIFE IN 44 VOICES

Unless otherwise stated, all comments are taken from interviews conducted with the author between 1998 and 2002.

John Berger   The first thing that I would remember about him is how handsome he was. In his face, a lot of the richness of his interior was visible. It wasn't just that it was sculpted – he had a presence. It's perhaps the first thing that comes back to me when I think about him. Maybe, like us all, the image he saw in the mirror was not the same image as you see outside.

Zulfikar Ghose   The first thing I saw of him when I opened the door was his eyes. Not their colour, which in the shadow of the threshold appeared a greyish blue, but their look that struck me as sad and *afraid*. Perhaps it was merely the apprehension of meeting someone for the first time with whom previously he had only corresponded; perhaps it was fear of a door opening to beckon him to enter an unknown world.[1]

Alan Burns   I didn't get to know him well enough to take in his character, his personality or his intellect. I just had the sense that here, clearly, was a writer: I was going to say a real writer, which sounds silly but that is the way I would have put it. One might just say a real professional. But quite an impressive presence. Not just his physical presence – I would say a little bit more than that. I would say that I was struck by his intelligence, his eloquence and his lack of pomposity – his downrightness – all clearly 'Johnsonian' qualities that you would be familiar with.

Alan Brownjohn   He's always in my memory of him physically the same: big, chubby, red-faced with a kind of combined expression of ruefulness and cheerfulness. Sometimes a melancholy look but very often a jocular melancholy look.

Judy Cooke   Yes, my first memory of him is of this large, lugubrious person sitting next to me in a lecture and he and I agreeing how awful life was. At the same time he was so entertaining and terrific, you know, but *very* serious.

Marta Szabados   I knew *him* before I knew his work, so I had my first impression of him as a man – not as a man, as a person – completely separated from this work which I got to know later; and I thought ... I had the impression that he was a moody person, someone who is not easy-going. Not inhibited but looking – not sad, or worried – but not quite at ease. But he was so amiable.

Joebear Webb*   He has been described as Tony Hancock, and you couldn't help seeing that: this combination of tragedy and comedy. Of course I don't think a comparison ought to be or could be stretched very far, but there was a physical similarity, facial, and a vocal similarity, as you know. I think that would have appealed to him, there was that robust side of him that was really London, that was really Sam Johnson. I think he probably would have recognized himself as a Tony Hancock type of character, I think he would have been happy with that.

Julia Trevelyan Oman   He was so enormous. He went into the room and the whole room was taken up by him. And you always felt he'd washed, and you always felt he was clean. Women are very susceptible to that sort of thing, and you always felt that he'd had a bath and all the rest of it – whereas, you know, some men, when girls meet them, they absolutely stink. But with Bryan one always felt he'd shaved and bathed and combed his hair and everything of that sort.

Alan Brownjohn   Yes, the size of the man! He was a most devoted eater. And not a food specialist, he just loved very good and large meals. And a good Indian restaurant would do him as well as Rules, for instance. But after a meeting that say ended rather early, his first thought would not be, 'What are the opening hours, shall we stroll around and wait for a drink?' he would say, 'Well, let's go off and have a pastry somewhere in Soho and *then* have a drink.' I don't think he ever came to terms with the weight problem – I don't know how much he tried.

Zulfikar Ghose†   For some reason (e.g., going into different shops) we would part, and looking for him I invariably found him in the *patisserie* devouring considerable quantities of cakes. Even in London, he had been a compulsive eater between meals; when we left pubs at closing time, he

---

*   Friend and correspondent of Johnson's. They did some work together on the *Albert Angelo* screenplay. Now a lecturer in computing and multimedia at Birkbeck College, London.
†   Reminiscing about his holiday with Johnson in Spain.

would make for a fish and chips shop, or, when in Soho, the shop in Great Windmill Street that sold salt beef sandwiches. But I had never seen him eat so many sweets before. And when I received the news of his death, one of the images that came to my mind was seeing him in one of those *patisseries*, gluttonously thrusting a large quantity of cream, sugar and pastry into his mouth, almost as if his body were driving him to make up some obscure chemical deficiency ...[2]

Meic Stephens   He did have a thing about his weight. He was convinced that it was going to kill him.

Gordon Williams   I once went with him to Derby to see a football match. I remember that on the way Bryan took a bag of food to eat with him on the train, and then on the way to the ground he stopped at a corner shop to buy a packet of sliced ham and a chunk of cheese. There was a huge police presence, and at one point he rushed over to rescue someone who was being searched by the police. I had to restrain him – he was mad, mad to even think of it. And then at halftime, he spotted the place where they were selling pies and buys two big pasties for himself. I wasn't in any way psychologically aware at the time, but I could tell that this guy was eating far too much. And it wasn't for the pleasure of eating, it was some compulsion ...

Alison Paice*   Yeah, he was a big man. I mean it wasn't just that he was fat, he had a big frame ... I can't remember, is it in one of the books, he says this thing about how comforting it was having his mother cook him a big fried egg breakfast. Either that or it was something I heard him say, but certainly, the lusciousness of the yolk of the fried egg, I remember him either writing or speaking about this. This thing about the fried breakfast with the luscious yolk.

Joyce Yates   He was always tending to be overweight because in those days women's only desire was to shove as much food down their children as they could and his mother just fed him up. That was her way of giving him love.

Giles Gordon   I think there was huge insecurity in this vast, elephantine frame. This great figure who was sweating the whole time – it was like a sort of waterfall – because he was so big, there was a lot of liquid to get out. My guess is that he hated his physical form, because he was ... he was huge, and his neck was thicker than the top of his head, and I think he found his body quite difficult to live with – and yet he had this *ravishingly* attractive wife.

---

* Knew Johnson in the early 1960s through mutual friends at King's College London.

Gloria Cigman All I knew of Bryan was that this was a man who felt that he was ugly, I think, and he was very self-conscious about his weight and very touchy about it. I remember a conversation across the dinner table at home – somebody had said something, it may even have been me, about dieting or 'You are what you eat' or something – or maybe even Stephen had said it – and Bryan was very explosive and said, 'Some people just have a glandular problem.'

Jeremy Hooker Physically, he was built a bit like a bull, you know, one sort of felt that he would go his own way, and it didn't matter whether he had to go through a door or a window to get there, but he would just do it, and that is one of the things that I liked about him and retrospectively like even more. Yes, he was built like a bull and he had something of that strength and determination and probably blindness, you know, to go his own way, irrespective of what . . .

Alan Burns It was an extraordinary thing, but again you see it goes to the irrepressible integrity of the man – that he would find himself driven to adopt what would clearly, in some cases, be a quite crazy attitude, and then he would go through with it like a bull, as if to say, 'Here I am and here I stand and take it or leave it.'

This relates to another area which again I can only touch on, and not authoritatively, which is Bryan's regard for himself as a writer of quality, which again is a most important aspect of him because it genuinely was there. He did believe in himself as a very considerable writer of genuine and very substantial talent. I am sort of measuring my words to some extent, and I'm avoiding the word genius, but there he was, an admirer of Joyce and a friend of Beckett, and he did feel himself up there. So to that extent he had a general feeling of not getting fully what he deserved in every way. Bryan was very money conscious – it was a measure of his success, it was like his everyday battle, and he would to some extent measure his success in those terms and fight like mad for it: Diana will testify to the way he would put the screws on his agent to make sure his agent fought for him. So to the general question, Did Bryan get his desserts?, the answer is, Certainly not in money, of that he deserved more.

Ben Glazebrook Yes, he had this tremendous belief in himself as a writer.

Jeremy Hooker But then I have to say I have yet to meet a writer, however famous, who feels that he or she has received adequate recognition, and Bryan certainly wasn't one of them and he probably had more reason than some that I have met.

John Berger When he died, I remember also feeling a sense of injustice.

That's to say there was also somewhere a kind of anger, not against him but against how – one could say how *life* but one could also say how the fucking literary establishment and all those cunts writing in those papers – had treated him. And although, first of all, one said to oneself, 'I didn't do enough,' but after that I also felt that there was this injustice in relation to what he was trying to do and what he had achieved. I suppose at that moment – this would no longer be true but at *that* time, and in the years before, it was certainly true – you know I could begin to make a little list of the people who the literary establishment had in one way or another assassinated: and he was on that list.

John Horder*

'Unsatisfied Author'

He went around all the publishers
Asking for more money
When what he really wanted was more tit (at birth)
And the publishers just hadn't got any.
He was thought (by the publishers) to be
A most awkward specimen of humanity.

Convinced in himself of his own genius,
He demanded that the world recognise him for what he was.
But the world just hadn't got any. Tit, of course.
He hadn't recognised that it was just far, far too late in the day.

Francis King   I admired Johnson's novels but never felt at my ease with him. In his company, it was always as though the seat-belt light had come on during a previously tranquil flight. I sensed a profound dissatisfaction in him and guessed that its primary cause was his conviction that he was a more important writer than even his admirers acknowledged him to be. He and I served together on a Society of Authors committee on PLR and, though we never fell out, I found that any sort of calm, rational discussion with him was extremely difficult. One had only mildly to disagree to get a blast of indignation or even rage.[3]

Philip Ziegler   In one letter he accused me of trickery and blackmail and ... quite clearly he was demented when he wrote it. I popped it in an envelope and sent it straight back and said I have not read this letter, if you wish to terminate our relationship finally and abruptly send it back to me again. Which he didn't. He apologized not abjectly, but ... he had a great charm, Bryan. He could be so nice, and he did realize he had gone a bit too

---

*   Poet and literary journalist who interviewed Johnson several times. This poem is from his collection *Meher Baba and the Nothingness*, published by the Menard Press in 1981.

far, I think. And his more hysterical letters I assume were related to periods of depression. But often one could see there was a pressure building up, like a pressure cooker and out would zoom this jet of steam, out it would gush.

John Boothe Bryan always had this slightly angry atmosphere about him. He *could* be very funny, he could laugh and joke, but I suppose in my mind looking back he did seem to be angry quite a lot of the time about *something*.

Diana Tyler It was always said that he was a man people were frightened of, and he terrorized people. I never found that to be true. He could be quite frightening ... He was a big man, so if he was really angry about something that anger came out, perhaps more than it would with someone else. He made his feelings known. If you were out for dinner with him and you got into an argument and he'd had a few drinks, he could be very belligerent. But I didn't take that as him being rude, I just took it as being his way, and I don't think people often understood Bryan's way. He could get on the phone and he could be really angry about something, but although he made people think the anger was directed personally it wasn't, really: he was angry about a situation. He was angry about a book, he was angry about a programme, he was angry about reviewers who had seen his work – but that was his way, and if people didn't accept it ... well, you have to accept people as they are. I don't know anybody who was deeply offended by Bryan.

Julia Trevelyan Oman I'm sure he must have had remorse over an awful lot of things that he did, people he'd hurt. He was usually trying to hurt people who he thought superior to him. I never think that he'd have been unkind to somebody who he thought was lesser than him. He was really trying to put people in their place, wasn't he?

Alan Sapper* On our delegation to Hungary, he was terribly behaved, and I told him off. He was nasty to people who weren't creative. Other people in the delegation. I was amazed to experience his vicious character, when he felt threatened, by other, talented people. 'What do *you* know?' would be his attitude towards them. He could be very generous in his dealings with people: but usually people who were less talented than him.

Zulfikar Ghose Bryan always declared that because he had a large body, he therefore possessed a higher tolerance level than others; but when drunk, he would grow obstreperous and, losing his inhibitions, become somewhat rude. At one of [Joe] McCrindle's parties, Bryan and I were having a long conversation about the form of the novel he was then beginning to work on, *The Unfortunates*; he had only just begun to see the possibility of having

---

* General Secretary of the ACTT in the early 1970s.

loose sheets instead of a bound book and was describing with considerable animation the form he had discovered that would perfectly match the subject matter of his book; but suddenly, he broke off, and turning to another guest, a man who was an editor at a publishing house, shouted at him, 'You know what you are, you are a cunt!' And he proceeded to abuse this man at the top of his voice for several minutes, so that the roomful of people stared in amazement at the incredible performance. The person in question did not deserve any of the abuse, but he was not the only one over the years to have been the object of such a public outburst from Bryan. In a letter Bryan wrote to me when I had moved to Texas, he described how he had given someone (a critic and editor) a 'dressing down' at a party at Edward Lucie-Smith's.

Both these men whom Bryan abused belonged to a particular class, socially much higher than Bryan's; they are of that group of gifted or fortunate people whose class, together with an Oxbridge education, assures them of a privileged position in London's literary power struggle. Bryan despised them: perhaps because they were what he could not be, or because they acquired so easily what he, with his great talent, was denied.[4]

Anthony Smith   At root Bryan was a very insecure man. That's why he needed theories and rules and positions and why he was dogmatic and not a good arguer because he wouldn't leave from any position he took up. And yet, like anybody who is paradoxical, occasionally in conversation he would say something which was very funny and really throwaway, but he wouldn't let that bit get anywhere near the bit of him that was a serious novelist. The other point about this is how very much it mattered to him that he must be taken seriously as a writer. I've always thought that part of what drove Bryan to kill himself was a sort of an impatience, or maybe even despair, that the world was never going to give him the valuation that he thought he needed as a writer, he must have thought he deserved. I don't think he had quite deserved it yet: he might have achieved it one day, but he couldn't go on living long enough to wait and see if it was going to happen, which I find very sad. When he would put forward this argument that 'Life is chaos. Each life a series of accidents, so telling stories is telling lies: imposing patterns on chaos', I always argued back that we are driven (by a sense of identity/ dignity) to make stories of whatever happens, like Greek myths. If you ask people to explain the principles of something, they give you examples, they tell you stories. We communicate through stories, by metaphor. But Bryan had the arrogance of a certain sort of autodidact. I would quote George Eliot to him: 'Extremism is the resource of the weak.' Or a joke of my own: 'Beware of the dogma.'

Alison Paice   Yes, he was definitely a bit arrogant towards others, in a way.

He liked professionalism in anybody and he couldn't be bothered with anybody who wasn't giving him something worthwhile to listen to: you know, he was never frivolous. I remember him as being never frivolous, I was going to say a bit cold but I don't know whether that's the right word. Perhaps a bit ungiving.

Barry Cole   He could get hold of the wrong end of the stick very very easily. And once he'd got hold of it, he wouldn't be shifted. It once ruined a whole evening together when I turned up late. He thought I'd done it on purpose to annoy him.

Roma Crampin   I think there was an ambivalence in Bryan because he was very kind and he didn't hurt people's feelings, yet sometimes he would be a bit bolshie and if he thought people were being ... well, usually it was people he didn't know – he would perhaps be rude, whereas if they were people he'd known from way back he wouldn't put them down. He wouldn't ever put me down in public at all, whatever he thought.

Gloria Cigman   I remember another of our confrontations. I was reading Solzhenitsyn, *The First Circle* I think, and I was just very impressed with it. Bryan was furious: he said, 'Oh, so you want to read a Victorian novel – as far as you're concerned the novel hasn't moved anywhere.' I don't know why he was quite so aggressive with me, I think because he liked me. But he saw me as someone who was in the other camp and he wanted me in his camp.

Gordon Williams   If Bryan could make an enemy, he would. I used to see the way he behaved with newspaper editors: if he met them the first thing he would tell them was what shits they were; but then he'd expect them to smile and say, 'Bryan, you're a genius – it's an honour to be insulted by the Laurence Sterne of his time.'

Joebear Webb   Bryan had this absolute commitment to the *evolution* of the novel, and it was wonderful discussing it with him, but there were things in his books that you felt were kind of not him, and when you tried to look at it from that point of view he became defensive, and he would retreat a bit, so you always had to concentrate on what was good. But of course he wasn't egotistic at all, I never found him in the least bit immodest or egotistic, everything that he said about his writing or anyone else's writing was just focused narrowly on this one beam of light – *the novel must evolve.*

John Boothe   He wasn't aggressive in the sense that he was offensive and would put you off – from our very first meeting, the feeling was that one warmed to him and didn't mind in the least, even when one walked away with a slight feeling of guilt after having been ticked off for something.

Thelma Fisher   He was very emotionally demanding, and that would be what was scary because you would sense that there was a huge pent-up thing and if you put a foot wrong you would get the lot, and that you'd be kind of on sufferance for not taking life seriously enough. Probably because of what had happened to you – his sense that you hadn't had to work for or suffer for what you'd got, and he'd be impatient about that. The same with religion: he felt that if you're religious then you'd better be serious about it. It was no use just being religious because in the 1950s people were. Nothing like that was good enough, you had to have thought it out and really worked at it. He was a bit obsessive.

Gianni Zambardi-Mall   He could be rather eccentric at times. I remember we used to drink, go for a drink in Wardour Street and you know if the glass wasn't full to the brim he'd just leave it there and walk straight out, much to the surprise of the barmaid.

Alan Burns   I have got this quite shameful and silly characteristic – before I meet someone, I make notes of topics that I'm going to talk about. And once when we were in an Indian restaurant, Bryan was in the toilet and I took out my cheque book and looked at the list of things that I had decided to talk about with him – not important business matters but just chitchat, maybe politics, I don't know – and he came back a bit sooner than I expected and saw me looking at this list and I was sort of driven to tell what it was and he was outraged. This must have confirmed his sense that I was not very good at socializing and so he said, 'You're out with me, your mate,' – he used the word 'mate' but not the word 'pal' – 'and you're making a fucking list, for God's sake!' And again he showed one of his characteristics, which is to say that on the one hand he would joke about it and also there is a little grain of genuine resentment there. You know what I mean? In a way he was genuinely cross.

Joebear Webb   He once said to me his famous thing about experimental writing: he got very angry and said, 'I make experiments but I don't show them to anybody,' and so on, as if to say, What were his critics talking about? He was still very angry about it afterwards, stressing it was *not* experimental writing: that was something else, these words, strange little words like imagination and experimental, they were like red rags to him. He was incredibly emotional about it, not intellectual at all. Passionate rather than intellectual. And with these emotional things about his work you couldn't really tread further than that, because you knew it would hurt him and that was the last thing you wanted to do, he was such a lovely man.

Harry West* He could get on with people, and at the Greater London Arts Association he hit it off ever so well with the rest of the panel. You know, there was no side to him – Margaret Drabble was just Maggie to him! He was very direct but never impolite or anything like that. He was forthright and related well to other people.

Alan Brownjohn As chairman of that panel he was blunt and to the point, and he moved the business on, and he knew what he wanted, and he very often got it, but he gave people the opportunity to speak, he didn't browbeat or overrule – he was good. And he always ensured we got a very good lunch – if we were interviewing for writers' fellowships, starting say at eleven, we would go on till one and see perhaps three or four people, and then the ones coming in the afternoon would see us anything up to an hour late. From Southampton Street at the top of the Strand to the left, it was only a three minute walk to Rules Restaurant, and we lunched on the GLAA most lavishly at Rules. If Bryan could organize that sort of lunch to lighten a long day, he would do that.

Meic Stephens The other odd thing I can remember about him is that he was always stopping to pick up paper clips in the street – I don't know what a biographer can make of that! I remember walking round the streets of London with him and he obviously had a detailed and intimate knowledge of the streets of London, almost like a taxi driver. But I remember him picking up paper clips and saying that he was going to give them a good home, which I thought was a bit whimsical, you know, at the time.

Michael Bakewell I was much more aware of his compassion for people who were sick or ill or lame or who'd fallen down in the street. He always thought that these people were placed in his way and he would have to go and dust them down and sort them out. He felt that they were predestined to come in his way somehow.

Stuart Crampin He was extremely kind to me after I had my accident.

Alan Burns Again that brings us to another characteristic of Bryan as a writer and a friend, that he was very loyal and, as they say, a doughty fighter not just for his own work but also – I was going to say for his friends', but that's not quite the way to put it. He didn't fight for the writing of people he knew because they were his friends, but maybe they were his friends because he loved the work, rather than the other way round. And he would do his damnedest for such people. This was absolutely part of the man – partly it was loyalty, partly it was a natural humane generosity, partly it was

---

* Chairman of the Greater London Arts Association in the early 1970s.

generalship: you see, this was part of his campaign for the good stuff and we were his allies; I was his ally and he was mine.

Barry Cole If you were accepted by him as a friend, he just assumed automatically that you were his loyal friend. There were no two ways about it. His friends were always very loyal to him; and vice versa – it was a reciprocal thing.

William Hoyland I couldn't imagine Bryan exploiting me at all. If one of the films we'd made together had been a huge success and made millions of pounds, he would have given me my share, I have absolutely no doubt about that. I knew if there was money there I'd be paid properly. And if not, I enjoyed the work anyway. When *You're Human* won all its plaques and things, he made sure that, you know, it was 'You have this one, I'll have that one', sort of thing. He was always very fair.

Diana Tyler And indeed he needed to know that you were completely trustworthy and that you were more than on his side, that you were batting for him all the time in everything that you did. You had to go that one hundred per cent all the time and that was absolutely vital to Bryan because he did that too, he worked very hard and he was a perfectionist, so his feeling was that you've got to be too.

Joebear Webb He was remarkable – I mean, I would talk to him and he would remind me of something I had said three years ago in a conversation. An incredibly retentive memory. I think it was something to do with this obsession with order in life – which in itself was very paradoxical I found, with him, because he was such a Rabelaisian man, he would come out with all sorts of swear words, he was very boisterous, full of gusto.

Judy Cooke I remember lots of jokes, and he was a very meticulous swearer, Bryan. I think he said 'cunt' a lot of the time, which was fairly unusual in those days. But also I remember him finding out that the origin of 'bloody' was 'by our lady', and he used to say that a lot; you would be waiting at a bus stop for a 24, you know, and you would see a bus coming, and Bryan might say 'Oh, it's another by our lady 29'. He just loved language. That's my main memory of him.

Alan Brownjohn He was unpretentious and approachable, and he was not awesome intellectually in the way that some other friends were. Bryan came over as more approachable, natural, he certainly knew a hell of a lot but he was chummier to talk to. He had a kind of London humour – Cockney humour, I mean, not south London humour – one was always joking with him, and making the sort of joking exchanges that you wouldn't think of making, say, with Edward Lucie-Smith or Peter Porter or other people in that category.

Michael Bakewell   About the time we put on *B. S. Johnson vs God* in Greek Street we then did another week of Bryan, me and Diana reading his poetry. On one occasion we had an audience of one and we said, 'Do you want us to do the programme, or will you have a drink with us at the bar?' but we did the programme to this solitary chap and had a long drink at the bar afterwards. Bryan wasn't in the least bit upset about that – he took it in his stride. The fact that no one had come along to hear his poetry was just one of those facts of life, he didn't get depressed about it. He regarded it as rather amusing.

Alan Brownjohn   I do remember occasions swapping unseemly jokes with Bryan. At some gathering, I suppose around 1970/1971, we met at a party and I know we had a kind of contest in producing the second line of the perennial joke, 'She was only the tobacconist's daughter ...' – where the other person has got to provide an answer, as it might be, 'She sold the best shag in the shop.' 'She was only the postman's daughter but she got them all in through the slot.' And we were just throwing these at each other, and he won in straight sets, actually. He would give me one, like 'She was only the grocer's daughter,' and then *he* would supply the punch line – he was very fast on his feet. He was a man of earthy humour, earthy behaviour. No matter who he was with, or what business it was on, he would still do things like get out of a car and grimace, and say, 'Oh, Christ, I've done me bollocks in on the gear stick', or something. Which doesn't mean that he was loud or coarse, it was kind of rueful, that it should happen to *him*, just as he'd accepted a lift to go to an important Arts Council meeting, he was limping in because he'd injured himself getting out of the car. He was full of that natural, easy, rueful, earthy humour, which I liked very much.

Meic Stephens   I remember him telling me one that I've heard many times since, but it was from Bryan I heard it first: 'My mother made me a homosexual.' 'If I gave her the wool would she make me one?' He used to write these down, didn't he, he had a collection?* I remember watching football on television with him, as well, and noticing how excited he was getting!

Glyn Tegai Hughes   Yes, he even talked about Chelsea at his interview for

---

* Johnson did indeed keep a collection of graffiti, which he hoped to publish one day. Another favourite was the line 'Masturbation stunts your growth' – to which the writer would add, much lower down the wall, 'Now he tells us!'. In a macabre way, the layout of that joke was echoed in his suicide message.

the Gregynog Fellowship. I'm not really a football fan, myself, I'm a rugby man, but I did go with him to the Cup Final replay, the year when Leeds United and Chelsea drew at Wembley. And I've used this occasionally in lectures: here was this highly sophisticated, experimental writer, jumping up and down and effing and blinding at the referee. And he had some story about his father wanting his ashes strewn at Stamford Bridge, so that when a high wind was blowing and Chelsea were losing his ashes would go in the referee's eyes.

William Hoyland   You know one of the first things he did when he got his famous contract with Secker was to buy his dad a season ticket at Chelsea. And that was an absolutely typical gesture of Bryan's.

Joebear Webb   He spent money as soon as he got it, because you'd go out with him and he would be splashing out on drinks for everybody, never thinking to ask whose round it was. That was something you noticed about him. He'd take me out for meals several times and he would just pay, it was almost embarrassing, you really wanted to say, Look, I'm really happy just to be talking to you, Bryan. He wouldn't hear of it. He was so modest, as well; he didn't convey any impression that you might feel privileged to be with him, that was part of his wonderful, innocent charm and vulnerability. It was always just, 'How nice to see you.' I noticed it was like this with everybody.

Barry Cole   During the seamen's strike of ... 1966, was it?, he was very active, and went down to the docks to give his support, and we went to some pub in the East End afterwards with Rita [Cole] and Virginia. It was full of Lascars, I remember, and the looks we got were amazing. But he could get on with anybody, because he was so sincere, he was so open.

Frank Fisher   One felt inordinately proud of being associated with Bryan. He had that kind of presence about him, in a way.

Thelma Fisher   But it's the boyishness, the ridiculous side of Bryan that I remember. I must say my first, overriding impression was of this rather forbidding, morose, pent-up person who was going to explode – as of course he did. But then I found out about this absurdly funny person as well, with this laugh which had a real glee about it, a real 'teeheehee' kind of laugh. So the absurd was never far away.

Frank Fisher   It wasn't a guffaw.

Thelma Fisher   But it's the contrast, when you look back, between those two aspects of his character, which of course you also get in his books.

Marta Szabados   You know, there is this commonplace description of the

British person who is conservative, introvert, cultured, a little arrogant, maybe shy, a combination of all these. But Bryan was none of this: he was warm. You felt the warmth of his nature, he came down as a very warm person and it also became known that he was very much in love with Virginia and Virginia was everything, a cornerstone or the basis of his life.

Meic Stephens   He used to come and stay with us and was always very good with the children. We had at the time three little girls, and whenever he came he would unpack his bags, rather like Father Christmas, and would always have some unusual toy. I remember he would go down on all fours and play with them, or just entertain them in a way that most grown-ups are not able to do, really.

Roma Crampin   He was good with children, if he had the time he would sort of lollop around and act the fool for them. He seemed very good with his own children, certainly.

Gianni Zambardi-Mall   Yes, he was very sort of ... protective, really, with little Katie because she was so small, she used to stand between his legs when I was driving and look out, and he was very happy. Very strange that he did what he did, all things considered.

György Novák   I was sent this article by a Dutch friend, all about how he used to get drunk and thrown out of bars,* and I was very surprised when I read things like that. We didn't have the time to become intimate or go and get drunk together, but this was so much out of character with the person I knew, or thought I knew him to be. I just knew him as a father and as a very kind and polite person – very nice person. Nice person, yeah.

Roma Crampin   He did drink, he liked going to pubs but I don't think he was anything ever approaching an alcoholic.

Stuart Crampin   I would have thought, actually, that he would not like the thought of losing control. I don't think he drowned his sorrows very often.

John Boothe   Although Bryan drank a lot, in comparison to a lot of our authors, who used to arrive in the office paralytic, or be thrown out of the office by the receptionist paralytic, or would appear in the office at eleven o'clock in the morning to take us out for a drink – I mean, those drunken lunchtimes in Beak Street! – although I saw him drunk, he wasn't like the Jim Ballards or the Kingsley Amises. I mean, Kingsley Amis used to ruin

---

* 'The dangers of drinking with BSJ', by Stan Gebler Davies, *Evening Standard*, 12 February 1973.

some of my days. There was a whole raft of them who looking back were paralytic most of the time. But Bryan wasn't like that.

Meic Stephens Oh yes, he could drink quite well, but he was never drunk in our house, even though we plied him with wine and so on. And of course, he took me around some of the more disreputable joints, you know! But as I say, I never saw him the worse for wear, he was certainly never vicious or obscene, he never misbehaved himself under the influence of drink. He just got mellower and mellower, really – more and more genial.

Michael Bakewell Yes, of course, he drank a great deal, and this is another factor of great importance: he became very angry and bitter through drink. He could also be a convivial drunk, but others experienced the anger and bitterness and resentment.

Bill Holdsworth Sometimes when he was drunk he would use his body almost as a weapon. He used his uncouthness as a weapon. In his books and his poems, and when dealing with kids, he was as sensitive as hell, and he was so charming. And yet there was this other side to him. And he had this beautiful woman, and when I saw her my mouth would fall open. And she would see that, and he would see that: but he would never say, 'Do you fancy my wife?' Another thing, we both had that working-class side – we never cut across a mate's lady. Point of honour. You never did. It was against the code – and Bryan was full of codes. He wasn't at all part of the sixties counterculture: we were still the kids of the war. He was a fifties man, really – with the hope of a better world, but also the disillusionment that the post-war Labour government hadn't delivered on its promises, and then the slow collapse of the old socialist ideas.

István Bart I think he lived in an imaginary world of pre-war working-class values to which he was very much attached. Singing the songs and so on, when he got drunk. (Which he did very fast.) I don't know why he made such a point of introducing me to this world, but he did: he introduced me to his father and his friends, we all went to a greyhound race together; these friends were wearing cloth caps, they looked very much out of touch, like relics – which they were at the time.

Ferenc Takács He took us out the night we arrived to his local which was the Old Parr's Head. It's now changed utterly, although Islington in those days already had a touch of the left-wing gentry. (They had Lenin's statue in Islington town hall, I remember.) But he took us to the Old Parr's Head and had to explain to us what was going on: there was a lady playing the piano there on Sunday night, singing 'Buggered if I know' and this sort of stuff,* and there was a raffle with a bottle of whisky as the prize. We were sitting in the public bar and Bryan told me that the barman who runs this thing always cheats and makes sure the prize is given to one of the old-age pensioners. So we found this absolute sense of old-style local working-class culture; and Bryan was obviously party to all this. So he actually hated this whole late '60s/early '70s thing, drugs and pop music and so on ...

István Bart   That was hateful for him. I don't think it ever touched him. It never touched him.

Joebear Webb   I remember in 1967, when he was in Paris – so this would have been the summer of love and all that – he had his hair cut really short, it was almost a pudding bowl thing. He would wear blazers as well. I mean, I would turn up to meetings with him, in the latter part – 1968, 1969 – with bell-bottom velvet trousers and floral shirts and not quite kaftans, but almost: that silly but very trendy gear. I would turn up with my hair really long and there he would be with his great long trousers, sitting there with a tie, white shirt and blazer and I thought, Oh man, you are so square.

Gianni Zambardi-mall   He was always well dressed, that was another thing.

Joebear Webb   But that was him, you were so glad to see him, but when he talked it almost contradicted what he was wearing, because he didn't talk like an estate agent, or a managing clerk or something like that, he didn't talk the way he dressed at all.

Barry Cole   One thing you noticed about him was that he was on friendly terms with all the pub landlords, which was very unusual. He carried this aura of a certain respectability about him, or solidarity, I don't know what it was, but there was something there, in his personality, that made these very highly professional people like him. You know, if he hadn't been there for week or so, they would ask.

John Boothe   He never took pot and I suspect he didn't approve of it. He had a slightly puritanical, working-class side to him. And you know, there are some authors you had to admonish for shouting at secretaries and being rude and that sort of thing. We never had to do that with Bryan.

William Hoyland   Bryan wasn't a hedonist at all – he was a very moral man. But he couldn't see anything wrong with having a drink and a bit of fun as well.

---

* I must confess that I've been unable to locate a song with this particular title.

Alan Burns   I remember an event at the ICA which was the launch of a short-lived group called Writers Reading. One of the other readers was Ann Quin, who was a close friend of myself and Carol my wife; and Bryan was quite strongly aware of her and respectful of her talent. She was very rocky mentally and to cut a long story short, at this ICA event, we all gave our readings and it was all going in a very jolly way and then Ann Quin's turn came and she did her Quin thing, that is to say she came onto the stage and she just sat and looked at people, she wouldn't say a goddam word! She just stared, she either implied or she actually stated that we sort of 'think-communicate', we can communicate more in silence than with someone actually putting the words across: which I was really quite intrigued by, it seemed to be sort of radical and provocative and interesting, whereas Bryan was simply pissed off, he was furious with her.

I regard that as perhaps the key quality of Bryan – integrity, or, if you like, truth-telling, he would not simply go with the fashion or the tide even if it was sixties and lefty and all of that, he just wouldn't. Also it was maybe a class thing in that he was less free in a way, he was more – not respectful of tradition, he would really get cross if he heard one say that – but he had some regard for the elementary structures and some awareness of them. Now some of the sillier sixties folk hadn't and he would express a view about that.

Of course politically we were in general agreement, we were socialists, but I remember him once, for instance, dismissing the whole of the Irish question as 'a scrap between the Micks', just saying, Well, the Protestants hate the Catholics, to hell with both of them, I don't give a damn. Whereas I would get all Marxist and talk about Imperialism and he would say to hell with it. On that case I think he is wrong but on the other hand he could be profoundly right and I will give you an example of that. This was at another conference at Harrogate and one of the topics that arose was the family and there was a vocal group of which I was at least a member, if not a leader, which was arguing that we should abolish the family and all the stuff that goes with it. I sort of assumed that my lefty friend Bryan would be with me – but absolutely not. He was adamant that not only can't you scrap the family, you can't oppose the family, it's all we've got, so let's try and make it prosper, for God's sake. He spoke up very strongly about that, and was always quite prepared to be a lone voice, not only a lone voice among the right-wingers but among the lefties as well. And I now know what an idiot I was and how right he was!

Philip Ziegler   He liked to stress his working-class ancestry and talk about you toffee-nosed gits from public school, and so on, but it was all quite light-hearted, and he rather enjoyed being taken to a stuffy sort of club for lunch. He liked all that.

Alison Paice He would always say he was a peasant, which I always thought was absolute nonsense, as we all lived a middle-class life. With Virginia he was a classic case of someone marrying into the middle classes but never letting you forget where he came from!

Ben Glazebrook I remember going to dinner with him at his flat in Myddelton Square. I went informally dressed, and he had thought that I would come in a suit, so he was wearing a suit. So after the soup course he got up to clear away the plates, and came back in informal dress – he'd taken his suit off. If he'd been more confident he would have just worn what he wanted to wear.

Gloria Cigman I remember with the BBC crew everybody liked him, he was 'one of the chaps' – kind of aggressively working class, I suppose, but that was his background, wasn't it? And that was all part of his anti-grammar school, anti-university attitude. I think he failed the eleven-plus, didn't he? And then he went to King's and got a 2.2 and was scornful about the whole system. And yet I've got a letter which reminds me that at one point he wanted to be a writer-in-residence at Warwick University. Having it both ways! So you have this paradox of a man who would aspire towards certain things that he claimed to despise – like that kind of wife, like academics and so on. That's why I think that if he'd got into the establishment, if he'd got a writer's fellowship, I don't think he'd have been a fighter, I think he'd have loved it. Politically and culturally in those days there were people who were anti-establishment, often just for the sake of it. Which is not as negative as it may sound, because there was something wrong with the establishment, and this was a generation of intellectuals who didn't know what to put in its place but knew they didn't like what was there. I think Bryan was in that category. He didn't know what he wanted, but he was just disgruntled, you know – a kid going round kicking Coca-Cola tins.

Alan Sapper The other delegates who came with us to Hungary didn't like him at all, and were very critical, so he was critical in return. He just didn't like the class that they were representing, because *they* were working class.

Helen Sapper It's got something to do with his being highly educated, starting to like words, to like the things that the working class might label as 'middle-class attributes'. Bryan liked nice things – his wife was ravishing, almost aristocratic really. Bryan liked those kinds of things, and that might have been what started to make him uncomfortable with those people.

Alan Sapper He had a really good understanding of people – but not of class. I don't think he knew what politics were. He didn't know the confines of a political ideology. All his politics were completely personal.

István Bart He had very strong communist sympathies, but he was not a party man, in any sense of the word. But his intellectual sympathies and his moral sympathies were with anything that was oppositional. He preferred the old left. Michael Foot would be a key figure – I learned about Michael Foot through him. He was bitterly complaining about the British Labour movement losing the intellectual stance of Michael Foot, losing all the intellectual hinterland. I clearly remember that.

Barry Cole He was never on the Communist side, but he was certainly a Tony Benn kind of socialist, I would have thought.

István Bart He saw his avant-gardism as a political statement. The trouble was that the rest of Britain was not thinking in the same terms. So his whole attitude was European, as against British. He would have been a natural figure in either France or Germany, where he would have got the right response. In Britain he was simply ignored, not seen as a threat. In France or Germany the establishment would have looked upon him as a threat and reacted accordingly. In Britain he was made into a nonentity. And that was the deepest blow he could ever get, of course. But all his models, the kind of people he was craving to become, were French writers, German writers, Hungarian writers.

Jeremy Hooker And Welsh, of course! And yes, it's not uncommon for English writers, for writers outside Wales, to have rather an idealized portrait of the Welsh writer and the Welsh writer's situation, so I'm sure that Bryan, who only came here for a fairly short time, was very much prone to it. I think he did have a sense of the poet as Bard, the spokesperson for his community with a very strong role to play, and I guess that some of the Welsh people that he knew would have tended to confirm that view. If, for example, he had read Ned Thomas's book *The Welsh Extremist,* and talked with Ned about his interest in Gwenallt – he would be one of the archetypal modern Welsh poets, very much a voice coming out of a strong sense of community and I think Bryan did value that and also idealized it.

Michael Bakewell I think there's possibly a spiritual dimension to this – his commitment to Welsh Nationalism (although he had no Welsh blood). Wales was tremendously important to him, partly because of the time he spent as a writer in residence at Gregynog, and Bryan was very seriously devoted to Glyn Tegai Hughes, who ran the place. Celtic religion he was particularly prepared to embrace.

John Berger It seems to me he was essentially an urban character and his zone is an urban zone, but at the same time I can well understand that the dimensions of his sadness would find an enormous echo under Celtic skies.

Michael Bakewell   But then the whole spiritual question is so complicated, in his case – although he was an atheist he needed God's existence to shout at (or somebody to blame for it all). But there *is* a spiritual dimension and there's also a strong superstitious dimension to Bryan, like worrying what might happen to his fingernails – that he might expose himself to forces of evil. You see, witches use fingernails, you put them into a clay doll and it gives you power over the person. He was interested in witches, as was I at that time. An interesting side, as a contrast to the solid, real, very unspiritual aspect that he usually pushes in his work.

Frank Fisher   I always thought it was quite interesting that Ginnie wasn't unattached to the church. Her mother was secretary to the vicar of St John's Wood.

Thelma Fisher   She was a good church lady.

Frank Fisher   Rather like Bryan's father being with the SPCK.

Joebear Webb   I often got a suspicion from Bryan that he really was quite superstitious in many ways. He didn't want to know, on the one hand, but on the other he did *want* God – or not God himself, maybe, but at any rate 'nothing from the bargain basement'. He did want something – who doesn't? – I mean he wanted there to be something, but he felt a peculiar relationship with this absence of something because he wrote about it, it was central to his being and central to his activity, so I think it must have concerned him an awful lot. The moon I do remember; when my child was just born, he was asking me did I follow where the moon was, and all this sort of thing. We were talking about Moon Goddesses and I'm still interested in all that stuff. I think he did try and address this in spite of himself, he had an enormously active subconscious, you only have to watch the ending of *Fat Man on a Beach*. He had these preoccupations with the moon and with the sea: these are all elemental.

Michael Bakewell   Of course, he was capable of a great deal of self-dramatization . . .

István Bart   All the time he was actually building a narrative, of which the working-class origins were very much part – and the drama of his trying to make it and break out of the working-class barriers, and behaving like the European avant-garde behaves, in an environment which was so unreceptive to anything European in the cultural sense. He thought he was revolution-izing the English novel – that was his ambition, to bring over something of the European avant-garde to Britain. That was his great frustration, that he never succeeded in doing so, he never got the right response, because he was fighting against an environment which was made of wool, and you could never confront anyone. That was his main ambition, to find somebody who would confront him, somebody he could fight with – there was nobody he could fight with. He got into a soft environment that would not react.

Ferenc Takács Yes, the *TLS* sort of response: 'Mr Johnson's interesting little novel' and so on.

Philip Ziegler I thought he was very much – though this is an awful phrase – a writer's writer. The general public were not aware of him. And if you were aware of him you thought he was cranky and exhibitionist. At the moment I'm writing a book about Rupert Hart-Davis, and Rupert would have been outraged by him, he would have thought he was silly and vulgar. And on the whole the more sedate literary establishment would have felt that. People like Rupert, who can take with equanimity the experimentalism and over-the-topness of *Tristram Shandy*, look with horror at B. S. Johnson and consider it to be the most meretricious kind of exhibitionism. I suppose simply because *Tristram Shandy* was 200 years ago, and it's become respectable with time!

István Bart He didn't know much about Germany. If he would have known more about the German avant-garde, I think he would have identified with the socialist, communist avant-garde of the 1920s. He was a reincarnation of that period. It's correct that he worshipped Brecht: but he knew very little else about it. He was not widely read. He was not a cultivated man. He was not cultivated in an academic sense. He refused also to be drawn into the system. Doing that while acquiring the cultivated attitudes of an intellectual society would have been being swallowed by society, to which he was resisting. Resistance is a very important word. He didn't want to be incorporated.

Bryan may look like an avant-garde writer, but what turns out, after so many years, to be his contribution is that in fact all the time he was writing a folklore, a folklore of a whole society, of this working-class past: attitudes that simply disappeared and will never come back and are gone. Even at the time he was making this world up: it was not real at the time. It was dead. There were just relics of it. He was making up a lore for himself, on which to fall back. It was quite obvious that this was the past, this was gone. Replaced by the sixties, seventies, non-partisan, non-political life where all the old working-class values were being broken down.

Joebear Webb Yes, and he did have this view – I mean, I was brought up with the same view, actually, I think it is a very working-class view – of fidelity and the hearth and home. I don't think anyone in the streets where I grew up would have been unfaithful, for example, any woman would have been unfaithful and I think she would have been slapped around the street and everyone would have known about it. I think that was Bryan's background, you see it a lot in the North still because I have a number of Northern friends who have got this absolutely inflexible view of fidelity, nothing like middle-class novels or TV drama.

Diana Tyler   I think in his family life, I think his marriage was absolutely vital to him, oh yes, and it didn't fit into the scheme of things that that should go wrong.

Bill Holdsworth   Bryan and I were both men who loved women, but neither of us were very good at dealing with them in the way that they'd want. We were scared to be a bit earthy, but when we were, we went too far. Or we were hypersensitive.

Francis King   I always suspected a repressed homosexuality in Bryan.[5]

John Horder   Most people were taken in by Bryan's tragic desire to 'pass as straight'. I was at the time. If Bryan had been less closeted, he might be alive today.[6]

Claire Andrews   There was absolutely nothing of that sort of thing with Bryan – he struck me as totally straight: *except* it did strike me he didn't have the faintest idea about women.

Keith Andrews   He put them on a pedestal.

Barry Cole   Bryan was very much a masculine society person. I don't think he had much respect for women. He'd fall in love with them, but I don't think he had much respect for them. But he was always polite to women. Always.

Julia Trevelyan Oman   I never in any way felt that he would abuse one's friendship, I never felt unsafe with him. OK, he was such a huge man that he could have knocked one over in two seconds, but I never felt anything other than safe with him, which spoke very well for him. Because people might have thought he'd have been hands-on, but he wasn't in any way. I think Virginia would never have had any worry over that sort of thing, absolutely none. And one's conversations never strayed that sort of way at all. One's conversation was always to do with work.

Gloria Cigman   He chose Virginia – this classy girl – who had a posh mum who couldn't stand Bryan – is that coming back to me...? So she held the purse strings – which he would have resented – other grounds for resentment. I certainly remember the poshness of Virginia in contrast with the deliberate peasant persona of Bryan. This was a syndrome, a person who decides, I suspect, that he feels he's not going to make it into the other image so he's going to milk this one for all he can get. Whenever I think of them, I remember Virginia as very beautiful, but always very nice and friendly. There was no sense that she was in his shadow. If anything, I have the sense of him as a bit of a bully, but what went with that was a feeling that he felt as though *he* was in *her* shadow. I may be wrong about that. That's my recollection: he dressed scruffily and she was elegant (we're not talking Harrods but we're talking someone with a flair which I suspect she still has) and I remember big eyes and an oval face and very classy, that's what comes to mind. What comes to mind are two essential differences in this couple: one of class and one of physical beauty. And that, to me, characterized them as a couple and I suppose I saw Bryan as the intimidated one.

Marta Szabados   I remember he bought a winter coat for himself when he first came to Budapest because he was told this was a cold country, and it was a nice black winter coat and he looked very good in it. He bought it in England and took it to Budapest and he was tall with a good movement of the body, a certain confidence (so the confidence he lacked was more to do probably with his work that he was struggling with – well, that's what I assume). And this confidence was because anyone who can marry a woman like Virginia must be *somebody*, because Virginia was looking very good and spoke French and Virginia said yes to Bryan Johnson, and so Bryan Johnson had to be *some kind of a man*!

Thelma Fisher   How, with Bryan, could you have retained your own personality as a woman? That's how I would put it. I don't know what I'm basing that on apart from an intuitive feeling. It would have been very difficult to be a whole person with him because of the emotional burden he appeared to put on you. It didn't leave you any space and I've always admired Ginnie for coping with that, especially as my first impression of her was that she wasn't strongly an individual. (Now, looking back, Muriel quite clearly *was* a very strongly formed person, so that must have been a collision of giants, really.) Ginnie has just had a lot to cope with. Just to live with Bryan for that long with all his restrictions, and his obsession for writing his own autobiography – the pressure that would create on somebody would be immense. And then to have to bring up two perfectly ordinary children in that environment, cope with her mother as well down in the basement with Bryan up in the attic writing. Then the dreadful circumstances of his getting violent and his death . . .

William Hoyland Virginia absolutely saved his life, and got him to write in the sense that he then felt life was worth living, even though the human condition weighed so heavily down upon him. And he was devoted to her. And although he was an intelligent and aware man and knew that couples can move apart, I don't think it occurred to him ever that it might happen to him, and I think the realization of that was too much for him to bear. If he had a weakness of perception, that was probably it. And that's what made it so tragic, really, because he should have been able to change a bit, and see that Virginia was a woman and maybe he was investing too much in her, and it's a fairly common syndrome, after all, people feel so much weight on them that they actually want to escape or take a break, from being that complete bedrock.

Gordon Williams Bryan struck me as a lonely person, who knew a lot of people only in the sense of having met them. Met them in some place, always the fashionable places where he wanted to hang out. The thing is, everybody in this business is on the hustle one way or another. And I think poor Bryan couldn't quite understand that: you know, it's a merry hell, this life, do your bit, take it easy, have a laugh, why are you so sad, and again we come up against the dead end – it's a psychological problem we're talking about, not an *attitude*, not an intellectual position.

John Berger There was something about him that you immediately or fairly quickly felt and you can say that this was his tragedy: he had something about a tragic destiny in him, and I'm not saying that because he killed himself. And of course you could see that, on the other side, he was incredibly difficult. But it was the kind of difficulty which comes from suffering and which also provokes suffering. By which I'm not saying that he brought everything upon himself or anything as stupid as that, but he was like a wounded soldier. And I say soldier because he was in fact involved all the time in a kind of war and he *had* been wounded, and this also gave him something heroic which connects with what I call his beauty.

Philip Ziegler The first time Bryan came in to the office, my secretary, who had these moments of wisdom, came in to see me straight afterwards and said, 'That man's going to kill himself.' I think it was just his demeanour . . .

Alison Paice I think he was very sad.

Ron Verney He didn't smile much.

Ferenc Takács In many ways he was terribly isolated and lonely.

Helen Sapper Bryan used to come to our home and sit in the chair where you're sitting now, and barely open his mouth often for the whole of the evening. I think he was very introspective.

István Bart   He was not a very jolly fellow. Never.

Judy Cooke   He could be really depressed, you know, sort of taking it for granted that life is hell. *Unassuageable* is the word that always comes to mind with Bryan.

Stuart Crampin   You know he was an evacuee and he hated that, I think, and he resented the fact that his parents thought it was too dangerous for him to stay in London whereas the parents he loved were happy to stay there themselves. He couldn't see why he should be shipped away. That was certainly disruptive for his relationship with them.

Marjorie Verney   Well, it was for safety, they thought. Which figures because him and his mum were so, so close. Especially an only child, when you've got an only child you're even closer, aren't you?

Ron Verney   So that means he must have been six when the war broke out, would that be right? Because we were fifteen.

Marjorie Verney   He was only a baby then.

Ron Verney   Well, just beginning to understand a little bit what was going on.

Marjorie Verney   It must have been heartbreaking being taken away from his mother.

Gloria Cigman   He hated being an evacuee – and that's one of the things I remember we did discuss, because as I say in my piece in that book, for me it was a very positive experience. OK, bombs were falling down in London and my parents could have been killed, but I adapted. But I think Bryan – don't you think it's just that what people are they always are, really? That people modify and adapt but there's something solid at the core and I think Bryan was always kicking things around, always quarrelling ... It's interesting that what emerges about this man is that everything he was defined by was something negative: Negative attitude to evacuation; negative attitude to school, to universities ... I think he was one of those people who somehow managed to go through an arts degree, a literature degree and out the other side, without it doing what one always hopes it will do at best, which is to teach people *how* to think rather than what to think. He didn't really learn how to think.

Jeremy Hooker   Well, that takes us again back to the bull image, which I didn't mean disrespectfully: on the contrary, I mean that was part of his strength, part of his toughness – he knew what he believed. He had this sense of absolute materiality, and the principle of decay in all material life: his obsession with that was absolute, but also it seemed to me it was very dangerous. He says something towards the end of *Trawl*, he is having a relationship with a woman and he says something like, 'I'm going to give life one last chance', and that means *her*, and when I read it I thought what a terrible thing to say and what a terrible thing to believe – giving life a chance. I just find the whole idea of that appallingly narrow and dangerous. But he knew what was real and what wasn't real, and what was real is that we are all material beings, and we live in a material universe and it decays – people get cancer, they die and that is it, that is it. That was his subject, and that was the difference between us, because I liked Bryan but his views to me seemed so desperately limited: but maybe that is where the strength of his vision comes, maybe to have that kind of passionate conviction about things is a spring, for him it was a creative spring. It made him the writer he was. And also I had to respect it because I knew that in his case it was based upon personal experience, and that's another reason why, had the opportunity to argue arisen, I wouldn't have pursued it, because at the back of his conviction was the death of his friend and then the death of his mother – that is what it was all about. One doesn't argue with that kind of experience.

Glyn Tegai Hughes There was an undercurrent of interest in death which came out in conversation and I think in some talks to students. It wasn't anything like a formulated doctrine but it was a background interest.

Thelma Fisher We were very ordinary, middle-class, church people, so I sometimes ask myself why on earth would he bother with people like us? And the answer must be in this feeling that you don't let anything go. Because he seems to have been a hoarder of people, maybe, as well as pieces of paper and experience, and if you suffered severe loss as a child, as he clearly had through that evacuation experience, the fact that his mother was the world to him, then allowing yourself to be close to a woman and experiencing the loss would make you hang on, and that looks as if it was a theme . . .

Frank Fisher It's connected, somehow, with the White Goddess in his case. I'm not sure how.

John Berger It seems to me survival was so difficult for him – it took all his attention. And by survival I mean his survival as a man and as a writer (and the survival of his writing, if you wish). There are people – sometimes one sees this in cases of people who are actually physically handicapped or ill in some way or another – for such people it is an hour-to-hour struggle to get comfortable, to find the energy and then to go on. In fact they can go on for years but it means that there is very little energy left for anything outside that struggle. I felt Bryan to be like that, but it wasn't physical in his case. And yet that makes him sound like a victim and he didn't seem like a victim, there was nothing pathetic about him at all, and he could be quite aggressive. He lacked the sort of protective carapace that other people have, but one has to add that his achievement wouldn't have been possible if he'd had that carapace. So that the lack of a carapace was intimately related – was the same thing, almost – as his talent and his vision and his originality. It's as though in the remorseless tide of life, as *he* saw it, there are moments of respite, when some small hope can be constructed, some exchange can take place and the poignancy of this also comes from this lack of protection.

Anthony Smith I knew that there had been this woman, Zulf probably knew much more than I did, and that Bryan didn't seem to have got over her, and that is of a piece, I'm afraid. That chip-on-the-shoulder thing, very – not paranoid, that's too strong a word, but it's the foothills of the same formation, which is also to do with 'Why aren't things in the world arranged in the way that I think they should be? I ought to be with Muriel...' He couldn't loosen up, to use a more modern phrase. There are people, and Bryan was one I think, who can't ever get over things like that. They remain open wounds that won't form scar tissue.

Joebear Webb There was agonizing self-doubt, bless him, you could see the self-doubt all over him, even when he was totally boisterous and Rabelaisian, you could still see his vulnerability. You could hurt him very easily. You could hurt him by treading on areas he didn't want to talk about, especially with his work. You always got this impression: Bryan was a very, very big man but he was walking a tightrope and the bigger they are ... you always know that he only has to fall off this tightrope and he actually hasn't got much to fall back on. If the critics really slaughtered the last thing he did and if he hadn't done what he really wanted ... The ones who had the knives out for him were really going to have a feast and he possibly knew that.

Bill Holdsworth He didn't seem to have enough defences. That's all I can say, really.

István Bart It's amazing that Bryan's work keeps evoking responses. He thought the opposite. He thought that this was it. He regarded himself as a complete failure. He said that. His books, his life – a complete failure. That was his last phone call. I'm talking about the moment he committed suicide. Oh yes, he was convinced that he was there to renew the British novel, but he simply gave up – well, as a human person he gave up, and saw himself rejected: rejected by Virginia, rejected by the world, a complete failure, a life that was destined to end in disaster. He was building this up. And he created a scenario for himself where what he was trying to do was hopeless to achieve.

Gordon Williams   That last year, when Bryan and I were sharing an office, he couldn't handle it. He couldn't handle it because he could not get from me the reaction that he wanted, which was rejection. He wanted me to reject him *because that would prove that he was right.* That he was always going to be rejected. Later on after I'd known him I became rather alcoholic so I gave up and went to a place down in Fulham, for about ten years, just Tuesday and Thursday nights. It was amateurish, but just enough to start reading about these things, and to see patterns. And I would say now, looking at it, Bryan's problem would be a problem with the father, somewhere, something between him and his father: absence of the father, that would be my way of looking at it. To me, he was a walking example of father problems. What was his relationship with his father? He never talked about him much. I don't remember anything ... Was he kind of genteel, lower-middle class? Well, that would have been the worst thing. If he'd been a gorblimey brute, that would have been great. Or if he'd been a peer of the realm. But I've known people who were raging alcoholics in their fifties, distinguished people, academics and lecturers and so on, and what it would come down to is that their fathers had never touched them, never given them a hug or told them that they loved them.

Alison Paice   Had he died? Was he there? I thought he didn't have a father there? Do you know, I always imagined Bryan fatherless, I thought he was fatherless, how strange. I thought he had either been killed in the war or left home or I didn't even know he was around. I never, never heard a word about him at all.

Diana Tyler   He was a sweet, gentle man, his father. I met him on several occasions, once at the house. A very quiet man, I mean quite clearly here they have a wonderful, intelligent, talented son and they really didn't know what they'd got in a way, but he was very proud of him, and Bryan was very proud of his parents. He loved his parents.

Gianni Zambardi-mall   Bryan was very much like his mother, the looks and fair hair. His father was rather passive, and very quiet ...

Marjorie Verney   Bryan's dad used to work in a Christian bible shop – he worked there all his life, didn't he? Oh, he was extremely quiet, he never said hardly a word, yeah, very quiet, and this is what makes it difficult when you can't get conversation with people as they get older, as we all get older, and because Stan was so quiet it didn't register much, did it?

István Bart   His father was a silent, tired old man, who never understood a thing of what Bryan was doing, and Bryan was very much aware of this. His mother died soon before I met his father, and it was sort of obvious that his father was going to die soon, I don't know why, but it was clear he wasn't going to live much longer. He was lovingly taking care of his father but never ever trying to explain anything to him.

Gordon Williams   That's what I would ask, anyway. What was his relationship with his father?

B. S. Johnson*   'The first match I reported this season happened to be a major one at Stamford Bridge [...] and immediately after I'd phoned my early report through I met my father for a few moments. Chelsea had won well and easily, but he was still pessimistic and cast severe doubts on the parentage of two of the forwards.

I left him to go back and write another report for the later editions. From the unpopulated terraces came the strange undercurrent of scratchiness caused by plastic beakers blowing about. By the time the preoccupied evening dog-racing crowds had begun to straggle in, I'd finished what was my longest and to me, my most important report so far.

When I saw my father a week later, he hadn't even read it.'

*

Anthony Smith   I can't remember how I heard he was dead but when I did hear I had the classic stereotype reaction which was anger.

Alan Burns   I recall inevitably the moment that I heard the news of Bryan's death – I was in my work room in the basement of Patrick Gardens where we lived and the phone rang and I stood up to pick it up and it was from Diana and I remember as it were I buckled at the knees and fell into an armchair. I did actually fall. Or did I find that maybe this is just my characteristic, as some years previously when I heard the news of Kennedy's death, I happened to be at the top of the stairs and I sort of fell down the stairs, so maybe that's just something in me.

Gloria Cigman   Anger is a very usual reaction to suicide. I wasn't close enough, it wasn't anger I felt but sorrow, really, it was, 'Poor Bryan'. I understood what Virginia felt in relation to her children, but I've learnt more about suicide since then – learnt that the person who's suicidal just has no sense of anybody else. It really is the end of the road, it's absolute despair. But I thought it was sad because he was somebody who was likeable.

---

*   Writing in the *Observer*, 18 April 1965: a reminiscence of his early football-going days with his father, the first half of which has been quoted above, Fragment 8, pp. 52–3.

Zulfikar Ghose   When I received the cable BRYAN DIED SUICIDE I said Fuck you Bryan and went out to the garden and found things to do muttering Fuck you Bryan and I could not look at his books again gave away his letters to the university could not phone Virginia did not see her on subsequent visit to London because I did not want to see him not there and remained pissed off with him for ten years always muttering Fuck you Bryan and then writing this going to the library to look at his letters again ten years later the sight of them the humour the passion the rage ten years later taking down his books from the shelf and then writing this suddenly at last I am crying like a bleeding child Fuck you Bryan.[7]

Gianni Zambardi-Mall   Of course I never really understood why Bryan did what he did. It was my father who told me, I was in Turin by then, teaching, and my father phoned me up and told me the news. I couldn't understand why, it knocked me off for two days, I didn't sort of ... I just lay in the dark for two days, it was so upsetting.

John Berger   Of course I was very shocked and very pained. And as always when you know somebody who kills himself, you say to yourself, even if you are not really very intimate with them (and of course if you're intimate with them it's even worse) but you say to yourself, probably I didn't do enough. At the same time, I wasn't so surprised – shocked, but not so surprised. When other people I've known killed themselves (I can think of one immediately) I was very shocked and also absolutely amazed because it revealed an aspect of him that I hadn't felt or known and the circumstances contradicted the act incredibly. But in Bryan's case, there was a kind of configuration and it wasn't difficult in a way to imagine that end.

*

Alan Burns   When I spoke at the funeral, the other thing I remember is sort of agonizing over what I would say, and I decided to risk a joke: I was going through what his characteristics were and I said how he had a great circle of friends – although not all the friends were friends of each other – so he had a talent for friendship and he certainly must have liked publishers, too, he must have because he had so many of them! Finally, my recollection of that time is something I absolutely again will not forget. Virginia was sitting in front and there came the time where the curtains open and the coffin was being taken out, and as that happens, normally one just waits for that to happen but Virginia got up and walked past me, behind me, and there was a tiny click and what it was, she was touching the brass inlay of the coffin with her gold wedding ring as a sort of goodbye.

Alison Paice   I dreamed Bryan's suicide before we heard about it. I don't know whether you believe in this kind of thing, but I'll tell you what I dreamed because I've never forgotten this dream. I dreamed that he was standing in a corner and the blood was flowing out of him, he was standing in this dark corner but the main thing about the dream was this terrible sense of regret, that he couldn't undo what he'd done, and this was the whole feeling of the dream, a really overpowering sense of regret and mistake. It was really awful, as if he'd suddenly realized that he shouldn't have done this, that it was more or less a gesture, a stupid gesture and now he couldn't reverse it and it was too late. I told Eric about the dream in the morning and it was later during that day that we heard that it had happened. I think it was that same day, yes ...

Marta Szabados   It is no one's fault, really, and as you say we are not talking about Bryan killing himself because of Virginia, but I understand that as long as she lives this will be with her.

Alan Brownjohn   When he came round the door into a party or a poetry reading he was such a huge, physically big presence – maybe he was only about five foot nine or ten – but he brought a kind of strong presence with him, and at the same time a sort of amiable presence, but not extrovert or cheerful, jovial but rueful, jovial but sad, a sadness in the lines of the face under the sort of robust, cheerful look, there was a sadness in the eyes. One felt this before he did what he did. So that, for a long time I used to think he could still be going to come round the door, a little bit late for a meeting, and apologizing, or I would suddenly spot him at the other side of a party, that kind of thing. He was one of those people who kind of gave you criteria: and for a couple of years I would think in the chair at those meetings, What would Bryan have said about this? I could imagine Bryan saying, 'Oh, bollocks, we can't do that, why don't we try so and so?' Because he was so full of ideas, and he'd wanted to do so much ...

Marjorie Verney   It's sad really because he had so much to give to the world didn't he? He really did. There's no two ways about it. His books are very very unique, aren't they?

Virginia Johnson   He was great fun, very physical, a great liver of life, always a strong presence in a room whether he was joining in the conversation or not. He could be possessive and jealous, intensely demanding and adamant, sometimes sure of himself and at times deeply unsure, charming and funny, soft voiced but overbearing and dogmatic if one of his bêtes noires happened to surface. A memorable, lovable and comic, vulnerable man, intensely missed by those who were close to him.

CODA

FRAGMENT 46

The subtitle of this book, as you will have noticed, is *The Story of B. S. Johnson*. But even that might need qualification, as far as these final pages are concerned. What follows, I must declare at the outset, is merely '*a* story about B. S. Johnson'. It's not the only story I could tell about him; it might not enlighten us very much about him, when all is said and done; hand on heart, it might not even be a true story. But it's the story that took hold of my imagination, and came to tantalize and preoccupy me above all others, as I reached the closing stages of my work on this book. You might end up thinking (anything is possible!) that this tells you more about me than it does about him.

Anyway. Let's begin with a quotation or two:

'It gives some indication of the tremendous, bitter anger that was raging in him, that in the middle of writing a book that was more important to him than any other book he'd written, and before he'd finished making a film which had great personal importance to him, he should just suddenly tear himself away from all this.'

This was one of the things that Michael Bakewell said to me about B. S. Johnson during the course of our interview. And then he added something which would haunt me for years.

He said:

'*And in the end, there is something inexplicable, that the events don't quite account for.*'

*

I'm no expert in the psychology of suicide; but I know enough to understand that you cannot explain or 'account for' someone's suicide by pointing to

421

one single, decisive factor. There will always be a matrix of reasons. More importantly, it's not the purpose of this book – or even one of its purposes – to explain why B. S. Johnson killed himself. That would be both an impossibility and an impertinence.

However, the industrious biographer should be conscientious about unravelling mysteries, and tying up loose ends, and however many people I spoke to there were still a few things I'd been told about Johnson – both his early life and his last few months – that left me feeling curious. These did not necessarily have any bearing on his suicide: they were just part of the picture I was trying to reconstruct, and it was frustrating that I didn't know where to place them. There was, for instance, a remark made by Thelma Fisher, when she mentioned 'that awful story of Ginnie's about that bloke following them in his later years' – to which her husband added, 'it was as if this guy was trying to persuade Bryan to do something, and that in a sense was what was haunting him'. Gordon Bowker's assertion that 'in his last months, Bryan had fallen in with an occultist, who seemed to exercise a strange power over him'. A memory from Alan Brownjohn, as well: 'there was another thing that surprised me very greatly, which I just know from a sentence someone told me, that Bryan was being pursued by someone who had homosexual interests that he was not going to involve himself in'. And that strange episode related by John Furse, which gave him the title for his memoir of Johnson: the unnamed heckler who had risen to his feet at some far-off British Council meeting to declaim to the audience, 'B. S. Johnson is a porcine lout'. A story which might well have been funny if Johnson himself had not seemed to be so weirdly scared by it.

There was one thing that bugged me more than anything else, though. In Diana Tyler's memory of her final Sunday with Johnson, there was a significant gap. At the end of their day together, she remembers driving him to an appointment with somebody, a 'friend from Paris' with whom he was going to have dinner. She dropped him at the corner of Holland Park, and that was the last she saw of him. The last that anybody saw of him.

When she told me this, I had no idea who the friend could be. Diana Tyler had no idea either. A thorough search through Johnson's address books showed that he didn't appear to have any friends who lived in Holland Park. Nobody seemed to have a clue, in other words, who had been the last person to see B. S. Johnson alive.

That was the big conundrum of his final days, as far as I was concerned. Rewinding back to his twenties, to the days when he had discovered his vocation and was just beginning to find his voice as a poet, I recalled that there was another seemingly insoluble riddle: Johnson's belief that he had received some sort of visitation from Graves's White Goddess:

Jan 55: *Physical manifestation of Goddess; indicates my servitude to her; death at 29; never able to have happy love/marriage as She was so jealous; but reward as writer; poetry really starts from then; NO BLACK MAGIC – BUT EQUALLY CERTAINLY NOT XTIAN. (Mar 55) Meeting with Michael; confirmation of all this; unified concept of art and life; M on life, I on art – conflict; M wanted to go too deep and I was too scared to follow him; (Aug 55) break which freed me, broke him; real conflict; Bach; went to Rome; own version; pursued own art-course; went to college as my way of following; directed first by Joyce then by Muriel.*

Homosexuality would be such an affront to the Goddess that I am tempted, merely to see if she would destroy me.

If only I could prove Her wrong by finding a woman who would love me completely, then Her spell would be broken: time is so short (there are four months left of my 29th year) and that is why I talk about Kate as the last chance.

The 'devil' I 'saw' was her punishment for not serving her in Wales. A vision of punishment, now made real.

Again, I seemed to be confronted by a gap in my narrative which could never be filled in. The facts were simply lost, lost beyond recovery. I wondered if it might be helpful, all the same, to find out what a psychiatrist might make of Johnson's belief. Had he actually been so depressed, when he wrote those words, that his mind had given in and he had started hallucinating? Was there a terminology to describe his state of mind at that point – words like 'psychotic' or 'delusional'? I realized that, as a layman, I didn't really know what these terms meant: so I sent off an email to my friend Andrew Hodgkiss, a consultant in psychiatry at St Thomas's Hospital, London. I attached an extract from Johnson's 1961 diary – a longer one than I've quoted earlier in the book, and including some of his reflections on the reasons why his latest girlfriend might have rejected him. 'My "analytical" habit of mind,' he had written there, 'makes me weigh everything, and give consciously in the expectation of getting something back. I see farther than others: I saw Kate (or "apprehended" Kate) as one of *us*: this makes her all the more inexplicable – she must be denying or unfaithful to herself. While I can analyse, it does not make me exempt from pain: in fact, it makes it worse.'

— Original Message—
From: Jonathan Coe
To: Andrew Hodgkiss
Sent: Thursday, February 28, 2002 6:17 PM
Subject: Favour

Hi Andrew

Now I know you're busy, and there's no hurry with this one, but
could you maybe do something for me? Printed below is an extract
from one of B. S. Johnson's diaries, from September 1961. What I
need – only in a few words – is a psychiatric verdict on it. How
would you classify his state of mind when he wrote this entry?

No hurry for this at all – some time in the next few weeks
maybe . . .

Jonathan.

— Original Message —
From: Andrew Hodgkiss
To: Jonathan Coe
Sent: Tuesday, March 05, 2002 10:34 PM
Subject: Diaries of BSJ

Jon

This man was simply depressed and suicidal (with at least one
specific method, the rifle, in mind). There is no evidence of
psychosis (ie no delusions or hallucinations or other phenomena of
schizophrenia). He seems to have markedly obsessional personality
traits (that he dubs 'my analytical habit of mind') and this
personality structure is thought to predispose to depressive illness
(because, in Freudian terms, the person has an overdeveloped
superego which judges and finds the subject imperfect). Such
personalities find making decisions or commitments very difficult.
Hence his anger that, he having been decisive with difficulty, she
is not interested. Finally I think it is worth pondering whether he
also has narcissistic personality traits. He admits to some problems
accepting, or even really believing in, the alterity and autonomy of
the woman, Kate. He insists that he has 'apprehended her as one of
us' and concludes therefore that she must be 'denying or
unfaithful to herself' in rejecting him. In short he finds her
rejection inexplicable because he can't get past his assumption that
she is very like him. He can't accept, never mind enjoy, the
otherness of the other.

That's as far as mainstream psychiatry and my psychoanalytic leanings can take this I'm afraid. You will probably conclude that there is a lack of richness or development in this sort of nomenclature and way of writing compared to literary approaches. I think that would be fair. 'Depressed and suicidal' hardly does justice to BSJ's condition but that is what we shrinks would call it.

Best wishes & see you soon
Andrew H.

— Original Message —
From: Jonathan Coe
To: Andrew Hodgkiss
Sent: Wednesday, March 06, 2002 3:28 PM
Subject: Re: Diaries of BSJ

Dear Andrew
Many thanks for getting back to me. That was very helpful. But – can I just double check this: you say there are 'no delusions or hallucinations or other phenomena of schizophrenia'. But doesn't this bit (below) suggest that he was (or had been) delusional? He claims to have physically seen a 'Goddess' (his muse); to be in 'servitude' to her; to have been told by her that he would die when he was 29; to be prevented from having a successful relationship because 'She' was jealous? etc. etc. Surely there must be some element of delusion in all this?

Thanks again.
Jonathan

— Original Message —
From: Andrew Hodgkiss
To: Jonathan Coe
Sent: Thursday, March 07, 2002 9:23 PM
Subject: Re: Diaries of BSJ

No. There is not enough in those extracts to support a psychotic state. Possible alternative explanations include participation in fortune telling practices (and belief in them, which is considered culturally appropriate in some sections of our community) and/or conjuring up a vision by an effort of volition (which is called 'imagery' and is not psychopathological). Surely this is just a man who was freaked out by predictions about his future (like tarot cards). A delusional belief has to be held with pathological certainty and incomprehensible in terms of the person's cultural/religious milieu. If BSJ was heavily influenced by a close friend interested in the occult/spiritualism then the belief that a visionary woman has predicted and owns his fate becomes understandable and, quite possibly, shared by others. This is why members of religious cults, no matter how bizarre their beliefs and practices, are not usually considered to be psychotic. The syntax of his writing and the precision of meaning in most of the diary extracts you sent me are not consistent with schizophrenia.

Finally, the fact that he put the 'saw' in inverted commas in the last extract implies a degree of insight into the unreality of any vision of a woman he might have had. From a psychopathology textbook perspective this makes the phenomenon at most a pseudohallucination. A pseudohallucination is a percept without an object that the subject recognises as a product of their own mind rather than a real object in external space.
Pseudohallucinations have little diagnostic specificity (ie would not clinch a distinction between normality and psychosis). That's not to say the person isn't fascinated, preoccupied or worried by the experience.
I hope this helps.
Andrew.

Andrew had one more second thought about this, which he emailed me a few minutes later:

> — Original Message —
> From: Andrew Hodgkiss
> To: Jonathan Coe
> Sent: Thursday, March 07, 2002 9:30 PM
> Subject: Re: Diaries of BSJ
>
> Jon
> Looking again, more closely, the final experience mentioned, of seeing a devil which BSJ concludes was a punishment from his Goddess/Muse, could support a diagnosis of psychotic depression. In this condition there can be delusions of punishment and mood-congruent hallucinations (either auditory or visual). OK – I would accept the POSSIBILITY of that.
> Andrew

I found this exchange satisfying in some ways and unsatisfying in others. Whatever Andrew's reservations about 'the lack of richness or development in this sort of nomenclature', his language struck me as curiously reassuring: 'depressed and suicidal' are, at any rate, terms that we can all understand, and his observation that Johnson experienced 'some problems accepting, or even really believing in, the alterity and autonomy of the woman' rang resoundingly true with everything I had been told by his former partners and girlfriends.* But I had, of course, been looking for something more than that. I'd been hoping for some magic formula that would unlock the mystery of Johnson's mystical encounter. In all probability, I would never find it: and in any case, I was going to have to keep looking elsewhere.

So, what about the enigmatic 'Michael', who figures so importantly in these diaries? If Johnson's meeting with him in 1955 had provided the 'confirmation of all this' ('this' being the whole Muse/Goddess/romantic failure/death-at-twenty-nine scenario) then surely he was at the centre of the riddle? Who was he? – where was he? – and how much could I find out about him?

When it came to the subject of Michael Bannard, Virginia was guarded, but helpful. She told me that he had died, she believed, in a car accident some time in the 1980s. Another time she mentioned something that Michael Bakewell had said about him, comparing him – rather astonishingly – to Aleister Crowley: which at least chimed with the 'occult' connection. She also gave me the telephone number of Doug Davies, who had lived in the flat beneath Johnson's at Claremont Square in the early 1960s, and who she seemed to remember had known Bannard quite well.

So, in February 2002 I continued my investigations, beginning with a phone call to Michael Bakewell who told me that he had only met Bannard once or twice, but had picked up the sense that he had a 'whiff of sulphur about him' and was the kind of person 'who establishes a hold over you'. This was intriguing, but didn't seem to get me very far. Doug Davies had quite a lot more to say: he told me, for instance, that the flat in Claremont Square had in fact been occupied by Michael Bannard before Johnson moved in there, and described him to me as a 'Peter Pan', and 'a child: a hedonistic little boy who had not grown up, and was used to being indulged'. He rather pooh-poohed the idea of Bannard appearing sinister or establishing a hold on people. 'If anybody was going to be taken over by him I would have to say that the victim would have to be a willing victim, and would have had to have had plenty of insecurities of his own. You'd have to be fairly fragile.'

Well, Johnson was certainly that: as we know.

Next, Doug Davies pointed me in the direction of Claire Andrews (née Latham), whose mother had been the landlady at Claremont Square and who had lived there herself for some years, along with her husband Keith: they had both got to know Johnson very well in that time. When I interviewed them on 27 February 2002 they painted a vivid and surprisingly

---

* e.g. Virginia's remark to me one day that their marriage had started to fail because 'the roles seemed to be set in stone'; also Jean Nicholson's comment that 'Bryan didn't see me as *me*: he saw me as the person he would like me to be, or as the person he could make me into. That was one of the reasons it didn't work.'

attractive portrait of Michael Bannard: bohemian, homosexual, culturally omnivorous, overbearing, exasperating, a man with a huge appetite for his favourite things in life (food, art and sex: not necessarily in that order). The man they described to me sounded, in some ways at least, not dissimilar to B. S. Johnson himself.

Claire and Keith Andrews were understandably puzzled by some of my questions. Somehow, a suspicion – or intuition – had entered my head that Bannard might *himself* have been the mystery heckler at the British Council meeting who rose to his feet and described B. S. Johnson as a 'porcine lout'. (Where did John Furse tell me this had taken place? Bangkok?) I asked them, therefore, whether he was the sort of person who heckled at public events, and Claire Andrews immediately recalled a concert at the V&A where he stood up and shouted criticism at the performers the moment it finished: 'Oh yes, Michael certainly heckled. He was very, very exhibitionist. After that he came floating down the staircase, swirling his cape around him – he was very dandyish in those days.' Her brother James Latham, whom I interviewed a few weeks later, confirmed this story, and recalled going with Bannard to a rare 1950s performance of *The Rite of Spring* at Sadler's Wells, where the whole performance was done in modern dress and the dancers wore dungarees: Bannard stormed out halfway through, declaring that it was a travesty. 'That was Michael at his most extreme. English good manners were not Michael's thing. In fact, flouting them was.'

All of which supported my suspicion; but was hardly conclusive. And in any case, my image of Michael Bannard as a satanic, sulphur-trailing Svengali-figure was beginning to evaporate. (Apart from the cape, that is.)

As I concluded the interview, Claire Andrews asked me whether I had spoken to Peter Dunsmore. This was a name I had never heard before. 'Oh, you must,' she insisted. Dunsmore, apparently, had been Michael Bannard's closest friend in England for the last twenty years of his life. 'As you know, Michael was hardly ever in the country during that time,' she told me. 'But whenever he came back to England, he always stayed with Peter. Always.' Then she rooted around in her diary, and gave me his address. Which was in Holland Park.

*

Of course, the overwhelming balance of probability was that this was simply a coincidence. That was what I tried to make myself to believe, in the two or three days (only) that passed before I received a reply from Peter Dunsmore to the letter I had immediately written:

'I shall do my best to help you in your researches,' he wrote back (on 1 March 2002), 'but I fear that what I have to offer may not amount to much.'

His letter described Michael Bannard as 'a man who kept his cards close to his chest and his friendships ... very much compartmentalized'. 'His energy was awesome,' he added. 'He behaved as if time was running out for him, as indeed it was.'

My eye skimmed over these lines until I came to the passage I had been waiting for and which I seemed to know, by now, that I would find:

'I met Bryan Johnson only once, a day or so before his death. Michael brought him here and he was clearly not in a happy frame of mind...'

*

I didn't know what this meant, but it certainly told me one thing. This friendship which had – on some level or other – disturbed Johnson so deeply back in the mid-1950s, and which I had assumed was over and done with by 1961, had actually continued right up to the very end of his life. The friend who had 'wanted to go too deep' with him when they were both in their twenties (leading to 'real conflict') had not gone away. And Johnson had chosen (or felt compelled?) to see him the day before he died.

Why?

Because he happened to be in the country? But how would Johnson have known that?

*

I found Peter Dunsmore to be a quiet, courteous, extremely cultivated Scotsman whose initially rather dry and severe manner masked a considerable generosity of spirit. He was as helpful to me, I believe, as he possibly could be: photocopying letters from Michael Bannard (often ones of considerable personal significance), photocopying his CV, playing me tapes of Bannard reading English poetry (recorded in Japan where he spent many years of his life as a teacher of English language and literature). It was not his fault, by any means, that I left his flat on the morning of 12 March 2002 feeling almost as unsatisfied as when I arrived. There had been no momentous revelations. An encounter with a man he had never met before, almost thirty years ago, had not left him with many solid memories.

'Bryan must have been having serious domestic problems, because on that particular day he walked out of the house, and Michael brought him back here, and he wanted to crash somewhere for the night. [He stayed the night here?, I asked, and Dunsmore nodded, and pointed to the leather couch where I was sitting. With a start I realized that I was sitting on the very spot where Johnson had had his last night's sleep.] It would have been quite out of character for Michael to have brought him back here under normal circumstances: I'm quite sure I would never have met him. Michael would have met him in town and they would have had a meal in a restaurant, but I think it was only because of those peculiar circumstances that I managed to meet him at all. The next thing I heard was that he had committed suicide, I think it was either the next day or the day after, something like that. I felt so bad – although it was nothing to do with me at all, I felt as though I had failed the guy in some way, you know? As if I hadn't given him some reason to live or inspired him in any way. I rather think that Michael had to go abroad again just a couple of days later – whether he stayed for a funeral or not I don't remember.' (I'm pretty sure he didn't.)

There were two things I particularly wanted to know: the first of which was (obviously enough), What had they talked about?

Peter Dunsmore sighed. 'It was nearly thirty years ago, and I met the poor man for only a few hours. All I remember is – I mean, he wasn't talking to *me* about his marital problems, it was Michael who told me that. He stayed the night here and left in the morning and the next thing I knew I was reading his obituary in the papers.' He considered for a moment, and added: 'If you read his [Johnson's] poetry he's obviously someone for whom his emotional life would have been all-important: of whom you would say *"liebe schlecht, alle schlecht"*, you know? Michael did not have a very exalted view of women, and he would have deplored that squandering of emotional energy. I don't know what the reason for Bryan's suicide was, but for Michael, to die for love would have been the ultimate absurdity. He saw woman perhaps as being the inspiration for creativity, but ultimately the destroyer. They weren't really deserving of adulation.'

And did he have any sense of how close their friendship was, in those last days? Had they been in touch by telephone? By letter? Dunsmore couldn't say: he reiterated his point that, 'It was not accidental that Michael compartmentalized his friendships. I don't think he wanted his friends and acquaintances to start comparing notes. I think his cover would have been blown, to a certain extent. I don't mean that in any kind of sinister way – there was something almost silly about it, instead.' He had the impression, that night, that the two men had not seen each other for some time. Certainly Bannard had been out of the country almost constantly since 1968. (Although not in Paris: I'm not sure where Diana Tyler got that impression from. For most of the time he had, in fact, been employed as a teacher of English to private students at the International Language Centre in ... Bangkok.)

So I left with only the outlines of a plausible scenario. Peter Dunsmore surmised that Johnson and Michael Bannard might have met at a local restaurant, and then, seeing that his friend was in such a bad way and did not want to be alone that night, Bannard would have brought him back to Dunsmore's flat, unannounced. After that, if Johnson *had* attempted to ask for advice about his marital problems, Bannard would have given him a fairly dusty answer: that he had been 'squandering emotional energy' by getting married in the first place. Hardly something that was going to reduce his sense of failure.

And yet, once again, I came away with a strong sense of Michael Bannard as a benign, maddening but life-enhancing figure: a man for whom Peter Dunsmore had obviously held the tenderest feelings of friendship. Perhaps the simple truth was that Johnson had loved him. Adolescence frequently includes a homosexual phase, and for Johnson (as for many of us) adolescence could be said to have lasted well into his twenties. Perhaps the overwhelming sensation – the 'confirmation of all this' – that Johnson described himself as having felt when he first met Bannard in March 1955, was first love. (And wasn't this very much on his mind at the moment? Wasn't it one of his last professional acts to send out commissioning letters for an anthology called *You Always Remember the First Time*?) Of course, he had never wanted to consummate it, physically – that had been the ruination of the friendship. But still, in this overweight, overbearing, larger-than-life, Falstaffian personality, he might well have found something more than a kindred spirit; he might have found both his soulmate and his opposite; his homosexual doppelgänger. And so the fact that Michael Bannard was, in all probability, the very last person to see B. S. Johnson alive had a wonderful sense of symmetry to it. A real closing of the circle had taken place.

I came back from Holland Park, sat down in the office I was then renting on the Fulham Road, and continued to think about this. The way it was taking shape in my head now, my story about B. S. Johnson almost had a happy ending, with this unexpected reunion between two long-separated friends. It was annoying, though, that there seemed to be no surviving letters to support this version of events. For the hundredth time I looked through the 'B' file of Johnson's correspondence (I knew what Michael Bannard's handwriting looked like now) to see if there was anything from him. Nothing at all. Then I tried 'L', thinking that there might be letters from James Latham in there. But instead I became distracted by something else: the immense volume of correspondence from Frank Lissauer.

*

Frank Lissauer's letters had been on my conscience for some time. He was the librarian at King's when Johnson was a student there. Being a good deal older than the undergraduates, and a published poet, he seems to have struck up an intense friendship with Johnson from his very earliest days at King's. Lissauer's side of their correspondence – the only side I had been able to find – ran to hundreds of pages, and I had never read it all. Somewhere there must be (or must have been) an equal volume of correspondence on Johnson's side, which is a maddening thought: it would certainly be revelatory. Although they wrote to each other mostly about poetry, there seems to have been a candour, even a confessional quality to this correspondence which was unique in Johnson's case. From Frank Lissauer's replies we can tell that Johnson felt able to discuss matters of faith with him which he didn't dare raise with anybody else: the letters are full of references to the Muse, the White Goddess, the White Lady. And we can see, I think, why Johnson was so confiding: Lissauer was an extremely generous, thoughtful, kind and perceptive correspondent. His comments on the manuscript of *Travelling People* run to thousands of closely argued, constructively critical words.

That afternoon, for the first time, I started reading Frank Lissauer's letters systematically. They were arranged in reverse chronological order, and I began by reading his comments on the newly published *Albert Angelo*. Much of what he wrote was so good that it should be collected and published as a gloss on Johnson's early novels and poems, but that isn't what concerns us here. Eventually, I worked my way back to the letters dated September and October 1961: the time when Johnson had been feeling so confused and unhappy.

Clearly, he had written to Frank Lissauer giving him full details of his state of mind during those days. He had told him about the rifle. He had told him about his desire (or, again, was it a compulsion?) to go and visit Michael Bannard's parental home in Banbury (even though Bannard himself was no longer in the country). This was how Frank Lissauer replied:

5 October 1961: Thank you for your nice letter: I am greatly relieved to hear that you are feeling better but sorry to know that you persist in following a seemingly false destiny by persisting in your intention of going to MB's home. I do believe you make yourself vulnerable [. . .]

2 October 1961: . . . in spite of forgetting to phone you at a crucial moment, I am really concerned for you. I am surprised myself at the affection I feel for you and I dislike being so explicit but I am completely at a loss for really helpful suggestions [. . .] All the encouraging things I can say with sincerity are these: [. . .] I should feel genuinely impoverished without you; and I urge you as strongly as I can to hand your bloody gun to the police or wrap it up and throw it in the river. I think you are too wise to use it but it is a potential danger & temptation to all those who know of it. It could even happen that a burglar found it & surprised by you, used it. And while I can make no useful suggestions about Kate I do again pray you to defer your curiosity about MB's home and shun it like a portent. With your premonitions & fears and general state of being run-down – in all, amounting to a kind of superstition – you are very vulnerable; prone to accidents; and the slightest event at

MB's home, out of the ordinary, may give you infinite pain & prolong your unhappiness. Whereas in view of your recent recovery, accompanied by the successful completion of your novel, acceptance of poems, promising interview etc., you should be in a position to stick your tongue out at MB and tell him to go bake in hell while you fornicate with the Muse. Try by not trying, and don't go to MB's home. Who's he, after all, to order you around like a mistress?

A few months before this, early in May 1961, Johnson seems to have spent an evening with Frank Lissauer during which they had had a long, intimate, confidential conversation. Johnson gave him a full account of his superstitious fears: his belief that he would die at twenty-nine, that he would never have a successful romantic relationship (with a woman), the 'physical manifestation of the Goddess' and his subsequent bondage to the life of a poet. He also discussed his relationship with Michael Bannard, and asked Lissauer for advice as to what should be considered 'normal' and 'abnormal'. On 15 May, after he had had time to digest the conversation, Lissauer replied:

Thank you for your card. It is not for you to be thanking me for listening, rather for me to thank you for confiding in me. I cannot keep my promise (did I promise?) not to make a few remarks about your story: if you would rather not read them you will not hurt me in the least by tearing this letter up now – but before you do, let me hasten to say that my remarks are in no sense judgments, except possibly on myself. I accept your story as true and credible.

[...] while I accept a certain inevitable isolation and positively seek solitude, I do not classify myself 'normal' or 'abnormal' (leaving that to others more interested in that aspect); I do believe, at the same time, that the poetry, such as it is, is the product of a friction of myself as I really am and as I choose to see myself in the context of human society. I am sorry if this is rather involved, but what I am trying to get at (in terms of mental economy, a concept very dear to me) is that for me it is more fruitful to think of myself in this way than to think of myself as possibly abnormal.

May I suggest you try to retell your story to yourself in this light, event by event, coincidence by coincidence? As you told it, it was not good fiction, either for verse or prose, being too true, and I cannot think how in itself it could serve as a very fruitful set of images. (Oh I know it's not concerned in this way and I do not mean to reduce it, except for the sake of talking about it.) I think your Goddess is an inspiration of the first importance (I should say a godsend) and would in no way detract from her or disbelieve you that you have seen her and know her. But I do believe your relations with girls may bear reinterpretation, for the benefit of your greater fruit of mind, in terms of *their* failures, and in terms of actual time. I think you may have become prejudiced and hardened by a sense of failure and by the mockery of MB who does not seem entirely a friend. I think it is also worth referring back to childhood and finding out why you should be so deeply influenced by a man like MB. I have always taken you for a person of great character and individuality, sceptical of all authority and attempts at domination; and you have surprised me often by your submission in face of criticisms, say, of your poems, and now submission to MB, and even more, to the idea that you should die within two years.

Now this is very serious and I beg you at least to pretend that you won't die so soon. Although you say you now feel well and happy, I do not believe that such an idea can be of any use to you either to living or writing. Go, by all means, to a doctor and have a really thorough examination. But chiefly re-examine your coincidences and see if you cannot dissipate the image of the hand of fate. I think you are worn down by the failure of so many excellent ventures, after the success of your acquiring by your own unaided efforts the education you wanted. Publication and fame are very slow and hard in coming, and it is not sufficient for your friends to testify to the quality of your work – you simply must finish the novel and test it against the resistance of publishers, or you will end up in a miserable state of frightened indecision where it is easier to live in the glow of reluctant rejections than to make the effort to convert a try [. . .]

Is this any use? I have talked about both of us simultaneously although I have mostly written 'you' and 'you'. In my own life, a story such as yours would have become at the moment of its crystallisation either untrue, proved wrong by subsequent experience; or a finer crystallisation in art. Don't let it be static in yours. MB is mercifully far away and Muriel doesn't deserve a thought. Please type your novel.

*

All of which, coming hard on the heels of my interview with Peter Dunsmore, rapidly undid most of the theories I had been contentedly spinning. Clearly – just as I had suspected at the outset – we were in fact dealing with a very complicated friendship, something much more fraught than the simple love affair between two men which I had been starting to construct in my mind. Why the talk of 'submission to MB'? Why was Johnson being advised to try 'referring back to childhood and finding out why you should be so deeply influenced by a man like MB'? What does Frank Lissauer mean by Bannard's ability to 'order you around like a mistress'? How could Bannard have 'ordered' Johnson to visit the family home when he wasn't even in the country? And why the occult imagery ('shun it like a portent', 'tell him to go bake in hell while you fornicate with the Muse')?

It was almost starting to sound as if Michael Bannard might be the self-same 'occultist' who in Gordon Bowker's (obviously distorted, second- or third-hand) version of events 'seemed to exercise a strange power over him. He might jump up in the middle of a family meal and leave the house saying that he "knew" this man wanted him'. If so, we might be looking at something akin to 'delusions of control' in Johnson's case: a sense of powerlessness, brought on by depression, in which the sufferer helplessly believes that all action is ultimately futile because his destiny is being determined by a force (or personality) much stronger than his own. This seems to have been what he felt in 1961. Was it what he felt in 1973?

The trail went cold at this point. I got on with the business of writing the central sections of this book. But my curiosity about Johnson's friendship with Michael Bannard wouldn't go away, and as it simmered at the back of my mind, it started to turn into something else, something unexpected. I became angry with Johnson. In my head I started talking to him, and saying: 'Look, Bryan.' (We were on first name terms by now.) 'You were the great advocate of honesty in the novel, right? You were the one who said that "Writers can extract a story from life only by strict, close selection, and this must mean falsification". You were the one who told us that you wrote to exorcise (an interesting choice of word!), to heal yourself of the pain of your most bruising experiences. So where is it, then? *Why did you never write about your friendship with this guy?* It's obvious that this was one of the most important and disturbing experiences of your life. Did you write about it and then destroy it, perhaps? And does that make things any better?'

Unfair, probably. It seems to me, from the reference in his 'Matrix Trilogy' notes to the 'Bannard letters' (which, if they existed, I never found), and 'the White Goddess experience' that Johnson must have been intending to write about these episodes in the second and third volumes, *Buried Although* and *Amongst Those Left Are You*. Perhaps that was why (or one of the reasons) he was so daunted by the whole project; why it defeated him, in the end. It would have taken phenomenal courage. Not that he was ever lacking in that quality.

In any case, a few months later, I made a discovery.

I had begun to see the Johnson archive – a vast construct of cardboard boxes and plastic bags, which for some years now had been shunted from room to room in Virginia's house at my whimsical behest – as a sort of large-scale version of *The Unfortunates*. That is, a narrative, not entirely lacking in order (remember the sections marked 'First' and 'Last'), but never intended to be read in a strictly linear sequence: rather, something to be shuffled and arranged randomly by the reader, as a way of replicating the chaos of life and the unstructured human consciousness. And I must admit that, although I'd done my best to catalogue, roughly, everything in the different boxes, and to go through their contents methodically, I had tended to favour the most personally revelatory material, at the expense of things that seemed largely of academic interest. *Travelling People*, for instance, exists in several different manuscript and typescript versions, and I have never collated them all: some tenured Johnson scholar can tackle that one in the future. Similarly, I had not read, from start to finish, the handwritten manuscript of *Albert Angelo*. A dereliction of duty on my part, I know. But I'm human like the rest of them.

It was Claire Andrews who pointed out to me that *Albert Angelo* contains the only reference to Michael Bannard in all of Johnson's published work. He is mentioned in passing, on the very first page, as the 'Graham' who used to inhabit Albert's flat in Percy Circus. (For which, read 'Claremont Square'.) We are told that he was 'bleeding round the twist', used to listen to strange music, and could often be heard 'groaning and saying his prayers with beads'. And that's about it. The briefest, most derisory of cameo appearances. Probably Johnson's revenge on him for all that 'mockery' of his ambitions that he had to put up with.

Except that there was, I realized, more. A whole lot more. One sunny morning in August 2002, surrounded yet again by all those bloody boxes, defeated by the sheer volume of paperwork I was supposed to absorb and steer my way through, I reached out for the closest thing to hand and found it was a plastic carrier bag containing the *Albert Angelo* manuscript. And there it was, tucked away at the back, deleted, never used: the original opening of the novel, which appeared to tell nothing less than the story of Bryan Johnson and Michael Bannard, from start to (almost) finish.

Johnson wrote this narrative at Joe McCrindle's cottage in Winchelsea, in December 1962. I shall present it here, and you can make of it what you will. Decide for yourselves whether it answers any of my questions. I have not tidied it up in any way, so you must bear the following things in mind:

1. The gaps are Johnson's own – details he was going to fill in later. Likewise, the words in brackets reflect his own uncertainty about using them.
2. 'Graham' is Michael Bannard; 'Samuel' (not re-named 'Albert' until Johnson typed the novel) is B. S. Johnson.
3. Scenes set in Winchelsea are based on events which actually took place in Banbury.
4. As a novelist, Johnson was not fully committed to 'truth' yet, so, as in the published book, there is a certain amount of fictionalizing. 'Samuel' has been made an aspiring architect (not, like Johnson, an aspiring poet), so the scenes where Samuel and Graham discuss

architecture cannot be read as true recollections of discussions between Johnson and Michael Bannard. Nonetheless, I'm convinced that the bulk of this narrative is truth, not fiction.

5. This section was supposed to begin on the first page of the novel, immediately after the words, 'Oh, yes, I knew Graham. Well.'

46: DELETED EPISODE FROM *ALBERT ANGELO*

(The narrative begins in March 1955)

Oh, yes, Samuel knew Graham. Well. If anyone ever knew anyone well, Samuel knew Graham well. Graham knew Samuel well. Well. There was an electric unspeakable inexplicable knowing between them, like the blood-bond of Siamese twins.

Samuel and Graham had both worked for Amalgamated-Consolidated,* a giant American-owned (multipod) which spread its overgrown weight deadeningly but profitably across the Free World in defiance of humanity and the anti-trust laws.

On Samuel's first day at Amalcon, Graham had come (sweeping) into Samuel's part of the office, floating a sheet of pastel pink paper and walking quickly with long strides in counterpoint to the rhythm of a (snatch) of modern music he was humming:

His head jerked to either side to a further counterpoint rhythm seemingly not connected. He stopped, and when he spoke to Samuel about some point on which their employments coincided, it was archly, arrogantly: then their eyes met and a strange thing happened. It was as if they had exchanged minds for a second, synchronously. Graham had then turned, ignoring what he had come in for, resumed his whistling, to the intense annoyance of controller Dubois, and had swept out.

Later, on the same day, Samuel received a note by the inter-office messenger service: "RFH – 7 – Tonight. Coming?" Without asking who had sent it, but sensing, knowing, who it was, he had written 'Yes' on it and directed the messenger to return it.

Graham knew infinitely more about music than Samuel did. A small string ensemble played a programme of pre-Bach baroque, and Graham spent all of the interval telling Samuel about its aims in (striving) to

---

* i.e. the Standard-Vacuum Oil Company (Stanvac).

perform the music as its composer intended, and with exactly the instrumentation for which it was written. During the performance Graham was completely absorbed, eyes closed, head swaying (to crescendo rhythms). Samuel was less than absorbed (concentration on music comes only with considerable practice), and often glanced at Graham's face. His attention was as much on the architecture of the hall as on the music, and after the concert, to speak about something he knew about, he tried to tell Graham of his admiration for the RFH. Graham dismissed his enthusiasm, however, saying that the boxes reminded him irresistibly of the open drawers of chocolate (vending) machines (on tube stations) and ridiculing the lavatory splash guards which shielded only the centre and not the sides, where he considered naturally-splayed feet should stand. Samuel found that he could not argue with Graham, or have him admit the good points. Graham was always like this: his desire was to score points and to pass on quickly to something else. He talked constantly about the music, and Samuel found himself listening in spite of himself, and learning, too. He was not required to say anything, it seemed.

Samuel could connect nothing he did at Amalcon with the real world: this world of paper and requisitions and transfers and invoices had nothing to do with any world he knew. The people there, too, were inhuman. Samuel saw, for instance, only one touch of humanity in controller Dubois during the whole of his 2 years there: this was when, Samuel once having cramp from the position he had taken up in his Naturo-Posture chair, Dubois told him that he used to wake up every morning with cramp in his upper arm where his wife had lain on it during the night; he added that this was early in the marriage, before the child came.

It was the utter deadness of Amalcon that drew Samuel and Graham into an alliance. They used the place, Graham much more daringly than Samuel: they would send each other interdepartmental memos several times a day on such important matters as the methods of reproduction commonly employed by worms, and each kept his own file of these memos. They used the callup system to remind themselves of concerts and theatres for which they had booked, and, later when they had been found out, for fictitious events like Royal Garden Parties.

Samuel often wondered why he and Graham were not dismissed, until he realised that Amalcon prided itself on its employee selection procedure and any dismissal was regarded as an indictment of it. They said you had to rape a typist, twice, before they would consider sacking you.

Samuel had a highly developed conscience: but it did not elude [*sic*] him for taking his eight pounds a week from Amalcon for relatively little work. He saw himself as giving more than eight pounds' worth of work, though not as much as the company exploited from most [of] the other employees. And in any case he thought that since society in general had refused to give him the chance to do what he was interested in, he owed it nothing; and the nearest thing he could epitomise society by was Amalcon.

Graham made great demands on Samuel's time: not that Samuel resented it, for he did not, but that it left him little time for anything else. They went to concerts four or five times a week: to the RFH, to the Albert Hall (which Samuel respected and laughed at, as a building, at the same time), to Wigmore Hall (which Samuel just laughed at) and to all sort of churches with musical incumbents and drawing-rooms with musical daises. When they did not go to concerts they went to the theatre or to opera or ballet.

Always it was Graham who was leading, teaching Samuel: not that Samuel minded this, either, for he did not, either, for he did not mind learning from anyone, anyone, but that it created in him a huge debt of obligation which he felt he would rather not bear, rather not bear, and he had after all much of his own to give, to teach Graham. As when, for instance, he saw for himself for the first time the essential nature of an octagon, perceived it in its eightsidedness, realised, apprehended its unique itness, and tried to share it with Graham: who was strangely resentful, and aggressively changed the subject, chattering on illogically about music; Samuel felt he had not been listening even, and stored the eightsidedness of an octagon carefully within himself never to show it again.

Later, however, Graham realised that not to appear to let Samuel teach him something would ruin his own need to impose his own teaching, destroy his audience. Therefore they would now visit places of Samuel's choosing, for the architecture, Syon House with its

Lancaster House with its

Best of all, Samuel would take Graham to Sir John Soane's House in Lincoln's Inn Fields, not far from Amalcon's offices, and talk to him about the architect's home, and try to communicate his enthusiasm about architecture. The two of them would go into the picture room (cunningly designed by Soane to accommodate three times as many pictures as any other room its size) and swing back the huge hinged frames to look at the drawings of Piranesi and Clérisseau and at Soane's composite paintings of buildings he had designed or dreamed of design-ing, usually to the annoyance of tourists and other non-Londoners who wanted to look at Hogarth's *Rake's Progress* and nothing else. One lunch-hour Graham had stood at the door refusing to let anyone else enter while Samuel gazed at his favourite picture: '*Architectural Visions of early fancy in the Gay Morning of youth – and dreams in the evening of life*'. For this Graham was banned from the museum: but for twenty minutes Samuel had managed to be alone with Soane's visions of domes and cupolas, collonnades and porticos, flights of steps and . And Graham was pleased to have done that for Samuel.

They would spend hours discussing their ideal building. Graham's contribution was a composite of all the features he enjoyed: the coffered dome of St Stephen's Walbrook over the hall, the 4-pillared canopy over the altar of Westminster Cathedral in his chief bedroom, a long library like that at Syon, the double-cube room at Wilton House for a living-room, and a collonnaded courtyard round three sides of an area the size of a football pitch. This composite demand he presented to Samuel to design.

Samuel's solution was to set the whole on a vast ferro-concrete raft which was pivoted at the north to swing daily through a hundred and eighty degrees with the sun, so that the shadows in the double cube room were always at nearly the same lateral angle, and the sun never reached the calf-bound books in the library. Outside this raft were balustraded terraces, and, to east and west, revolving homes based on Nervi, for the servants, each revolving at a different speed according to the servant's status.

Samuel had been interested at school in becoming an architect, but no one at school had been interested in Samuel becoming an architect. And since, because the system is on the side of inertia, Samuel was not strong enough to fight it himself, he had been pipelined into Amalcon.

When they began to demolish the Holborn Restaurant, Graham and Samuel went in every lunch-hour. Auction of the contents was going on at the same time. They could wander freely through all the rooms. In one there was a piano; Graham played a piece he had composed, loudly and frenetically, and dedicated it to Samuel. In another there were Masonic robes; Samuel put one on and intoned a mock spell at which Graham was suddenly horrified and brutal. They found their way to the gallery of a blackened bombed-out hall, and were startled by the appearance of a woman who said she had worked there before the war, gazing nostalgically at the tiled debris-strewn floor and smutted mosaic walls and pillars. The last time they had gone there they had turned on a gas-tap in a deserted room and hurried out: all that afternoon at Amalcon they had sat there waiting for the explosion, and at about four there had been a dull thud. Graham came into Samuel, sank his eyes into his for a moment, and left. But when they went out at five-thirty the building was still there.

Graham hated women: it was not that he was homosexual, for he was not. He just hated women. He loved his mother. He told Samuel he was impotent. The closeness of their relationship was always of the mind. Indeed, their bodies touched only twice. The first time when they sat back to back on a hot summer evening in the arena at a prom and the points of contact seemed to burn together so that they thought they might never come apart; and the second time when, crossing a road, Graham caught at Samuel's hand to save him from stepping in front of a lorry and an intense feeling transmitted itself to them both, at once exhilarating and terrifying. It was as though God had made another ballsup and had made Samuel's other half almost a man instead of wholly a woman. But Graham was not homosexual, just neuter.

This was why it was so funny when the head of London Amalcon hauled Graham over the coals for his allegedly adulterous relationship with a married woman on the staff. Graham defended with spirit his right to true love and adultery with whomsoever he pleased, as long as it was not in the company's time, and only Samuel knew how impossible it was. Graham was friendly with the woman only because she was a neuter like himself, and needed his friendship.

Sometimes Graham would go off for days at a time, alone, just vanish from Amalcon, and meet Samuel as if by some uncanny method of detection, as he was descending an escalator, or going into Flo's for lunch.

On one such occasion Samuel was in Southampton Row trying to get into the closed train (tunnel viaduct) to the Embankment when he saw Graham, very tired and dishevelled, standing on an island, just standing, and beckoning. And they had started walking north, up Southampton Row, across Euston Road, up until they came to Kenwood. Graham found a toad, kissed it on the head and commanded Samuel to do the same. Samuel did. It was raining. They crashed wildly through azaleas and laurels and rhododendrons until they reached the duelling-ground. Taking up positions, they duelled with horror-words: Samuel finally won, 'Tchaikovsky' crumpling up Graham into a damp, scream-ing heap on the stunted turf. They were both very young.

In the house, a concert began two minutes after they arrived: a great Russian woman singing sad Ukrainian songs at the right-angled intersection of two series of rooms. Samuel sat bemused by the facets of the crystal chandeliers, pendant liquid light and fire reflected by angled mirrors into a holocaust of feeling within him. Between two songs they noticed how strangely alike their left hands were.

The toad was waiting for them. It was nearly dark. Graham circled slowly and fearfully round it and then he thrust something into Sam-uel's hand and ran across the heath crying and screaming. Samuel saw that it was a voluted, gnarled shell. He walked home.

It was not the same after that. Samuel suspected everything Graham said, began to find out things that he had accepted as true from Graham were not, resented his glib generalisations and snap aesthetic judgements. Not that anything was said, for it was not; but they both sensed a new tension. Graham's reaction was to give in more to Samuel, to appease him, seek less to dominate him. He took him down Hungerford Lane, for instance, delighting in showing him the whitewashed vaults, and the roofs and fire-escapes forming a kind of chaotic clerestory on one side. Samuel thought that this must be a surviving part of the complex of the Adelphi, and was pleased with it, but careful not to show his pleasure to Graham. Most of the time they were together there was now a sullen silence between them. Yet still there was a mystical oneness, connection. Samuel began less and less to see him, and became friendly with a brunette in the office whom Graham spitefully referred to as the blackhead.

There had been a long-standing arrangement to visit Graham's parents one weekend that Samuel felt he ought to honour. Graham had built up a tremendous picture of his mother and his home for Samuel. She lived at Rye, and they went from Charing Cross one Friday evening to the

(image)

Graham's mother ran a pub in a back street. She was dumpy, with grey hair tensed into a bun, and aged about seventy. She had enormous energy and was devoted to her son: Graham responded to her with a synthetic show of love which sickened Samuel. The home was very little as Samuel had been led to expect. So was Graham's room, the holy of sanctuaries talked about so much. His reaction was to go to the other extreme and allow nothing connected with Graham to be good, in his severe disillusionment. The cat there was the only thing Samuel allowed himself to like, a proud, warm cat upon whom he spitefully lavished the affection and communication he denied to Graham. Only at one point was it suddenly like it was, when they discovered a common interest in fishing: but Samuel brutally and brusquely changed the subject. Graham took Samuel walking towards Winchelsea; awkwardly climbing over a wire fence he fell towards Samuel and clutched at him to save himself, grasping the loose flesh on his arm and making him wince disgustedly. Samuel was disgusted, and did not speak again. That evening they caught the wrong train through a mistake by Graham, and had to wait two hours to catch one back; Samuel was speechless with fury and misery and trudged off without a word when they reached London.

As if in revenge, Samuel plunged into a wild, incongruous affair with the Blackhead, whose name (was) (can be) Doreen, and at the same time he was trying to find a school of architecture which would accept him as a student. Someone advised him to try applying to teacher training colleges as well, so he did. Samuel's strength in thus trying to overcome the inertia which had landed him at Amalcon was almost entirely due to knowing Graham, and he felt guiltily indebted to him for it. No architectural school would take him for at least 2 years ahead, and Samuel felt that he could not wait that long to leave Amalcon. He therefore accepted the place offered him by a X X college at Norwich, which seemed the most architecturally interesting town of those who did reply favourably to his application.

In the lunch-hour of his last day at Amalcon, he found himself walking down High Holborn behind Graham. Mischievously, elated by the fact that he was opting out of the ratrace, he whistled the fragment from *Sacre* to which he and Graham had given especial significance:

Graham turned round, furious, his eyes wide in a kind of curse, hating Samuel. He turned his head round again, and Samuel could see how red his neck had gone, and he hated himself.

That afternoon Graham came bouncing into Samuel's part of the office and in a frenzied, shouting attack said that Samuel would never be an architect, that he had treacherously betrayed all that was good in him and in the world, that he would now be earthbound, of the earth, and that his small spark of spirit would prick and burn him still. And that he would die at 29. A lot more of this hysterical shouting Samuel could not understand at all. Graham stumbled out before Dubois could decide whether to call the police or tackle him himself. Samuel felt highly embarrassed, and left at once without completing the afternoon. A collection for him by Doreen raised 7/1d, and the girl had added enough herself to buy a 7/6d Boots token which she gave him on behalf of [*sic*] when she saw him that evening; Samuel bought contraceptives with it; he felt it was appropriate.

I don't know how important you think all this rubbish about Samuel and Graham, or how much you want to know; but I'm going to take a chance and skip a few years.

Graham was malevolently regarding the splashguards in the west firstfloor lavatory of the RFH when Samuel saw him again. Suddenly he felt the unity between them again; so did Graham, for he turned and their eyes locked as they had done the first time.

After the concert they walked at random north, talking: over Waterloo Bridge, half round Aldwych, up Kingsway, along Holborn, then

round by (State House) (where Graham introduced Samuel to the —
piece of sculpture by Barbara Hepworth), along Theobald's Road, past
Gray's Inn, along King's X Road. Then Graham turned uphill right
towards the Angel, saying that this was where he lived.

The first thing about Percy Circus is that it is on a hill, sideways.
Then the next thing is that half of it is not there. There are trees in the
circular patch in the middle – planes mostly, but some — as well. Some
of the houses have patches where new London stocks show up yellow
against the old blackened ones, and Samuel realised what had happened
to the rest of the Circus. He accurately dated it as early Victorian by the
windows, which had stucco frames as wide as the reveals were deep,
with a scroll ornamentation at the top. The houses' proportions were
quite good, though the move away from Georgian was obvious except
in the top and lead-flashed dormer windows. There was stucco channelled jointing up to the bottom of the first floor windows, which were
graced by little castiron balconies which swelled enceintly. The paint-
work everywhere was brown and old and peeling.

Samuel was enchanted. Graham invited him in for coffee. The
proportions of the rooms seemed perfect to him: (give details)
Graham had two rooms on the ground floor, looking out and upwards
across the circus.

Graham was leaving for India in a few weeks' time. He still worked,
surprisingly to Samuel, for Amalcon, using them and exploiting them
more than they him, he said. He felt the answer to everything, for him,
was to be found in India, and he had engineered his (life) so that
Amalcon paid for him to go there. Both of them at once had the idea
that Samuel should take over the flat when Graham left: suddenly there
was the same bond restored between them as it was at Kenwood, the
same mystical one-ness. Both knew it would not be the less for their
being physically apart, Graham in India, Samuel in London.

On Graham's last evening they went to a wine-cellar forming part
of the Adelphi. The Greek meaning of the word hit Samuel: and he
remembered all the coincidences of this nature in connection with
Graham, and now believed he saw that they were not coincidences.

They walked up Hungerford Lane together, under the arches' groins
past the crazy clerestory above: and Samuel confessed that he had
brought Jenny* the girl he loved through here once and had shown her
what Graham had shown him, and was guilty about it. Graham knew
somehow already, and said there was nothing to be done about past
betrayal, nothing at all: that it was at least easier to know it. He said that
Samuel would be, was being, punished for it, and would not cease to be

---

*   i.e. Muriel.

until his death. And reminded Samuel that this would be when he was twenty-nine. Samuel had sensed, had known, this since Graham had made it spoken between them that afternoon six years before; but had refused to accept it; it was too ludicrous. Now he told Graham he accepted it, while he was with him, but would not feel it was true afterwards.

Graham said they would not meet again. Samuel gave him back the — shell as they parted.

* * * * *

And there it ends. Johnson seems to have cut the passage even from his earliest drafts of *Albert Angelo*: a later sentence was to have explained that 'There was a long section about Graham just here, but I cut it out because Graham bored me.' Further on he lamented that, 'I needn't have written it at all. I wasted all that time. And shed no tears because you know little (and will hear no more) of Graham. I assure you he was boring.' But in the end, he cut even that.

Cuts! Yes, cuts!

It seems to me, now, that here we have the significance of the famous holes in the pages of *Albert Angelo*. Just as the boxed format of *The Unfortunates* was a 'physical, tangible metaphor for randomness', so the holes in the pages of *Albert Angelo* are richly symbolic (whether Johnson intended it or not) of the profound *absence* at the heart of the novel. The absence of the crucial section which explains...

Well, what does it explain, exactly?

When the poet and critic John Horder wrote to me (some years ago now, on 19 February 1997) to share his belief that B. S. Johnson was basically homosexual, with a 'tragic desire to pass as straight', he warned me that one or two of Johnson's surviving friends – whom he described as 'raving heterosexuals' – would laugh the idea out of court. And indeed, for my own part, I think that Horder massively overstates his case. But surely not even the most raving heterosexual could deny the homoerotic undertones of this deleted section. It's there from the very beginning in the reference to 'the electric unspeakable inexplicable knowing between them, like the blood-bond of Siamese twins'. Also: 'their eyes met and a strange thing happened. It was as if they had exchanged minds for a second, synchronously'; 'they sat back to back on a hot summer evening in the arena at a prom and the points of contact seemed to burn together so that they thought they might never come apart'; 'Graham caught at Samuel's hand to save him from stepping in front of a lorry and an intense feeling transmitted itself to them both, at once exhilarating and terrifying'; 'light and fire reflected by angled mirrors into a holocaust of feeling within him'; 'Between two songs they noticed how strangely alike their left hands were'; and, of course, most tellingly of all, 'It was as though God had made another ballsup and had made Samuel's other half almost a man instead of wholly a woman.'

I would deduce from all this, certainly, taking this section as a piece of autobiography, that Johnson had felt quite powerful (and disturbing) homo-erotic feelings for Michael Bannard in 1955, but had decided not to act upon them.

M wanted to go too deep and I was too scared to follow him

> Recalling your intense obliqueness,
> the unsaid things we knew together,
> you would disapprove; whether
> you are right I cannot say,
> but you would call it treacherous weakness
> that I thus take the normal way.

In his (also unpublished) play *The Proper End*, Johnson wrote about 'the double-entry theory of love: love automatically creates a force of hatred which is its opposite, its equal, its complement, its corollary'. This would equally seem to apply to whatever happened between him and Michael Bannard on that rainy day at Kenwood. But even here, in writing this scene, Johnson himself showed such 'intense obliqueness' that it's not really clear what is going on. Where has 'Graham' produced this 'voluted, gnarled shell' from, and why does he thrust it into 'Samuel's' hand? Samuel returns the shell at the end of the section, so presumably – in real life – Johnson gave it back to Bannard in April 1961, and that was why it was waiting for him in the bedroom of Bannard's parents' house in Banbury when he went there in October that year: *'M's room –* the *shell first thing to catch my eye – it seems to be central thing in room – did he ask her to put it there? Or is it intended to be the centre?'* (And just now, re-typing those words, I realize the significance of the question 'did he ask her to put it there?' Johnson thinks Michael Bannard might have asked his mother to arrange the room in a certain way; in other words, Bannard knows that Johnson is making this visit – *he has gone there at his behest.*)

Even more extraordinary is the way that 'Samuel' makes 'Graham' *kiss a toad* while they are at Kenwood together. Did such a scene *really* take place, between B. S. Johnson and Michael Bannard, in 1955? I believe that it must have done. What does it mean, then? Well, it refers to witchcraft, apparently. This is supposed to be one of the methods by which witches are anointed into the coven:

1. The members or novices were marked by the prick of a needle while they renounced their Maker.

2. They were compelled to kiss a toad.
3. They must abjure God and promise to obey the commands of the devil.
etc.*

So, unlikely though it seems, it may be that sometimes, when he was feeling at his most vulnerable and depressed, Johnson believed that there was some sort of occult bond between himself and Michael Bannard; that Bannard had supernatural power over him; that the pact between them had sinister ('they noticed how strangely alike their left hands were'), even Satanic overtones. (As he wrote in his diary on 14 October 1961: '*The forces who control my life know my needs, whether I conjure them or not; and since I do not know their true identity, I might well be messing about with something dangerous and evil.*')

Perhaps what really scared him, in all of this, was the thought that he might be being offered the possibility of escape: of escaping from his very nature, and finding a different sexual identity. Perhaps that was just one uncertainty too many.

But of course, we can never know something like that. Not for certain. It's a good story, that's all: and that's probably why it appeals to the novelist in me.

There is also something touching about this deleted section, however. I like the idea of Johnson and Bannard as 'adelphi' – brothers: it makes him seem less alone, at the end. He was so depressed by the Rhesus negative story, the thought that he might have been responsible for his sister's death in the womb. He hated being an only child. So of course, on that last night, with his wife gone and nobody to talk to, it was natural that he should seek out his 'brother'.

This brother had been cruel to him, all the same. Throughout his life, Johnson had continually suffered rejection, of one sort or another: Michael Bannard had been the only person *he* had ever rejected, and he was hated for it, and made to suffer for it. That night in April 1961, when Johnson took over his flat, Bannard had reminded him again that he had 'betrayed' him by taking the 'normal way', and told him that he 'would be, was being, punished for it, and would not cease to be until his death'.

Did he believe that, I wonder? Did he ever really believe it?

I'm sure Michael Bannard didn't say it to him on the night of 11 November 1973. Or at least, not in so many words. But he might well have said something (I am speculating here, but carefully) along the lines of 'I

---

* My source for this is a website, www.red4.co.uk/Folklore/trevelyan/welshfolklore/chapt16. htm, which deals mainly with witchcraft in Wales.

told you so.' 'Graham hated women,' Johnson states, bluntly, in the deleted section. Peter Dunsmore, more tactfully, told me that Bannard believed 'that woman was on the one hand the possible inspiration for creative work, and ultimately its destroyer, through failure to understand, through trivializing, not being on the same high plane of intellectual and creative life. He was always complaining about friends who got married.' Tormented by this theory, and by the domineering conviction with which his friend expressed it and lived according to it, Johnson had been determined to prove him wrong: he *could* be a successful writer and still have a beautiful wife and children and a happy domestic life. It *was* possible. And indeed, for some years, it had been. Everything had been going so well. But now here he was, his domestic life (apparently) fracturing, his latest novel (apparently) rejected, coming back to his friend and pleading for a bed for the night. *I told you so* ... Could he have resisted saying it? Or making it clear that he thought it?

Let's see what *The White Goddess* has to say about poetry and domesticity. Here we are – page 449 of the 1961 Faber edition:

> The reason why so remarkably few young poets continue nowadays to publish poetry after their early twenties is not necessarily – as I used to think – the decay of patronage and the impossibility of earning a decent living by the profession of poetry [...] The reason is that something dies in the poet. Perhaps he has compromised his poetic integrity by valuing some range of experience or other – literary, religious, philosophical, dramatic, political or social – above the poetic. But perhaps also he has lost his sense of the White Goddess: the woman whom he took to be a Muse, or who was a Muse, turns into a domestic woman and would have him turn similarly into a domesticated man. Loyalty prevents him from parting company with her, especially if she is the mother of his children and is proud to be reckoned a good housewife; and as the Muse fades out, so does the poet [...] The White Goddess is anti-domestic; she is the perpetual 'other woman', and her part is difficult indeed for a woman of sensibility to play for more than a few years, because the temptation to commit suicide in simple domesticity lurks in every maenad's and muse's heart.

Ah. That strikes a few chords, as well.

But of course there is (again) another way of looking at it.

*

I have several favourite images of B. S. Johnson. I love the thought of him being slapped on the back by Jacques Tati at that film festival dinner, glowing with pride but still scarcely able to raise a smile. Or being carried up from a Budapest wine cellar, all seventeen stone of him – drunk as a skunk – by two Hungarians, while Bill Holdsworth and his friend sing the ballad of Harry Pollitt. But my absolute favourite is another Hungarian image: Johnson in the village of Szentlőrinc, on a hot summer's afternoon, happily reading his poetry to a crowd of teenagers when all he had been expecting was a long lazy lunch with György Novák.

Novák never heard from Johnson again after receiving the letter in which he had described himself as a 'fat foolish man'. He assumed that he was busy, that he had things on his mind, that another letter would come in a month or two. Then, in the January 1974 edition of a Hungarian literary magazine called *Nagyvilág*, he read the news of his death. Devastated, bewildered, he wrote to Philip Pacey, another of Johnson's close friends (was ever a suicide more surrounded by close, loving friends?). Pacey had also been one of the first academics to publish something about Johnson, in *Stand* magazine. He wrote a long letter back to Novák on 15 January 1974, explaining some of the factors, as he saw them, behind the suicide.

> [...] The tragedy is that it was all so unnecessary: if they had both worked at it they could have mended the marriage. Bryan gave in too soon – because of his lack of confidence. I feel quite certain that *that* is to blame.
>
> It is my belief that Bryan's lack of self-confidence goes back to his early life. In *Trawl* he seemed to trace it back to the experience of being separated from his mother when he was evacuated in the war: the first of the 'betrayals' which he writes about there and in the poems, of which, in his eyes, Virginia's must have been the last and the one he could not bear. I am sure he is right to go back to his childhood and his relationship with his mother, but possibly he would have to have gone further back to get at the real origin of his troubles. The 'object relations' psychology of Klein, Guntrip, and Winnicott may throw light on this: they say that the source of our confidence in the outside world lies in our infant relationships with the world in the person of our mother, who at first *is* the world to us. As you know, Bryan was working on a trilogy of novels to be called 'Matrix', in which he was going to write about his mother and the mother-goddess, the earth-mother. I think this must have been an intuitive attempt to get to the root of the problem and exorcise it once and for all. It is probably significant that, after completing the first volume, he said that he thought he might not be able to go on with it. It must have been a difficult and painful challenge; I believe it was something he simply had to do *if* he was going to break out of his self-imposed limits as a novelist, and if he was going to break out of his self-imposed limits as a person, and heal himself. These limits were his defence; he could not believe because he

dared not believe; he retired into his own shell and wrote inside that, because he dared not be open to the world. And he rationalised his position by saying that 'all is chaos', so there is no reason to be open to it, and every reason to close oneself up.

What strikes me now, re-reading Bryan's books as I have been doing since he died, is that they are full of signs pointing to the likelihood of what actually happened. This is especially true of *Trawl*: you remember he comes back from that voyage looking forward to getting married to Virginia (Ginnie) – but he says to himself that this is the *last chance* he is going to give life; or in other words, if this marriage doesn't work, he will kill himself. It seems to me that in those circumstances, with that clearly written in the book (whatever he may have said to her), it was very brave of Virginia to marry him and to try to give him the home which would help him survive [. . .] Probably we should be thanking her for the books Bryan did write when he was with her. She tried and, I think, very nearly succeeded, not only to keep Bryan alive but to let him cure the trouble through his own creativity. It is my feeling that if *Matrix* could have been completed, all might have been well.

A good statement, I think, of the case against Graves (and Bannard): the case for domesticity as the saviour of art.

*

Is it true, what Philip Pacey says in this letter about Johnson's 'self-imposed limits as a novelist' and the way he 'retired into his own shell and wrote inside that'? This is not just a question of subject matter ('telling stories is telling lies') but also form and technique. Many of the people I interviewed about Johnson, while full of admiration for most aspects of his writing, felt that he had driven himself into a theoretical cul-de-sac, and that his dogmatic insistence on high modernist innovation as the only way forward for the novel was not really a serious literary aesthetic at all – more of a defensive posture, adopted to mask his insecurities. These were class insecurities, as much as anything. You can see why he so hated the gentlemen amateur novelists who thronged the literary salons of 1960s London: the ones who in turn looked down on *him* for insisting that he was paid like a professional, the people Giles Gordon called 'upperclass toffs who were writing for pin money because they could afford to do so'; but he was also scared, in a way, that he couldn't compete with them on their own turf. To be sure of winning, to be sure of being the *best* novelist in the country, better than any of those Oxbridge bastards, he had to move the goalposts – had to move onto a different pitch altogether, in fact, a pitch where he was almost the only player, so that he could say to them, 'Not only are your novels not as good as mine, but you haven't even *started*, you're not even writing *the right kind of novel'*.

In Chapter Five of *The White Goddess*, 'Gwion's Riddle', Robert Graves discussed a Welsh romance in which

> someone who styled himself Little Gwion [...] a person of no import-ance, accidentally lighted on certain ancient mysteries and, becoming an adept, began to despise the professional bards of his time because they did not understand the rudiments of their traditional poetic lore.

That's Johnson, isn't it? Bryan = Little Gwion. Even the name seems to fit. Acting on a hunch, I consulted his own copy of *The White Goddess* – not the one he must have read as a teenager (I was never able to find that), but the one Zulfikar Ghose gave him in 1961 – and sure enough, there was that same passage, on page 75, underlined by Johnson himself. He must have seen the parallel.

Oh, yes. I know him pretty well by now.

*

But how well, exactly?

If the eight years I've spent writing this book have taught me anything, they've taught me that biographers enter into a strange relationship with their subjects: at once very intimate, and very distant. Sometimes I think that no one could understand B. S. Johnson as thoroughly as I do now, having had the privilege of seeing him from so many different angles, through the filter of so many different people's impressions and memories. Then again, I never met the man, let alone lived with him, or had him for a father. You can't argue with that kind of first-hand knowledge. Can you? And in the same way, my own relationship to him as a writer is oblique, ambiguous. I've had many dreams about Johnson in the last few years, and in all of those dreams (which invariably find him alive, well, and choosing to live in secrecy a few miles from his family home in north London), he has been perfectly friendly to me, but behind that, I've sensed an antagonism. Despite the fact that I come from a fairly ordinary middle-class family, and had a routine suburban upbringing in which books never loomed very large – never for a moment felt, in other words, the sense which I've occasionally noticed in some English writers of my generation, the sense of having *inherited* the right to literary eminence, and public attention – despite all of this, I had a fairly easy run of it from the age of eleven onwards, when I was sent to a selective, direct-grant school, and Cambridge seemed to follow almost as a matter of course. To be sure, I've got a fair stack of rejection slips dating from my mid-twenties, and three unpublished manuscripts tucked away in a bottom drawer, and when I did get published it was after being dug out from the slush pile: but still – 'There's never going to be an article called "Jonathan Coe – My Struggle", is there?', as a (working-class, state-educated) novelist said to me only semi-teasingly a few years ago. Johnson would probably have agreed, and seen me as 'one of that group of gifted or fortunate people' (the words, already quoted in this book, are from Zulfikar Ghose) 'whose class, together with an Oxbridge education, assures them of a privileged position in London's literary power struggle. Bryan despised them: perhaps because they were what he could not be, or because they acquired so easily what he, with his great talent, was denied.'

Slowly, as I continued work on the book, this antagonism of Johnson's – which I had intuited and which then wormed its way into my dreams – bred something similar on my side. My attitude towards him became more and more combative. Perhaps this needs to happen when you're writing biography. Perhaps (like the best double acts, or the best screenwriting partnerships) the form thrives on prickliness and tension. Perhaps a biography written out of pure love and admiration would become flaccid, inert, having no friction to power it along. For a while, anyway, he could do nothing right, as far as I was concerned. I found fault wherever I could. His theories were untenable; the novels themselves were weakened by the theories underpinning them; his own estimation of himself was inflated, and so on. It wasn't until I had finished the book, and been forced to lay it aside and stay away from it for a few months, that my feelings about him started to cool down. And in the end, I found myself coming full circle: rediscovering the excitement I had felt about him as a Warwick postgraduate, all those years ago.

But it's a different sort of excitement, now. How could it be otherwise, now that I know him so much better? At the very beginning of this book I wrote that it was only when I sensed Johnson's capacity for *doubt* ('confusion' might have been an even better word) that I felt him flicker into life. One of the interviewees who spoke most warmly, most lovingly about Johnson (Joebear Webb) also laid a special emphasis on this quality: 'There was agonizing self-doubt, bless him, you could see the self-doubt all over him, even when he was totally boisterous and Rabelaisian, you could still see his vulnerability.' Self-doubt, and vulnerability: these were the things, I've come to realize, that made B. S. Johnson the artist he was. The kind of self-certainty he affects in the introduction to *Aren't You Rather Young To Be Writing Your Memoirs?* is in fact the enemy of art. On the contrary, it was because he *agonized* over those novels, hovered endlessly on the brink of thinking them completely worthless, that they quiver with nervous energy even now; pulse with doubts about their own legitimacy. There may be a quality of 'QED' to his formal experiments but beneath that, at a much deeper level, there is a layer of insecurity which gives them an astonishing rawness, a self-questioning urgency that keeps them thrillingly alive. As

John Berger pointed out, both as a man and as a writer B. S. Johnson 'lacked the sort of protective carapace that other people have, but one has to add that his achievement wouldn't have been possible if he'd had that carapace. So that the lack of a carapace was intimately related – was the same thing, almost – as his talent and his vision and his originality.'

> And now I am curious to look
> Into the blinkered mind
> Of one who wants to write a book
> In a world of such a kind.

Robert Graves, in the book that Johnson revered above all others, wrote that 'The test of a poet's vision, one might say, is the accuracy of his portrayal of the White Goddess and of the island over which she rules.' By the same token, one might say that the test of a real novelist is that he or she will recognize the self-doubt, the paralysing uncertainty about the worth of their own vocation, that lie behind those lines of Thomas Hardy's. They are presumed to be spoken, of course, by the moon – the dedicatee of Johnson's last published novel, repeatedly identified by Robert Graves with the Goddess Johnson both worshipped and feared, and by whom he believed himself to have been visited.* Real novelists, picking up their pens in the morning, booting up their computers, ask themselves this question every day: Is it worth it? Is there any point? Without that bedrock of doubt, nothing that you write will have any value. Novel-writing is not a hobby (although we're allowed to find it enjoyable); it is not a form of therapy (although it can be therapeutic). It's an *intervention*, if it is anything: an act of lunatic faith in the notion that by adding something to the world we might somehow be improving it. The stakes are that high, and taking our lead from B. S. Johnson we should occasionally throw off our wretched middle-class English self-deprecation (with which he was so thoroughly unencumbered) and say as much. Not many novelists are prepared to do that: to own up to their *responsibilities* – to the form, to their readers, to the tradition that they are inheriting. *That* is what B. S. Johnson meant by 'writing as though it mattered, as though they meant it, as though they meant it to matter'.

I can't help seeing an analogy with religion here. B. S. Johnson did not, I think, have any real problem with religious belief, as long as it was held with seriousness, with honesty. The people he felt contempt for were the ones who flirted with religion, paid lip service to it because it was the decorous or respectable thing to do. As Thelma Fisher said: 'He felt that if you're religious then you'd better be serious about it. It was no use just being religious

---

* My thanks to Peter Dunsmore for drawing my attention to Hardy's poem in the first place. I don't know if Johnson himself ever knew it.

because in the 1950s people were. Nothing like that was good enough, you had to have thought it out and really worked at it.' It was the same with literature: there was no point in writing novels just because in the 1960s people did (and still do in the 2000s); if you were going to do it properly, you had to do it with real faith. And faith in the novel has this, at least, in common with faith in God: in both cases, you can always tell the genuine article because it will always be riddled with doubt. Which means that it's often the heretic who is closer to God than the regular, unquestioning churchgoer; and as I said before, probably the best way to think about B. S. Johnson's novels is to conceive of them not as experiments, but as literary heresies.

Like all heresies, his novels challenge our most fundamental beliefs: our belief in the moral integrity of 'fiction', our belief in the usefulness of storytelling when the daily truths thrown up by our misbegotten world cry out for immediate, practical attention. The challenge is posed not just by his work as a whole, but by each novel individually. We could ask ourselves whether we are 'writing as though it mattered', or we could be more specific than that, and ask ourselves: Is my first novel as adventurous, as risk-taking, as *Travelling People*? Have I ever written, or will I ever write, anything as ruthlessly self-interrogating as *Albert Angelo*? Could I ever match *Trawl* for a sustained feat of muscular lyricism and unsparing scrutiny of the past? Have I ever memorialized any of my own friendships as movingly as *The Unfortunates* does? Could I stare the worst of the human condition as rudely in the face as Johnson does in *House Mother Normal*? Do I have it in me to write a comedy as black and unsentimental as *Christie Malry's Own Double-Entry*? Could I walk right to the very edge of the novel's possibilities, and even put one foot suicidally over the precipice, as Johnson dared to do in *See the Old Lady Decently*? These are the questions that B. S. Johnson's novels should be forcing subsequent generations of writers to ask themselves. *Amongst Those Left Are We.* Here is the baton: do we have the courage to run with it?

And those are the last words I intend to write about B. S. Johnson. I write them, appropriately enough, late at night in the kitchen of my parents' house, at the same table where I can remember writing the final paragraph of my first published novel, in the same house where, even earlier than that, twenty-nine years ago, I watched *Fat Man on a Beach* with my uncomprehending family, and the image of that strange, compelling man burned itself onto my thirteen-year-old mind, although I had no idea where it was going to lead me. The same house ... the same table..... *I, always with I..... one always starts with I........ And ends with I.*

Birmingham
23 October 2003
12.39 a.m.

NOTES

Introduction

1. Zulfikar Ghose, 'Bryan', *Review of Contemporary Fiction*, vol. 5, no. 2 (Summer 1985), p. 23.
2. Press release for *The Unfortunates*, February 1969.
3. Introduction to *Aren't You Rather Young To Be Writing Your Memoirs?* (Hutchinson, 1973), p. 30.
4. *Travelling People* (Constable, 1963) p. 12.
5. Introduction to *Aren't You Rather Young To Be Writing Your Memoirs?*, p. 14.
6. Milan Kundera, *The Art of the Novel*, translated by Linda Asher (Faber & Faber, 1988), pp. 144–5.
7. Introduction to *Aren't You Rather Young To Be Writing Your Memoirs?*, pp. 18–19.

A Life in Seven Novels

1. Letter to Gordon Williams, 21 October 1966.
2. Introduction to *Aren't You Rather Young To Be Writing Your Memoirs?* (Hutchinson, 1973), p. 22.
3. Ibid., p. 14.
4. Ibid, p. 25.
5. Christine Brooke-Rose, *A Rhetoric of the Unreal* (Cambridge University Press, 1981), p. 358.
6. Introduction to *Aren't You Rather Young To Be Writing Your Memoirs?*, p. 26.
7. *Christie Malry's Own Double-Entry* (Delux Productions, Movie Masters, The Kassander Film Company and Woodline Films), directed by Paul Tickell, written by Simon Bent and starring Nick Moran as Christie.
8. Johnson, quoted in Michael Bakewell, Introduction to *See the Old Lady Decently* (Hutchinson, 1975), p. 8.
9. Jonathan Coe, Introduction to B. S. Johnson, *The Unfortunates* (Picador, 1999), p. viii.

The Goddess

1. Robert Graves, *The White Goddess* (Faber & Faber, 1961), p. 24.
2. 'Sheela-na-gig' in *Statement Against Corpses* (Constable, 1964), pp. 95–100.

Solitude

1. *See the Old Lady Decently* (Hutchinson, 1975) p. 46.
2. All quotations from *Trawl* so far have been from pp. 44–53 in the Secker & Warburg edition (1966), included in the *B. S. Johnson Omnibus* (Picador, 2004).
3. Ibid., pp. 53–4.
4. Ibid., p. 55.
5. From an unpublished article for the *Sunday Times* Magazine, special World Cup issue, written on 8 February 1966.
6. *Trawl*, pp. 162, 164.
7. *Statement Against Corpses* (Constable, 1964), p. 26.
8. Ibid., p. 21.
9. Letters to Anthony Smith, 1 July 1962.

Rather an Elderly Student

1. Letter to the author, 1 March 2002.
2. Letter to Stuart Crampin, 23 September 1957.
3. Letter to Lucia Glanville, 17 March 1960.
4. Zulfikar Ghose, 'Bryan', *Review of Contemporary Fiction*, vol. 5, no. 2 (Summer 1985), p. 32.
5. Ibid., p. 24.
6. Letter to Stuart Crampin, 5 April 1961.
7. Zulfikar Ghose, op. cit., p. 29.

Claremont Square

1. *Albert Angelo* (Constable, 1964), p. 103, also included in the *B. S. Johnson Omnibus* (Picador, 2004).
2. Letter to Stuart Crampin, 12 January 1962.
3. Letter to Anthony Smith, 29 March 1962.
4. Introduction to *Aren't You Rather Young To Be Writing Your Memoirs?* (Hutchinson, 1973), p. 17.

5. Source: www.roy-hart.com/awe.htm
6. Letter to Stuart Crampin, 23 December 1962.
7. Letter to Christine Brooke-Rose, 25 June 1965.
8. Letter to Roma Crampin (Williams), 26 March 1963.
9. *The Unfortunates* (Picador, 1999), 'Just as it seemed things were going his way', p. 4.
10. Ibid.
11. Ibid., p. 5.
12. Letter to Roma Crampin, 24 April 1963.

Ginnie and Albert

1. *Aren't You Rather Young To Be Writing Your Memoirs?* (Hutchinson, 1973), p. 85.
2. Letter to George Macbeth, 6 June 1963.
3. Introduction to *Aren't You Rather Young To Be Writing Your Memoirs?*, p. 14.
4. Zulfikar Ghose, 'Bryan' in *Review of Contemporary Fiction*, vol. 5, no. 2 (Summer 1985), p. 29.
5. Letter to Patrick Snaith, 22 January 1964.
6. Email to the author, 15 September 2002.

'Value This Man'

1. *The Unfortunates* (Picador, 1999), 'At least once he visited us', pp. 1–2.
2. Gordon Bowker, 'Remembering B. S. Johnson', *London Magazine*, vol. 40, nos. 7/8 (October–November 2000, pp. 45–54), p. 50.
3. *The Unfortunates*, 'June rang on the Saturday', p. 1.
4. Gordon Bowker, op. cit., p. 46.

The Pleasuretripper

1. David Farrer, *The Warburgs* (Michael Joseph, 1975), p. 233.
2. Email to Will Buckley, 23 October 1999, copied in to the author.
3. Ibid.
4. *London Life*, 29 January 1966, p. 4.
5. Letter to Zulfikar Ghose, 5 November 1965.
6. Letter to Ruth Liepman, 29 September 1965.
7. 'A Plea for the Minor Art of Playing on Pin-Tables', *London Life*, 30 April 1966.

The Laureate of Scunthorpe-on-Loire

1. Letter to Zulfikar Ghose, 19 December 1967.
2. Letter to Zulfikar Ghose, 28 January 1967.
3. Zulfikar Ghose, 'Bryan', in *Review of Contemporary Fiction*, vol. 5, no. 2 (Summer 1985), p. 26.
4. Letter to Johnson, 19 January 1968.
5. Email to Will Buckley, 23 October 1999, copied in to the author.
6. *Scene*, 7 (25 October 1962), p. 9.
7. An edited version was published in the *Listener* (23 March 1967), pp. 391–2.
8. Letter to Roma and Stuart Crampin, 23 November 1966.
9. Letter to Zulfikar Ghose, 15 March 1967.
10. Ibid.
11. Letter to Zulfikar Ghose, 26 July 1967.
12. Letter to Jeremy Brooks, 17 July 1967.
13. Letter to Jeremy Brooks, 18 July 1967.
14. Letter to Zulfikar Ghose, 26 July 1967.
15. Letter to Anthony Smith, 22 August 1967.
16. Letter to Zulfikar Ghose, 21 August 1967.
17. Letter to Zulfikar Ghose, 16 October 1967.
18. *Albert Angelo* (Constable, 1964), pp. 64–97
19. Letter to John Furse, 1 December 1967.
20. Ibid.
21. Letter to Barry Cole, 12 December 1967.
22. Undated postcard to Zulfikar Ghose.
23. Letter to John Furse, 15 December 1967.
24. Ibid.
25. Letter to Zulfikar Ghose, 16 January 1968.
26. Letter to Zulfikar Ghose, 16 January 1968.
27. Letter to Zulfikar Ghose, 2 February 1968.
28. These quotations are taken from a 1968 British Film Institute press release.

Hungary and Wales

1. Letter to Zulfikar Ghose, 19 February 1968.
2. Letter to John Furse, 19 February 1968.
3. Undated letter to Bob Hamilton, organizer of the ACTT.
4. Gordon Bowker, 'Remembering B S Johnson', *London Magazine*, vol. 40, nos. 7/8 (October–November 2000, pp. 45–54), p. 48.
5. Letter from Lorna Pegram, 26 October 1967.

6. Letter to John Furse, 18 August 1968.
7. Review for *Bookcase*, broadcast on the BBC World Service, 13 February 1969.
8. Ibid., 22 January 1969.
9. Letter to Joebear Webb, 3 August 1969.
10. Letter to the author, 22 July 2002.
11. Letter to Philip O'Connor, 30 July 1972.
12. Letter to Alison and Peter Smithson, 17 February 1970.
13. Letter to John Furse, 17 February 1970.
14. Letter to Rosemarie and Peter Buckman, 8 March 1970.
15. Letter to Zulfikar Ghose, 28 June 1970.
16. Letter to Zulfikar Ghose, 25 September 1970.
17. Introduction to *Aren't You Rather Young To Be Writing Your Memoirs?* (Hutchinson, 1973), p. 26.
18. The Gregynog Press and the Gregynog Fellowship, *The Private Library*, second series, vol. 6:1 (Spring 1973), pp. 4–15.

Bloody Doing Something about It

1. Letters to Zulfikar Ghose (28 June 1970) and Joebear Webb (29 July 1970).
2. Letter to Zulfikar Ghose, 25 September 1970.
3. Letter to Zulfikar Ghose, 28 June 1970.
4. Letter to Zulfikar Ghose, 21 December 1970.
5. George P. Garrett, 'B. S. Johnson (1933–1973)' in the *Dictionary of Literary Biography*, vol. 40, *Poets of Great Britain and Ireland since 1960*, ed. Vincent B. Sherry, Jr. (Detroit, Gale Research, 1985, pp. 277–82) p. 280.
6. David Dutton, *British Politics since 1945: The Rise and Fall of Consensus* (Oxford, Blackwell, 1991), p. 68.
7. All quotations are from the teleplay as published in *Transatlantic Review*, 45 (Spring 1973), pp. 55–75.

Disintegration

1. Letter from Zulfikar Ghose, 18 December 1972.
2. Letter to 'Mr Rathbone', Secretary, The Royal Town Planning Institute, 31 December 1972.
3. Letter to Zulfikar Ghose, 4 March 1973.
4. Eva Figes, 'B S Johnson', *Review of Contemporary Fiction*, vol. 5, no. 2 (Summer 1985), p. 71.
5. Zulfikar Ghose, 'Bryan', *Review of Contemporary Fiction*, vol. 5, no. 2 (Summer 1985), p. 26.

6. Letter to Zulfikar Ghose, 4 March 1973.
7. Letter to Zulfikar Ghose, 9 May 1973.
8. Letter to Zulfikar Ghose, 6 September 1973.
9. Ibid.
10. Eva Figes, op. cit., p. 71.
11. 'Everyone Knows Somebody Who's Dead', in *Aren't You Rather Young To Be Writing Your Memoirs?* (Hutchinson, 1973), p. 133.
12. Gordon Bowker, 'Remembering B S Johnson', *London Magazine,* Vol. 40, Nos. 7/8 (October–November 2000, pp. 45–54), p. 53.
13. Ibid.
14. Letter to Zulfikar Ghose, 12 December 1972.
15. Gordon Bowker, op. cit., p. 52.
16. Ibid., p. 51.
17. Peter Ackroyd, 'Fads' in *Spectator,* 3 May 1975, p. 545.
18. Letter to the author, 28 January 1997.

A Life in 44 Voices

1. Zulfikar Ghose, 'Bryan', *Review of Contemporary Fiction,* vol. 5, no. 2 (Summer 1985), p. 23.
2. Ibid., p. 31.
3. Letter to the author, 1 March 2002.
4. Zulfikar Ghose, op. cit., p. 26.
5. Letter to the author, 1 March 2002.
6. Postcard to the author, 19 February 1997.
7. Zulfikar Ghose, op. cit., p. 34.

A B.S. JOHNSON CHECKLIST

The aim of this checklist is to provide a comprehensive record of Johnson's published work, along with any significant completed works that were not published. Uncompleted works are not listed.

Johnson was a prolific journalist, and he wrote for a wide variety of literary and political magazines, some of them obscure even at the time. My procedure has generally been to work through his own file copies, checking them wherever possible against the published versions. However, inevitably some omissions will have occurred, and I would be grateful if they could be brought to my attention for correction in any future editions.

My thanks to Artemis Gause and Michael Seeney for research assistance with this checklist.

NOVELS

(UK editions only are noted)

Travelling People, London, Constable (1963); London, Transworld (1964); London, Panther (1967).

Albert Angelo, London, Constable (1964); London, Panther (1967); New York, New Directions (1987); London, Picador (2004) (as part of *B. S. Johnson Omnibus*).

Trawl, London, Secker & Warburg (1966); London, Panther (1968); London, Picador (2004) (as part of *B. S. Johnson Omnibus*).

The Unfortunates, London, Panther Books in association with Secker & Warburg (1969); London, Picador (1999) (revised edition, with an introduction by Jonathan Coe).

House Mother Normal: A Geriatric Comedy, London, Collins (1971); London, Trigram Press (1971); London, Quartet (1973); Newcastle upon Tyne, Bloodaxe (1984); New York, New Directions (1986); London, Picador (2004) (as part of *B. S. Johnson Omnibus*).

Christie Malry's Own Double-Entry, London, Collins (1973); Harmondsworth, Penguin (1984); New York, New Directions (1985); London, Picador (2001) (with an introduction by John Lanchester).

See the Old Lady Decently, London, Hutchinson (1975).

SHORTER PROSE

Published

Street Children (photographs by Julia Trevelyan Oman), London, Hodder & Stoughton (1964).

Statement Against Corpses (with Zulfikar Ghose), London, Constable (1964). Contains: 'Clean Living Is the Real Safeguard', 'Perhaps It's These Hormones', 'Statement', 'Kindly State Your Motive', 'Broad Thoughts from a Home', 'On Supply', 'Never Heard it Called That Before', 'Sheela-na-Gig' and 'Only the Stones'.

Penguin Modern Stories 7 (with Anthony Burgess, Susan Hill, Yehuda Amichai), edited by Judith Burnley, Harmondsworth, Penguin (1971). Contains: 'Instructions for the Use of Women *or* Here, You've Been Done', 'For Bolocks Please Read Blocks Throughout' and 'Mean Point of Impact'.

Aren't You Rather Young To Be Writing Your Memoirs?, London, Hutchinson (1973). Contains: 'Introduction', 'Aren't You Rather Young To Be Writing Your Memoirs?', 'Mean Point of Impact', 'What Did You Say the Name of the Place Was?', 'Never Heard It Called That Before', 'A Few Selected Sentences', 'Instructions for the Use of Women; or, Here, You've Been Done!', 'Broad Thoughts from a Home', 'These Count As Fictions' and 'Everyone Knows Somebody Who's Dead'.

'Everyone Knows Somebody Who's Dead', London, Covent Garden Press (1973).

Uncollected

'The Frog and the Golden Ball', *Lucifer*, vol. 55, no. 2 (spring 1958), p. 19 (under the pseudonym Henry Wriothesley).

'Male Tale', *Lucifer*, vol. 55, no. 3 (spring 1958), p. 29 (under the pseudonym Henry Wriothesley).

'Grimm for Our Times', *Lucifer*, vol. 56, no. 2 (January 1959), p. 3.

'The Rook Rifle' [semi-autobiographical story; some overlap of material with 'Clean Living Is the Real Safeguard'], *Lucifer*, vol. 56, no. 3 (summer 1959), pp. 8–10.

Unpublished

Prepar-a-Tory. Written with Zulfikar Ghose (1960).

'In Here'. Written for *Winter's Tales for Children: Three* (Macmillan, 1967); rejected.

POEMS

Collected

Poems, London, Constable (1964).

Poems Two, London, Trigram Press (1972).

Penguin Modern Poets 25, Harmondsworth, Penguin (1975). Selection from the above two volumes, together with poems by Gavin Ewart and Zulfikar Ghose.

Uncollected

'Solitude' (translation from the French of Alphonse de Lamartine) in the *Chronicle* ['The Magazine of the Commercial Department of the Hinchley Wood County Secondary School'] (1949), pp. 31–2.

'Villanelle in January', *Lucifer*, vol. 55, no. 1 (autumn 1957), p. 3.

'Irregular Villanelle', *Universities Poetry*, no. 1 (March 1958), p. 46.

'For Daphne', *Lucifer*, vol. 55, no. 2 (spring 1958), p. 26.

'A Broader Ballad' [parody, with mock-annotations], *Lucifer*, vol. 56, no. 1 (autumn 1958), p. 27.

'Hafod a Hendref', *Planet*, 10 (February–March 1972), pp. 47–54.

'*Beyond Concorde*', Dawn [published by the Port Talbot Literary Society] 2 (1974), p. 1.

Unpublished

'All in the Same Race (being Rough Notes for Secondary Modern Kids)' [long poem in rhyming couplets; some overlap of material with *You're Human Like the Rest of Them*]. (Written 1964).

Poems of Gwenallt. [Five poems from the Welsh of David James Jones, adapted from literal translations by Ned Thomas: '*Colomennod*' ('Pigeons'), '*Sir Forgannwg a Sir Gaerfyrddin*' ('Glamorganshire and Carmarthenshire'), '*Y Dirwasgiad*' ('The Depression'), '*Cymdogion*' ('Neighbours'), '*Y Meirwon*' ('The Dead'). More were to have been attempted.] (Written 1971–3.)

Special editions

Three Gregynog Englynion ('Fern', 'Broom' and 'Beech'), Newtown, Gregynog Press (1970).

A Dublin Unicorn, Nottingham, Byron Press pamphlet series, 5 (1973).

ANTHOLOGIES

(As editor)

The Evacuees, London, Gollancz (1968).

London Consequences: A Novel, London, Greater London Arts Association (1972). (Edited with Margaret Drabble; containing unattributed chapters by Paul Ableman, John Bowen, Melvyn Bragg, Vincent Brome, Peter Buckman, Alan Burns, Barry Cole, Eva Figes, Gillian Freeman, Jane Gaskell, Wilson Harris, Rayner Heppenstall, Olivia Manning, Adrian Mitchell, Julian Mitchell, Andrea Newman, Piers Paul Read, Stefan Themerson.)

All Bull: The National Servicemen, London, Allison & Busby (1973).

You Always Remember the First Time, London, Quartet (1975). (Editorial work completed after Johnson's death by Michael Bakewell and Giles Gordon.)

DRAMA

Stage

Cinderella. A pantomime for children, written in 1960 or 1961. Unpublished, unperformed.

Double Trouble, a new play for children. Written 1962. Revised 1969, and published in *Play: Young People and the Creative Arts*, vol. 1, no. 5 (November 1969), pp. 8–10.

Scenes from the Pathetic Old Age of George Offord Murrain, Boundary Group (1963). Unpublished, unperformed.

You're Human Like the Rest of Them, Royal Shakespeare Company (1964). Published in *Transatlantic Review*, 19 (autumn 1965), pp. 37–43, and *New English Dramatists 14*, Harmondsworth, Penguin (1970), introduced by Edwin Morgan, pp. 221–32. Later performed as part of *B. S. Johnson vs God.*

Whose Dog Are You?, Royal Shakespeare Company (1967). Unpublished. Extracts later performed as part of *B. S. Johnson vs God.*

One Sodding Thing After Another, Royal Court (1967). Unpublished, unperformed.

B. S. Johnson vs God. Performed at the Basement Theatre, London, 18–29 January 1971. Containing two extracts from *Whose Dog Are You?* and the complete *You're Human Like the Rest of Them.*

Down Red Lane. Published in *Stand*, vol. 15, no. 2 (1974), pp. 8–18. Performed at the Open Space Theatre, London, 1974. Radio adaptation broadcast on BBC Radio Three, 5 May 2002.

Radio

(All unpublished, and all unperformed except for *)

Arrow to the Heart. Adaptation of the novel by Albrecht Goes, translated by
C. Fitzgibbon (1959).

'The Great Welsh Harp Abduction Mystery'. Specimen script for *The Goon Show*,
written with Michael Baker (1960).

It May Be Just What We Need: A Fantasy for Radio. Written with Michael Baker
(1960).

The Proper End. A play for the Wolfsohn voice of Roy Hart (1962).

* *Entry.* Broadcast 13 January 1965, BBC Third Programme.

* *Christie Malry's Own Double-Entry.* Semi-dramatized reading of entire novel.
Broadcast 30 January 1973, BBC Radio London.

Television

Turkish Delight. Sample episode of 'television comedy series based on university life',
written with Michael Baker (1960). Unpublished, unproduced.

What Is the Right Thing and Am I Doing It? (1971). Unpublished, unproduced.

Not Counting the Savages. Published in *Transatlantic Review*, 45 (spring 1973),
pp. 55–75. Broadcast on BBC Two, 3 January 1972.

Compressor (1973). Unpublished, unproduced.

Cinema

(* Also as director)

The Savage Canary. First draft of screenplay, written with John Paxton, from a
treatment by John Burke, based on the book by David Lampe (1965).
Unpublished, unproduced.

* *You're Human Like the Rest of Them.* BFI (1967).

Albert Angelo. Several draft screenplays (1967–70). Unpublished, unproduced.

The Perfect Tickle. First draft of screenplay, from a story by C. Scott Forbes (1968).
Substantially different version produced by Sunnymede Films in 1970 as *The
Perfect Friday.*

* *Up Yours Too, Guillaume Apollinaire.* ICA (1968).

* *Paradigm.* Elisabeth Films (1969). Screenplay published in *Transatlantic Review*, 30
(autumn 1968), pp. 99–100.

DOCUMENTARY

(All as writer and director unless otherwise stated)

Television

The Evacuees. Broadcast as part of *Release,* BBC Two, 24 October 1968. Extended
  version broadcast BBC Two, 31 August 1969.
The Unfortunates (writer only). Broadcast as part of *Release,* BBC Two, 22 February
  1969.
Charlie Whildon Talking, Singing and Playing. Made for BBC Two's *Release,* but
  apparently not broadcast. No print survives.
This City Is Dying – Look to Your Heads!. Broadcast as part of *Release,* BBC Two,
  14 June 1969.
The Smithsons on Housing. Broadcast on BBC Two, 10 July 1970.
On Reflection: Samuel Johnson. Broadcast on ITV, 31 January 1971.
On Reflection: Alexander Herzen (director only). Broadcast on ITV, 4 April 1971.
Hafod a Hendref (writer only). Broadcast as part of *Gallery,* ITV, 25 May 1972.
Fat Man on a Beach (writer only). Broadcast on ITV, 12 November 1974. Screenplay
  published in *Beyond the Words: Eleven Writers in Search of a New Fiction,* edited
  by Giles Gordon, London, Hutchinson (1975), pp. 149–81.

Cinema

(* Also as director)
Goal! CIPHAS Films (1966). Treatment and first-draft screenplay. Not used in
  completed film.
* *Unfair.* ACT Films (1970).
* *March!.* ACT Films (1971).
Here Comes Everybody! ACT Films (1971). First-draft screenplay. Not used.

JOURNALISM

*(This section lists pieces written for print media only; and only those which are not
otherwise available in volume form)*

General

'Restatement' [joint statement of editorial policy, written with Stuart Crampin],
  Lucifer, vol. 55, no. 1 (autumn 1957), p. 41.
'Adventures in the Straits' [on editorial visit to Nottingham], *Lucifer,* vol. 55, no. 2
  (spring 1958), p. iv.

'Editorials: One, Two, Three', *Lucifer*, vol. 55, no. 3 (spring 1958), p. 3.

'Editorial', *Lucifer*, vol. 56, no. 1 (autumn 1958), p. 3.

'Consumer Persuasion' [on the advertising business], *Lucifer*, vol. 56, no. 1 (autumn 1958), pp. 14–15.

'Departures Will Be Delayed: Live New Departures', *Western Daily Press* (4 December 1961), p. 8.

'A Comic in the Terrible Silence: Samuel Beckett', *Western Daily Press* (22 October 1962), p. 4.

'Key to Beckett – Who Doesn't Give a Damn', *Scene*, 7 (25 October 1962), p. 9.

'Opinion' [discussion of *Steptoe and Son*], *Scene*, 17 (26 January 1963), pp. 10–11.

'Bard in the Boozer' [on poetry readings organized by the Dulwich Group], *Scene*, 22 (6 April 1963), pp. 26–7.

'The Travails of *Travelling People*', *Smith's Trade News* (20 April 1963), pp. 24–5.

'Anti or Ultra', *Books and Bookmen*, vol. 9, no. 8 (May 1963), p. 25.

'Discoverers of New Talent' [survey of literary magazines], *Observer* (12 January 1964), p. 24.

'The Child's Reading', *Western Mail* (7 November 1964), p. 7.

'Same Old Chelsea' [childhood memories of football-watching], *Observer* (18 April 1965), p. 18.

'Writing and Publishing: or, Wickedness Reveal'd', *Socialist Commentary* (June 1965), pp. 33–5.

'Pi Printers', *Censorship*, 3 (summer 1965), pp. 43–5.

'Bricks and Mortar, and also the Pen', *Western Mail* (5 June 1965), p. 7.

'London: The Moron-Made City, or, Just a Load of Old Buildings with Cars in Between' [profile of Peter and Alison Smithson], *London Life* (23–9 October 1965), pp. 45–51.

'The Demolition Man' [profile of Frank Valori], *London Life* (11–17 November 1965), pp. 28–31.

'Holes, Syllabics, and the Succussations of the Intercostal and Abdominal Muscles', *Northern Review*, vol. 1, no. 2 (1966), pp. 75–89.

'Poets Who Must Pay for a Public' [on the economics of the poetry business], *London Life* (16 April 1966), pp. 8–9.

'A Plea for the Minor Art of Playing on Pin-Tables', *London Life* (30 April 1966), pp. 16–17.

'Views/Reviews: "Telling Stories is Telling Lies"', *Vogue*, vol. 123, no. 13 (October 1966), p. 18.

'Festivals' [report on the 5th International Short-Film Festival, Cracow, and the 8th Polish National Short-Film Festival], *Guardian* (15 June 1968), p. 7.

'A Living for Writers', *New Society* (9 January 1969), p. 58.

'Moment of Truth – and Birth of a New Novel', *Morning Star* (13 February 1969), p. 4.

'The Professional Viewpoint' [on the treatment of sex in his novels], *20th Century Studies*, 2 (November 1969), pp. 117–18.

'The Disintegrating Novel (2)', *Books and Bookmen*, vol. 15, no. 12 (September 1970), p. 8.

'Soho Square' [on Rupert Murdoch], *Film & Television Technician* (February/March 1971), p. 13.

'Soho Square' [on the British film industry], *Film & Television Technician* (August 1971), p. 14.

'Uncle Tom's Cobblers: or Where Are They Now?' [attack on British film producers], *Film & Television Technician* (December 1971), pp. 12–13.

Introduction to 'A Retrospective of Recent Anglo-Welsh Poetry', *Transatlantic Review*, 42/43 (spring–summer 1972), p. 66.

'Good Evening, Mr Kadar' [account of ACTT delegation to Hungary], *Film & Television Technician* (June 1972), pp. 26–7.

'Soho Square' [reflections on the Angry Brigade], *Film & Television Technician* (January 1973), p. 15.

'The Gregynog Press and the Gregynog Fellowship', *The Private Library*, Second series, vol. 6:1 (spring 1973), pp. 4–15.

'The Happiest Days?', *Education & Training* (March 1973), pp. 92–3.

'Writers' Column' [on the role of writers in the film industry], *Film & Television Technician* (April 1973), p. 15.

'The Author's Plight – the Need for a Union', *Tribune*, vol. 37, no. 24 (15 June 1973), p. 7.

'Opinion' [on working as poetry editor for the *Transatlantic Review*], *Poet*, 2 (summer 1974), pp. 1–4.

Theatre reviews and other writings on theatre

'The Royal Road and the Real Road' [reviews of *Camino Real* by Tennessee Williams and *Summer of the Seventeenth Doll* by Ray Lawler], *Lucifer*, vol. 55, no. 1 (autumn 1957), pp. 19–22.

'Theatre Workshop', *Lucifer*, vol. 55, no. 2 (spring 1958), pp. 13–17.

Saint Joan [Shaw] [review of King's College production], *Lucifer*, vol. 55, no. 2 (spring 1958), p. 35.

Nekrassov [Sartre] [review of Royal Court production], *Lucifer*, vol. 55, no. 2 (spring 1958), p. 37.

The Kidders [Donald Ogden Stewart] [review of St Martin's Theatre production], *Lucifer*, vol. 55, no. 3 (spring 1958), p. 41.

Epitaph for George Dillon [Osborne and Creighton] [review of Royal Court production], *Lucifer*, vol. 55, no. 3 (spring 1958), p. 43.

The Chairs and *The Lesson* [Ionesco] [review of Royal Court production], *Lucifer*, vol. 56, no. 1 (autumn 1958), p. 35.

The Hamlet of Stepney Green [Kops] [review of Lyric, Hammersmith production], *Lucifer*, vol. 56, no. 1 (autumn 1958), p. 36.

The Hostage [Behan] [review of Theatre Royal production], *Lucifer*, vol. 56, no. 2 (January 1959), pp. 31–2.

Happy As Larry [MacDonagh] [review of King's College production], *Lucifer*, vol. 56, no. 2 (January 1959), pp. 35–6.

Creditors [Strindberg] and *The Cheats of Scapin* [Otway] [review of Lyric, Hammersmith productions], *Lucifer*, vol. 56, no. 3 (summer 1959), pp. 33–4.

'Cavorting in the Bogs' [overview of recent London theatrical productions], *Umbrella*, vol. 2, no. 7 (1961), pp. 125–130.

'The Criminal and the Saint: Jean Genet', *Western Daily Press* (31 May 1961), p. 9.

'Don't Tell Me How It Feels – *Show* Me: Bertolt Brecht', *Western Daily Press* (13 November 1961), p. 8.

Happy Days [review of Royal Court production], *Western Daily Press* (5 November 1962), p. 6.

'On the Boundary', *Scene*, 9 (8 November 1962), p. 19.

'Martyr at the Winch' [on Strindberg], *Spectator* (24 May 1963), pp. 672–3.

'Interview with Walter Hall of the Basement Theatre', *Transatlantic Review*, 44 (autumn–winter 1972), pp. 39–42.

Book reviews

Brecht, by Ronald Gray, *Western Daily Press* (3 May 1961), p. 8.

Pantaloon, by Philip Toynbee, *Western Daily Press* (11 December 1961), p. 10.

A B C of Reading, by Ezra Pound, *Western Daily Press* (18 December 1961), p. 8.

The Hard Life, by Flann O'Brien, and *The Dark Labyrinth*, by Lawrence Durrell, *Western Daily Press* (22 January 1962), p. 8.

Milton's God, by William Empson, *Western Daily Press* (29 January 1962), p. 9.

An Experiment in Criticism, by C. S. Lewis, and *The Romantic Imagination*, by Sir Maurice Bowra, *Western Daily Press* (5 February 1962), p. 8.

Dun Karm: Poet of Malta, translated by A. J. Arberry, and *One Hundred Poems by Kabir*, translated by Rabindranath Tagore, *Western Daily Press* (12 February 1962), p. 8.

Juvenilia I, by Robert Nye, *Love Me, Lambeth*, by Michael Hastings, and *Ode to the Shadows*, by David Bulwer Lutyens, *Western Daily Press* (26 February 1962), p. 8.

The John Fletcher Plays, by Clifford Leech, *Western Daily Press* (5 March 1962), p. 8.

Selected Prose, by A. E. Housman, edited by John Carter, *Western Daily Press* (12 March 1962), p. 4.

The White Goddess, by Robert Graves, *Western Daily Press* (19 March 1962), p. 4.

Llareggub Revisited, by David Holbrook, *Western Daily Press* (26 March 1962), p. 8.

Unicorn (spring 1962 issue), edited by Norman Harvey, *Western Daily Press* (2 April 1962), p. 8.

Tales from the Calendar, by Bertolt Brecht, *Western Daily Press* (16 April 1962), p. 8.

Poems in English, by Samuel Beckett, *Western Daily Press* (7 May 1962), p. 8.

Auto-da-fé, by Elias Canetti, translated by C. V. Wedgwood, *Western Daily Press* (4 June 1962), p. 8.

Happy Days, by Samuel Beckett, *Spectator* (20 July 1962), p. 92.

Poems, by Alan Dugan, *A Durable Fire,* by Patric Dickinson, *Control Tower,* by Richard Kell, *The Secret Sea,* by Hugo Manning, *Green Hunger,* by Louis Newman, and *So I Looked Down to Camelot,* by Rosamund Stanhope, *Outposts,* 54 (autumn 1962), pp. 20–2.

The Riddle of Shakespeare's Sonnets, edited by Edward Hubler, *Spectator* (28 September 1962), p. 444.

Our Exagmination Round His Factification for Incamination of Work in Progress, by Samuel Beckett et al., and *Introducing James Joyce,* edited by T. S. Eliot, *Western Daily Press* (1 October 1962), p. 6.

Round-up of forty-six paperbacks by T. S. Eliot, Anthony Blunt et al., *Spectator* (26 October 1962), pp. 654–5.

The Manoeuvring Sun, edited by Alan Crang, *Western Daily Press* (5 November 1962), p. 6.

The Otters' Tale, by Gavin Maxwell, *Finn the Wolfhound,* by A. J. Dawson, *Bruno, King of the Wild,* by Michel-Aimé Baudony, and *Mountain-Lion: A Puma Called Rusty,* by John B. Prescott, *Spectator* (9 November 1962), p. 732.

Round-up of fourteen books for children by Michael Bond, Dorothy Whipple et al., *Spectator* (23 November 1962), p. 834 (under the pseudonym Henry Wriothesley).

Samuel Beckett: A Critical Study, by Hugh Kenner, and *Beckett and Behan and a Theatre in Dublin,* by Alan Simpson, *Spectator* (23 November 1962), pp. 816–18.

Prohibition: The Era of Excess, by Andrew Sinclair, *Spectator* (7 December 1962), pp. 900–1.

Lord Byron's Wife, by Malcolm Elwin, *Spectator* (14 December 1962), p. 938.

London: City of Any Dream, by Colin MacInnes and Erwin Fieger, *Spectator* (21 December 1962), p. 970.

Earls of Creation, by James Lees-Milne, *Les Pavillons,* by Cyril Connolly and Jerome Zerbe, and *Architecture: The Indispensable Art,* by W. R. Dalzell, *Spectator* (11 January 1963), pp. 47–8.

The Irish Comic Tradition, by Vivian Mercier, *Spectator* (25 January 1963), pp. 103–4.

Rails through the Clay, by Alan A. Jackson and Desmond F. Croome, *Spectator* (25 January 1963), p. 103 (under the pseudonym Henry Wriothesley).

Samuel Beckett: A Critical Study, by Hugh Kenner, and *Beckett and Behan and a Theatre in Dublin,* by Alan Simpson, *Western Daily Press* (28 January 1963), p. 6 (signed 'G.V.B.')

The Pattern of English Building, by Alec Clifton-Taylor, *Spectator* (15 February 1963), p. 204.

Unicorn (autumn and winter 1962 issues), edited by Norman Harvey, *Western Daily Press* (18 February 1963), p. 6.

The Whale Killers, by Douglas Liversidge, *Hunting the Desert Whale,* by Erle Stanley Gardner, and *Freshwater Fishes of the World,* by Günther Sterba, *Spectator* (22 March 1963), p. 367 (under the pseudonym Henry Wriothesley).

Cinnamon Shops and Other Stories, by Bruno Schulz, *The Director's Wife and Other Stories*, by Brian Glanville, *The Saucer of Larks*, by Brian Friel, and *A Piece of Land*, by Noel Hilliard, *Spectator* (29 March 1963), pp. 402–3.

Experimental Drama, edited by William A. Armstrong, and *Karel Capek*, by William E. Harkins, *Spectator* (11 April 1963), p. 474.

A Reader's Guide to the Contemporary English Novel, by Frederick R. Karl, and *Postwar British Fiction*, by James Gindin, *Spectator* (3 May 1963), p. 578.

Round-up of seven books by Asa Briggs, Nikolaus Pevsner et al., *Spectator* (24 May 1963), p. 680 (under the pseudonym Henry Wriothesley).

Round-up of seven books by T. S. Eliot, Tennessee Williams et al., *Spectator* (24 May 1963), p. 679 (under the pseudonym Jeremy Purdue).

Penguin Modern Poets 3: George Barker, Martin Bell, Charles Causley, Countermoves, by Charles Edward Eaton, *Alcaic Poems*, by Friedrich Hölderlin, and *The Lightning Makes a Difference*, by Hubert Witheford, *Outposts*, 57 (summer 1963), pp. 22–4.

Round-up of eighteen non-fiction books for children by Noel Streatfield, Bryan Morgan et al., *Spectator* (7 June 1963), p. 748.

A Group Anthology, edited by Edward Lucie-Smith and Philip Hobsbaum, and *Contemporary American Poetry*, selected and introduced by Donald Hall, *Outposts*, 58 (autumn 1963), pp. 22–3.

What Is Remembered, by Alice B. Toklas, *Spectator* (6 December 1963), p. 759.

Murphy and *Watt*, by Samuel Beckett, *Flight of the Bat*, by Donald Gordon, *The Cunninghams*, by David Ballantyne, and *The Run of Night*, by Peter de Polnay, *Spectator* (13 December 1963), p. 800.

The Trial of Marie Besnard, by Marie Besnard, *The Unknown Citizen*, by Tony Parker, and *Prison*, edited by George Mikes, *Spectator* (27 December 1963), pp. 857–8.

A Kingdom for My Horse, by B. L. Jacot, *Say Not Goodnight*, by Olga Hesky, and *Sundry Debtors*, by John McGhee, *Spectator* (17 January 1964), p. 84.

A Shadow Backwards, by Martha Wiley Emmett, *The Whistling Zone*, by Herbert Kubly, *Joby*, by Stan Barstow, *O Stranger, the World*, by Christopher Leach, and *The Water-Castle*, by Brenda Chamberlain, *Spectator* (14 February 1964), p. 221.

An Edge of Pride, by Deane Narayn, *The Other Kingdom*, by Victor Price, *Geraldine Bradshaw*, by Calder Willingham, *A Man Beside Himself*, by Andrew Shonfield, and *The Biggest Picture*, by Stanley Price, *Spectator* (13 March 1964), p. 352.

A Fine Madness, by Elliott Baker, *Tom and Jenny*, by Kenneth Warner, *The Narrow Shore*, by Louis Battye, *The Hand of Mary Constable*, by Paul Gallico, and *The Face of a Madonna*, by Thomas Armstrong, *Spectator* (10 April 1964), p. 493.

The Tenants of Moonbloom, by Edward L. Wallant, *The Carib Sands*, by Terence Kelly, *The Director's Dinner*, by Charles W. Chapman, *Nuts in May*, by Richard Gordon, and *Weep Not, Child*, by James Ngugi, *Spectator* (8 May 1964), p. 641.

To Build a Ship, by Don Berry, *Town Parole*, by Alex Hamilton, *Quick, Before It Melts*, by Philip Benjamin, *Reach for the Ground*, by R. F. de la Reguera, and *Mercenary Prince*, by Charles Durbin, *Spectator* (5 June 1964), p. 762.

Round-up of eleven non-fiction books for children by Warren Armstrong, Gabriel Seal et al., *Spectator* (5 June 1964), pp. 767–8.

How It Is and *Play, Words and Music and Cascando*, by Samuel Beckett, *Spectator* (26 June 1964), p. 858.

The Novels of Samuel Beckett, by John Fletcher, *The Lamp and the Lute*, by Bonamy Dobrée, *The Guns of Elsinore*, by Martin Holmes, and *Wordsworth and the Poetry of Sincerity*, by David Perkins, *Spectator* (28 August 1964), p. 280.

The F.A. Book for Boys, Observer (30 August 1964), p. 14.

Festival Night, by Cesare Pavese, *Beggar My Neighbour*, by Dan Jacobson, *Lost Upon the Roundabouts*, by A. L. Barker, *Stories from the* London Magazine, edited by Alan Ross, *To Catch a Spy*, edited by Eric Ambler, and *The Neighbour's Wife*, edited by James Turner, *Spectator* (16 October 1964), p. 516.

Late Call, by Angus Wilson, *Spectator* (13 November 1964), p. 644.

The Lost City, by John Gunther, *Twelve Months, Mrs. Brown*, by Kathleen J. Smith, *The Monkey Game*, by Graeme Kent, *The Paper Dolls*, by L. P. Davies, and *Deep Is the Blue*, by Max Ehrlich, *Spectator* (20 November 1964), p. 686.

The Assassination Bureau, Ltd., by Jack London, *Tales of the Five Towns*, by Arnold Bennett, *The Hornblower Companion*, by C. S. Forester, and *Modern African Stories*, edited by Ellis Ayitey Komey and Ezekiel Mphahlele, *Spectator* (18 December 1964), pp. 849–50.

The Classical Language of Architecture, by John Summerson, *Western Mail* (31 December 1964), p. 4.

The Flag, by Robert Shaw, *How Many Miles to Babylon?*, by Ann Borowick, *Professor Descending*, by Ramona Stewart, and *The Fly*, by Richard Chopping, *Spectator* (15 January 1965), p. 75.

Measures, by Norman MacCaig, *Ariel*, by Sylvia Plath, and *Adam at Evening*, by David Wright, *Ambit*, 24 (1965), pp. 45–6.

A Spaniard in the Works by John Lennon, *Guardian* (9 July 1965), p. 8.

A History of English Architecture, by Peter Kidson, Peter Murray and Paul Thompson, *Western Mail* (29 January 1966), p. 8.

Three, by Ann Quin, *Tremor of Intent*, by Anthony Burgess, *The Partnership*, by Barry Unsworth, and *The Early Life of Stephen Hind*, by Storm Jameson, *Sunday Times* (5 June 1966), p. 27.

All Day Saturday, by Colin MacInnes, *Caliban's Wooing*, by Victor Price, *The Train Ride*, by Peter Loughran, and *In Praise of Older Women*, by Stephen Vizinczey, *Sunday Times* (14 August 1966), p. 31.

Almost a Gentleman by Mark Benney, *Sunday Times* (30 October 1966), p. 48.

The New Brutalism, by Rayner Banham, and *A Portrait of the Female Mind As a Young Girl*, by Alison Smithson, *Western Mail* (31 December 1966), p. 8.

Death of a Naturalist, by Seamus Heaney, and *Cages*, by Ruth Fainlight, *Outposts*, 72 (spring 1967), pp. 29–30.

Giles Goat-Boy, by John Barth, *Books and Bookmen*, vol. 12, no. 7 (April 1967), pp. 60–1.

Giles Goat-Boy, by John Barth, *Western Mail* (1 April 1967), p. 8 (under the pseudonym Henry Wriothesley).

No's Knife and *Eh Joe and Other Writings*, by Samuel Beckett, and *Beckett at Sixty: A Festschrift*, *New Statesman* (14 July 1967), p. 54.

Celebrations, by Alan Burns, and *The Self-Devoted Friend*, by Marvin Cohen, *New Statesman* (17 November 1967), p. 684.

The Euston Arch and the Growth of the London, Midland & Scottish Railway, by Alison and Peter Smithson, *Guardian* (27 December 1968), p. 10.

B, by Eva Figes, *Evening Standard* (28 March 1972), p. 25.

Dreamerika!, by Alan Burns, *Evening Standard* (23 May 1972), p. 28.

Balcony of Europe, by Aidan Higgins, *New Statesman* (29 September 1972), p. 442.

Pasmore, by David Storey, *Evening Standard* (10 October 1972), p. 27.

Raw Material, by Alan Sillitoe, *New Statesman* (27 October 1972), pp. 608–9.

Cleopatra, by Michael Grant, *Evening Standard* (30 November 1972), p. 25.

Black Marsden, by Wilson Harris, and *Natives of My Person*, by George Lamming, *New Statesman* (1 December 1972), p. 832.

Numbers: A Further Autobiography, by Jakov Lind, *Evening Standard* (13 February 1973), p. 24.

A State of Heat, by Sheilah Graham, *Evening Standard* (20 March 1973), p. 25.

Football Mania, by Gerhard Vinnai, *Evening Standard* (10 April 1973), p. 24.

Transparent Things, by Vladimir Nabokov, *Evening Standard* (29 May 1973), p. 27.

The Region's Violence, by Ruth Fainlight, and *Urban Gorilla*, by Wes Magee, *Outposts*, 99 (winter 1973), pp. 23–4.

Sports reporting

Between 16 September 1963 and 20 November 1965, Johnson filed some forty league and FA cup reports for the *Observer*.

Between 11 July 1966 and 31 July 1966, he filed thirty-two World Cup match reports for the *Times of India*.

Also for the *Times of India*, he covered two Wimbledon tennis championships (20 June 1965–3 July 1965 and 18 June 1966–2 July 1966) and one Davis Cup (November 1965).

PUBLISHED INTERVIEWS WITH B. S. JOHNSON

(This listing is confined to stand-alone interviews, and does not include short news pieces in which Johnson's comments were briefly quoted.)

Scotsman (8 August 1964), p. 2.

Tatler, vol. 256, no. 3324 (12 May 1965), p. 322.

Guardian (7 November 1966), p. 7.

London Life (12 November 1966), p. 45.

Morning Star (15 June 1967), p. 4.

Books and Bookmen, vol. 13, no. 9 (June 1968), pp. 12–13.

Evening News (25 October 1968), p. 4.

Evening Standard (16 January 1969), p. 10.

Sunday Times (2 February 1969), (Atticus), p. 15.

Guardian (15 March 1969), p. 9.

The Imagination on Trial: British and American Writers Discuss Their Working Methods, edited by Alan Burns and Charles Sugnet (London and New York, Allison & Busby, 1981), pp. 83–94. [Interview conducted by Alan Burns in 1973.]

FURTHER READING

The most substantial academic book on Johnson to have appeared so far is *B. S. Johnson: A Critical Reading*, by Philip Tew (Manchester University Press, 2001). A concise and readable introduction is also provided by *Fighting Fictions: The Novels of B. S. Johnson*, by Nicolas Tredell (Pauper's Press, 2000). Both books contain full bibliographies which will direct readers to the growing body of academic writing about Johnson.

Mention must also be made of two numbers of the *Review of Contemporary Fiction*. Half of vol. 5, no. 2 (summer 1985) was devoted to B. S. Johnson: it included reminiscences by Zulfikar Ghose and Eva Figes, along with ten critical essays. And half of vol. 17, no. 2 (summer 1997) was devoted to Alan Burns. Among the pieces included here are 'Two Chapters from a book provisionally titled *Human Like the Rest of Us: A Life of B. S. Johnson*' in which Burns gives his own account of Johnson's last few weeks. This extract starts with the shooting of *Fat Man on a Beach* and ends with Johnson's suicide. It includes comments from Michael Bakewell, Peter Buckman, Barry Cole and others.

Johnson's death in 1973 provoked a number of poetic responses. Among the most notable are Alan Tucker's 'BSJ: A Monody to the Plan of Milton on the Death by Suicide of B. S. Johnson' (Keepsake Press, 1974), 'Last Days (i.m. BSJ)' by Ruth Fainlight, available in her *Selected Poems* (Sinclair-Stevenson, 1995) and 'Odds Against (IM BSJ)' by Barry Cole, from his collection *Inside Outside* (Shoestring Press, 1998). Judy Cooke's novel *New Road* (Gollancz, 1975) also contains an account of an artist's suicide partly based on the death of B. S. Johnson.

However, the most sustained and remarkable imaginative response to Johnson's work so far has been the novel *Drift*, by Brian Castro, published by William Heinemann Australia in 1994. This is best described as a fantasy upon, and free continuation of, Johnson's uncompleted Matrix trilogy, relocated to Tasmania and featuring a central character called Byron Shelley Johnson. It has not been published in the UK.

A comprehensive B. S. Johnson website can be found at www.bsjohnson.co.uk.

ACKNOWLEDGEMENTS

This is an authorized biography, written with the full cooperation of B. S. Johnson's widow, Virginia, his son Steve and his daughter Kate. I am conscious that it has been a difficult and demanding undertaking for them. Virginia in particular has lived, for several years, with my frequent – at times almost daily – presence in her house, accompanied by a constant barrage of questions, even the most casual of which have often stirred up painful memories. Without her patience, forbearing and generosity, this book could not have been written.

It should be emphasized, however, that responsibility for the opinions expressed in the book, the emphasis laid on certain facts and the interpretations given to them, rests entirely with myself. The portrait of B. S. Johnson drawn in this biography is my own.

*

Many other people helped with the writing of the book.

For agreeing to take part in taped interviews, my thanks go to: Claire Andrews, Keith Andrews, Michael Baker, Michael Bakewell, István Bart, John Berger, John Boothe, Sir Edward Britton, Alan Brownjohn, Alan Burns, Charles Clark, Gloria Cigman, Barry Cole, Judy Cooke, Roma Crampin, Stuart Crampin, Doug Davies, Peter Dunsmore, Frank Fisher, Thelma Fisher, John Furse, Ben Glazebrook, the late Giles Gordon, Barbara Hardy, Bill Holdsworth, Jeremy Hooker, William Hoyland, Glyn Tegai Hughes, Michael Joseph, Stephen Joseph, Trev Leggett, Alan Marshfield, Jean Nicholson, Gyorgy Novak, the late Julia Trevelyan Oman, Alison Paice, Alan Sapper, Helen Sapper, Anthony Smith, Patrick Snaith, Wendy Stacey, Meic Stephens, Marta Szabados, Ferenc Takács, Ned Thomas, Lucia Turner, Diana Tyler, Marjorie Verney, Ron Verney, Joebear Webb, Harry West, Gordon Williams, the late Joyce Yates, Gianni Zambardi-Mall and Philip Ziegler.

For talking to me informally, corresponding with me about B. S. Johnson by letter and email, and sharing information, my thanks go to: Brian Aldiss, Anthony Barnett, Bernard Bergonzi, I. E. Bloom, J. T. Boulton, Gordon Bowker, Dennis Brown, Will Buckley, Peter Buckman, Rosemarie Buckman, Val Butler, Carmen Callil, David Crow, Peter Dempsey, Maureen Duffy, Howard Erskine-Hill, Ruth Fainlight, Eva Figes, Anne

Fine, John Furnival, Zulfikar Ghose, Robert Gill, Dr Rüdiger Görner, Gordon Gridley, Bryn Griffiths, Andrew Hodgkiss, John Horder, Marie Ingram, Clive James, Ray John, John Idris Jones, Julian Joseph, Francis King, Tony Lamb, Jean Lissauer, John Lucas, Edward Lucie-Smith, Paul Magrath, Michael Pennie, Deborah Rogers, Richard and Jeannette Seaver, Michael Seeney, Marion Spicer, Sir Tom Stoppard, Sir Roy Strong, June Tillinghast, Kelvin Tillinghast, Alan Tucker, John Powell Ward, Colin Wiles and Adèle Winston.

Special thanks must also go to Alan Burns, who generously gave me all the material he had amassed while researching his own, unfinished biography of B. S. Johnson. This included copies of papers originally provided by Patrick Taylor Galleries of Dublin.

Dan Mitchell, Library Assistant in the Little Magazines section of the UCL Special Collections Library, helped to fill some difficult gaps in the bibliography. Staff at the Harry Ransom Center at the University of Austin, Texas, were most helpful in facilitating access to the B. S. Johnson papers held there. Zulfikar and Helena Ghose were generous and welcoming hosts during my visit to Texas.

Artemis Gause proved herself a trusty researcher and Girl Friday; she can now probably claim (should she so desire) to be a world expert on B. S. Johnson. Excellent transcripts of my taped interviews were provided by Sarah Sambles, Kate Shaw and, latterly, Rachel Hewlett Office Services.

My gratitude also goes to the people who read the book in manuscript. Julie and Jonathan Myerson made time to read some early chapters: Julie was wonderfully encouraging at a time when my confidence in the project was at a low ebb; Jonathan made some useful criticisms. Ian Higgins and Phil Tew were swift and responsive readers of the first draft. Invaluable feedback later came from Anthony Smith, John Furse, Zulfikar and Helena Ghose, Diana Tyler and Philip Pacey. And Carol Watts gave the next draft a brilliantly alert and (in the best sense of the word) academic going-over.

Thanks to Laura Cumming for many sympathetic discussions; to Philippe Anclair for French translations; to Annabel Giles for inspired suggestions; to Phil Tew (again) for uplifting chat over any number of artery-busting breakfasts in a variety of Johnsonian locations; and to Roger Lewis for always being at the other end of the telephone with his caustic, knowledgeable and – how shall I put this? – idiosyncratic advice on every aspect of the biographer's art.

Peter Straus commissioned the book in 1995. It was his passion for B. S. Johnson – a shared passion, as we discovered sixteen years ago – that made the whole thing possible. Andrew Kidd inherited the project at Picador and proved himself a supportive and tactful editor. Tony Peake, as always, has been much more than an agent: he is also my first and best reader. And Janine McKeown took B. S. Johnson on board as the third party in our marriage (did she have any choice?) and put up with the fallout, which was not always pleasant. As BSJ himself said of *The Unfortunates*: 'Certainly I know very well that this one cost me more of myself than anything else I have ever written.'

Text Acknowledgements

The author and publisher gratefully acknowledge permission to reproduce copyright material in this book.

Extracts from the published and unpublished works of B. S. Johnson are reproduced by permission of Virginia Johnson and the MBA literary agency. Extracts from the letters of Samuel Beckett are quoted by permission of the Samuel Beckett Estate. An extract from a letter by Michael Legat is quoted by permission of Michael Legat. Extracts from a memo by Sir Michael Balcon are used by kind permission of Jill Balcon. An extract from a letter by Sir John Drummond is quoted by permission of Peters, Fraser and Dunlop on behalf of Sir John Drummond. An extract from *Tea with Mrs Goodman* by Philip Toynbee is reproduced by permission of Jason Toynbee. An extract from a letter by Philip Pacey is quoted by permission of Philip Pacey. Extracts from *Memoirs of a Porcine Lout* by John Furse are reproduced by permission of John Furse. A card to the author from Carol Burns is reproduced by permission of Carol Burns. John Horder's poem 'Unsatisfied author', from his collection *Maher Baba and the Nothingness*, © John Horder 1981, is reproduced by permission of the author. Extracts from emails by Dr Andrew Hodgkiss are reproduced by permission of Dr Hodgkiss.

Picture Acknowledgements

All the photographs in the plate section were supplied by Virginia Johnson except:

— BSJ with Joyce Yates and her son Stephen, supplied by Michael Joseph
— the unveiling of a statue at the Glyn Club, 1959
— BSJ with Tony Tillinghast, supplied by Kevin Tillinghast
— BSJ reading for György Novák's students in Hungary, 1973, supplied by György Novák.

Every effort has been made to contact copyright holders of material reproduced in this book. If any have been inadvertently overlooked, the publishers will be pleased to make restitution at the earliest opportunity.

INDEX